A PARTISAN
Century

Columbia University Press

New York

Political Writings from Partisan Review

A PARTISAN

Century

Edith Kurzweil, Editor

Columbia University Press

Publishers Since 1893

New York   Chichester, West Sussex

Copyright © 1996 Edith Kurzweil

Library of Congress Cataloging-in-Publication Data

A partisan century : political writings from Partisan review / Edith
  Kurzweil, editor.
    p.   cm.
  Includes index.
  ISBN 0–231–10330–1 (cl.: alk. paper).— ISBN 0–231–10331–x (pbk.: alk. paper)
  1. Press and politics—United States.   I. Kurzweil, Edith.
  II. Partisan review (New York, N.Y. : 1936)
  PN4888.P6P38   1996
  071'.3—dc20   96–982
                                                   CIP

Casebound editions of Columbia University Press books are printed on
permanent and durable acid-free paper.

Printed in the United States of America
c 10 9 8 7 6 5 4 3 2 1
p 10 9 8 7 6 5 4 3 2 1

Contents

"Second Thoughts on the U.S.S.R." by André Gide. Reprinted with permission of Editions Gallimard.

"Art and Politics" by Leon Trotsky. Reprinted with permission of Pathfinder Press. Copyright 1970 by Pathfinder Press.

"September Journal" by Stephen Spender. Reprinted with permission of Stephen Spender.

"Leon Trotsky" by James T. Farrell. Reprinted with permission of the Estate of James T. Farrell.

"Ten Propositions on the War" and "Reply" by Clement Greenberg and Dwight Macdonald. Reprinted with permission of the Estate of Clement Greenberg.

"A London Letter" by George Orwell. Excerpt from *The Collected Essays, Journalism and Letters of George Orwell, Volume II: My Country Right or Left 1940–1943*, copyright 1968 by Sonia Brownell Orwell, reprinted by permission of Harcourt Brace & Company.

"Ten Propositions and Eight Errors" and "The Sense and Nonsense of Whittaker Chambers" by Philip Rahv. Reprinted with permission of the Philip Rahv Estate.

"Paris Letter" and "Sartre versus Camus: A Political Quarrel" by Nicola Chiaromonte. Reprinted with permission of Miriam Chiaromonte.

"The Culture Conference" by Irving Howe. Reprinted with permission of Nicholas Howe, literary executor of Irving Howe.

"Report on the International Day Against Dictatorship and War" and "The Berlin Congress for Cultural Freedom" by Sidney Hook. Reprinted with permission of Ernest B. Hook.

Acknowledgments

Our Country, Our Culture

Norman Mailer (Comment). Reprinted with permission of Norman Mailer.

David Riesman (Comment). Reprinted with permission of David Riesman.

Lionel Trilling (Comment). Reprinted with permission of Diana Trilling.

Arthur Schlesinger Jr. (Comment) Reprinted with permission of Arthur Schlesinger Jr.

"The Oppenheimer Case: A Reading of the Testimony" by Diana Trilling. Reprinted with permission of Diana Trilling.

"Coexistence: The End of Ideology" by Raymond Aron. Reprinted with permission of Dominique Schnapper.

"Letter from the South: Nobody Knows My Name" originally appeared in *Nobody Knows My Name*, published by Vintage Books. Copyright 1959 by James Baldwin. Copyright renewed. Reprinted with permission of the James Baldwin Estate.

THE COLD WAR AND THE WEST

Hannah Arendt (Comment). Reprinted with permission of the Hannah Arendt Literary Trust.

Mary McCarthy (Comment). Reprinted with permission of the Mary McCarthy Literary Trust.

Hans J. Morgenthau (Comment) and "The Decline of the West." Reprinted with permission of Susanna Morgenthau and Matthew Morgenthau.

Norman Podhoretz (Comment). Reprinted with permission of Norman Podhoretz.

"National Style and the Radical Right" by Daniel Bell. Reprinted with permission of Daniel Bell.

"Notes on Camp" from *Against Interpretation* by Susan Sontag. Copyright 1964, 1966 and renewed 1994 by Susan Sontag. Reprinted by permission of Farrar, Straus & Giroux, Inc.

THE NEW RADICALISM

Nat Hentoff (Comment). Reprinted with permission of Nat Hentoff.

Michael Harrington (Comment). Reprinted with permission of the Estate of Michael Harrington.

"What's Happening to America" by H. Stuart Hughes. Reprinted with permission of H. Stuart Hughes.

AMERICA TODAY: AN EXCHANGE

Norman Birnbaum (Comment). Reprinted with permission of Norman Birnbaum.

"The Neoconservatives" by Amitai Etzioni. Reprinted with permission of Amitai Etzioni.

"The Responsibility of Scientists" copyright 1981 by Andrei Sakharov. English translation courtesy of Khronika Press.

"Thunder on the Left" by Morris Dickstein. Reprinted with permission of Morris Dickstein.

"Letter from Israel" by Shlomo Avineri. Reprinted with permission of Shlomo Avineri.

"Israeli Letter" by Robert S. Wistrich. Reprinted with permission of Robert S. Wistrich.

"Gratitude to Our Former Rulers" by Vassily Aksyonov. Reprinted with permission of Vassily Aksyonov.

"The Polish Spring" by Jeffrey Herf. Reprinted with permission of Jeffrey Herf.

"No Third Way" by Ralph Dahrendorf. Reprinted with permission of Ralph Dahrendorf.

"The End of Communism?" by Paul Hollander. Reprinted with permission of Paul Hollander.

"Intellectuals and the Failure of Communism" by Walter Laqueur. Reprinted with permission of Walter Laqueur.

"Soft Totalitarianism" by Steven Marcus. Reprinted with permission of Steven Marcus.

"American Identities" by Conor Cruise O'Brien. Reprinted with permission of Conor Cruise O'Brien.

"Romania's Mystical Revolutionaries" by Vladimir Tismaneanu. Reprinted with permission of Vladimir Tismaneanu.

Partisan Review has been the most influential American literary cultural journal for much of the 20th century. Throughout, its circulation was small, but it has been read by every leading intellectual and opinion maker, and by quite a few academics; it never was financially safe, but has continued to survive; it stayed away from all party affiliation but has been read, however reluctantly, by pundits of all stripes; it eschewed trendy politics, but was scrutinized by partisans of both the left and the right. Although the magazine never focuses on everyday politics, the editors have always considered politics in its deepest, theoretical sense. When it was unfashionable to critically explore left-liberal beliefs, *Partisan Review* lent its page to the discussion of such questions as communist practices, repression in the Soviet Union, the Moscow trials, World War II, Vietnam, the successive new radicalisms, and the differing nuances of conservatism. The editors braved many an attack by both the left and the right. And they never expected to be proven correct so soon by the disintegration of the Soviet Union—when all they had said about communism was borne out by events. In other words, they went against the grain, and were vindicated.

William Phillips and Philip Rahv, the magazine's founding fathers, were convinced that political interests should not affect literary values. Because they were certain that, ultimately, the voice of the intellect would win out, that momentary expedience might prevail in the short run but not over the long haul, they paid attention to large forces and movements. They always were on the lookout for astute, nonconformist opinions. These might be expressed in fiction and poetry as well as in polemical essays. But they were adamant in keeping art and politics apart because they had

Introduction

become painfully aware of the lethal effect of socialist realism on the creativity of writers and artists. They made sure that the magazine would maintain its own sense of direction while keeping its pages open to conflicting views.

To indicate the gist of these views and concerns, I have assembled here a sampling of the political essays *Partisan Review* has published over the past sixty years. In that time, the magazine has served as a political barometer of our age. Phillips and Rahv met at the offices of New York's John Reed Club in 1934, where they had gone to meet other writers. The John Reed Clubs were under the umbrella of the Communist Party, though officially independent of it, and aimed to enlist artists and writers in furthering the cause. Like many others during the Depression, Phillips and Rahv were in favor of drastic economic, social, and political reforms; and they set out to explore the possibility of advancing their radical, Marxist ideals, of inducing readers to think more openly, with the help of inventive writing. To do so, they started *Partisan Review* in 1934. They raised the necessary funds by arranging a lecture by John Strachey, a prominent British Communist, which netted them $800—enough to keep them going for the first year. Soon, however, they realized that some members of the party expected them, for the most part, to print material that would further the party line—by explicitly rallying the working classes. But they were drawn to issues posed by modernism—by T. S. Eliot, Kafka, Thomas Mann—and eschewed socialist realism and propaganda. Their disenchantment coincided more or less with the dissolution of the John Reed Clubs throughout the country in 1936. Phillips and Rahv were close enough to the inner circle of the party to be aware that the orders had come from Moscow. (Kremlin policy had shifted to creating a "Popular Front" of all leftist and socialist parties.)

This alerted Phillips and Rahv to the secret and subversive domination by the Communist International—the Comintern—of Communist parties around the world and to the ruthless tactics their people were wont to use. They became anti-communist and were determined that the new *Partisan Review* would be a wholly independent publication. Their 1937 *Editorial Statement*, the first selection in this anthology, best describes how they expected to carve out their autonomous, anticommunist position, to avoid conformities on both the right and the left, and to further both modernism and Marxism.

From Phillips's *A Partisan View: Five Decades of the Literary Life* (1983) as well as from Dwight Macdonald's papers in the Yale University Library we learn that Phillips and Rahv resolved to collaborate and publish this independent magazine after a raucous discussion that lasted an entire Sunday, at Phillips's house. Phillips and Rahv were joined by an editorial board consisting of Dwight Macdonald, a journalist, Mary McCarthy, a young, talented writer just out of Vassar, Fred Dupee, a literary critic, and George L. K. Morris, a painter who was in a position to help finance the venture.

Contrary to current lore, they did not embark on a publication by or for "New York Jewish intellectuals," but were reaching out to new, modern talents, and especially to European writers and thinkers. Except for Phillips and Rahv, the editors were not Jewish, and they all wanted to explore and advance modernism, to deprovincialize American letters. All of them had had their own love-hate relationships with the communists. They were young, full of enthusiasm, and none of them imagined that they were launching a magazine that would last for over sixty years, or that either they themselves or the magazine might become the subjects for scores of dissertations, books and articles.

The December 1937 issue is an example of what was to follow: a striking mixture of literary expressions—from stories by Delmore Schwartz, "In Dreams Begin Responsibilities" and James T. Farrell, "Mrs. O'Flaherty and Lizz," to poems by Wallace Stevens, "The Dwarf," and James Agee, "Lyrics," to theater criticism by Mary McCarthy and serious evaluations of "Flaubert's Politics" by Edmund Wilson and of Ignazio Silone's *Fontamara* by Lionel Abel. Macdonald's "Laugh and Lie Down" takes on the *New Yorker* for its philistinism, its writers who "prune their talents into a certain shape," and its "cocktail party tone," set by editors who "would have considered Mark Twain too crude and Heine too high-brow." The trenchant book reviews that follow undercut literary and political superficialities. Among others, Sidney Hook concludes that Kenneth Burke's writing is "in the style in which weak men of minor talent make a bid for acceptance to the side they think will win"; Philip Rahv judges that *To Have and Have Not* is Ernest Hemingway's "least successful novel. . . . emancipation from the most elementary bourgeois illusions is in itself no great achievement, unless it is but the first step in a development that leads one to perceive the world of materialist relations, and of men themselves"; and Lionel Trilling demonstrates why the novels by Robert Briffault, which "try to educate both his hero and ourselves to revolution" are vulgar, splenetic and ultimately dangerous: because he "wants not so much a liberated humanity as a sterilized humanity and it would gladly make a wasteland if it could call the silence peace."

I have indicated the flavor of this first issue to suggest to the reader of this anthology that *Partisan Review* then—and even more so later—was not what we now understand as a political publication, even though its editors were staunchly anticommunist while remaining critical of the excesses of capitalism. However, the politics of anticommunism were made explicit in the last two pages of this issue, in the "Ripostes," answers to slander of the editors by the Communist Party that convey the virulent political polemics that prevailed in the 1930s.

Between 1937 and 1940, Hans Arp, Elizabeth Bishop, R. P. Blackmur, Louise Bogan, Max Brod, James Burnham, Eleanor Clark, John Dos Passos, Paul Goodman, Randall Jarrell, Victor Serge, Ignazio Silone and Gertrude Stein were among the growing list of contributors, some of them on a regular basis. The magazine printed a number of Rosa Luxemburg's "Letters from Prison" (translated by Eleanor Clark), Franz Kafka's "Bloomfeld, An Elderly Bachelor" (translated by Philip Norton) and "In the Penal Colony" (translated by Eugene Jolas), and "Second Thoughts on the USSR" by André Gide. George L. K. Morris regularly covered the art scene; Macdonald the movies; and McCarthy the theater. Phillips, Rahv, and Dupee continued to treat diverse aspects of contemporary literary works and the prevailing politics. Dupee's essay "The English Literary Left" is an early example of the sort of cultural comparisons the magazine would continue to further. "Ripostes" to the ad hominem attacks on *Partisan Review* and its editors appeared in nearly every issue. The *New Masses* perceived the magazine to be as formidable an opponent as fascism. Katherine Anne Porter commented: "I am not convinced that everyone who has a quarrel with the *New Masses* is per se a Trotskyist or indeed anti-Soviet" 4(4): 60. The *New Masses*, however, kept up their vile attacks in the name of the working classes, and worked to destroy all enemies on its left. The editors were sensitive to Trotsky's plight and to his exile in Mexico. Except for Macdonald, they did not become Trotskyist, although they printed his literary and political criticism.

By 1939, Harold Rosenberg with "Myth and History" and Clement Greenberg with "Avant-garde and Kitsch" began to write art and cultural criticism and the editors began to debate politics in every issue, in a section called "This Quarter." Only one of these contributions states that it is written by Rahv. Most of the others appear to explore the different positions held by the editors: they all were opinionated armchair politicians, and their polemics reflect the ways in which each of them assessed the political realities in his or her way during a dangerous and explosive period—not reaching consensus but exploring all the options and possible consequences. "A Letter to *The New Republic*" exemplifies their ongoing fight against closet Communists. Stephen Spender's "September Journal" is an example of their attempts to stay in touch with the democratic forces in Europe. And James Farrell's "Leon Trotsky" is a tribute to the man murdered by the Soviets.

Even before 1940 the editors strongly condemned German fascism; they commented on fascist elements in France; and they criticized the excesses of capitalism in America. After the Stalin-Hitler pact and again after the Russo-German division of Poland, the editors clearly lumped the Soviets with the German aggressors. They continued to distrust the Communists at home, marveling at the flexibility with which the Communists moved, overnight, from their militant antifascism to pacifism and a neutral stance, and after Hitler's invasion of the Soviet Union to all-out support of the war. By the time the Germans had overrun Czechoslovakia, Denmark, Norway, Holland, Belgium and France, and England was being bombarded nightly, the editors agreed with President Roosevelt that Hitler must be stopped. But Macdonald argued that we ought to stay out of the war while also maintaining that he was not an isolationist, and that fascism would spread to America unless "the present democratic capitalist system is replaced by a democratic socialist government of the working classes" 7(4): 250. He also held that "the present German economy cannot be called 'capitalistic' [but] is a new and different kind of system" 8(3): 198–220. Phillips recalls that Rahv said ironically that if Germany had abandoned capitalism the newspapers would have reported it. "Ten Propositions on the War" indicates Macdonald's and Clement Greeenberg's thinking. Rahv felt strongly that Hitler had to be defeated and argued against Macdonald in "Ten Propositions and Eight Errors." By 1942, the editors printed a "Statement" to the effect that they "have no editorial line on the war, only individual positions." Basically, Phillips agreed with Rahv, but he said that he hesitated to send young men to be killed (he had had polio as a child and knew he would not be drafted). By the summer of 1943, the editors came to blows over this issue. Soon after, Macdonald left *Partisan Review* for personal and political reasons, arguing that the magazine wasn't political enough. Between 1944 and 1949 he published *Politics*.

The editors were intellectually attuned to Europe, especially to England and France. In addition to Spender, they invited other contributions from abroad. George Orwell wrote the first of many "London Letters" in April 1941, which informed *Partisan Review* readers of how the English were faring during the Blitz—when military defeat seemed in the offing. The following issue contained two "Anonymous" contributions about political and cultural tendencies in Paris by recent emigrés. (Among other items, T. S. Eliot's poem, "The Dry Salvages," art criticism by Paul Klee, and Saul Bellow's story, "Two Morning Monologues," also appeared in that issue.) Now the editors chose to review a preponderance of books dealing with fascism and capitalism by such renowned figures as Karl Korsch, C. Wright Mills, and Melvin Lasky, as well as by the editors themselves. As they disagreed more and more about what positions to take on the European debacle, they continued to fill the pages of the magazine with excellent fiction, art, literary and theater criticism, and poetry. Of course, the war was their major concern.

Some of the Europeans who had been contacts moved to New York. Among them were Parisian painters and sculptors, and emigré intellectuals such as Hannah Arendt and Victor Serge. Talented young writers and artists such as Saul Bellow, Isaac Rosenfeld, Lionel Abel, and Robert Motherwell also entered the original circle around the magazine.

By 1944, the editorial board consisted of only Phillips, Rahv, and Delmore Schwartz. (All along, some collaborators were kept on the masthead long after they stopped collaborating, while volunteers contributed without having their names on the masthead.) Political pieces, except in the form of book reviews, Orwell's letters, and an occasional essay on Marxism, such as "Lenin's Heir" by James Burnham, became rare. Moreover, ever since Hitler had declared war on

Stalin and the Soviet Union became our ally, the *New Masses* was supporting the war effort, so that this ideological enemy was for a time on the same side, and there were no more occasions for "Ripostes."

Immediately after the Germans were ousted from France, the magazine printed Sartre's "Case for Responsible Literature" and a "Paris Letter" by H. J. Kaplan—both of these on writing rather than politics. By the end of 1945, Freud's "Dostoevsky and Parricide" was for the first time made available in English. Stephen Spender reported on his impressions of the Germany he had just revisited; H. J. Kaplan sent another "Letter from Paris" describing the political landscape; and Hannah Arendt introduced Heidegger's philosophy. A section of Sartre's *La Nausée* appeared in the first issue of 1946, and a good part of the second issue was devoted to French writing by, among others, Camus, Valéry, Malraux, Genet, Queneau, and Leiris, as well as Sartre. In the third issue of that year, the editors collaborated on an editorial, "The Liberal Fifth Column," which lays out their views of the American political landscape and warns against the dangers of trusting the Communists. A rejoinder by Heinz Eulau followed.

During 1947, the editors solicited articles on "The Future of Socialism," by Sidney Hook, Granville Hicks, Arthur Schlesinger, George Orwell, and Victor Serge, as well as a "London Letter" by Arthur Koestler, and a "Paris Letter" by Nicola Chiaromonte. The latter, as well as Melvin Lasky's "Letter from Berlin," deal with politics rather than the literary and art scenes. In 1948, at the suggestion of an "angel" who provided funding, *Partisan Review* started to come out monthly for two and a half years, and then bimonthly, and now included more criticism on art as well as on architecture and music. In 1949, Irving Howe wrote on "The Culture Conference" of the Communists and fellow-travelers held at New York's Waldorf Hotel, and Sidney Hook published a "Report on the International Day Against Dictatorship and War." These were the first signs that the impending Cold War was also to be fought on the cultural front. "The Berlin Congress for Cultural Freedom," commented on by Sidney Hook, was held as a counterpoint to the Russians' endeavors.

At the beginning of the 1950s, *Partisan Review* printed a lecture by Diana Trilling on "A Communist and His Ideals," Raymond Aron's "The Leninist Myth of Imperialism," and introduced Czeslaw Milosz's much-reproduced novelistic indictment of communism, "Murti Bing," just after he left his post as Poland's cultural attaché and remained in the West. The book reviews contained the usual political bite; James Baldwin wrote on Negro life, and Ralph Ellison's "Invisible Man: Prologue to a Novel," appeared. Starting with the May/June issue of 1952, the editors printed replies to the questions they had been asking themselves, and then had posed to prominent American thinkers, on "Our Country and Our Culture." Most of the answers inevitably addressed cultural rather than political issues. The responses of Norman Mailer, David Riesman, Lionel Trilling, C. Wright Mills, and Arthur Schlesinger, Jr. are among the most political.

In 1954, the magazine published an attack on "This Age of Conformity" by Irving Howe during Joseph McCarthy's crusades against communists. James Burnham was asked to resign from the Advisory Board of the magazine because he was pro-McCarthy; Macdonald criticized two pro-McCarthy books; and Phillips and Rahv refused to disclose information about the John Reed Club when called before a grand jury in Washington: they were both anti-McCarthy *and* anticommunist. Diana Trilling's essay on "The Oppenheimer Case" explores the complexities of these issues, particularly as they appeared in the thinking of the famous scientist who had been accused of disloyalty.

In the fall of 1956, *Partisan Review* published "Communism Now: Three Views" by Isaac Deutscher, G. L. Arnold (George Lichtheim's early pseudonym), and Irving Howe. During the following years, there were a few accounts commenting on the decline of American educational standards, and a number of contributions about the politics and dilemmas of writing under totalitarian rule behind the iron curtain. James Baldwin's "Letter From the South" is one of the major intimations that intellectuals' political questions were starting to focus less on Communism and more on racism. Macdonald's now classic "Masscult and Midcult" appraised the changes that had taken place in American culture, and essays on psychoanalysis continued to be printed. Richard Crossman provided a British perspective on "Socialism and the Cold War," and Jean Bloch-Michel reported on "Frenchmen's Division Over Algeria."

In 1960, Doris Lessing started to offer stories to the magazine. In the first issue of 1962, the editors organized a symposium on "The Cold War and the West" with fifteen contributors, among them Hannah Arendt, Mary McCarthy, Hans Morgenthau, and Norman Podhoretz. And Norman Birnbaum commented on "The Coming End of Anti-Communism." This essay led the American Committee for Cultural Freedom to sever its relations with the magazine. Daniel Bell explained "The National Style of the American Right."

In the fall of 1963, Phillips took *Partisan Review* to Rutgers University (Rahv already had been at Brandeis University for nearly a decade), and Richard Poirier, then Department Chair of English at Rutgers, was made a senior editor. This move from New York to New Brunswick, New Jersey, however, did not alter the previous focus on literature, poetry, and the arts nor the general tenor of contributions. Still, Poirier's softer views of left-wing currents, which at least in part led him to write a rather negative review of Podhoretz's *Making It* in the following year, inevitably caused certain underlying tensions among the editors (later exacerbated by Poirier's scathing review of Saul Bellow's *Herzog*). Then, too, Lionel Abel's review of Hannah Arendt's *Eichmann in Jerusalem* provoked a bevy of attacks and counterattacks, all of them inspired by political stances.

In the fall of 1964, *Partisan Review* printed twelve comments on the significance of Senator Goldwater as a presidential candidate; an essay by R. H. S.
Crossman on "Radicals of the Right"; and Susan Sontag's "Notes on Camp"—
which named a theretofore unnamed sensibility, "a certain mode of estheti-
cism," that had become part of American culture and, however indirectly, was
an indication of an as yet not explicit politics, and, in part, announced the onset
of postmodernism.

The move to Rutgers coincided with a lessening of the magazine's anticommunism. Now, the interest of the country, and of intellectuals, shifted to
American policy on Vietnam and students' opposition to it. For a short time,
Phillips did not totally resist the tide. He sympathized with the students, especially with their high spirits. In the following issues of the magazine during 1965,
there were contributions on "Is There New Radicalism?" by Nat Hentoff and
Michael Harrington, and a short position statement on Vietnam—with agreements and disagreements with this view in the subsequent issue. By 1967, the editors invited a symposium on "What's Happening in America." Among the
responses H. Stuart Hughes's was the most leftist; Susan Sontag's the most pessimistic; and Sidney Hook's the most optimistic. The positions taken by the
respondents to this symposium clearly presage the inescapable split between the
so-called left and right—which at first would demarcate opposing opinions and
later would end up in loud polemics. By focusing on these issues in *Partisan
Review*, the magazine was deemed to be on the right by the left and on the left by
the right. That was the moment too, when it was revealed that the CIA had been
funding intellectual magazines in Europe; the editors objected to such funding.
In "Learning from the Beatles," Richard Poirier put the Beatles on nearly the
same plane as T. S. Eliot. Soon thereafter, Phillips began to get annoyed at not
having opposed this sort of fusion, although he too was pulled along by the irresistible tug of the now overwhelming wave of the politics of culture.

Partisan Review opened 1968 with Robert J. Lifton's "Protean Man"—the
modern individual he deemed to be forever responsive to forces outside himself.
The magazine also printed a piece on French structuralism; a symposium on
American black power; and "Seven Interviews" on the Columbia University student rebellion—whose shortcomings and anomalies, as Lionel Trilling concluded, were not synonymous with the conflicts of society or of a particular government. And Phillips wrote a short comment about the assassination of Senator
Robert F. Kennedy. In 1969, Peter Brooks reported on the aftermath of the student uprisings in France. But an anonymous piece by "A.J." on the Soviet invasion of Czechoslovakia and the consequences of repression served as a reminder
that politics can be more than just aspects of culture.

A year later, in 1970, Phillips began to print short "Remarks" on political topics in nearly every issue. He commented, for instance, on the fact that Israel was

being attacked by both the left and the right, and on the "Politics of Polemics." Around that time, Richard Poirier decided to take a less active role. Philip Rahv, who after his move to Brandeis University had gradually drifted away, started another magazine, *Modern Occasions*.

In 1972, the editors held a symposium on "The New Cultural Conservatism" which was summarized by Phillips in "Looking Backward." At that time, too, dissident writers from behind the Iron Curtain (who often were not trusted by either the American left or the right) such as the pseudonymous V. Nadaje started to appear more and more frequently. Among them were Leszek Kolakowski and Vadim Belotserkovsky. Still, few political pieces were being submitted. Experimental fiction as well as literature, criticism, and art remained center stage.

In 1975, Hans Morgenthau wrote on "The Decline of the West" and the following year saw Robert Lekachman on "Capitalism: The End of the Journey," Lewis Coser on "A View From England," and Alain Touraine on "From Crisis to Critique." All these pieces were appraisals of a general malaise rather than the sort of political engagement that had prevailed in earlier decades. An exchange of letters between William Phillips and William Barrett, "While America Burns," is an assessment of what happened in the interim.

In 1978, the magazine moved to Boston University; the editors and other writers endorsed Jimmy Carter for President; they arranged a discussion among Irving Howe, Morris Dickstein, and Hilton Kramer on "New York and the National Culture" moderated by William Phillips; and they published a comment on "The Neoconservatives" by Amitai Etzioni. In the following year, we find the proceedings of a heated meeting on "Eurocommunism," which focused on whether or not, and to what extent, the various European communist parties were independent of the Soviet Union. (We now know that they all were financed by Moscow.) Soon thereafter, the editors arranged yet another symposium — on the meaning of the emerging neoconservatism.

In this period, the opinionated debates that years before had been held, for the most part, in Phillips's living room, were now being conducted between magazines, as the split between "left-wing" and "right-wing" intellectuals became too sharp to tolerate under one roof. However, as most intellectuals were by then employed by universities, and some by the media, they were influenced by the leftist turn these institutions had taken ever since the late 1960s. Increasingly the left held sway and continued to make inroads in the culture even as the American presidency went to the Republicans.

Partisan Review remained committed to pointing to the totalitarian danger of communism while also providing a middle ground for debates, and not tipping too much to either side. As Phillips put it, we had to "keep our sanity." Dennis Wrong's essay on "The Rise and Fall(?) of Neoconservatism" summed up many of the dilemmas. Jan Kavan's "Czech Letter" showed in stark contrast the more practical preoccupations by Europeans with communism. Andrei Sakharov wrote on "The Responsibility of Scientists," and I reported, in a "Letter from Italy," on the underlying connections that motivated the attempt on Pope John Paul II's life. In 1982, in addition to Shlomo Avinieri's "Letter from Israel," the magazine solicited a number of essays on "New Polish Writing," printed Fritz Stern's "Clio in China," and Gerald Graff's "Criticism of Textual Leftism"—the cultural politics he would so insistently advocate a few years later. Morris Dickstein wrote on "Thunder on the Left" and in 1983, Robert Wistrich sent in an "Israeli Letter."

A conference of Soviet and East European dissidents, "Writers in Exile," whom *Partisan Review* brought together for the first time, cannot be reproduced here, except for the leading contribution by Vassily Aksyonov. This contact with intellectuals who had been persecuted for voicing their ideas taught us that even American anticommunists did not fully grasp what lasting damage life under a totalitarian regime can do to individuals. As more and more dissident writers were able to leave the Soviet Union and its satellites, *Partisan Review* brought out their fiction and thereby called attention to the many abuses of communism which in America even long after Stalin were being downplayed or ignored.

During the 1980s, political opinion among intellectuals ran high, but reflection was at a low. The editors decided to air the strong disagreements among themselves in print. In 1985, William Phillips commented on "Stalinism of the Right" and soon thereafter on "The Death of Socialism." In the following year, Ronald Radosh reported on the conflict in Nicaragua. The editors organized a symposium on the "Star Wars" antimissile defense program a year later, and printed two accounts of the political disaster in Lebanon. Subsequently, they published an assessment of Mexican politics by Enrique Krauze, and the transcript of a talk on "The Politics of French Intellectuals" by Dominique Schnapper, as well as her "Letter from Paris." "Hungary After Glasnost," in 1989, was yet another symposium.

After the fall of the Berlin wall, in November 1989, it seemed that communism had come to an end, and the central political debates in the magazine tended to focus on "post-communism." Craig Calhoun, for instance, commented on the Chinese students' revolt, Jeffrey Herf on "The Polish Spring," and Ralf Dahrendorf argued that there was "No Third Way"—which some Europeans, especially the German left, had been advocating for years, and which equated the problems of Eastern communism with those of Western consumerism.

By 1990, Paul Hollander speculated on "The End of Communism," and Walter Laqueur commented on "Intellectuals and the Failure of Communism." A number of others gave various accounts of the economic, social, and political problems Central Europe was facing after the collapse of the communist experiment. The magazine also published a special issue on "The Culture of the

University," which brought together the so-called right and left in order to debate the dominance of leftist pieties that had taken over American educational institutions.

In 1992, the editors again organized a symposium to delve into issues of American schooling, "Education Beyond Politics." They were searching for a means of stopping the drift toward mediocrity, the downward slide of intellectual culture. The last and expanded issue of 1992 was dedicated to a conference I organized at Rutgers University on "Intellectuals and Social Change in Central and Eastern Europe." During the first session the speakers were Czeslaw Milosz, Saul Bellow, Ralph Ellison, and Joseph Brodsky. George Konrad, Doris Lessing, Susan Sontag, Adam Michnick, Hans Magnus Enzensberger, Tatyana Tolstaya, and Adam Zagajewski were among the others at later sessions. These writers discussed sharply the political questions related to the future of their countries and they explained the nearly insuperable predicaments they all found themselves in after the fall of the Soviet empire. Now that the blinkers had been removed from the eyes of the American left, it not only was easier to receive information about what used to happen behind the iron curtain, and how alignments were changing, but also to get people to write about these subjects which until recently had been obscured by rose-tinted glasses.

At the end of 1993, *Partisan Review* assembled a symposium on "The Politics of Political Correctness" which, once again, dealt with academic politics and its debilitating, anti-intellectual consequences, as discussed in Steven Marcus's essay, "Soft Totalitarianism." In the following issue, Stephen Koch's "Bloomsbury and Espionage" exposed the international network of Soviet spying which could not be fully proven during the Cold War while all "hard" information was kept secret. Slavenka Drakulic described the underlying reasons for the political and military battles in the former Yugoslavia. Now that Communism seems to have been licked, more contributions focused on American cultural politics, which over the years had become nastier and more polarized. Among these was a symposium, "Is There a Cure for Anti-Semitism?," my own comment on the National Endowment for the Humanities, Conor Cruise O'Brien on "American Identities," and Irving Louis Horowitz's critique of American sociology.

In this brief overview, I have indicated that even after the outbreak of World War II in Europe, the editors of *Partisan Review* did not forget what they had learned during their brush with communism. At the same time, a general benevolent attitude toward leftist thought, bolstered by American liberalism, concern for the underdog, populism, and a genuine interest in furthering the ideals of America's Founding Fathers, dominated the culture of the country. All of these influences have been reflected in a variety of ways in the thinking and interests of many in the universities. *Partisan Review* tried to remain on top of all these strands of thought—by sharply analyzing what did not readily meet the eye. As political and cultural concerns in the country changed and the threat of communism was replaced by various intellectual fashions, academic specialties, and therapeutic preoccupations, and as the politics of culture moved to the fore, the *Partisan Review* editors' focus shifted and they printed material reflecting these changes. Changing with the times, the magazine succeeded in staying the course between the right and the left (terms which themselves have become less clear), to hold on to what might best be described as the critical edge, and to the ambiguities which distinguish intellectuals from politicians.

This anthology of political commentary from *Partisan Review* represents only about one percent of all the contributions the magazine has published during its first sixty years. I have necessarily left out selections belonging to other genres—fiction, poetry, reviews, and interviews. And I could choose no more than the shortest contribution on politics by any one person, and regretfully had to omit many an important commentator. I have had to ignore that the magazine discovered many of the century's most talented writers, and published the most outstanding literary and art criticism, as well as such poets as T. S. Eliot, Spender, Berryman, Auden, and Lowell.

In fact, being published in *Partisan Review* frequently has lent cachet. For some it has become a stepping stone to recognition; for others, it has led to tenure in a university. Intellectuals behind the Iron Curtain read *Partisan Review* in *samizdat*, as many later told us. The magazine has stayed on top of new thought while being critical of trendiness. For instance, it introduced French ideas to America after 1945, and again in the 1960s, but turned into an early critic of these ideas when they were being simplified and misapplied, or led to excesses in our universities. And it paid attention to dissident writing from the former Eastern bloc. Throughout, the editors have been on the alert to detect sham, to expose thinking that might lead to dangerous, irresponsible politics. The editors as well as those European contributors to the magazine who had first-hand experiences of communism did not hesitate to go against the tide when it was modish to praise the Soviet Union. They rejected the facile slogan, "the personal is the political," which reduces the larger political issues to individual preferences. For *Partisan Review*'s explicit reaching out to all of intellectual life remains anathema to interest-based, factional politics. *Partisan Review* continues to create a viable ground—not centrist, but one that we hope will hold.

Edith Kurzweil
July 19, 1995

A PARTISAN
Century

Editorial Statement

As our readers know, the tradition of aestheticism has given way to a literature which, for its origin and final justification, looks beyond itself and deep into the historic process. But the forms of literary editorship, at once exacting and adventurous, which characterized the magazines of the aesthetic revolt, were of definite cultural value; and these forms *Partisan Review* will wish to adapt to the literature of the new period.

Any magazine, we believe, that aspires to a place in the vanguard of literature today, will be revolutionary in tendency; but we are also convinced that any such magazine will be unequivocally independent. *Partisan Review* is aware of its responsibility to the revolutionary movement in general, but we disclaim obligation to any of its organized political expressions. Indeed we think that the cause of revolutionary literature is best served by a policy of no commitments to any political party. Thus our underscoring of the factor of independence is based, not primarily on our differences with any one group, but on the conviction that literature in our period should be free of all factional dependence.

There is already a tendency in America for the more conscious social writers to identify themselves with a single organization, the Communist Party; with the result that they grow automatic in their political responses but increasingly less responsible in an artistic sense. And the Party literary critics, equipped with the zeal of vigilantes, begin to consolidate into aggressive political-literary amalgams as many tendencies as possible and to outlaw all dissenting opinion. This projection on the cultural field of factionalism in politics makes for literary cleavages which, in most instances, have little to do with literary issues, and which are more and more provocative of a ruinous bitterness among writers. Formerly associated with the Communist Party, *Partisan Review* strove from the first against its drive to equate the interests of literature with those of factional politics. Our reappearance on an independent basis signifies our conviction that the totalitarian trend is inherent in that movement and that it can no longer be combatted from within.

But many other tendencies exist in American letters, and these, we think, are turning from the senseless disciplines of the official Left to shape a new movement. The old movement will continue and, to judge by present indications, it will be reinforced more and more by academicians from the universities, by yesterday's celebrities and today's philistines. Armed to the teeth with slogans of revolutionary prudence, its official critics will revive the petty-bourgeois tradition of gentility, and with each new tragedy on the historic level they will call the louder for a literature of good cheer. Weak in genuine literary authority but equipped with all the economic and publicity powers of an authentic cultural bureaucracy, the old regime will seek to isolate the new by performing upon it the easy surgery of political falsification. Because the writers of the new grouping aspire to independence in politics as well as in art, they will be identified with fascism, sometimes directly, sometimes through the convenient medium of "Trotskyism." Every effort, in short, will be made to excommunicate the new generation, so that their writing and their politics may be regarded as making up a kind of diabolic totality; which would render unnecessary any sort of rational discussion of the merits of either.

Do we exaggerate? On the contrary, our prediction as to the line the old regime will take is based on the first maneuvers of a campaign which has already begun. Already, before it has appeared, *Partisan Review* has been subjected to a series of attacks in the Communist Party press; already, with no regard for fact—without, indeed, any relevant facts to go by—they have attributed gratuitous political designs to *Partisan Review* in an effort to confuse the primarily literary issue between us.

But *Partisan Review* aspires to represent a new and dissident generation in American letters; it will not be dislodged from its independent position by any political campaign against it. And without ignoring the importance of the official movement as a sign of the times we shall know how to estimate its authority in literature. But we shall also distinguish, wherever possible, between the tendencies of this faction itself and the work of writers associated with it. For our editorial accent falls chiefly on culture and its broader social determinants. Conformity to a given social ideology or to a prescribed attitude or technique will not be asked of our writers. On the contrary, our pages will be open to any tendency which is relevant to literature in our time. Marxism in culture, we think, is first of all an instrument of analysis and evaluation; and if, in the last instance, it prevails over other disciplines, it does so through the medium of democratic controversy. Such is the medium that *Partisan Review* will want to provide in its pages.   December 1937

• Ripostes

Independence Plus Literature Equals Fascism

Since the first announcement of the new *Partisan Review*—and, of course, long before anything could be known of its character or contents—the press of the Communist Party has savagely, at times hysterically, attacked the magazine and its editors. These polemics have been entirely political in nature. Their cultural level is suggested by their headings: "Falsely Labeled Goods" (*New Masses*), "A Literary Snake Sheds His Skin for Trotsky" (*Daily Worker*, Oct. 12),

"Trotskyist Schemers Exposed" (*Daily Worker*, Oct. 19), "No Quarter to Trotskyists—Literary or Otherwise" (*Daily Worker*, Oct. 20). In the language of V. J. Jerome, one of the Party's deviation experts, we are "of the same ilk that murdered Kirov, that turned the guns on the backs of Loyalist civilians in Spain and betrayed the Army's front line, that have been caught red-handed in plots with the Gestapo and Japanese militarists to dismember the Soviet Union." What we, in our innocence, conceived of as a literary magazine has become the organ of the murderers of Kirov. Such is the result of refusing to accept the party line in literature.

It would be tedious to examine in detail the "charges" hurled at us by the Party press. They are based in each case either on misconception or falsification. Two examples of the latter may be given. The *Daily Worker* charged that our colleague, F. W. Dupee, while he was literary editor of the *New Masses* last winter "had the gall to demand freedom of expression for attacks against the Soviet Union and against the Communist movement." This is a reference to Dupee's efforts to relax the pressure of the party line in the book review section. Our fellow editor, Philip Rahv, in an unpublished essay which the Party somehow laid hands on, wrote: "The literary Left-wing movement is particularly native to New York, for its underlying philosophy, Marxism, is a product of European thought." This observation, accurate to the point of being positively banal, the *Daily Worker* quotes, taking the precaution to omit the word "literary" and thus extend its scope to include the New Deal and the C.I.O. Nor does it fail to point out the moral: "This is a typical counter-revolutionary line, which unites its exponent with Hearst and the Liberty Leaguers, who also try to smear Communism as 'foreign.' Rahv's services to the fascists should brand him and his undertakings for what they are in the eyes of all true workers and of all honest writers." According to this line of reasoning, the real friend of fascism was Marx himself who, not foreseeing that Communism would become twentieth century Americanism, was gauche enough not to be born in a Kentucky log cabin.

The second category—misconception—is best represented by Comrade V. J. Jerome, who blasts away for three apoplectic columns at *Partisan Review*, which he conceives to be a fortress, a veritable bristling arsenal of fascism. His attack he bases on the same unsound premise that all these attacks rest on: that the professed literary aims of *Partisan Review* are merely a smoke screen for its "real" object, which is to spread Trotskyist propaganda. That we do not consider ourselves "Trotskyists" and that Partisan Review has been founded precisely to fight the tendency to confuse literature and party politics—these facts Comrade Jerome chooses to ignore. He prefers namecalling—and what names! "Slanderers of the working class . . . turncoats . . . great revolutionaries (irony here) . . . scribblers . . . amateur literati . . . tyros . . . agents provocateurs . . . strikebreakers. . . ."

In one passage Comrade Jerome, with his peculiar flair for melodrama, pictured us as being "wined and dined as high personalities" by the appreciative bourgeoisie. This puzzles us. We respect Comrade Jerome as an expert in wining and dining, considering his past services as Commissar to Hollywood, where he was, as we hear, lavishly entertained. But nothing so glamorous has yet happened to any of us. We hope the bourgeoisie will realize the value of our services before long and do its duty. When the gay round of cocktail parties and buffet suppers begins, we shall be glad to ask Comrade Jerome along. Of course, he mustn't expect too much—New York isn't Hollywood.

One must smile at the sweating, blundering zeal of the Party's commissars of culture, who bring to bear against *Partisan Review* such a ponderous machinery of polemic. But there is more in the situation than humor. It is painful to us, as radicals, to realize the intellectual bankruptcy of the Communist Party leadership. One of our motives in reviving *Partisan Review* was to struggle against the "partyization" of leftwing letters. We hoped to demonstrate the degenerative effect of imposing a Party Line on Literature. The press of the Communist Party is supplying us, gratis, with some excellent examples of just what we mean.

THAT MAN IS HERE AGAIN

Ever since Granville Hicks made his debut as a Marxist critic, he seems to have regarded himself as a superintendent of American writing. No sooner had he announced his own conversion than he proceeded to submit American writers since the Civil War to an examination in Marxism, which, of course, most of them flunked. Subsequently he brought his critical method up to date by evaluating contemporary writers according to their proximity to the official Communist Party; he banished to a literary Siberia those who had other political beliefs or were truly independent; he laid down a series of rules for young and newly converted novelists, and set a quota for the number of magazines which might publish leftwing writing.

One of his chief tasks, however, was to deliver pep-talks to those writers who did not share his blatant cheerfulness—his theory being that the class struggle is expressed in literature as a struggle between pessimism and optimism; and identifying optimism with the future of mankind, he set out on a crusade against gloom in American writing. Thus in a recent review (*New Masses*, October 4) of *New Letters in America*, Hicks stated that he was very much disappointed in this collection because hope was not its keynote. "They could scarcely write more bleakly," says Hicks, "if they were avowed Spenglerians, or felt, with Joseph Wood Krutch, that the triumph of the proletariat would mean the end of civilization"; and "the prose writers express disgust, bitterness, pity, cynicism, but seldom hope." And when you consider that the Spenglerians have in their ranks not only younger writers, but, as Hicks later adds, such well-known figures as Dos Passos, Farrell, Cantwell, and Caldwell, the menace of gloom is very great indeed. True, Hicks does admit that the Spenglerians are by far the more talented writers, and he advocates, therefore, that they be tolerated, but so far as the direction of literature is concerned Hicks takes an unequivocal stand on the side of optimism.

Naturally, no one could be opposed in principle to optimism, so long as it is not mere ideological cheerleading, and it is not difficult to understand why Hicks, whose passion for pigeonholing experience offered him but two alternatives, should have chosen hope in preference to despair. But it requires a critic of Mr. Hicks's simpleminded fanaticism to squeeze the qualities and meanings of literature into such naive categories, and to persuade his readers that the hope of American literature is in such writers as Jack Conroy and Fielding Burke, whom he lists among the apostles of optimism. Then, too, there arises the problem of deviations, for writers who are not pessimists may still not be out-and-out optimists. Would Granville Hicks say that the optimism of Bruce Barton, for example, is good in form but bad in content?

CULTURE AS CONSPIRATOR

Garcia Lorca's career as poet, collector of Spanish folk music and impresario of the native drama was brought to an abrupt and shocking end by a fascist firing-squad in Granada in the early weeks of the Spanish war. Lorca died in his middle thirties: he was already an accomplished poet, in a vein of popular and indigenous expression which contrasted markedly with the Europeanizing tendency of the Madrid intellectuals. And the high degree of sophistication in his work promised a still more mature poetry to come. (For examples of Lorca's work see *Lament for the Death of a Bullfighter*, by Federico Garcia Lorca.) The democratic character of Lorca's poetry leaves in little doubt the general tendency of his political sympathies; yet, at the time of his death, he was not known to have any very definite political convictions. His execution appears, then, to have been the result of some brutal bureaucratic "error" on the part of the Granada fascists. A possible clue to the means by which he became implicated in the antifascist cause has been supplied by Rolfe Humphries (*The Nation*, September 18): Lorca's sister lived in a house owned by the Popular Front mayor of Granada! But, as Mr. Humphries adds, "More probably the fascists recognized in him the kind of person they were eager to get rid of." And whatever the exact circumstances of Lorca's death, we are at liberty to see in it something more than a grievous individual tragedy. If a single poet may be shot down as a political conspirator, so, in effect, may a whole culture.

(Ripostes is a department devoted to brief editorial comment and to communications. Readers are invited to contribute.)   December 1937

• Second Thoughts on the USSR
André Gide

The publication of my book, *Return from the USSR*, has won me a good deal of abuse. Romain Rolland's part in it pained me. Though I have never had much taste for his writing, his moral character, at least, commands my respect. I was distressed because the incident demonstrated how rare it is for a man to reach the end of his life without having previously reached the limit of his powers. The author of *Above the Battle*, would, I believe, pass a harsh judgment on Rolland grown old. This eagle has made his nest, and there he lies.

Besides the vituperation there were a few criticisms made in good faith. It is to answer them that I am writing this. . . .

A superficial survey, a hasty judgment, my book has been called. As if it were not precisely on first sight that the Soviet Union is so attractive! As if one did not have to go deeper before catching sight of the worst!

In the heart of the fruit the worm hides. But when I told you this apple of yours was wormy, you accused me of poor vision, or of not liking apples.

If I had been satisfied to be an admirer, you would certainly not have reproached me with superficiality. Then, however, I would have deserved it.

I have met your criticisms before. They are practically identical with those provoked by my *Trip to the Congo* and my *Return from the Chad*. Then I was found fault with on the grounds that:

(1) the abuses to which I called attention were exceptional and irrelevant;
(2) there was every reason for admiring the present regime, if one would only compare it to the previous regime, to the days before the conquest (I almost said, before the Revolution);
(3) everything I deplored had its profound *raison d'être*, which I had not been equipped to understand—was but a temporary evil in anticipation of a greater good.

At that time, the criticisms, the attacks, the abuse all came from the right; and you, adherents of the left, did not for a minute dream of making a to-do about my confessed "incompetence." You were only too happy to seize upon my statements as long as they fitted in with your ideas, as long as you could make capital of them. And in the same way, today, this incompetence of mine you would never have held against me had I only praised the USSR, and declared that everything there was going rapturously well.

All of this in no way alters the fact (and this is the only thing that matters to me) that subsequently the commissions of inquiry set up in the Congo confirmed all my observations. So now, the quantity of evidence which keeps coming my way, the reports which I have been able to read, the stories of impartial observers (however great "friends of the Soviet Union" they are, or were before they went there to look at it), together bear witness to the reality of my picture of the Soviet Union, together reinforce my fears for it. . . .

One of the most legitimate objections made to my *Return from the USSR* is that it seems to lay too much stress on intellectual questions, which one must be willing to see relegated to second place, so long as other, more pressing problems remain unsolved. The reason for this is that I had felt obliged to include the few speeches I had been persuaded to make in Russia, and which had given rise to some controversy. In such a little book these speeches took up too much space and drew attention to themselves. They date for the most part from the beginning of my trip, from a time when I still believed (yes, I was that naive) that in the Soviet Union it was possible to speak seriously about culture and to debate straightforwardly, from a time when I did not yet realize how primitive and uncertain the social equilibrium was.

But I protest the attitude which has insisted on regarding what I said as the mere special pleading of a literary man. When I spoke of intellectual freedom, I meant something much more general. Science is compromising itself quite as badly as literature by its complaisance to authority.

Such-and-such a scholar finds himself forced to repudiate a theory in which he believed but which had a not-quite-orthodox look. Such-and-such a member of the Academy of Science disavows "his former errors," since they "were susceptible of being used by fascism"—so he himself has just declared in public (*Izvestia*, December 28, 1936). Such a man is compelled to admit the veracity of charges launched, under orders, by a journal like *Izvestia*, which smells out in his researches the dreadful symptoms of "counter-revolutionary delirium."

Eisenstein is halted in the middle of his work. He must acknowledge his "errors," admit that he has made a mistake and that the new film, which he has been two years getting ready and on which two million roubles have already been spent, does not measure up to doctrinal requirements, and was therefore quite rightly banned.

As for justice! Do you think that the last trials in Moscow and Novosibirsk are going to make me regret having written that sentence that infuriates you: "I doubt whether in any other country today, even in Hitler's Germany, the spirit is less free, more cramped, more fearful (terrorized), more enserfed"?

I had for three years been too thoroughly steeped in the literature of Marxism to feel very much out of my element in the Soviet Union. Besides I had read too many accounts of trips, enthusiastic descriptions, apologies. My great mistake was that I believed too willingly in the hymns of praise. This was partly due to the fact that everything I came upon which might have put me on my guard was so clearly bad-tempered in tone. . . . I would more willingly trust love than hate. Yes, I subscribed; I had faith. Likewise, in the Soviet Union I was never so much disturbed to find imperfection as I was to encounter straight off the very prerogatives I wanted to get away from, the privileges I hoped were abolished. Certainly, it seemed natural to me that they would try to treat a guest as well as possible, to give him the best of everything. But what amazed me was the enormous disparity between this "best," and the common lot, that such excessive privilege should exist side by side with a mass standard of living so mediocre or so bad.

Perhaps this is an eccentricity peculiar to my mind and its Protestant conditioning, but at any rate I distrust ideas that pay dividends, and "comfortable" opinions; I mean opinions by which the holder can hope personally to profit.

And I can see very well indeed how much the Soviet government stands to gain from doing the handsome thing by artists and writers, by everybody who could possibly sing its praises—though there may be no definite attempt at corruption. But also I see only too well how the writer stands to gain by endorsing the government and a constitution which favors him to this extent. And so at once I am on my guard. I am afraid of letting myself be bribed. The unheard-of profits they offer me in Russia actually terrify me. I don't go to the Soviet Union to rediscover privileges. Those that were waiting for me there were scandalous.

And why shouldn't I say that?

The Moscow newspapers had informed me that in a few months more than 400,000 copies of my books were sold. I leave it to the reader to calculate the author's royalties. And the fat pay for magazine articles! Had I written a dithyramb on the USSR and on Stalin, what a fortune would have been mine!

Such considerations could not have made me withhold my praise; no more will they silence my criticism. Yet I confess the extraordinary favoritism (greater than in any other country in Europe) shown to everybody who wields a pen, provided they write grammatically, did more than a little to put me on my guard. Of all the workers and craftsmen of the Soviet Union the writer is by far the most pampered. Two of my traveling companions (each had a translated book on the press) scoured the antique shops, the curiosity shops, the secondhand stores, not knowing how to spend the advance of several million roubles they had just received and which they knew they could not take out of Russia. As for my own case, I could hardly make a dent on an enormous bank account, for everything there was given me free of charge. Yes, everything, from the trip itself to packages of cigarettes. And whenever I would take out my wallet to settle a restaurant or hotel bill, to pay an account, to buy stamps or a newspaper, the exquisite smile and imperious gesture of our guide would stop me: "You're joking! You are our guest, you and your five companions too."

Indeed I had nothing to complain of during the course of my trip through the Soviet Union, and of all the malicious explanations that were concocted to invalidate my criticisms, the one that tries to pass them off as the expression of a personal dissatisfaction is by far the most absurd. Never before have I traveled in such ostentatious style. If by train in a private car, otherwise in the best automobiles, always the best rooms in the best hotels, the most plentiful and select tablefare. And what a reception I got! What pains were taken! What attentions were paid me! Everywhere cheered, flattered, pampered, fêted. Nothing was considered too good, too exquisite for me. I would have been graceless indeed to have repulsed these advances; I could not; and I retain a marvelous memory of them, and a lively gratitude. But these very favors continually conjured up the idea of privileges, of differences, where I thought to find equality.

When, having escaped with great difficulty from the supervised world of officialdom, I had rubbed elbows with some piece-workers whose earnings were no more than four or five roubles a day, how was I expected to feel about the banquet given in my honor, which I could not avoid attending? An almost daily banquet, where there was such a quantity of hors d'oeuvres alone that one was three times surfeited before starting on the meal proper, a six-course repast which lasted over two hours and left one absolutely stunned. What an outlay! Since I was never allowed to see a bill, I cannot be specific about the cost. But one of my fellow travelers, well informed about prices, estimates that each banquet must have come to more than three hundred roubles a head with the wines and the liqueurs. Now there were six of us, seven, counting the guide, and there were often as many hosts and guests, sometimes many more.

Throughout the whole trip we were not, properly speaking, guests of the government, but of the rich Union of Soviet Writers. When I think of the expense they went to for us, I doubt whether the goldmine of my author's royalties, which I now resign to them, can possibly suffice to reimburse them.

Evidently they were counting on a different return from such generous advances. And I think that part of the spite I am conscious of in *Pravda* comes from the fact that I was a rather bad investment.

I insist that there is something tragic in this Soviet adventure of mine. I had come as an enthusiast, I was totally convinced, I was prepared to admire a new world, and they offered me, *as seductions, mind you*, all the prerogatives I abominated in the old.

—But you don't understand, an excellent Marxist told me. Communism is opposed only to the exploitation of man by man; how many times must I tell you that? Once exploitation is ended you can be as rich as Alexis Tolstoy or a great opera singer if only you acquire your fortune by your personal work. In your scorn and hatred for wealth and possessions I detect a very regrettable trace of your early Christian ideas.

—That may well be.
—Which, let me tell you, have nothing in common with Marxism.
—Alas! . . .

As long as man is under the yoke, as long as the repression of socially vicious forces keeps him prostate, one correctly keeps on hoping for a future flowering of all that he carries in him. One similarly expects great things of children who grow up quite ordinary. One has often the illusion that man in the mass is made up of individuals superior to the rest of humanity. I believe only that he is less spoiled; but money will rot him quickly enough. And look what is happening in the USSR: the new bourgeoisie forming there has all the faults of ours. No sooner has it escaped from misery than it scorns the miserable. Avid of all the good things of which it was for so long deprived, it knows how to go about acquiring them and protecting them. "Are these really the people who made the Revolution? No, these are the people who profit from it," I wrote in my book, *Return from the USSR.* They may be Party members but there is nothing of communism in their hearts.

But the fact is that the Russian people appear to be very happy. I am entirely in accord with the testimony to this happiness made by Vildrac and Jean Pons, whose books on Russia I cannot read without nostalgia. Because, and I too have said so, nowhere except in the USSR do the masses of people, the people you meet in the street (at least the young people), the workers in the factories you visit, the crowds who swarm the places for rest, culture, amusement, present so smiling an appearance. How to reconcile this appearance with the frightful poverty in which the great masses are plunged?

Those who have travelled widely in the USSR tell me that Vildrac, Pons, and myself would have been quickly disenchanted had we quit the big centers and the beaten paths of tourists. They speak of whole districts where misery hits you in the face. And where . . .

Misery in the Soviet Union is difficult to find. It hides itself like a guilty thing. It cannot attract pity or charity, it is exposed only to scorn. Those who exhibit themselves are those whose wellbeing depends on this misery. When one does come across numbers of people who are obviously starving, they are smiling too, and their happiness, as I said, is made "of confidence, ignorance, and hope."[*]

---

[*] It is necessary to remark once more on the Russian people's prodigious capacity for life. Astonished at having endured inconceivable vicissitudes, having suffered so greatly without being diminished by suffering, Dostoyevsky attributed to himself the "vitality of a cat." A love of life which conquers pain as readily as indifference or apathy, a welling up of amusement and lyricism, of unexplained, inexplicable joy; no matter when, where, how. . . . I shall have to call it an extraordinary propensity for happiness. And in spite of everything. It is this quality which makes Dostoyevsky so representative of Russia. It is this quality which attracts me so profoundly and fraternally, and which, through him, directs me to the whole Russian people. It is doubtful whether any other people would have given themselves so generously to so tragic an experience.

If everyone we see in the Soviet Union appears to be spirited, it is equally true that anyone who has the audacity to lack spirit is immediately suspected. It is extremely dangerous to be sad, or to indicate that you are sad. A complaint cannot be lodged in Russia—it goes to Siberia.

Russia is prolific enough not to show the terrible depredations among her human herds. These ravages are all the more terrible for being hardly noticeable. And those who disappear, who are spirited away, are very likely the most worthy, if not with respect to their practical capacity then insofar as they dare to disagree, differ, distinguish themselves from a mass which insures its unity only by means of a mediocrity which becomes more and more ignoble.

In the Soviet Union what is called "opposition" is in reality courageous criticism, freedom of thought. Stalin demands applause and treats those who do not join in as enemies. Often enough it happens that Stalin adopts as his own some measure suggested by somebody else; but first, the better to appropriate the proposal, he gets rid of the proposer. This is Stalin's way of being right. So that very soon he shall find himself surrounded exclusively by men who can hardly annoy him with critical ideas since they shall have no ideas at all. Such is the traditional fate of despots: to be surrounded not by values but by an empty servility.

Whatever the issue which brings before any Soviet court workers of any category, whatever the justice may be of the workers' cause, where is the lawyer who will dare defend them if the rulers have decided on condemnation?

And the thousands deported . . . those who have not bowed in the way prescribed.

I do not have to imagine myself in their boots as M., the other day, was saying, "The devil! It could happen to me, too. . . ." These victims I see, I hear, I feel right near me. It is their gagging cries which wake me in the night; it is their silence which today dictates these lines. Because I have dreamed about these martyrs I have had to write words against which you protest, and whatever assistance my book can bring them means far more to me than all the praises and imprecations of *Pravda*.

Nobody intervenes on their behalf. All the right-wing journals simply exploit their fate to censure a regime which the reactionaries detest; the Barbusses and Rollands, those who love liberty and justice, who fight in behalf of men like Thaelmann, are silent; around the martyrs to criticism the immense proletarian mass is blind.

But when I become indignant, you explain (and still in the name of Marx!) that these definite and undeniable evils (I refer not only to the deportations but also to the profound poverty of the workers, the enormous disproportion of incomes, the reconstituted privileges, the furtive reestablishment of classes, the liquidation of Soviets, the progressive liquidation of everything conquered by

1917) you show great skill in explanations as you point out that these evils are inevitable, and that you yourself, as an intellectual inured to the contradictions (the sophistries) of the dialectic, regard the evils as provisional pauses on the road to a greater good. You, the intelligent communist, know of these evils and deem it best to hide them from those who, being less intelligent than yourself, are very likely to disapprove. . . .

I cannot prevent people from finding my writings useful to them, and if I could I should not want to do so. But to write anything at all in the direct interests of a particular political party—no, that I cannot do. I warned my new Communist friends at the very beginning of our relations: I would never be a satisfied recruit, a recruit to repose.

I have read a statement somewhere to the effect that "intellectuals" who come over to communism ought to be regarded by the Party as "unstable elements" useful on occasions but not entirely to be trusted. How true, how very true! I said the same thing many times to Vaillant-Couturier; but he would not believe it.

There is no party which can keep my loyalty—which can prevent me from preferring truth to the Party itself. When falsehoods intervene I am ill at ease; my role is to denounce them. I attach myself only to truth; if the Party rejects truth then I must reject the Party.

I know well (and you have instructed me often enough in this matter) that from the "Marxist point of view" Truth does not exist; at least not in an absolute sense; that there are only relative truths; but it is precisely these relative truths which are here in question; which you falsify. And I believe that in questions of such weight and import one only deceives oneself by seeking to deceive others. For whom are you fooling now? Those you pretend to serve: the people. One serves the people ill by blinding them.

It is necessary to see things as they are, not as one would have liked them to be:

The USSR is not what we hoped it would be, what it gave promise of being, what it still tries to appear to be; it has betrayed our hopes. If we do not want our hopes to fail too, we must attach them elsewhere.

But we shall not turn our face from you, O glorious and grieving Russia. If first you were an example to us, now, alas! you show into what engulfing sands a revolution can sink.   1937, vol. 4, no. 2

• Art and Politics: A Letter to the Editors of *Partisan Review*
Leon Trotsky

You have been kind enough to invite me to express my views on the state of present-day arts and letters. I do this not without some hesitation. Since my book

Literature and Revolution (1923), I have not once returned to the problem of artistic creation and only occasionally have I been able to follow the latest developments in this sphere. I am far from pretending to offer an exhaustive reply. The task of this letter is to correctly pose the question.

Generally speaking, art is an expression of man's need for an harmonious and complete life, that is to say, his need for those major benefits of which a society of classes has deprived him. That is why a protest against reality, either conscious or unconscious, active or passive, optimistic or pessimistic, always forms part of a really creative piece of work. Every new tendency in art has begun with rebellion. Bourgeois society showed its strength throughout long periods of history in the fact that, combining repression and encouragement, boycott and flattery, it was able to control and assimilate every "rebel" movement in art and raise it to the level of official "recognition." But each time this "recognition" betokened, when all is said and done, the approach of trouble. It was then that from the left wing of the academic school or below it—i.e. from the ranks of a new generation of bohemian artists—a fresher revolt would surge up to attain in its turn, after a decent interval, the steps of the academy. Through these stages passed classicism, romanticism, realism, naturalism, symbolism, impressionism, cubism, futurism . . . Nevertheless, the union of art and the bourgeoisie remained stable, even if not happy, only so long as the bourgeoisie itself took the initiative and was capable of maintaining a regime both politically and morally "democratic." This was a question of not only giving free rein to artists and playing up to them in every possible way, but also of granting special privileges to the top layer of the working class, and of mastering and subduing the bureaucracy of the unions and workers' parties. All these phenomena exist in the same historical plane.

The decline of bourgeois society means an intolerable exacerbation of social contradictions, which are transformed inevitably into personal contradictions, calling forth an ever more burning need for a liberating art. Furthermore, a declining capitalism already finds itself completely incapable of offering the minimum conditions for the development of tendencies in art which correspond, however little, to our epoch. It fears superstitiously every new word, for it is no longer a matter of corrections and reforms for capitalism but of life and death. The oppressed masses live their own life. Bohemianism offers too limited a social base. Hence new tendencies take on a more and more violent character, alternating between hope and despair. The artistic schools of the last few decades— cubism, futurism, dadaism, surrealism—follow each other without reaching a complete development. Art, which is the most complex part of culture, the most sensitive and at the same time the least protected, suffers most from the decline and decay of bourgeois society.

To find a solution to this impasse through art itself is impossible. It is a crisis which concerns all culture, beginning at its economic base and ending in the highest spheres of ideology. Art can neither escape the crisis nor partition itself off. Art cannot save itself. It will rot away inevitably—as Grecian art rotted beneath the ruins of a culture founded on slavery—unless present-day society is able to rebuild itself. This task is essentially revolutionary in character. For these reasons the function of art in our epoch is determined by its relation to the revolution.

But precisely in this path history has set a formidable snare for the artist. A whole generation of "leftist" intelligentsia has turned its eyes for the last ten or fifteen years to the East and has bound its lot, in varying degrees, to a victorious revolution, if not to a revolutionary proletariat. Now, this is by no means one and the same thing. In the victorious revolution there is not only the revolution, but there is also the new privileged class which raises itself on the shoulders of the revolution. In reality, the "leftist" intelligentsia has tried to change masters. What has it gained?

The October revolution gave a magnificent impetus to all types of Soviet art. The bureaucratic reaction, on the contrary, has stifled artistic creation with a totalitarian hand. Nothing surprising here! Art is basically a function of the nerves and demands complete sincerity. Even the art of the court of absolute monarchies was based on idealization but not on falsification. The official art of the Soviet Union—and there is no other over there—resembles totalitarian justice, that is to say, it is based on lies and deceit. The goal of justice, as of art, is to exalt the "leader," to fabricate a heroic myth. Human history has never seen anything to equal this in scope and impudence. A few examples will not be superfluous.

The well known Soviet writer, Vsevolod Ivanov, recently broke his silence to proclaim eagerly his solidarity with the justice of Vyshinsky. The general extermination of the old Bolsheviks, "those putrid emanations of capitalism," stimulates in the artists a "creative hatred" in Ivanov's words. Romantic, cautious by nature, lyrical, none too outspoken, Ivanov recalls Gorki in many ways, but in miniature. Not a prostitute by nature, he preferred to remain quiet as long as possible but the time came when silence meant civil and perhaps even physical annihilation. It is not a "creative hatred" that guides the pen of these writers but paralyzing fear.

Alexis Tolstoy, who has finally permitted the courtesan to master the artist, has written a novel expressly to glorify the military exploits of Stalin and Voroshilov at Tsaritsin. In reality, as impartial documents bear witness, the army of Tsaritsin—one of the two dozen armies of the revolution—played a rather sorry role. The two "heroes" were relieved of their posts. If the honest and simple Chapayev, one of the real heroes of the civil war, is glorified in a Soviet film, it is only because he did not live until the "epoch of Stalin" which would have shot him as a Fascist agent. The same Alexis Tolstoy is now writing a drama on the theme of the year 1919: "The Campaign of the Fourteen Powers." The principal heroes of this piece, according to the words of the author, are Lenin, Stalin, and Voroshilov. "Their images [of Stalin and Voroshilov!] haloed in glory and heroism, will pervade the whole drama." Thus, a talented writer who bears the name of the greatest and most truthful Russian realist has become a manufacturer of "myths" to order!

Very recently, the 27th of April of this year, the official government paper *Izvestia* printed a reproduction of a new painting representing Stalin as the organizer of the Tiflis strike in March 1902. However, it appears from documents long known to the public that Stalin was in prison at that time and besides not in Tiflis but in Batum. This time the lie was too glaring! *Izvestia* was forced to excuse itself the next day for its deplorable blunder. No one knows what happened to the unfortunate picture, which was paid for from State funds.

Dozens, hundreds, thousands of books, films, canvases, sculptures immortalize and glorify such historic "episodes." Thus the numerous pictures devoted to the October revolution do not fail to represent a revolutionary "Center," with Stalin at its head, which never existed. It is necessary to say a few words concerning the gradual preparation of this falsification. Leonid Serebriakov, shot after the Piatakov-Radek trial, drew my attention in 1924 to the publication in *Pravda*, without explanation, of extracts from the minutes of the Central Committee of the latter part of 1917. An old secretary of the Central Committee, Serebriakov had numerous contacts behind the scenes with the Party apparatus, and he knew well enough the object of this unexpected publication: it was the first step, still a cautious one, towards the principal Stalinist myth, which now occupies so great a place in Soviet art.

From a historical distance the October insurrection seems much more planned and monolithic than what it proved to be in reality. In fact, there were lacking neither vacillations, search for solutions, nor impulsive beginnings which led nowhere. Thus, at the meeting of the Central Committee on the 16th of October, improvised in one night, in the absence of the most active leaders of the Petrograd Soviets, it was decided to round out the general staff of the insurrection with an auxiliary "Center" created by the party and composed of Sverdlov, Stalin, Bubnov, Uritzky, and Djerjinsky. At the very same time at the meeting of the Petrograd Soviet, a Revolutionary Military Committee was formed which from the moment of its appearance did so much work towards the preparation of the insurrection that the "Center," appointed the night before, was forgotten by everybody, even by its own members. There were more than a few such improvisations in the whirlwind of this period. Stalin never belonged to the Military Revolutionary Committee, did not appear at Smolny, staff headquarters of the revolution, had nothing to do with the practical preparation of the insurrection, but was to be found editing *Pravda* and writing drab articles which were very little read. During the following years nobody once mentioned the "Practical

Center." In memoirs of participants in the insurrection—and there is no short-age of these—the name of Stalin is not once mentioned. Stalin himself, in an article on the anniversary of the October insurrection, in the *Pravda* of November 7, 1918, describing all the groups and individuals who took part in the insurrection, does not say a word about the "Practical Center." Nevertheless, the old minutes, discovered by chance in 1924 and falsely interpreted, have served as a base for the bureaucratic legend. In every compilation, bibliographical guide, even in recently edited school books, the revolutionary "Center" has a prominent place with Stalin at its head. Furthermore, no one has tried, not even out of a sense of decency, to explain where and how this "Center" established its head-quarters, to whom it gave orders and what they were, and if minutes were taken where they are. We have here all the features of the Moscow trials.

With the docility which distinguishes it, Soviet art, so-called, has made this bureaucratic myth into one of its favorite subjects for artistic creation. Sverdlov, Djerjinsky, Uritsky, and Bubnov are represented in oils or in tempera, seated or standing around Stalin and following his words with rapt attention. The building where the "Center" has headquarters is intentionally depicted in a vague fashion in order to avoid the embarrassing question of the address. What can one hope for or demand of artists who are forced to follow with their brushes the crude lines of what they themselves realize is a historical falsification?

The style of present-day official Soviet painting is called "socialist realism." The name itself has evidently been invented by some high functionary in the department of the arts. This "realism" consists in the imitation of provincial daguerreotypes of the third quarter of the last century; the "socialist" character apparently consists in representing, in the manner of pretentious photography, events which never took place. It is impossible to read Soviet verse and prose without physical disgust mixed with horror, or to look at reproductions of paint-ings and sculpture in which functionaries armed with pens, brushes, and scissors, under the supervision of functionaries armed with Mausers, glorify the "great" and "brilliant" leaders actually devoid of the least spark of genius or greatness. The art of the Stalinist period will remain as the frankest expression of the pro-found decline of the proletarian revolution.

This state of things is not confined, however, within the frontiers of the USSR. Under the guise of a belated recognition of the October revolution, the "left" wing of the Western intelligentsia has fallen on its knees before the Soviet bureaucracy. As a rule, those artists with some character and talent have kept aloof. But the appearance in the first ranks of the failures, careerists, and nobod-ies is all the more unfortunate. A rash of Centers and Committees of all sorts has broken out, of secretaries of both sexes, inevitable letters from Romain Rolland, subsidized editions, banquets and congresses, in which it is difficult to trace the line of demarcation between art and the GPU. Despite this vast spread of activity, this militarized movement has not produced one single work that was able to outlive its author or its inspirers of the Kremlin.

In the field of painting, the October revolution has found her greatest interpreter not in the USSR but in faraway Mexico, not among the official "friends," but in the person of a so-called "enemy of the people" whom the Fourth International is proud to number in its ranks. Nurtured in the artistic cultures of all peoples, all epochs, Diego Rivera has remained Mexican in the most profound fibers of his genius. But that which inspired him in these magnificent frescoes, which lifted him up above the artistic tradition, above contemporary art—in a certain sense, above himself—is the mighty blast of the proletarian revolution. Without October, his power of creative penetration into the epic of work, oppression, and insurrection would never have attained such breadth and profundity. Do you wish to see with your own eyes the hidden springs of the social revolution? Look at the frescoes of Rivera. Do you wish to know what revolutionary art is like? Look at the frescoes of Rivera.

Come a little closer and you will see clearly enough gashes and spots made by vandals: Catholics and other reactionaries, including, of course, Stalinists. These cuts and gashes give even greater life to the frescoes. You have before you not simply a "painting," an object of passive esthetic contemplation, but a living part of the class struggle. And it is at the same time a masterpiece!

Only the historical youth of a country which has not yet emerged from the stage of struggle for national independence has allowed Rivera's revolutionary brush to be used on the walls of the public buildings of Mexico. In the United States it was more difficult. Just as the monks in the Middle Ages, through ignorance, it is true, erased antique literary productions from parchments to cover them with their scholastic ravings, just so Rockefeller's lackeys, but this time maliciously, covered the frescoes of the talented Mexican with their decorative banalities. This recent palimpsest will conclusively show future generations the fate of art degraded in a decaying bourgeois society.

The situation is no better, however, in the country of the October revolution. Incredible as it seemed at first sight, there was no place for the art of Diego Rivera, either in Moscow, or in Leningrad, or in any other section of the USSR where the bureaucracy born of the revolution was erecting grandiose palaces and monuments to itself. And how could the Kremlin clique tolerate in its kingdom an artist who paints neither icons representing the "leader" nor lifesize portraits of Voroshilov's horse? The closing of the Soviet doors to Rivera will brand forever with an ineffaceable shame the totalitarian dictatorship.

Will it go on much longer—this stifling, this trampling underfoot and muddying of everything on which the future of humanity depends? Reliable indications say no. The shameful and pitiable collapse of the cowardly and reactionary politics of the Popular Fronts in Spain and France, on the one hand, and the judicial frame-ups of Moscow, on the other, portend the approach of a major turning point not only in the political sphere, but also in the broader sphere of revolutionary ideology. Even the unfortunate "friends"—but evidently not the intellectual and moral shallows of *The New Republic* and *Nation*—are beginning to tire of the yoke and whip. Art, culture, politics need a new perspective. Without it humanity will not develop. But never before has the prospect been as menacing and catastrophic as now. That is the reason why panic is the dominant state of mind of the bewildered intelligentsia. Those who oppose an irresponsible skepticism to the yoke of Moscow do not weigh heavy in the balance of history. Skepticism is only another form, and not the best, of demoralization. Behind the act, so popular now, of impartially keeping aloof from the Stalinist bureaucracy as well as its revolutionary adversaries, is hidden nine times out of ten a wretched prostration before the difficulties and dangers of history. Nevertheless, verbal subterfuges and petty maneuvers will be of no use. No one will be granted either pardon or respite. In the face of the era of wars and revolutions which is drawing near, everyone will have to give an answer: philosophers, poets, painters, as well as simple mortals.

In the June issue of your magazine I found a curious letter from an editor of a Chicago magazine unknown to me. Expressing (by mistake, I hope) his sympathy for your publication, he writes: "I can see no hope however [?] from the Trotskyites or other anemic splinters which have no mass base." These arrogant words tell more about the author than he perhaps wanted to say. They show above all that the laws of development of society have remained a seven times sealed book for him. Not a single progressive idea has begun with a "mass base," otherwise it would not have been a progressive idea. It is only in its last stage that the idea finds its masses—if, of course, it answers the needs of progress. All great movements have begun as "splinters" of older movements. In the beginning, Christianity was only a "splinter" of Judaism; Protestantism a "splinter" of Catholicism, that is to say decayed Christianity. The group of Marx and Engels came into existence as a "splinter" of the Hegelian Left. The Communist International germinated during the war from the "splinters" of the Social Democratic International. If these pioneers found themselves able to create a mass base, it was precisely because they did not fear isolation. They knew beforehand that the quality of their ideas would be transformed into quantity. These "splinters" did not suffer from anemia; on the contrary, they carried within themselves the germs of the great historical movements of tomorrow.

In very much the same way, to repeat, a progressive movement occurs in art. When an artistic tendency has exhausted its creative resources, creative "splinters" separate from it, which are able to look at the world with new eyes. The more daring the pioneers show in their ideas and actions, the more bitterly they oppose themselves to established authority which rests on a conservative "mass base," the more conventional souls, skeptics, and snobs are inclined to see in the pioneers, impotent eccentrics, or "anemic splinters." But in the last analysis it is the conventional souls, skeptics, and snobs who are wrong—and life passes them by.

The Thermidorian bureaucracy, to whom one cannot deny either a certain animal sense of danger or a strong instinct of self-preservation, is not at all inclined to estimate its revolutionary adversaries with such wholehearted disdain, a disdain which is often coupled with lightness and inconsistency. In the Moscow trials, Stalin, who is not a venturesome player by nature, staked on the struggle against "Trotskyism" the fate of the Kremlin oligarchy as well as his own personal destiny. How can one explain this fact? The furious international campaign against "Trotskyism," for which a parallel in history will be difficult to find, would be absolutely inexplicable if the "splinters" were not endowed with an enormous vitality. He who does not see this today will see it better tomorrow.

As if to complete his self-portrait with one brilliant stroke, your Chicago correspondent vows—what bravery!—to meet you in a future concentration camp—either fascist or "communist." A fine program! To tremble at the thought of a concentration camp is certainly not admirable. But is it much better to foredoom oneself and one's ideas to this grim hospitality? With the Bolshevik "amoralism" which is characteristic of us, we are ready to suggest that gentlemen—by no means anemic—who capitulate before the fight and without a fight really deserve nothing better than the concentration camp.

It would be a different matter if your correspondent simply said: in the sphere of literature and art we wish no supervision on the part of "Trotskyists" any more than from the Stalinists. This protest would be, in essence, absolutely just. One can only retort that to aim it at those who are termed "Trotskyists" would be to batter in an open door. The ideological base of the conflict between the Fourth and Third Internationals is the profound disagreement not only on the tasks of the party but in general on the entire material and spiritual life of mankind.

The real crisis of civilization is above all the crisis of revolutionary leadership. Stalinism is the greatest element of reaction in this crisis. Without a new flag and a new program it is impossible to create a *revolutionary* mass base; consequently it is impossible to rescue society from its dilemma. But a truly revolutionary party is neither able nor willing to take upon itself the task of "leading" and even less of commanding art, either before or after the conquest of power. Such a pretension could only enter the head of a bureaucracy—ignorant and impudent, intoxicated with its totalitarian power—which has become the antithesis of the proletarian revolution. Art can become a strong ally of revolution only insofar as it remains faithful to itself. Poets, painters, sculptors, and musicians will themselves find their own approach and methods, if the struggle for freedom of oppressed classes and peoples scatters the clouds of skepticism and of pessimism which cover the horizon of mankind. The first condition of this regeneration is the over-throw of the domination of the Kremlin bureaucracy.

May your magazine take its place in the victorious army of socialism and not in a concentration camp!

Leon Trotsky

Coyoacan, D. F.

June 18, 1938

(Translated by Nancy and Dwight Macdonald)

1938, vol. 5, no. 3

• The English Literary Left
F. W. Dupee

In France and America left-wing literature has been largely a prose literature. In England, however, the novelists (Hanley, Calder-Marshall, Hampson) are negligible in comparison with the group of poets gathered around W. H. Auden. The one prose writer of importance is Christopher Isherwood, who belongs to the Auden circle. Comparatively negligible too are the critics and journalists associated with *Left Review*. Edgell Rickword, Montagu Slater, Alick West—these writers comprise the official, the Communist Party Left, with which the Auden circle is linked through Stephen Spender and C. Day Lewis, its political wing. Its other wing, literary in the traditional sense, opposed to the pamphlet-poem and the politically inflated reputation, is made up of Geoffrey Grigson, who edits the small bimonthly *New Verse*, and Louis MacNeice, its chief contributor. In the center of the Auden circle, looking both ways, is W. H. Auden himself.

THE ENGLISH RENAISSANCE

In the light of the American Left, there is a great deal that is ambiguous about the Auden circle. Politically they fall short of the specifications for a left-wing group, and in a literary sense they tend to exceed them. Orientated though they are towards the Communist Party, there yet has been little direct transposition of party politics into their writing; and as poets they have much in common with the purely literary avant-garde movements of the twenties. No such ambivalence can be ascribed to the American Left. In the United States the bohemian esthetic tradition of the twenties was largely played out when the Depression came, and little friction was encountered by the Communist Party in its literary operations, for it was working in a cultural vacuum. For this reason, and because the party was able to divert writers back to a venerable literary populism which had survived through the twenties as a thin, secondary current, the program for a "proletarian literature" succeeded in America—succeeded, that is, in influencing enough writers to produce an organized movement. Among English writers, however, no such swift and radical adjustment to the Stalinist program was possible. The available literary tradition in Britain was aristocratic; it was, moreover, still comparatively vigorous. And the young English poets glanced back towards that tradition quite as often as they looked ahead towards any other.

A comparison of Stephen Spender's *The Destructive Element* with Granville Hicks's *The Great Tradition* will reveal the crux of the difference between the two Lefts. Both Hicks and Spender torture the literary past in order to compel it to yield the justification for a contemporary literature of politics and class struggle. But Hicks leaves the past in ruins and the Communist Party in solitary possession of the present. Spender on the other hand is enormously respectful towards the older writers; and after, as it were, extorting from them the admission that they were individualists, he turns the weapon of individual integrity—*their* weapon—on the Communists. Spender is, of course, a sensitive and valuable critic; and his superiority over Granville Hicks is a measure of the greater literacy of the English movement.

Yet the writers whom Spender so respectfully salutes as "ancestors" were not in most cases English. Henry James and T. S. Eliot were Americans; Joyce and Yeats were Irish. England had produced in the twenties several modern personalities (D. H. Lawrence, Wyndham Lewis) but no organized modernist movement; and the Auden circle has had the task of realizing such a movement in the thirties. In architecture, the theater, and the plastic arts England had likewise missed the boat; and only in the present decade have abstract and surrealist painting, a functional architecture, and an expressionist theater begun to appear in force on the English scene. The poetry of the Auden circle is thus but one feature of a tardy cultural awakening which extends to several fields.

England's belated modernism came to birth, however, under conditions which have curiously modified both its character and its mission. Not a boom, but a depression, had prepared its coming. For a century English society had permitted no really rebellious esthetic movement to cling for long to its monolithic crags; but, shaken a little by the Depression, it developed rifts in which a modern culture might take precarious root. And this culture could hardly fail to take note of its environment, could not but draw conclusions, political and economic, from the conditions which alone had made it possible. So the esthetic program of the New Poetry was reinforced by a messianic purpose unknown to such movements in the past; and the heritage of symbolism, surrealism, and expressionism was expended on a literature of propaganda. In W. H. Auden virtuosity unites with didacticism.

With its miscellany of styles and ideas, its shifting points of view and its incredible contradictions, the world of the New Poetry seems a veritable fantasia of modern art and ideology. It has had many jobs to do, and often it has confused them one with another. In addition to the task of erecting on English soil the technical machinery of modernist literature, it has had the mission of enlightening benighted Britain on sex. A revolt against "puritanism"—that is to say, against bourgeois family morality—has figured in the majority of postwar literary movements. In England, however, the belated reformers were faced not only with a neurotic family life but with a prostrated society. Hence they could not be satisfied to derive from the new psychology merely a literary program and a bohemian ethic. The Freudian perspective was raised to a social gospel, sometimes competing with the historical perspective of Marxism, but more often simply melting into it.

So long as psychology was not confused with politics, but operated as an alternative and a foil, it proved in many cases an effective instrument of literary creation. The Healer who figures as a hero in Auden's early work is not only a nonpolitical but an antipolitical conception; yet Auden's most militant, brilliant, and self-consistent poetry is built around it. But the big extravaganzas of a later period, *The Dog Beneath the Skin* and *The Ascent of F6*, indiscriminately tap both psychology and politics, and are essentially incoherent. Where Auden went, the others followed. The proletariat became, for many a writer of the English Left, the social embodiment of libido; in Charles Madge's "darksome working man" and Sylvia Warner's "kiln-man" the gypsies of D. H. Lawrence had a new incarnation; in the floods, the steamrollers, and other dream symbols which were invoked to represent it, the revolution acquired the character of emancipator for the inhibited middle classes; and in *The Wild Goose Chase*, Rex Warner's interminable "fable," the ambition to "synthesize Marx and Freud" was finally reduced to its essential absurdity. Yet the failure of so many of these writings, like the failure of Auden's later plays, cannot be attributed to ideological confusion alone, for this confusion is only symptomatic of a meager, confused, and synthetic experience.

In their early period Auden and some of his fellow poets had another important mission; one which they have since dropped. The economic crisis, coinciding with the longstanding crisis in English culture, called forth in the first instance not a socialist but a nationalist reaction from the young poets; and Auden was intensely conscious of himself as the prophet of a resurgent Britain. His early verse is vibrant with the sense of an England depressed, inert, helmless and looking for a sign. In this doggerel poem, "Get there if you can and see the land you once were proud to own," he ran through the symptoms of national decadence and complained that "they quietly undersold us with their cheaper trade abroad." And at the end of *The Orators* (1932) he invoked the leader who should restore

To England's story
The directed calm, the actual glory.

The concern for England's glory thus re-entered serious poetry, from which it had been absent for a generation. T. S. Eliot, to be sure, had tried to foster certain institutional revivals; but these were directed not towards a strictly English resurgence but towards implicating Britain in a renaissance of the Latin internationalism of the medieval system. Auden was not interested in institutions but in *inspiration*; in the revival of libidinal energy as a cure for English crime, disease, and fear of life. The healer replaced the priest in his conception, and for the Dantesque spirituality of Eliot he would have substituted the primitive Anglo-Saxon stoicism of Gisli the Outlaw. Rejecting Eliot's tradition, he also discarded the international style and working from Skelton and the sagas he developed the hard, compact, de-latinized austerities of his early manner. Day Lewis also showed nationalistic tendencies in that period, but he was far less radical than Auden. He merely sought to restore England's glory through reviving the cult of fresh air and natural magic; and from Hopkins and the English Romantics he compounded his famous nougat-paste style. Other writers who have since become identified with Auden's circle had no traffic with this English revivalism. Louis MacNeice was too much the cosmopolitan Irishman, and Stephen Spender too deeply rooted in a family tradition of liberal idealism. And in 1933 the antifascist movement intervened to arrest the nationalistic tendencies of Auden and Lewis and to bring the group together on a common political basis.

"THE RUPERT BROOKE OF THE DEPRESSION"

Stephen Spender and his fellow poets have ranged through English literature in search of "ancestors"; but the Freudian censor appears to have been at work in them, for they have studiously ignored Shaw, Wells, and Rupert Brooke, who are in so many respects their true antecedents.

From their early writings it is clear that Communism first appealed to them as a possible solution for their own intellectual dilemmas. Politically, Stephen Spender matured more rapidly than the others. Somewhat *manqué* as a poet, he has nevertheless the gift of logic, of drawing general conclusions from his experience, and of discarding ideas when they no longer fit in with what he observes. Where MacNeice, ideologically speaking, exhibits no progression whatever, and Auden shuttles continually back and forth between two fixed points, Spender's work falls readily into a pattern of development, simple but pronounced.

His earliest verse, invoking Time, Death, and Frustration, speaks the usual language of introversion. His first social emotion appears in such poems as "The Port" and "The Prisoners": it is an emotion of pity: pity for the mad, the poor, the confined. He is trying to bring to bear on the Crisis the detached compassion with which Wilfred Owen had endured the War. But as Spender himself has said, writing of Owen: "The difficulty is that poetry inspired by pity is dependent on that repeated stimulus for its inspiration." But this is impossible: the alternative is some ponderable link with reality: love, Communism, immersion in the external world. He begins accordingly to celebrate sexual health and comradeship, the new social order, the world of machines and workers. And finally, in *Vienna* (1934) he contrasts the "stalking inner worlds" of a corrupted individuality with the revolutionary heroism of the Vienna workers. "These," he decides, "are our ancestors." He had accepted, *as a poet*, the revolutionary imperative.

Vienna was written as the result of a trip to Austria. Like the visits which Auden and Isherwood had paid to Berlin a few years earlier, Spender's stay in Vienna provided a fund of experience enormously important to his creative work and his political development.

After 1934 his work was largely done in prose. He was seeking some basis on which he could cooperate with, or even join, the Communist Party. At first his approach to Stalinism was a literary one; it revolved around the question of "proletarian literature"; and Spender feared, rightly enough, that to accept the Stalinist program meant to surrender his rights and his integrity to party control and to "RAPPism." He failed, however, to examine "proletarian literature" as a theory, or to connect the theory and the excesses of RAPPism with the bureaucratic emergencies which had occasioned them. By 1936, however, he had already found a broader base for his essentially personal Communism; a base which permitted him to draw closer to the Communist Party. In that year he published *Forward from Liberalism*. This characteristically candid and well-intentioned book stated with much eloquence the case against capitalism and for socialism; but it developed a blind spot as to ways and means. He had come to socialism, he admitted, as a liberal, and because it was a stage through which the liberal mind must pass en route towards the ultimate fulfillment of its ideals of freedom. The unconscious class egotism of this view—as though the proletariat's function were to realize for certain righteous bourgeois types the lofty plans which their own class had somehow bungled—was strictly in the tradition of English social dilettantism. It was possible only in a country where the bourgeoisie, having lived unchallenged for generations, could regard their world as the field in which historical questions were all finally decided. Thus the Fabianism of Shaw and Squire, of Brooke and Lady Warwick, made its reappearance in a young poet of the thirties, assuming new forms in keeping with the new epoch. The social democracy on which the older Fabians had leaned was now discredited; the new Fabians discovered the Comintern. And at the same time, of course, the Comintern began to seek out the Fabians. English reformism thus acquired what it had badly needed: the tradition of a successful revolution; and Stalinism possessed itself of a respectable facade for its adventures in class collaboration. For Stephen Spender the emergency maneuvers of the Soviet foreign office became the norms of socialist action; the People's Fronts of Spain and

France he accepted as full-fledged socialist governments; and the injustices, the tyrannies, the crimes of the Soviet regime were put down as misdemeanors which the new "democratic constitution" would correct. Spender's authorities on the Soviet Union, needless to say, were the indispensable Sidney and Beatrice Webb, in whose ancient persons the Fabianism of two epochs was united.

In *Forward from Liberalism* Spender declared that it was a "betrayal of his function" for the intellectual to become the apologist for a political party. The intellectual, he said, must "judge and criticize" the party line from the viewpoint of absolute justice, the final end of politics. However, in the two-odd years of his membership in the Communist Party (he joined it shortly after the appearance of *Forward from Liberalism*) Spender has found no occasion to exercise publicly the right to "judge and criticize."

He has recently published a verse play written for the Group Theatre in London. *Trial of a Judge* is not strong either as poetry or as drama. The characters are poorly contrived effigies of types popularized by the antifascist movement; the situations are as banal as the editorials of the *Daily Worker*; and the infusion of T. S. Eliot has given the verse no more than a factitious "atmosphere." But the play is curious as a comment on Spender's ideological development since 1934. With its Central European setting, it shows him still clinging to his early experiences. It is as though the present line of the Comintern had conspired with the meagerness of his own English experience to convince him that the tragic political subject is confined to Central Europe. But from his memories of the Vienna journey he now draws rather different conclusions. *Trial of a Judge* is an attempt to construct a tragedy out of the predicament of a liberal faced with the choice between Communism and Fascism. The play is probably an accurate reflection of history as it looks to supporters of the People's Front, for the fate of society is made to hinge on the liberal's decision, and the Communists in the play are reduced to the role of suppliants. Thus for Spender the locus of tragedy has moved up a step in the social scale since he composed *Vienna*. In that poem the heroes were workers tragically betrayed by their leaders—and by liberals.

THE HEALER

Where Spender, as a poet, remains the captive of his reasoning mind with its abstract data and its memories of other literature, Auden, drawing on latent memories of the ruined Midlands of his childhood, is able to build around his emotions an entire landscape of images fearful in their grotesque materiality. Among his fellow writers Auden is really the *poet*: he alone is really sensitive to the zeitgeist; the others are merely sensitive to him.

His powers of literary assimilation are not unconnected with this mediumistic faculty. Among the innumerable writers he has tapped, he obviously owes most to Lawrence and Eliot (his early rejection of Eliot did not prevent his being greatly influenced by him both then and later on). Different as these two writers are, yet Auden reconciled them by incorporating them as part of the living experience of his time. A wasteland which has acquired the features of the depressed areas, the landscape of his early poems is peopled with spectral neurasthenics which resemble Lawrence characters stripped of their sex, their mannerisms, their personalities—of everything but their "symptoms."

We must remember, however, that Eliot and Lawrence were children of the static prewar system: for all the intensity of their beliefs they could not but see the world as fixed in its agony. Auden's world on the contrary is one in which change is implied in the very immobility of the old order. On one side are arrayed the "Holders of one position, wrong for years"; on the other side is the Adversary who is waiting and plotting to blow them off the map.

> The falling leaves know it, the children,
> At play on the fuming alkali-tip
> Or by the flooded football ground, know it—
> This is the dragon's day, the devourer's . . .

While Spender imports the tragic subject from abroad, Auden makes capital out of poverty at home, uncovers the kernel of violence in the husk of inertia, the tragedy in the pathos of England, where

> No one will ever know
> For what conversion brilliant capital is waiting,
> What ugly feast may village band be celebrating;
> For no one goes
> Further than railhead or the ends of piers,
> Will neither go nor send his son
> Further through foothills than the rotting stack
> Where gaitered gamekeeper with dog and gun
> Will shout 'Turn back.'

These lines belong to the period (1928–34) when Auden was a genuinely subversive force in English poetry, his vision unimpaired by loyalties to friend or party. Day Lewis was at that time still seeking private norms in marriage and fatherhood. Today Lewis salutes each new repulse of history with a fresh gust of "democratic" optimism. And Auden? A *Left Review* critic complains that he has drifted into "the simple exploration of individuality": look at the plaintive lyrics, the rueful public clowning, the growing tendency to challenge the pamphlet in the name of the poem, Marxism in the name of Love. This is a retreat! True, but is it not possible that Auden's mood reflects, obscurely, the bankruptcy of the English Left and its ideals—that obvious bankruptcy which nobody dares declare?

Auden is the creative leader of his group—that is acknowledged. But in other respects he is their captive. He lacks a critical intelligence; and one cannot always be sure whether the hub is turning the spokes or the spokes the hub. At present we may guess that Auden is the captive of his friends' reformist gentility, their politically fostered blindness, the rationalized prudence of their democratic front against Fascism—as though Fascism were a respecter of prudence, of democracy!

The *Left Review* critic, although he stops short of a prescription, is nevertheless right in his diagnosis of Auden's present state of mind. The poet who began as the impersonal voice of a generation, whose greatest merit was the power to generalize his experience, seems, like Eliot before him, in his later work to have been thrust deeper and deeper into his own ego. In order to retrace the stages by which Auden arrived where he is today, we may follow the evolution of his favorite conception: the figure of the Healer. In his ambiguities and his successive incarnations, this transfigured scientist, who talks the clipped jargon of the clinic and views the world as a psychiatric ward, embodies the poet's shifting attitudes towards the fact of social change.

The idea of the Healer seems to have been suggested to Auden by two actual psychiatrists: Homer Lane and Georg Walther Groddeck, with whose teachings he came in contact in Berlin in 1929. "Teachings" rather than "theories" because, in addition to sharing a similar conviction as to the functional nature of disease and crime, both men strove to unite belief and practice in their own lives, and both endeavored to cure by example. Homer Lane, who experimented in progressive penology, was fiercely antiauthoritarian. And Groddeck, a practicing psychiatrist, underwent at one point in his career a dramatic conversion from hypnotic methods of therapy, which brought into play the will of the physician, to a technique of suggestion and reeducation. From the ideas and experiences of these men, Auden appears to have derived his repugnance to the will and all forms of coercive change, and, conversely, his doctrine of Love—"What can be loved (he has said) can be cured."

In any case, the Healer is a kind of psychiatric saint or redeemer; but in order to emphasize his benign aspects Auden has given him a terroristic alter ego; and the Healer is always undergoing transformations from one self to the other.

His earliest appearance seems to have been in certain of the *Poems* (1930). He is here invoked as the Enemy, and if he foreshadows the new order he also signifies the unqualified extinction of the old. "Death, death of the grain, our death, Death of the old gang." In later poems we shall see him transformed into Eros Paidogogus, the embodiment of love in its "reeducative" aspects. But for the present he is love the avenger, with a hawk's vision of the undifferentiated loveless and neurasthenic mass: he is Anteros who punishes with death those who from greed or fear, egotism or false shame, pervert the norms of sexuality and deny the affection of others. Yet suddenly in the very last poem in the volume the Enemy becomes a friend: "Sir, no man's enemy, forgiving all." And he is called on to

> Send to us power and light, a sovereign touch
> Curing the intolerable neural itch,
> The exhaustion of weaning, the liar's quinsy . . .

The Enemy thus stands forth in his counter-role as the psychiatric saint.

The next appearance of the Healer is in *The Orator* (1932). Here, as the Airman, he has acquired a profession in keeping with his hawk's eye vision. And we are now taken into his confidence and introduced to his journals: not he, but the old order, is now the Enemy. The Airman is a young man who, operating with a few friends from a country house called "The Hollies," is plotting to overthrow "society." His plan of attack, while it simulates a political insurrection, consists essentially in undermining the old order through disrupting its habitual thought associations. These are accordingly analyzed, plotted and diagrammed in the Airman's journal, as the defenses of some well-fortified country might be studied by an army that proposed to invade it. At the very last, however, when the great attack is in its seventh day, the Airman has a sudden change of heart, paralleling the abrupt transformation of the Enemy at the end of the earlier volume. "Do not imagine," he says to himself, "that you, no more than any other conqueror, can escape the mark of grossness." And he repudiates coercion and violence for humility and understanding.

Yet in 1933, just a year after the appearance of *The Orators*, Auden writes the play *The Dance of Death* and in the central figure of the Dancer revives his former hero—only to slay him summarily with the apparition of Karl Marx. Caricatured and discredited, the specter of the psychological redeemer appears to be laid for good. But in reality he is not. In *The Ascent of F6* (1936) the old problem of coercion is resuscitated in a new form and the Healer has yet another incarnation, this time sympathetic, in the character of the Abbott. But, devoid alike of scientific professions and a terroristic alter ego, the Abbott simply realizes all the devout and ritualistic tendencies inherent in the Healer type from the beginning. In later lyrics the type becomes merged with the Dioscuri—which are merely a literary symbol for astronomical benevolence—or more often with the poet himself, who now preaches love and forbearance in his own voice.

Psychology or politics? Inner reform or social revolution? Such are the issues implied in those writings of Auden's that center around the figure of the Healer. And the survival of this unreal dilemma is a curious reflection not only on Auden but on the English Left itself. As Spender in *Vienna* had declared the revolutionary tradition his own, so Auden in *The Dance of Death* had banished the psychiatrist for Marx. It is hardly necessary to point out that the militant period of Auden and Spender corresponded to the years of hope and struggle in the revolutionary movement itself. But as the movement deteriorated, sowing reformist maneuvers and reaping disasters, so there emerged once more that vast vague Atlantis of idealist illusion on which, so long as it is visible, the intelligentsia will set their hopes. And the poets returned to the timeless world of Freud and the "liberal mind." It is true that, even in the years 1932–34, Auden and Spender had reservations when it came to Marxist politics. Nor can *Vienna* and *The Dance of Death* be described as formidable contributions to revolutionary literature. They were the products of a mood—solemn in Spender's case, breezy in Auden's—a mood of discovery; but the emotion was no less real for being immature. It needed experience to deepen and confirm it: experience of the class struggle in their own land, among their own people, their old associations. Yet hardly had Spender returned from Austria and Auden slain the Healer, than the Comintern discovered that English capitalism was "progressive." The class struggle was promptly exported to Central Europe and Spain, and the poets were invited to make their peace with labor politicians, titled democrats, and lady novelists with a passion for humanity. To be sure, the Stalinist critics continued to lecture them, to recommend them to "join the workers"; but what good were their sermons when the workers had to all appearances joined the bourgeoisie?

In Spender's case the changed political situation merely meant that his poetry was brought into line with his politics, and the militancy of *Vienna* dissolved into the People's Front perspective of *Trial of a Judge*. But Auden is less responsive to the programs of political parties than he is to his general environment; and after 1935 that environment could only be conducive to *anxiety*. Auden became as a man afflicted with a dual identity: Auden the Public Figure gave support to Stalinist causes, wrote accomplished poems for the Medical Aid fund, visited the scenes of democracy's holy wars and reported them for the liberal weeklies. The private Auden envisioned socialism more and more as a dream of the future, gave expression to his fears for the present in long, melancholy, personal lyrics (*Look, Stranger*), which seem to be patterned on Matthew Arnold's *Dover Beach*, and endeavored, with a rather ineffectual spirituality, to counteract the obviously disastrous trend of the zeitgeist.

> In the houses
> The little pianos are closed, and the clock strikes.
> And all sway forward on the dangerous flood
> Of history, that never sleeps or dies,
> And, held one moment, burns the hand.

Such lines, and there are many such in the later poems, can only be interpreted as *warnings*.

POLITICS AND BOHEMIA

A few years ago, in "A Hope for Poetry," Day Lewis cited as models for the Auden circle those rare poets of modern Britain who, rooting themselves in monasteries or universities, had refused to be plucked up, transplanted to the gardens of popular culture, and there domesticated. Today this disciple of Gerard Hopkins occupies a post on the Book Society with Sir Hugh Walpole and J. B. Priestley. Lewis is an extreme case, and he has perhaps landed in the place reserved for him by his essential talents. But Auden as playwright, parodist, and author of amusing travel books has a foot in Bloomsbury too, and Spender is the intensely busy poet and publicist of petit-bourgeois democracy.

In recoiling from the years of militancy into the variegated social and psychological reformism of the present, they have made a political truce with the bourgeoisie; and a younger literary generation in England already suspects them of having made an esthetic truce as well. Politics has razed Bohemia and replaced its strict taboos with the rough and ready touchstones of parties engaged in the struggle for power and influence. So long as the Stalinist grouping for which the Auden circle writes preserved its revolutionary and class character, it constituted a collectivity with homogeneous social values to which the Auden circle were free to bring their own esthetic. Both camps gained from the connection: *New Verse* was a "little magazine" with a social conscience, and *Left Review* a political journal with a mature attitude towards the arts. But as the Stalinist grouping, in quest of the Democratic Front, expands beyond its original base, cutting across lines of class, interest, and value, the Auden circle finds itself addressing an audience which embraces a social field so large that it is practically commensurate with society as a whole. And what is society as a whole but capitalist society, what are its values but the values of the bourgeoisie?   1938, vol. 5, no. 3

A Letter to *The New Republic*

In the October 19 [1938] issue of the *New Republic*, Malcolm Cowley published a lengthy article abusing *Partisan Review* as "factional," "anti-Soviet," a perpetrator of "literary crimes" and "hardly" distinguishable from the *American Mercury*. As we go to press, the *New Republic* has promised to print our reply in an early issue. Pleading limitations of space, however, the *New Republic* insisted that we cut down our original letter to 1,000 words—although Mr. Cowley's attack ran over 1,700 words. (The only specific omission they stipulated was the sentence: "Isn't this the same Malcolm Cowley whose use of his position on the *New Republic* to play Communist Party politics has long been a literary scandal?"

This, Bruce Bliven wrote us, "obviously transcends the legitimate boundaries of public controversy"—though Mr. Cowley was apparently within those bounds when he implied that *Partisan Review* is a quasi-Fascist organ.) For the interest of our readers, we print below the full text of our original letter. It may be regarded as a restatement of our political position as well as an answer to Mr. Cowley.

Editor, The New Republic
Sir:

We sympathize with Malcolm Cowley's growing impatience with *Partisan Review*, whose literary and political values are at drastic variance with his own. But we must point out that his article on our magazine is a malicious and politically motivated attack masquerading as a matter of literary differences. These are strong words. We think we can show they are justified.

Mr. Cowley makes two main charges against *Partisan Review*. (1) We have proclaimed that literature should not be degraded to an instrument of political factionalism, and yet we devote much space to what Mr. Cowley calls "anti-Soviet articles." (2) This secret addiction to politics has reduced *Partisan Review* to the literary level of the *New Masses*.

To support his first charge, Mr. Cowley quotes from our opening Editorial Statement, which announced a policy of "no commitments to any political party." This he interprets to mean that *Partisan Review* had forsworn politics and was going to devote itself to an above-the-battle kind of Pure Literature, such as the *Dial* once stood for. And so he points triumphantly to the fact that we have actually paid a good deal of attention to politics. But we have never aspired to stand for Pure Literature. We have always agreed with Mr. Cowley that the contemporary writer must concern himself with politics if his work is to have any deep meaning for our time. Mr. Cowley's quotations from our editorial were, to say the least, very selective. One sentence he did *not* quote was: "Any magazine, we believe, that aspires to a place in the vanguard of literature today will be revolutionary in tendency." That is clear enough, surely.

But Mr. Cowley also objects to the *kind* of political approach we have had, insisting that to attack the Communist Party's cultural line is to play factional politics. This we deny. The struggle between Stalinism and revolutionary Marxism seems to us to go far beyond party or factional issues. By this time, Stalinism has ceased to be a revolutionary tendency and in fact is rapidly turning into the opposite. We do not consider our struggle against it as committing us to any party line, any more than we consider our constant criticism of capitalist values—whether "democratic" or fascist—a matter of factional politics. Many radical groups, from the Fourth International to the Social Democratic Federation, oppose Stalinism for much the same reasons we do. We have never endorsed the political line of any of these groups—which obviously on other subjects have deep-rooted differences among themselves—nor have we excluded any contributor from our pages because he belonged to or didn't belong to any of these groups. And if the literary sympathizers of the Communist Party have not appeared in our pages, it is because they have yielded to a well-organized boycott campaign.

Mr. Cowley quotes extensively from two paragraphs of our six paragraph Editorial Statement. But he neither quotes from nor mentions the three central paragraphs, and for the very good reason that to do so would explode his main charge: that we are running under false colors. These paragraphs were devoted to a single theme: our reasons for considering the influence of the Communist Party a major threat to both literature and revolution in our time, and our determination to fight against this influence. Mr. Cowley is simply misrepresenting when he implies we have made any secret of our position on this issue. We must also object, in passing, to his expression, "anti-Soviet articles." He may identify the Kremlin with the Soviet Union. We don't, any more than we identify any particular administration with the United States of America.

Mr. Cowley's other charge—of inferior literary quality—he is careful to make almost wholly in the form of innuendo. Thus he implies but does not state that *Partisan Review* is on the same cultural level as the *New Masses*. (Our lawyers assure us that, although calculated to injure our business, this is an expression of opinion and so not libelous.) He implies but does not state that, for political reasons, we have shut the door on talented young unknowns. (We might note that our $100 short story prize was divided between two young writers whose prose we were the first to print, and that we have printed work by James Agee, Delmore Schwartz, Mary King, E. S. Bley, Jackson Matthews, Parker Tyler, Elizabeth Bishop, and many other young and comparatively unknown writers.) Mr. Cowley accuses us of substituting political for esthetic criteria—and also objects to our poetry and stories as "second-hand" Kafka and Mallarmé. Does this imply that Kafka and Mallarmé followed a Trotskyist-Bukharinist line? He also charges that "factional politics has got into the book review." To date, we have printed thirty-one reviews, in only one of which—Sidney Hook's review of Kenneth Burke's book—is the Stalinist issue raised explicitly. At least two books by writers close to the Communist Party—Richard Wright and Ernest Hemingway—were praised.

Mr. Cowley states: "F. W. Dupee . . . wrote a long essay on André Malraux and ended up by dismissing him as 'the type of liberal Comintern lobbyist thrown up by the stooge politics of people's frontism.' " This is a flat misquotation: Mr. Dupee applied these words not to Malraux, but to Garcia, the central character in *L'Espoir*. His article on Malraux, furthermore, is not a simpleminded political diatribe against a writer with whom he is in political disagreement, but a precise and painstaking analysis which attempts to correlate the literary and political qualities of Malraux's work. Mr. Cowley may or may not agree with Mr. Dupee's conclusions, but he has no right to imply the article is a mere piece of abuse such as — shall we say? — Mike Gold might have written.

It seems odd to us that Mr. Cowley, whose passion for Pure Literature burns in every line of his article, has never criticized the *New Masses* — which, with a great show of being fairminded, he admits is "more timid and conventional in literary matters than it used to be" — as he now attacks *Partisan Review*. It also seems odd that Mr. Cowley should find our literary standards so low when such non-political and exclusively literary magazines as *Poetry*, *New Directions*, and *The Criterion* have printed flattering notices of *Partisan Review*.

Who is this Galahad of Pure Literature who is demanding that *Partisan Review* emasculate itself politically and who can say a kind word for neo-Catholic literary magazines and Southern Agrarian literary magazines but not for anti-Stalinist literary magazines? (His position amounts to this: if you're going to touch on politics, be Stalinist; if you can't be Stalinist, then back to the Ivory Tower with you!) Who is this belated mourner at the bier of the *Dial* and the *Hound & Horn*? (According to those who followed his writing when those magazines were still alive, Mr. Cowley's admission that he "saw both of them go without much sorrow" is a masterpiece of understatement.) Isn't this the Mr. Cowley who not so long ago wrote an article defending the political censorship of literature? Isn't this the same Mr. Cowley we remember exhorting us at Writers' Congresses to climb up on the bandwagon of revolution? Isn't this the same Malcolm Cowley whose use of his position on the *New Republic* to play Communist Party politics has long been a literary scandal? And could we have mistaken the name signed to a review in the *New Republic* a few weeks ago which argued that Yeats was saved from "a broken career and an early death" by his political interests, even though he had "in many cases the wrong opinions"? "Some other week," concluded Mr. Cowley, "I should like to talk about Yeats and political criticism, as it is represented in this country by magazines like *Partisan Review*." But when he came to writing the article, he said nothing about Yeats. Perhaps he realized the cases were hardly parallel. Yeats was "wrong" on Irish political issues which have only an academic interest here today, and so his political interests enriched his poetry. But *Partisan Review* is "wrong" on issues which very intimately and tenderly concern Mr. Cowley, and so *our* political interests have destroyed and corrupted our literary perceptions.

Mr. Cowley concludes his highminded defense of literary values by remarking of *Partisan Review*: "Put a green cover on it, and today you could hardly tell it from the *American Mercury*." This is Red-baiting, C.P. style, no more and no less.

The Editors of *Partisan Review*

October 17, 1938.

1939, vol. 6, no. 1

• September Journal
Stephen Spender

September 6th

I want to go on about Germany, about my landlord in Berlin, about Curtius, but I feel too tired, I can't go on. The first thing about any war is that everyone is tired, countries at war are countries of tiredness, fatigue becomes a spiritual experience. It becomes an illumination: fetters of habit which make one wash and shave every day, which make one preface every contact with one's neighbor with embarrassment, fall away, and one enters into a more easy relationship with one's fellow beings, an exhausted simplified state of being oneself. The wrong words which come into one's mind, which the rigid discipline of wakefulness would reject, are suddenly the right ones, everything flows freely and nervously, one does not even resent the heavy weight on one's eyes, because one sees so much light.

There was an air raid warning last night. A— seems so far away now, I imagine her in her red dressing gown and she looks pale and dazed. I don't imagine her happily. But I imagine her tenderly. Perhaps in a few days I'll be able to think about her without reproach. Perhaps I'll get tired enough during this war to forgive her.

I remember again the water, the flowing line of the hills, the rich harvest quality of Germany. Immediately, of course, I suspect it of a certain falsity, a certain coarseness and thickness and monotony of texture, but still it is there, there like Wordsworth's poem about the peasant girl. E. took me all over the place. He had a little car, and when he wasn't watching the road, his eyes were on me watching the effect of the storks on the roofs of North German villages, of monkeys playing at the Hagenbeck Zoo, of the Harz mountains. "If you like music we shall have a great deal in common," he said when we first met, and if ever I admitted for one moment that I appreciated anything, his eyes were ready to smile: "Ah, we have a great deal in common."

So we went to the Harz mountains, stopping on our way at Brunswick where we saw in a very dusty and deserted gallery one of the finest Rembrandts I have ever seen. We visited some people called Harman who had a house in the Harz mountains. Like everyone else they had lost their money and all they had was the property itself and, I suppose, the salary of Professor Harman. The whole family, grandmother, son, daughter-in-law, a grandson, two daughters, and a brother and sister who were fellow-students of Wolfgang, the son, at — University, were there. Like nearly everyone I met in Germany at this time, they were obviously living from hand to mouth, they spent what they had, they laughed and talked a great deal, and yet they had an air of having lost everything. Wolfgang had rather pinched, vague features which had a certain pallid, distracted beauty which attracted me at the time.

Several years later, after Hitler's rise to power, Wolfgang came to visit me in London. Earnest, and pale as ever, he had a mission: he wanted to convert me to Nazism. "Of course, there are things I do not like about the Nazis," he said. "I do not agree with their views on literature and art. I do not sympathize with the persecution of the Jews. I do not accept their explanation of the Reichstag fire (though there is more in it than you would think). I do not like Goebbels' propaganda. In fact, I dislike everything nasty about them. But all they same, they have a Faith." Here his fists clenched and his eyes burned with a dubious mystery. "They have restored to us our belief in Germany and Life. Some of them are Idealists. There is a good deal of socialism in their economy." I raged as I had done before. I told him that the most dangerous propagandists of Nazism were people like himself who pretended that they did not approve of its bad qualities and yet had accepted it. I told him he was a dupe, and that the Nazis wouldn't care a damn about his footling little qualifications to satisfy his own conscience, so long as they had got him where they had got him. I said: "If I were a German, as I well might be, I would by now either be in a Concentration Camp or else deprived of every means of earning my living. You can't expect me to be fair. I don't care about your reasons." And I am ashamed to say that I kicked him out of the house.

This was an unnecessary piece of self-righteousness on my part, because I heard later that he became disillusioned about the Nazis and was one of those unhappy, pained, gentle creatures who represent the heart of another Germany and do not understand what is happening to them. I have touched a deeper chord than I knew here, for have I not met two or three of them, don't I know very well the peculiar whiteness and stillness of their eyes, which seem to have been drained of pigment? These poor ghosts are really beautiful in a sexless way, because if one is a young man of another era, naturally one cannot expect to be virile. How closely I press now upon a secret! Why am I always attracted by these desolate spirits? There was one whom I met on the Hook of Holland boat once shortly before Hitler's rise to power. He was the son of a general, and now that at least four names crowd on to me, I remember that they are all aristocrats and often close to the higher ranks of the army. I cannot remember the names exactly—oh yes, this boy was called Horst. He had a round face with very well-formed features, delicate lips, china blue eyes, a tender complexion and brown hair of an almost feathery lightness. He was quiet and polite, and he had some small out-of-the-way interest (just as Wolfgang had a card index in which he "collected" Shakespeare's imagery)—Horst's hobby was playing the flute or making musical instruments or something. There's really nothing much more to it than that. He had a Rhodes scholarship at Oxford and I used to call on him there and we went for walks and I introduced him to Isaiah Berlin because he didn't seem to know anybody. But he never became part of the life at Oxford. He was always just as gentle, just as isolated, and gradually one saw beyond the varnish of his interest in the musical instrument—or whatever—to a distress and restlessness of spirit that never ceased. Isaiah saw him several times and then confessed to me that the sustained slight sense of his unhappiness was too much: he no longer cared to see him.

Another such was surely Jowo von M— who wandered about Europe looking at pictures. They all had some mild objective interest which obviously was not their life but which covered their refusal ever to speak about Germany. Perhaps, like Wolfgang, when the Nazis first came to power they flamed with a momentary hope which soon disappeared as they reverted to their former hobbies. Werner von L— was a more energetic variation on this type of German. When I first met him he was an ardent Social Democrat, in fact he was literally holding up in his rooms at Oxford a red banner which a Jewish girl with whom he lived had embroidered for a Peace Procession. When the Nazis came into power he took the complicated view that this after all was perhaps the socialism he had been fighting for. He was a law student and he pretended to admire enormously the legal code which the Nazis introduced with their revolution. He forced, rather cruelly, the Jewish girl (who still used to visit Germany and camp with him in the woods) to admire this masterpiece. She told me that although she did not agree with the treatment of the Jews, etc., nevertheless, the documents in which the new laws were codified were marvelous. It was pathetic. I showed my lack of understanding again by fulminating.

September 8th

When I come to think of it, the trouble with all the nice people I knew in Germany is that they were either tired or weak. The young people in Hamburg were tired, the young Nationalist aristocrats were weak. How are the people of good will today to avoid weakness and fatigue?

September 9th

Yesterday morning while I was waiting for a bus, some soldiers passed down the road singing "It's a long way to Tipperary." An unshaved and very ragged old tramp wearing the ribbons of several medals so loosely attached to his coat that they were almost falling off said to me: "They're singing now, but they won't be singing when they come back. Hearing 'em sing reminds me of when I went out to fight in them trenches. We went out singing, but we didn't sing for long."

In the afternoon I got a taxi to Waterloo before going into the country. We were stopped near Southampton Row by five Frenchmen carrying a flag and singing the Marseillaise. The taxi man said to me: "They won't be doing that for long."

Peter Watson travelled from Paris to Calais a few days ago in a troop train. The compartment was crowded with soldiers. They sat all the way in absolute silence, no one saying a word.

September 10th

The best lack all conviction, while the worst
Are full of passionate intensity.

W. B. Yeats, who wrote these lines, himself became a Fascist sympathizer. He was prepared to accept the worst. He wanted strength at any price.

Why were the gentle and kind people I knew in Germany tired or weak?

The tiredness of our generation consists in exploring unimportant and superficial aspects of the idea of freedom, without trying to discover the strong basis on which any really free life must be built. Freedom, the young people in Hamburg said, is sexual freedom primarily, then freedom to enjoy yourself, to wander, not to make money, not to have the responsibility of a family, or the duties of a citizen generally. Freedom is one long holiday. They were tired. What they wanted, in fact, was a holiday.

Beware of people who explain themselves in terms of the difficult childhood they have had, the economic conditions of their country since the war, and everything in short that they have been through. Beware of people who say: "You don't understand me."

After 1929, it became obvious that the world of these irresponsible Germans was threatened.

New styles of architecture, a change of heart.

The architecture was mostly swimming baths built with money raised from American loans. The change of heart, sunbathing and sexual freedom, was almost as uneconomical an investment as the new architecture. That's to say, although it produced a charming little shoot, it didn't take root in the stony and barren soil of the difficult postwar years.

I feel uneasy about discussing these things in an airy, Left Book Club manner, suddenly identifying myself with the Workers, in order to sneer at the people with whom I spend my weekends, and dismissing my own promiscuous past as though I have renounced it finally. The fact is that I have just had a first class failure in my personal life, and I am so full of regret and bitterness that I cannot stay in the country because I dream of nothing else.

However, important as these things are, the first sign of the "German tiredness" is to treat them as though nothing else were more important. My friends in Hamburg behaved as though nothing mattered in life except sex and personal relationships, and at the same time they kept these problems in a state of perpetual, unsolved, pleasurable suspense.

But if a human relationship becomes more important than anything else in two people's lives, it simply means that there is a lack of trust between these two people. A relationship is not a way of entering into a kind of dual subjectivity, a redoubled and reciprocal egotism, it is an alliance of two people who form a united front to deal with the problems of the outside world and who understand that their trust in each other will not be broken up by impertinent outsiders. The problem of married people is not to become absorbed in each other, but how not to become absorbed in each other, how, in a word, to trust one another, in order to enter into a strong and satisfactory relationship with the society in which they live.

A great cause of weakness today is people putting less important things before those that are more important, for example, personal relationships before work and an objective philosophy of life, sex before love. People who put personal relationships before their work become parasites on each other, form mutual admiration societies, agree to do nothing that may make one jealous of the success in the world of the other. People who put sex before love flee from one marital relationship to another, using love as their excuse; because, for them, sex has become a thing in itself, dissociated from personal relationships. They have an image in their minds of one hundred per cent sexual satisfaction, and when they are in love, they are continually asking themselves "Am I satisfied?" and they are continually tormented by the thought that perhaps they are not. For them love, at first an opportunity, soon becomes a trap, forcing them to give something instead of taking all the time, and preventing them from grasping at the possibly greater delights they might get elsewhere.

Satisfactory personal relationships exist when the people who enjoy them have a satisfactory relation with society. They exist within society, they are not a conspiracy against society. In the same way, satisfactory sex exists within love and can be attained through love, which means patience and loyalty and understanding.

Another cause of weakness is not to admit but to pursue our failures blindly. There is such a thing as real failure in personal relationships and in sex. How easily then, that which symbolizes failure, the poor substitute improvised for love, becomes the most important thing in life! How people build it up and call the scars of failure their dazzling successes! Masturbation, homosexuality, following people in the streets, breaking up relationships because one has failed in one's own, all these compensatory activities form a circle of Hell in which people can never rest from proving that their failures are the same as love. Yet the lives of countless men and women show that the great compensation lies in accepting failures as failures, and recognizing substitutes as substitutes, and making the most of the rest of one's life. In fact the great artists and poets have almost without exception been failures in life. By this I mean that their relations with their fellow beings were really and truly at some point unsatisfactory, that most of them were fully conscious of this, and that their honesty in admitting a defect restored to their lives a sense of scale which hopelessly neurotic people lack. Baudelaire's relationship with a Negress, the breakdown of Gauguin's marriage which led him to go to the South Seas, Van Gogh's failures in love, Rilke's wanderings and sense of being *outside* love, to mention only a few examples which immediately come to mind, were all real failures in life and to "the man of genius" the failure to be a complete man must always be a humiliation. The compensations of genius are so dazzling that it is difficult to realize that Beethoven and Balzac paid so great a price, when they yet had the infinite privilege of being Beethoven and Balzac. They suffered as men, they rejoiced as creators.

The creative artist realizes that art is not a complete life, otherwise he would be self-sufficient, he would isolate himself from the world of ordinary living, and there would be happy, unreal artists creating a truly pure art. Some people who are not artists, or who are bad artists, think that art is like this, a world cut off from the world, where aesthetic experience is everything. These are the virtuosi of art and of appreciation: spirits which have flowed completely into an aesthetic medium, without the friction of living their lives.

Of all the arts, music provides the most self-sufficient alternative world removed from the real world. Painting is the most objective of the arts because visual imagery always has a direct reference to real objects, and in order to get away from the broad day, painters have deliberately to paint visual experiences remembered from sleep—dreams. But music is not a dream that imitates our sleep, it is a world of its own, full of abstract aural patterns which are not recognizably related to the noises we hear in everyday life. At the same time it creates a world of tremendous conviction. The absolute ideas which have such a wavering meaning in words and which it puzzles us to attach to human behavior have their fixed places in music. Schiller's "Ode to Liberty" is a work which conveys little more to us today than a sense of enthusiasm for ideas which meant a great deal to Schiller but which the time between him and us has cast a doubt if not a slur upon. But in the music of the last movement of Beethoven's Ninth Symphony these ideas are fixed in a world of their own which one can enter without referring it back to the real world and the disillusion of the past hundred years.

Actually, the value of the music lies in the fact that it does nevertheless refer back to the real world of experience. The triumph of art is not merely a triumph over technical difficulties, but the triumph of resolving the conflicts of life into a more enduring form of acceptance and contemplation. To regard these great acts of acceptance—the masterpieces of art—as acts of rejection and escape is simply a way of losing grip, it is letting the engine run without the wheels turning. If one looks at the faces of people in a concert one can see the difference between those who use music as a form of living and those who use it as a form of dying. The virtuoso of listening is, like the virtuoso of performing, a wonderful child, one who has never grown up but melted himself on the furnace of great works of art where he continually flows away. The people who are not virtuosi have a certain sculptural rigidity—the face of Schnabel or Toscanini—because they are always discovering a unity between the experiences of life and art.

The young aristocratic sons of German militarists whom I call "weak" were trying, without much conviction, it is true, to use the appreciation of art as a complete way of living and as an escape from their despair about Germany. But this does not work. You go to the concert and music offers an interior life of sounds inside your head which is as complete as anything you have experienced. You read a play of Shakespeare and you enter into a love and a courage of feeling completer because more explicit and final than anything that your own life may provide. "This is where I live most intensely," you think. "This is real for me. Everything else can be put aside and forgotten." But it can't. The felt life in the work of art is only intense, and often painful, because it actually touches the life of deep and terrible experience. Without this experience, art would simply express a frictionless tendency towards a vacuous perfection. But in true art there is a real conflict of life, a real breaking up and melting down of intractable material, feelings and sensations which seem incapable of expression until they have been thus transformed. A work of art doesn't say "I am life, I offer you the opportunity of becoming me." On the contrary, it says: "This is what life is like. It is even realer, less to be evaded, than you thought. But I offer you an example of acceptance and understanding. Now, go back and live!"   1940, vol. 7, no. 1

• The Cultural Front: Leon Trotsky
James T. Farrell

The life of Leon Trotsky is one of the great tragic dramas of modern history. Pitting his brain and will against the despotic rulers of a great empire, fully conscious of the power, the resources, the cunning and cruelty of his enemy, Trotsky had one weapon at his command—his ideas. His courage never faltered; his will never broke. His children were murdered or driven to suicide; his friends, his coworkers, and secretaries were killed. His entire generation was annihilated. He lived the life of a prisoner, continually exposed to the blow of an assassin. He was fatalistic enough to know that he would probably not live to see his ideas triumph. Nevertheless, he accepted without a moment's hesitation all the risks involved in the propagation of his doctrines. Finally, unable to refute his ideas, they drove a pick axe into his brain.

During the last forty years Leon Trotsky's life was consecrated to one end—the socialist revolution. It was with the greatest of contempt that he looked upon the men in power who had traded their historic roles for portfolios. And how did their conduct compare with his when they too lost power and were forced into exile? Nomadic statesmen, they traveled from capital to capital begging favors from bourgeois public opinion, intriguing, maneuvering, manipulating, with the hope that perhaps the Quai d'Orsay, Downing Street, or the White House might restore their portfolios. But Trotsky was big enough to stand alone, always rising to the level of his historic position. In exile he produced book after book, a brilliant series of works unmatched in our time that, even more than the example of his life, remain the legacy of future generations. And you cannot drive a pick axe into ideas.

I admired Trotsky as a historical figure, and Trotsky the man inspired me with affection. Even his critics have recognized Trotsky's brilliance as a writer; but his work is more than brilliant—it is fertile, suggestive, illuminating. Compared to its method, acuteness, and high seriousness, the productions of our American political scientists and journalists seem morally flabby, spineless, full of facile improvisations. No political writer alive today can rival his record of almost clairvoyant predictions of later events.

Most of Trotsky's critics have presented him as a modern Machiavelli, hungry for personal power, who even in exile was desperately seeking to recapture it. This conception of Trotsky as a power-hungry Machiavellian falsifies his life. Trotsky the materialist took ideas with the greatest seriousness. He defended Marxism dogmatically. He defended dialectical materialism at times when neither its defense nor its rejection involved questions of power. His policies were based on his ideas. His decisions were in harmony with his premises and his principles. It is noteworthy that anecdotes about Trotsky, reminiscences of personal discussions, and his letters do not contain a single cynical statement about the methods necessary to attain power which one inevitably finds in the records of genuine Machiavellians like Napoleon. He had supreme confidence in the validity of his ideas. To hold to the conception of Trotsky as a Machiavellian one must argue that almost his entire life, his voluminous books, and his numberless letters were all a false front to mask a secret motive which he hid from his closest friends and collaborators.

For Trotsky all intellectual questions were practical and concrete. His test for the validity of ideas was how they worked out in practice, in the actual framework of history. In this respect he was close to the pragmatists. While Trotsky upheld some dogmas and was sometimes even schematic in his thinking, he was a relativist in his handling of ideas. He had an acute sense of the involvement of events in each other, of their interrelationships. I recall how, during the course of a disagreement with him, he emphasized the necessity of conceiving a fact not merely as something which exists but also as something which is in process of becoming. This sense of becoming in events, of the relational character of events to each other, was one of his most remarkable intellectual traits. He never isolated political events; he saw them consistently in their international setting. He was no crude empiricist, nor did he indulge in easy psychological interpretations as a substitute for objective analysis. Some of us thought that our general theories were at times more sound than Trotsky's. We even took delight in proofs that his philosophical formulations were not modern and could easily be refuted through logical analysis. Yet Trotsky was more creative with his bad epistemology than we were with our good epistemology.

Trotsky was a harsh opponent, never hesitating to break with friend after friend on issues of principle and policy. In this regard he did not differ from most men of strong convictions. In his thinking he was more inclined to draw sharp distinctions than to conciliate differences. These temperamental traits were, in a sense, psychological adaptations to his chosen way of life. Moreover, a man less intransigent than he could not have endured the blows he received in his days of exile. In public, Trotsky was often sharp, alert, metallic. Under questioning he was guarded and suspicious, inclined to break out in sharp invective or ironic statements. But his adamant side did not exhaust his personality. Many of his friends and disciples knew him as a warm and generous man. I think he wanted friends and tended to be excessively trusting with them, so much so that he often regarded people whom he had met only a few times as friends. In his personal relations he was simple and charming—a man of singular grace.

Highly disciplined, Trotsky was unsparing of himself, subordinating all his impulses to his central purpose. I have never known another man whose very organism was so completely under the control of his will and intelligence. What he hated most was stupidity. In fact, he so hated it that he could not even listen to stories about the stupidity of his enemies. He was also impatient of incompetence. I recall how on a picnic Trotsky watched a friend try to start a fire clumsily. This friend had broken with him politically. In a bantering way Trotsky suggested that his friend's politics matched his ability to start a fire. Finally he made the fire himself quickly and efficiently.

One of Trotsky's traits that I admired most was his capacity for contempt. He knew how to despise those liberal intellectuals who, behind a set of pretentious gestures, invariably reflected the hypocrisy of bourgeois public opinion. At the same time such people puzzled him. A New York editor who had printed attacks on Trotsky which virtually called him an assassin requested to see him while vacationing in Mexico. He refused the request. But he was no snob. While intolerant of people who wished to visit him purely for curiosity's sake, he was hospitable to more serious visitors, regardless of their reputations or achievements. Thus he devoted as much care and thought to a letter to an unknown worker as he would to an article directed against a famous figure. He saw in everyone the representative of a class or of a social group, and in everyone's ideas he perceived their political consequences. His estimates of character, despite the charges of his critics, were generally not personal: they were political and intellectual. His brilliant character vignettes in *The History of the Russian Revolution* are actually social studies in miniature. In answering questions put to him by the Dewey Commission he was most balanced in his evaluation of Stalin. He pointed out that Stalin did not become what he is today all at once, and at one time even Stalin was a good revolutionary. But to Lenin Trotsky had a personal relation. Even more than Marx, Lenin was (I think) his teacher. I would categorically discount the charge that Trotsky was really jealous of Lenin and used his memory to justify himself. On the contrary, his attitude to Lenin was one of reverence.

Some have been disconcerted by Trotsky's optimism and faith. But this faith, even if one cannot share it, is easily understood when one considers that they are necessary elements in any practical activity. What was to him a series of practical issues was to his intellectualistic critics purely a set of formal questions. In formal intellectual activity we are not optimistic and believing but skeptical; and in some of Trotsky's theoretical opponents this skepticism sometimes results in irresponsibility. While he was risking his life for his ideas, they are risking a syllogism.

Neither Stalinism nor the capitalist world can forgive Leon Trotsky. They will hate his memory, but they will never succeed in erasing it. History will know how to preserve it.

One of the best tributes we can pay Trotsky is to understand him. These notes are an effort toward such an understanding. I offer them in tribute to the memory of the Old Man.   1940, vol. 7. no. 5

- ## Ten Propositions on the War
Clement Greenberg and Dwight Macdonald

1. *This war is different from the last one.*

This war is not essentially a repetition of the 1914–1918 conflict. There are decisive differences—in economy, politics, war aims—between the two sides. The writers are not agreed as to whether these differences go so far as to constitute a new kind of society in Germany, but they do agree on their existence. The Kaiser's victory would not have meant a *break* in our civilization. Hitler's would.

2. *Fascism is less desirable than democratic capitalism.*

Fascism in general and Nazism in particular do not represent the kind of revolution the bourgeoisie led against feudalism, but a union of advanced technology with reactionary social concepts. A Nazi-dominated Europe will be politically enslaved, economically impoverished, culturally barbarous.

3. *The issue—not war but revolution.*

Modern politics revolve on the axis of War. But the real issue is not the war itself—"for?" "against?"—but the war in relation to social revolution. The choice is not whether to Defend America by Aiding the Allies or to Keep America out of War. Neither formula *in itself* will advance us one step nearer the only real solution, which is to deflect the current of history from Fascism to socialism. ("Socialism" we define as collectivized property plus political democracy.) In the war or out of it, the United States faces only one future under capitalism: Fascism. The socialist alternative: i.e., to win the war without losing democracy, can be realized only by revolutionary mass action.

4. *Isolationism is provincial inanity.*

The argument of the Keep America out of War Committee, which unites pacifists, liberals, and Norman Thomas socialists on an isolationist platform, is that if we go in, we will go totalitarian *ourselves*. Agreed. But if we keep out and Hitler wins, how does the future look? Immediate: competition in the world market with a totalitarian Europe, building a huge "defensive" war machine—undertakings which, under capitalism (and the Committee takes no stand on an alternative system), also demand totalitarian controls. Long range (five to ten years): the third, and climactic, World War, the final showdown between German and American imperialism. This can be postponed, but it is provincial idiocy to think, as Thomas and his KAOW seem to, that the America of 1941 could turn its back on the world and peacefully cultivate its own back yard. Assuming the persistence of capitalism in this country, the left interventionists have all the better of the argument. And it is just here that Thomas offers the same old program of peaceful, respectable, "evolutionary" progress whose last pretensions were shattered in 1914.

5. *To support the Roosevelt-Churchill war regimes clears the road for fascism from within and blocks the organization of an effective war effort against fascism outside.*

The line which most of the left today favors (liberal weeklies, top labor bureaucracy, Committee for Democratic Action, such ex-Marxists as Eastman, Corey, and Hook) is to support the Roosevelt-Churchill war regime as the lesser evil to Hitlerism. But hasn't the experience of the last decade shown clearly that the very most democratic capitalism can do is *retard* the advance of fascism (and even that only under exceptionally favorable circumstances) and that it cannot negate or destroy fascism? Haven't we yet learned that this is a period when the greater evil yields not to the lesser evil, but only to the positive good? (The Brüning regime was a 'lesser evil' to fascism in its day.) But now the social system of Churchill and Roosevelt is so incompetent to plan large scale production whether for war or peace, so lacking in appeal to the masses, that it is a weapon which is breaking in the hands of those who would turn it against Hitlerism.

The war party proclaims theirs as the only "realistic" antifascist program. They reject a revolutionary struggle for socialism during the war as quixotic, if not worse. We say *theirs* is the unrealistic course, we say *they* are the true Don Quixotes, foolishly dreaming of defending an antiquated way of life.* If the isolationists are provincial, the interventionists lack a historical sense. No deficiency could be more fatal today.

The experience of the British labor movement after a year of "realistic" collaboration with Churchill and the Tories against Hitler should teach us something. As has been the case for half a century, from Millerand to MacDonald and Blum, this "collaboration" really means submission of the ruled to their rulers. To the increasing dismay of liberals, the center of gravity of the Churchill-Labour government has shifted steadily to the *right* in the past year. Similar effects are beginning to appear in this country: the use of the Army to break the North American Aviation strike. In both countries, the logic of politics has turned the present governments against the greatest living force against fascism: the labor movement.

All this might be stomached as a lesser evil to a Nazi victory—but it is just the point that all this is making such a victory increasingly likely. Thus in England the political suicide of the Labour Party, in restoring to power the Tories, has given back the conduct of the war precisely to those who can never win it.

The lesser evil policy means toleration of the existing social system. But capitalism is *intolerable* in a functional as well as a moral sense. It has become archaic to the point where the ruling class can no longer defend its own interests within that form. Evidence: the failure of England, even after a year of total war, to create a real war economy; our own increasing difficulties along that line; the political ineptness of the "democracies" in the war to date; the lack of war aims; the constant indications that almost no one, *including the capitalists*, any longer seriously believes that the old order will survive this war. The alternatives the lesser evil policy of supporting Roosevelt-Churchill presents are: military defeat owing to the superiority of fascism in total warfare; or victory under a fascist system of our own.

6. *The working class alone can lead a successful fight against Nazism because it alone can overmatch the Nazis in (1) military methods, (2) war production, (3) war aims.*

(1) Hitler's advanced methods of waging war reflect his advanced politics—advanced in the sense that they manifest a greater awareness of the present state

---

* Quixote's delusion was to overestimate his antagonists, seeing windmills as giants, sheep as armies. His modern similars see giants as windmills and Nazis as simple lunatics. They show, however, as great a capacity of idealization, as cf. the Dulcinea of Churchill-Roosevelt democracy, the Rosinante of the Anglo-American war machine.

of the world and a more serious resolution to meet its problems than shown by the bourgeois democracies. A social revolution throwing a new class—the proletariat—into power would produce even more advanced methods of waging war, since this new class would be under a minimum of illusions and would have no interest in salvaging the status quo with all its impediments. It would be able to act with a directness and a realism and therefore an efficiency even Hitler—after all, only a pseudo-revolutionary—could not match; it would open up opportunities to the new talents we now so urgently need.

(2) In this war you see a new phenomenon. The British and American bourgeoisie, tied to a system of private property hopelessly archaic vis-à-vis the economic demands of modern warfare, are unable to organize production efficiently enough to win their own imperialist war. Such planning as we have seen has come from the working class. The British did not even begin to create a modern war economy until the Labour Party took over the key economic posts last year. In this country, the CIO Industrial Councils plan and the Reuther plan for mass production of aircraft by the automobile industry are much the boldest and most reasonable proposals for all-out war production. It is true that the reformist *political* line of the British and American labor chiefs who put forward these plans, based as it is on the perpetuation of capitalism and hence the subordination of labor to the bourgeoisie, has made it easy for the ruling class to sabotage them. The significance of the plans remains, however. In putting them forward, Bevin and Morrison, Murray and Reuther are speaking as representatives of a class whose interests are in congruence and not in conflict with the organization of a planned economy. Nothing less than this will beat Hitler.

(3) As even the conservatives are beginning to realize, this is a political war. The lack of any inspiring—or even sensible—war aims is therefore the greatest weakness of the capitalist democracies. The Churchillian defenders of democracy agree with the appeasers in that they cannot conceive of any war aims more desirable than the preservation of the social status quo. (They differ only as to whether Hitler or the British Empire would be the better preserver.) Thus in Nazi-occupied countries where native revolutions could win the war for England, Churchill's propaganda arouses little response. Actually, the rulers of Great Britain were afraid to encourage a revolution in Italy at the time of the Libyan reverses because they knew that such a revolt could only come from the Left, under the banners of socialism. And so British airplanes dropped leaflets on the Italian countryside which read: "REMEMBER GARIBALDI'S CURSE: WOE TO HIME WHO FIGHTS AGAINST ENGLAND!" (Those dropped in Germany are most likely copies of Schiller's poem on the defeat of the Spanish Armada.)

As long as Churchill-Roosevelt and their class conduct the war against Hitler, the masses everywhere can hope for little *for themselves* from Hitler's defeat. Only a program which promises a real reorganization of society can inspire the peoples in the conquered countries to dare to revolt, to take the risks involved by widespread and constant sabotage. And only working-class socialism can offer them such a program.

7. *The involvement of Russia in the war does not change the issues.*

Now that Hitler has attacked Russia, we may expect to see one more indication that the political line of the American Communist Party is simply a reflex of Soviet foreign policy. Already the Stalinists' fraudulent antiwar propaganda is yielding to ever louder calls for all aid to the "workers' fatherland." Tomorrow they will be the most ardent supporters of Roosevelt's war policy—if he gives such aid. But the issues of the war are still the same in the sense that without socialist revolution, fascism will triumph in one form or another. The writers disagree as to whether or not Soviet Russia should be supported against Hitler, but they agree that the struggle against the present conduct of the war and for socialism in this country cannot be relaxed one jot, regardless of the effect on aid to Russia.*

8. *Social revolution in England or America would not necessarily open the gates to Hitler. It would most probably be short and relatively peaceful and lead to an immediate intensification of the war effort.*

It is likely that the revolution, if it comes at all during this war, will be neither a protracted nor an especially violent struggle.

Its chief opposition will be a ruling class so discredited by its military incapacity and so demoralized by its own mistakes as to be unable to offer serious resistance for some time to come. As in the French and Russian revolutions, the *ancien régime* will surprise everybody with the suddenness and completeness of its collapse. Even in England, and certainly in this country, the actual transfer of power need not offer Hitler any open door. The real revolutionary struggle will come considerably later, when the counterrevolution has had time to organize itself. (This, by the way, may also be expected to take place *abroad*, as in the French and Russian experiences, with Hitler backing the counterrevolution à la Pitt-Clemenceau.) The revolutionary cause, calling for a more efficient, energetic, and uncompromising fight against Hitler, will immediately become the patriotic cause *par excellence*. Counterrevolutionaries would be open to the charge of treason and by their very least acts would identify themselves with the foreign enemy. As in the great French revolution, the fight against the enemy within would only intensify the struggle against the enemy without.

9. *There exists today no organized leadership for such a revolutionary policy as we advocate. But while this is a serious lack, it is not a fatal one. New organizational forms must and will be found.*

We can learn valuable lessons, of course, from the Russian revolution, but it is not the pattern for all revolutions. Many of those who today deprecate most violently the practicability of a successful revolution conceive of the socialist revo-

---

*My position here, I admit, is a difficult one and open to serious misunderstanding, but no matter: as Trotsky said, "If we theoretically admit war [involving the Soviet Union] without revolution, then the defeat of the Soviet Union is inevitable." If we admit this present war without revolution, the defeat of humanity is inevitable. —C.G.

lution exclusively in terms of Bolshevism, arguing that since such a party is necessary, and since no such party of any significance exists today, therefore the
prospect is hopeless. They are Leninists in reverse.

A tightly disciplined and trained organization was a necessity in Russia
because of the extremely low cultural level of the masses. This backwardness was
such as to require, as midwives of the revolution, a "general staff" of Bolshevist
experts who had to take every initiative themselves and were unable to delegate
responsibility or authority in a democratic way. Here in the West it is quite otherwise. The technical competence and relatively high cultural level of the individual worker would make for a much wider distribution of initiative and authority, thus making possible, indeed necessary, a quite different kind of party from
the Bolshevik model: a looser party reflecting the diversity of a more highly developed society, perhaps a grouping of parties rather than The Party.

It is wrong to look at the question of political parties *sub specie eternitas*: the
great French revolution was not made by any one party, nor was the 1905 Russian
revolution. While it is true that *some* form of organization is necessary and does
not exist today, this deficiency does not of itself invalidate the general line of these
propositions. And if this line of development is correct, if the capitalist order in
England and America is as unequal to the problems of this war period as we think
it is, then we can at least today propagandize such ideas and support such tendencies as seem to lead towards the formation of a party or movement which will
be able to take advantage of the revolutionary situations we believe will develop
in the future. Parties sometimes make history, but history also makes parties.

10. *To win the war against fascism, we must work for the replacement of the present governments in England and the United States by working-class governments
committed to a program of democratic socialism. All support of whatever kind must
be withheld from Churchill and Roosevelt.*

Otherwise we are lost. They can only lead us to disaster. The attack upon them
and what they represent should take the form of constant and radical criticism of
their conduct of the war. This criticism must be coupled with demands for the
greatest possible mass participation in the leadership and guidance of the state,
referenda upon crucial issues, working class control of economic planning, public diplomacy, democratization of the army, equality for Negroes, etc., etc.* These
demands are by their very nature an attack upon the existing social order, and it

---

* There are those who will say that these demands per se are so impracticable as to cancel themselves
out in the public consciousness: there won't be enough time to put such demands into effect, and even
should they be put into effect the machinery of the state and the army would become so cumbersome
and slow as to be ruinous to the prosecution of the war. As for (1), this war has so far consisted of long
periods of comparative inactivity punctuated by short bursts of fighting, which would have given Great
Britain and France ample time to reorganize themselves along the lines proposed. Such changes can
take place more speedily in wartime than in peace. The British still have time. As for (2), democratization of the state and the army does not exclude the limited delegation of authority in emergencies, and
it is debatable whether referenda would take more time than the deliberations of bourgeois statesmen.

is inconceivable that Churchill or Roosevelt would or could grant them. The policy of Laski, Strachey, Bevan, Williams, and the left wing of the British Labour Party of supporting the present government and at the same time pressing for such demands, therefore, means in practice giving up these demands and acquiescing in the status quo. The choice is inescapable: which do you put first, your support or your demands? Laski & Co. put their support first, we put our demands first. The conclusion is equally inescapable: opposition to any government which cannot grant such demands. The experience of the last year in England, to delve no deeper into history, seems to indicate that the fight for an all-out socialist war effort can be prosecuted only from *outside* the present regimes in England and this country. Only socialism can win this war. Only uncompromising, unambiguous, and unflagging opposition to Churchill and Roosevelt can win socialism.

Roosevelt-Churchill have a simple, all too simple formula for victory: kill enough Germans. Aside from the fact that the cost of such a victory would make it an empty one, entailing the destruction of as much that we love as that we hate, the truth is that the democracies cannot defeat Hitler by force. They cannot get close enough to slug it out—even assuming they are better at slugging than the Germans. And so for years to come they must content themselves with long-range attrition, warfare that exhausts and kills but does not decide. What future does this hold out to our civilization?

The only way this conflict can be won in the interests of mankind as a whole is by some method of warfare that will transfer the struggle from the flesh of humanity to its mind. Such a method is offered only by the cause of the socialist revolution.   1941, vol. 8, no. 4

- **London Letter**
  George Orwell

April 15, 1941

Dear Editors,
As you see by the above date, I only received your letter a month after it was sent, so there is not much hope of my getting a reply to you by April 20th. I expect this will reach you before June, however. I will try to make some sort of answer to all your questions, but I should go over the allotted space if I answered them all in full, so I will concentrate on the ones I know most about. You don't mention anything in my previous letter having been blacked out by the censor, so I presume I can speak fairly freely. [Neither in this nor in Mr. Orwell's last letter did the British censor make any deletions.—ED.]

1. *What is the level and tone of the popular press these days? How much real information about the war effort comes out? How fully are strikes and labor troubles reported? Debates in Parliament? How dominant is the propaganda note? Is this propaganda mostly anti-Hun and jingoistic flag waving as in the last war, or is it more antifascist? What about the radio? Cinema?*

The tone of the popular press has improved out of recognition during the last year. This is especially notable in the *Daily Mirror* and *Sunday Pictorial* (tabloid papers of vast circulation, read largely by the army), and the Beaverbrook papers, the *Daily Express, Sunday Express,* and *Evening Standard.* Except for the *Daily Mail* and certain Sunday papers, these used to be the most lowbrow section of the press, but they have all grown politically serious while preserving their "stunt" make-up, with screaming headlines, etc. All of them print articles which would have been considered hopelessly above their readers' heads a couple of years ago, and the *Mirror* and the *Standard* are noticeably "left." The *Standard* is the least important of Beaverbrook's three papers, and he has apparently taken his eye off it and left its direction almost entirely to young journalists of left-wing views who are allowed to say what they like so long as they don't attack the boss directly. Nearly the whole of the press is now "left" compared with what it was before Dunkirk—even the *Times* mumbles about the need for centralized ownership and greater social equality—and to find any straightforward expression of reactionary opinions, i.e. reactionary in the old pre-Fascist sense, you now have to go to obscure weekly and monthly papers, mostly Catholic papers. There is an element of eyewash in all this, but it is partly due to the fact that the decline in the trade in consumption goods has robbed the advertisers of much of their power over editorial policy. Ultimately this will bankrupt the newspapers and compel the state to take them over, but at the moment they are in an interim period when they are controlled by journalists rather than advertisers, which is all to the good for the short time it will last.

As to accuracy of news, I believe this is the most truthful war that has been fought in modern times. Of course one only sees enemy newspapers very rarely, but in our own papers there is certainly nothing to compare with the frightful lies that were told on both sides in 1914–18 or in the Spanish civil war. I believe that the radio, especially in countries where listening to foreign broadcasts is not forbidden, is making large-scale lying more and more difficult. The Germans have now sunk the British Navy several times over in their published pronouncements, but don't otherwise seem to have lied much about major events. When things are going badly our own government lies in a rather stupid way, withholding information and being vaguely optimistic, but generally has to come out with the truth within a few days. I have it on very good authority that reports of air battles, etc., issued by the Air Ministry are substantially truthful, though of course favorably colored. As to the other two fighting services I can't speak. I doubt whether labor troubles are really fully reported. News of a large-scale strike would probably never be suppressed, but I think you can take it that there is a strong tendency to pipe down on labor friction and also on the discontent caused by billeting, evacuation, separation allowances for soldiers' wives, etc., etc. Debates in Parliament are probably not misrepresented in the press, but with a House full of deadheads they are growing less and less interesting and only about four newspapers now give them prominence.

Propaganda enters into our lives more than it did a year ago, but not so grossly as it might. The flag waving and Hun-hating is absolutely nothing to what it was in 1914–18, but it is growing. I think the majority opinion would now be that we are fighting the German people and not merely the Nazis. Vansittart's hate-Germany pamphlet, *Black Record*, sold like hot cakes. It is idle to pretend that this is simply something peculiar to the bourgeoisie. There have been very ugly manifestations of it among the common people. Still, as wars go, there has been remarkably little hatred so far, at any rate in this country. Nor is "antifascism" of the kind that was fashionable during the Popular Front period a strong force yet. The English people have never caught up with that. Their war morale depends more on old-fashioned patriotism, unwillingness to be governed by foreigners, and simple inability to grasp when they are in danger.

I believe that the BBC, in spite of the stupidity of its foreign propaganda and the unbearable voices of its announcers, is very truthful. It is generally regarded here as more reliable than the press. The movies seem almost unaffected by the war, i.e., in technique and subject matter. They go on and on with the same treacly rubbish, and when they do touch on politics they are years behind the popular press and decades behind the average book.

2. *Is there any serious writing being done? Is there any antiwar literature like Barbusse, etc., in the last war? Over here we hear there is a tendency towards romanticism and escapism in current British writing. Is this true?*

So far as I know, nothing of consequence is being written, except in fragmentary form, diaries and short sketches for instance. The best novels I have read during the past year were either American or translations of foreign books written several years earlier. There is much production of antiwar literature, but of a one-eyed irresponsible kind. There is nothing corresponding to the characteristic war books of 1914–18. All of those in their different ways depended on a belief in the unity of European civilization, and generally on a belief in international working-class solidarity. That doesn't exist any longer—Fascism has killed it. No one believes any longer that a war can be stopped by the workers on both sides simultaneously refusing to fight. To be effectively antiwar in England now one has to be pro-Hitler, and few people have the intellectual courage to be that, at any rate wholeheartedly. I don't see why good books shouldn't be written from the pro-Hitler angle, but none are appearing as yet.

I don't see any tendency to escapism in current literature, but I believe that if any major work were now produced it *would* be escapist, or at any rate subjective. I infer this from looking into my own mind. If I could get the time and mental peace to write a novel now, I should want to write about the past, the pre-1914 period, which I suppose comes under the heading of "escapism."

3. *What is the morale of the regular army like? Is there any tendency towards more democracy? Is it, so to speak, a* British *army primarily, or an* anti-Fascist *army—like the Loyalist army in Spain?*

I believe that the morale of the army is very good in a fighting sense but that there is much discontent about low separation allowances and class privilege in the matter of promotion, and that the troops in England are horribly bored by the long inaction, the dully muddy camps where they have spent the winter while their families were being bombed in the big towns, and the stupidity of a military system which was designed for illiterate mercenaries and is now being applied to fairly well-educated conscripts. It is still primarily a "nonpolitical" British army. But there are now regular classes in political instruction, and subject to local variation, depending on the commander of the unit, there seems to be a good deal of freedom of discussion. As to "tendency towards democracy." I should say that there is probably less than there was a year ago, but that if one looks back five years the advance is enormous. On active service the officers now wear almost the same uniform as the men (battle dress), and some of them habitually wear this on home service. The practice of saluting officers in the street has largely lapsed. New drafts of recruits all have to pass through the ranks and promotion is theoretically on merit alone, but the official claim based on this, that the army is now entirely democratic, should not be taken seriously. The framework of regular officers is still there and newcomers tend to be promoted on social grounds, with no doubt an eye to political reliability. But all this will gradually change if the war goes on. The need for able men will be too great, and the difference between the middle class and the better-paid working class is now too small for at any rate the lower ranks of the army to remain on a class basis. The disasters now probably ahead of us may push the process of democratization forward, as the disaster in Flanders did a year ago.

4. *We read your interesting article in a recent* Tribune *on the Home Guards. Could you tell us something of the present status of the movement? Is Wintringham the moving force behind it still? Is it mostly a middle-class or a working-class army? How democratic is it today?*

The Home Guard is the most anti-Fascist body existing in England at this moment, and at the same time is an astonishing phenomenon, a sort of People's Army officered by Blimps. The rank and file are predominantly working class, with a strong middle-class seasoning, but practically all the commands are held by wealthy elderly men, a lot of whom are utterly incompetent. The Home

Guard is a part-time force, practically unpaid, and at the beginning it was organized, I think consciously and intentionally, in such a way that a working class person would never have enough spare time to hold any post above that of sergeant. Just recently the higher positions have been stuffed with retired generals, admirals, and titled dugouts of all kinds. Principal age groups of the rank and file are between thirty-five and fifty or under twenty. Officers from Company Commander (captain) upwards are much older on average, sometimes as old as seventy.

Given this set-up you can imagine the struggle that has gone on between the Blimpocracy, wanting a parade ground army of pre-1914 type, and the rank and file wanting, though less articulately, a more democratic type of force specializing in guerrilla methods and weapons. The controversy has never been overtly political but has turned upon technical points of organization, discipline, and tactics, all of which, of course, have political implications which are half-consciously grasped on both sides. The War Office has been fairly open-minded and helpful, but I think it is true to say that the higher ranks within the Home Guard have fought steadily against a realistic view of war and that all experimentation and attempts at serious training have been due to proddings from below. Wintringham and some of his associates are still at the Home Guard training school (started unofficially by the weekly *Picture Post* and afterwards taken over by the War Office), but the Wintringham ("People's Army") school of thought has lost ground during the past six months. It or something like it will probably gain ground again during the coming months, and Wintringham has had very great influence, as thousands of men from all parts of the country have passed through his hands in three-day training courses. Although the Home Guard is now more similar to the regular army, or rather to the prewar Territorials, than it was when it began, it is much more democratic and consciously anti-Fascist than some of its commanders would wish. It has several times been rumored that the government was growing nervous about it and contemplated disbanding it, but no move has been made to do this. A very important point, technically necessary to a force of this kind but only obtained after a struggle, is that the men keep their rifles and usually some ammunition in their own homes. The officers wear practically the same uniform as the men and there is no saluting off parade. Although the class nature of the command is widely grasped there has not been much friction. Within the lower ranks the spirit is extremely democratic and comradely, with an absence of snobbishness and class-uneasiness that would have been unthinkable ten years ago. I speak from experience here as I serve in a mixed residential area where factory workers and quite rich men march in the ranks together. In general the political outlook of the men is old-fashioned patriotism mixed up with ill-defined but genuine hatred of the Nazis. Jews are numerous in the London units. In general, I think the danger of the Home Guard being turned into a reactionary middle-class militia still exists, but that this is not now likely to happen.

5. *How aggressive and articulate is big business reaction today (not Mosley's black shirts, but the more solid and serious forces of big capital)? You mention a political swing to the right in the Churchill government of late months. Does this mean the forces of organized business are climbing back into the saddle?*

I don't know what is going on behind the scenes and can only answer this question very generally, thus: Laissez-faire capitalism is dead in England and can't revive unless the war ends within the next few months. Centralized ownership and planned production are bound to come. The whole question is who is to be in control. The recent rightward swing means that we are being regimented by wealthy men and aristocrats rather than by representatives of the common people. They will use their power to keep the structure of government on a class basis, manipulate taxation and rationing in their own favor, and avoid a revolutionary war strategy; but not to return to capitalism of the old chaotic kind. The swing of the past six months hasn't meant more economic freedom or profits for the individual businessman—quite the contrary; but it has meant that you are less likely to get an important job unless you have been to one of the right schools. I have given elsewhere my reasons for thinking that this tendency will change, but that *has* been the tendency since last autumn.

6. *Would you say that Bevin and Morrison still command the support of the British working class? Are there any other Labour Party politicians who have taken on new dimensions in the course of the war—assuming those two have? Is the shop steward movement still growing?*

I know very little of industrial matters. I should say that Bevin does command working class support and Morrison probably not. There is a widespread feeling that the Labour Party as a whole has simply abdicated. The only other Labour man whose reputation has grown is Cripps. If Churchill should go, Cripps and Bevin are tipped as the likeliest men for the premiership, with Bevin evidently favorite.

7. *How do you explain what, over here, seems to be the remarkable amount of democracy and civil liberties preserved during the war? Labor pressure? British tradition? Weakness of the upper classes?*

"British tradition" is a vague phrase, but I think it is the nearest answer. I suppose I shall seem to be giving myself a free advert, but may I draw attention to a recent book of mine, *The Lion and the Unicorn* (I believe copies have reached the U.S.A.)? In it I pointed out that there is in England a certain feeling of family loyalty which cuts across the class system (also makes it easier for the class system to survive, I am afraid) and checks the growth of political hatred. There *could*, I suppose, be a civil war in England, but I have never met any English person able to imagine one. At the same time one ought not to overrate the amount of freedom of the intellect existing here. The position is that in England there is a great respect for freedom of speech but very little for freedom of the press. During the past twenty years there has been much tampering, direct and indirect, with the freedom of the press, and this has never raised a flicker of popular protest. This is a lowbrow country and it is felt that the printed word doesn't matter greatly and that writers and such people don't deserve much sympathy. On the other hand the sort of atmosphere in which you daren't talk politics for fear that the Gestapo may be listening isn't thinkable in England. Any attempt to produce it would be broken not so much by conscious resistance as by the inability of ordinary people to grasp what was wanted of them. With the working classes, in particular, grumbling is so habitual that they don't know when they are grumbling. Where unemployment can be used as a screw, men are often afraid of expressing "red" opinions which might get round to the overseer or the boss, but hardly anyone would bother, for instance, about being overheard by a policeman. I believe that an organization now exists for political espionage in factories, pubs, etc., and of course in the army, but I doubt whether it can do more than report on the state of public opinion and occasionally victimize some individual held to be dangerous. A foolish law was passed some time back making it a punishable offense to say anything "likely to cause alarm and despondency" (or words to that effect). There have been prosecutions under it, a few score I should say, but it is practically a dead letter and probably the majority of people don't know of its existence. You can hardly go into a pub or railway carriage without hearing it technically infringed, for obviously one can't discuss the war seriously without making statements which *might* cause alarm. Possibly at some time a law will be passed forbidding people to listen to foreign radio stations, but it will never be enforcible.

The British ruling class believe in democracy and civil liberty in a narrow and partly hypocritical way. At any rate they believe in the *letter* of the law and will sometimes keep to it when it is not to their advantage. They show no sign of developing a genuinely Fascist mentality. Liberty of every kind must obviously decline as a result of war, but given the present structure of society and social atmosphere there is a point beyond which the decline cannot go. Britain may be fascized from without or as a result of some internal revolution, but the old ruling class can't, in my opinion, produce a genuine totalitarianism of their own. Not to put it on any other grounds, they are too stupid. It is largely because they have been unable to grasp the first thing about the nature of Fascism that we are in this mess at all.

8. *From over here, it looks as though there had been a very rapid advance towards a totalitarian war economy in the last few months—rationing spreading*

wider, Bevin's conscription of certain classes of workers, extension of government controls over business. Is this impression correct? Is the tempo growing more or less rapid? How does the man in the street feel about the efficiency of the war effort? How much does he feel in his daily life the effect of these measures?

Yes, the thing is already happening at great speed and will accelerate enormously in the coming months. In a very little while we shall all be in uniform or doing some kind of compulsory labor, and probably eating communally. I don't believe it will meet with much opposition so long as it hits all classes equally. The rich will squeal, of course—at present they are manifestly evading taxation, and the rationing barely affects them—but they will be brought to heel if the predicament is really desperate. I don't believe that the ordinary man cares a damn about the totalitarianization of our economy, as such. People like small manufacturers, farmers, and shopkeepers seem to accept their transition from small capitalists to state employees without much protest, provided that their livelihood is safeguarded. People in England hate the idea of a Gestapo and there has been a lot of opposition, some of it successful, to official snooping and persecution of political dissidents, but I don't believe economic liberty has much appeal any longer. The changeover to a centralized economy doesn't seem to be altering people's way of life nearly so much as the shift of population and mingling of classes consequent on conscription and the bombing. But this may be less true in the industrial North, where on the whole people are working much harder in more trying conditions, and unemployment has practically ceased. What the reaction will be when we begin to experience hunger, as we may within the next few months, I don't prophecy. Apart from the bombing, and the overworking of certain categories of workers, one cannot honestly say that this war has caused much hardship as yet. The people still have more to eat than most European peoples would have in peacetime.

9. *What war aims does the left-and-labour movement now agree on? How sanguine are you about these aims being carried out? How much pressure is there now on the government to proclaim socialist war aims? On the question of war aims, of policy towards Europe and Germany in the event of victory, does there seem to be any radical difference between the Labour and Tory members of the Churchill government? How definite are the plans for the "social rebuilding" of England after the war?*

I haven't space to answer this question properly, but I think you can take it that the Labour Party, as such, has now no policy genuinely independent of the government. Some people even think that the left Conservatives (Eden, and possibly Churchill) are more likely to adopt a socialist policy than the Labour men. There are constant appeals to the government to declare its war aims, but these come from individuals and are not the official act of the Labour Party.

There is no sign that the government has any detailed or even general postwar plan. Nevertheless the feeling that after the war "things will be different" is so widespread that though, of course, the future England may be *worse* than that of the past, a return to Chamberlain's England is not thinkable even if it is technically possible.

10. *Would you say that the masses, working class and middle class, are more or less enthusiastically behind the present government than in May 1940? Are they more or less behind the war effort in general?*

So far as the government goes, less enthusiastically, but not very greatly so. This government came in with a degree of popular support which is quite unusual. In its home policy it has disappointed expectations, but not so grossly as governments usually do. Churchill's personal popularity will have waned somewhat, but he still has a bigger following than any premier of the last twenty years. As to the war, I don't believe there is much variation. People are fed up, but nothing to what one might expect. But one can't speak with certainty of this till after the coming crisis, which will be of a different nature, less intelligible, perhaps harder to bear, than that of a year ago.

I hope that answers your questions. It is a bit over the length you allowed me, I am afraid. All well here, or fairly well. We had hell's own bombing last night, huge fires raging all over the place and a racket of guns that kept one awake half the night. But it doesn't matter, the hits were chiefly on theatres and fashionable shops, and this morning it is a beautiful spring day, the almond trees are in blossom, postmen and milk carts wandering to and fro as usual, and down at the corner the inevitable pair of fat women gossiping beside the pillar-box. The best of luck to you all.

Postscript, May 15, 1941

The chief events since I wrote on April 15th have been the British defeats in Libya and Greece and the general worsening of the situation in the Middle East, with Iraq in revolt, Stalin evidently preparing to go into closer partnership with Hitler and Darlan getting ready to let German troops into Syria. There has also, within the last two days, been the mysterious arrival of Hess, which has caused much amusement and speculation but which it is too early to comment on.

The question that matters is whether the disastrous turn the war has taken will lead to a further growth of democratic sentiment, as happened last year. I am afraid one must say that the chances are against this. The reason why the Dunkirk campaign and the collapse of France impressed public opinion and did a great deal of good was that these things were happening close at hand. There was the immediate threat of invasion, and there were the soldiers coming home in hundreds of thousands to tell their families how they had been let down. This time the thing is happening far away, in countries that the average person neither knows nor cares anything about—the ordinary British working man hasn't the faintest notion that the Suez canal has anything to do with his own standard of living—and if the troops who got away from Greece have tales to tell they are telling them in Egypt and Palestine. Also, no one expected the Greek campaign to be anything but a disaster. Long before any official announcement was made it was known that we had troops in Greece and I could find no one of whatever kind who believed that the expedition would be successful; on the other hand, nearly everyone felt that it was our duty to intervene. It is generally recognized that as yet, i.e. until we have an up-to-date army, we can't fight the Germans on the continent of Europe, but at the same time "we couldn't let the Greeks down." The English people have never been infected with power-worship and don't feel the futility of this sort of gesture as a continental people probably would. I can see no sign anywhere of any big swing of opinion. In the parliamentary debate on the Greek campaign the attack on the government was led by envious throw-outs like Lloyd George and instead of being a proper discussion the debate was easily twisted into a demand for a vote of confidence, which on the whole the government deserves—at any rate it deserves it in the sense that no alternative government is at present possible. The repercussions which are probably happening in Australia, however, may do something towards democratizing the conduct of the war. People here are beginning to say that the next leftward push must come from America. It is suggested, for instance, that Roosevelt might make it a condition of further help that the British government do something about India. You are better able than I am to judge whether this is likely.

The air raids continue. To the ordinary people this is the part of the war that matters, in fact it *is* the war, but their stolidity is surprising. There was a sidelight on the popular mind which probably did not get into the American press and which may interest you, in a recent by-election in Birmingham. A dissident Conservative who called himself a "reprisals candidate" ran against the government's nominee. His claim was that we should concentrate on bombing German civilians to avenge what has been done here. Canon Stuart Morris, one of the leading lights in the Peace Pledge Union, also ran on a pacifist ticket. The respective slogans of the three candidates were "Bomb Berlin," "Stop the War," and "Back Churchill." The government man got about 15,000 votes and the other two about 1,500 each. The whole poll was probably low, but considering the times we live in I think these figures are encouraging.

George Orwell

1941, vol. 8, no. 4

• Ten Propositions and Eight Errors
Philip Rahv

In their *Ten Propositions on the War* (July–August issue) my fellow editors Greenberg and Macdonald seem to me to have put themselves into a snug sectarian hole. Their dicta outline a position which I cannot adopt as my own because I regard it as morally absolutist and as politically representative of a kind of academic revolutionism which we should have learned to discard long ago. Despite the shattering surprises of the past two years, Greenberg and Macdonald are still sure they know all the answers. But the answers turn out to be nothing more than the same old orthodox recommendations. Again we read that the social revolution is around the corner and that imperialism is tottering on the edge of the abyss, and again we fail to recognize the world as we know it.

Speaking for no movement, no party, certainly not for the working class, nor even for any influential grouping of intellectuals, the authors of the *Ten Propositions* nevertheless write as if they are backed up by masses of people and as if what has been happening is daily confirming their prognosis. They refuse to see anything which does not fit into their apocalyptic vision of a single cleansing and overpowering event which will once and for all clear away the existing social system in Britain and in America, administer the coup de grace to the Hitler regime, and forthwith usher in socialism. A splendid program, to be sure, a program of maximum beneficence, but unfortunately its proponents fail to outline even the initial steps to its realization.

The fact is that by his swift conquests Hitler has removed one country after another from the area of possible revolutionary action. Thus the war has evolved in such a way as to exclude more and more the prospect of a socialist way out from the catastrophe. Now we have reached the stage where the war will either be won by the combined might of the Anglo-American imperialism and Stalin's Red Army, or else it won't be won at all; and the military defeat of Germany remains the indispensable precondition of any progressive action in the future. Such calculations naturally prove disappointing to Marxists accustomed to look forward to this war as the final act in the drama of the class struggle. But reality has utterly belied this agreeable perspective.

The orthodox Marxists thought that the imperialists of both camps will exhaust themselves and then they will take over. However, things have turned out otherwise. The exhaustion of imperialist Poland did not lead to any "taking over" by the Left but to its immediate fall to the Nazis; and the combined exhaustion and betrayal of France produced identical results. There has been no stalemate; England has survived, but her continental allies have all suffered total defeat. Now Russia is next, and if Stalin fails to stem the invasion it won't be a Trotskyite but Hitler's Gauleiter who will be installed in the Kremlin.

Actually, Greenberg and Macdonald's ideas are just as Utopian as the ideas propagated in England by people like Harold Laski and Francis Williams, who appeal to the British capitalists to abdicate, to commit social and political suicide, so as to build up the morale of the antifascist peoples and give the war a "creative meaning." Laski and Williams look to the Churchill government to execute and supervise this "revolution by consent." Now one must really possess an ultra-metaphysical faith in the goodness of human nature to adopt such a program! For if anything can be learned from historical experience, it is surely this: that no ruling class hesitates to put its class interests above its national interests. The conduct in this war of the bourgeois strata in France is the perfect confirmation of this insight into class behavior. There is no reason to doubt that if it were not for the promise of American aid the British conservatives would have long ago forced a negotiated peace with Hitler. American intervention is the only brand of "socialism" those people want and understand—it is Churchill's "socialism" and, I am afraid, Bevin's and Morrison's too. And at that, looking at it strictly from their point of view, it is by no means such a bad substitute.

No, declare the extremists, democratic capitalism will never do away with itself in order to speed the day of victory; hence it must be overthrown, and this is the only way to win the war. Well, all one can say in reply is that if this is true then the war is as good as lost. For consider this: since they concede—tacitly at least—the futility of counting on an internal upheaval against the Hitler regime so long as the Nazi armies have not been defeated, they have perforce narrowed down their revolutionary expectations to the two democracies. But these are precisely the countries where the working class is least schooled in independent political traditions and where reformism is the sole norm of labor action. Economic conditions in America and the relations between the social classes being what they are, is it not sheer romanticism to believe that basic revolutionary changes are likely to occur here in the near future? And, remember, we are not speaking of a revolution anytime, sometime, but right now, not later at any rate than within the next two or three years, before the situation is irretrievably lost through a definitive Hitler victory.

Revolutions, however, are not made to facilitate a fight against a distant enemy—especially not when a good part of the population, as in this country, holds that this fight is none of their concern—but only when the masses are convinced that there is absolutely no other way out from the impasse in which they find themselves. Moreover, even such a conviction will in itself come to nothing unless the top sections of society are at the same time thrown into a state of confusion and the armed forces guarding their interests have been successfully exposed to disintegrating propaganda. Plainly no such prerequisites exist, nor is there any real evidence that they are in process of formation, either in the United States or in Britain. And this being the case, the categorical "must" employed in the *Ten Propositions* reduces itself to mere braggadocio.

Both the revolutionaries by class war and the revolutionaries by "consent" approach situations abstractly, in terms of what is unconditionally desirable, not in terms of what can actually be accomplished within a given period. And in this connection I would like to quote the concluding sentences from Macdonald's review (September–October issue) of Francis Williams' book, *War by Revolution*. "Mr. Williams' book was published a year ago," Macdonald writes tauntingly. "India is still not free, the British government has moved steadily to the right, and, instead of the democratic manifesto he urges on Mr. Churchill, we have the famous Eight Points. To Mr. Williams must be addressed the question: how much longer can you continue to believe that Messrs. Churchill and Roosevelt are on your team?" This is surely correct. By the same token, however, one can address a similar question to Macdonald. Since the war began, we must say to him, you have advocated the policies embodied in the *Ten Propositions*. Now, after two years, can you cite a single political turn of any significance that substantiates your expectations? Is it not true that the labor movement here as in England, especially now that the Stalinists have returned to the fold, is more than ever committed to supporting the war effort of Messrs. Churchill and Roosevelt? Politics is a game ruled by empirical considerations. If it is quite fair to subject Mr. Williams' notions to the test of reality, why not test your own in the same manner?

Today's War and Yesterday's Strategy

Greenberg and Macdonald's first two propositions declare that (1) "This war is 'different' from the last one" and (2) that "Fascism is less desirable than democratic capitalism." The Kaiser's victory, they contend, "would not have meant a *break* in our civilization. Hitler's would." Agreed. But the remaining eight propositions, which seem to me an amalgam of Leninist and Luxemburgian strategies of the last war literally applied to this one, tend to cancel out, if not altogether to refute, the first two. It appears that the opening gambit—"this war is different"— is a mere argumentative concession leading to no revision of policy. Take proposition No. 3: "The issue—not war but revolution." Even winning the war, they write, will not advance us "one step nearer the only real solution, which is to deflect the current of history from fascism to socialism. In the war or out of it, the United States faces only one future under capitalism: fascism." Here we have a series of bald assertions that wholly ignore the element of time, which is the one element one can least afford to overlook in political calculations. Greenberg and Macdonald forget that an issue becomes real only insofar as it takes hold of the mind of the masses; and since the issue of revolution has so far failed to take hold, shall we therefore say that the outcome of the war is a matter of indifference to us?

Moreover, it is wholly gratuitous to dismiss a bourgeois-democratic victory as meaningless. While in itself it will not bring socialism, it will, on the other hand, bring us quite a few steps nearer "the only real solution" by giving the labor movement an opportunity to take stock of itself, to regroup its forces, and, if so minded, to resume the struggle for a fundamental reconstruction of society. Hitlerism in collapse would most probably pull down with it the structure of fascism the world over, thus eliminating, for a time at least, the most effective instrument of class and national terror that modern imperialism has yet been able to devise. In short, whereas a Nazi victory would bury the revolution for good, the chances are that a Nazi defeat would recreate the conditions for progressive action. At all events, we no longer have any real alternative to supporting the democratic war effort. Fascism is very strong; the accumulated betrayals of Stalinism have caused millions of people to lose their faith in the socialist program; and the Comintern and Social Democratic experiences have eaten up entire generations of revolutionary leaders and activists. Under such circumstances if we can save anything substantial through piecemeal solutions we ought to count ourselves fortunate indeed.

As for the idea that by going into a shooting war this country would automatically turn fascist, that is one of those abysmal clichés that have done infinite harm to the antifascist cause. After all, it is not Roosevelt who now looms up as the potential Führer but the isolationist Lindbergh; and it is not the various interventionist committees but the America First outfit which is today the leading proto-fascist organization in the United States. Having lost its character of a provincial movement rooted in the populist traditions of the farm communities, isolationism has undergone a sea change. It has been seized upon by the native fascists, who, emerging from the back alleys of the political world, have finally discovered the true-blue "American" issue they have long been seeking. At last they have come in contact with wealth, power, and respectability; and if Hitler has his way in Europe they will have their way in America. This danger, however, is overlooked by the authors of the *Ten Propositions*, who are compelled by the peculiar logic of their political line to see in the Roosevelt administration the mainstay of reaction.

Though formulated differently, with Luxemburgian interpolations, Greenberg and Macdonald's program reduces itself in practice to the Leninist policy of revolutionary defeatism. But the trouble is that our impetuous proposition-makers do not quite understand the conditions that gave Lenin's policy its political stamina and consistency. Lenin saw in the defeat of one's own country the chance for revolutionary action. In this he was correct, for the collapse of the Eastern front led to the February and October revolutions and, later, the collapse of the Central powers led to the abortive revolutions in Germany, Austria, and Hungary. Lenin's reasoning, however, was based on two premises: first, the approximate identity of the social system in all the belligerent states and, second, the expectation that the defeat of a country would not result in the loss of its national independence, in its being swallowed up by the victor. Only on the basis of these premises can one justify, from a Marxist point of view, the risks of a defeatist policy. The Versailles powers did not set up a puppet regime in Berlin; they exacted reparations and sliced off certain territories, but essentially they left the German people free to choose, and if necessary to fight, for whatever internal regime they preferred. At Brest-Litovsk the Kaiser's generals did not demand the complete surrender of Russian sovereignty; and the signing of that onerous treaty still left the Bolsheviks plenty of room for their Soviets. But today neither premise of Lenin's strategy holds good any longer. The defeat of Poland, Norway, France, etc., has brought about their total extinction as independent states—and obviously a proletarian revolution in the face of Gestapo rule and Nazi garrisons is unthinkable. The Kaiser fought for a re-partition of the world's colonies and natural resources, whereas Hitler is fighting to convert Europe itself into a colony. And a colonial status for Europe puts an end to all Marxist hopes.

The Chances of an Anglo-American Victory

But the crux of Greenberg and Macdonald's argument is that the Churchill and Roosevelt governments are incapable of organizing "an effective war effort against fascism outside" and that, therefore, the actual choice is between socialism and Hitlerism. I venture to say that this prediction of an Anglo-American rout unless socialism comes to the rescue is not a little intermixed with wishful thinking. The fact is that Hitler is now further away from winning than he was a year ago, and American aid is beginning to flow in measurable quantities. It is true that the Nazis have at their disposal a wholly centralized and efficient economy, but this advantage is largely canceled out by the indisputable American superiority in industrial plant and raw materials. There is every reason to believe that once America is fully drawn into the struggle its offensive power will astound the world. If we should stay out, however, the Nazi plans are likely to be fulfilled; and it is hard to grasp just how, under conditions of all-around ruin, any last-minute attempt to refurbish social and property relations in Britain or Russia can save either country from disaster. The victorious Nazi soldiers are immune to socialist propaganda; only when beaten down will they heed the voices of dissent.

Greenberg and Macdonald complain that in the Nazi-occupied countries "Churchill's propaganda arouses little response. . . . Only a program which promises a real reorganization of society can inspire the peoples in the conquered countries to revolt, to take the risks involved in widespread and constant sabotage." This, mind you, was written just three months ago, but today, without the benefit of any socialist promises from Churchill or even the semblance of an ulti-mate program, all of occupied Europe is in a state of latent revolt. No sooner did the German setbacks in Russia become known than the conquered nations were swept by a wave of sabotage, arson, terrorism, and guerrilla warfare. Clearly, what the masses in the conquered countries find intolerable is precisely the Nazi occu-pation and they do not need to be artificially provided by the British with reasons for hating their alien masters. Their suffering in the hands of the Nazis is a suffi-cient incitement to hatred and, should the opportunity come at last, to armed rebellion. But if these oppressed peoples finally regain their national indepen-dence, they will doubtless learn from their own experience that there is no road back to the pre-Hitler world—and one can expect that at this historical turning point socialism will again become a concrete issue. This whole process, however, must be lived through: the consciousness of the masses knows of no short cuts.

The Bonanza of a "Peaceful" Revolution

To speak seriously of a revolution without taking into account the very real haz-ards of a civil war is the height of political frivolity. But it is exactly to such frivo-lity that Greenberg and Macdonald are driven when they actually go so far as to "promise," as it were, that a social revolution in England or America, if it comes at all during this war, "would probably be short and relatively peaceful." Nor would it "necessarily" open the gates to Hitler through a *belated* civil war, they claim. Not necessarily, to be sure, but it is quite likely that in case of a grave rev-olutionary threat the British rulers would know how to strike a bargain with Hitler at the expense of the rebels. At any rate, this is not a matter to be dismissed airily, by means of a frail historical analogy with the French revolution, which ran its course under totally different circumstances. A ruthlessly logical revolutionary would openly accept the risk of a civil war and the consequent danger of "open-ing the gates" to the foreign enemy; but Greenberg and Macdonald want to have their cake and eat it too.

This blithely optimistic theory of a "short and relatively peaceful revolution" anticipates that the ruling class would be "so discredited by its military incapac-ity and so demoralized by its own mistakes as to be unable to offer serious resis-tance for some time to come." But this is pure speculation, and one cannot build a realistic policy on the basis of episodic contingencies. Do you want the British workers, then, to sabotage the war effort of the Churchill government, thus exposing themselves to mortal danger, in order to prepare for a problematical sit-uation that might never arise? Such a course of action might be worthwhile if there were little to choose between Hitlerism and the existing order in Britain; but this primary condition of a Leninist antiwar strategy is no longer available. A militarily decisive and demoralizing defeat for the British would most probably be followed by a successful invasion, and in such a crisis a zero-hour revolution in London would be a futile gesture of despair. Another variant: a change of government is possible in case Churchill bungles some extremely important campaign; the Labour Party might then be charged with exclusive responsibility for the conduct of the war, but this is a far cry from the classic Marxist uprising that our left-wing irreconcilables have in mind. As for the prospect of an American revolution in the near future, the logic of a sanguine outlook in this respect escapes me altogether.

The Fatal Lack

But throughout Greenberg and Macdonald assume that their program is in no sense invalidated by the absence of an organized movement to shape and lead such a revolution. Proposition No. 9 reads: "There exists today no organized leadership for such a revolutionary policy as we advocate. But, while this is a serious lack, it is not a fatal one. New organizational forms must and will be found." Now I am not in the least impressed by the categorical phrase, "must and will be found." During the past decade we have all encountered this rhetoric of confidence too often in Marxist brochures to mistake it for anything more than a ritualistic invocation, a kind of *leitmotif* of History on the March. What is fatal, in my opinion, is precisely this lack of a revolutionary movement. (For in this article I am not arguing against a revolutionary policy in principle; I am arguing that in the absence of a revolutionary movement and also because certain other essential conditions are wanting such a policy is illusory.) The fascists are not going to withhold their blows until the leftists have finally discovered the "new organizational forms" and filled them with the proper political content. It's all very well to write: "Parties sometimes make history, but history also makes parties." Yes, but in our epoch history has undone before our very eyes quite a number of parties—the degeneration of the Comintern is one example and the breakup of the Fourth International into splinter groups is another. At bottom all that Greenberg and Macdonald are really saying is that if a revolutionary party existed it would not fail to act in a revolutionary manner. But that is a tautology, not an insight.

In Proposition No. 9 it is further assumed that the American workers are now ready to undertake a struggle for socialism and all that remains to be solved is the seemingly "technical" problem of leadership. But the workers are by no means ready, nor is leadership by and large a "technical" problem. It is closely related, rather, to our estimate of the political capacities of the workers as a class and to our whole conception of the tasks and functions of a revolutionary vanguard. Do Greenberg and Macdonald still believe in the doctrine of the dictatorship of the proletariat, for instance, and do they still see in this class the kind of social instrument that the founders of Marxism saw in it? It is meaningless to say, as they do, that we want a "loose" party instead of a tight one on the

Bolshevik model. Loose or tight, what are the working principles and organizational methods of this party?

No, what has been lost in the past two decades through an uninterrupted series of blunders, betrayals, and defeats cannot so easily be regained. Oracular appeals to history and a mere show of will on the part of a few literary intransigents will avail us nothing. Life is running so low in the revolutionary movement that only a top to bottom transformation, on a world scale, of our entire moral and political environment can possibly bring about its recovery. In the meantime let us not lull ourselves with illusions about the war aims of the bourgeois democracies on the one hand, or about the ability of the workers to fulfill the Marxist prophecies on the other. I am not suggesting that Greenberg and Macdonald and their political friends should rush to join the war party. Doubtless they have other things to do. In a sense this war, even if it accomplishes the destruction of fascism, is not yet *our* war. But this fact in itself does not permit us to take for granted that the salvation of mankind has been entrusted to us and that we alone know how to achieve it.

Reply by Greenberg and Macdonald

Without attempting to match rhetoric with our fellow editor, we want to make the following points.

1. Distortions of our position

1. Rahv identifies our position with Lenin's revolutionary defeatism, and claims we view the outcome of the war with indifference. On the contrary, we emphasize our concern with beating Hitler and fascism; we present socialism as the means; and our "transitional demands" show concretely the first steps to be taken. If this is "Leninism," Lenin never heard about it. The propositions trace their paternity rather to Rosa Luxemburg's "revolutionary defensism."

2. It is not true that we claim that "the social revolution is around the corner," or that we expect Churchill to be overthrown by "a classic Marxist uprising" (which Rahv apparently misconceives as a sudden, violent putsch rather than a social process). There is no evidence for either statement in the propositions. We agree with Orwell that there was a "revolutionary situation" in England after Dunkirk, and we can imagine this happening again. While we hold no fixed conceptions as to how the revolution is to be effected, we are certain that it will not be done by supporting Roosevelt-Churchill.

3. Rahv charges we "assume" the American working class is ready to fight for socialism today and that only the problem of leadership has to be solved. We stated that the *objective* factors for socialism have matured, not that the American

masses are now *subjectively* in a revolutionary mood. We "assumed" only that the solution of the problem of leadership would itself have an effect on the total revolutionary process—and also depend on its development.

2. Rebuttals

1. Rahv asks if we can "cite a single political turn" since the war began that supports our interpretation. We can cite the following: (a) the low army and civilian morale in this country; (b) the poor showing to date of British and American war production; (c) Churchill's inability to take advantage of Hitler's involvement in Russia; (d) the persistence of widespread strikes in "defense" industries; (e) the inability of Roosevelt-Churchill to put forth any war aims that are either politically meaningful or propagandistically effective; (f) above all, the fact that the only army able to cope with the Reichswehr so far in morale, equipment, and strategy is the Red Army, product of a society that, whatever it is, certainly is not bourgeois-democratic. (We can't help noting that the basic defect of Rahv's approach to the war is its naive idealism and romantic optimism. He apparently takes seriously Roosevelt's fireside chats.)

2. Rahv writes that the British ruling class would make a deal with Hitler if revolution threatened. But if there was a revolutionary situation—and we neither expect nor advocate revolutionary action *without* such a situation, Rahv to the contrary notwithstanding—then an attempt to make peace with Hitler would simply precipitate the overthrow of the rulers and enormously speed up the revolutionary process.

3. We concede that we underestimated the strength of anti-Nazi feeling on the continent and that "without the benefit of any socialist promises from Churchill . . . all of occupied Europe is in a state of latent revolt." (Rahv forgets he has written earlier that "by his swift conquests Hitler has removed one country after another from the area of possible revolutionary action"—a typical exaggeration of Hitler's strength and underestimation of the masses, which he himself here contradicts.) But these very events strikingly confirm our *general* analysis. (1) We claimed that Churchill could neither lead nor exploit the continent's deep hatred of the Nazis, and these recent acts of violence have remained sporadic and historically sterile precisely because they lack *political* leadership. (2) Don't these outbursts, above all, show that the European working class is *not* the corpse Rahv thinks it is, that revolution is still a factor with which Hitler's "New Order" must reckon?

4. Rahv asks us if we still see the working class as the social force Marx and Engels did. We believe the workers must take the lead in any revolutionary social change, and that their class interests express the general interests of society more fully than do those of any other existing class.

3. And what about Rahv's own position?

1. "Greenberg and Macdonald forget that an issue becomes real only insofar as it takes hold of the minds of the masses." But it is precisely the job of politically-minded writers, including Rahv, to see things a bit *ahead* of the masses, not merely to follow along after events. Rahv seems to ignore the factor of *change* in history; he simply projects the present balance of forces into the future.

2. In line with the above, Rahv assumes that the forces arrayed against Hitler at present assure us within a reasonable amount of time a neat, orderly military victory over Hitler, and that such a victory will be a solution. We think a military victory can be achieved by the Allies only as the result of profound changes in their present social structure, and that these changes will add up to either fascism or socialism. It's quite likely that Rahv will refuse his victory by the time it's ready to be presented to him, that he will then be clamoring for unconditional support of a status quo threatened by an even greater evil than Hitler.

3. Rahv's approach to history is that of the homeowning commuter. He makes great play with such terms as "pure speculation," "episodic contingencies," and "problematical situations"; he wants his revolution covered by 5% gold bonds and insured at Lloyds against failure. But *any* policy that looks to the future—Lenin's in 1910, Hitler's in 1925—instead of merely paraphrasing, as Rahv's does, the status quo, must "speculate" on "contingencies," and *all* future situations are "problematical." Social change is always a gamble.

4. Rahv is extremely vague about his own concrete program—which is, of course, of considerable polemical advantage to him, since he can measure the weaknesses of our program against an ideal program instead of an actual one. In politics, no program but has defects and faces obstacles. The question must always be: what is the best policy *relative to other possible policies* to achieve the end in view? Rahv seems to agree, by implication rather than direct statement, with our end, namely, socialism. His program for getting there—also merely hinted at here and there—seems to be prostration before the status quo on this side of the battle line. He rejects *both* the revolutionary and the reformist programs for moving in the direction of socialism, and argues for concentrating entirely on winning the war, after which the masses "if so minded" will have that famous "breathing spell" in which to resume the struggle for "a fundamental reconstruction of society." (We think the pace of social change is too fast for any such breathing spell to materialize; and even if it should, Rahv's war policy seems to insure that the masses will *not* then be "so minded.") All this would indicate that Rahv is for this war and for unconditional support of Roosevelt-Churchill in it. But in his penultimate sentence he remarks that this war "in a sense . . . is not yet *our* war." In what sense? "Not yet"—then when? *Whose* war, then?

What exactly is our co-editor's position? It is a position for which he refuses to take any moral or intellectual responsibility. He knows only too well upon what he is relying to protect us from Hitler. He realizes the emptiness, the shabby hypocrisy of the present British and American war aims. Like Macbeth, he would like to profit by the crime without committing it.   1941, vol. 8, no. 6

A Statement by the Editors

The country is now actually at war. *Partisan Review*, while primarily a cultural magazine, has always been concerned with politics. A question, therefore, as to our future editorial policy naturally arises.

For some time, as recent issues of the magazine have made clear, the editors have disagreed on major political questions. The complexity of the world situation, indeed, is reflected in the fact that no two editors hold the same position on all major issues. The actual outbreak of hostilities has not altered this line-up. It is clear, therefore, that *Partisan Review* can have no editorial line on the war. Its editors will continue to express themselves on the issue as individuals.

We believe that a magazine like *Partisan Review* cannot undertake to present the kind of programmatic guidance one expects of a political party. Our main task now is to preserve cultural values against all types of pressure and coercion. Obviously we cannot even speak of the survival of democratic civilization apart from the survival of our entire cultural tradition. This includes the fullest freedom of expression on political matters. All of us can at least agree on this: that in times like these it is a necessity, not a luxury, for *Partisan Review* to continue to give space to radical—in the literal sense of "going to the roots"—analysis of social issues and the war. No intelligent decisions can be made without a full consideration of alternatives.

Clement Greenberg
Dwight Macdonald
George L. K. Morris
William Phillips
Philip Rahv
1942, vol. 9, no. 1

• The "Liberal" Fifth Column
Editorial Statement

It is time that the United States awoke to the truth that nothing is gained for us vis-à-vis Russia by "getting tough."
Editorial, *The New Republic*

The New Republic proclaimed this oracular "truth" on April 22, 1946. Several weeks earlier the German Social Democrats in the Allied zones voted seven to one against fusion with the Communists; the fusion was later forced in the Russian zone without any vote. Two weeks after the editorial appeared, the French people administered a smashing defeat to the Communist Party by rejecting the proposed Constitution. The French referendum cannot be interpreted as a swing to the right, since many Socialists voted no, against their own party leadership. Moreover the vote called out the thirty percent absentees from the last election, who, had they been Rightists, could have voted for the parties of the Right at that time. The French people wanted democracy and their nose was keen enough to smell out the totalitarian odor of the Constitution; their referendum cannot be twisted to show any other meanings. Both French and German votes indicate that there are millions on the continent with genuine democratic longings—even though many (for example, the French absentees) are not yet expressed completely by any party. If these democratic longings do not exist in Europe, we can write off European civilization right now; if they do exist, they will certainly not grow stronger by being fed the bread and water of a feeble American foreign policy. As long as American policy is weak and halting, the peoples of Europe will persist in believing that the United States intends to withdraw altogether from Europe, and they will gravitate helplessly—and under the threat of terror—into the Russian orbit.

Meanwhile in New York a journal which calls itself "liberal" is advocating a policy to sell out these millions into Stalinist slavery. When *The New Republic* published this editorial, it was actually helping to herd Social Democrats into concentration camps in Germany; helping to shoot democrats, of every shade and color, in Germany, Poland, Romania, Bulgaria, Hungary, Austria; helping to strengthen the French Communist Party's reign of terror over public opinion—a terror which will wax or wane with the position of Russia in Western Europe.

These are not metaphors of political rhetoric, but a literal description of the consequences that follow from the political behavior of *The New Republic*'s editors. The juxtaposition of their editorial statement with political reality could scarcely be more pointed, and the direction in which it points has now become unmistakable: that we have in our midst a powerfully vocal lobby willing to override all concerns of international democracy and decency in the interests of a foreign power. The foci of this infection are the newspaper *PM* and the liberal weeklies *The Nation* and *The New Republic*. Insofar as the advantage of this foreign power becomes an exclusive end in itself, this lobby functions, as we shall show, as a virtual Fifth Column. Whether those who march always know where they are going, whether they are confused about their purposes or really taken in by sham purposes, they are not any the less a Fifth Column. Political positions are weighed by objective consequences and not by subjective intentions. This is a well-worn truism by now, but it seems it has to be dinned afresh into these "liberal" ears. But when intentions fall out so persistently and shrewdly in one pattern, may we not also conclude that they have a pretty shrewd glimpse of the objective direction?

How has this Fifth Column arisen? And in what forms does it exert its pressures? To answer these questions we must look briefly at its genesis: the process step by step by which the column has been recruited in our midst during one year of peace.

II

The European war had hardly ended in May 1945 when the rumblings in the Communist Party were announcing preparations for a new line and a new ideological offensive. These had to remain, for a while, preparations only: the war had not yet become entirely imperialist again, as in 1939–41, for Russia had still to play its part in the Japanese war, having in fact to hasten into Manchuria ahead of schedule lest the United States finish the war before Stalin had won it for us. The explosion of the atomic bomb was the dramatic end of the war. The two events were also a simultaneous political explosion which blew the war honeymoon to bits, ushering in the new groupings in world politics and opinion.

Humanity had good reason to be afraid now that the atomic bomb had arrived. But in the first rush of journalistic panic it was not always easy to distinguish those afflicted with fear and trembling from those who were merely glad of an occasion to don the robes of prophecy and pontification. The "liberals" seized upon the occasion to launch a new campaign of war hysteria. "War in 90 days!" *The New Republic* screamed on the first page of one of its issues—which appeared, by the way, more than ninety days ago. The "liberals" fell all over themselves to violate elementary logic: the bomb was no secret, therefore the secret should be given immediately to Russia; or to violate common sense: the secret itself would explode—as if the secret were a ticking infernal machine, and human hands, with definite political purposes, were not required to make a bomb and set it off. *But behind all these antics the essential point of the "liberal" attack was simply that the United States had the bomb and Russia did not.* Here was the first clearcut indication that a new standard of judgment for all political and social questions had been found: the potential advantage or disadvantage to Soviet Russia. The "liberal" distrust of the United States was as unbounded as their confidence in Russia: in American hands the atomic bomb constituted a threat to the peace of the world, but of course, if Russia had possession of it, the world could rest secure. The millions of Stalin's political victims, if they could speak from the grave, might have a wry comment to make upon this.

The Fifth Column developed steadily through the period of the first meeting of prime ministers in London. Molotov wrecked that conference on a legal technicality, which brought an enormous advantage to Russia. The longer Europe remains unsettled by treaty, the longer it remains prey to the occupying Red Army and the Soviet secret police. Stalin can be counted upon to continue this delaying tactic as long as he can get away with it. (The Russian evasiveness when Byrnes recently offered a security pact which would take the Red Army out of certain parts of Europe was another illustration of this tactic.) Molotov also began to fiddle another tune to which our "liberals" were soon jigging. He accused the United States of playing "atomic power politics," although up to that point Byrnes—considerably to Bevin's disgust—had been giving a remarkable imitation of a diplomatic Caspar Milquetoast. But this did not bother the "liberals." They were showing that they could dance just as eagerly as the Communist Party to the official tunes of Russian propaganda—and with just as much disregard of the facts, too.

When the UN Security Council met at London, Russia pulled another tactic out of its bag of tricks which has since been worked by the "liberals" for all it is worth. To forestall inquiry into Russian operations in Europe—at that time in Manchuria too—Vishinsky launched a prompt attack upon British actions in Greece and Indonesia. This is Stalin's game of international chess. When a piece in an advanced attacking position is threatened, he relieves by attacking elsewhere, maintaining thus a continuing but shifting pressure. Again the "liberals" showed they knew how to take the cue. It was their signal to launch an all-out campaign to hate Britain. Some of PM's cartoons on the theme of Perfidious Albion became a match for those of the Hearst-McCormick press, when these latter were conducting their anti-British campaign in the interest of isolationism and Hitler. It used to be considered a liberal principle to attack imperialism wherever it showed its head. But now if Russian imperialism is attacked, the "liberals" rise as one man to shout: "what about Britain?"

This dazzling piece of "liberal" logic may be summed up as: *Two wrongs make a right—and it is always Russia's right.*

The dizzy corruption of logic and morals was to reach new depths in the handling of the Iran case by the "liberal" press. The same day that the *New York Times* carried the first reports of the continued presence of Soviet troops in Iran, I. F. Stone produced in *PM* a masterpiece of journalistic insinuation. Stone turned what purported to be an account of the Iranian situation into a minute description of his own confusions as a reporter in getting the news. Before he had finished, he had managed to convey the impression that the illegal presence of the Red Army in Iran was just a concoction of rumor and innuendo, and probably of British origin at that! Stone does not impress us as one of the innocents; he is a clever enough reporter to know what he is about, and the fact that he has subsequently hewed persistently and bitterly to the anti-British line shows very well what he is about.

All of *PM*'s staff were promptly mobilized for the defense of the Socialist Fatherland. Max Lerner, who had already played so many comic roles in his career hitherto that one more could not matter, rushed before the footlights in the role of the Ambassador of Iran: he knew better than Hussein Ala what the situation and policy of Iran should be. *PM* transformed the question into a struggle between Britain and Russia for Iranian oil and the onus of guilt was shifted, as one would expect, to perfidious Britain. "We have become tools," I. F. Stone wrote, "in the hands of the British who are intent on maintaining a status quo that would deny Russia additional oil and an outlet to the Mediterranean." What folly for the United States to take Britain's side in this criminal struggle to deny Russia the oil of Iran! From this hackneyed anti-British perspective, the facts that Russia had broken a treaty and that her troops were in a foreign country against that country's will disappeared from the canvas beneath the deft coloring of *PM*'s apologists.

History was making strange bedfellows when Nicholas Murray Butler and Henry Wallace raised their voices together in support of a new-found common friend, Joseph Stalin. Butler, old and ailing, had reached the ripe, overripe, fruit of wisdom, to see that Russia had a right to foreign oil. (In official publications Soviet scientists have stated that Russia has some 58.7 percent of the world's oil resources—and most as yet undeveloped!) The doddering capitalist was delighted to think this might be just good old-fashioned "respectable" imperialism after all. The fellow travelers, Wendell Wilkie style, would love to believe that Russia is capitalist at heart, and so no worse, and therefore just as good—by God!—as anybody else. In a speech in the Midwest Henry Wallace pleaded that even if Russia were wrong on every point, we should give in for the sake of world peace. At last, a frank and open appeal for appeasement! The hotheaded patriot who screams "My country, right or wrong!" could hardly be more partisan and unreasoning than Wallace in the interests of Russia.

This from a Secretary of Commerce—who, but for a maneuver of party politics, might now be President of the United States. Never during the disastrous period of fellow traveling in the thirties were the Russian zealots so highly placed in American life. On the floor of the Senate itself, Claude Pepper, senator from Florida, made the startling and impassioned accusation that in its foreign policy the United States was pushing Britain's imperialist cart and "ganging up" with Britain against Russia. The corruption of language could scarcely go much beyond this. "Ganging up" had suddenly become the expression for an inquiry (which would have had to remain at most an inquiry, since the Russian veto would have prohibited any action) into the illegal occupation of one country by another. Meanwhile the tireless Eleanor Roosevelt continued her tiresome pleas for "cooperation" with Russia in order to insure Russian "security."

Yes indeed, Russia must be secure even if we have to sacrifice the security of all her neighbors. What about Iran's security? The "liberals" were too busy to raise that question. Besides, as everyone knew, certain reactionary groups in Iran were a distinct threat to Russia. A nation of fifteen million a threat to a nation of one hundred eighty million! When *Izvestia* made this fantastic charge, it was following precisely Hitler's tactic towards a country he had designated for absorption or conquest—and Hitler had never been more preposterous in his claims of imaginary aggression.

Russia may not gobble up Iran, and the Iranian case may subside into a relatively minor incident; in which case you can expect the "liberals" to set up a shrill hue and cry that the matter was a tempest in a teapot engineered by reactionaries over a few months' longer occupation by the Red Army—a few months being, as we all know, but a moment in world history. *PM* has already hinted at this high-historical piece of apologetics. Certainly Russia's operations in Europe are *at this time* immensely more important, however rich in oil Iran be and however decisive Middle Eastern politics will shortly be in the total international picture. Stalin's pressure on Iran eliminates the possibility of opposing pressure against Russian operations in Germany, Poland, and the Balkans. Above all he gains time, which is so important for him. The longer he can operate unchecked in Europe, the more democrats he can shoot. Even if forced to pull back entirely from Iran, he has still won a point, since the Council has been unable meanwhile to bring up the other situations. The Russian game of chess again, and so far working beautifully. Thanks in large part to his various Fifth Columns abroad who consciously or unconsciously succeed in misleading public opinion.

But whatever happens, the Iranian case cannot be considered a "minor" incident if for no other reason than that it showed beyond any shadow of doubt what Stalin thinks of the UN. When Gromyko walked out of the Council, his gesture epitomized perfectly the essential *rudeness* of Stalin's regime. Russia—with whom its foreign advocates have persistently demanded "cooperation"—showed itself unwilling to cooperate on anything but its own terms. Protected by its veto, Russia knows it has nothing to fear, and indeed everything to gain from the UN. Stalin will continue to use the UN as a front organization, while he carries on his own brand of politics behind the scenes. A few more such walkouts and the UN will be revealed to the world for the farce it is.

Even the diehard "liberal" apologists became a little hard-pressed as the Iran affair dragged on, and were glad to draw a breath of relief when the Russian satellite, Poland, brought up the Spanish question before the Council. A breathing spell at last! Once again they could wrap themselves in the toga of self-righteousness and parade as aggressive champions of democracy all over the world. The "liberals" of *PM*, *The Nation*, and *The New Republic* have always required easy whipping boys; this permits an uninterrupted glow of self-righteousness without at the same time exacting the stiff price of intelligence and courage, two qualities they have shown little trace of for the last dozen years. But the very fury of their attack upon Franco is a self-betrayal: they are really for democracy except when and where the interests of the Soviet Union are involved.

Every argument they use to justify intervention in Spain is a valid argument for intervention in Russia. Spain is totalitarian? Beside Stalin's monolithic police state Franco's fascism is a petty and amateur affair. Spain is antidemocratic? Stalin has not only extinguished all traces of democratic liberties among his own people but is engaged in snuffing out these liberties wherever the Red Army has spread. Spain gave aid to Hitler during the war? By the Russo-German Treaty of 1939 Russia gave the indispensable aid which was the very possibility of launching the war; that treaty was further supplemented by an economic pact under which, during 1939–41, Stalin gave considerable economic aid to Hitler while the latter was fighting the western democracies; and Franco never gave Hitler such outright military aid as the Russian invasion of Poland in 1939. Franco is a menace to world peace? The comparison here becomes laughable when we consider that Spain is a fifth- or tenth-rate military power, while Russia maintains the largest standing army in the world, spread at this moment over vast areas outside its own territories; and when we consider too that every recent international tension which has made the peoples of the world think fearfully of war has resulted from one or several aggressive maneuvers on the part of Stalin.

If the "liberals" are uncompromisingly for democracy throughout the world, why not then be for it in Russia too? If they are still in doubt as to the facts about Russia, why not ask the UN for an international commission of inquiry, as in the case of Spain? But the expectation that they will struggle for any such policy is vain. The "liberals" will continue to evade comparisons between Spain and Russia. They will continue to think that Stalin's totalitarianism is somehow different from Franco's, different from Hitler's. Alas yes; the considerable difference is that the former is able to enlist "liberal" support.

III

It is clear from this outline of their recent behavior that the "liberals" are embarked upon nothing less than a policy of *appeasement of Russia*. This may exist as a confusion and a fear in many "liberal" minds, but it is nonetheless a policy for all that. A policy is simply the effective direction in which one throws all one's available political weight.

We are not surprised to find appeasement repeating itself, and the new instance already shows all the features familiar from the appeasement of Hitler. It involves first, as we have already said, a campaign to hate Britain, conducted with a new subtlety but with infinitely more political viciousness than that of the Bund and America First groups. When Henry Wallace publicly declares: *"We have no more in common with imperialist England than with Communist Russia,"* he is playing exactly the same game as the appeasers who shouted: *"We have no more in common with imperialist England than with National Socialist Germany."* But those appeasers were at least more honest: they did not masquerade as champions of democracy and they did not have the effrontery to label themselves "liberals." By a well-timed coincidence Ralph Ingersoll's *Top Secret*, which portrays the British as secret villains of World War II, appeared during the Iran case. One step further and Ingersoll himself would have been openly accusing (in effect, he made the accusation at a rally at Madison Square Garden on May 16) the British of working for the defeat of Russia in World War II.

A second feature of this new appeasement is the consistent attack upon the State Department. The discrediting of the State Department very shrewdly paves the way for the kind of attack in *The New Republic* from which we have quoted at the head of this article. Not the least dishonest aspect of that attack was its pretending to assume that the State Department had in fact already got sufficiently tough against Russia. Instead of trying to needle this timidly conservative department into a more aggressively democratic policy, the "liberals" are trying to make it stoop lower to the despicable service of pulling Stalin's chestnuts out of the fire for him. Bad as the State Department may be, to treat it as a greater menace to world peace than Stalin's Politburo, to criticize it violently and consistently while Russia is criticized, if at all, only lackadaisically and inconsistently—is a piece of sheer idiocy or sheer knavery.

But perhaps the grossest ingredient in this new dish of appeasement is the constant "liberal" shout of war. They accuse certain groups of talking in a way that can only lead to war, but in fact nobody is beating the drums of war more loudly than they. Nobody else has been staging public rallies (complete with Frank Sinatra, Olivia de Havilland and the indispensable Pepper) for or against the next war; nobody else has been working with quite such political cunning on the veterans—that particular segment of the population which is most disaffected with war and therefore the easiest prey to propaganda for appeasement—transforming mass meetings, ostensibly for veterans' housing, into rallies to sanction Russian aggressions.

At this point it is hard to believe we are not being confronted with a piece of conscious deception. Obviously the American people does not want and could not now be mobilized into war. War cannot therefore be a political issue. To cry it up as such is to conceal the issues which are really now at stake. If Stalin believed that war were an issue now, he would very quickly change from lion to lamb and pull back from his aggressions. *Pravda* bleated towards Nazi Germany during 1939–41 like the gentlest of lambs because Stalin knew Hitler would not have stood for the kind of treatment now being given the Allies. Stalin knows that neither Britain nor America is ready for a new war, and he strikes while the iron is hot, grabbing off as much as he can now while there is no prospect of armed opposition. This is the immediate compulsion behind present Russian aggression. The "liberals" have been so persuaded that Stalin does not have Hitler's economic compulsions to expand that they will continue to believe whatever he does is done only for "security." How far does he have to go before they will believe it is aggression and not security that is at issue? To the Rhine? the Bay of Biscay? perhaps when Stalin starts to cross the English Channel? But beside the economic reason of plunder, there may be political reasons for expansion—a specifically totalitarian dynamic of expansion to survive. The dictatorship has always been rationalized by keeping the Russian masses in a state of mobilized hostility towards the capitalist world outside Russia. But whatever Stalin's ultimate purposes (and for the present we can only speculate about them), there can be no doubt about what he has done. *We do not have to establish a motive to prove a crime when the crime has been publicly committed before the eyes of the world.*

But granted (which we do not believe) that the situation is as hopeless as "liberals" make out, and any consistent criticism of Russia will necessarily lead to war; will appeasement, then, do any better? If war is that inevitable, does it not become a man's duty to cry stinking fish and face up to the inevitability? Was war against Hitler avoided by appeasement? On the contrary, Hitler might have been permanently checked had he been firmly opposed at his very first steps towards aggression. If war between Russia and the United States is not inevitable, then perhaps the only way to avoid it is to stop licking Stalin's boots. After the disastrous record of a whole decade's appeasement of Hitler, surely it is the depth of folly and self-degradation to cast sheep's eyes at appeasement as the way out of war.

IV

But what, then, do the "liberals" really want? Their program is clearly appeasement, but are there any principles, political or human, behind it?

If you are an international revolutionary, you may override the interests of your government for the sake of some principle you regard as higher—international socialism, for example. You may, on the other hand, be a patriot in the specific sense that in a given international situation you think the political values of your government—however imperfect or circumscribed—are worth preserving. You may, finally, persistently override the interests of the government under which you live for the sake of some foreign government from no general principle except that . . . well, you are for that foreign government. The three available political alternatives thus boil down, without needless division into subspecies, to three: you are an international revolutionary, or an American patriot, or—a Russian patriot.

To which category do our "liberals" belong?

International revolutionaries? They have certainly been keeping the secret very well hidden all these years. Have they ever committed themselves even to socialism against capitalism? Well, on the other hand, they have never committed themselves to capitalism against socialism. By being neither fish nor fowl, the "liberals" think to confound their critics, who will not know whether to take them with hook or gun. But taking them as fish *and* fowl, and allowing them moreover to shift their ambiguous biology wherever convenient, we still cannot make them come out right with either logic or principle. If they were socialists, they could not be loyal partisans of the regime which has paralyzed or destroyed every genuine socialist movement in our time. Perhaps they are the most incorrigible of myth addicts as still to believe that Russia is socialist in fact or tendency? Then they put themselves beyond the pale of serious consideration, they lose authority to speak seriously on any issue, since they will obviously be immune to any and all facts whenever convenient for them. When J. A. del Vayo recently stated that "after all, Russia *is* socialist," he demonstrated only that *The Nation*, which is currently paying his expenses for a European tour, might keep a tighter fist on its checkbook. Nobody is going to believe that a man who makes this statement will be able to report on even the most obvious political matters abroad. But if Russia were really socialist "after all" (after what? one wonders; even del Vayo cannot make the statement without some repressed demurrer) and the "liberals" are pro-Russian because they are socialists, then why shouldn't they be unequivocally and openly for Russian expansion? Why stop at their present mealy-mouthed and squirming rationalizations instead of declaring openly they want Stalinism to engulf Iran; the Balkans; Europe to the Rhine; yes, to the Atlantic—and then why stop there? Instead of smirking slyly at their discomfitures, the "liberals" should root openly for the checkmate of Byrnes and Bevin whenever this pair goes into conference against Molotov. "But you really ask too much of me," the "liberal" pops up at this point, "you ask me to be *unequivocal!* We know that Stalinism is 'after all' socialism, and we 'liberals' are all secretly socialist at heart, and that is why we condone Stalin's socialist imperialism; (Stalin showed us there can be 'proletarian millionaires,' and why not then 'socialist imperialism'?); but we distinguish between condoning and declaring openly for expansion, we are careful only to condone Russian expansion because 'after all' Stalinism may not be socialism and how can we be sure we are really socialists?"

No; however you try to cast up the "liberal" accounts, you cannot make them come out right, you can find no consistent principle behind their support of Russia. We are left with the third category (their behavior obviously removes them from the second): the "liberals" can only be described as Russian patriots.

We therefore call them a Fifth Column. We do not mean by this that they are officially designated and paid by this foreign power; nor do we claim to say what the term of their services will be. Their services are probably altogether too spontaneous and "pure." But this does not mitigate their guilt for a campaign of concealment, misrepresentation, and deception in the interest of a foreign power—all the more reprehensible in being without any other discoverable principle than the devotion itself to that power. We are long since familiar with the fact that the Communist Party is a Fifth Column, since it proposes no other end for all its actions but the advantage of the Soviet Union. The "liberals" have become a more potent and dangerous Fifth Column since they succeed in deceiving a good many more people.

It would take a very obtuse intelligence to miss the Stalinist sympathies of *PM*, but the methods of *The Nation* and *The New Republic* are at once more confused and more subtle. *PM* is the plebeian wing of the "liberal" admirers of Russian totalitarianism and its methods are therefore far cruder and more obvious. But many readers of *The New Republic* and *The Nation* probably miss the subtle internal politics of book reviewing that goes on week by week. When *The New Republic* wished a reviewer for Victor Kravchenko's *I Chose Freedom*, what happy stroke of editorial inspiration led them to select Frederick Schuman? Is it possible they did not know the kind of review they would get? There is a point beyond which the hypothesis of innocence cannot be stretched. Does the editor know anything about his reviewers beforehand or does he hand his books out to any chance comer in the street? Schuman did not disappoint: for vilification and innuendo his review might almost have adorned the pages of *The Daily Worker*. Among other things, he defended Stalin's terror by pointing to gangsters, lynchings, and strikes in the United States; without mentioning, however, that gangsters and lynchings are not the official program of our government as their equivalents are in Russia. As for strikes, perhaps Schuman would prefer the situation (no doubt, "after all, socialist") in Russia, where striking is a capital offense. The "liberal" weeklies will maintain they are conducting their reviews on the principle of freedom of opinion—remarkable that the "freedom" seems to run so consistently one way. Why didn't they allow such "freedom of opinion" in their reviews of Hitler and Mussolini? Schuman himself is scarcely worth noticing except that his choice as reviewer and his review itself afford a particularly startling whiff of the "liberal" putrescence. Schuman justifies the Russian terror as the necessary price for rapid industrialization; apart from the fact that this argument has been refuted time and again, all evidence pointing to the continual disruption of industry by the political dictatorship—we might analogously justify Hitler for having reduced unemployment and built magnificent roads in Germany, and Mussolini for cleaning Italian cities and making the trains run on time. From the vantage point of Mars or of history five hundred years from now, some scholarly dilettante might draw up a list balancing favorable and unfavorable aspects of Hitler. But for those who had to confront it politically in their lifetime, a pro and con attitude would have been absolutely without political content: Hitler's regime was essentially vicious and had to be opposed politically. This point is capital and I dwell on it because the "liberals" somehow think they can salve their conscience by various sad remarks from time to time—which prove their "impartiality," no less!—acknowledging that political liberty is not all it should be in Russia. Are they too stupid or too knavish not to understand that an attitude neatly balanced of pros and cons toward a criminal dictatorship is absolutely without political meaning? Or, rather, that it has only one political meaning: sanction of that dictatorship? The ineffable Ingersoll, again, tells us: "We must be neither for nor against Russia, but we must try to understand her." Analogously, we should have been neither for nor against Hitler, but simply have tried to understand him.

If some "liberals" are slightly taken aback at being called a Fifth Column, they should learn from Victor Kravchenko that the Russian employees in the Soviet Embassy at Washington were allowed to read, of American publications, only *The Daily Worker, PM, The Nation,* and *The New Republic.* During the appeasement of Hitler, these "liberal" publications pointed loudly to every praise the Hearst-McCormick press received in Berlin as proof that these publications were virtual Fifth Columns. Is it likely Stalin is any less shrewd than Hitler in knowing who his friends are?

How far, after all, can we go in excusing people as being unconscious of their motives? When Ralph Ingersoll likened (*PM,* May 6) our military and diplomatic position to Nazi Germany's vis-à-vis Russia, perhaps he was not aware that he was very definitely implying that the United States, and not Russia, is most like Hitler. Perhaps not; but to gauge the effect of such an editorial we must take into account the distinct frame of reference established by the newspaper for its day-to-day reader—the fact, among many, that Ingersoll's statements appeared in a newspaper whose cartoons have already evolved a snarling bullying type of U.S. Army officer as an American counterpart to the familiar caricature of the ramrod monocled Prussian. And Ingersoll himself gave his cartoons a speaking voice when he declared (at Madison Square Garden, May 16) that the American military were even now engineering a war against Russia—precisely as if we had here a German High Command operating *as a political force* behind the back of the people. We are not writing this editorial from Kansas or Texas, where we have only the printed words of *The Nation* or *The New Republic* before us, but from New York City, where our frame of reference is also further established by the conversations in which we occasionally engage these people. In conversation certain "liberals" become more open or more unwary (it is hard to say which), and when pushed to the point of the alternative, "You must choose between the United States or Russia," they will occasionally break down and admit: "Well, then I choose

Russia." Here the Fifth Column confesses itself, but do not expect such frankness from a "liberal" unless you have pushed him to it.

Yet what do "liberals" really stand to gain from their present frenetic support of Russia except their own political death? A worldwide victory of Stalin would mean their immediate extinction. On the other hand they would fall as the first victims of a terror of the Right as American public opinion becomes solidly mobilized against Russian aggressions. Such a mass movement in America would be condemned to fall into reactionary hands by the "liberals" themselves because they have failed to provide their own leadership. In a situation of impending or existing hostility between America and Russia, the Communists will be dealt with for what they are, outright foreign agents; but reactionaries, never remarkable for niceties of discrimination, have always been a little colorblind to the difference between pink and red friends of Russia, and the reaction, when it comes, would thus clamp a tight lid on all political liberties and perhaps even bring a ruthless suppression of civil liberties. If certain "liberals" insist on digging their own graves, that might seem to be their private affair; but we hope they are not past pleading with that they are dragging down in their own ruin everyone else who genuinely desires the values that have been an essential part of traditional liberalism.

Of course, Stalin may go too far, and the "liberals" will be forced to pull in their horns. At the moment, they are already giving signs of pulling back: Stalin has already gone so far that they are hard put for rationalizations to defend him. These days *PM* can defend Russia only by keeping silent and switching the spotlight to the threat from German rearmament due to the evil laxness of—the British. But do not be deceived, reader. Stalin has only to pull back a little, make a few beneficent remarks about peace and the UN, and his American well-wishers will be on the bandwagon again, shouting what a fine fellow he is, and how slanderous, criminal, and endangering to international relations were such criticisms of him as this.

V

The "liberals" will not lack for other evasions meanwhile. Their fecundity for rationalizations has already shown itself bottomless. No doubt they will accuse the views of this editorial as expressing an attitude of hatred towards Russia or Stalin (they do not bother to distinguish)—and probably a "pathological" hatred too, if you please. (Lately they have taken to using a debased and comic version of Freud for what they imagine is an avant-garde weapon of vilification.) But it is they who really hate the Russians, since they do everything within their power to further Stalin's oppression of this people. And is it so pathological to hate a criminal dictator? Was it pathological to hate Hitler? Then it was also pathological for Locke to hate the Stuarts, Voltaire to hate the Bourbons, Beethoven to hate

Napoleon, Marx to hate Louis-Napoleon, Lenin to hate the Tsar. The "liberals" will also have other worn and tattered scarecrows to shake—any opportunism that comes to hand, anything indeed to avoid the issue of democracy against totalitarianism. Unlike the "liberals," we have no secret and ambivalent longings to "escape from freedom" which we mask under one rationalization or another; and having no totalitarian commitments anywhere in the world, we insist that no compromise be made with totalitarianism.

Until they take at least this minimum position, the "liberals" are obviously usurping a name which they have despoiled of every vestige of its original meaning. The word "liberal" now retains nothing but a denotative value, and that is why we have persisted in keeping it in quotation marks throughout. Whether or not the "liberals" here spoken of will ever earn the removal of quotation marks from their "liberalism," they have already made themselves a long past to live down.   1946, vol. 13, no. 3

• The "Liberal" Fifth Column: A Rejoinder
Heinz Eulau

In publishing their ill-tempered editorial, "The 'Liberal' Fifth Column" (Summer 1946), the editors of *Partisan Review* have done themselves an injustice because they have lost an opportunity. If it was their intention to come to grips with the present dilemma of American liberals vis-à-vis the reality of Sovietism, they utterly failed. This is the more deplorable as the effort at a critique of American liberals attempted in the editorial was worth undertaking, and because the editorial contained some valid censures.

The reason for this failure, I believe, lay in the editorial's exclusive emphasis on the problem of the liberal attitude toward Russia. This, I will undoubtedly be told, was its purpose. But it would have been justified only if the editorial had concerned itself solely with substantive charges instead of also seeking to discover motivations for the liberal position. However, this position cannot be appraised satisfactorily within the narrow limits set in the editorial. Had it discussed present-day liberal attitudes generally, it would not have found it impossible to see any consistent principle behind the liberal approach to Russia except the potential advantage or disadvantage of the Soviet Union.

The editorial touched a desirable explanation when it pointed out that the liberals have never committed themselves to socialism against capitalism, or to capitalism against socialism. But this line of reasoning was dropped, and the editorial reverted to the rather tiresome because repetitive harping on the theme of "fifth columnism."

For some reason which I do not quite understand the editorial saw in the liberal demand for the internationalization of atomic energy control—and this they want rather than that "the secret should be given immediately to Russia"—the "first clear-cut indication that a new standard of judgment for all political and social questions had been found." Now, I am sure, the editors of *Partisan Review* do not really believe *this*—even if they believe Victor Kravchenko that "the Russian employees in the Soviet Embassy at Washington were allowed to read, of American publications, only *The Daily Worker*, *PM*, *The Nation*, and *The New Republic*." Certainly, the friendly attitude of the liberals toward Russia is older than the bomb. The charge that the liberals suddenly became "Russian patriots" can readily be thrown where it belongs—in the garbage can of political slogans.

More interesting, on the other hand, was the intimation that Stalin may go too far, forcing the liberals to pull in their horns, and that they are already giving signs of pulling back. In spite of *Partisan Review*'s warning that all that is needed to reverse this trend are a few benevolent remarks about peace and the UN from Stalin, it may be appropriate in this connection to call attention to another editorial entitled "To the 'Neutral' Liberals" in the June–July 1946 issue of *The Protestant*. *Partisan Review* charged the liberals with saying that "in American hands the atomic bomb constituted a threat to the peace of the world, but of course, if Russia had possession of it, the world could rest secure." *The Protestant*, on the other hand, discovered that "the attitude of some liberals toward this war is tragic. Apparently these liberals would prefer atomic war to the spread of communism beyond the borders of the Soviet Union." And it accused the liberals of preparing "to support the war against the Soviet Union."

I don't quite know what variety of liberals the two journals are talking about, whether with or without quotation marks. But I have a hunch that it is the same species. In any case, I would not bring up the editorial in *The Protestant* if it had not dealt, like that of *Partisan Review*, with political motivations. *Partisan Review*, as a matter of fact, had sanctified its vitriolics with the strange axiom that "political positions are weighed by objective consequences and not by subjective intentions." The editorial surely proved it. If intentions, even though they are good, are obviated by "objective consequences," it is indeed unnecessary to examine or at least present truthfully "subjective intentions."

Falsification of "subjective intentions" can only result in the most bizarre interpretation of "objective consequences." This the juxtaposition of the *Partisan Review* and *The Protestant* editorials with their diametrically opposed conclusions as to "objective consequences"—"appeasement" in the former, "war against the Soviet Union" in the latter—amply demonstrates. But is it not actual behavior and not arbitrarily discovered "objective consequences" which is the socially effective and decisive reality in political life? This, I think, was partly, if inadvertently, recognized in *Partisan Review*'s statement that the liberals are neither fish nor fowl as far as the issue of capitalism vs. socialism is concerned. It may explain the liberal attitude toward Soviet Russia.

Liberal behavior toward Russia is essentially ambivalent. Because they are not socialists, the liberals can look upon certain features of Soviet reality rather uncritically. Their lack of proper socialist standards of judgment—mistaking, for instance, a nationalized economy for socialism in spite of its being controlled by a bureaucratic elite—permits the liberals to think of Russia as a socialist state. Hence their hope for the eventual liberalization of the Soviet regime (in addition to their incurable optimism which stems from their failure to break with the notion of continual progress).

On the other hand their devotion to democratic and liberal values—"subjective intentions"—makes them critical of the illiberal and undemocratic features of the Soviet regime. *Partisan Review* is blatantly unfair in omitting this side of the liberal ambivalence. It is this omission of not seeing the liberal as ambivalent, but selecting only one side of his ambivalence, that leads to such distorted inferences as presented in *Partisan Review* and *The Protestant*. The former, in its admitted hatred of Stalinism, cannot conceive of any manifestation of friendliness toward Soviet Russia, however reluctant, but as "fifth column" activity. The latter, manifestly Stalinist, cannot bear any criticism, however well-justified, without noting a plot against Russia. Neither journal can quite grasp what makes the liberals tick.

The major political disease of the liberal in recent times is the lack of a self-critical attitude as well as the lack of functioning as a critic in general. Liberals could speak of the Roosevelt administration and of the Stalinist regime as the two great centers of dynamic energy because they were essentially uncritical. As a matter of fact, it has become quite fashionable for liberals to pride themselves on being different from the liberal of the twenties who, as one spokesman said, "was more likely to be a critic than a man of action," and who—it was rather gracelessly put—"was brought up in a world where other people did things and he sat back and complained about them." As a result of this professed abdication of the critical function, the liberals found it difficult to resist the bandwagon mentality which first developed with the New Deal and later crystallized in their uncritical support of the policies of the Anglo-American-Russian coalition. Loyalty to the White House meant, in line with the Roosevelt program, getting on with the Kremlin.

When the liberals uncritically accepted the anomalous decisions made at Teheran and Yalta, they invited the anomalous situation in which they now find themselves. Their lack of critical imagination can only have the effect of keeping them in a continual state of surprise. They are surprised when Stalin suddenly blames the war on capitalism, and they are surprised when "Big Three Unity" turns out to be a myth. A further result of the abdication of the critical function is the opportune feeling that the latest is the best. And from this concession to complacency it is only a small step to the equally convenient belief that present trends will continue indefinitely into the future.

I believe that the friendliness of American liberals toward Russia during the war, and even now, stems primarily from their uncritical worship at the shrine of political power—the fictitious power of "Big Three Unity," for instance, and not, as *Partisan Review* suggested, from subservience to the whims and wishes of the Kremlin. Had the liberals been less enthusiastic about Teheran and Yalta, they would not have had to face their present dilemma of having to defend an untenable position.

Finally, it is the shock of disillusionment, I believe, rather than *Partisan Review*'s impugned "fifth columnism" on behalf of Russia, that is largely responsible for the liberal attacks on the State Department, the domestic war party, and British imperialism. I do not have the slightest doubt that the liberals will also resume attacks on Russia (as during the Nazi-Soviet Pact period). For they are now pinning their hopes on the workability of the United Nations which, I think, is anything but a "front organization" of Stalin, as *Partisan Review* put it. It is so clearly an institutionalization of the contemporary complex of international power politics that sooner or later the liberals alone will find themselves in the unenviable spot of being the sole defenders of its nobler objectives.

Heinz Eulau

1946, vol. 13, no. 5

• Paris Letter
Nicola Chiaromonte

"Would you call the present situation an *extreme* one?" I asked a historian friend of mine. "It seems to me," he answered, "that an extreme situation is characterized by the fact that the individual is there confronted with, or crushed by, clear-cut alternatives. In mortal danger, in the middle of a revolutionary upsurge, in the ignominy of a concentration camp, a man at least knows where he stands. But, if there is any extremity in the condition of the European individual today, it is an extremity of unclarity and ambiguity.

" '*Either* America *or* Stalin, *either* Communism *or* Gaullism,' they tell him, 'you must choose.' And does he choose? I don't think so. I think that it is a mere figure of speech to call choice the act by which a French citizen today acquiesces to the inevitability of the dilemma, and eventually *follows* one kind of crowd or the other. He follows, while being convinced that *neither* America *nor* Stalin, *neither* Communism *nor* Gaullism, is really the answer. To use Koestler's image (which contrary to what Koestler thinks, can work both ways), very little perspicacity is needed to realize that there is no black and white, only different shades of gray. In fact, the arguments used by the different political groups, the way in which they state their dilemmas, implies that the either/or alternative is intended for public use, while in reality the choice is between lesser evils, shades of gray, expedients.

"No shrewd Stalinist propagandist today argues that one must be a Communist because the Soviet state is a model for socialist construction, but rather that one should stick to the CP because it is the *only available* instrument in the struggle against capitalism. Similarly, the real argument of the Gaullists is not that de Gaulle is a second Joan of Arc, but that he is the *only available* man under whose authority the French state can be rescued from the quagmire of Third Force fickleness. Such arguments surely permit the individual to remain distraught and perplexed, even though he may straggle along with the parade. There is nothing desperate, nothing extreme, in such a state of mind. It is not evident to people at large that some other political choice does not exist.

"At the bottom of all this I can see social stagnation and apathy, but I don't see that people are possessed by the feeling of a dire emergency threatening them, which requires a miracle of energy on their part. People today don't believe in miracles of any kind any longer, much less in political messianism. What they really feel is that history is being made without them anyway, and that performing some symbolic act of worship to some traditional idol, like the Revolution or the Fatherland, is about all they can do to assert their presence on the scene. That is why Europe today resembles a ghetto, rather than a gallant three-master tossed by a storm."

I must say that the type of arguments I had heard from a number of people, especially Gaullists and Communists, tended to confirm my friend's diagnosis. I asked, for example, a well-known French scholar and publicist who has recently joined the Rassemblement du Peuple Français, what reasons he would give to prove that de Gaulle does not mean fascism. He answered that, in his opinion, a fascist ideology contains four ingredients: 1) anti-Communism; 2) reinforcement of the state; 3) nationalism; 4) a war of conquest as the final issue. "Now," argued this intellectual, "de Gaulle certainly stands for the first two points, but not for the other two. He accepts the idea of a united Europe, and when he thinks of war, he simply thinks of the necessity to do everything possible to make France ready to withstand Stalin's probable onslaught."

"But," I retorted, "are you sure that de Gaulle is not a nationalist in the sense that he conceives of France as a monarchic entity requiring a certain type of behavior and rejecting certain others, and whose commands can finally be interpreted only by the leader? After all, this is the essence of nationalism. Besides, don't you think that de Gaulle's insistence, whenever he speaks of Europe, on the notion that Europe's unity can be achieved only under French leadership, reveals more than a little national egocentrism? As for war, does it really matter whether the war one prepares for is a defensive or an offensive one, once the danger of war is considered to create a state of emergency and authorize a methodically drastic action on the part of the government?"

"I won't deny," said my interlocutor, "what everybody knows, namely that de Gaulle has a somewhat hermetic, and possibly outdated, notion of France's mission, as well as of his own with regard to France. But what is politically relevant is the fact that this notion gives him the singlemindedness which is needed to break the present political stalemate. I might even agree that de Gaulle is a poor politician, and not really a statesman, except in the classical sense of a man who wants to make new fundamental laws. Still, he is the only man who can keep France united while operating a series of drastic but inevitable changes."

"What about the social program of the RPF?" I asked.

"Frankly, all I can say is that we are trying to have one," was the answer, "and it is not an easy job. There are too many old-fashioned conservatives among us. If only the Socialists could understand that the choice is between us and the CP. But all they do is be afraid that if they don't call us fascists the Stalinists will call them "social traitors," which they do anyway. Hence, in spite of the great influence of such men as Soustelle, Vallon, and Malraux, the left wing of the RPF remains rather weak. If you want to know what I personally think, I can tell you that I am a Gaullist because I think that Gaullism is a chance for conservatism. By conservatism, I mean a principle of government which allows for specific progress and definite changes. At the opposite pole there is the ideology of revolution, which is that of the Communists, namely the will to seize power in order to change everything. Since I don't believe in changing 'everything,' and since I don't see any force in France today capable of introducing the partial reforms that are needed, except the RPF, I am with the RPF. I don't expect any miracles. What I expect is a minimum of rationality and realism, more especially I expect de Gaulle to give us a state which will be strong and limited, instead of being both impotent and omnipresent, like the one we have today. As for the rest, I am an old-fashioned liberal. Only I think that today civil liberties cannot be saved except through a period of emergency powers. Even if de Gaulle should establish a kind of dictatorship, it would only last a couple of years. In any case, de Gaulle will do no worse than the Third Force."

"Do you feel confident of it?" I asked.

"Not quite, I must say," answered this intellectual, "but the risk must be taken, since we have no choice."

So here was a man who had joined a movement which claims to stand for nothing if not for "energy, clarity, and firmness of purpose," and who at the same time was aware that 1) the leader of the movement is a symbol rather than a political man; 2) the movement itself gives no guarantee as to the direction it may take, and has no program on the crucial issue of the day, which happens to be also the one on which the enemy (i.e., the Stalinists) is strongest; 3) the whole enterprise, if successful, might have no better effects than the ones that are being denounced as the worst imaginable. Only in France, I felt, the will not to be a dupe can play such tricks.

The day of the Bedell Smith — Molotov affair I saw a young man whom I have known for many years, and toward whom personally I feel very friendly. He is a CP member and, because of the outstanding role he has played in the resistance movement, occupies now a rather important position. That day he appeared to be immensely amused by the trap sprung on that dope of an American ambassador by Comrade Molotov. I told him that maybe the joke was not so funny, and that, in any case, I didn't feel that it took us nearer a state of peace. My friend didn't agree: Molotov's was a master stroke, and it would force America to accept negotiations instead of being so irresponsibly "tough." He went on to say that the real obstacle to an understanding between America and the Soviet Union were Messrs. Bidault and Bevin, with their ridiculous claim that, before making peace, Moscow and Washington should listen to British and French quibbling. "In other words," I said, "you would like America and Russia to get together." "I certainly would," he said, "otherwise we haven't got a chance." "And on what basis do you think they could agree?" I insisted. "On the very good basis of our backs, my dear," answered my Stalinist friend, with a hearty laugh.

Earlier in the conversation, he had explained to me the Stalinist line of "chauvinism in every country," and its systematic opposition to any idea whatsoever of a United Europe, by saying that European capitalism was selling countries wholesale to its American masters, and couldn't carry out its schemes without the cover of Europeanism. Hence, the defense of national interests had become one of the main tasks of the working class.

This, it now appeared, was a theory for the possibly transitory period of the "cold war." As soon as the atomic lightning of naked power politics struck, however, dialectics would automatically be put out of action, and the only rational thing to do would be to resign oneself to naked force, with no illusions as to the softening effects of ideologies on it. Which is, after all, what Europeans are doing right now. They hardly need Marxist indoctrination in this, since their backs are already sore enough from the burden of geopolitics. What is the use of improvising cumbersome theories if they can't even hide the fact that they finally serve no purpose, and the fundamental question remains the same for everybody? — I could have asked my friend. But I didn't, and just took notice that, for him too, black and white were colors for public use, while in private he saw gray, like everybody else.

The gray became even darker for this particular Communist when the Tito affair burst into the headlines. The ideological hocus-pocus of the Cominform he didn't find hard to swallow, except for the style, which, he agreed, was depressing. But he was seriously bothered by the procedure adopted by comrade Zhdanov. As Tito promptly pointed out, the Yugoslav party had been excommunicated directly by its brother, the Russian party, and all that Duclos, Togliatti, and the rest of the gang, had been allowed to do was to decorate with their signatures the Russian ukase after it had already been sent to Belgrade. That was a dark foreboding. It was the *official* notice broadcast to all and sundry, capitalists and proletarians, faithful and faithless, that there could not be anything like an indigenous policy of this or that CP. Up to now, in France as well as in Italy, the Communist propaganda line has not been that "we are going to do just what they did in Russia," but, on the contrary, that Communism would take different, and autonomous, forms in each country, and especially in the highly civilized West. At the same time, the conviction has been common among the militants, that "when it comes to France (or Italy), the Russians will not be able to just push us around like Bulgarians, they will have to reckon with *us* (the base)." The hammer that hit Tito left little standing of such hopes. It was another cause for resignation to *force majeure* added to many others. "So, you are going to hold your nose and gulp down this one too," I told my friend. "What else can we do? There is no alternative," he answered.

If their party's day-to-day tactics gave them some ground for believing that they are headed for something like revolution the Stalinists would probably be the only ones today who could successfully entertain a mood of extreme situation. But they can't. The brightest political perspective that is offered them is that of a Soviet invasion of Western Europe. "What would you do if the Red Army occupied France?" I asked my friend. "It would be a damn rotten business," was his answer. To such an eventuality, no doubt, the most ardent and most sincere militants would vastly prefer that of an underground struggle against "home reactionaries and American imperialism" in case of war. This would at least involve some idealism. But they can hardly *hope* for such a thing to happen.

The fact is that, after the Czechoslovakian coup, the Italian election, and the Tito affair, and after the failure of last winter's political strikes, the CPs are condemned to a policy of systematic and politically schizophrenic agitation deprived of any intelligible prospect. In reality, the Cominform and their leadership have maneuvered them into a position in which they can do little else except push defensive actions in all possible directions. Only the mistakes of their adversaries, the establishment of a dictatorship, or war, can get them out of their present fix. A good party member will of course be able to explain away a dozen Himalayas. Sympathizers, however, are less well trained, and less ready to look like indoctrinated dunces. You can put a French CP sympathizer to a crucial test by asking him two questions: 1) Do you think that the CP policy is a policy *for* peace? 2) Do you see any other outcome of present CP domestic policies than a strong reaction? After a greater or lesser amount of shuffling, and sometimes right away, the answer will be "no" on both counts. As of today, the French Communists expect some favorable development from three directions. First, in October, when the elections for the Council of the Republic (the almost purely nominal legislative body which has taken the place of the old Senate) will be held, the RPF, which runs nearly forty percent of the municipalities, while having no representatives in the National Assembly is sure to win a considerable victory. At that moment, the Communists hope to be able to take the lead of a movement for the "defense of the Republic." Secondly, thanks to the blithe ineffectiveness of the government, the social question, which today simply means the question of the relation between prices and wages, remains as bitter as ever. Thirdly, the Communists think (and their view is supported by a number of experts) that the Marshall Plan will have no visible effects on the French economy. To these three reasons for optimism, the Communists add a fourth one, which is the noticeable comeback of "clericalism" into French life, especially in the school system. Here too the CP, helped by the fact that the Socialists are the allies of the Catholics in the government, might well try to organize the exploitation of traditional French anticlericalism, which remains a strong social factor.

These calculations are certainly not unfounded. It is, however, hard to conceive how, even under the most favorable (i.e., the worst) political circumstances, the Stalinists could go beyond the stage of demagogic agitation, as long as they are obliged to adopt Stalin's contraceptive measures, which they certainly will be as long as there is no war. The amazing thing is that CP tactics still seem to be based on the notion that the proletariat must *almost* make the revolution in order to allow Messrs. Duclos and Thorez to get back into the government. And this is the most resplendent victory that can be promised to the suffering French masses today by the party of Marx-Lenin-Stalin. Even if such a triumph were possible, it is hard to see how the aforesaid gentlemen could repeat for the second time the performance which consists in exploiting ministerial advantages while making the other fellow responsible for all mismanagement and unpopular measures.

The most revealing symptom of Stalinist weakness seems to me the fact that they still feel obliged to stick to the Popular Front idea: "the rally of all progressive forces against reaction and for the defense of French independence." This when even the "anti-anti-Stalinists" feel that accepting Communist company is about as safe as keeping a copperhead under your shirt—which feeling is one of the main reasons for the undeniable decline of Stalinism. Stalinism was strong as long as it could win over and control non-Stalinist elements, seduce them into believing that it was the last refuge of political idealism, and that, in spite of all the circuitousness, the CP would take them *somewhere*. With the incalculably precious help of the Kremlin, such illusions have by now been dispelled. "I don't like them. But if they are persecuted I will be on their side," is the boldest pronouncement an "anti-anti-Stalinist" is willing to make at present. Once again, such ways of speaking, especially when resorted to by intellectuals, express a last mulish reluctance to relinquish certain ideological habits, rather than a conviction, or a choice. If I were a Communist, I would not put much trust in any such resolve.

The main contribution of a certain kind of intellectual to the CP cause (as, in earlier times, to the cause of Fascism) is the spinning out of verbal justifications. I heard a French professor, the holder of a number of state sinecures, say of the Cominform edict against Tito: "How beautiful. A true Church style. You can think what you please, but in our time only the Communists are in a position to talk such a language." An utterance which my Stalinist friend would have considered perfectly ludicrous. Seriously speaking, however, on the level of culture and intellectual life, the Stalinists have by now suffered a complete loss of face, which was not the case two years ago, when the Communist position was still being discussed with consideration, if not with awe.

Among the latest symptoms of the wearing out of Communist witchery, one can certainly count the unexpectedly great success of Camus' *The Plague* (over one hundred thousand copies sold, at a moment when buying a book is a luxury) and the equally great success of Sartre's *Les Mains Sales* which has been playing for four months to sold out houses. (The play has now closed, but will open again in the fall.) Camus' novel is neither faultless nor written to please, but the general public have apparently found in it an answer to their yearning for ordinary humaneness and good sense. The moral of *The Plague* is that the only adequate answer to an extreme situation is to stick to normal human behavior. The book is not specifically directed against Communism and yet it has been interpreted in this sense by both the Communists and their adversaries. As for Sartre's play (an intellectual product so curious, and so curiously ambiguous, that it would deserve a detailed analysis), it has no moral at all, and is not really an anti-Communist play. In spite of its tragic plot, it is a comedy, the reduction to absurdity of Communist logic with no particular conclusions drawn from it. But from the point of view of the public, *Les Mains Sales* inevitably appears as a savage attack on Communist mentality and tactics. An irresistible piece of theatrical engineering in the good old-fashioned nineteenth-century tradition, the play certainly owes a great deal of its success to the moment in which it was produced. Sartre knows a lot about timing. Such a public undressing of the "Stalinist situation" as his latest play could hardly have been conceivable in 1946, when the CP was still "the party of the executed."

The decline of the CP does not mean at all that light is beginning to shine over France. It simply suggests that, in an atmosphere of political freedom and peace in which people would at least begin to have the feeling that their urgent needs are being reasonably taken care of, the CP would constantly lose ground. For the time being, however, the rabid anti-Communism of the right (which intends to make the defeat of the CP a victory for nationalism, colonialism, and social conservatism), together with the ineptitude of the Socialists, tend to slow down, rather than accelerate, the process. So that up to now the most efficient agent of Communist disintegration remains Comrade Stalin.

Nicola Chiaromonte
1948, vol. 15, no. 9

• The Culture Conference
Irving Howe

Nothing at the "Cultural and Scientific Conference for World Peace" happened quite as one expected; consequently it had an importance beyond its attendant flare of headlines and picket lines. From it one could learn something about the current condition of Stalinism, the possible appearance of a new political tendency in the U.S., and perhaps even the behavior of certain American intellectuals. Since *Partisan Review* readers have by now no doubt seen detailed reports of the conference proceedings, I shall largely confine myself to general observations and conclusions.

Outside the Waldorf, the Catholic War Veterans were picketing aggressively; inside, some three thousand middle-class Wallaceites, braced by the usual strategically placed party fraction, sat passively listening to speeches. It was interesting and important to observe that the percentage of young people seemed smaller than at previous conferences of this sort; apparently the Stalinists are not doing well on the campus. It was also interesting that in addition to the breathless middlebrows, half grasping and half fearful in their culture-hunger (*did you* see Shostakovich?), there were untainted innocents who really thought the conference had some genuine relation to working for peace. Somehow the Stalinists always find new innocents, each batch on a lower cultural level.

At the very first session there were significant divergences from previous Stalinist-front conferences. None of the speakers was either a prominent or a serious intellectual; no official representative from the Communist Party of the U.S. appeared; each speaker deplored, if only in passing, the absence of democracy in Russia. None of these things would have been possible ten years ago.

Few commentators on the conference have said anything about the first speaker, a retired bishop from Utah who nearly broke up the whole affair by talking forever, but to me his speech and its enthusiastic reception were particularly revealing. Apparently not having enjoyed so receptive a congregation for some time, the bishop indulged in every conceivable pulpit witticism and rhetorical flourish. To watch the Stalinists on the stage grin knowingly (the Poles were particularly amused) and then applaud vigorously his peroration on behalf of God's path as the only way to peace, was to see in miniature the maddening absurdities of our political-cultural situation. What preposterous reasoning could have led a retired clergyman from Utah to share, with beaming self-delight, a platform with a commissar from Russia? And the worst of it was that the poor man (*he looks so much like the Dean*) seemed totally oblivious to the indecency of the farce in which he played the pious jester.

The other speakers, Harlow Shapley, O. John Rogge, and T. O. Thackrey, then editor of *The New York Post*, began with slurred criticisms of Russian "restrictions on liberty" and then launched detailed denunciations of U.S. foreign policy. This political line, while extremely useful to Stalinism, is not to be identified with it. It is something rather new, and on the following day received its most sophisticated intellectual development by Frederick Schuman.

If, as seems probable, there will not be a war in the next two or three years, and if, as also seems probable, the Marshall Plan does not solve the fundamental problem of the European economy, the Schuman-Rogge position may become a serious factor in American political life. The cold war rankles—why not reach a cold agreement? Why not divide the world on a bluntly imperial basis, allowing the Russians free reign in "their" sphere of influence in order to be rid of the annoyances of the western Communist Parties? The idea of formalizing the world's split—in the name, of course, of one world—will be attractive to those who fear war and feel no sense of rebellion against either Stalinism or capitalism. Hence the Schuman-Rogge position, half a cynical imperialist proposal for the U.S. and half a proposal for the appeasement of Russia, could be advanced alternately or simultaneously in the name of peace and *realpolitik*. To gain large popular support, such a position would have to be presented by politicians untainted with Stalinist associations; various new leaders or semi-isolationists might find useful the position Schuman and Rogge have prepared for them. The Russians might then find powerful new allies in the U.S.—allies, not apologists. For Fadeyev's polemic against Schuman notwithstanding, they are likely to feel that powerful allies are more useful than powerless apologists. The possibility of such a new political formation a few years hence may have been one reason why the Stalinists tolerated the anti-Russian remarks of the conference speakers to an extent that would have been impossible during the thirties.

Then again, the Stalinists had no alternative. Few prominent American intellectuals are now willing to work with them, some because of intellectual conviction and others because it is no longer safe or fashionable; the only literary highbrow of wide reputation who spoke at the conference was F. O. Matthiessen. Having lost most of its support in both intellectual circles and the labor movement, the C.P. retains strength only in the urban middle classes, particularly the professions and the mass culture and amusement industries. There can be for it no adequate compensation for losses in the unions, but in some ways the C.P. finds Hollywood and Broadway a profitable substitute for the intelligentsia. The Broadway people are less troublesome, ask fewer questions than the intellectuals; they are less prone to fool with notions about independent thought; and they have much more money to contribute. Yet this shift from quality has certain disadvantages: the Stalinists could find no "big name" intellectual—no Dos Passos or Richard Wright or Edmund Wilson—to lead off at the conference. That they were forced to use such intellectual flyweights as Rogge and Thackrey is a telling indication of how serious has been their recent decline.

The two ideologies at the conference, the outright Stalinist one and the other which, for lack of a better label, I have called the Schuman-Rogge position, were not in conflict but neither were they in complete harmony. Fadeyev, head of the Russian delegation and the warden who runs the Russian "Writers Union," severely and with obvious pleasure chastised Schuman for his unfavorable remarks about Russia. (Behind Fadeyev's behavior there was probably a certain nonpolitical factor: how the commissar loves to lord it over the deviating "civilized" foreigners.) Officially, however, the two ideologies melted into one emotional whine: a call for "cultural understanding" and "peace." The phrase "cultural understanding" is one of the more vicious bits of obscurantist political verbiage. We are supposed to believe that the international crisis arose from a misunderstanding—the reception on the phone was bad, perhaps, and the Americans and Russians did not hear each other rightly—if only the Americans read a few more Russian novels and the Russians realized that there *are* good Americans who want to share sincerely—to share in what?—well, in cultural understanding. Similarly, the word "peace" was repeated endlessly, as if in some desperate incantation. Yet what did the word refer to at this conference, other than the Stalinists' program for Russian conquest and the all too legitimate fears and yearnings of the innocents?

The audience, one felt, was uneasy. Picket lines outside, oppositionist intellectuals both in the hotel and the conference, attacks on Russia by *our* speakers—was this the emotional solace and bolstering for which the fellow-travelers come to such conferences? To get together in one room, to hear authoritative voices ringing with confirmation of one's hopes, to see and perhaps for a moment talk to the leaders after their oratorical performances, to be reassured by the august trustees of the faith from overseas—this was the attraction of the conference. Now it may be objected that all political movements must engage in such ritual procedures, which is true; but the distinctive feature of Stalinism, as of all total-itarian movements, is that these procedures become the essence of the convoca-tion of followers. For this ritual to be satisfying to the participants, the managers of such a conference must make certain that it moves with a minimum of distur-bance and dissent, a maximum of pleasant and smooth unanimity. The fellow-traveler's half-totalitarian mind wants to be soothed, to be immersed in a warm bath of rhetorical reassurance. And this the conference managers could not quite provide—the bath was there, but the temperature was erratic. Which is why the audience applauded the Russians so hysterically: they at least were reliable, undeviating, the real thing.

For the party fraction working behind the scenes, organizational control of the conference was a quite easy matter. The larger the conference, the less trouble a small minority has in controlling it. By its very nature, such a conference attracts people who have neither the intention nor the ability to raise serious problems or to participate actively; they come for passive delights. Bound together by the Russian myth, the participants are infinitely pliable; were they not, they would not have come at all. (How can three thousand people hold a conference, any-way?) For the Stalinist managers the problem was not the mass of participants, but the unpredictable speakers. So long as they can bank on the Russian myth and so long as they have cadres of hardworking anonymous members, the Stalinists will always be able to control the mechanical side of such conferences.

Besides, they have developed in the past twenty years a series of highly skilled manipulative devices. The conference chairman, Harlow Shapley, appointed a resolutions committee—and which delegate would have thought to disturb the atmosphere of unity by suggesting that the committee be elected? Shapley ran the conference as if he were an old party factionalist; how curious the way in which the fellow-traveler delights in the vicarious sensations of regularity and dis-cipline. At Princeton I have argued with scientists who furiously insist that Shapley is an independent intellectual and not a fellow-traveler, but if his behav-ior at the Waldorf was not fellow-traveling, it was, for the Stalinists, a most con-venient kind of intellectual independence.

At the heart of such conferences, and in fact of the whole Stalinist movement, lies the Russian myth. How deeply the hope of socialism must have sunk into the Western mind can be seen by the fanatical insistence with which millions of peo-ple in Europe and America (not, after all, the worst people in the world) cling to the fantasy that in Russia socialism is, in one or another way, being built. To admit that the slave society of Russia is a cruel distortion of the original socialist hope is to face a terrifying world in which all the trodden paths of history seem only to lead to destruction. One often wonders why the European worker and the

American middle-class fellow-traveler cling to the Russian myth. There is certainly no one answer to that question, but perhaps one of the answers is itself a question: what must they face if they abandon the myth?

In the meantime, the conference's sense of unanimity was severely disturbed by the presence of an opposition of several hundred anti-Stalinist intellectuals headed by George Counts and Sidney Hook. Hurriedly organized but supported by intellectuals of various anti-Stalinist persuasions (including liberal supporters of capitalism, pacifists, and various kinds of socialists), the Americans for Intellectual Freedom was a committee which largely confined itself to several specific immediate issues: a disclosure of the true sponsorship of the Waldorf conference, a challenge of the Russians' claim to be free intellectual agents, and an exposure of the conference sponsors' failure to include any known anti-Stalinists among its speakers. The AIF issued informative press releases on these points, held a public meeting, and gained the support of writers from abroad, among them T. S. Eliot, Ignazio Silone, Arthur Koestler, and Bertrand Russell.

Its effectiveness in combating the Stalinists was at least partly due, I think, to not having tried to work up any kind of general political program. As soon as questions of program are raised—the sociological meaning of Stalinism, how to oppose it politically, with whom alliances against Stalinism are permissible and profitable—there must undoubtedly appear sharp disagreements. (As it was, there were a few remarks in one AIF statement in support of U.S. foreign policy which some anti-Stalinists, including myself, could not accept, as, I imagine, might not even some of those who signed the AIF releases or were active in its work. Nonetheless, on the specific issues raised by the conference, it was possible for those who support and do not support U.S. foreign policy to work together.) At the AIF meeting there was expressed a considerable range of political opinion, including that of the pacifist A. J. Muste. (No pacifists were invited to the Waldorf "peace conference.") I cite these differences of opinion, not of course to deplore them, but to indicate that such a rallying of intellectuals, being without programmatic agreement, is most effective when confined to matters of specific action. At the Waldorf it was possible for anti-Stalinists of various liberal and radical hues to work together on the basis of one common denominator: a defense of democratic rights and intellectual freedom. This basis has been used in the past for civil liberties cases, and can be used for demarcated action against the Stalinists as well as other opponents of democratic liberties. Apparently, some sort of similar cooperation among anti-Stalinist intellectuals is to be organized in France to oppose the much more dangerous "peace conference" soon to be held there.

At the panels into which the conference divided, it was possible to study the behavior of both Stalinists and fellow-travelers when confronted by radical or democratic opposition. Several anti-Stalinist intellectuals, some affiliated with the AIF and some not—Peter Blake, George Counts, Robert Lowell, Dwight

Macdonald, Mary McCarthy, Jean Malaquais, and Nicholas Nabokov—spoke for two minutes each. Not all were effective; it takes considerable skill to be able to express a political opinion in two minutes, and most intellectuals, accustomed to more indulgent audiences, lack that skill. Counts began to document his charge that there was no intellectual freedom in Russia, but could not finish. Macdonald asked Fadeyev several sharp questions about the fate of Russian writers. McCarthy asked F. O. Matthiessen if he approved of Fadeyev's answers. Malaquais told how the French Stalinists had abused André Gide after his book on Russia appeared.

Fadeyev spoke with the shrill ferocity and brutality of a bureaucrat who, at the moment, lacks prisons and labor camps and must therefore confine himself to less persuasive means of action. There is no reason to believe that he is any sort of intellectual, even of the unhappy variety of which the rest of the Russian delegation was composed; he is simply a privileged bureaucrat; and it is remarkable that he looked, behaved, and spoke so very much like the bureaucrat of one's imagination. Fadayev seemed to enjoy himself more than anyone else at the conference; he did not have to worry about maintaining good relations with Schuman or Rogge and just let loose berating those stupid Americans.

At the beginning of the writers' panel, F. O. Matthiessen had made an incredibly simplistic speech about "the American tradition," quite worse than anything concocted by Granville Hicks. (He had praised Melville for making the hero of *Moby Dick* a "common man.") When forced to comment on Fadeyev's remarks, he did not take the easy out of pleading ignorance of Russian literary conditions. As if driven by some compulsion to extreme commitment or "martyrdom," he plunged into a defense of Fadeyev, saying that he found the Russian's remarks to be "direct and forthright." That was all: no qualifications about censorship and state pressure, not even of the sort present in his book.

And then Shostakovich. I confess myself somewhat at a loss to formulate a definite attitude towards the Russian composer. At the writers' panel he confined himself to a brief ritualistic statement: Russian criticism had helped his music go forward. (He did not say to what.) The next morning he delivered a long speech attacking "formalism" in music and repeating the stock Stalinist phrases about culture. One wondered then: was he, as he sometimes seemed, a pathetic little man, obviously ill at ease and wishing to be away from these painful discussions? Or did we think him pathetic because we expected him to be so? There was no way of knowing whether he wrote his speech himself or delivered it under pressure. Was he a victim, as we liked to think, or had he too become calloused by the alternate privileges and rebukes of the Stalin regime? No one could answer these questions, for in the Waldorf too the Iron Curtain hung.

Finally, Norman Mailer, in response to cries from the floor, spoke. Mailer's hesitant, painful, but obviously deeply felt talk was a perfect illustration of a politically inexperienced mind freeing itself from Stalinist influence. A supporter of Wallace in the last election, Mailer now said that he thought both the U.S. and Russia were drifting to state capitalism, that he saw little hope for peace, and that he regretted his pessimism but could not honestly avoid it. The audience listened quietly, with emotions one can imagine.

The conference, on the whole, was a failure. It aroused articulate and aggressive oppositions; it was disturbed by deviant speeches from among its own spokesmen; it could hardly have offered its supporters much reassurance. My final impression is that the Stalinists must soon decide to enter a new political phase in which they will largely abandon their independence and, following a Browder policy, work only through front groups—or face disintegration and destruction. I must also record my perplexity with regard to the behavior of certain American intellectuals. I think I understand Fadeyev and Howard Fast. But Shapley and Matthiessen: what shall one make of them? How can a man like Matthiessen, cultivated and intelligent, lend his support to a creature of a slave state like Fadeyev? What are the drives to self-destruction that can lead a serious intellectual to support a movement whose victory could mean only the end of free intellectual life?   1949, vol. 16, no. 5

• Report on the International Day Against Dictatorship and War
Sidney Hook

The idea of the International Day of Resistance to Dictatorship and War, held in Paris on April 30, 1949, was suggested to David Rousset, its chief initiator, by the meeting conducted at Freedom House in New York City on March 26, by Americans for Intellectual Freedom.

The project was supported by the Executive Committee of the *Rassemblement Democratique Revolutionnaire* and by the editorial staff of the daily newspaper *Franc-Tireur* in whose joint name invitations were issued.

The RDR is a group of left-wing writers, critics, and artists—the most notable of whom is Jean-Paul Sartre—whose political sentiments range from near-Communist to democratic socialist. It conceives its mission as a regrouping and integration of "left" forces in French life. For practical purposes, it defines the left as almost all elements who regard de Gaulle rather than the Communist Party as the main enemy of freedom and socialism in France. The Communist Party of France is regarded by the RDR as a genuine working-class party with bureaucratic deformations, too subservient to the Kremlin, but capable, together with the Socialist Party, of being influenced by genuinely revolutionary socialist ideas. The RDR is devoid of any mass influence but has a strong following among the footloose Paris intelligentsia who are excited by ideological novelties but are politically very immature. Because of the prestige of ideas and literary personalities in French culture, the RDR has considerable snob appeal.

The *Franc-Tireur*, one of whose editors is Rousset, until recently followed the Communist Party line rather faithfully but with greater sensationalism and demagogy. As a result of a schism with the Party stalwarts and a visit by Rousset and Altman, its chief editor, to the United States, where they discovered that the U.S. was neither decadent nor neo-Fascist, that Negroes are not lynched on every street corner, and that a strong trade-union movement was leading the struggle for progressive social legislation, the *Franc-Tireur* dropped its exclusively anti-American line. Now, without ceasing to denounce American foreign policy, it also ventures to ask rhetorical questions about the existence of democracy in the Soviet Union. Recently it has had several sharp exchanges with *l'Humanité*. So far it has kept its three hundred thousand readers, who only a few months ago were hardly distinguishable from the readers of *l'Humanité*. The editors are convinced that their reading public must be spoon-fed with mild injections of anti-Stalinist criticism until they build up a tolerance to stronger doses. Since the Communist Party has already denounced them as agents of American imperialism, they lean over backward to appear as vigorous critics of American policy, particularly the Atlantic Pact. They no longer criticize the Marshall Plan.

The sponsors of the International Day set themselves a very ambitious task — nothing more than the preparation of a World Congress Against Dictatorship and War to be held in Europe next fall. The only conditions for participation in the preparatory April 30th meeting were (1) recognition that the struggle for freedom against all forms of totalitarianism is bound up with the struggle for peace, and (2) acceptance of *freedom of inquiry* for all participants to present solutions to make this struggle effective. No one was to be choked with a predetermined party line.

If allowance is made for the shortness of time, the slender resources, and the peculiar character of the initiating committee — which although at odds with the Stalinists often talks like them to the discomfiture of some socialist groups — a rather large but *far from representative* group of participants gathered in Paris. There were delegates from England, the United States, Holland, Belgium, Italy, West Germany, and democratic Spain. Among the delegates were Silone, Carlo Levi, Borkenau, Tarnov, Brockway, De Kadt, the English geneticist Darlington, Bourdet, Pivert. Expressions of support were received from Julian Huxley, Crossman, Dos Passos, Sinclair, and many others. The bulk of the delegates consisted of Frenchmen and an extraordinary number of spokesmen for colonial peoples. The most important organizations officially represented were the Socialist Party of the Seine, the autonomous unions, and the Paris region of the Force Ouvriére. There were a baker's dozen of other French organizations, represented either officially or by self-delegated individuals, on the order of the Mouvement Socialiste des Etats-Unis d'Europe and the Ligue Internationale contre le Racisme et l'Antisemitisme.

What gave the International Day importance was that it followed hard on the heels of the Congress of World Partisans for Peace—a Cominform affair from start to finish. That there were two peace meetings weakened the force of the first and revealed more clearly its Communist character. The placarding of the walls of Paris with posters advertising the International Day undoubtedly had some limited educational effect.

Nonetheless the initiators of the Day were careful *not* to call it a counter-demonstration to the Stalinist meeting, among other reasons for fear of antagonizing a considerable number of persons who although not sufficiently sympathetic to the Communist Party to accept the role of public fellow-travelers are not sufficiently courageous to appear in open opposition to it.

The cultural and political climate of opinion in France until recently has been such that it required more courage in non-Communist left circles to be openly critical of the Communist Party and the Soviet Union than is required for an individual to become a Communist Party fellow-traveler in the U.S. Last summer I had already observed this obsessive fear among avowed non-Communists in France, particularly in French literary and intellectual circles, to challenge in any fundamental way the Soviet myth. Ignorance of conditions in the Soviet Union was matched only by ignorance of conditions in the United States, about which the Communists and their fellow-travelers had sold them a misleading bill of goods unwittingly helped by American novels of social criticism like those of Steinbeck, Lewis, and Wright. (The French read these books as sober sociological reports about the current state of American culture.) The Communist Party was regarded not as the French fifth column of the Kremlin, something which the Party itself hardly troubles to conceal, but as an organization of brothers in the class war against capitalism—erring only in impatience and unnecessary dogmatism. This is still the predominant spirit among the so-called left, and raises several problems I shall discuss later.

It is this mood which explains the astonishing fact that the initiators of the International Day offered a place on their program to official representatives of the Communist Partisans for Peace—which might have been tactically legitimate under certain circumstances—but refused to invite men like Koestler, Burnham, and Raymond Aron, who whatever else may be said of them, towered intellectually above most of the other participants present, particularly the French. Raymond Aron, e.g., former resistance leader, sympathizer but not a member of de Gaulle's RPF to which he is perceptibly cooling, more clearly fulfilled the conditions of participation laid down by the organizing group—opposition to war and dictatorship, and willingness to consider all proposals to prevent both—than the Stalinists to whom an invitation had been extended but who scorned it.

II

The International Day consisted of two meetings—an afternoon meeting in the Grand Amphitheater of the Sorbonne, and an evening mass meeting at the Velodrome d'Hiver, the Madison Square Garden of Paris. The first was jammed full to the rafters, the second was attended by about 12,000. Both meetings revealed that the organizers were woefully inexperienced. They did not know how to space speakers, and when to conclude the meeting.

In the evening both organizers and the audience let themselves be intimidated by a handful of noisy anarchists and Trotskyists who had shrewdly appraised the extent to which pacifist sentiment was a disguise for moral irresoluteness. Seizing on the remarks of the innocent Karl Compton, who was as much at home in this environment as a Yankee in Tibet, they tried to snatch the mike and were pacified only when they were given the rostrum to denounce the organizers, delegates, and the whole conception of the International Day. Some of the Americans seemed appalled by the interruptions, but the Frenchmen and the French press generally seemed to shrug it off as *une affaire Parisienne.*

Incidentally, the anarchists and Trotskyists, who between them numbered no more than a hundred, had refused to participate in the organization of the Day. But they demanded the right to attack it despite the fact that their points of view had been amply presented at the Sorbonne meeting by speakers from the Congress of Peoples and other participating organizations. Perhaps the wildest speech of the day was made by a Trotskyist from Ceylon who was given the floor because he claimed he had come all the way from Ceylon to attend the meeting. It later turned out he had come to attend the Communist Congress of Partisans for World Peace at the Salle Pleyel but had been barred. Neither he nor his fellows tried to snatch the mike *there*. His main theme at the Sorbonne, as expressed in his concluding sentence, was: "The only way to insure peace is to turn the cold war against the Soviet Union into a civil war against the West!"

There would have been nothing objectionable in giving the psychopathic ward on the left a place on the program. After all, the International Day was a cross between a political fair and a political bedlam. But it was cowardice to yield to a show of force. Everyone knew, and none better than the anarchists and Trotskyists, that if they had attempted to disrupt a Communist meeting or a de Gaullist meeting they would have been carried out dead. That is why they carefully stayed away from the six-day Communist talkfest at the Partisans Congress for Peace. But here was a chance too good to miss. It involved no risks.

III

With few exceptions the speeches were on an incredibly low political level—and I am not now referring to the line—in tone, expression, and content. Not since I was a boy thirty years ago listening to the soap-boxers in Madison Square have I heard such banalities and empty rhetoric. There was no attempt at serious analysis. No one answered anyone else. There was no discussion. This was as true at the Sorbonne as at the Velodrome. The statues of Descartes, Pascal, and other eminent French men of thought looked down on the proceedings. If they had come to life I am sure they would never have been convinced that they were in France listening to Frenchmen. For whatever seems to be left of logic in Paris has apparently taken refuge in the subways with their clear and precise charts. It would not be an exaggeration to say that the "underground man" in Paris is one who believes that evidence and logic are still relevant in reaching responsible political positions.

If those who attended were actually representative of the non-Communist left, it is testimony of the devastating effect of the war and Nazi occupation on its political education. It is hard to determine how representative the gathering was in political *feeling*. Certainly its rhetoric did not square with the practices of either the Socialist Party or the non-Communist trade unions. As far as the audience is concerned it seemed to be composed mainly of pacifists—the kind of people who would turn out to hear Garry Davis—sprinkled with infantile revolutionary sectarians who in reality are Stalinists *manqué*.

But several things were clear. The prevailing mood, both among the speakers and audience, was as anti-American as it was anti-Soviet. The anti-Americanism, I gathered, was not new; the anti-Stalinism was. The effect was rather odd. In order to win the right to say a critical word—usually by indirection—about the Soviet Union, the speakers would attack even more vehemently and quite explicitly American imperialism. It was as if, fearful of being attacked by the Communists as American agents, they sought to ward off the criticism by showing that they could be as extreme and reckless as the Communists in their comments on the United States.

Most of the speakers were quite outspoken in their opposition to the Atlantic Pact and pleaded for a neutrality between what they called the two blocs, as if the liberties of Western Europe were threatened equally by the Soviet Union and the United States. It was interesting to note that most of the Frenchmen who criticized the Atlantic Pact said very little or nothing against the Marshall Plan although last summer they had been very hostile to it. When I asked for an explanation of this one Frenchman dryly remarked that they had all put on some weight as a result of it. More significant was the admission many were prepared to make in private but not in public that the Marshall Plan had saved France from the Communists and de Gaullists.

The criticisms of the Atlantic Pact were not made on the basis of an analysis of its specific provisions and of any realistic alternative but in terms of abstract formulas about expanding American capitalism. One got the impression that they believed that the Atlantic Pact was imposed upon the governments of Western Europe in the same way as Vishinsky set up a government in Romania. In a statement read to the Sorbonne audience, Sartre, Merleau-Ponty, and Wright drew an explicit equation between the terroristic annexations of the Soviet Union in the East and the Atlantic Pact in the West, condemning both "equally and for the same reason." In the case of Sartre reference to the Atlantic Pact was purely formal. He spoke substantially the same way a year ago, before there was an Atlantic Pact, about the Marshall Plan. And he held the same view even prior to the Marshall Plan. From the standpoint that the current cold war is nothing but an opposition between two forms of economy—capitalism and socialism—apparently no particular analysis of anything is necessary. Last summer when I asked one of the leading figures of Sartre's group in what specific ways the Marshall Plan threatened the French economy, the only reply I received was the vulgar psychological *a priorism*: "Everyone knows that no nation helps another except out of economic self-interest." As if the self-interest of two groups cannot sometimes coincide!

This primitivism in economic and political matters is not surprising because it is based on ignorance of complex matters and a kind of exhibitionism by subtle men, too impatient to study something which they feel is alien to their "essence" but in relation to which they wish to take a brave "independent" stand. Primitivism in cultural matters, however, by people with developed sensibilities is something else again. Sartre's statement, developing the simple equation between Soviet and American culture, admits that the Soviet Union is a terroristic police state but then goes on to add "But neither is the United States a paradise of liberty." Since the United States is not a paradise of liberty—as if anyone, anywhere, at any time had even faintly suggested it was!—there is no difference between it and the cultural hell of the Soviet Union sufficiently important to justify engaging oneself in the common fight of all democratic elements to prevent the Iron Curtain from advancing West—*a fight that cannot be won without American help.*

I do not know what a "paradise of liberty" would be, and I suspect I would not enjoy many of its liberties if it were occupied by fanatical people with widely different tastes. But I grant that the Weimar Republic was no paradise of liberty. Neither was the Loyalist regime in Spain. Nor Czechoslovakia in 1938, Poland in 1939, Finland and Holland and Belgium in 1940. Will anyone who wishes to breathe the air of a free culture therefore strike an attitude of neutrality between what is short of paradise and the totalitarian Inferno which threatens to replace it? Were the unhappy occasion ever to arise I can imagine no more convenient premise for the Pétainists of a Russian occupation than Sartre's foolish equation. I am confident he would be the first to repudiate it—if his erring brothers in the Communist Party let him live long enough.   .

No speaker at the sessions who opposed the Atlantic Pact made the legitimate distinction between the rearming of Western Europe, which is a highly debatable proposition even on the basis of military strategy, and its guarantee of protection to European countries that they could continue their program of social reconstruction; even, as in the case of England, the building of a socialist economy, without suffering the fate of Poland or Czechoslovakia. To be against the Atlantic Pact simply followed from their opposition to American imperialism, which was just as bad—to the splinter and crackpot groups even worse—as the expansion of the Soviet terror state. As to the concrete meaning of American imperialism in the present historical conjuncture, no coherent or consistent account could be elicited. It was hard to separate opposition to chewing gum, Coca-Cola, the *Reader's Digest* (bestselling periodical in France) from condemnation of segregation, the monopoly of the atom bomb, and the "colonialization" of Europe achieved by the Machiavellian device of sending bread and machinery to rebuild Europe.

De Kadt, member of the Dutch parliament and the leading figure in the left wing of the Dutch Labor Party, began his five-minute speech with a condemnation of Dutch policy in Indonesia. This brought tumultuous applause. But when he went on to explain in simple words why the Dutch workers firmly supported the Atlantic Pact, the audience—or what was left of it by the time he spoke—turned hostile. De Kadt remained unmoved. In the calm voice of a sober man speaking among drunkards—and by this time many in the audience seemed word-drunk as a result of the sloganized speeches: "If you want peace, prepare the revolution," "If you want bread, prepare the revolution"—De Kadt reminded them that if it were not for the Marshall Plan and the Atlantic Pact, they would not even have the freedom to sit in the Sorbonne and criticize American imperialism. This so infuriated some of his auditors that the Chair had to appeal to them to let the speaker finish.

At the Velodrome, Silone talked for almost an hour to an audience which seemed a little disappointed that he did not go beyond vague and commonplace generalities about a socialist Europe. He was followed by a French scientist, M. Perrin. Karl Compton, who through some misunderstanding appeared instead of his brother, Arthur Compton, then spoke about the history of atomic research, the race against Hitler's scientists, the considerations which led to its use in Hiroshima, and the prospects of peaceful applications of nuclear energy. After he finished, the fracas around the mike took place. Garry Davis, world citizen, got a big hand when he intervened to read a message the Communists had prevented him from reading at their Congress. Rousset then delivered a powerful speech, with the voice and manners of a mass orator, in which he skillfully sought to placate the political surrealists. He criticized the Atlantic Pact but carefully avoided making the same kind of equation between the U.S. and the USSR which Sartre and his friends had done. Politically, he is a man of quite a different kidney from Sartre.

The meeting dragged to a close with the reading of resolutions which were adopted by acclamation.

IV

To American liberals the most difficult thing to understand is the reluctance of the non-Communist left to speak out openly and with appropriate vigor against the regime of terror in the Soviet Union, its betrayal of every socialist ideal, and its foreign policy of annexation and subversion through fifth column specialists in national sabotage in other countries. This difficulty in assessing the situation is aggravated by the indiscriminate use of belligerent rhetoric against the United States despite the facts that French ideology and traditions are certainly closer to those of the U.S. than to those of the USSR and that the foreign policy of the French government, which this section of French opinion prefers either to the regime of de Gaulle or the Communist Party, is in general agreement with that of the United States. These two points, although somewhat related, must be discussed differently.

Despite the myths and legends which sprang up after the liberation, there was not much of a resistance movement to the Nazis in France. In 1940 when the war seemed irretrievably lost, almost the entire population collaborated in some form or other with the Vichy government and passively accepted the occupation. The Resistance consisted of a handful around de Gaulle, the Jews, and after June 22, 1941, the Communists, who on orders from the Kremlin were able to acquire strategic posts, organize nonparty groups under their command, and carry on incessant propaganda which pictured the desperate defense of the Soviet Union against its erstwhile partner as a defense of France. After the liberation the Communists exploited their position of prestige very cleverly. Since mid-1941 on, their opposition had been total, they could intimidate the vast majority which had adjusted itself at one time or another to what seemed to be the irrevocable decisions of history. They were aided in this by the natural tendency of many Frenchmen to extenuate and reinterpret their behavior under the Vichy regime in order to escape punitive measures, and by the almost universally shared hope that the Soviet Union would alter its policy as a result of the common struggle against Hitlerism from which it had suffered so much. Since the most overtly reactionary and conservative groups in France had been most conspicuously identified with Vichy, there was little opposition to those aspects of the domestic program of the Communists, even by the de Gaullists, which sought to strip reactionaries of the right of their power.

The eloquent and, if properly construed, damning fact that the Soviet Union and the Communists everywhere had actively collaborated with the Nazis, that the French Communists had sabotaged the war effort until Hitler took the initiative against Stalin, that the French Communists were in reality Soviet Maquis, not French patriots, could not be used against the Communists because of the bad conscience of most Frenchmen and the seeming futility of raking up the past. De Gaulle, who immediately after the liberation was in a position to brand them for what they in effect were—a Soviet fifth column—out of ignorance or policy failed to do so, and when he later turned against them he had already alienated other groups in France. By this time Communist propaganda had already done its work in selling many non-Communists the Soviet myth despite the fact, perhaps because of the fact, that France had been liberated by the Americans and English and not by the Red Army.

How powerful the Communist position was in France can be gathered from the rights of extra-territoriality which the Soviet Union enjoyed until recently, including the existence of its own concentration camps to which kidnapped men and women who had acquired French citizenship were taken. So pervasive at the time was the process of Communist infiltration into all government positions and other strategic posts that Koestler's observation that the Communist Party of France could have taken over the country by a telephone call was hardly an exaggeration.

The legacy of fear, blackmail, and silly hope in a new Soviet turn has only slowly worn off—not in virtue of any counter-propaganda but as a result of Communist intransigence in sacrificing the interests of France on the altar of Soviet foreign policy. The postwar French intellectuals were completely devoid of any political experience. Large numbers of them had been newly converted to revolutionary socialism and blossomed into full-fledged Marxists almost overnight not as a result of study but of enthusiasm. To this day they have very little understanding of what Leninism and Stalinism mean. Although they feel hurt that the French Communists "have gone too far" and "have been unfair" to their opponents, they still regard them as part of the French community. The translation of Koestler's *Darkness at Noon* came as a shock to them. The Kravchenko trial was another. In terms of the past, their *public* participation in the International Day marked an advance for them, particularly in view of the reaction of the Communists to their support of any affair in which some harsh truths about the Soviet Union were expressed.

This evolution of opinion is related in a distinctive way to the anti-Americanism of the non-Communist French left which is in turn related to the anti-Americanism of the French public generally. For long-range purposes this last point is most important. The French public, by and large, is shockingly ignorant of the character of American life and culture. Its picture of America is a composite of impressions derived from reading the novels of social protest and revolt

(Steinbeck's *Grapes of Wrath* is taken as a faithful and *representative* account), the novels of American degeneracy (Faulkner) and inanity (Sinclair Lewis), from seeing American movies, and from exposure to an incessant Communist barrage which seeps into the non-Communist press. *The informational reeducation of the French public seems to me to be the most fundamental as well as most pressing task of American democratic policy in France, toward which almost nothing along effective lines has been done.* This does not require a propaganda campaign. If the sober facts about American life in all their nakedness, good and bad, were communicated to the French public it would be sufficient to produce a revolution in this attitude.

The non-Communist left absorbs its anti-Americanism from the general milieu. But in its case this is reinforced by several special factors. First, like all political neophytes its spokesmen feel that they can only criticize the Communist Party by competing with it in revolutionary phrasemongery. No matter what they do its spokesmen talk "ultra-left." Second, as primitive Marxists the basic conflict appears to them today to be between capitalism and socialism, and although they dispute among themselves as to whether the Soviet Union is socialist, they are unanimous in thinking of the U.S. as an expanding imperialist capitalist power. Since capitalism is the main evil, the existence of cultural and political freedom by which capitalism can be transformed is dismissed as a sham. Many among them are convinced that the American political regime is not far away from fascism. It was instructive that Rousset felt called upon to assure his audience that he had seen with his own eyes the freedom with which Americans walk the streets and associate with each other. Farrell got the close attention of the audience when he denied that the U.S. had a fascist government. He was bringing news. (Whereupon the Trotskyists, who are postgraduates of the Stalin school of falsification and the source of the most fantastic reports about what transpired at the meeting, tagged him as a flag-waving American imperialist.) The American literary expatriates either contribute to this kind of information by puffing up some of the shameful episodes in American life or remain silent for fear of being tagged as apologists of America and losing some of their "existentialist" friends.*

---

* The case of Richard Wright is a curious one. Having broken with Stalinism more on personal than on political grounds, he has no understanding of its true nature. He is flattered by the use which Sartre makes of him as a kind of club against American culture analogous to the use the Communists make of Robeson. Although he joined Sartre in his statement, in a recent interview he sought to dissociate himself from Robeson's view that the American Negroes would not fight for "American imperialism" in the event of a conflict with the Soviet Union. According to Wright they would and should. But if he believes the statement he signed, such a position makes no sense. Only Robeson's position is consistent with Sartre's simpleminded formulas.

In the same interview—which since it appeared in the Trotskyist press may have been edited according to Bolshevik ethics—Wright pretended he had discussed his position with me in Paris. I have never exchanged two words with him on politics or anything else. He also refers to me as one "who proclaims to high heaven that he is an orthodox Marxist." This means that he has not read a line—but not a line!—of anything I have ever written about Marx or Marxism. If any additional commentary were needed about the character of left-wing French political thought, the emergence of Wright and Garry Davis as political figures would be sufficient.

Finally, it costs nothing—there are absolutely no risks—in denouncing American culture and foreign policy, whereas naggingly present in the consciousness of these Frenchmen, and not only them, is an awareness that the borders of France are only a short march from the Soviet outposts in Europe. And the sad fact is that at present the fears of France are deeper than its hopes and courage.   1949, vol. 15, no. 7

• The Berlin Congress for Cultural Freedom
Sidney Hook

The Congress for Cultural Freedom which met in Berlin from June 25th to June 30th was an exciting affair. The news of the invasion of Korea broke just before the first session when it seemed uncertain whether the Russians would march in Germany too, in which event every delegate would have been a prisoner of the M.V.D. in a few hours. West Berlin, defenseless in an iron ring of Soviet armor, remained outwardly calm. Nor was there any overt sign of nervousness or anxiety among the Congress members. On the contrary. The militant tone taken toward the Soviet version of culture, the appeal of Professor Ernst Reuter, the elected Mayor of West Berlin and an active participant in the sessions, to the peoples of the satellite countries to support the program of the Congress, the Message of Solidarity sent by Western intellectuals to their confréres in the East, indicated that the Korean events, if anything, had given a fillip to the spirit of the delegates.

Theodore Plivier, author of *Stalingrad* who had broken with the Communists and was hiding out from them in Stuttgart, had originally recorded his message to the Congress on tape. As soon as he learned of the invasion of Korea, he flew to Berlin in order to emphasize by a public appearance his denunciation of the Soviet practice of "total unfreedom." A security watch had to be placed on him as on several other delegates from satellite countries to circumvent attempts at kidnapping. To discuss cultural freedom in Berlin might cost something. It was clear to almost all the delegates that in the nature of the case this was no ordinary meeting of a learned society in a city like Lausanne but also a political affirmation. The analytic quality of some of the discussions left something to be desired. But considering the atmosphere and the fact that the sessions were held before audiences that ran sometimes to thousands, many of the presented papers, and at times the discussions, were extremely good.

More than a hundred delegates from twenty different countries were present. Among the French were Jules Romains, David Rousset, Henri Frenay, and André Philip; among the Germans, Alfred Weber, Eugen Kogon, Carlo Schmid; Denis de Rougement and François Bondy from Switzerland; Haakon Lie from Norway; Charles Plisnier from Belgium; Ignazio Silone, Lombardi, Spinelli from Italy; Herbert Read, A. J. Ayer, J. Amery, Trevor-Roper from England; and a sizable contingent from the United States including H. J. Muller, the geneticist, Arthur Schlesinger Jr., Burnham, Farrell, George Schuyler. The outstanding figure at the Congress was Arthur Koestler, mainly because of the provocative character of his speeches, partly because of his linguistic abilities, and partly because he was so cordially detested by some of the English delegates, one of whom (Trevor-Roper) has since denounced the Congress as a plot concocted by warmongering "rootless European ex-Communists" abetted by their American allies.

Several dramatic incidents highlighted the sessions. Hans Thirring, the Austrian theoretical physicist now turned psychologist, had been invited to attend the Congress and had presented a paper which was a criticism of the foreign policy of the Western powers. Previously he had courageously criticized the position of the Soviet Union at a Communist peace conference in Vienna. His paper had already been distributed to the press and delegates. When his turn came to speak, he withdrew his paper "The Responsibility of Intellectuals" because two of its assumptions had become untenable as a result of the Korea incident, viz., that Soviet political aggression would not develop into military aggression and that the United Nations was an effective instrument in preventing military outbreaks.

At the same session Professor Nachtsheim of the Free University of Berlin gave an account of the fate of science in the universities of the East and described the recent evolution of the famous Deutsche Academie der Wissenschaft originally founded by Leibnitz. On the occasion of Stalin's seventieth birthday, a telegram was sent to him in the name of the membership of the society which hailed him in the most fawning and Byzantine way for his scientific achievements. As soon as Professor Nachtsheim disclosed this fact, Alfred Weber, the famous Heidelberg sociologist, demanded the floor and announced his immediate resignation from the Academy. Weber in the opening plenary session had delivered a searching critique of the German failure to develop an indigenous liberalism. Before a vast audience that overflowed into the streets, Weber concluded his eloquent and shrewd appraisal of the German past with a *nostra culpa, nostra maxima culpa*. (I had heard Weber twenty-two years ago at Heidelberg where every one of his lectures was like an act of parturition. In Berlin he spoke with unwonted fluency. He was one of the few remaining links with the culture of the Weimar Republic.)

At a subsequent session, after a particularly lively give and take, a student who had secretly traveled from the University of Leipzig to listen to the discussion asked for permission to address the Congress. He described briefly the enforced uniformity of belief which was officially imposed on students in the East, his delight at witnessing the free exchange of opinion, and declared his intention never to return to East Germany.

The Congress wound up with a mass meeting in the Summergarden of the Funkturm before an audience of 15,000 at which the Manifesto of Freedom and Message to the East were read. Among the speakers was Boris Nicolaevsky who spoke of peace and freedom to the Russian people over the heads of their government.

II

West Berlin of course is not West Germany. It is not stuffy, self-pitying, or conservative. Although predominantly Social-Democratic, the Social-Democratic party there is not a conventional one based on fixed economic dogmas. Despite its programmatic differences with the other two major parties, it recognizes that the basic issue which unites them all is whether freedom is to survive. And islanded in the Soviet sea, everyone knows what freedom is. The material situation in Berlin had vastly improved over the period of 1948 when I was last there at the height of the blockade. But the spirit was the same—the toughness, sense of humor, bitterness towards everything Nazi and disdain towards everything Communist, not Russian. These people believe that they suffer a common oppression with the Russian masses at the hands of the men in the Kremlin. If there is a democratic center in Germany, it is here. Its leaders are anti-Nazis who spent the Hitler period either in prison or in exile and are free of any German nationalist taint. Without them the West could not have held Berlin. Their lives will be immediately forfeit if the Soviets march. For many months a Communist whispering campaign had circulated the rumor that the West would withdraw from Berlin. It was finally scotched by the U.S. action in Korea. The thousands of people who crowded the sessions of the Congress were the vanguard of the democratic resistance of West Berlin. One could not forget their presence for a moment, and the points they punctuated with their applause showed they were listening intelligently. With few exceptions, about which more later, all the delegates realized that Mayor Reuter's opening remark "We greet you as fellow fighters in the cause of freedom" was no mere rhetoric. The people of West Berlin were part of the Congress.

III

Since almost every delegate presented a paper, I can give an account only of those that precipitated general discussion. There was a brace of papers by Koestler around which a good deal of the discussion crystallized. The first was on "Two Methods of Action." Its basic thesis was that at certain times and in respect to certain crucial issues, instead of saying "Neither-Nor" and looking for other viable alternatives, we must recognize an "Either-Or" and take one stand or another. It was obviously directed against the type of intellectual who today says "I am neither a Communist nor an anti-Communist" just as fifteen years ago he said "I am neither a Nazi nor an anti-Nazi." Partly because his formulations were literary rather than pointedly political, he was criticized sharply for oversimplification. Lombardi suggested that to demand a Yes or No answer was itself to fall victim to a totalitarian mentality. Some other participants seemed to be under the impression that Koestler was denying the validity of any other type of approach, that he was saying our choice was always between white and black—"our side" being white—something that Koestler has always denied. The choice between Hitler and the democracies, he once said, is inescapable but it is a choice between a lie and a half-truth. Sartre and Merleau-Ponty, who refused to attend the Congress even to defend their point of view there, were quite aware of French and American injustices to Negroes when they supported the Resistance to Hitler. But they can see no justice in the Western defense against Communist aggression because the Negroes have not yet won equality of treatment.

One might have generalized Koestler's position and shown that the recognition of the possibility of many alternatives always proceeds on the assumption that, in respect to some value or goal or method, a choice of the either-or type is involved. For example, either you are looking for the truth in science or you are not. There are no two ways about it. But once you have decided to look for the truth, then any particular truth may lie on a scale in which there are so many alternatives that it is absurd to have to choose between particular contraries (as distinct from formal contradictories). In the face of a totalitarian threat either you decide to oppose or appease; but having decided to oppose, the alternative may not be either this method of opposition or its contrary.

The very title of Koestler's second paper—"The False Dilemma"—indicated how far he was from universalizing dilemmatic situations. He denied that the choice between "Left" and "Right" was any longer cognitively meaningful because of their varying emotive effects. He denied that we are confronted by a genuine choice between capitalism and socialism, not as conceptual structures, but as historical movements. He claimed that on a number of vital issues, the so-called capitalist opponents of socialism have adopted a more socialist policy than the existing socialist parties. He showed that the nonsocialist governments of France, Italy, and Germany are in some respects more "internationalist" than socialist Britain. He criticized England for creating obstacles to European unity and drove his point home by quoting from the Labour Party statement, "No socialist government in Europe could submit to the authority of a body whose policies were decided by an anti-Socialist majority."

This criticism was unfortunate because it was misinterpreted, despite Koestler's warnings, as an attack on socialism and an apology for capitalism instead of a plea for the abandonment of the antithesis. Koestler also overlooked the fact that greater equality had been produced in England under a Socialist regime than elsewhere.

To an audience rapidly growing restive, Koestler then went on to assert that insofar as domestic freedom, civil rights, and even economics were concerned there is no relevant difference between capitalist United States and socialist Britain. "The alternative is no longer nationalization or the private economy in the abstract: the real problem is to find the proper balance of state ownership, control, planning, and free enterprise. And this is an empirical question." He concluded by summing up the present conflict between Communism and democracy as "total tyranny against relative freedom."

Except for the unfortunate historical references to England, which provoked Mr. Trevor-Roper to fury, there was little in what Koestler said that had not been previously said in this country by Lewis Corey, Reinhold Niebuhr, myself, and sometimes even Norman Thomas. But Koestler can recite the truths of the multiplication table in a way to make some people indignant with him. He also overlooked the fact that although all large terms have been kidnapped by the enemies of freedom, one could still justify historically the use of the phrase "democratic socialism" for the economic set-up he advocated.

The discussion was quite heated and, up to the point that a Herr Grimme spoke, on a high plane. Haakon Lie replied to Koestler and reminded him that he had neglected to take the achievements of Scandinavian socialism into account. He was pursuing this fruitful line of argument when he suddenly veered to emphasize (against the claims of Communist propaganda) that the American working class enjoyed more rights and privileges and a higher standard of living and degree of participation in economic life than the workers in any European country—which left Koestler grinning like a Cheshire cat. Mayor Reuter also rejoined with a reference to the goals and activity of the Berlin socialist movement. Spinelli took the floor and needled Koestler about not emphasizing sufficiently the dependence of political freedom on economic security. Several of the discussion speakers, since Koestler had not advocated specific social reforms in his speech, charged him with overlooking their importance as a method of combating Communism and positively contributing to a free society.

Then a Herr Grimme arose, a parson of sorts with a voice like a foghorn, to argue that all these concrete questions were basically religious. He spoke with an eloquent emptiness and became concrete only at the end when he descended to personalities and made some contemptuous remark about Koestler being a "political convert" who now was fervently opposing what once he had fervently supported, thus showing he had never surrendered his dialectical materialism.

The reference to his former Communism left Koestler unmoved as it did Mayor Reuter, another political convert from way back. But it aroused Franz Borkenau. His delivery left a great deal to be desired for he was obviously nettled. He forcefully defended the political converts from Communism, of which he was proud to be one, and asserted that because of their experience in the Communist movement, they understood the enemy better than most others, that Communism made all truly human existence impossible, and that its leaders were prepared "to go to the end" in forcing their program upon the world. Borkenau would have been more effective if he had not been so overwrought and had repeated what Plisnier said earlier at the Congress in explaining the conversions of the few "old Bolsheviks" present: "It is not because we surrendered our revolutionary ideas that we left the Communist movement but because we were and remain revolutionists devoted to the welfare of mankind who realize that not all means are justified in the struggle, that bloody and dirty hands infect with mortal disease the new society we wish to see born."

In the course of his remarks Borkenau told his audience that despite all their doubts and criticisms of the United States, each one of them knew that in his heart he was glad to get the news that the United States, instead of appeasing Stalin, had come to the defense of the South Koreans. The applause was tumultuous. Of this applause Trevor-Roper, who hates all ex-Communists and regards Togliatti as a "humanist," in a garbled report to the *Manchester Guardian* wrote: "It was an echo of Hitler's Nuremberg"—unconsciously revealing his own judgment of American foreign policy.

Burnham's paper, in his customary provocative style, drove home with relentless logic the absurdity of contemporary pacifism and the self-defeating character of the position that a Europe devoted to the ideals of freedom and human welfare could remain neutral in the crusade of the Kremlin for world power. Burnham asserted that he was not opposed "under any and all circumstances" to the use of atomic bombs. "I am against those bombs now stored or to be stored in Siberia which are designed for the destruction of Paris, London, Rome, New York, and of Western civilization generally. I am, yesterday and today at any rate, *for* those bombs made in Los Alamos, Hanford, and Oak Ridge and guarded I know not where, which for five years have defended—have been the sole defense of—the liberties of Western Europe."

To which André Philip replied, with the approval of the audience, that when atom bombs fall, they do not distinguish between friend and foe, enemy or lover of freedom—a proposition which, of course, is true for all bombs, not merely atomic ones. Philip called for the economic unification of Europe as soon as possible, and compared Europe to a sick man kept alive by American penicillin against the pathogenic bacteria with which the Soviet Union was infecting him. Because Burnham had not mentioned what measures on the domestic front had to be taken to build up the immunity of the patient, Philip and some others assumed, with little logical justification, that he did not regard them as necessary. Kogon underscored Philip's position by saying that the Soviet Union would not attack the West if Europe became, with American help, an economically healthy, federated, socialized community. Mayor Reuter and Melvin Lasky closed the discussions by pointing out that the two approaches—a strong military defense and a strong welfare economy—were complementary to each other.

The panel on "Art, Artists, and Freedom" was jammed, the papers were interesting and had varied viewpoints but there was no opposition to the positions taken by Silone, Robert Montgomery, de Rougement, Herbert Read, Borghese, Nabokov, Schuyler and others. The session terminated with a denunciation of Franco and Spanish totalitarianism by a Basque priest.

It is hard to estimate the achievements of the Congress because many of its projects have yet to be realized.

The first great achievement is to have held the Congress in Berlin and to have strengthened the feeling of solidarity with those still struggling for freedom under conditions hard to imagine by Western intellectuals.

The second is to have created a nucleus for a Western community of intellectuals who will have no truck with "neutrality" in the struggle for freedom either at home or abroad.

Its Manifesto of Freedom expresses the least common denominator of democratic faith for individuals who differ about specific political and economic programs.

Its Message to the East brings assurance to intellectuals beyond the Iron Curtain that they are not forgotten, that the conflict of our time as seen by their colleagues on this side is not a conflict between East and West but between free thought and enslavement.

An international committee of twenty-five under an executive committee of five: Silone, Koestler, Rousset, Schmid, and Brown, plans to organize the Congress on a permanent basis to do, among other things, the following:

1. Issue a series of White Books along the lines proposed by Silone, giving a documented picture of the Writer, Artist, and Scientist in countries behind the Iron Curtain.

2. Organize aid for those intellectuals who escape from totalitarian countries.

3. Inaugurate a special series of radio talks, "Dialogues Across the Curtain," consisting of open letters to the Communist leaders of cultural fronts in satellite countries.

4. Aid in the establishment of a university center, somewhere in Europe, for exiled Eastern professors and students.

A half-dozen other projects of a practical kind have been outlined whose fulfillment depends upon the extent to which intellectuals of the West rally to the call of the Congress.

The weaknesses of the Congress are obvious. It is not yet sufficiently representative. More literary men and scientists must be drawn into the struggle for freedom. It must concern itself not only with the main danger to free culture from the Communist East but also to the dangers in the imperfectly free cultures of the democratic West. Without ceasing to be political in the basic Aristotelian sense, its work must be more analytical. It must dramatize its existence until not only the intellectuals of the world become aware of it but also the statesmen of the free countries, whose policies on cultural matters the Congress should evaluate in an independent and critical spirit.   1950, vol. 17, no. 7

• Our Country and Our Culture
Editors

The purpose of this symposium is to examine the apparent fact that American intellectuals now regard America and its institutions in a new way. Until little more than a decade ago, America was commonly thought to be hostile to art and culture. Since then, however, the tide has begun to turn, and many writers and intellectuals now feel closer to their country and its culture. The following quotations illustrate the earlier pattern and the change that has recently occurred.

Here, for example, is the artist-hero of a James story speaking in 1879:

> We are the disinherited of art! We are condemned to be superficial. We are excluded from the magic circle. The soil of American perception is a poor, little, barren, artificial deposit. Yes! We are wedded to imperfection. An American, to excel, has just ten times as much to learn as a European. We lack the deeper sense: we have neither taste, nor tact, nor force. How should we have them? Our crude and garish climate, our silent past, our deafening present, the constant pressure about us of unlovely circumstances are as void of all that nourishes and prompts and inspires the artist as my sad heart is void of bitterness in saying so! We poor aspirants must live in perpetual exile.   *The Madonna of the Future*

Ezra Pound in 1913:

> O helpless few in my country,
> O remnant enslaved!
> Artists broken against her,

Astray, lost in the villages,
Mistrusted, spoken against . . .

Van Wyck Brooks in 1918:

How, then, can our literature be anything but impotent? It is inevitably so, since
it springs from a national mind that has been sealed against that experience from
which literature derives all its values. *Letters and Leadership*

John Dos Passos in 1937:

The business of the day . . . was to buttress property and profits with anything
usable in the debris of Christian ethics and eighteenth century economics that
cluttered the minds of college professors, and to reinforce the sacred, already
shaky edifice with the new strong girderwork of science Herbert Spencer was
throwing up for the benefit of the bosses. *The Big Money*

And, finally, Edmund Wilson in 1947:

My optimistic opinion is that the United States at the present time is politically
more advanced than any other part of the world. . . . We have seen in the last fifty
years a revival of the democratic creativeness which presided at the birth of the
Republic and flourished up through the Civil War. This began to assert itself
strongly during the first two decades of this century, was stimulated by the
depression that followed the blowing-up of the Stock Market, and culminated in
the New Deal. It was accompanied by a remarkable renascence of American arts
and letters. *Europe Without Baedeker*

The American artist and intellectual no longer feels "disinherited" as Henry
James did, or "astray" as Ezra Pound did in 1913. Van Wyck Brooks himself has by
now entirely repudiated the view that "the national mind has been sealed against
that experience from which literature derives its values." John Dos Passos in 1951
would deny precisely what he affirmed in 1937. And what Edmund Wilson wrote
in the conclusion to his book describing a visit to postwar Europe represents a
new judgment of American civilization. It is a judgment that would have been
inconceivable twenty-five years ago, yet it is one which seems natural to most serious writers today. We have obviously come a long way from the earlier rejection
of America as spiritually barren, from the attacks of Mencken on the "booboisie,"
and the Marxist picture of America in the thirties as a land of capitalist reaction.

Essential in the shift of attitudes is the relationship of America to Europe. For
more than a hundred years, America was culturally dependent on Europe; now

Europe is economically dependent upon America. And America is no longer the raw and unformed land of promise from which men of superior gifts like James, Santayana, and Eliot departed, seeking in Europe what they found lacking in America. Europe is no longer regarded as a sanctuary; it no longer assures that rich experience of culture which inspired and justified a criticism of American life. The wheel has come full circle, and now America has become the protector of Western civilization, at least in a military and economic sense.

Obviously, this overwhelming change involves a new image of America. Politically there is a recognition that the kind of democracy which exists in America has an intrinsic and positive value: it is not merely a capitalist myth but a reality which must be defended against Russian totalitarianism. The cultural consequences are bound to be far-reaching and complex, but some of them have already become apparent. For better or worse, most writers no longer accept alienation as the artist's fate in America; on the contrary, they want very much to be a part of American life. More and more writers have ceased to think of themselves as rebels and exiles. They now believe that their values, if they are to be realized at all, must be realized in America and in relation to the actuality of American life. In one way or another, this change has involved us all, but it has not yet been the subject of critical reflection and evaluation. Hence we think there is much to be gained by the exchange of impressions which a symposium fosters.

The problem as we see it is this: the affirmative attitude toward America which has emerged since the Second World War may be a necessary corrective of the earlier extreme negation, but the affirmation cannot be unequivocal. For American economic and political institutions have not suddenly become ideally beneficent, and many intellectuals are not prepared to give up all criticism of them. In addition, the enormous and ever-increasing growth of mass culture confronts the artist and the intellectual with a new phenomenon and creates a new obstacle: the artist and intellectual who wants to be a part of American life is faced with a mass culture which makes him feel that he is still outside looking in. Ortega y Gasset has formulated the difficulty in an extreme way: "The mass crushes beneath it everything that is different, everything that is excellent, individual, qualified, and select. Anybody who is not like everybody, who does not think like everybody, runs the risk of being eliminated." By "mass" Ortega y Gasset does not mean any social or economic class of society. "By mass," says Ortega y Gasset, "is not to be specially understood the workers; it does not indicate a social class, but a kind of man to be found today in all social classes, who consequently represents our age, in which he is the predominant ruling power."

We cannot however accept the views of Ortega y Gasset without serious qualifications, for he ignores the fact that political democracy seems to coexist with the domination of the "masses." Whatever the cultural consequences may be, the democratic values which America either embodies or promises are desirable in purely human terms. We are certain that these values are necessary conditions for civilization and represent the only immediate alternative as long as Russian totalitarianism threatens world domination. Nevertheless, there are serious cultural consequences: mass culture not only weakens the position of the artist and the intellectual profoundly by separating him from his natural audience, but it also removes the mass of people from the kind of art which might express their human and aesthetic needs. Its tendency is to exclude everything that does not conform to popular norms; it creates and satisfies artificial appetites in the entire populace; it has grown into a major industry which converts culture into a commodity. Its overshadowing presence cannot be disregarded in any evaluation of the future of American art and thought. Its increasing power is one of the chief causes of the spiritual and economic insecurity of the intellectual minority.

Apparently cultural democracy is an outgrowth of political democracy under conditions of modern industrial development. And the democratization of culture involves an inevitable dislocation, though it may in the end produce a higher culture and demonstrate that a political democracy can nourish great art and thought. But whatever the future may promise, we cannot evade the fact that at present America is a nation where at the same time cultural freedom is promised and mass culture produced. This paradox, we think, creates many difficulties for American writers and intellectuals who are trying to realize themselves in relation to their country and its cultural life.

1. To what extent have American intellectuals actually changed their attitude toward America and its institutions?
2. Must the American intellectual and writer adapt himself to mass culture? If he must, what forms can his adaptation take? Or do you believe that a democratic society necessarily leads to a leveling of culture, to a mass culture which will overrun intellectual and aesthetic values traditional to Western civilization?
3. Where in American life can artists and intellectuals find the basis of strength, renewal, and recognition now that they can no longer depend fully on Europe as a cultural example and a source of vitality?
4. If a reaffirmation and rediscovery of America is under way, can the tradition of critical nonconformism (going back to Thoreau and Melville and embracing some of the major expressions of American intellectual history) be maintained as strongly as ever?

Norman Mailer

I think I ought to declare straightaway that I am in almost total disagreement with the assumptions of this symposium. My answer, then, can hardly contribute much in an affirmative way, but perhaps it may serve the value of not allowing the question to be begged.

At any rate, one has to admit that the older American intellectuals and writers have changed their attitude toward this country and its culture. The New Criticism seems to have triumphed pretty generally, *Partisan Review*'s view of American life is indeed partisan, and a large proportion of writers, intellectuals, critics—whatever we may care to include in the omnibus—have moved their economic luggage from the WPA to the Luce chain, as a writer for *Time* or *Life* once remarked. Among the major novelists, Dos Passos, Farrell, Faulkner, Steinbeck, and Hemingway have traveled from alienation to varying degrees of acceptance, if not outright proselytizing, for the American Century. Dare one mention that their work since the Second World War has been singularly barren and flatulent? Is it entirely a coincidence that they sound now like a collective *pater familias*?

A symposium of this sort I find shocking. One expects a J. Donald Adams to initiate it, a John Chamberlain to bristle with editorials in its support, a Bernard De Voto to flex his muscles. This period smacks of healthy manifestos. Everywhere the American writer is being dunned to become healthy, to grow up, to accept the American reality, to integrate himself, to eschew disease, to re-value institutions. Is there nothing to remind us that the writer does not need to be integrated into his society and often works best in opposition to it? I would propose that the artist feels most alienated when he loses the sharp sense of what he is alienated from. In this context, I wonder if there has been a time in the last fifty years when the American artist has felt more alienated. He cannot enjoy the old battles against censorship; in lieu of a Comstock or a Sumner, there is an editorial bureaucracy which uses the language of taste in the service of repression. He does not have the naïveté of the twenties with its sure pleasure of *épater les bourgeois*; he can no longer believe in the social art of the Depression; he is left only with the warmed-over sentimentality of the war years. One can agree with Edmund Wilson that the last fifty years represent a revival of American arts and letters, vigorous and enthusiastic, but with almost no exceptions it is a literature of alienation and protest, disgust and rebellion. The writer had a sense of his enemy and it could nourish him.

Today, the enemy is vague, the work seems done, the audience more sophisticated than the writer. Society has been rationalized, and the expert encroaches on the artist. Belief in the efficacy of attacking his society has been lost, but nothing has replaced the need for attack. If, then, a number of important intellectuals and writers now see it as their function to interpret American society from within (the curious space relations of politics which equates right to within and left to without), must one necessarily assume that the motives are more serious than exhaustion?

Possibly. What seems never to be discussed are the alternatives. Every intellectual who is now "within" seems to regard his conversion as a result of the application of pure thought upon moral purity. The fact that there is a society outside himself which threatens, suggests, nudges, and promises, is dismissed as mere mechanical leftism. It is considered the worst of bad taste to imply that the artist or intellectual who does not make his way "within" can find no community "without," and must suffer if he is first-rate the exercise of his abilities in obscurity, or if he is second-rate must incur the even more painful condition of being not at all chic.

Really, the history of the twentieth century seems made to be ignored. No one of the intellectuals who find themselves now in the American grain ever discuss—at least in print—the needs of modern war. One does not ever say that total war and the total war economy predicate a total regimentation of thought. Rather it is suggested that society is too difficult to understand and history impossible to predict. It has become as fashionable to sneer at economics and emphasize "the human dilemma" as it was fashionable to do the reverse in the thirties. Economics is now for experts and the crisis of world capitalism is considered dull enough to be on a par with the proletarian novel. One never hears about the disappearance of the world market, nor is it polite to suggest that the prosperity of America depends upon the production of means of destruction and it is not only the Soviet Union which is driven toward war as an answer to insoluble problems.

The symposium posed questions about mass culture and democratic society without seriously debating how much freedom there is to find the *effective* publication of one's ideas if they are dissenting ideas, without wondering whether democracy becomes more attenuated and may cease to exist when the war comes, and without considering how America may change in the future. Everything is viewed in a static way. We are democratic, we support the West, and the American artistic caravan is no longer isolated. The important work is to search out the healthy aspects of American life, and decide whether we can work with the movies.

I have said that none of the older American writers and intellectuals have produced anything of note since the war. The literary history of this last period has been made, for better or worse, by the younger writers, who seem inevitably to arrive as barbarians or decadents. Does not this, in itself, answer the question? John Aldridge in *After the Lost Generation* could come up with only one prescription—a genius is needed. If and when he arrives may I speculate that he will be more concerned with "silence, exile, and cunning" than a strapping participation in the vigors of American life. It is worth something to remind ourselves that the great artists—certainly the moderns—are almost always in opposition to their society, and that integration, acceptance, nonalienation, etc. etc. has been more conducive to propaganda than art.

David Riesman

I think it is America, and not only some of its intellectuals (or the relative cultural balance between America and Europe), that has changed. In the sphere of economic development I don't believe it necessary to argue the point in these pages, but a word might be said concerning our political institutions. The two spheres are of course related, and our steadily rising productivity has made it possible for politicians to pay off their promises in jobs and coin of the realm rather than in a fanatical search for scapegoats; indeed, even a demagogue like Huey Long or Townsend could hardly keep ahead of the social services which were coming anyway. Despite the current outcry over apathy and corruption, Americans possess increasingly competent government without having to spend much energy getting it. Many intellectuals and nonintellectuals feel uncomfortable in this situation and wish for parties and programs that would provide election Armageddons and "meaningful" issues—as many once "found" such issues by applying Marxist stereotypes to events. But here, as in the economic area, the European model has been quite misleading and has caused us to regard as vices such things as lack of doctrine, "racial balance" on municipal tickets, and noncabinet government that in a different perspective may appear as actually suited to our big country which, like other big modern countries, has had to face a civil war.

In the area of mass culture, evaluation is difficult; we have an enormous country, much is going on, and only a tiny fraction comes to our attention. Even the term "mass culture" may beg the question; it is better to speak of "class-mass culture," because what I think we have is a series of audiences, stratified by taste and class, each (even that of *Partisan Review* devotees) large enough to constitute, in psychological terms, a "mass." Moreover, I believe there is more critical judgment, at more of these levels, than is generally realized. And on one level there is perhaps too much. Our intellectuals do not, for instance, allow themselves to praise Hollywood movies as much as, in my opinion, they deserve; they are like psychiatrists who do not dare give a patient a clean bill of health lest some other doctor find a hidden flaw.

Moreover, I see no evidence of the alleged increasing power of the mass media producers. The American cultural spectrum seems more interesting and no less diverse today than at earlier times. The various audiences are not so manipulated as often supposed: they fight back by refusing to "understand," by selective interpretation, by apathy. Conformity there surely is, but we cannot assume its existence from the standardization of the commodities themselves (in many areas a steadily diminishing standardization) without knowledge of how individuals and groups *interpret* the commodities and endow them with meanings. In fact, the really menacing conformity lies in the ability of particular peer-groups and subcultures to supply such meanings and to extirpate idiosyncratic ones. At the same time, such cultural commodities as movies and periodical fiction have the potentiality of dissolving as well as reinforcing these group ties—for instance, by creating imaginary peers with whom one can identify as against one's actual peers.

Indeed, American culture constantly outdistances its interpreters. The moguls of Madison Avenue and Hollywood feel alienated from the avant-garde on the one hand and the "grass roots" on the other; they are vulnerable both to pressure and to formulae. But the avant-garde, too, are often subtly frightened by the huge unmalleability of America, and since understanding is our stock in trade, we may respond by formulae about "mass culture" at the price of increasing our own alienation and feelings of oppression. Paradoxically, many intellectuals have failed to keep up with their own changing status within America: they have arrived, they count (among all the other "veto groups" who have an "in" on the American scene), they are recognized by those representatives of the lower-middle class who make use of them as convenient enemies.

At the same time, many of the former enemies of the intellectuals from the upper social strata have succumbed to them: men in industry and in the popular culture business, lawyers and doctors, and many other large groups have become bored with their daily work (in some part because of the way it has been described to them by intellectuals), and are taking up "culture" and becoming not only patrons but aficionados of art, thus moving into roles and motivations once delegated to the womenfolk, to "imports" from Europe, and to a few native highbrows. But neither his new friends nor his new enemies give the intellectual much feeling of poise and assurance.

For one thing, he fears the shifts in middlebrow taste which might leave him in the position of liking something also liked by a *New Yorker* or *Harper's* audience. He cannot allow himself to enjoy what, in the eyes of some perhaps European taste-leader, might seem vulgar or second-rate; he behaves as if his patent to his status depends more on a widening circle of dislikes than on a widening circle of sympathies. In my judgment, the intellectual needs more pleasure and more self-esteem deriving from the activities of his mind and imagination so that he can stop being afraid of liking people and cultural objects which do not fit some momentary critical canon, and stop also fearing the popularization among America's vastly increasing number of amateur intellectuals of "his" ideas and tastes. For some, however, it may still be necessary to go through a novitiate of emotional expatriation in order to establish securely a claim to the intellectual's function—as we can see in a somewhat analogous case when we ask: how soon can the descendants of immigrants again eat garlic and other savory foods after a bland, self-inhibited period of "Americanization"? As we get second- and third-generation intellectuals, these problems may for many become less intense.

I am saying that an endless process of discovering ourselves, our burgeoning audiences, and our country may prove life-giving; it may also help us avoid the recurrent error, in a rapidly changing culture, of entrenching prejudices while still thinking of ourselves as heretics. Yet this is only possible if we are not too frantic in our search for originality, for sure conviction, and for good conscience. We will often find that our discovery has been made by others. We will often find that we need to take a stand against being forced to take a stand; that we have a right to be vague, confused, and indecisive. And if we are too concerned with making our views appear incorruptible and intrepid, we will be victims of those among us who can always manifest a stance of even greater righteousness and severity. The thinker who takes the outré position, the violent posture, the contemptuous tone still, in this country as in Europe, carries moral suasion; he may or may not, depending on the concrete details of his view, deserve it.

This hegemony of the self-styled extreme is not unrelated to the problem of the intellectuals' attitude toward America. If we confuse complacency with contentment we will fail to appreciate many qualities of American bourgeois existence. We will continue — in our literature, in our erotic dreams, in our romantic admiration for upper-class insouciance and lower-class uninhibited aggression — to pay homage to the cult of violence.

Yet it is particularly hard for us as intellectuals to change our view of America at the very moment when our country has risen to world predominance. Germans, Frenchmen, and Jews can testify that it is hard to detach one's loyalties from a weak, threatened, or defeated nation; it is perhaps even harder to attach one's loyalties to a newly powerful one. It is hard for us not to feel we are selling out when our views (let us say, our discovery of the virtues of our bourgeois "capitalism") not only keep us out of trouble but open up jobs or audiences for us. Indeed, it is our bad luck as intellectuals that we have had to recognize our country's growing intellectual and cultural differentiation and emancipation at the same moment that our world role has grown and Europe's lessened — especially as we have such a long tradition of mindless or defensive boasting to live down.

For there can be no doubt that the job of the intellectual — to some extent of anyone — is to remain in some tension with his audience and his immediate milieu. As every sect tends to become a church, so our new stance toward America even before it is well launched should take account of the risks of engendering new complacencies. Here the great variety of American audiences may aid us in maintaining a continuous self-scrutiny and renovation. We will find, for instance, that the attitude of the "new highbrows" who are curious about and sympathetic to industry, business, and popular culture will offend both the "old highbrows" and their pupils, the self-emancipating middlebrows who have been taught to despise commerce, the middle class, and television as vulgar. Once aware of these shifts, we intellectuals must speak in such a way as to challenge our friends while refusing comfort to our enemies—still telling the truth. And this requires us to search for the shadings and ambiguities, the crosscurrents and diversities, that *are* the truth about America.

There is an obvious danger in this course, namely that we will mistake shock on the part of our audiences for evidence that we are telling the truth—and we may form a tropism for the shock rather than for the truth. But I see no way of avoiding the moral and intellectual complexities of communication to an audience not all of which is at the same level of sophistication, complacency, or receptivity; and only by listening for this ambiguity and what it signifies can we flexibly protect our cultural role as Socratic questioners and skeptics.

So far I have spoken as if the problem of cultural evaluation were special to the modern intellectual. But as with most problems of moment, the roots lie in existential dilemmas. Every gossip who tells a story on a close friend faces an issue akin to that of "national loyalty." The writer, whether he is a social scientist, a novelist, essayist, or journalist, must constantly fight the feeling that he gains access to the facts he criticizes by what amounts to espionage. (By defining himself as "alienated," he acquires an easy alibi: they hit first; they exclude him.) Even if we praise what we are writing about, we are still, in some senses, exploiting it. And when we read ruthless comments about our country and its culture, we are in the position of the person who listens to a tale about his friend, attacked for faults he undoubtedly has—but do we deny the justice of the portrait, or attack its creator for lack of charity? The varieties of satire are ways of resolving these dilemmas creatively.

Once we realize that these problems of stance are more broadly human than otherwise we may become less insistent on an immediate solution and on the necessity of finding it in *American* life rather than in life itself. We may be able to see that the assurance we have admired in the European intellectual has had its roots in certain class conventions that are by no means unmixed blessings to the artistic life. The British intellectual in Fry's *A Sleep of Prisoners*, for example, is allowed to torment the consciousness of a less gifted soldier, but not vice versa: the soldier is physically strong enough to choke the intellectual but not humanly impressive enough to shake him morally. "Abel" in other words only takes account of "Cain" as either a useful or a dangerous thing, whereas American versions of the pastoral are more complex and less patronizing: democracy implies that intellectuals, whatever their social class position, can be not only choked but also shaken by nonintellectuals and their ways of life. While this delays our achieving the assurance whose absence now makes us so intemperate with our country, our culture, and ourselves, it also means that, once we gain it in our more difficult setting, we will also have gained a somewhat broader understanding and a wider gamut of topics for art and thought than has been characteristic of our models either at home or abroad.

Lionel Trilling

It is certainly true that in recent years—say the last ten—American intellectuals have radically revised their attitude toward America. An avowed aloofness from national feeling is no longer the first ceremonial step into the life of thought.

A prime reason for the change, and a material and an obvious one, is America's new relation with the other nations of the world. Even the most disaffected intellectual must respond, if only in the way of personal interestedness, to the growing isolation of his country amid the hostility that is directed against it. He has become aware of the virtual uniqueness of American security and well-being, and, at the same time, of the danger in which they stand. Perhaps for the first time in his life he has associated his native land with the not inconsiderable advantages of a whole skin, a full stomach, and the right to wag his tongue as he pleases.

He also responds to the fact that there is now no longer any foreign cultural ideal to which he can possibly fly from the American stupidity and vulgarity, the awareness of which was once likely to have been the mainspring of his mental life. The ideal of the workers' fatherland systematically destroyed itself some time back. Even the dullest intellectual now knows better than to look for a foster-father in Thyestes. Nor can he any longer entertain the idea of the bright cosmopolis of artists and intellectuals. The political situation, the commanding position of Stalinism in French cultural life, does not prevent our having the old affinity with certain elements of that life, but it makes the artistic and intellectual leadership of France unthinkable.

For the first time in the history of the modern American intellectual, America is not to be conceived of as a priori the vulgarest and stupidest nation of the world. And this is not only because other nations are exercising as never before the inalienable right of nations to be stupid and vulgar. The American situation has changed in a way that is not merely relative. There is an unmistakable improvement in the present American cultural situation over that of, say, thirty years ago. This statement is, of course, much too simple and I make it with the awareness that no cultural situation is ever really good. Yet as against the state of affairs of three decades ago, we are notably better off.

The improvement is manifold. I shall choose only one aspect of it, and remark the change in the relation of wealth to intellect. In many civilizations there comes a point at which wealth shows a tendency to submit itself to the rule of mind and imagination, to refine itself, and apologize for its existence by a show of taste and sensitivity. In America the tendency to this submission has for some time been apparent. For assignable reasons which cannot here be enumerated, wealth inclines to be uneasy about itself. I do not think that in a commercial civilization the acquisition of money can be anything but a prime goal, but I do think that acquisition as a way of life has become conscious of the effective competition of other ways of life.

And one of the chief competitors is intellect. We cannot, to be sure, put money and mind in perfect opposition to each other. Indeed, in a certain sense, the intellect of a society may be thought of as a function of the money of a society (specifically of the money, not merely of the wealth in general). But this symbiosis may be attenuated or suspended, or the two parties may not be aware of it, and the appearance or even the reality of opposition may develop between them. In such an opposition as formerly obtained in this country, money was the stronger of the parties. But now the needs of our society have brought close to the top of the social hierarchy a large class of people of considerable force and complexity of mind.

This is to be observed in most of the agencies of our society, in, for example, journalism, finance, industry, government. Intellect has associated itself with power as perhaps never before in history, and is now conceded to be itself a kind of power. The American populist feeling against mind, against the expert and the braintruster, is no doubt still strong. But it has not prevented the entry into our political and social life of an ever-growing class which we have to call intellectual, although it is not necessarily a class of "intellectuals."

This new intellectual class is to be accounted for not only by the growing complexity of the administering of our society but also by the necessity of providing a new means of social mobility, of social ascent. Our many bureaus and authorities were created not only as a response to the social needs which they serve, but also as a response to the social desires of their personnel. They have the function of making jobs and careers for a large class of people whose minds are their only property. The social principle here at work may be observed in the policy of the powerful labor unions, which are consciously attracting and carefully training college graduates to carry out their increasingly complex undertakings. It may also be observed in the increased prestige of the universities. The university teacher now occupies a place in our hierarchy which is considerably higher than he could have claimed three decades ago, and the academic career is now far more attractive to members of all classes than it used to be.

I do not believe that a high incidence of conscious professional intellect in a society necessarily makes for a good culture. It is even possible to imagine that a personnel of considerable intellectual power would have little interest in what is called the intellectual life, and even less interest in art. But this is not at present the case. The members of the newly expanded intellectual class that I have been describing, partly by reason of the education they receive, partly by reason of old cultural sanctions which may operate only as a kind of snobbery but which still do operate, and partly because they know that the mental life of practical reality really does have a relation to the mental life of theory and free imagination, are at least potentially supporters and consumers of high culture. They do not necessarily demand the best, but they demand what is called the best; they demand something. The haste and overcrowding of their lives prevents them from getting as much as they might want and need. So does the stupidity of the entrepreneurs of culture, such as publishers, who, in this country, have not had a new idea since they invented the cocktail party. So does the nature of the commitment of the people who produce the cultural commodity, that is, the actual "intellectuals." Yet it seems to me that art and thought are more generally and happily received and recognized—if still not wholly loved—than they have ever before been in America.

A country like ours, so big as ours, compounded of so many elements of a heterogeneous sort, makes it difficult for us to think that ideas such as might be entertained by anything like an elite can have any direct influence. And it is undoubtedly true that there is a considerable inertia that must be taken into account as we calculate the place of mind in our national life. But we should be wrong to conclude that the inertia is wholly definitive of our cultural situation. This is a characteristic mistake of the American intellectual, particularly the literary intellectual, with whom I am naturally most concerned. He is a man who is likely to be unaware of the channels through which opinion flows. He does not, for example, know anything about the existence and the training and the influence of, say, high school teachers, or ministers, or social workers, the people of the minor intellectual professions, whose stock in trade is ideas of some kind. His sense of an inert American mass resistant to ideas, entirely unenlightened and hating enlightenment, is part of the pathos of liberalism in the twenties and thirties, which is maintained despite the fact that the liberal ideas of the twenties and thirties are, I will not say dominant—this might, at the present juncture of affairs, be misleading—but strongly established, truly powerful. That the resistance to these ideas often takes an ugly, mindless form I should not think of denying, but this must not blind us to the power of ideas among us, to the existence of a very considerable class which is moved by ideas.

From what I have said about the increased power of mind in the nation, something of my answer to the question about mass culture may be inferred. Although mass culture is no doubt a very considerable threat to high culture, there is a countervailing condition in the class I have been describing. As for mass culture itself, one never knows, of course, what may happen in any kind of cultural situation. It is possible that mass culture, if it is not fixed and made static, might become a better thing than it now is, that it might attract genius and discover that it has an inherent law of development. But at the moment I am chiefly interested in the continuation of the traditional culture in the traditional forms. I am therefore concerned with the existence and effect of the large intellectual elite I have described. This group will not be—is not—content with mass culture as we now have it because for its very existence it requires new ideas, or at the least the simulacra of new ideas.

The social complexion of this new large intellectual class must be taken fully into account as we estimate the cultural situation it makes. The intellectual and quasi-intellectual classes of contemporary America characteristically push up from the bottom. They are always new. Very little is taken for granted by them; very little can be taken for granted in instructing them or trying to influence them. In some ways this is deplorable, making it difficult to think of the refinement of ideas, making it almost impossible to hope for grace and vivacity in the intellectual life. But in some ways it is an advantage, for it assures for the intellectual life a certain simplicity and actuality, an ever-renewed energy of discovery.

From this would seem to follow my answer to the question, Where in American life can the artists and intellectuals find the basis of strength, renewal, and recognition, now that they can't depend on Europe as a cultural example?

In attempting an answer, I shall not speak of the artist, only of the intellectual. For purposes of his salvation, it is best to think of the artist as crazy, foolish, inspired—as an unconditionable kind of man—and to make no provision for him until he appears in person and demands it. Our attitude to the artist is deteriorating as our sense of his needs increases. It seems to me that the more we undertake to provide for the artist, the more we incline to think of the artist as Postulant or Apprentice, and the less we think of the artist as Master. Indeed, it may be coming to be true that for us the Master is not the artist himself but the Foundation, whose creative act the artist is.

But intellectuals are in a different case. They can be trained. They can, I believe, be taught to think. They can even be taught to write. It is not improper to discuss what kind of work they should be doing, and their manner of doing it, and the conditions of their doing it, and the influences to which they might submit.

It is in a way wrong or merely academic to talk of the *influence* of European thought on American thought since the latter is continuous with the former. But insofar as the American intellectual conceived of the continuity as being an influence, it no doubt was exactly that, and in being that it was useful and liberating. Yet now it seems to me that if the European influence, as a conscious thing, has come to an end, this is, at the moment, all to the good (except, of course, as it implies the reason for its coming to an end, and as it may suggest a diminution of free intercourse, of which we can never have enough).

The American intellectual never so fully expressed his provincialism as in the way he submitted to the influence of Europe. He was provincial in that he thought of culture as an abstraction and as an absolute. So long as Marxism exercised its direct influence on him, he thought of politics as an absolute. So long as French art exercised its direct influence upon him, he thought of art as an absolute. To put it another way, he understood himself to be involved primarily with the mental discipline he had elected. To be sure, the times being what they were, he did not make the mistake of supposing that the elected discipline was not connected with reality. But the reality that he conceived was abstractly conceived—he never quite saw that it was conditioned by the local circumstance in which the discipline to deal with it had been developed. The "society" which the American intellectual learned about from Europe was in large part a construct of Marxism, or a construct of the long war of the French intellectual with the French bourgeoisie. Ideas, of course, are transferable; there is no reason why the American intellectual might not have transferred what he had learned to America, why he should not have directed the impatience, the contempt, the demand, the resistance, which are necessary elements of the life of the critical intellect—and, as I think, of a large part of the creative life as well—upon the immediate, the local, and the concrete phenomena of American life. I do not say that he did not display impatience, contempt, demand, and resistance, but only that he did not direct them where they should have gone, that he was general and abstract where he should have been specific and concrete.

The literary mind, more precisely the historical-literary mind, seems to be the best kind of critical and constructive mind that we have, better than the philosophic, better than the theological, better than the scientific and the social-scientific. But the literary intellectuals, possibly because they are still fascinated by certain foreign traditions, still do not look at our culture with anything like the precise critical attention it must have. If we are to maintain the organic pluralism we have come to value more highly than ever before, it is not enough to think of it in its abstract totality—we must be aware of it in its multifarious, tendentious, competitive details.

For example, it is a truism that universal education is one of the essential characteristics of modern democracy and that the quality and tendency of the education provided is a clear indication of the quality and tendency of the democracy that provide it. What, then, is the condition of American education? The question has been allowed to fall into the hands of reactionaries of the most vicious kind, and of progressives and liberals whose ideas may evoke sympathy and whose goals are probably right in general but who live in a cave of self-commiseration and self-congratulation into which no ray of true criticism ever penetrates. Who among us intellectuals really knows what is being taught in the great teachers' colleges? Who knows what is the practice among the schools of the big cities or the small ones? Who knows what the directives are that are being issued by the superintendents? Who among us is even aware that these directives are based on the most elaborate theories of society and the individual? Who knows anything about the quality of the teaching staffs of the schools? What is the literary curriculum of the high schools? What is taught in "Social Studies"? What actually happens in a "progressive" school—I mean apart from what everybody jokes about? What happens in colleges? These are questions which the intellectuals have been content to leave to the education editor of the *New York Times.* With the result that Dr. Benjamin Fine, a man with, properly enough, his own ax to grind and his own tears to shed, is far more influential in an actual way in our culture than any intellectual who reads this, or writes it, is ever likely to be.

Psychology is a science to which literary intellectuals feel affinity. But who knows just what is happening in psychology? Dr. Fromm and Dr. Horney and the late Dr. Sullivan, and their disciples, have great influence upon many members of the elite. What, actually, do they say? What is what they say worth? What is happening in the development of Freud's ideas by those who are called orthodox Freudians—is anything happening? Departments of psychology in the universities are detaching themselves from the faculties of philosophy in order to enter the faculties of pure science, on the ground that their science is wholly experimental. What is the value of the considerable vested interests of this academic psychology? Colleges nowadays give courses in Marriage and Sex—presumably *not* on an experimental basis—and who knows what is the received doctrine in these courses?

I could go on with these questions at very great length, for I have chosen my two examples quite at random from among an inexhaustible number. But there is no need for me to go on. My simple point is surely plain. As I make it, I see that it answers the last question, about how a reaffirmation and rediscovery of America can go hand in hand with the tradition of critical nonconformism. The editors, to identify the great American tradition of critical nonconformism, speak of it as "going back to Thoreau and Melville." I am glad that they have done so, for it saves me the trouble of defending myself from those to whom it will seem that I recommend an elaborate prostitution of the literary mind to trivialities, to whom it will seem that I have suppressed and betrayed art by my emphasis on the local particularities of culture and, if not art, which I expressly exempted from consideration, then those larger and finer and more transcendent matters to which the most gifted intellectuals are naturally drawn. The recollection of Thoreau and Melville will sustain me in my certitude that the kind of critical interest I am asking the intellectual to take in the life around him is a proper interest of the literary mind, and that it is the right ground on which to approach transcendent things. More: it is the right ground for art to grow in—for satire, for humor, for irony, for despair, for tragedy, for the personal vision affirming itself against the institutional with the peculiar passionateness of art. Art, strange and sad as it may be to have to say it again, really is the criticism of life.

C. Wright Mills

Your questions direct me first to an assessment of changes in the attitudes intellectuals hold of America and second to my own attitudes toward this country. I take the questions in this double way because I do not believe they are answerable on the first interpretation without the second intruding. It's a matter of whether or not you're aware of their inevitable interpenetration. Nevertheless, I am going to try to keep them distinct.

1

1. American intellectuals do seem quite decisively to have shifted their attitudes toward America. One minor token of the shift is available to those who try to imagine "the old *Partisan Review*" running the title "Our Country . . ." in 1939. You would have cringed. Don't you want to ask from what and to what the shift has occurred? From a political and critical orientation toward life and letters to a more literary and less politically critical view. Or: generally to a shrinking deference to the status quo; often to a soft and anxious compliance, and always a synthetic, feeble search to justify this intellectual conduct, without searching for alternatives, and sometimes without even political good sense. The several phases of this development I've recently tried to document and explain elsewhere.

2. Of course intellectuals *need* not adapt themselves to "mass culture" as it is now set up; but many of them have, doubtless others will, maybe some won't. We must remember that this is a tricky question to answer, because some might exclude from "the intelligentsia" those who do "adapt" to these media contents, believing that they thereby become technicians, maybe brilliant ones, but technicians.

3. One key thing about American mass culture, as Hans Gerth once commented, is that it is not an "escape" from the strains of routine, but another routine, which in its murky formulations and prefabricated moods (Type one: Hot; Type two: Sad) deprive the individual of his own fantasy life, and in fact often empty him of the possibilities of having such a life. So if your questions mean should intellectuals adapt to *that*, I suppose I have to say they can't.

4. The "nonconformism" tradition to which you make reference has faded and, in my opinion, will continue to fade. Who, as a group or even as a clique, publicly represents it today? Nobody who isn't so genteel and muted about it that it is practically a secret set of beliefs, or so mechanical and untalented about it

that it is publicly irrelevant. Besides, I certainly am not aware of any "reaffirmation and rediscovery of America" going on, outside the Voice of America. The attempt to *understand* "America" has, in my opinion, been largely given up by many intellectuals. Of course it's possible, especially for those who have given up the attempt, to "reaffirm" at will.

2

The Englishman John Morley, in his profound essay *On Compromise*, distinguished deference to the existing state of affairs in (1) forming opinions, (2) in expressing them, and (3) in trying to realize them. With him, I believe there is no reason for such deference in the first and at least not yet in the second of these three spheres. The third is another matter: choices are often necessary, even if they are morally corrupting. What is happening is that many intellectuals have had to give up some of the ideas that made their impatience for change palatable, and moreover have lived under conditions that affect their freedom in the first and second spheres. What is happening in the United States is that three is out of the question (no movement), so two tends to dry up (no audience), and so in one, people adapt (no individual opinion). Without a movement to which they might address political ideas, intellectuals in due course cease to express such ideas, and so in time, shifting their interests, they become indifferent.

They can no longer take heart by functioning only in the second area (that is, as intellectuals per se) because they no longer believe, as firmly as Morley did, that in the end opinion rules and that therefore small groups of thinkers may take the lead in historic change. They no longer believe that existing institutions and policies are held provisionally—until new and better ideas about them are available as replacements. They no longer believe that the prosperity, or even the chance, of an idea depends upon its intrinsic merits, but rather that its medium and conditions are usually more important to its fate. And they now know that ideas and force do not "belong to different elements"—as nineteenth-century liberals were wont to believe; but rather that movements, established and on the make, use force to modify ideas and ideas to justify force. This presence of coercion, actual or threatened or even unconsciously felt to be threatening, is one important meaning of the dwindling of liberty.

What would presumably clear up a lot of "confusion" and "drift" to which many intellectuals publicly "confess" is some urgent moral orientation which they could embrace and babble over; the sort of thing some of them have found and lost at least three different times—with little intellectual continuity between them—since the middle thirties. But one should not let such people interfere with the serious and important task of understanding the main drift of modern society.

The reason one feels foolish making programmatic statements today is that there is now in the United States no real audience for such statements. Such an audience (1) would have, in greater or lesser degree, to be connected with some sort of movement or party having a chance to influence the course of affairs and the decisions being made. It would also (2) have to contain people who are at least attentive, even if not receptive, to ideas—people among whom one has a chance to get a hearing. When these two conditions are available one can be programmatic in a "realistic" political way. When these conditions are not available, then one has this choice:

To modify the ideas or at least file them and hence, in effect and at least temporarily, to take up new allegiances for which conditions do exist that make working for them realistic.

Or: To retain the ideals and hence by definition to hold them in a utopian way, while waiting. Of course these two ways can be combined in various sorts of tentative holding actions. Nevertheless, they present a clear-cut choice.

There are reasons for taking the first way: one might judge that dangers are so great one has to fight with whatever means are at hand, so if Truman and company are the only ones around, then support them and try to defeat the Tafts or MacArthurs. Bore from within for so long as you can breathe down in the old wormy wood. Well, my judgment is that world conditions and domestic affairs are not yet that perilous.

"A principle, if it be sound," wrote Morley, "represents one of the larger expediences. To abandon that for the sake of some seeming expediency of the hour is to sacrifice the greater good for the less, on no more creditable ground than that the less is nearer. It is better to wait, and to defer the realization of our ideas until we can realize them fully, than to defraud the future by truncating them, if truncate them we must, in order to secure a partial triumph for them in the immediate present. It is better to bear the burden of impracticableness than to stifle conviction and pare away principle until it becomes hollowness and triviality."

I suppose this is the direction in which I go. In my own thinking and writing I have deliberately allowed certain implicit values which I hold to remain, because even though they are quite unrealizable in the immediate future, they still seem to me worth displaying. They seem worthwhile in another way too: they sensitize one to a clearer view of what is happening in the world. One tries by one's work to issue a call to thinking to anyone now around or anyone who might later come into view and who might listen. There are times when clear-headed analysis is more important and more relevant than the most engaging shout for action. I think this is such a time. Of course, "frank presentation of ominous facts," as the late German-trained Joseph Schumpeter once remarked, is open to the terrible charge of "defeatism," but then, as he pointed out, "the report that a given ship is sinking is not defeatist" and "this is one of those situations in which optimism is nothing but a form of defection."

I also believe, as an amateur historian, that one should never allow one's values to be overwhelmed in short runs of time: that is the way of the literary faddist and the technician of the cultural chic. One just has to wait, as others before one have, while remembering that what in one decade is utopian may in the next be implementable. Surely after the thirties and the forties, we have all learned how very rapidly events can occur, how swiftly whole nations can turn over, how soon fashionable orientations, especially as presented in magazines like yours, can become outmoded.

In the meantime, we must bear with the fact that in many circles impatience with things as they are in America is judged to be either mutinous or utopian.

Arthur Schlesinger Jr.

There seem to me two main issues raised by the *Partisan Review* statement: (1) the change of attitude toward America on the part of American intellectuals; and (2) the prospects for culture in a mass society.

Of course, American intellectuals have vastly changed their attitude toward American institutions in the last generation (or perhaps it would be better to say that bitter experience has forced them to summon up resources within themselves and within the American tradition to whose existence they had previously been indifferent). The twenties had placed the American intellectual in a singular dilemma. He lived in a society which seemed to work fine economically, but whose leaders were clearly hostile to art and intelligence. He therefore went through the dramatic motions of "rejecting" this business-dominated and business-oriented society without really rejecting the deep sense of security it gave him. The social framework, though suffocating and repugnant, seemed stable and enduring. The rejection of business rule was accompanied by an unquestioning belief in the permanence of that rule. With the economic (and, one must add, military) foundations of life thus secure, the intellectual could luxuriate, a bit irresponsibly, in the mood of being in a wasteland, a member of a lost generation, a hollow man with headpiece filled with straw, etc., while at the same time losing himself in the creative exuberance of a brilliant period. And, in the rejection of business rule, a rejection somewhat delighted and self-conscious, the intellectual identified business with America and rejected America too. Like Calvin Coolidge, he really believed that the business of America was business.

Then came the Depression; and the intellectual realized with a shock that the foundations were not solid, that the framework was very fragile indeed. With the chips really down, he needed every source of support he could find. The

Depression thus brought about a serious—even a desperate—inventory of American resources. "In times of change and danger," wrote Dos Passos, "when there is a quicksand of fear under men's reasoning, a sense of continuity with generations gone before can stretch like a lifeline across the scary present." The intellectual, his fantasy life of the twenties tumbling around him, sought ground to stand on. Hence the great move to repossess the American past—a move led by such men as Van Wyck Brooks who had previously done their best to discredit and disown that past.

More than that, America rose to the crisis. The brilliant artistic exuberance of the twenties was followed by the brilliant political exuberance of the thirties. It is fashionable today among ex-liberal intellectuals to forget the extraordinary revival of confidence and recovery of nerve that the New Deal produced in this country. These intellectuals should consult their own writings of the early thirties to see how frantic was their fright, how deep their sense of panic; and they might have the grace today to recognize how much more correct Roosevelt and the New Dealers were in assessing the resources of democracy.

The Depression was the first impetus to a revaluation of America. Then the rise of Fascism abroad thrust the problem of American culture into a new dimension. Next to Himmler, even Babbitt began to look good (see *The Prodigal Parents*, 1938). For all its faults, the United States was an open society, unfinished, with a plenitude of possibilities, while Fascism meant the death of culture.

We confront the same situation today. Since a live foe is always more dangerous than a dead one, Communism appears to carry an even more implacable threat to culture than fascism. The intellectual knows now, as he did not know in the twenties, that the economic and military foundations of life are insecure. He knows too that the chief hope of survival lies in the capacity of the American government and the strength of American society. Naturally he has changed his mind about American institutions.

Still, this has been primarily a political transformation. The open society, at best, contains cultural *possibilities*: it guarantees nothing. The first priority, even for the intellectual, is the survival of the open society. But more complex problems lie beyond survival—the problems of the fate of culture in "mass society."

The intellectual probably tends to approach these problems in too catastrophic terms. Yet the rise of what Gilbert Seldes has called the Great Audience is one of the awful facts of our modern life. As Frank Stanton, the president of CBS, put it: "A mass medium must concern itself with the common denominator of mass interest. . . it can only achieve its great audience. . . by giving the majority of people what they want." The presupposition of the mass media is that Americans constitute a uniform audience. The more the mass media act on this presupposition, the more they tend to manufacture this uniform audience and thus strike at the roots of democracy.

The only answer to mass culture, of course, lies in the affirmation of America not as a uniform society, but as a various and pluralistic society made up of many groups with diverse interests. The immediate problem is to conserve cultural pluralism in the face of the threat of the mass media. In many cases, this becomes a technical problem—the problem of developing markets for cultural "minorities"; the problem of devising means by which media geared to mass consumption can shift over to the satisfaction of more specialized interests; the problem of getting at the economics of book and magazine publishing so that a 10,000 copy sale or a 20,000 circulation is not essential for survival. One would hope (rather feebly) that the foundations might try to tackle these problems; but they are more likely to press on with their policy of forcing the collective approach into the remotest corners of our intellectual life.

The task of maintaining and enlarging our cultural pluralism is not perhaps hopeless. Still, the situation can be bettered only if a number of people make a deliberate and sustained attempt to better it. There can be no final solution, of course; and who would want one? A moderate degree of "alienation" is indispensable to the artist and writer.

Above all, the survival of cultural pluralism depends on the preservation of an atmosphere congenial to free inquiry. We can maintain the American "tradition of critical nonconformism"; but only if we determine to do so. The trouble is that intellectuals today are not united in that determination. Some have forgotten the wisdom of Tocqueville when a century ago he identified the antidote to the new power that democratic equality bestowed upon mass opinion. "Many people in France consider equality of conditions as one evil," he wrote, "and political freedom as a second. When they are obliged to yield to the former, they strive at least to escape from the latter. But I contend that in order to combat the evils which equality may produce, there is only one effectual remedy—namely, political freedom."

Tocqueville could not have been more right; political freedom is the indispensable preliminary to any effective defense against the leveling of culture. That is why McCarthyism seems to me as much a cultural as a political problem. I cannot go along with those who profess a belief in cultural freedom, on the one hand, and refuse to condemn McCarthyism, on the other—those who argue, apparently, that McCarthyism is a genial excess of political zeal, a Washington matter with no larger reverberations in our culture. The real *trahison des clercs* lies, in my judgment, with those who collaborate with the foes of the mind— whether they are the demonic foes of the mind, like Hitler and Stalin, or the gangster foes, like McCarthy and McCarran. We cannot hope to preserve cultural freedom and cultural pluralism in a society where political freedom and political pluralism become impossible.   1952, vol. 19, nos. 3–5

• The Sense and Nonsense of Whittaker Chambers
Philip Rahv

What chiefly caught my interest when I first encountered Whittaker Chambers back in the early thirties, not long before the "underground" claimed him, was something in his talk and manner, a vibration, an accent, that I can only describe as Dostoevskyean in essence. I thought at the time that he was far from unconscious of the effect he produced. He had the air of a man who took more pleasure in the stylized than in the natural qualities of his personality. Still, whether aware or not, it was distinctly the Dostoevskyean note that he struck—that peculiar note of personal intensity and spiritual truculence, of commitment to the "Idea" so absolute as to suggest that life had no meaning apart from it, all oddly combined with a flair for mystification and melodrama. That early impression, since confirmed by other people, is now reaffirmed in his book.

Witness is in the main a fully convincing account of the role its author played in the Hiss case. It is also a heady mixture of autobiography, politics, and apocalyptic prophecy; and it contains a good many of the characteristic elements of a production à la Dostoevsky, above all the atmosphere of scandal and monstrous imputation, the furtive meetings and the secret agents, the spies, informers, and policemen, desperate collisions, extreme ideas, suffering, pity, and remorse, the entire action moving inexorably toward the typical dénouement of a judicial trial in the course of which heroes and victims alike are exposed as living prey to the crowds and all the secrets come tumbling out.

The influence of the Russian novelist is literally everywhere in the book, in the action as in the moral import, in the plot no less than in the ideology. And Chambers goes in for ideology without stint or limit. Even his Maryland farm, of which he writes at great length, is at once a real place and a piece of ideology pure and simple. And the ideology is fashioned in accordance with the precepts of the Russian master from whom he borrows some of his key terms and characteristic turns of thought. Thus Chambers seems to have appropriated, lock, stock, and barrel, the entire Dostoevskyean polemic against socialism as the culminating movement of Western rationalism and secularism, leading through the rejection of God to the deification of man. He accuses the radicals of worshiping "Almighty man," just as the creator of Ivan Karamazov accused them of worshiping the "man-god," and refuses to distinguish in principle between liberals, socialists, and party-line communists, whatever the divergences among them. Regardless of their political practice at any given time, in theory they are all equally committed to unbelief, to the elevation of man above God—the supreme act of rebellion converting man into a monster.

That is exactly the approach of Dostoevsky, who also saw no reason to discriminate among the varieties of free thought. (He did not hesitate, for instance, to lay the blame for the criminal acts of Nechayev—the model for the sinister figure of Pyotr Verhovensky in *The Possessed*—not only upon such revolutionary theorists as Belinsky and Herzen but also upon the far more moderate liberal idealists of the type of Granovsky, a Moscow professor who taught his students scarcely anything more virulent than that man was a creature endowed with a mind and that it was his duty to use it.) Science and reason are the enemy. And what is socialism? According to Dostoevsky it is "not merely the labor question, it is before all else the atheistic question, the question of the form taken by atheism today, the question of the tower of Babel built without God, not to mount from earth to Heaven, but to set up Heaven on earth." This, indeed, is the *locus classicus*. It is the pivotal thought of Chambers's book. But there are other ideas in Dostoevsky which he entirely ignores; and with good reason, for they emphatically call into question his view of religion as the one secure basis of freedom. Perhaps he would not be so certain of their "indivisible" union if he had been more attentive to the important historical lesson contained in the legend of the Grand Inquisitor—a lesson which belies the national-religious thesis of Dostoevsky's work as a whole and which is a deadly critique of the shallow doctrine that if men but believed they would soon enter the promised spiritual kingdom. In that legend Dostoevsky tells us that religion too, yes, even the religion of Christ, can be transformed into an instrument of power in the hands of a self-chosen elite bent on depriving men of their freedom and organizing a "universal human ant heap." And it is precisely men's readiness to believe and their irresistible craving for "community of worship," the principal source of bigotry and intolerance, that induces them to accept the total claims of their rulers.

The Russian writer's influence on Chambers is one-sided but very real. In the biographical chapters, too, the story is sometimes given a Dostoevskyean twist. Consider the following brief passage in which, while recalling his student days at Columbia, Chambers portrays himself for all the world as if he were writing not about a boy from Long Island but a blood brother of Shatov or Raskolnikov, brooding in the Russian cold about the ultimate problems of existence. "One day, early in 1925, I sat down on a concrete bench on the Columbia campus, facing a little Greek shrine and the statue of my old political hero, Alexander Hamilton. The sun was shining, but it was chilly, and I sat huddled in my overcoat. I was there to answer once for all two questions: Can a man go on living in a world that is dying? If he can, what should he do in the crisis of the twentieth century?" The "huddled in my overcoat" is a good touch; but the peremptory "to answer *once for all* two questions" (and what questions!) is really priceless. Here, histrionics aside, it is not only the inflection of the narrative line which reminds us of the author of *Crime and Punishment*; even more suggestive is the thoroughly *ideologized* conceptions of life it reveals. Essentially it is the idea that in order to live at all one must first ascertain the answer to the ultimate questions—an idea so utterly unpragmatic that one is almost tempted to call it "un-American."

However, in spite of Chambers's wonderful aptitude for turning ideas into dramatic motives, in its lack of humor and irony his book is anything but Dostoevskyean. His seriousness is of that portentous kind which in a novelist we would at once recognize as a failure of sensibility. For Chambers eliminates from his account anything that might conceivably be taken as ambiguous or incongruous in his own motives and convictions, and this permits him to bear down all the more heavily on those of his opponents. No sense of humor or irony can survive that sort of attack. He is a splendid satirist; the mordant phrase, manipulated with ease and perfect timing, is ever at his disposal; but of that true irony which implicates the person writing no less than other people, the subject as well as the object, there is not a trace in his pages. This deficiency makes it hard for him both to modulate his ideas and to relate himself to them without pomposity and self-conceit. Perhaps that will explain the occasional lapses in taste and the tone of heroic self-dramatization which is sometimes indistinguishable from sheer bathos, as when he writes that at issue in the Hiss case was "the question whether this sick society, which we call Western civilization, could in its extremity still cast up a man whose faith in it was so great that he would voluntarily abandon those things which men hold good, including life, to defend it."

And his prose is open to criticism on related grounds. He is a born writer, greatly accomplished in a technical sense. Yet his prose, for all its unusual merit, is not very adaptable to confessional writing. Tightly organized and controlled, even streamlined, though in the best sense of that much-abused word, it is hardly an appropriate medium for the expression of intimate personal truth or the exploration of inner life. It shuns the spontaneous and repels subjectivity.

The fact is that when we are through reading this enormously long book, with its masses of detail, we are still left with very little knowledge of the author as a person. We have been instructed in his politics and in his philosophy; we have learned much about his childhood years, so fearfully depressing and ill-making; and we have learned to know him in his successive adult roles—Communist Party member, Soviet agent, editor of *Time*, Maryland farmer, convert, and witness. Nonetheless he remains shielded from us to the very end, encased in his "character-armor." We communicate almost exclusively with the externalized Chambers, a man apparently bent on transforming his life into a public destiny, incapable of projecting himself on any level but that of objectified meaning, and possessed by a lust for the Absolute (the ultimate and unqualified pledge of objective Being). He is certain of its existence; and he finds it—invariably. First History, now God. For he repented of his unbelief even before he openly emerged from the Communist underground, thus insuring himself of uninterrupted contact with the Absolute.

One wishes that Chambers had absorbed less of Dostoevsky's political ideology—a sphere in which he is assuredly a false guide—and had instead absorbed more of his insight into unconscious motivation and the cunning maneuvers of the battered ego in reaching out for self-esteem, pleasure, and power. He might then not be quite so intent on dissolving the concrete existence of men in their specific conditions of life into the abstractions of the impersonal Idea, whether in its idealist or materialist version. (The difference between the two versions is not half so great as the devotees of metaphysics imagine.) Nor would he take it for granted, as he now does, that behavior can be directly deduced from ideology, thus overlooking the fact that the relation between them is frequently not only indirect but devious and thoroughly distorted.

But to Chambers the Idea is everything; men nothing. The role of personality in history is abolished. For instance, he absolves Stalin of responsibility for any and all of the evils of Communism, and even goes so far as to characterize him as a "revolutionary statesman" for carrying through the Great Purge. ("From the Communist viewpoint, Stalin could have taken no other course, so long as he believed he was right. . . . That was the horror of the Purge—that acting as a Communist, Stalin had acted rightly.") This is sheer fantasy. What evidence is there that the Purge advanced the cause of Communism, that it was in any sense "objectively necessary," or that Stalin was under any illusions as to its effect? It should be obvious that the Purge strengthened Stalin's personal dictatorship at the cost of considerably weakening the Communist movement the world over. It shook the faith of millions in the Soviet myth. (For that matter, Chambers himself might still be numbered among the faithful if not for the Purge, the direct cause of his break.) After all, no policy that Stalin promulgated *after* the Purge could have been seriously resisted, let alone blocked, by the abject and beaten Old Guard of the Revolution. Not the necessities, real or imaginary, of the revolutionary cause but the drive for unlimited power on the part of Stalin and his faction, who have never hesitated to sacrifice the good of the cause for their own advantage, is the one plausible explanation of the Purge.

Chambers appears to have quit the Communist Party cherishing some of the same illusions with which he entered it. He was certainly close enough to the Stalinist oligarchy to have learned that it has long ago ceased to regard power merely as a means—least of all as a means of bringing to realization "the vision of man," as he calls it—but as an end in itself. The present Stalinist elite, which raised its leader to the supreme heights and which he, in turn, organized and disciplined in his own inimitable fashion, no longer cares to remember the socialist idealism of the generation that made the Revolution. It has been taught to despise that idealism; and Chambers's portrait of Colonel Bykov, his Russian superior in the "apparatus," is perfectly illustrative of this psychology. Whatever the nature of their rationalizations, those people now act more and more like the totalitarians in George Orwell's novel 1984, whose program comes to only one thing: power entirely for its own sake. "Power is not a means; it is an end. . . . The object of persecution is persecution. The object of torture is torture. The object of power is power."

The original idea of Communism accounts for the behavior of real live Communists no more and no less than the original idea of Christianity can account for the behavior of real live Christians in the centuries when they wielded temporal power; the Great Purge, the slave-labor camps and the other horrors of the Soviet system can no more be deduced from the classic texts of socialism than the murderous Albigensian Crusade and the practices of the Holy Inquisition can be deduced from the Sermon on the Mount. Chambers denies that there is any phase or single event in the history of Bolshevism, like the Kronstadt rebellion for example, that can be taken as a turning point in its degeneration. Its fascist character, he writes, was "inherent in it from the beginning." That is true in a sense, but scarcely in a meaningful way. It is equally true that besides the totalitarian potential a good many other things were inherent in the Revolution which came to nothing by reason of the power in the hands of certain men and the irreducibly tragic nature of the circumstances under which they exercised it, such as Russia's isolation and ruinous poverty and the fusion of the absolutist element in the Marxist dialectic with the caesaro-papist heritage of the Russian mind. Chambers is so obsessed with the "atheistic question" that he is willing to absolve the very worst men of responsibility for their crimes in order all the more justifiably to implicate the values and ideas they profess. He forgets that men in general, not only the worst among them, tend to honor such values and ideas more in the breach than in the observance. At one time Lenin warned his followers that there is no idea or movement that cannot be turned into its exact opposite. If that is true, it is because ideas and movements have no reality except insofar as they derive it from living men. No ideology, whether secular or religious, exists in some ghostlike fashion apart from the men who believe in it or merely use it for their own ends; and since its one lodging place is in the powermongering human mind, it can never be immune to corruption.

Though disappointing in its character as a work of ideas, Witness is still of the first importance as an authentic expression of historical crisis and as a presentation of crucial facts. And by far the most crucial is the fact that the Soviet Military Intelligence, by winning to its service men of the type of Harry Dexter White and Alger Hiss, came very close to penetrating the top headquarters of the U.S. government: "It was not yet in the Cabinet room, but it was not far outside the door." The stealing of secret documents was, of course, of little consequence compared to the power that the infiltrators acquired to influence policy. This infiltration was not simply the exploit of clever spies; the spy-thriller aspect of their performance is of negligible interest. What is of commanding interest is the lesson it enforces; and that lesson is that the infiltration, which was more extensive, probably, than we shall ever know, was intrinsically the result of the political attitudes that prevailed in this country for a whole decade, if not longer, at the very least between 1938 and 1948.

Chambers may be exaggerating in saying that in those years it was the Popular Front mind that dominated American life, but he is hardly exaggerating when he specifies that it was that mind which then dominated most "avenues of communication between the intellectuals and the nation. It told the nation what it should believe; it made up the nation's mind for it. The Popular Fronters had made themselves the 'experts.' They controlled the narrows of news and opinion. . . . The nation . . . could not grasp or believe that a conspiracy on the scale of Communism was possible or that it had already made so deep a penetration." And the fierce resistance which Chambers encountered when he finally broke through with his testimony to the nation at large was essentially a symptom of the anguish of the Popular Front mind and its unreasoning anger at being made to confront the facts of political life. The importance of the Hiss case was precisely that it dramatized that mind's struggle for survival and its vindictiveness under attack. That mind is above all terrified of the disorder and evil of history, and it flees the harsh choices which history so often imposes. It fought to save Hiss in order to safeguard its own illusions and to escape the knowledge of its gullibility and chronic refusal of reality.

Where Chambers goes wrong, I think, is in his attempt to implicate that mind in the revolutionary ethos. Hence his distorted picture of the New Deal as a "genuine revolution, whose deepest purpose was not simply reform within existing conditions, but a basic change in the social and, above all, the power relationships within the nation." The proof? The New Deal was bent on replacing the power of business with that of politics. But this notion is altogether too narrow, too onesided. Of course the New Deal was bound to increase the power of government in its effort to pull the economy out of depression and to save business from its own follies. The New Deal is unrecognizable in Chambers's description of it. Here again he proceeds in accordance with the method of pure ideological deduction, this time deducing the New Deal from the revolutionary intention he imputes to the Popular Front mind. He is in error, it seems to me, in his evaluation of that mind. I see that mind not only as unrevolutionary but as profoundly bourgeois in its political amorphousness, evasion of historical choice, and search for formulas of empty reassurance. It is the bourgeois mind in its mood of good will and vague liberal aspiration, the mind of degenerated humanism glowing with the false militancy of universal political uplift. It wishes to maintain its loyalty to free institutions and at the same time to accommodate itself to the Communists, particularly so when the latter oblige by playing the game of not being "real Communists" at all but democrats of the extreme left. It wanted to be and was duly sold on the theory of Chinese Stalinism as a movement of agrarian reform; and it never wanted to know the truth about Soviet Russia, even though for many years now, certainly since the Great Purge in the mid-thirties, it has not been very difficult to discover what that truth was. The Communist mind, on the other hand, while Utopian in its faith in the "science of history" and the materialist dogmas, is crassly realistic to the point of cynicism in its grasping sense of power and in the choice of means to attain it; its will is always armed and, whenever feasible, it prefers constraint to compromise in settling issues. If the New Dealers, insofar as they can be identified with the Popular Front mind (and the identification is by no means complete), failed to recognize the Communists in their midst, it was not, as Chambers asserts, because they lived in the same mental world with them but because at bottom they had almost nothing in common with the agents of the police state.

The dynamism of the New Deal in its early years should not mislead us as to its objectives, which were in reality very limited. Chambers invests that indigenous reform movement with sinister qualities, thus justifying his present allegiance to the far right. I do not believe that the explanation for his political behavior is to be sought in any love he has of late acquired for laissez-faire economics and the division of society into warring classes. It must be his dread and hatred of Communism that impel him to reject precipitantly all ideas of social reform and innovation. But if Communism is so overwhelming an issue, what does the far right actually offer by way of leadership in the struggle against it? As I see it, it provides neither a fundamental understanding of Communism nor the moral, intellectual, or political weapons with which to conduct that struggle to a successful conclusion. That withered conservatism, which invariably mistakes all social adjustments, however necessary and belated, for wild plunges into the sinful economics of "statism," and which looks to a reduction in taxes and a balanced budget for salvation, has simply ceased to count in the world of today. It is really another form of nihilism, by far the most mediocre and boring of all. Whatever the material force which this withered conservatism may still command in some countries, the Stalinist aggressors know well that it presents no serious obstacle to their worldwide sweep. Chambers, who can hardly be called an optimist, surely understands that this is the case, as he virtually despairs of "the world outside Communism, which lacks a faith and a vision." What, then, is the answer? His answer is religion.

It is at this juncture that Chambers ceases to think politically, giving in entirely to his mystic proclivities. One doubts that he has ever been really at home in politics, if we take politics to be a delimited form of social thought and action. It was in the course of his search for wholeness and identity that he joined the Communists, reading a transcendent meaning into their political passions.

He admits that while in the Party he avoided reading all "books critical of Communism" and also that he had never sought to influence policy. Nor did his activity as spy-courier in the Party's secret apparatus make any urgent claims upon his political sense. Unconcerned with politics in its hard empirical aspects, he is essentially a mystic swept into the world of parties and movements by the crazy pressures of the age.

What he is unable to see in his present mood is that the appeal to religion, however valid in its own sphere, turns into the merest surrogate when made to do the work of politics. It is well known that the religious consciousness is reconcilable to so many contradictory and even antagonistic concepts of society that the attempt to hold it to any particular social or political orientation is nearly useless. There is no substitute for politics, just as for those who must have it there is no substitute for religion. It is true that religious believers have every reason to be hostile to Communism; yet the motive of belief forms but one strand in a complex of motives. Believers, like all men, live in the real world of varied and pressing needs and interests, of which the material interest is surely the last that we can afford to underrate; and all too frequently the predominant concerns of men are such that the acknowledged duty to their faith is easily thrust aside. In 1917 the Russian peasants, though traditionally far from irreligious, backed the Bolsheviks despite all churchly admonition—the petitions of orthodoxy counted as nothing against the promise of peace, bread, and land. Clearly, Lenin's professed atheism in no way deterred the peasants in their support of the Revolution; and now large sections of the peasantry of Italy and other countries show the same lack of inhibition in voting the Communist ticket. The breakup of traditional societies is a salient feature of our time, and no impromptu summons can recall these societies to the ancient faith. Of what relevance are the propositions of Christian theology in China or India, or in areas like the Middle East, where the crumbling of the social order unlooses the rage of masses and Stalinist ambition feeds on hunger and despair?

It is futile to expect religion to undertake the radical task of reorganizing the world. Its institutional practices are remote from such aims, and its doctrines have hardened in the mold of otherworldliness. In truth, we have nothing to go on but the rational disciplines of the secular mind as, alone and imperiled, it confronts its freedom in a universe stripped of supernatural sanctions. Chambers's melodramatic formula—God or Stalin?—is of no help to us in our modern predicament. He reproaches Western civilization for its "three centuries of rationalism." Now rationalism has its fallacies, to be sure, but is it fair to hold it to account for the horrors of the Russian police state, which has behind it not even one, much less three, centuries of rationalism? Soviet society bears the indelible stamp of the long Russian past of feudal-bureaucratic rule, an absolutist rule of the mind as of the body. Of course, the Marxist teaching is not exempt from censure for the consequences of the Revolution. It should be added, however, that this teaching, Western in its main origins and holding a heavy charge of Judaeo-Christian ethics, has suffered a strange metamorphosis in its Muscovite captivity. And now, in its movement deeper into the East, it is seized upon, with all the fervor of native absolutism, by the backward, semi-mendicant intelligentsia of the Asian countries. This intelligentsia, untrained in habits of social responsibility and unformed in the traditions of humanist and rationalist thought, has converted Marxism into a dogma of nothing less than incendiary content. Its detachment from the West is virtually complete.

Chambers allows for no modulations in his attacks on the rationalist and naturalist trends in Western culture. For him the only issue is atheism, even where the disorder is patently economic and social. His religious-political plea is made unconvincing by the very terms it is cast in, terms belonging to that type of religious conservatism which ordinarily finds its complement in political reaction. It may well be that the religious mind has a significant part to play in "the crisis of history," but the intervention of that mind will do religion no good if the Christian credentials are used to no better purpose than to consecrate, as the late Emmanuel Mounier put it, "the appeal to pre-existing ideas and established powers."

Mounier, a French Catholic thinker of radical tendency, saw with uncommon lucidity the dangers that threaten the religious mind in its turn to political projects. He protested against the idealist habit of thought by which the activity of men in nature and society is reduced to no more than a reflection of the spirit, and he warned against enlisting the religious tradition in defense of the conservative cult of the past—a defense by prestige which sooner or later exposes the defenders to vengeful blows. Not at all alarmed by the fact that his analysis of the present crisis coincided in some respects with that of the secular radicals, he kept a tight hold on the obvious truth which religionists generally appear to have great difficulty in keeping in mind—the inescapable truth that economic and social ills can only be cured by economic and social means, even if not by those means exclusively. "Christianity no longer holds the field," he wrote in his last book, *Personalism*. "There are other massive realities; undeniable values are emerging apparently without its help, arousing moral forces, heroisms, and even kinds of saintliness. It does not seem, for its own part, able to combine with the modern world . . . in a marriage such as it consummated with the medieval world. Is it, indeed, approaching its end? . . . . Perhaps the decomposing hulk of a world that Christianity built, that has now slipped its moorings, is drifting away, and leaving behind it the pioneers of a new Christianity."

Whether Mounier's hope for a "new Christianity" will be historically justified or not we do not know, but that he had a deep understanding of the discords experienced by the modern consciousness in relating itself to religious life there can be no doubt. He corrects the excesses of a writer like Chambers, whose illusion it is that he is serving religion by pulling down the image of man.

• Sartre versus Camus: A Political Quarrel

Nicola Chiaromonte

The news in Paris is the public break between Albert Camus and Jean-Paul Sartre on the issue of Communism. I hope *Partisan Review* readers will not think the fact that these two famous Parisian intellectuals could be aroused by such an issue to the point of ending a ten-year-old friendship is another sign of European belatedness. This polemic and this break are in fact a sign that in France ideas still count, and, more particularly, that French intellectuals cannot easily reconcile themselves to the divorce between principles and political life which has been the mark of the postwar years all over Europe. Moreover, the arguments exchanged between Camus and Sartre touch upon questions of general intellectual import. Finally, the Communist issue will be a live and significant one in Europe as long as the Communist parties retain their strength. The fact that they are still strong is not the fault of the intellectuals. And while the Communist issue is alive, it is worth the trouble to study its phenomenology.

At the origin of the Sartre-Camus clash, which occupies a good part of the August issue of *Les Temps Modernes*, there is *L'Homme Révolté*. With this book, Albert Camus attempted to do something that Jean-Paul Sartre has never found the time to do, namely to give an account of the reasons which led him to take the position he has taken with regard to the political ideologies of our time, and more particularly Communism. Camus had taken part in the Resistance as a writer and a journalist, he had been the editor of a daily paper after the Liberation; during this period he played a public role and took political stands. Having withdrawn from public life in order to devote himself to his writing, he felt that he was under the obligation of thinking through the ideas that he had been expressing in articles and speeches. In other words, he felt intellectually responsible for his political commitments, and attempted to live up to this responsibility. For this, if for nothing else, he deserves credit.

In the author's own words, *L'Homme Révolté* is intended to be "a study of the *ideological* aspect of revolutions." This has to be stressed because, as we shall see, the attack launched upon the book by *Les Temps Modernes* is all based on the assumption that Camus had meant his work to be primarily a political manifesto, if not a new *Das Kapital*. Briefly summarized, the main thesis of *L'Homme Révolté* runs as follows: (1) Nihilism, already implicit in the Jacobin myth of terroristic violence, has been brought to its extreme consequences by contemporary Communism. But nihilism is not exclusively a political phenomenon. It is rooted in the history of modern consciousness, and its origins can be traced back to such strange "revolts" against reality as Sade's, Lautréamont's, and Rimbaud's. Philosophically, the Hegelian notion of reality as "history" and of human action as a dialectical series of "historical tasks" knowing of no other law than their real-ization is one of the main sources of ideological nihilism. From Hegel, in fact, Marxist prophecy is derived, with the vision of a "happy end" of history for the sake of which, in Goethe's words, "everything that exists deserves to be annihi-lated." This is the aspect of Marx emphasized by Communist fanaticism at the expense of Marx's critical thought, simply because apocalyptic prophecy, being as it is beyond the pale of proof, is the surest foundation of a ruthless orthodoxy. (2) At this point, the revolutionary myth finds itself in absolute contradiction with man's impulse to revolt against oppression, leading to systematic enslavement rather than liberation. (3) By denying that human life can have a meaning aside from the "historical task" to which it must be made subservient, the "nihilist" must inevitably bring about and justify systematic murder. The contradiction between the revolutionist who accepts such a logic and the man who revolts against injustice in the name of the absolute value of human life is radical. And the very absurdity of this contradiction should convince the man who insists on acting for the sake of real humanity that he cannot escape the classical question of the "limit." To begin with, the limit of the idea of "revolt" is, according to Camus, the point where the idea becomes murderous. Contemporary ideologies, the revolutionary as well as the reactionary ones, are essentially murderous. Hence they must be refused once and for all, at the cost of one's being forced into what the ideologists call "inaction," but which in fact (except for the self-satisfied and the philistine) is a refusal of automatic action and an insistence on choice, real commitments, and the freedom to act according to authentic convictions on the basis of definite situations, rather than follow ideological deductions and organizational discipline.

This is a rather crude simplification of Camus' thesis. It should, however, be sufficient to indicate that, no matter how debatable the arguments and the con-clusions, the question raised by Camus is a serious one, and deserves to be dis-cussed seriously at least by those people today who, while not pretending to have at their disposal any new systematic certainty, are aware of the sterility of the old political dogmas. Let's notice in passing that until recently Jean-Paul Sartre was not unwilling to recognize that he belonged in the company of these people. As a matter of fact, he went so far as to write that the biggest party in France was that of those who abstained from voting, which proved how deep among the people was the disgust with the old parties, their methods, and their ideologies; a new Left, he added, should try to reach those masses.

An attentive reader of *L'Homme Révolté* will not fail to notice that, in his own peculiar language, and in terms of general ideas rather than of specific moral problems, Camus formulates against the modern world the same indictment as Tolstoy. For Camus, as for Tolstoy, modern society does not recognize any other norm than violence and the accomplished fact; hence it can legitimately be said that it is founded on murder. Which is tantamount to saying that human life in it has become a senseless affair. Tolstoy, however, believed that, besides retaining an "eternal" value, Christianity was still alive in the depths of our society among the humble; hence he thought that a radical Christian morality—nonviolence—could offer a way out. Camus is not religious, and much more skeptical than Tolstoy as to the moral resources of the modern world. He does not advocate nonviolence. He simply points out the reappearance, through nihilistic reduction to absurdity, of the need for a new sense of limit and of "nature."

No matter how uncertain one might consider Camus' conclusions, his attack on the modern ideological craze appears both strong and eloquent. Of course, if one believes in progress, one might still maintain that Nazism and Stalinism were the result of contingencies, factual errors, and residual wickedness. But progressive optimism is precisely the notion that Camus vigorously questions. His arguments cannot be easily dismissed by a philosophy like existentialism, which stresses so resolutely the discontinuity between human consciousness and any "process" whatsoever, and which in any case makes it very difficult to go back to the notion that man's ethical task is to "change the world" through historical action. This not only because the idea of "changing the world" is a radically optimistic one in that it presupposes precisely that fundamental harmony between man and the world which existentialism denies; but because only if man is "historical" through and through (as Hegel and Marx assumed) is the definition of a "historical task" possible at all. Now, the main existentialist claim was the rediscovery of an essential structure of human consciousness beyond historical contingencies. From this, going back to Hegel and Marx seems a rather difficult enterprise, one, in any case, that requires a lot of explaining.

Yet, lo and behold, in the first attack against *L'Homme Révolté* launched in the June issue of *Les Temps Modernes* by one of Sartre's faithful disciples, Francis Jeanson, this critic found no better line of attack than to accuse Camus of "antihistoricism." His arguments can be summarized as follows: (1) by rejecting the cult of History which seems to him characteristic of the nihilistic revolutions of our time, Camus places himself "outside of history" in the position of the Hegelian "beautiful Soul" which wants to remain pure of all contact with reality, and is satisfied with the reiteration of an abstract Idea void of all dialectical energy; (2) by criticizing Marxism and Stalinism, Camus accomplishes an "objectively" reactionary task, as proved by the favorable reviews of his book in the bourgeois press; (3) intellectual disquisitions are a fine thing, but the task (the "choice") of the moment makes it imperative to struggle in favor of the emancipation of the Indochinese and the Tunisians, as well as in defense of peace; this cannot be done effectively if one attacks the CP, which, at this particular moment, is the only force capable of mobilizing the masses behind such a struggle.

This was bad enough. Much worse and much sadder is the fact that, in his answer to Camus's "Letter to the Editor of *Les Temps Modernes*," Sartre himself did little more than restate his disciple's arguments.

In his "Letter," Albert Camus had addressed the following remarks, among others, to Sartre: "To legitimate the position he takes toward my book, your critic should demonstrate, against the whole collection of *Les Temps Modernes*, that history has a necessary meaning and a final outcome; that the frightful and disorderly aspect that it offers us today is sheer appearance, and that, on the contrary, in spite of its ups and downs, progress toward that moment of final reconciliation which will be the jump into ultimate freedom, is inevitable. . . . Only prophetic Marxism (or a philosophy of eternity) could justify the pure and simple rejection of my thesis. But how can such views be upheld in your magazine without contradiction? Because, after all, if there is no human end that can be made into a norm of value, how can history have a definable meaning? On the other hand, if history has meaning why shouldn't man make of it his end? If he did that, however, how could he remain in the state of frightful and unceasing freedom of which you speak? . . . . The truth is that your contributor would like us to revolt against everything but the Communist Party and the Communist state. He is, in fact, in favor of revolt, which is as it should be, in the condition (of absolute freedom) described by his philosophy. However, he is tempted by the kind of revolt which takes the most despotic historical form, and how could it be otherwise, since for the time being his philosophy does not give either form or name to this wild independence? If he wants to revolt, he must do it in the name of the same nature which existentialism denies. Hence, he must do it theoretically in the name of history. But since one cannot revolt in the name of an abstraction, his history must be endowed with a global meaning. As soon as this is accepted, history becomes a sort of God, and, while he revolts, man must abdicate before those who pretend to be the priests and the Church of such a God. Existential freedom and adventure is by the same token denied. As long as you have not clarified or eliminated this contradiction, defined your notion of history, assimilated Marxism or rejected it, how can we be deprived of the right to contend that, no matter what you do, you remain within the boundaries of nihilism?"

This is a stringent argument. Sartre did not answer it, except by insisting that "our freedom today is nothing but the free choice to struggle in order to become free," and that if Camus really wanted "to prevent a popular movement from degenerating into tyranny," he should not "start by condemning it without appeal." "In order to deserve the right to influence men who struggle," Sartre admonished, "one must start by participating in their battle. One must start by accepting a lot of things, if one wants to attempt to change a few." Which is, among other things, a theory of conformism, or at least of reformism, not of revolution and drastic change. Because if one "must start by accepting a lot of things" in order to change "a few," then why not begin by giving up wholesale notions such as "capitalism," "communism," the "masses," etcetera? If he had cared to answer further, Camus could easily have retorted that it was precisely the awareness that "one must start by accepting a lot of things" if one wants to obtain real changes that had persuaded him to give up ideological radicalism. While Sartre, for the sake of changing "a few things," is ready to swallow a totalitarian ideology plus a totalitarian organization.

One thing is certain: Sartre is more intelligent than that and knows much better. How can he then, in polemic with a man like Camus, imagine that he can get away with taking over the most ordinary kind of journalistic arguments?

The answer, I believe, must be found in the phenomenology of the amateur Communist, a type widespread in Europe today, especially among the intellectuals.

The first thing to say about the amateur Communist is that he is by no means a "fellow traveler." He does not receive either orders or suggestions from the Party; he does not belong to any "front organization," and, except for an occasional signature, he does not give any particular help to the Communist cause. What he is interested in is the defeat of the bourgeoisie and the victory of the proletariat. A truly independent Communist and, within the framework of the Communist *ideal*, a liberal, that is what he is. His points of contact with official Communism are two: (1) he considers it obvious that the Soviet Union is a socialist, that is, a fundamentally just, state; (2) for him, it is self-evident that the CP, being the party of the "masses," is also at bottom the party of social justice and peace. Hence he supports both these institutions in principle, but by no means on all counts. The totalitarian mentality is utterly foreign to him. As for the difficulties and ambiguities of his position, he is perfectly aware of them. But, precisely, "one must accept a lot of things, if one wants to change a few."

One would surmise that, being neither a Communist nor an anti-Communist, neither a totalitarian nor a liberal, and insisting as he does on the difficulty, if not the illegitimacy, of a resolute political stand, the amateur Communist should be a rather Hamletic character. At this point, however, we witness a remarkable phenomenon: the fact of participating (at a variable distance) in the massive intellectual universe of Communism (of being able, i.e., to use Communist arguments without subjecting himself to the rigid rules by which the militant Communist must abide) gives the amateur Communist a singular kind of assurance. Far from feeling uncertain, he feels very certain, and behaves as if his position were not only politically sound, but also guaranteed by the laws of logic, ethics, and philosophy in general, not to speak of history. Which amounts to saying that he enjoys both the prestige of the Communist uniform which he shuns and the advantages of the civilian clothes which he ostensibly wears. He considers himself "objectively" a Communist insofar as he embraces the proletarian cause, but "subjectively" a free man, since he does not obey any order from above. The last, and most refined, touch of such a character is the conviction he often expresses that, in case of a Communist victory, he will be among the first to be "liquidated." His heretical orthodoxy will thus receive even the crown of the martyrs. In what substantial way these refinements can further the cause of the oppressed is, on the other hand, a question that should not be asked. The important thing here is that the unhappy consciousness of this believer without faith should continue to feed on contradictions, since contradictions are to him *the* sign that he has a firm grip on real life.

A man of Sartre's talent cannot be forced into a "type." But the fact is that, since 1945, every time they took a stand on contemporary politics, he and his friends have been behaving more and more like amateur Communists. Worse still, they have been more and more satisfied with taking over the usual arguments of the Communist catechism, and this with an arrogant refusal to justify their position in terms of the philosophical tenets with which they fare so well. They have been behaving, that is, as if, once they had declared themselves in favor of the proletariat, the consistency of their ideas was a matter of automatic adjustment of which no account was due to "others." By so behaving, these philosophers have obviously fallen victim to the most intolerably dogmatic aspect of Communist mentality: the idea that being a resolute partisan can make short work of all questions.

The crudeness of the arguments used by Sartre against Camus cannot be explained if one does not assume that, having established an intellectual connection with the Marxist-Leninist-Stalinist mentality, he is intellectually dominated by it. Personally, of course, he remains independent. That is precisely why he, an intellectual, can be a victim of the delusion that intellectual assent has no intellectual consequences. But having reached the conclusion that "participation" in the Communist system is the most effective way to pacify his political conscience, it follows that the philosopher of "anguished freedom" participates in the moral smugness which the system guarantees to its proselytes. From moral smugness to intellectual arrogance the step is short indeed. Once one has adopted a certain logical system, it is of course absurd not to avail oneself of the arguments that, from such a point of view, are the most effective.

It remains that Jean-Paul Sartre has not answered Albert Camus.

The latest news has it that *Lettres Françaises* has offered the excommunicated Sartre a political alliance. It is unlikely that the editor of *Les Temps Modernes* will accept such an offer. He prizes independence too much. He will not give any direct help and comfort to the Communist Party. He will simply continue to spread the intellectual confusion by which the Communist Party benefits.

1952, vol. 19. no. 6

• The Oppenheimer Case: A Reading of the Testimony
Diana Trilling

Between June 2, 1954, when the Gray Board announced its findings in the Oppenheimer case, and June 30, when the Atomic Energy Commission published its decision not to grant clearance to Dr. Oppenheimer, the transcript of Dr. Oppenheimer's lengthy hearings before the Gray Board was unexpectedly released to the public [*In the Matter of J. Robert Oppenheimer: Transcript of Hearing Before Personnel Security Board*]. A gigantic volume, some thousand oversized pages of minute type, it is a document which asks for untold hours of close reading. Yet no one who has not studied it carefully can properly evaluate the final verdict which was passed upon Dr. Oppenheimer. It is not only that the evidence on the specific charges put forward by the Atomic Energy Commission cannot be assessed without recourse to the record. Even more important, it is impossible to form a sound judgment of Dr. Oppenheimer's situation without acquaintance with at least what the transcript tells us of the highly complicated context in which these charges were raised and explored.

First, there is the adversary nature of the hearings themselves. No loyalty inquiry is a trial, but neither was this inquiry a neutral investigation in which the Atomic Energy Commission, having been apprised of certain derogatory information about one of its employees, undertook to the best of its ability to command the whole evidence of his guilt or innocence. I am not implying that Dr. Oppenheimer was not given his full day in court—he most surely was. I am merely calling attention to the fact that the approach of the Atomic Energy Commission to the case was that of a prosecution. For instance, while all the defense witnesses appeared voluntarily or perhaps at the request of Dr. Oppenheimer's counsel, all the witnesses against Dr. Oppenheimer appeared by order of the Commission or of their superior officers in government service. That is, the Commission concerned itself to produce only such testimony as would help prove that Dr. Oppenheimer should be refused clearance. And Mr. Robb, lawyer for the Commission, addressed himself to the case entirely in this adversary spirit: it was his effort to elicit from his witnesses not the whole truth, whichever side it might serve, but solely such evidence as would discredit the defense. Ruthless and brilliant, Mr. Robb was a prosecuting attorney with a single-minded purpose, to achieve Dr. Oppenheimer's defeat.

In addition, the procedure employed in the hearings gave a large advantage to the Commission. In a trial, the prosecution would have to state its case first and the burden of proof would lie with it. In this inquiry, as, I gather, in all loyalty hearings, the defense bore the burden of proof. The defense was on the stand first and had to make its case without exact knowledge of the evidence that might be produced against it. Counsel for the Commission had access to all govern-ment files and documents, including Dr. Oppenheimer's own files from the period of his government service, and was allowed to produce them at will with-out first acquainting the defense with their existence and content. Then, when Dr. Oppenheimer's lawyers raised the conventional legal objections to this pro-cedure, they were made to seem unfriendly, even petulant and unreasonable: friendliness was demanded only of their side. Repeatedly and humiliatingly, Mr. Garrison and Mr. Silverman were reminded of the many courtesies to which they were responding with an insufficient gratitude.

The courtesies were of course there. It is not to be denied that Mr. Gray, as Chairman of the Board, not only made constant scrupulous reference to the rules under which the Board operated but was also explicitly conscious of the desirability of a certain generosity to the defense. In essence, however, the pro-cedural framework within which the Board worked made a mockery of cour-tesy—or so it seems to the reader like myself who has no legal training. It is also my impression that, for all his rather too-elaborate caution, Mr. Gray did not always succeed in rising above the ambiguous circumstances in which he had been placed. The procedural latitude permitted him by the legally unconven-tional circumstances of the inquiry inevitably licensed a large play of his per-sonality, and almost from the start of the hearings there appears a certain note of moral advantage in Mr. Gray's dealings with the defense which is not to be heard in his dealings with Mr. Robb. This unfortunate tone intensifies with the passage of the days until, near the close of the sessions, when Dr. Vannevar Bush is recalled as a rebuttal witness, Mr. Gray not only allows Mr. Robb to badger Dr. Bush as if he were a witness in a criminal trial but himself so far exceeds the situation as to address a distinguished member of the community as if he were a schoolboy.

As the Chairman, Mr. Gray was the most exposed member of the Board. The behavior of the other two members must be differently characterized. Mr. Morgan spoke scarcely a word throughout the inquiry; we know him only through the majority opinion in which he concurred. As to Dr. Evans, his ques-tions and remarks are hardly the more cogent for so obviously proceeding from a struggling mind and heart. His often comic and touching awkwardness before the momentous problem he is asked to consider are not reflected in his minority report, but they must be taken to account for its weakness.

No doubt it was necessary to have a scientist on the Board, and manifestly it must have been difficult to find a reputable member of the profession, other than Dr. Evans, who was sufficiently remote from the persons and issues in the con-troversy to qualify as without bias. For this is another, and surely the most signif-icant, element in Dr. Oppenheimer's investigation which cannot be appreciated without knowledge of the record—the professional in-fighting involved in it.

Thirty-nine witnesses appeared for and against Dr. Oppenheimer in the hearings and gave many long hours of testimony. Of the thirty-nine, only his wife was not professionally concerned in the affairs which concerned Dr. Oppenheimer. All the rest were either themselves scientists who had worked on government programs which also involved Dr. Oppenheimer, or military or other official persons closely connected with the scientific-military projects and policies which have engaged Dr. Oppenheimer over the last eleven years—in this latter group I include, of course, security officers who had had dealings with him, and government officials like Mr. Lilienthal and former Ambassador Kennan. There were no nonprofessional friends and acquaintances such as even the most dedicated man of science must number in his circle. There were no associates from the days of Dr. Oppenheimer's admitted Communist sympathies. (Curiously enough, Haakon Chevalier, who figures so largely in one of the major charges against Dr. Oppenheimer, was never called by either side.) Of the thirty-eight witnesses other than Mrs. Oppenheimer, only the three or four security officers had not either worked for or with Dr. Oppenheimer, or made policy with him, or tried to make policy in opposition to his views, or been professionally affirmed or hampered by his scientific-political attitudes. And even the security officers, having once had to formulate judgment on him, had positions to defend.

And this is to speak only of the witnesses we confront directly and not of the crucial part which, we learn, must have been played in Dr. Oppenheimer's case by persons who are never presented in the inquiry—Roosevelt, Truman, Senator MacMahon, General Vandenberg, General Doolittle, Air Force Secretary Finletter, Acheson, Bernard Baruch, Commissioner Strauss, Commissioner Murray: to name some of the most notable of them—and by professional groups who have no official spokesman before the Board. Even in advance of the hearings one had heard of considerable conflict between Admiral Strauss, Chairman of the Atomic Energy Commission, and Dr. Oppenheimer on the H-bomb issue and one had naturally assumed that Dr. Oppenheimer's situation involved disagreements at high policy levels. What the record adds to such elementary information while still leaving one with the conviction that the full inside story of the Oppenheimer case has not even begun to be disclosed and may indeed never be known to the public, is the realization that it was not alone one grave policy conflict in which Dr. Oppenheimer was caught but a whole vast tangle of personal, professional, and political animosities. The conflict between the H-bomb proponents and the H-bomb opponents is undoubtedly the climax of dissension but we cannot fail to be aware of the multitude of alignments and groupings, commitments and cross-purposes, all of which are unmistakably bound up with Dr. Oppenheimer's predicament. The scientific "ins" versus the scientific "outs," the friends of Dr. Oppenheimer versus the friends of Dr. Teller, the military versus the academics, the Air Force versus the Army and versus the Navy, the Strategic

Air Command versus the Air Defense Command, Los Alamos versus Livermore, MIT versus the University of Chicago, Dr. Oppenheimer the individual versus individuals of a dramatically different disposition of mind—scarcely a witness appears before the Board whose testimony does not point to one or more of the myriad oppositions whose existence and resolution must surely have been decisive in Dr. Oppenheimer's fate.

As good an example as any is the testimony of David Tressel Griggs, a geophysicist and witness for the Commission, who was chief scientific consultant to the Air Force and a close associate of Air Force Secretary Finletter from the fall of 1951 through June of 1952—the period in which Dr. Oppenheimer is accused by the Commission's witnesses of having in various ways demonstrated his advocacy of a military program that concentrated on continental defense at the sacrifice of our striking power against a foreign enemy, and of having failed to support a second laboratory, in addition to Los Alamos, for thermonuclear research but, instead, put his influence on the side of such enterprises as the Lincoln Summer Study which concerned itself with defensive warning systems and antisubmarine warfare. We do not have to assess the merit or lack of merit in a defensive military policy or even determine whether this is an accurate description of Dr. Oppenheimer's position—actually it is not—to recognize that if Mr. Griggs *thought* this was Dr. Oppenheimer's emphasis he would naturally and immediately be worried by its threat to the prestige of the Air Force. And if Mr. Griggs is quick to testify that the reason he watched Dr. Oppenheimer's views so closely was because both General Vandenberg and Mr. Finletter had told him that they had serious question of Oppenheimer's loyalty, he is equally unhesitant to discuss the more pressing cause for his worry about the Lincoln Summer Study. Himself an Air Force man, Mr. Griggs was deeply concerned because the Summer Study was being promoted and participated in by people who did not share his allegiance to that branch of the service. He was worried because the way it was being administered suggested the unhappy possibility that it might venture into such matters as budgetary allocation between the Strategic Air Command and the Air Defense Command and that its results might be reported directly to the National Security Council instead of to his chiefs. He was deeply disturbed that despite the fact that the Lincoln Project, of which the Study was a kind of offshoot, took 80 to 90 percent of its financial support from the Air Force, the Study planned in part to devote itself to submarine warfare.

But this barely suggests the nature of the professional and personal biases involved in Dr. Oppenheimer's case as they reveal themselves in the testimony of only a single witness. For example, there is the moment when Mr. Griggs is being crossexamined about the membership of a certain State Department panel with whose recommendations he differed. Citing the minutes of the panel as the source of his information, first Mr. Griggs mentions "Dr. Oppenheimer, Dr.

DuBridge, Dr. Bush, and others" as members. Asked to repeat the names, he mentions "Dr. Oppenheimer, Dr. DuBridge, Dr. Conant and others." (These are all, of course, defense witnesses.) Asked to repeat the names yet again, this time Mr. Griggs omits Dr. Conant's name and, questioned about the omission, acknowledges that his memory is not clear. Finally he is confronted with the information that Dr. DuBridge was not a member and that there are no minutes of the panel. As I shall presently indicate, Dr. Oppenheimer's own memory is no less fallible than Mr. Griggs's, though there will be an observable difference between the kind of judgment passed on Dr. Oppenheimer for his mistakes of recollection and the kind passed on Mr. Griggs for his. It is the pattern of error in Mr. Griggs's faulty memory that I call attention to here. Because the conclusions of the panel were of a sort with which he did not agree, Mr. Griggs gives the panel a composition of the sort with which he would not agree—the sort like Dr. DuBridge and Dr. Conant who could be presumed to have opinions like Dr. Oppenheimer's.

Or there is Mr. Griggs's testimony, under oath, that it was Dr. Zacharias (who initiated the Lincoln Summer Study) who told him what patently is a grave distortion of Dr. Oppenheimer's position, that Dr. Oppenheimer advocated giving up the Strategic Air Arm for the sake of world peace and, too, that it was Dr. Zacharias who wrote on the blackboard of a public meeting the letters ZORC to indicate that Zacharias, Oppenheimer, Rabi, and Charles Lauritsen were in such agreement that they could be thought of in this cabalistic form. Not only does Dr. Zacharias, also under oath, deny the fact that he ever wrote these letters on a blackboard but, of the fifty to a hundred persons supposedly present at the meeting, not one is produced by the prosecution to support Mr. Griggs's testimony.

Or there is Mr. Griggs's disconcerting evidence that in conversations with Commissioner Murray, Murray confirmed his suspicion that roadblocks were being put in the way of a second laboratory by Dr. Oppenheimer. One of Dr. Oppenheimer's final judges, Commissioner Murray was also—we keep it in mind—among the persons who launched the present investigation of Dr. Oppenheimer's loyalty. While there are witnesses for the defense, such as Mr. Gordon Dean or General McCormack Jr. or Professor Von Neumann of Princeton, who disagreed with Dr. Oppenheimer about the H-bomb but who yet firmly believe in his loyalty, there is not a single witness for the Commission who favored a second laboratory for H-bomb research who is also not flatly in the anti-Oppenheimer camp. The inference to be drawn must be obvious as to where at least this one of his judges stood in relation to Dr. Oppenheimer even before the hearings were held.

That, with this much *parti-pris*, there should be any objectivity at all on the part of the witnesses is, I suppose, a miracle. That, as I have indicated, the miracle occurs only among the witnesses for the defense is not surprising in view of their generally superior human quality. The reader must be warned, of course, against confusing amenity with disinterestedness. Still, style is its own form of morality and if the style of the defense witnesses—their taste and intellectual manners; the informing tone of their testimony—is by so much more impressive than the style of the Commission's witnesses, this cannot be dismissed as without bearing on their credibility. On Dr. Oppenheimer's side there is no one guilty of behavior like that, say, of Dr. Teller who, of all Dr. Oppenheimer's opponents, has most to gain in public prestige from Dr. Oppenheimer's downfall but who yet can permit himself to agree with the suggestion of Mr. Robb that Dr. Oppenheimer could go fishing for the rest of his life without being missed! There is no one, among the defense witnesses, to balance out the ugly impression left by the appearance of Mr. Borden for the purpose of reading into the record the letter he wrote to the FBI—a copy of which was received by the Atomic Energy Commission shortly before it suspended Dr. Oppenheimer's clearance—in which, without a shred of evidence to support it, Mr. Borden announced his opinion that Dr. Oppenheimer was a spy. Mr. Borden's letter includes this extraordinary statement: "While J. Robert Oppenheimer has not made major contributions to the advancement of science, he holds a respected professional standing among the second rank of American physicists." In an opposition of such low quality inevitably we remark a bottom-dog hostility which may once have been matched by the top-dog arrogance which we hear ascribed to Dr. Oppenheimer. But hostility intimates, as arrogance never does, a motivation too personal to be trusted. And if indeed Dr. Oppenheimer was once arrogant, this is no longer observable in the record. Perhaps he has been much chastened, but now all we read in his behavior is a decent pride.

Of course in any society, and particularly in our own, a distinction like Dr. Oppenheimer's is not easily borne, not even by the person who is himself so generously endowed—there is more than a trace of apology for his unique gifts in Dr. Oppenheimer's autobiographical letter in reply to Mr. Nichols' letter of notification suspending his clearance. It is expectable enough that the witnesses who appear at the inquiry on Dr. Oppenheimer's behalf are themselves, most of them, greatly distinguished men well known far beyond their own professions—Vannevar Bush, James Conant, Gordon Dean, Oliver Buckley, K. T. Compton, John J. McCloy, ex-Ambassador Kennan, Fermi, Rabi, Von Neumann. But what is no less expectable, I suppose, and yet peculiarly dismaying is the fact that Dr. Oppenheimer's personal powers, his influence on his associates and his persuasiveness, are offered by those who oppose him as supporting evidence of his dangerousness to the national security, and especially as we come to see the degree to which the investigation of his loyalty rests, not so much on factual evidence, as on interpretation—and I mean interpretation by the witnesses as well as by the judges: there is scarcely a witness in the hearings who does not tell us what Dr. Oppenheimer must have been thinking or what he would necessarily think under given circumstances. In Dr. Oppenheimer's situation, that is, the unhappier human motives are not merely a comment on the human disposition but also an important clue to the nature of the dilemma.

As I say, one had heard reports of a sharp cleavage between Commissioner Strauss and Dr. Oppenheimer on the H-bomb decision. One had even heard that the loyalty charge against Dr. Oppenheimer had been revived by powerful adversaries in and around the Atomic Energy Commission in order to destroy his power. Rumor is now given most uncomfortable substance as we study the record and begin to understand the kind of interest Dr. Oppenheimer challenged, both as a personality and a policy maker, and the strength of personal and professional feeling which might very well have dictated his elimination from the scientific-military community. After all, the fact of Dr. Oppenheimer's past association with Communist activities was hardly news in 1953 and '54. It was no news even in 1943, when Dr. Oppenheimer was put in charge of Los Alamos. And the record frequently reminds us that in 1947 there was another loyalty check-up on him, and Dr. Oppenheimer was cleared by the Atomic Energy Commission. Yet now, more than six years later, his case is reopened and not on the basis of significant new evidence against him—most of what is new and significant that can now be charged against Dr. Oppenheimer was discovered or established in the hearings and was not sufficiently known to the Commission to have compelled a reinvestigation—but, at best, on the basis of making security doubly sure according to the latest security rulings. Inevitably, seeking an explanation of why what might have been handled as a routine check-up was launched like a full-scale manhunt, we are returned to the history of the last six years of scientific-military development in the United States and, most crucially, to the year 1949 when our scientific-military community broke into the two warring camps which would seem now to have met in final battle.

It was in the fall of 1949, we remember, that Russia exploded an A-bomb and that a group of distinguished physicists, Dr. Teller chief among them, immediately sprang into action with a program for pursuit of a superweapon with which to outdistance the Soviet Union. They were supported by a certain section of the academic world and certain branches and persons in the military and in government. On the other side, opposed to a crash program for the H-bomb, was a group of scientists of whom Dr. Oppenheimer is described as "the most experienced, most powerful, and most effective"; this group also had the support of certain government persons. Dr. Oppenheimer was then Chairman of the General Advisory Committee of the Atomic Energy Commission. In October 1949 this Committee met and although it encouraged further research into thermonuclear reactions, it made strong recommendation against a hydrogen weapon. This was a tremendous blow to the H-bomb proponents. They had to wait for a presidential decision before being able to carry forward their program, and even then, according to the allegations in Mr. Nichols's letter of notification and of the Teller group in the hearings, although Dr. Oppenheimer no longer voiced opposition to the pursuit of a hydrogen weapon, he failed to support the effort with sufficient enthusiasm and therefore seriously hampered its progress. President Truman's order to proceed with the crash program came in January 1950. A few months later Dr. Oppenheimer, because he felt that it was perhaps not appropriate for him to continue as chairman of a committee engaged on a program which he had disapproved, offered his resignation as Chairman of the General Advisory Committee to Mr. Gordon Dean, then Chairman of the Commission. Mr. Dean refused the resignation. In company with other members of the Committee who had shared his position on the H-bomb, Dr. Oppenheimer continued as adviser to a program in which he had not concurred but which was now ordered by the President.

This, most briefly and in terms only of the public record, is what is behind the Oppenheimer case. In barest outline, it summarizes a policy division the statement and interpretation of whose details take up, I should say, some two-thirds of the transcript of the Gray Board investigation. The history of Dr. Oppenheimer's attitudes toward thermonuclear research ever since the start of Los Alamos; the degree to which Dr. Oppenheimer might have been responsible for the attitudes of his colleagues and the extent to which his disagreements might conceivably have hampered the efforts of the thermonuclear group; the projects on which Dr. Oppenheimer engaged himself which can be interpreted as diversions from the main thermonuclear goal; the military policies which Dr. Oppenheimer is said to have advocated which differed from the policies of other scientific advisers to the military—all these are the subject of many long days of reasoning and conjecture before the Gray Board, the testimony in which we discover the conflicting scientific and military views and the personal and professional friendships and animosities which are at once the fascination and the horror of Dr. Oppenheimer's peculiar tragedy.

We recall that in Mr. Nichols's letter of notification there were some two dozen specific items of derogatory information about Dr. Oppenheimer—that he had been a sponsor of the Friends of the Chinese People, that he had been a member of the Western Council of the Consumers Union, that his wife had been formerly married to a Communist and herself briefly a member of the Communist Party, that his brother had been a Communist, that his brother's wife had been a Communist, etc., etc. Among these allegations we remember there appeared a group of four or five points which dealt with Dr. Oppenheimer's relation to the H-bomb. Quite properly, I think, when the Gray Board announced its findings, it took up each of these specific items seriatim, including those which had reference to the H-bomb issue. In fact, the Gray report devoted what looked at the time, before the transcript of the inquiry was available to the public, like a rather disproportionate amount of space to Dr. Oppenheimer's attitudes on the hydrogen weapon. The public reaction to this part of the Gray report was intensely unfavorable. Liberal sentiment was outraged that in a democracy a man should be condemned because his opinions differed from what came to be ruling opinion—for this was how the public interpreted the Gray Board's evaluation of Dr. Oppenheimer's attitudes in the H-bomb controversy.

This experience of the public response to the Gray report behind it, the Atomic Energy Commission was far more cautious than the Gray Board had thought to be. With an impressive show of democratic conscience, it ruled the matter of Dr. Oppenheimer's opinions on the H-bomb out of the discussion of his fitness for clearance. It is nevertheless my belief, on my reading of the record, that whatever pitfalls the Gray Board was led into by its attempt to deal with Dr. Oppenheimer's attitude toward the H-bomb, it was at least honest in trying to reach a conclusion on this most considerable aspect of the case. On the other hand, the Atomic Energy Commission, in steering clear of the disagreeable charge of punishing a man for his opinions, evaded the very issue in which, I believe, its differences with Dr. Oppenheimer and its suspicions of him had crystallized. For while the two parts of the Commission's case against Dr. Oppenheimer—(1) his Communist associations, his character, and his discretion and (2) his attitude toward the H-bomb—can now be separated as the Commission has separated them, the record of the inquiry leaves no doubt in my mind but that the two parts were intimately connected in the Commission's formulation of its action against Dr. Oppenheimer. Indeed, I am wholly persuaded that it was precisely because of Dr. Oppenheimer's differences with the H-bomb enthusiasts, with all the conflicts of personality that this dissension aggravated, that his Communist past was reopened and the question of his loyalty revived.

Now, if this is so, it is obvious that motive is immediately and most importantly called into question. Is there, we must ask, anything in Dr. Oppenheimer's Communist past to account for his opposition to the H-bomb and to warrant the suspicion that his scientific-military opinions were improperly motivated? Or is improper motive to be ascribed, not to Dr. Oppenheimer, but to those who oppose him?

I am frank to confess that from the preconceptions of a conventional anti-Stalinist position, the view I first took of this aspect of Dr. Oppenheimer's case was that Dr. Oppenheimer, once an admitted fellow-traveler, had favored the fiercest possible weapon which would presumably be used against Germany or Japan but had opposed the fiercest possible weapon which would presumably be used against Russia. On this line of reasoning I had concluded that Dr.

Oppenheimer's opposition to the H-bomb was wrongly motivated. The transcript has now profoundly altered this earlier view. It is now my opinion that Dr. Oppenheimer's former political attitudes are wholly irrelevant to his H-bomb position, and that the reason he was reinvestigated was because he represented a way of thinking and perhaps even of being which was antipathetic to a dominant faction and because the political climate of our times had prepared an appropriate ground for his defeat.

In large part this change in my view is dictated by the knowledge which the record gives us, which I have already tried to suggest, of the intense factionalism involved in Dr. Oppenheimer's case and of the range and quality of the hostilities which surrounded the professional divisions. But it is also influenced by the clear light which the record sheds on the nature of Dr. Oppenheimer's opposition to a thermonuclear weapon and its evidence of the variety both of judgments and political backgrounds which could meet on his side of the controversy.

The allegation in Mr. Nichols's letter that Dr. Oppenheimer opposed the H-bomb on moral grounds by claiming that it was not feasible, by claiming that there were insufficient facilities and scientific personnel to carry on the development, and on the ground that is was not politically desirable, is misleadingly simple. Actually, Dr. Oppenheimer's position involved a combination of very complex and subtle moral, political, strategic, and technical considerations, none of which can be understood except in relation to the others and to the state of scientific development at the time of the dispute. In 1949, although development in the fission field had far surpassed our accomplishments during the war, there was no knowledge of whether a thermonuclear weapon was even possible within the laws of nature. In order to follow the few poor leads which were then available in the fusion field, it looked as if there would have to be diverted from the further perfecting and production of fission weapons so much material and personnel that this area of development would be seriously damaged—and in the pursuit of an idea which one did not know would ever be feasible. Added to this question of whether the concerted effort to reach so uncertain a goal was worth its cost in diminished strength in the A-bomb field there was a question whether the super-weapon, *if* it could be produced, was in itself a sufficient addition to our arsenal to have validated its pursuit. Would it be deliverable in terms that made it strategically useful, against what kind of target would it be effective, what would it accomplish that could not as well or better be accomplished by a large enough number of varied atomic weapons such as we were already producing so efficiently? It was Dr. Oppenheimer's opinion, shared by many experts, that from a purely technological-strategic point of view, the gamble was a bad one.

And this scientific-military position was implemented by a moral-political position. Our efforts for the international control of atomic weapons, in which Dr. Oppenheimer had played a major role, had failed. Was the answer to start a race with Russia for even more destructive weapons? It was Dr. Oppenheimer's reasoning that if atomic weapons were ever to be outlawed, certainly this was less likely to be accomplished in the atmosphere of prodigious new research for a still worse bomb than the A-bomb; and in the meanwhile we might lose our present lead over Russia in the A-bomb field. Further—and this was an aspect of the argument which was stressed even more by former Ambassador Kennan and other defense witnesses than by Dr. Oppenheimer himself—the result of a crash program for a thermonuclear weapon would be that both the public and the government would tend to substitute military thinking for political thinking, with disastrous effect on our democratic allies.

In other words, neither pacifism nor tenderness for the Soviet Union animated Dr. Oppenheimer's moral and political considerations. And in every reason for his opposition to the crash program he was supported by persons of the greatest variety of political attitudes and background. Whereas before I read the transcript I had supposed that it was only the "liberal-progressives" among the scientists, all of them more or less formed by the same political culture which had bred Dr. Oppenheimer, who joined him in his opposition to the super weapon, the record convinces me that this was not so. There was Oliver Buckley, for instance, the now retired Chairman of the Board of the Bell Telephone Laboratories and previously President of the Bell Telephone Laboratories, who opposed production of the H-bomb in 1949 solely on the ground that you do not pursue a production program before you know there is something producible. There was Dr. Robert Bacher, an upstate Republican, who after helping assess the Russian atomic explosion still believed that an H-bomb was little addition to our arsenal. There was Hartley Rowe, Vice President and Director of the United Fruit Company, who opposed a crash program for the superweapon until we should more nearly have perfected the military potentialities of the A-weapons and who also took the position that no people can go from one awful weapon to another without losing all normal perspective on their relations with other countries. There was Sumner T. Pike, Chairman of the Public Utilities Commission of Maine, who was against the H-bomb because at the time we had no knowledge the military needed such a weapon, because of the cost of producing tritium, because a smaller weapon might get more efficiency, and because there are benefits as well as destruction to be got from fission but only destruction from fusion. The list can be extended.

The weight of evidence, in short, is conclusive that it was perfectly possible to oppose the H-bomb without being influenced either by Dr. Oppenheimer himself, great as his powers of persuasion are said to be, or by Soviet sympathy. This is not to say, of course, that Dr. Oppenheimer *could* not have come to his own views for the wrong reasons. But this would have to be proved, and it is never proved in the record. We can be sure that, had it been, the Atomic Energy Commission would not have dropped this aspect of the case from its final decision. We remember, indeed, that even the Gray Board was able only to affirm the nature of Dr. Oppenheimer's opinions in this area and disapprove of Dr. Oppenheimer for holding them. While the Gray report leaves the impression that perhaps there was a tie between Dr. Oppenheimer's Communist past and his dissident scientific-military views, it does not even describe, let alone prove, a connection.

Thus the case against Dr. Oppenheimer's fitness for clearance which, it seems indicated, was reopened by the Atomic Energy Commission because of the fact and personal-professional consequences of his opposition to the H-bomb was closed by the Atomic Energy Commission on wholly other ground. It was closed on the ground only of Dr. Oppenheimer's character, discretion, and associations. We must turn, therefore, to what in point of evidential emphasis is so minor a part of the record but what is so major a part in point of the resolution of Dr. Oppenheimer's case, the items upon which the Commission finally rested its decision not to grant clearance to Dr. Oppenheimer.

II

While it was no surprise to the educated American public that Dr. Oppenheimer had at some time in his past, and perhaps even into the period of his highly sensitive government employment, been a fellow-traveler of the Communist Party, the publication of Mr. Nichols's letter of notification in the newspapers—it was of course released to the public by the defense—came as a considerable shock in even the most knowing anti-Communist liberal circles because of its disclosure of the apparent extent of Dr. Oppenheimer's Communist involvement. There was great force simply in the number of suggestive items mentioned in the Commission's notice. This first blow was much softened, however, by Dr. Oppenheimer's reply to Mr. Nichols, released to the public at the same time. To the sophisticated eye, Dr. Oppenheimer's autobiographical letter, with its careful account of his movement from an extreme of naïveté to political good sense, was far from reassuring on the score of his present political comprehension. Nevertheless, overriding the political story, there was the purely human story— dignified and poignant—which conspicuously confirmed his decency and probity, and this despite one or two taints of what looked like disingenuousness, such as his reference to *Harper's* and *Time* rather than *The Nation* and *New Republic* as typical of the magazines with which, in his remoteness from the world, Dr. Oppenheimer had had no acquaintance until the economic depression of the thirties brought him to political awareness.

Dr. Oppenheimer's letter also admirably sustained the Oppenheimer legend as it had grown up over the years. Ever since Los Alamos, Dr. Oppenheimer had of course been something of a culture hero for American intellectuals, especially for literary intellectuals—our contemporary scene does not offer many figures so exciting and sympathetic to the humanistic imagination as this most theoretical of physicists so apt for decisiveness in practical affairs, this genius of science who knows how to read and write English, this lean handsome aristocrat bred in the indulgent Jewish middle class, this remote man of civilization called from the academy into the fiercest of worlds—a world of inventions to destroy civilization—only to return at will into that purest of academies, the Institute for Advanced Study at Princeton. In identification with Oppenheimer, the American intellectual had been able to identify himself with a society whose most elaborate effort it had been to reconcile individual freedom with governmental responsibility, whose peculiar torment it had been to cherish the private gift while subduing it to the social need and will. And this identification remained unbroken, it was even fortified, by Dr. Oppenheimer's sketch of his life. From the story Dr. Oppenheimer told, the sensitive reader could already determine, even before the hearings had started, that its author was fated to suffer as much for his virtue as for his error, since they were so completely of a piece—which is always the character of the honest radical intellectual. The political history Dr. Oppenheimer traced in his autobiography was, indeed, the almost archetypical political history of the idealistic temperament of his generation: any number of its readers could find themselves in it.

Not that this was Dr. Oppenheimer's own view of his past. What is probably most special about his political story as Dr. Oppenheimer recounts it is his own belief that it is so very special. Dr. Oppenheimer tells us, for instance, that before his first essays into radicalism he was living so removed from the world that he had no telephone or radio and read no newspapers or magazines, and he proposes this as an unparalleled lack of preparation for his political awakening. But actually, nothing could be more typical of his time than the intellectual's separation from the concerns of his nation and the world—who among Dr. Oppenheimer's intellectual contemporaries, albeit he did have a radio and telephone and did take a daily newspaper, was better prepared than Dr. Oppenheimer for the political developments of the thirties? Dr. Oppenheimer may have exercised more literally than others of his generation the intellectual's right, so loudly enunciated in a previous decade, to be above the social battle, but he was no more politically handicapped and no more prone to the illusion of salvation by Communism. Here alter a date, there adjust the degree of leftist leaning, and Dr. Oppenheimer's political story is the story of countless highminded persons of liberal impulse who came to maturity with him.

Nor does the fact that Dr. Oppenheimer made his first affirmative political gestures at a time when there were those of his contemporaries who had already learned the whole miserable lesson of Communist perfidy—the part played by the German Communists in bringing Hitler to power; the part played by the

Communists in the Spanish Civil War—and that he was still a fellow-traveler when others of his generation had already learned that a staunch anti-Communism was the great moral-political imperative of our epoch, support any moral judgment against him. It merely attests to the different rates of evolution measurable in the lives of the modern liberal intellectual.

If we are moved to judge Dr. Oppenheimer harshly because he was so slow in seeing the error of the Communist way, it is well to remind ourselves that the speed with which a fellow-traveler breaks with Communism is not necessarily a guarantee of moral and intellectual superiority. A quick disillusionment with the Communist Party can reflect just the opposite of a person's innocence of intense connection with Communism; it can testify to his onetime closeness to the Party. It is the person who came late and who was *not* intimately associated with the Party who is likely to have stayed longest.

What I mean is this: Before the Spanish War, in the worst days of the Depression, it was the usual thing that a fellow-traveler thought of himself as in some degree a Marxist or as in some degree committed to the idea of proletarian revolution. His conviction need not be sufficiently strong to have carried him to Party membership. Nevertheless, he was soon close to the inner workings of the Communist Party, for in this period the Party overtly participated even in its inno-cents' groups. By the mid-thirties, however, the picture had altered. The worst days of our economic depression were past, and the fellow-traveler no longer thought in terms of revolution; a major renovation of our social-economic system no longer seemed mandatory. This was the period of the so-called Popular Front, when a fellow-traveler committed himself not to Marxism but only to antifascism or peace or some other decent abstract ideal virtually indistinguishable from the traditional ideals of liberalism, and this was the period in which the Communist Party learned to keep a safe distance from the gullible souls it was manipulating to its own purposes. Even the fellow-traveler who, like Dr. Oppenheimer, went to private meetings addressed by Communist functionaries or gave money directly to a Party person need know nothing of the Party in its actual function-ing. Indeed, he could be fully engaged in Communist-controlled affairs and yet be honestly persuaded that he was only a left-democrat, and it would not be until he came to a precise recognition of the nature of the Soviet Union and to the real-ization that his sympathy for the Spanish loyalists or for migratory workers or his antifascist activities were being used to serve the ends of the Soviet Union that he would learn the true import of his leftist associations.

It is of the utmost relevance to his defense and its greatest misfortune that Dr. Oppenheimer, who was *par excellence* the Popular Front fellow-traveler, seems to know so little of the various stages through which a fellow-traveler was likely to have passed and that he has such a poor comprehension of the inevitable part played in the evolution of the radicalized intellectual by idealization of the Soviet Union. As he tries to explain his past, both in his autobiographical letter and in the hearings, we see him floundering to make sense of what he feels *should* make sense but of which he has patently missed the main thread. Thus he tells us that first he disliked Russia and that then he slowly came to realize that the American Communist Party was controlled by Russia, when what he should really have said of himself is that although he was slow to realize that the American Communist Party was controlled by Russia and could therefore continue to think that it was free to pursue its stated objectives, he was even slower to recognize the truth about Russia. He cites his dislike of the Russian purges, the Nazi pact, the plight of the Russian people as evidence of his early disenchantment with Russia, without realizing that even the most profound disapproval of certain aspects of the Soviet performance does not constitute a proper knowledge of the nature of the Soviet Union—all fellow-travelers disapprove of certain aspects of the Soviet performance. He fails to understand that there is but a single criterion of a proper knowledge of the nature of the Soviet Union—the awareness that the Soviet Union is a totalitarianism as absolute as that of Nazi Germany—and that it is only when one knows that Russia is a totalitarianism that one also knows how impossible it is for a local Communist party to be free to pursue its own objectives or to have ascribed to it any decency of purpose.

Those who have been working closely with Dr. Oppenheimer in the last few years assure us—and his testimony amply supports this—that today he is perfectly clear that the Soviet Union is a totalitarianism and that whoever helps a Communist cause is helping totalitarianism. But he is completely ignorant of the slow stages by which his knowledge came to him, and this ignorance, shared by his lawyers, is the source of innumerable contradictions in the defense he offers. For instance at the start of the inquiry both Dr. Oppenheimer and his counsel speak at greatest length to try to establish the fact of his loyalty to America. Document after document is introduced to prove that the defendant is a patriotic citizen with a well-defined anti-Soviet position. Typical is an excerpt from an issue of *Foreign Affairs* in which Dr. Oppenheimer writes: "The second aspect of our policy which needs to be mentioned is that, while these proposals [about atomic control] were being developed and their soundness explored and understood, the very bases for international cooperation between the United States and the Soviet Union were being eradicated by a revelation of their deep conflicts of interest, the deep and apparently mutual repugnance of their ways of life, and the apparent conviction on the part of the Soviet Union of the inevitability of conflict." The date of this document is January 1948, and it is clear that the period Dr. Oppenheimer is discussing is the previous year and a half—the period since the autumn of 1946 when the Baruch plan was submitted to the United Nations Atomic Energy Commission and rejected by Russia and her satellites. But if this "revelation" came to Dr. Oppenheimer only so late, it must be obvious that the ground on which he would have assessed Communists and Communism during the war and immediately after the war was far from as firm as he now imagines it was. What kind of dislike of Russia is Dr. Oppenheimer alluding to, we must ask, which did not include an understanding that her interests were deeply in conflict with ours and that her way of life was deeply repugnant to the democratic way? How *could* a meaningful dislike of Russia such as Dr. Oppenheimer now ascribes to himself have predated his break with Communism, as he says it did, if he broke with Communism early in the forties and yet could be surprised by the behavior of the Soviet Union in 1946 and 1947?

These are not academic questions. They lie at the heart of the bad case Dr. Oppenheimer and his lawyers make for him. Political ignorance is the quintessential weakness of Dr. Oppenheimer's defense.

And this weakness is not lost on counsel for the Commission. In the first hours of crossexamination Mr. Robb has addressed enough questions to Dr. Oppenheimer on what he thought about Communists and Communism at what specific dates to get him into a trap from which he can never extricate himself. I do not mean that Mr. Robb, or, for that matter, any of Dr. Oppenheimer's judges, need be supposed to have a clearer understanding of Dr. Oppenheimer's political development than Dr. Oppenheimer himself has—as I shall presently indicate, much of United States policy and enlightened public opinion during the Roosevelt administration rested on misapprehensions of the nature of the Soviet Union similar to Dr. Oppenheimer's, and history has not yet adequately correlated for most politically conscientious Americans the connection between our lack of realism about Russia and the specific mistakes we made. But his own historical unawareness enables Mr. Robb, with honesty, to interpret Dr. Oppenheimer's confusion as evasion or downright untruthfulness and to take the fullest possible advantage of it.

And Dr. Oppenheimer's counsel are totally unequipped to help their client in this area where he desperately needs assistance; indeed, they confound confusion. The defense made by Mr. Garrison and his colleagues is certainly no pro-Communist defense. But neither is it an anti-Communist defense of a knowledgeableness such as the situation demands. It is a typical liberal-progressive defense with all this implies of unwillingness or unreadiness to make a close year-by-year appraisal of the evolving relationship, over the last two decades, between the typical liberalism of our time and the Soviet Union. The result of this political inadequacy, shared by Dr. Oppenheimer and his lawyers, is that Dr. Oppenheimer's honesty is impugned where it might have been most affirmed and his simplicity in confessing past mistakes, instead of ringing a note of sincerity, sounds like manipulation or inverse vanity. Most serious of all, because they lack the intellectual framework for comprehending his political conduct, Dr.

Oppenheimer and his lawyers are unable to defend him as they should against concrete charges.

We must keep it in mind that Dr. Oppenheimer's clearance was finally denied him on grounds of character and associations. On the issue of associations, the Commission rests the weight of its decision on the charge that Dr. Oppenheimer has continuing association with Communists, as evidenced by the fact that he has associated with Haakon Chevalier as recently as 1953. (I shall return to this point presently.) On the issue of character there are six charges:

1. In the matter of the Chevalier-Eltenton incident, he is charged with either having lied to Federal officers in 1943, as he says he did, or of lying today. (The implication being, of course, that he is lying today.) This incident concerns an approach to Dr. Oppenheimer in 1943 by Haakon Chevalier on behalf of George Eltenton for the purpose of obtaining scientific information for Russia. Dr. Oppenheimer rejected Chevalier's overture but did not report the approach until some months after it took place, and when he did finally speak of it to Colonel Pash of Military Intelligence and Colonel Lansdale, security officer at Los Alamos, he told a story which he now says was a tissue of lies except for the mention of Eltenton—he reported that an unnamed contact, operating for Eltenton and with access to microfilm and the Soviet consulate, had approached three persons on the project. That is, Dr. Oppenheimer suppressed Chevalier's part in the approach and his own, multiplied himself into three people, and mentioned only Eltenton. It was not until General Groves said he would order him to divulge the name of the contact that Dr. Oppenheimer identified Chevalier and even then he failed to correct his original story that the approach had been made to three people.

2. It is charged against him that although he now testifies that had he known in October 1943 that Lomanitz was a Communist he would not have supported his desire to return to the atomic project, official transcripts of earlier interviews show that in August 1943 he told Colonel Pash that Lomanitz had given information about the project and in September 1943 he told Colonel Lansdale he knew Lomanitz was a Communist.

3. It is charged against him that although he now testifies that he had met Rudy Lambert perhaps a half-dozen times prior to 1943, including one or two luncheon meetings in which he discussed with Lambert and another Communist functionary his contributions to the Communist cause, in 1943 he told Colonel Lansdale that he did not know Lambert or what he looked like.

4. It is charged against him that in 1949 Dr. Oppenheimer testified in a closed session of the Congressional Committee about the Communist activities of Dr. Peters but that when a summary of this testimony appeared in a Rochester

newspaper, Dr. Oppenheimer wrote a letter to that newspaper in effect contradicting his previous testimony.

5. It is charged against him that although before the meeting of the General Advisory Committee in October 1949 at which the Committee recommended against the H-bomb Dr. Oppenheimer had had a letter from Dr. Seaborg, the one absent member, voicing agreement with the thermonuclear program, he did not mention Dr. Seaborg's position in his report of this meeting to the Commission and now testifies that the Committee was "surprisingly unanimous" and that he had no way of knowing the opinion of Dr. Seaborg.

6. It is charged against him that although he told an FBI agent in 1950 that he had not known that Joseph Weinberg was a member of the Communist Party until that fact became public knowledge, there is proof that in 1943 he told Colonel Lansdale that Weinberg was a Communist Party member.

On first glance, perhaps even on second and third glance, it is not a pretty picture these charges paint. Even if we rule out of our minds, as the Commission ruled out of its decision, the entire matter of Dr. Oppenheimer's position on the H-bomb and confront only these specific points on which the Commission decided against clearance, the conclusion would seem warranted that Dr. Oppenheimer was condemned on rather substantial evidence against him. The Chevalier-Eltenton incident seems particularly damaging; and, indeed, it is this charge which has given the strongest support to popular sentiment where it has agreed with the decision of the Commission.

It is my own reaction to the Chevalier-Eltenton incident, however, that I find in it support not for the case against Dr. Oppenheimer but only for the case against the conduct of his defense. The record of the hearings leaves little doubt in my mind that Dr. Oppenheimer's sympathy with the Communist movement, in the period of his admitted participation in Communist activities, was rather greater than he now likes to think. But it leaves even less doubt in my mind that his sympathy, in whatever attenuated form, with both the Communist movement and the Soviet Union remained with him far longer than he now realizes. It is my belief that if Dr. Oppenheimer and his lawyers had fully comprehended these historical facts, the outcome of his hearings, at least so far as the findings of the Gray Board are concerned, might have been very different.

Let us supply, for a moment, certain background material to the Chevalier-Eltenton incident which is so disastrously missing from the record. The transcript shows us that in discussion of this episode, the Board frequently raised the question of whether a man is to be trusted with secret information who puts friendship above the security of his country: the point refers to Dr. Oppenheimer's explanation that, like an idiot, he withheld Chevalier's name from security officers and even fabricated a whole tissue of lies about Chevalier's approach to him because of his reluctance to implicate his friend and also himself. But Dr. Oppenheimer's explanation here seems to me to be clearly a misapprehension, or a seriously incomplete comprehension, of his own motives. Obviously he would have wanted to protect his friend and himself, but this does not necessarily mean that self-interest or friendship was his only or even major concern. It is my opinion that it was not loyalty to a friend which Dr. Oppenheimer put above loyalty to his country but loyalty to that amorphous but compelling entity called "the movement." It was, if you will, loyalty to his own still-recent past.

In 1943, America had been at war for two years, and Dr. Oppenheimer was completely identified with the patriotic effort. He no longer thought of himself as committed to the radical movement, he was committed to America. But still he must have retained, as every radical does in the long period of weaning himself away from his former ties, a certain loyalty to what he might have described as the radical spirit. Not unless his break with Communism is sudden and violent, and sometimes not even then, does the former Communist or fellow-traveler immediately free himself of all the emotions which once attached to the radical cause. In fact, there is nothing he fears more than that in his separation from his former commitments he will go to the other political extreme and become a reactionary. Almost inevitably, for a long time he retains an unfounded, unspecified loyalty to some generalized radical idea, if only to prove to himself that he has not betrayed that good part of his own past which first brought him to Communism.

This is very different, however, from a sympathy with one's own radical past which would embrace tolerance of overt anti-American action on the part of a Communist, such as was represented for Dr. Oppenheimer by George Eltenton. Dr. Oppenheimer did report Eltenton to the government because he suspected Eltenton of being a spy. He had no reason—he tells us—from his knowledge of Chevalier to suspect that Chevalier was a spy. It is my reconstruction of Dr. Oppenheimer as he was in 1943 that he would have considered himself not merely a disloyal friend—that would not have been so important to him—but a disloyal human being—disloyal, that is, to the idealistic aspect of his former radicalism and to himself—had he named Chevalier without being forced to. It is also my belief that he felt he had totally discharged the duties of patriotism and conscience while at the same time retaining his self-respect when, on his own initiative, he directed the Federal officers to Eltenton.

As to the embroidery around the story he told—the gratuitous mention of microfilm and the fanciful multiplication of himself into three persons—these additions I do not find either as inexplicable or as naive as they now seem to Dr. Oppenheimer. It is very likely that even on the periphery of the Communist Party, and at his innocent distance from spying, Dr. Oppenheimer had heard tales of microfilm and espionage chains which came to mind as an effective means of underscoring the reality of a spy danger while yet concealing what had actually happened. When we remember that less than two years before this Chevalier approach took place, Dr. Oppenheimer was still making his contributions to various causes he thought worthy directly through a Communist Party representative, and when we consider the extreme difficulty with which even the staunchest anti-Communist liberal, long years after he has entirely broken with the Party, reveals the names of former associates in the movement, perhaps what should surprise us is not that Dr. Oppenheimer suppressed Chevalier's name but that he had already progressed to the stage where he was able to name Eltenton.

But there is another point connected with Dr. Oppenheimer's attitudes in 1943 which makes his behavior in the Chevalier incident understandable even without this much subjective analysis—and that is the liberal culture of the time. Several witnesses for the defense, when they are asked their opinion of the Eltenton-Chevalier matter, call attention to the difference between our present feelings about security, especially vis à vis Russia, and those of 1943. Fortunately for our confidence in the historical memory, there are even some few who can recreate the general political-cultural context in which Dr. Oppenheimer committed the mistakes on which he is now judged. Notable among the latter is Colonel Lansdale, a defense witness, whose transcripts of conversations with Dr. Oppenheimer in the days when Lansdale was chief security officer for Los Alamos are, ironically enough, brought forward by the Commission as some of the chief evidence against Dr. Oppenheimer. Colonel Lansdale has been talking about the problem of Dr. Oppenheimer's questionable security clearance at Los Alamos, about the extra precautions the security people took because of his former Communist associations, and he goes on:

> At the same time over in the War Department I was being subjected to pressure from military superiors, from the White House, and from every other place because I dared to stop the commissioning of a group of 15 or 20 undoubted Communists. I was being vilified, being reviewed and re-reviewed by boards because of my efforts to get Communists out of the Army and being frustrated by the blind naive attitude of Mrs. Roosevelt and those around her in the White House, which resulted in serious and extreme damage to this country. . . .
>
> By golly, I stood up in front of General McNary, then Deputy Chief of Staff of the Army, and had him tell me that I was ruining peoples' careers and doing damage to the Army because I had stopped the commissioning of the political commissar of the Abraham Lincoln Brigade, and the guy was later commissioned on direct orders from the White House.

Nothing is made of Colonel Lansdale's helpful hints, either by Dr. Oppenheimer or his counsel. Indeed, between the lines of the record one reads the strained embarrassment of all of Colonel Lansdale's listeners as they have such a bitter dose of historical truth forced upon them. This aspect of Dr. Oppenheimer's situation is not to be overlooked, however, even though its pursuit gives comfort to those in our present administration who, for their own bleak purposes, refer to the Roosevelt regime in terms of twenty years of treason. Fairness to Dr. Oppenheimer requires that we remind ourselves that our current acute relations with Russia, of which the Oppenheimer case is only one relatively small result, would very likely never have reached their present point of crisis had not so much of the energy of liberalism been directed, in the very period in which Dr. Oppenheimer failed to report Chevalier, to persuading the American people that Russia was our great ally instead of the enemy of democracy and peace which she had already clearly demonstrated herself to be! If the dominant liberal sentiment of the time, from the White House down, could put its whole blind force on the side of protecting friends of the Soviet Union, why should Dr. Oppenheimer alone have been expected to see with the unclouded eyes of the future and promptly report his friend?

In short, Dr. Oppenheimer's defense should not have rested on trying to assimilate Dr. Oppenheimer's present temper and the temper of our present period to the temper of 1943—an effort which could only result in making Dr. Oppenheimer look like a liar. It should have rested on an unequivocal reconstruction of the situation, both objective and subjective, as it obtained in 1943. It should have comprehended and admitted the degree of sympathy with the radical movement, however ambiguous and however unconscious, Dr. Oppenheimer must inevitably have retained even after he supposed he was entirely through with Communism and even coincident with his great patriotic service to his nation. This would in no way have reflected on his present loyalty. On the contrary, it could only have affirmed both his loyalty and his honesty.

We recognize that the point at issue in all six character charges against Dr. Oppenheimer is his probity and we know the extent to which probity is a matter of cumulative effect. If we think we have caught a man in one lie, our trust is by that much diminished; if we suppose we have caught him in two or three lies, it is indeed the generous person who will thereafter give him the benefit of the doubt. In Dr. Oppenheimer's instance we peculiarly have a case where the cumulative effect of one seeming untruth after another goes all against our giving the defendant the benefit of the doubt. But suppose that in the Chevalier-Eltenton matter, the suspicion that Dr. Oppenheimer is presently lying had been eradicated by the defense supplying a coherent framework for his admission that he had lied in the past. Not only would this most telling of the charges against him have lost most of its impact but at least one other of the charges—the charge in the Lomanitz matter—would have wholly vanished and an atmosphere of candor would have been created which must surely have worked to Dr. Oppenheimer's advantage in the consideration of other discrepancies in his testimony. In Dr. Oppenheimer's response to questions about his relations with Lomanitz we have again a situation in which, instead of trying to persuade himself and the Board that in 1943 he would not have tolerated a Communist in atomic work, Dr. Oppenheimer should have understood and frankly admitted that at that period he saw no reason for alarm in employing a Communist, and that this was a point of view which was shared by any number of persons just as importantly engaged as he in the nation's business. He would then never have been in the position of saying in 1953 that he would not have sponsored Lomanitz in 1943 had he known Lomanitz was a Communist, only to have the Commission prove that in 1943 he did know Lomanitz was a Communist. And his counsel could then have advantageously recurred to the fact revealed in Colonel Lansdale's testimony, that it was Dr. Ernest Lawrence, one of Dr. Oppenheimer's chief opponents in the H-bomb controversy, who had "yelled and screamed louder than anybody else" when the security officers tried to rid the atomic project of Lomanitz by inducting him into the Army.

And two such confirmations of probity would have started the ball rolling in the direction of trusting Dr. Oppenheimer rather than distrusting him and permitted the generous but by no means strained interpretation of the contradiction between the fact that Dr. Oppenheimer told Lansdale in 1943 that Weinberg was a Communist and the fact that he told the FBI in 1950 that he knew Weinberg was a Communist only when it became public knowledge. After all, it is perfectly plausible that over seven years a man can forget the nature or source of information he once had. As to the charge that he told Lansdale in 1943 that he did not even know what Rudy Lambert looked like whereas in 1953 he admits to having seen him six or seven times, including one or two luncheon meetings at which he discussed with Lambert and another Party representative his contributions to Communist causes, surely Dr. Oppenheimer could only have strengthened his case if he had simply proposed, in rebuttal, the two likely and quite uncontradictory reasons for having told Lansdale what he once did—(1) that possibly such were still the remnants of his Communist partisanship and guilt in 1943 that he did not wish to incriminate either Lambert or himself by recollecting him and (2) that he may actually have forgotten Lambert in 1943 but recalled him to mind now through his recent intense searching of his past. This second explanation is, indeed, strongly suggested by Dr. Oppenheimer's testimony taken in conjunction with Mrs. Oppenheimer's: when Dr. Oppenheimer was preparing for these hearings he evidently and most naturally consulted his wife's recollection of persons and events on which his own memory was unsure. It is perfectly conceivable that Dr. Oppenheimer was telling the entire truth when he told Lansdale he had no recollection of Lambert, and that Lambert, among many other earlier associations, was recalled to him in his joint research into his Communist past with his wife. All married people have had this experience.

There remain, then, the charge in the Seaborg matter and the charge in the matter of Dr. Peters. Of all the charges on which the Commission rests its case, the worst-founded, it seems to me, is the charge that Dr. Oppenheimer is not a trustworthy character because he said that the recommendations of the meeting of the General Advisory Committee in October 1949 were "surprisingly unanimous" and that he did not know the opinion of the one absent member, Dr. Seaborg, whereas Dr. Seaborg had communicated his mildly dissenting opinion in advance of the meeting. There were nine members of the Committee, eight of whom were present and agreed. Who that has ever worked in committee would not call this surprising unanimity? As for Dr. Seaborg's letter stating his position on the H-bomb, this was produced from Dr. Oppenheimer's own files. Obviously, Dr. Oppenheimer could not have had any conscious intention of suppressing Dr. Seaborg's disagreement unless he remembered this letter which communicated Dr. Seaborg's views; and if he remembered it, nothing would have been easier than to destroy it. This explanation does not of course cover Dr. Oppenheimer's failure to include Dr. Seaborg's view in the report of the meeting which was given the Commission. In submitting, as he did, a majority and minority expression of the sentiments of the Committee without mentioning Dr. Seaborg's communication, Dr. Oppenheimer did, I suppose, fall short of his whole duty as Chairman. Perhaps this was purposeful, perhaps it was only careless, but whichever, the omission is fairly judged only in the light of Dr. Seaborg's own lack of firm conviction in the controversy, as revealed in his weak communication and by the fact that in the next meeting of the Committee Dr. Seaborg said he would prefer not to express his views.

In the Peters matter the Commission charges that Dr. Oppenheimer testified in one fashion about the Communist activities of Dr. Peters before a closed session of Congressional Committee and then in effect contradicted himself in a letter to a Rochester newspaper which had reported his testimony. Dr. Oppenheimer acknowledges that he made this shift; he tells us he wrote the letter because various people accused him of having been unfair to Peters and because Peters himself told him his facts were mistaken. Well, assuredly a political man would have been unmoved by this protest. Having put his opinion on record, he would have stuck to it at whatever risk of having done someone an injustice. But Dr. Oppenheimer, I think it has been sufficiently demonstrated, is not a political man—not even as intellectuals go. And he is a scientist, which is its own kind of intellectual. What the political man considers undue susceptibility to influence, someone of Dr. Oppenheimer's background and apparent temperament accepts as in the very nature of his business; it is his mark and his work to be available to correction. And while I would not wish to imply that Dr.

Oppenheimer's alteration of his stated opinion of Peters speaks well for his firmness of character, as firmness of character may necessarily be gauged in the conduct of the world's business, still this elasticity of judgment and the readiness to make amends where one may have done an injustice are of a kind which, in one's experience of intellectuals, is an everyday affair of the sensitive life of the mind and spirit, to be interpreted as an essential untrustworthiness only by those who place rigorousness and caution above the virtues of imagination and human feeling. The trouble may be that the intellectual does not belong in the active world of politics. But if the government presses the scientist into service, as it now must, it should at least heed the admonition of Mr. Kennan that virtually in the degree that an intellectual has special gifts to give his country, he must be recognized as a special instance of moral-intellectual development and not at each moment be held to account by the conventional criteria of behavior. In the sense that their conduct will not, by its very nature, always conform to the strictest requirements of military or political necessity, all gifted men and not alone Dr. Oppenheimer must be thought of as calculated risks.

General Groves and Colonel Lansdale, the two military officers whose knowledge of Los Alamos is most intimate, have much to tell us of the scientific temperament as it displayed itself during the tense days when the atom bomb was being sought for, especially of the almost willful flouting of security regulations by the top personnel of the project. Dr. Oppenheimer comes out considerably better from their report than most of his colleagues—so much better that it even seems something of a paradox that it is he alone who is now denied clearance. And furthermore, we keep it in mind that with the exception of Mr. Murray, none of Dr. Oppenheimer's judges considers Dr. Oppenheimer disloyal. We have several times been assured that Dr. Oppenheimer's lack of candor, his carelessness and susceptibility to influence and his continuing association with Communists* are not to be construed as evidence or even suspicion that Dr. Oppenheimer is now a man of divided political allegiance. But if the Commission sincerely believes that Dr. Oppenheimer's mistakes and indiscretions and discrepancies of testimony are unconnected with his Communist past, and if it truly believes that his conduct in the matter of the H-bomb is irrelevant to the disposition of his case, why has it not undertaken to reinvestigate all the people who have security clearance in order to determine whether they deserve to be considered better risks than Dr. Oppenheimer? Can their characters and

---

* The word is used in the plural but only a single instance is cited by the Commission—namely, Dr. Oppenheimer's continuing association with Chevalier. Specifically, this refers to the fact that Dr. Oppenheimer twice met with Chevalier in Paris in late 1953. One of these meetings, however, was for the purpose of going with Chevalier to visit Malraux, and anyone who knows Malraux's political history must have the gravest doubt that Malraux would receive Chevalier if he thought Chevalier was still a Communist. In other words, Dr. Oppenheimer would seem to have had Malraux's seasoned political judgment to support his own opinion that in continuing his association with Chevalier he was not continuing an association with a Communist.

conduct any more than Dr. Oppenheimer's sustain the kind of probing to which his has been submitted?

When we rid Dr. Oppenheimer's case of the personal-professional interests in which it is so thoroughly entangled and when we have eliminated from its consideration Dr. Oppenheimer's differences with present dominant military-scientific opinion, there remains of course only a single matter for decision: On the basis of the evidence which we have before us, is or is not Dr. Oppenheimer the kind of man whom we can now trust with our secrets? Clearly, this is not an absolute matter; anyone who is human is a risk. It is a relative matter; it is relative to what we have a right to expect of a man and what we expect of other men in whom we do place our trust. It seems to me that the very strict standards by which Dr. Oppenheimer is now judged are standards by which virtually anyone might fail. Is Mr. Griggs, who reports minutes of meetings where minutes apparently do not exist or who, apparently alone of some fifty to one hundred people, remembers that Dr. Zacharias wrote ZORC on a blackboard, a more reliable character than Dr. Oppenheimer who reports a fact differently in 1950 than he did in 1943 or who multiplies one person into three? Is Mr. Borden, who has accused a man of being a spy without evidence to support it, a better character than Dr. Oppenheimer who changed his evidence against a man when he was told it was mistaken? Or to take an example from the side of the defense: Is Dr. Conant, who does not remember a letter from Dr. Oppenheimer before the famous October 1949 meeting, any the less suspect for this lapse than Dr. Oppenheimer who does not remember a letter from Dr. Seaborg before the same meeting?

It is my guess that everyone around Dr. Oppenheimer has been much educated by Dr. Oppenheimer's experience. But so has Dr. Oppenheimer himself been educated, and not only by the experience of his own investigation but by his total political experience of recent years. There was a time, before Dr. Oppenheimer had come to understand the true nature of the Soviet Union, when surely it was the gravest of risks to trust him with secrets which the Soviet Union wanted so badly. But he never told those secrets then, and to have granted him clearance at that time only to take it away from him now, when at last he has learned the error of his way, seems to me at best to be tragic ineptitude. In effect, it constitutes a projection upon Dr. Oppenheimer of the punishment we perhaps owe to ourselves for having once been so careless with our nation's security.

I am afraid that in concentrating on what seem to me to be the main lines of investigation of Dr. Oppenheimer's situation, I have done but poor justice to the case in all its complexity of content and implication. I urge the readers of this article to read the transcript of the hearings for themselves—but carefully and fully, and not merely to find documentation for a preconceived judgment of Dr. Oppenheimer's deeds and motives.

• Communism Now

G. L. Arnold

"Communism now" is the sort of subject one would gladly leave to the special-ists, were it not that they have so frequently proved mistaken. This may be due to ordinary human frailty, but more probably it is a matter of being imperfectly aware of the peculiar mechanism which makes the Communist orbit what it is. The point can be illustrated by quoting a remark made in private not long ago by a Communist leader who holds a key position in an Eastern European country. He was discussing the prospects of de-Stalinization with a Western socialist and in the course of conversation he casually remarked that of course all this related only to Europe and perhaps the USSR: the Chinese Communist Party, by con-trast, was only now about to enter its Stalinist phase, "and since China is a more primitive country than Russia one must expect Chinese Stalinism to be worse than Russian." His interlocutor, being himself a Marxist, needed no elaboration of this point which some people might have found surprising: every Communist realizes (even if he does not say so) that Stalinism was the price the USSR had to pay for the policy of breakneck industrialization and wholesale collectivization to which the Russian Communist Party committed itself in the thirties. To deprive the peasant of his land and drive him into the factories an iron dictator-ship was needed, and since the Peking government seems determined to embark on the same experience—though admittedly with greater caution—it follows (at least if you are a Marxist) that it must in time produce its own variant of the Stalinist terror: if indeed it has not already done so.

Now it is possible to counter this line of reasoning by pointing to the unique-ness of the Soviet experience. The Russians after all were first in the field, and in principle it is open to the Chinese and others to avoid their worst and bloodiest mistakes. One may also, if one feels so inclined, draw some retrospective comfort from the revelations about Stalin's personal rule which have become orthodox since the Twentieth Party Congress last February. Although Khrushchev has not said so, it is conceivable that he and his colleagues now regard the wholesale mas-sacre and deportation of the *kulaks* as the greatest of Stalin's criminal blunders, and that Mao Tse-tung at any rate is determined to sidestep this particular pitfall. But taken by and large the major features of the Stalinist experience seem insep-arable from the attempt to telescope a century of industrial history into a decade, and to do it dictatorially and at the expense of the population. In its own way, the long-winded resolution of the CPSU's Central Committee published in *Pravda* on July 2nd gets to the bottom of the matter when it asserts that under the given conditions there was no alternative to letting Stalin govern dictatorially. The talk about "limitations of democracy" imposed by the need "to build socialism" under conditions of "capitalist encirclement" can be dismissed as the automatic paternoster of a regime committed to the defense of Stalin's heritage; but to Communists such phrases have an operational meaning when they are applied to the problems of backward countries where Communists have only recently (or not yet) come to power. What they suggest is a qualified defense of the Stalinist pattern as being rational—and so it is, if one subtracts the murderous and pathological aspects of the particular experience undergone by Russia in the thirties and forties. This, and not "Moscow control," is the real obstacle to genuine de-Stalinization among the East European satellites, and further afield in the fiefs now precariously occupied by Togliatti and Thorez. Reject the pattern, and what is left of the claim that Communism can industrialize faster than capitalism?

But the obverse also applies: accept the pattern, and there is no need to defend or justify what was peculiarly barbarous, murderous, and pathological about one man's personal rule. The essentials can be safeguarded. This is a recurring experience in revolutions: once a breakthrough to a new political and organizational level has taken place, the protagonist can be ditched. It is already clear that, if Moscow has its way, we are going to get Stalinism without Stalin. Of course Moscow may fail to have its way, even in the satellites, and for all one knows Mao Tse-tung may become the symbol of a somewhat less sanguinary method of depriving the peasant of his property. As against these possibilities one may note the evident reluctance with which so many Communists in Asian and Islamic countries approach the subject of de-Stalinization. It is not inconceivable that, even on the intellectual and moral-political level, Stalin will remain a hero to the average Communist in, say, Persia; just as it is probable that his reputation will suffer most among Communists imbued with the Latin, and especially the French, revolutionary tradition. Here there may be some belated conversions to the view that Trotsky was right about the man after all. But these shadings hardly affect the essential unity of the Communist movement as a worldwide attempt to impose by force a pattern of society modeled upon the USSR. Only if the Communists begin to realize that the attempt is hopeless and anachronistic will it be possible to say that the Stalinist inheritance has really been repudiated.

Traces of such an incipient revisionism have been detected in some recent utterances of the Italian Communist leadership, and it is at least conceivable that this mood may eventually spread to France. If it does, the two most important Communist parties in Europe will in effect have adopted the position already occupied for some years by the Yugoslavs; for it is the essence of the theoretical standpoint publicly and privately maintained by Tito, Kardelj, and their closest supporters that, since the entire world is gradually moving in a socialist direction, the Soviet doctrine on the existence of "two camps" is outmoded and politically dangerous. This attitude seems to have survived a succession of political maneuvers; it is evidently grounded in real conviction, and if it ever became the unspoken doctrine of West European Communism, it would be very difficult for the Kremlin to maintain its organizational hold over some of the mass movements it now controls. For that hold is in the last resort determined by a community of outlook which has hitherto been proof against the worst shocks administered to Communist loyalties by the sanguinary record of Stalinism at home and abroad. For practical purposes Communism since 1917 has implied not just belief in the "October Revolution" as the starting point of a new epoch in world history, but a commitment to the Soviet Union—and latterly the Sino-Soviet bloc—as the chosen instrument of global reconstruction. The socialist revolution is envisaged as a process in which a certain group of countries, having climbed onto the new historical level, confront and eventually absorb the shrinking capitalist remnant. This concept is central to Stalinism and it is all the more difficult for Communists to abandon since it is already implicit in Lenin's formulations on "uneven development" and the possibility of socialist revolutions in scattered areas of the globe. In its semi-conscious combination with Russian (and Chinese) nationalism cum imperialism it supplies a motive force so powerful that its abandonment could hardly fail to produce a first-class crisis of confidence among the inheritors of the Leninist tradition.

One is thus brought up against the problem of what is to happen to the Communists once they let go the theoretical certainties which have hitherto sustained them and armed them against doubt. Even the Yugoslavs have not traveled very far down this dangerous road, although one detects in their utterances a growing awareness that Leninism-Stalinism may turn out to be a political pattern suited only to certain backward countries in the throes of industrialization. ("It is our misfortune," they now tell the critical Western visitor, "that Communists have hitherto come to power only in poor and wretched countries.") From this admission to the realization that Communism is wholly unsuited to rich and progressive countries there is only one step, and some of the party leaders seem to have made it. But it is just on this point that the post-Stalin leadership in the USSR has proved most obdurate: backward Russia may have been, thirty years ago (and this is now indeed put forward as an excuse for Stalin's reign of terror), but today the Soviet Union is proclaimed at least the equal of the United States in all respects save material wealth, and tomorrow she is to excel in this domain too. And as for the notorious Tito-Kardelj doctrine on the gradual spread of socialist tendencies throughout the world and the consequent undesirability of political and doctrinal exclusiveness, only the new cult of politeness prevents Moscow from stigmatizing it as heresy.

For heresy it undoubtedly is. In technical terms it is an "Austro-Marxist" rather than a Leninist view, and if it ever comes to be adopted by a considerable number of Western Communists, the essential unity of the world Communist movement will be at an end. Togliatti's reputed vacillations on this subject are an infinitely more serious matter for the Kremlin than any number of workers' risings in Eastern Europe. Revolts can be suppressed, and will be, as long as the Soviet army stands ready to move against any serious threat, and as long as the satellite governments can draw on Soviet economic resources to get over their worst difficulties. Nationalist sentiment can be assuaged by half-serious promises to let Poland have the kind of relative independence enjoyed, say, by Mexico; and democratic stirrings can be appeased by intra-party "primaries" modeled on Western patterns; but let the worm of doubt creep into the theoretical fabric, and the political structure cannot hold. Communism stands and falls by what Communists believe to be the case about the relationship of their movement to the rest of the world. If ever they come to see it as only one tendency among many—and not the most important one at that, so far as the advanced countries are concerned—belief in victory will vanish, and with it the totalitarian drive to reshape the world. There will then remain little more than a gigantic pressure group held together by slogans no longer related to the will to make a complete break with tradition: one more political party competing for relative power within the framework of democratic society.

If this is the distant danger which threatens the Communist parties in the West, those in the East and in the Soviet orbit are confronted with the more immediate problem of effecting the transition to the post-Stalinist age under the slogan "back to Leninism." When one considers that the present "Soviet Thermidor" promises at the very least greater security and perhaps greater power for the managerial caste and the privileged upper crust generally, the current transmogrification of Stalinism into Leninism does not lack its humorous aspect. For what does Leninism imply if not a return to greater simplicity, equality, and doctrinal purity—everything, in fact, that the new ruling stratum abhors? And yet the regime can rid itself of the Stalinist encumbrance only by appealing to the authority of Lenin. It must do so even at the risk of arousing expectations it cannot fulfill, and in the knowledge that the Soviet elite will go on paying lip service to Leninism—as it has been doing for a generation—while intensifying its collective pressure for greater privileges. Lenin is too potent a symbol to be neglected at such a testing time. He would have to sanctify even so improbable (in the short run) an event as the effective displacement of the Party by the Army as the highest authority in the State. No military leader could rise to power without invoking the magic name, and in all probability this would be done with some degree of sincerity.

The present operation nonetheless has its dangers. What is a mere slogan to the Party leaders may be taken seriously by their followers, and perhaps by aspirants to power who would like to relegate the Party to second place. How these conflicting tendencies can be assembled under one roof is a problem that may well tax the ingenuity of the ruling stratum for years to come. "Back to Lenin" is a splendid slogan on condition that it is not taken literally. What if it becomes a rallying point for genuinely democratic tendencies? Lenin has not, after all, been dead long enough for pious evocations of his memory to be entirely harmless. If there is trouble in the near future it is likely to stem from this most impeccable of Communist saints.

The great unsolved problem, assuming that the retreat to "Leninism" can be executed without disaster to the ruling group, is the future role of the Party in a society which in some respects has outgrown its guidance. Totalitarianism means in practice that State and Party must be merged at the highest level; ideally they should meet in the person of a single autocratic ruler. It is arguable that in repudiating this pattern the present collective leadership has set itself in opposition to the logic of the system. If this is so, one must expect a new personal dictatorship to emerge from the present confused gropings of Stalin's heirs. Autocracy would seem to be required to harmonize relations between the Party and the Army: twin pillars of an overcentralized regime who must stand or fall together. It was not the least of Stalin's achievements that he was able to impose his authority upon both—at the cost, it is true, of terrorizing them into submission. Now that the remnants of his prestige are being shared out among political bosses and military leaders, each group may try to win the allegiance of an increasingly homogeneous privileged stratum. And this struggle must be waged in terms appropriate to a society which after almost forty years of Communist rule has become deeply committed to institutions whose real function is wholly at variance with the official ideology. Because the new integration appears to call for a renewed concentration of authority at the very topmost level of the hierarchy, even Communists who admire Lenin must feel that their trials are not yet over.

If these problems are urgent and difficult for the Soviet leaders, they are positively dramatic for the East European satellites, as the Poznan revolt showed. The obvious parallel to Poznan is the East Berlin rising of June 1953; the not so obvious but equally relevant comparison is with Kronstadt in 1921. After Kronstadt, Lenin introduced economic concessions but tightened the apparatus of political control and thus opened the way to Stalin. This is the orthodox Communist reaction to any challenge which has genuine mass support. It is difficult to see how the Polish Communists and the rest of the satellites can escape the logic of their single-party tyranny even were they to make economic concessions big enough to satisfy the workers. Comparisons with Russia in 1956 are deceptive. The Soviet economy is a going concern and the Soviet party is a powerful, well-established stratum which can afford to "liberalize" without losing control: Khrushchev's speech denouncing Stalin was a sign of self-confidence. The East European regimes are a thin crust over molten lava—a crust which itself consists of lava only a little less fiery than the underlying substance. Any crack on the surface threatens to release the accumulated pressures. That is why, paradoxically, the "thaw" is less dangerous in Russia, where it is absorbed by the privileged Soviet elite, than in the European satellites, with their recent memories of relative freedom. In Moscow, the end of terrorism is gratefully acknowledged. In Warsaw, Budapest, and Prague it stimulates demands for genuine liberty, or at the very least for a degree of self-government and decentralization that makes nonsense of single-party control and the planned economy as understood by Communists. Are the workers to have the right to strike? Is the price mechanism to be restored? Are the peasants to be relieved, once and for all, of the fear that they will be driven into collectives? What is left of Stalinism if these steps are taken—and if Stalinism is repudiated *in toto* and not just on paper and for the benefit of the ruling elite, how much is left of *Leninism*? These are questions that no Communist party has yet dared to face. They will have to be faced if the "thaw" is not to give way to another ice age.   1956, vol. 23, no. 4

• Coexistence: The End of Ideology
Raymond Aron

Coexistence is neither a doctrine nor a desire: it is first and foremost a *fact*. Communist and democratic countries live side by side or face to face on the same planet, on the same continent, without combating each other militarily and without renouncing the beliefs and ideologies which serve, on each side, to justify the existing regime and to disparage or condemn the regime established on the other side.

The anti-Communism of the free world cannot be rigorously equated with the *ideological* aggressiveness of the Communist states. Leninism-Stalinism proclaims the inevitable destruction of capitalism (and all Western countries are included in this term, whatever the degree or form of their socialism or the strength of their labor movements) and, in this perspective, enjoins the faithful to hasten the advent of the Last Judgment. Democratic doctrine—to the extent that the word doctrine can be applied to the ideas prevalent in the West—requires no declaration of war against the states which adhere to Leninism-Stalinism; it is essentially opposed to the universalist pretensions of the enemy ideology. Should the Soviets ever recognize that their regime is only one of a number of possible ways of organizing industrial societies, the majority of democrats—while continuing to regard certain practices of the Soviet regime as deplorable, inefficient, or inhuman—would no longer feel obliged to maintain an attitude of active hostility to the Soviet Union.

This proposition, that we of the West are committed to the destruction of the Soviet regime only to the extent that the latter seeks the destruction of our free societies, will be challenged or violently rejected by three categories of Westerners: extremists in anti-Communism (such as James Burnham), moralists, and representatives of Soviet-dominated countries. The opposition of the first group is based primarily on their refusal to believe in the reality or possibility of the hypothesis that Communism could abdicate its claim to universality, in other words that it could accept the existence of heretical or pagan states. What is the probability of such a conversion? This is a moot point. But logically a "Macchiavellian" should agree to peace between democratic Westerners and Russian Communism if ever and whenever the latter recognizes the right to exist of a welfare-minded capitalism such as we have in Scandinavia or the United States.

The moralists will object that the West would deny its own values if it ceased to believe in the universal validity of its ideas. We suggest no such denial. But a free press, political parties, and a parliamentary system cannot be propagated at bayonet point or by means of intercontinental rockets. In any case, the West cannot bring about a reform of the Soviet regime, much less a revolution that would destroy it. How can the West most effectively promote the evolution of the Soviet regime? The question is open, but it is a political and not a moral one. Sounding the anti-Communist trumpets will not bring the walls down. There is no particular merit in shouting one's distaste for Communism as loudly as possible.

There remains the case of the forcibly sovietized countries of Eastern Europe, whose plight we cannot recognize as definitive. Politically, the West rejects the European status quo so dear to Mr. Khrushchev's heart. In this sense and on this level, Western diplomacy is and must remain on the offensive. But we have neither the means nor the will to pursue this offensive by force. We know that our objective can be attained only through negotiation (the withdrawal of Soviet and American troops) or through a change in the ideas or in the methods of the Kremlin. If the Communists ceased to believe in the universal dissemination of their doctrine and their institutions, a relaxation of Russian domination over Eastern Europe would become less improbable.

There is no reason to believe, at this writing, that Soviet strategy has changed or that Mr. Khrushchev has abandoned the dogmas of the Leninist-Stalinist credo—to the effect that capitalism is bad and will die and that Soviet Communism is good and will triumph. Can this credo be equated with the formula: Mr. Khrushchev (or the Soviet Union) is seeking world domination? The situation is not as simple as that. If the United States were removed from the scene by the wave of a magic wand, Russia would no longer have an opponent in her class. In this sense, she would reign supreme over the world. But does this mean that she would be able to impose her every wish on China, India, or Europe, without encountering resistance? Nobody knows. The absence of a military rival is not the equivalent of omnipotence. If all the countries of the world were Communist, conflicts between Communist countries would become possible. Such speculations aside, the major fact of the present conjuncture is that the Soviet Union's hostility to capitalism is indistinguishable from her hostility to the only power mighty enough to oppose her: the United States. And the impossibility of a definitive or even a relatively definitive settlement of the Russian-American rivalry is neither more nor less evident under Khrushchev than it was under Stalin. Such a settlement is excluded for four basic reasons: the clash of ideologies prevents the two Great Powers from simply accepting each other or legitimizing the status quo; the division of Europe constitutes a permanent cause of insecurity; the anti-Western revolt in Asia, Africa, and the Middle East works to the advantage of the Soviets (even when they play no role in it) and threatens to isolate the white minority of Europe and America; and finally, the technological weapons race seems to rule out any stabilization or limitation of armaments.

Since a global settlement is excluded, the Soviet Union and the United States must choose between total war and the cold war. During the past twelve years their choice has gone clearly and constantly to the latter. The cold war is a form of coexistence. Rhetorical stress is laid on the term when the desire is to reject total war publicly and solemnly, but during the Korean war the effort to limit hostilities also implied the rejection of total war. Mr. Khrushchev's ultimate ambitions do not prevent this total non-war or coexistence. What they prevent, now as in the past, is a formal agreement on the terms of this mutual and hostile tolerance.

Is this more or less bellicose coexistence jeopardized by the launching of Sputnik, which symbolizes the progress of Soviet science and industry and suggests a probable Russian superiority in the realm of ballistic weapons? Is the West threatened with disaster if the power ratio is inexorably modified in favor of the Soviet Union?

The expression "balance of power," traditional in politico-military terminology, has been gradually replaced by the "balance of terror." This change in vocabulary strikes me as meaningful. Until recently the balance was calculated on the hypothesis of a possibly prolonged war: in the event of a trial of strength, what resources could be mobilized by a given state or coalition against another? This question has lost its point, since a few H-bombs would be enough to paralyze a medium-sized country and a few dozen would inflict tens of millions of casualties on a continental state like Russia or the U.S. Would total war come to an end in a few hours or a few days after an exchange of these monstrous projectiles? Nobody knows. All we do know is that such a war would be senseless for all concerned *unless it were waged unilaterally*. No political advantage obtained through victory could possibly match the cost of the war itself, unless one side had the technological means to protect itself from bombardment. In other words it would be utter lunacy for a ruler to touch off a total war at the present time if he were not virtually assured of destroying the enemy's entire capacity for reprisal at one blow. Such is the definition of the balance of terror. This balance exists as long as neither side has, or rather can be assured of having, the power to destroy all means of reprisal from the opposing side.

The balance of terror, thus defined, has not been upset by the fact that the Soviets have probably taken the lead in the field of ballistic weapons. It could be decisively upset in one way only: by a simultaneous superiority in offensive and defensive power. If the Soviet Union possessed an effective defense against air attack and a monopoly of ballistic weapons at the same time, while the United States were still vulnerable to the latter, then the United States would be at the mercy of its rival.

This is not the case at present. Even if Soviet intercontinental missiles are ready for military use at this very moment—an improbable supposition—American air power, thanks to the number and dispersion of its bases, is still capable of piercing the enemy's land-based rocket barrages. At least the percentage of aircraft that could get through would be sufficient to inflict enormous devastation. Supposing, on the other hand, that the American air forces could no longer get through the rocket barrages and that Soviet intercontinental missiles were already in use, the West could still employ medium-range weapons capable of reaching most Soviet cities. Thus, once again, the balance of terror is preserved.

We must therefore consider that a technological breakthrough in the fields of weapons, means of delivery, or defense, which would make it possible for one side to impose its will on the other, is not impossible but highly improbable. In the absence of such a breakthrough, war is not precisely excluded, since an accident or a misunderstanding of the enemy's intentions is conceivable (although accidents and misunderstandings are also becoming increasingly improbable); what is excluded is the possibility that a war will deliberately be unleashed by governments possessed of their senses.

This equilibrium of terror is an integral part of coexistence as we know it. Could there be a coexistence without some such approximate equality in destructive capacity? The question is pointless since this equality is a fact and will continue to be one. Both sides would probably prefer to avoid a costly and unpredictable total war even if it were fought without nuclear weapons. The latter, in any case, can only reinforce their will to peace (or rather, their will to non-war).

The fact remains that a number of new elements have recently emerged. As long as American territory was safe, or less vulnerable to air attack than Soviet territory, the U.S. could deter local aggressions by threatening to extend the hostilities: the "massive retaliation" doctrine. Since equality has more or less been restored one hears much less talk of massive reprisals; indeed, it would sometimes appear that it is the men in the Kremlin who have taken over the term.

In other words, the more war assumes the aspect of a collective suicide the less possible it becomes to use the threat of it to stop a local aggression or to settle a secondary conflict. The threat of collective suicide can protect Western Europe because the stakes are considerable and military invasion would be a highly risky affair, but it is doubtful that it could be used to protect Israel against an Egyptian-Syrian attack. Limited wars become all the more likely as total war becomes more horrible and absurd for all concerned. To be sure, the danger that a conflict might get out of hand deters the Great Powers from using their regular armies anywhere. But if their armies did become engaged in a non-vital theater, the opposing governments could *reasonably* be expected to attempt to keep such conflicts within limits and to avoid using a destructive power out of all proportion to their political purposes.

Since a general settlement is excluded and the preservation of the balance of terror is probable, what are the chances of partial agreements in one or another of the regions of the world where the interests, ambitions, and ideals of the two coalitions are in conflict? Let us briefly examine three of the diplomatic theaters of operations: Europe, the Middle East, and the Far East.

In Europe the situation has not fundamentally changed since 1945, except for the dissidence of Tito and the spectacular episode of the Berlin blockade. The countries liberated by the Soviet armies have been sovietized, the demarcation line drawn during the war by the diplomats in London has remained the frontier between the two worlds. The great event that has occurred in the meantime, however, will probably prove in the long run to be of decisive importance, although it is not visible on the map: Soviet Russia has failed in both phases of her dual undertaking in Eastern Europe. The subject peoples have not become resigned to Russification and the youth have not been converted to Communism. The tide of popular sentiment is running in favor of the democratic regimes and against Communism or any other sort of authoritarian regime. (In this respect, the old world is perhaps an exception, for elsewhere the new situation would seem rather to resemble that of Europe in the thirties.)

A fair-minded appraisal of George Kennan's views, as set forth in his Reith Lectures, published as *Russia, the Atom, and the West*, must first of all recall that they are based on one major premise: if the Europeans were free to determine their fate they would choose the West, democracy. Even the Communists in Hungary and Poland who would probably retain collective ownership of the factories would attempt to reintroduce free political institutions. The proposals of the former American ambassador to Moscow are designed to create a diplomatic situation within which the Europeans would manifest their preference. Such a situation, says Kennan, could be created by the withdrawal of the Russian and American armies.

In the long run it is hard to see how the unity of Europe could be restored except through some such diplomatic arrangement. The Western powers do not have the physical means to force the Soviet Union to give up Eastern Europe. They must therefore use persuasion, which implies some sort of exchange. One or another form of military "disengagement" would thus appear, in the long view, to be the indispensable condition of any peaceful, diplomatic "rollback" in Europe.

Having conceded this much, the fact remains that a negotiated European settlement is hardly around the corner. Mr. Kennan seemed to be suggesting that Europe, after the withdrawal of the Soviet and American troops, would be defended only by conventional armies, with respect to which he employed the term "militia." In point of fact he was thinking of the Swiss army, which is one of the toughest in Europe, although it is recruited according to a regional pattern. Furthermore, he seemed to be implying that the American commitment to come to the aid of Europe in the event of an aggression would remain absolute despite the withdrawal of troops from the continent. Here, however, we come to the weak point of this otherwise attractive proposal.

When the American continent was beyond the reach of Soviet bombs, it was conceivable that the United States could protect Europe without maintaining troops there. Once atomic or thermonuclear equality was established, such a guarantee from afar became practically worthless. Who could believe that the United States would consent to the destruction of its own cities in order to protect West Berlin? Besides, the question is not what the United States would do in such or such a case, but how the Soviet leaders would estimate American intentions. A misunderstanding or a faulty estimate of the American commitment is excluded by the physical presence of American troops in Europe. This is the primary reason for the hostility in European governmental circles toward the "nuclear vacuum."

Even supposing that the governments and peoples of Western Europe were willing to risk such a vacuum, they would demand, in return, some likelihood of a peaceful liberation of Eastern Europe. Such a liberation would be possible only if the Kremlin, after the mutual troop withdrawal, allowed a reform of the Soviet regimes, indeed perhaps even a revolution of the Hungarian type. But the Soviet spokesmen never tire of repeating that coexistence must be based on the political status quo. Thus we would have the following alternatives: either the negotiations leading to withdrawal would leave the political status of Europe in doubt, and in that case the ambiguity of the agreement would constitute a danger to world peace; or there would be a serious attempt to specify the political status of a reunified and militarily evacuated Europe, and there would be little chance of an accord.

Let us consider the first alternative. What would happen if after the departure of the Russian troops the Hungarians rose against their masters? Would the Kremlin passively absorb this defeat? What would the West do if the doctrine of the new Holy Alliance (the Russian right to intervene against counterrevolution) were applied? Make war? This would mean suicide. Would the United States then simply send its troops back to Germany? Even supposing that they could do so, the return to the status quo ante would merely mean that after the evacuation of Europe the Iron Curtain would continue invisibly to exist, since Soviet military operations west of the line would mean war and east of the line would not. If we are to have an Iron Curtain it would better be visible than invisible.

Let us now consider the second alternative. Prior to any military evacuation, the Russians, the Americans, and the Germans would attempt to settle the political status of Germany. Why should the wider framework make agreement any easier? For the moment, Mr. Khrushchev does not envisage the desovietization of Eastern Germany. The proof of this is simply that he has not proposed the one settlement which has occurred to everyone else. In return for desovietization he could easily force a reunified Germany out of the Atlantic Pact, since no government in Bonn could refuse neutrality if it were to be followed by democratic reunification.

The simple truth is that the West wants a military status quo and Moscow wants a political one. Compromise between these two contradictory purposes is, for the moment, improbable. Mr. Kennan's suggestions offer no way out of the impasse. The proposed evacuation implies a modification of the military situation which the West would accept only if it came with the quasi-assurance that the political situation in Eastern Europe would also change. Since this assurance cannot be had, the West will not agree to evacuation; at most (and even this is improbable) it might envisage a reduction of armaments in a limited zone.

A crisis may arise in Europe if Mr. Khrushchev, through the Pankow government, undertakes to blockade West Berlin. This is hardly probable at the moment although the possibility cannot be excluded. The situation is more ominous in the Middle East.

There we have an extremely violent revolutionary movement which will probably result, within a period of years, in forcing Iraq and Jordan into the so-called Unified State of Egypt and Syria. The rulers of the former two countries are attempting to defend themselves through a rival federation. But Nasser, unlike the Hashemite sovereigns, is supported by popular enthusiasm. This transformation is fraught with peril for Israel and the West. Europe will be dependent on Middle Eastern oil for another generation (unless the Sahara can be exploited on a large scale). What, one wonders, will be the attitude of Nasser's Arab State to Israel? The latter's security has been based on the superiority of its armed forces over the combined strength of its neighbors. Will this superiority last? And will the West be able to intervene if the Soviets support the Arabs?

Our concern here is not to speculate on the various possibilities. We have recalled the principal—and well-known—factors in the present situation in order to suggest a negative reply to the question of a Middle Eastern settlement. In Europe, a limited agreement is improbable because of the direct conflict between the Soviet insistence on the political status quo and the Western insistence on the military status quo. In the Middle East, agreement seems excluded by the revolutionary process which, although favored and partially manipulated by the Soviets, cannot be completely dominated by either side. Why should the men in the Kremlin agree to refrain from arming the "active neutralists"?

Nobody can predict the further developments of this crisis nor the extent to which the West will succeed in safeguarding its essential interests and coming to some sort of terms with the Arab nationalists. East-West negotiations would probably be sterile.

The prospect of limited agreement is hardly any brighter in the Far East. For the moment, the policy of Peking is not aggressive. Mao Tse-tung and Chou En-lai are seeking to reassure their neighbors in Southeast Asia. The Americans will eventually have to recognize the Chinese Communist regime. But the present situation can go on without change for years. Peking can scarcely *recognize* the fact of the Nationalist regime in Taiwan, and Washington cannot sacrifice the latter, nor deny its legitimacy, as long as it exists.

Is Western unity today more fragile, more threatened, than it has been in the past? Three factors—independent of each other but with cumulative effects—have given rise to the rather widespread feeling on both sides of the Atlantic that the Alliance is on the point of disintegrating: the present weakness of the Republican administration and of President Eisenhower himself, the progress of Soviet technology and military power, and the ill-disguised hostility of Washington and London towards French policy in North Africa.

How long can the Alliance hold together in the absence of effective leadership? It is difficult to say. Personally, I tend to believe that alliances between democratic countries are stronger than they seem. Their weaknesses are more visible than their factors of strength, but in the long run it is the latter that prevail. The majority of European statesmen are convinced that no alternative policy can afford as much security as the Atlantic Pact and NATO. This proposition is less obviously true in the era of ballistic weapons than in the era of American invulnerability; nevertheless, it remains true.

In Europe the Alliance can, with difficulty, arrive at a common policy with respect to the Soviet Union. Elsewhere in the world this is not the case. In the Middle East, the policies of the Western countries diverge not so much because their interests are contradictory as because the responsible officials—whether in Washington, London, or Paris—are incapable of defining an Arab policy. Each government lives from day to day, reacting to events as best it can. London clings to the Baghdad Pact and tries to keep control over the Arab princedoms of the Arabian peninsula. Washington tries to appease Arab nationalism without sacrificing the sovereigns. This pragmatism is perhaps inevitable, but it is not conducive to coordination. In Africa, the American and British governments have too little faith in the successful outcome of French policy in Algeria to support it; nor can they oppose it without setting forth an alternative policy. Being in doubt, they practice a semi-abstention, and thus earn the semi-indignation of both sides.

Between 1946 and 1956 the struggle of the Western democracies against Stalinist Communism in Europe had a sort of ideological purity. The Western intellectual knew what and whom he was combating. He could denounce the Communists and their allies with a clear conscience. As late as 1956, Khrushchev and his accomplices were presiding over the bloody suppression of the Hungarian revolution. But Communism in its post-Stalinist phase is less outwardly pathological, and it is armed with the H-bomb. The West cannot dispense with the threat of collective suicide, and the intellectuals can neither reject nor acclaim such a strategy.

Even more equivocal are the diplomatic conflicts outside of Europe. The independent states created since the war are certainly preferable to interminable warfare in Indochina and Africa, but they no sooner exist than they cease to stir the admiration or sympathy of the Western intellectual. It is all very well for the intellectual to become passionate over the "liberation" of the "colonized and oppressed" peoples, but the regimes created by these peoples are inevitably imitations of the Western (or Soviet) regimes. These improvised states should, we feel, receive Western aid. But it is hard to see why an intellectual should feel particularly committed to the adventure of a Nasser or of a Mohammed V. In other words, once the political domination of the Europeans over the Asians, the Arabs, and the Africans has been terminated—and, with the end of the Algerian war, the process will be nearing its conclusion—the new states will pose problems for the economists and the experts. Perhaps the rich white minority of Europe and America will feel isolated in a hostile world. The statesmen will have a great deal to do; the intellectuals will be hard put to find occasions for crusades.

Perhaps, in the field of world politics too, the era of ideology is coming to an end.

(Translated from the French by H. J. Kaplan)

1958, vol. 25, no. 2

• Letter from the South: Nobody Knows My Name
James Baldwin

> I walked down the street, didn't have on no hat,
> Asking everybody I meet, Where's my man at?
> Ma Rainey

Negroes in the North are right when they refer to the South as the Old Country. A Negro born in the North who finds himself in the South is in a position similar to that of the son of the Italian emigrant who finds himself in Italy, near the village where his father first saw the light of day. Both are in countries they have never seen but which they cannot fail to recognize. The landscape has always been familiar; the speech is archaic, but it rings a bell; and so do the ways of the people, though their ways are not his ways. Everywhere he turns, the revenant finds himself reflected. He sees himself as he was before he was born, perhaps; or as the man he would have become had he actually been born in this place. He sees the world, from an angle odd indeed, in which his fathers awaited his arrival, perhaps in the very house in which he narrowly avoided being born. He sees, in effect, his ancestors, who, in everything they do and are, proclaim his inescapable identity. And the Northern Negro in the South sees, whatever he or anyone else may wish to believe, that his ancestors are both white and black. The white men, flesh of his flesh, hate him for that very reason. On the other hand, there is scarcely any way for him to join the black community in the South: for both he and this community are in the grip of the immense illusion that their state is more miserable than his own.

This illusion owes everything to the great American illusion that our state is a state to be envied by other people: we are powerful, and we are rich. But our power makes us uncomfortable and we handle it very ineptly. The principal effect of our material well-being has been to set the children's teeth on edge. If we ourselves were not so fond of this illusion, we might understand ourselves and other peoples better than we do, and be enabled to help them understand us. I am very often tempted to believe that this illusion is all that is left of the great dream that was to have become America; whether this is so or not, this illusion certainly prevents us from making America what we say we want it to be.

But let us put aside, for the moment, these subversive speculations. In the fall of last year, my plane hovered over the rust-red earth of Georgia. I was past thirty, and I had never seen this land before. I pressed my face against the window, watching the earth come closer; soon we were just above the tops of trees. I could not suppress the thought that this earth had acquired its color from the blood that had dripped down from these trees. My mind was filled with the image of a black man, younger than I, perhaps, or my own age, hanging from a tree, while white men watched him and cut his sex from him with a knife.

My father must have seen such sights—he was very old when he died—or heard of them, or had this danger touch him. The Negro poet I talked to in Washington, much younger than my father, perhaps twenty years older than myself, remembered such things very vividly, had a long tale to tell, and counselled me to think back on those days as a means of steadying the soul. I was to remember that time, whatever else it had failed to do, nevertheless had passed, that the situation, whether or not it was better, was certainly no longer the same. I was to remember that Southern Negroes had endured things I could not imagine; but this did not really place me at such a great disadvantage, since they clearly had been unable to imagine what awaited them in Harlem. I remembered the Scottsboro case, which I had followed as a child. I remembered Angelo Herndon and wondered, again, whatever had become of him. I remembered the soldier in uniform blinded by an enraged white man just after the Second World War. There had been many such incidents after the First War, which was one of the reasons I had been born in Harlem. I remembered Willie McGhee, Emmett Till, and the others. My younger brothers had visited Atlanta some years before. I remembered what they had told me about it. One of my brothers, in uniform, had had his front teeth kicked out by a white officer. I remembered my mother telling us how she had wept and prayed and tried to kiss the venom out of her suicidally embittered son. (She managed to do it, too; heaven only knows what she herself was feeling, whose father and brothers had lived and died down here.) I remembered myself, as a very small boy, already so bitter about the pledge of allegiance that I could scarcely bring myself to say it, and never, never believed it.

I was, in short, but one generation removed from the South, which was now undergoing a new convulsion over whether black children had the same rights, or capacities, for education as did the children of white people. This is a criminally frivolous dispute, absolutely unworthy of this nation; and it is being carried on, in complete bad faith, by completely uneducated people. (We do not trust educated people and rarely, alas, produce them, for we do not trust the independence of mind which alone makes a genuine education possible.) Educated people, of any color, are so extremely rare that it is unquestionably one of the first tasks of a nation to open all of its schools to all of its citizens. But the dispute has actually nothing to do with education, as some among the eminently uneducated know. It has to do with political power and it has to do with sex. And this is a nation which, most unluckily, knows very little about either.

The city of Atlanta, according to my notes, is "big, wholly segregated, sprawling; population variously given as six hundred thousand or one million, depending on whether one goes beyond or remains within the city limits. Negroes twenty-five to thirty percent of the population. Racial relations, on the record, can be described as fair, considering that this is the state of Georgia. Growing industrial town. Racial relations manipulated by the Mayor and a fairly strong Negro middle class. This works mainly in the areas of compromise and concession and has very little effect on the bulk of the Negro population and none whatever on the rest of the state. No integration, pending or actual." Also, it seemed to me that the Negroes in Atlanta were "very vividly *city* Negroes"—they seemed less patient than their rural brethren, more dangerous, or at least more unpredictable. And: "Have seen one wealthy Negro section, very pretty, but with an unpaved road. . . . The section in which I am living is composed of frame houses in various stages of disrepair and neglect, in which two and three families live, often sharing a single toilet. This is the other side of the tracks, literally, I mean. It is located, as I am told is the case in many Southern cities, just beyond the underpass." Atlanta contains a high proportion of Negroes who own their own homes and exist, visibly anyway, independently of the white world. Southern towns distrust this class and do everything in their power to prevent its appearance. But it is a class which has a certain usefulness in Southern cities. There is an incipient war, in fact, between Southern cities and Southern towns—between the city, that is, and the state—which we will discuss later. Little Rock is an ominous example of this and it is likely—indeed, it is certain—that we will see many more such examples before the present crisis is over.

Before arriving in Atlanta I had spent several days in Charlotte, North Carolina. This is a bourgeois town, Presbyterian, pretty—if you like towns—and socially so hermetic that it contains scarcely a single decent restaurant. I was told that Negroes there are not even licensed to become electricians or plumbers. I was also told, several times, by white people, that "race relations" there were excellent. I failed to find a single Negro who agreed with this, which is the usual story of "race relations" in this country. Charlotte, a town of 165,000, was in a ferment when I was there because, of its 50,000 Negroes, four had been assigned to previously all-white schools, one to each school. In fact, by the time I got there, there were only three. Dorothy Counts, the daughter of a Presbyterian minister, after several days of being stoned and spat on by the mob—"spit," a woman told me, "was hanging from the hem of Dorothy's dress"—had withdrawn from Harding High. Several white students, I was told, had called—not called *on*— Miss Counts, to beg her to stick it out. Harry Golden, editor of *The Carolina Israelite*, suggested that the "hoodlum element" might not so have shamed the town and the nation if several of the town's leading businessmen had personally escorted Miss Counts to school.

I saw the Negro schools in Charlotte, saw, on street corners, several of their alumnae, and read about others who had been sentenced to the chain gang. This solved the mystery of just what made Negro parents send their children out to face mobs. White people do not understand this because they do not know, and do not want to know, that the alternative to this ordeal is nothing less than a lifelong ordeal. Those Negro parents who spend their days trembling for their children and the rest of their time praying that their children have not been too badly damaged inside, are not doing this out of "ideals" or "convictions" or because they are in the grip of a perverse desire to send their children where "they are not wanted." They are doing it because they want the child to receive the education which will allow him to defeat, possibly escape, and not impossibly help one day abolish the stifling environment in which they see, daily, so many children perish.

This is certainly not the purpose, still less the effect, of most Negro schools. It is hard enough, God knows, under the best of circumstances, to get an education in this country. White children are graduated yearly who can neither read, write, nor think, and who are in a state of the most abysmal ignorance concerning the world around them. But at least they are white. They are under the illusion—which, since they are so badly educated, sometimes has a fatal tenacity—that they can do whatever they want to do. Perhaps that is exactly what they *are* doing, in which case we had best all go down in prayer.

The level of Negro education, obviously, is even lower than the general level. The general level is low because, as I have said, Americans have so little respect for genuine intellectual effort. The Negro level is low because the education of Negroes occurs in, and is designed to perpetuate, a segregated society. This, in the first place, and no matter how much money the South boasts of spending on Negro schools, is utterly demoralizing. It creates a situation in which the Negro teacher is soon as powerless as his students. (There are exceptions among the teachers as there are among the students, but, in this country surely, schools have not been built for the exceptional. And, though white people often seem to expect Negroes to produce nothing but exceptions, the fact is that Negroes are really just like everybody else. Some of them are exceptional and most of them are not.)

The teachers are answerable to the Negro principal, whose power over the teachers is absolute but whose power with the school board is slight. As for this principal, he has arrived at the summit of his career; rarely indeed can he go any higher. He has his pension to look forward to, and he consoles himself, meanwhile, with his status among the "better class of Negroes." This class includes few, if any, of his students and by no means all of his teachers. The teachers, as long as they remain in this school system, and they certainly do not have much choice, can only aspire to become the principal one day. Since not all of them will make it, a great deal of the energy which ought to go into their vocation goes into the usual bitter, purposeless rivalry. They are underpaid and ill-treated by the white world and rubbed raw by it every day; and it is altogether understandable that they, very shortly, cannot bear the sight of their students. The children know this; it is hard to fool young people. They also know why they are going to an overcrowded, outmoded plant, in classes so large that even the most strictly attentive student, the most gifted teacher, cannot but feel himself slowly drowning in the sea of general helplessness.

It is not to be wondered at, therefore, that the violent distractions of puberty, occurring in such a cage, annually take their toll, sending female children into the maternity wards and male children into the streets. It is not to be wondered at that a boy, one day, decides that if all this studying is going to prepare him only to be a porter or an elevator boy—or his teacher—well, then, the hell with it. And there they go, with an overwhelming bitterness which they will dissemble all their lives, an unceasing effort which completes their ruin. They become the menial or the criminal or the shiftless, the Negroes whom segregation has produced and whom the South uses to prove that segregation is right.

In Charlotte, too, I received some notion of what the South means by "time to adjust." The NAACP there had been trying for six years before Black Monday to make the city fathers honor the "separate but equal" statute and do something about the situation in Negro schools. Nothing whatever was done. After Black Monday, Charlotte begged for "time": and what she did with this time was work out legal stratagems designed to get the least possible integration over the longest possible period. In August of 1955, Governor Hodges, a moderate, went on the air with the suggestion that Negroes segregate themselves voluntarily—for the good, as he put it, of both races. Negroes seeming to be unmoved by this moderate proposal, the Klan reappeared in the counties and was still active there when I left. So, no doubt, are the boys on the chain gang.

But "Charlotte," I was told, "is not the South." I was told, "You haven't seen the South yet." Charlotte seemed quite Southern enough for me, but, in fact, the people in Charlotte were right. One of the reasons for this is that the South is not the monolithic structure which, from the North, it appears to be, but a most various and divided region. It clings to the myth of its past but it is being inexorably changed, meanwhile, by an entirely unmythical present: its habits and its self-interest are at war. Everyone in the South feels this and this is why there is such panic on the bottom and such impotence on the top.

It must also be said that the racial setup in the South is not, for a Negro, very different from the racial setup in the North. It is the etiquette which is baffling, not the spirit. Segregation is unofficial in the North and official in the South, a crucial difference that does nothing, nevertheless, to alleviate the lot of most Northern Negroes. But we will return to this question when we discuss the relationship between the Southern cities and states.

Atlanta, however, *is* the South. It is the South in this respect, that it has a very bitter interracial history. This is written in the faces of the people and one feels it in the air. It was on the outskirts of Atlanta that I first felt how the Southern landscape—the trees, the silence, the liquid heat, and the fact that one always seems to be traveling great distances—seems designed for violence, seems, almost, to demand it. What passions cannot be unleashed on a dark road in a Southern night! Everything seems so sensual, so languid, and so private. Desire can be acted out here; over this fence, behind that tree, in the darkness, there; and no one will see, no one will ever know. Only the night is watching and the night was made for desire. Protestantism is the wrong religion for people in such climates; America is perhaps the last nation in which such a climate belongs. In the Southern night everything seems possible, the most private, unspeakable longings; but then arrives the Southern day, as hard and brazen as the night was soft and dark. It brings what was done in the dark to light. It must have seemed something like this for those people who made the region what it is today. It must have caused them great pain. Perhaps the master who had coupled with his slave saw his guilt in his wife's pale eyes in the morning. And the wife saw his children in the slave quarters, saw the way his concubine, the sensual-looking black girl, looked at her—a woman, after all, and scarcely less sensual, but white. The youth, nursed and raised by the black Mammy whose arms had then held all that there was of warmth and love and desire, and still confounded by the dreadful taboos set up between himself and her progeny, must have wondered, after his first experiment with black flesh, where, under the blazing heavens, he could hide. And the white man must have seen his guilt written somewhere else, seen it all the time, even if his sin was merely lust, even if his sin lay in nothing but his power: in the eyes of the black man. He may not have stolen his woman, but he had certainly stolen his freedom—this black man, who had a body like his, and passions like his, and a ruder, more erotic beauty. How many times has the Southern day come up to find that black man, sexless, hanging from a tree!

It was an old black man in Atlanta who looked into my eyes and directed me into my first segregated bus. I have spent a long time thinking about that man. I never saw him again. I cannot describe the look which passed between us, as I asked him for directions, but it made me think, at once, of Shakespeare's "the oldest have borne most." It made me think of the blues: *Now, when a woman gets the blues, Lord, she hangs her head and cries. But when a man gets the blues, Lord, he grabs a train and rides.* It was borne in on me, suddenly, just why these men had so often been grabbing freight trains as the evening sun went down. And it was, perhaps, because I was getting on a segregated bus, and wondering how Negroes had borne this, and other indignities for so long, that this man so struck me. He seemed to know what I was feeling. His eyes seemed to say that what I was feeling he had been feeling, at much higher pressure, all his life. But my eyes would never see the hell his eyes had seen. And this hell was, simply, that he had never in his life owned anything, not his wife, not his house, not his child, which could not, at any instant, be taken from him by the power of white people. This is what paternalism means. And for the rest of the time that I was in the South I watched the eyes of old black men.

Atlanta's well-to-do Negroes never take busses, for they all have cars. The section in which they live is quite far away from the poor Negro section. They own, or at least are paying for, their own homes. They drive to work and back, and have cocktails and dinner with each other. They see very little of the white world; but they are cut off from the black world, too.

Now, of course, this last statement is not literally true. The teachers teach Negroes, the lawyers defend them. The ministers preach to them and bury them, and others insure their lives, pull their teeth, and cure their ailments. Some of the lawyers work with the NAACP and help push test cases through the courts. (If anything, by the way, disproves the charge of "extremism" which has so often been made against this organization, it is the fantastic care and patience such legal efforts demand.) Many of the teachers work very hard to bolster the morale of their students, and prepare them for their new responsibilities; nor did those I met fool themselves about the hideous system under which they work. So when I say that they are cut off from the black world, I am not sneering, which, indeed, I scarcely have any right to do. I am talking about their position as a class—*if* they are a class—and their role in a very complex and shaky social structure.

The wealthier Negroes are, at the moment, very useful for the administration of the city of Atlanta, for they represent there the potential, at least, of interracial communication. That this phrase is a euphemism, in Atlanta as elsewhere, becomes clear when one considers how astonishingly little has been communicated in all these generations. What the phrase almost always has reference to is the fact that, in a given time and place, the Negro vote is of sufficient value to force politicians to bargain for it. What interracial communication also refers to is that Atlanta is really growing and thriving, and because it wants to make even more money, it would like to prevent incidents that disturb the peace, discourage investments, and permit test cases, which the city of Atlanta would certainly lose, to come to the courts. Once this happens, as it certainly will one day, the state of Georgia will be up in arms and the present administration of the city will be out of power. I did not meet a soul in Atlanta (I naturally did not meet any members of the White Citizen's Council, not, anyway, to talk to) who did not pray that the present Mayor would be re-elected. Not that they loved him particularly, but it is his administration which holds off the holocaust.

Now this places Atlanta's wealthy Negroes in a really quite sinister position. Though both they and the Mayor are devoted to keeping the peace, their aims and his are not, and cannot be, the same. Many of those lawyers are working day and night on test cases which the Mayor is doing his best to keep out of court. The teachers spend their working day attempting to destroy in their students— and it is not too much to say, in themselves—those habits of inferiority which form one of the principal cornerstones of segregation as it is practiced in the South. Many of the parents listen to speeches by people like Senator Russell and find themselves unable to sleep at night. They are in the extraordinary position of being compelled to work for the destruction of all they have bought so dearly—their homes, their comfort, the safety of their children. But the safety of their children is merely comparative; it is all that their comparative strength as a class has bought them so far; and they are not safe, really, as long as the bulk of Atlanta's Negroes live in such darkness. On any night, in that other part of town, a policeman may beat up one Negro too many, or some Negro or some white man may simply go berserk. This is all it takes to drive so delicately balanced a city mad. And the island on which these Negroes have built their handsome houses will simply disappear.

This is not at all in the interests of Atlanta, and almost everyone there knows it. Left to itself, the city might grudgingly work out compromises designed to reduce the tension and raise the level of Negro life. But it is not left to itself; it belongs to the state of Georgia. The Negro vote has no power in the state, and the Governor of Georgia—that "third-rate man," Atlantans call him—makes great political capital out of keeping the Negroes in their place. When six Negro ministers attempted to create a test case by ignoring the segregation ordinance on the busses, the Governor was ready to declare martial law and hold the ministers incommunicado. It was the Mayor who prevented this, who somehow squashed all publicity, treated the ministers with every outward sign of respect, and it is his office which is preventing the case from coming into court. And remember that it was the Governor of Arkansas, in an insane bid for political power, who created the present crisis in Little Rock—against the will of most of its citizens and against the will of the Mayor.

This war between the Southern cities and states is of the utmost importance, not only for the South, but for the nation. The Southern states are still very largely governed by people whose political lives, insofar, at least, as they are able to conceive of life or politics, are dependent on the people in the rural regions. It might, indeed, be more honorable to try to guide these people out of their pain and ignorance instead of locking them within it, and battening on it; but it is, admittedly, a difficult task to try to tell people the truth and it is clear that most Southern politicians have no intention of attempting it. The attitude of these people can only have the effect of stiffening the already implacable Negro resistance, and this attitude is absolutely certain, sooner or later, to create great trouble in the cities. When a race riot occurs in Atlanta, it will not spread merely to Birmingham, for example. (Birmingham is a doomed city.) The trouble will spread to every metropolitan center in the nation which has a significant Negro population. And this is not only because the ties between Northern and Southern Negroes are still very close. It is because the nation, the entire nation, has spent a hundred years avoiding the question of the place of the black man in it.

That this has done terrible things to black men is not even a question. "Integration," said a very light Negro to me in Alabama, "has always worked very well in the South, after the sun goes down." "It's not miscegenation," said another Negro to me, "unless a black man's involved." Now, I talked to many Southern liberals who were doing their best to bring integration about in the South, but met scarcely a single Southerner who did not weep for the passing of the old order. They were perfectly sincere, too, and, within their limits, they were right. They pointed out how Negroes and whites in the South had loved each other, they recounted to me tales of devotion and heroism which the old order had produced, and which, now, would never come again. But the old black men I looked at down there—those same black men that the Southern liberal had loved, for whom, until now, the Southern liberal and not only the liberal, has been willing to undergo great inconvenience and danger—they were not weeping. Men do not like to be protected, it emasculates them. This is what black men know, it is the reality they have lived with; it is what white men do not want to know. It is not a pretty thing to be a father and be ultimately dependent on the power and kindness of some other man for the well-being of your house.

But what this evasion of the Negro's humanity has done to the nation is not so well known. The really striking thing, for me, in the South was this dreadful paradox, that the black men were stronger than the white. I do not know how they did it, but it certainly has something to do with that, as yet, unwritten history of the Negro woman. What it comes to, finally, is that the nation has spent a large part of its time and energy looking away from one of the principal facts of its life. This failure to look reality in the face diminishes a nation as it diminishes a person, and it can only be described as unmanly. And in exactly the same way that the South imagines that it "knows" the Negro, the North imagines that it has set him free. Both camps are deluded. Human freedom is a complex, difficult—and private—thing. If we can liken life, for a moment, to a furnace, then freedom is the fire which burns away illusion. Any honest examination of the national life proves how far we are from the standard of human freedom with which we began. The recovery of this standard demands of everyone who loves this country a hard look at himself, for the greatest achievements must begin somewhere, and they always begin with the person. If we are not capable of this examination, we may yet become one of the most distinguished and monumental failures in the history of nations.   1959, vol. 26, no. 1

• The Cold War and the West

The contributions that appear here are replies to the following statements and questions.

As the situation becomes more critical, we think it important to reexamine some of the basic issues of the cold war which tend to become obscured by day-to-day politics even though they are expressed by them.

We feel that if these questions and their implications are not faced, we may find ourselves drifting from one position to another, always on the edge of nuclear destruction, reduced to a rhetoric of good will and indignation or to action taken blindly and without an adequate sense of history.

We would like you to participate in a symposium on these issues. The following questions are intended only as a guide, to provide a context for the discussion.

You are of course free to answer or ignore any of the questions or to discuss the problem in any way you choose.

1. What is your opinion of the position of the West in the cold war? Has the West been winning, losing, or holding its own? If you think it has been losing, or is likely to lose in the future, to what do you attribute this? Which features of the social and economic system prevailing in the West generally, and in the U.S. in particular, account for failures in coping with Soviet Communism?

2. To what degree is it desirable and possible for the U.S. so to reorient its policies as to identify with the movements and leaders of change throughout the world instead of supporting the opponents of radical social reform, as the U.S. has tended to do in the past? Do you think the present administration is making any decisive change in American policy in this respect?

3. Does the position of democratic socialism have any relevance, in the short or long run, to the cold war (not only in Europe and in the underdeveloped areas but in America as well)?

4. What are we defending in the West? Are the intellectual values and freedoms and the political and civil liberties we all affirm inseparable from the West's existing political and social institutions?

5. What has been the effect of the cold war on political thought and speculation in the Western world?

6. What are the objectives of the East and West? Are they ultimately negotiable? If the answer is yes, what are the chances of nuclear disarmament? And if some form of such disarmament were achieved, what would the West's prospects be in the ensuing political, economic, and ideological competition? If the answer is no, do you think the advance of Communism can be stopped without nuclear conflict?

7. Do you think the issues at stake in the cold war so decisive as to be worth a nuclear war?

Hannah Arendt

Wars and revolutions have thus far determined the physiognomy of the twentieth century; and in contrast to the ideologies which in the last twenty years have more and more degenerated into empty talk, war and revolution still constitute the two major political issues with which we are confronted. In actual fact, the two are interrelated in many ways, and yet for a clarification of these matters they must be kept apart. Historically, wars are among the oldest phenomena of recorded history while revolutions in the modern sense of the word probably did not exist prior to the end of the eighteenth century; they are the most recent of all major political data. Moreover, revolutions are very likely to stay with us into the foreseeable future whereas wars, if they should continue to threaten the existence of mankind and hence remain unjustifiable on rational grounds, might disappear, at least in their present form, even without a concomitant radical transformation of international relations. Hence—in anticipation of what I have to say—short of total annihilation and short of a decisive technical development in warfare, the present conflict between the two parts of the world may well be decided by the simple question of which side understands better what is involved and what is at stake in revolution.

In the following I would like to take up, almost at random, a few considerations which all seem to point in the same direction.

1. Obviously, Clausewitz's definition of war as the continuation of politics with other means, however appropriate it might have been for the limited warfare of European nation states in the eighteenth and nineteenth centuries, no longer applies to our situation. This would be true even without nuclear warfare. Since the First World War, we know that no government and no form of government can be expected to survive a defeat in war. A revolutionary change in government—either brought about by the people themselves, as after World War I, or enforced by the victorious powers through the demand of unconditional surrender and the establishment of War Trials—belongs among the most certain consequences of defeat even if we rule out total annihilation or complete chaos. Hence, even prior to nuclear warfare, wars had become politically, though not yet biologically, a matter of life and death.

At the moment when we are so preoccupied with the threat of total annihilation this may appear irrelevant. But it is not at all inconceivable that the next stage of technical advancement may bring us back to a kind of warfare which, though probably still horrible enough, will not be suicidal and, perhaps, not even spell complete annihilation to the defeated. Such a development seems to be within the range of definite possibilities for the simple reason that our present stage of international relationships, still based upon national sovereignty, cannot function without force or the threat of force as the *ultima ratio* of all foreign policy. Whether we like it or not, our present system of foreign affairs makes no sense without war as a last resort; and put before the alternative of either changing this system radically or making some technical discoveries which would bring war back into the political arena, the latter course may well turn out to be much easier and more feasible.

Politically, the point of the matter is that even under changed technical circumstances it is not likely that governments, no matter how well established and trusted by its citizens, could survive defeat in war, and such survival must be counted as one of the supreme tests of a government's strength and authority. In other words, under conditions of modern warfare even in its pre-nuclear stage, all governments have lived on borrowed time. Hence the war question—in its most extreme form a question of biological survival—is under any circumstances a question of political survival. Only if we succeed in ruling out war from politics altogether can we hope to achieve that minimum of stability and permanence of the body politic without which no political life and no political change are possible.

2. Confusion and inadequacy in the discussion of the war question are not surprising. The truth is that a rational debate is impossible as long as we find ourselves caught in a technical stage of development where the means of warfare are such as to exclude their rational use. To try and decide between "better dead than red" and "better red than dead" resembles nothing so much as trying to square the circle. For those who tell us better dead than red forget that it is a very different matter to risk one's own life for the life and freedom of one's country and for posterity than to risk the very existence of the human species for the same purposes. Moreover, the very formula goes back to antiquity and rests upon the ancient conviction that slaves are not human, that to lose one's freedom means to change one's nature and to become, as it were, dehumanized. None of us, I think, can say that he believes this, least of all those liberals who today try to avail themselves of the old formula. But this is not to say that its reversal has any more to recommend itself. When an old truth ceases to be applicable, it does not become any truer by being stood on its head. Within the framework of realities which we face, the slogan "better red than dead" can mean only the signing of one's own death sentence even before this sentence has been passed and decided upon.

Insofar as the discussion of the war question moves within the closed circle of this preposterous alternative, it is nearly always conducted with a mental reservation on both sides. Those who say "better dead than red" actually think: "The losses may not be as great as some anticipate, our civilization will survive"; while those who say "better red than dead" actually think: "slavery will not be so bad, man will not change his nature, freedom will not vanish from the earth forever." What should alarm us in these discussions is the reckless optimism on both sides—on one side, the readiness to count the losses in the tens and hundreds of millions, due in part, perhaps, to a simple failure of imagination but also in part to the frightful and frightening increase of population; and on the other side, the readiness to forget the concentration—and extermination—camps and with them the terrible prospect of freedom vanishing from the earth forever.

The only consoling aspect of this debate seems to lie in that all concerned by now are agreed, not only that war as such stands in need of justification, but that its only possible justification is freedom. This is not a matter of course for a number of reasons. First, freedom is implicitly recognized as the very center, the *raison d'être*, of politics by people who fifteen or twenty years ago would have thought this the utmost of political naiveté, if not a prejudice of the lower middle classes. More importantly, perhaps, justifications of war are at least as old as Roman antiquity, but, contrary to what we are inclined to think, it was not freedom but necessity upon which these justifications usually were based. "Just is a war which is necessary, and hallowed are the arms where no hope exists but in them," said Livy, and by necessity he and his successors throughout the centuries understood all the well-known realities of power politics—such as conquest and expansion, defense of vested interests and preservation of power or conservation of a power equilibrium, etc.—which we today would find quite sufficient to dub a war unjust rather than just, although we know, of course, that they caused the outbreak of most wars in history. Even our present-day notion that aggression is a crime has acquired its practical and theoretical significance only after the First World War had demonstrated the horribly destructive potentialities of warfare under conditions of modern technology.

3. Since the alliance which achieved victory in the Second World War was not strong enough to achieve peace as well, the whole postwar period has been spent by the two major powers in defining their spheres of interest and in jockeying for position in the rapidly changing power structure of a world in turmoil. This period has been called "cold war," and the term is accurate enough if we recall that fear of a major war has determined the actual conduct of foreign affairs and preoccupied public opinion more than any other issue. But in actual fact and despite occasional flare-ups, this whole period was much rather a time of cold and uneasy peace, and the reason why I insist on this is not that I am interested in semantics, but that I feel we should not cry wolf too soon.

In other words, what I am afraid of is that a cold war as a real substitute for a hot war may break out one day because it might constitute the only alternative in our present situation, in which we must avoid the threat of total annihilation without knowing how to exclude war as such from the realm of foreign politics. The recent and, let us hope, temporary resumption of nuclear tests has shown how a cold war actually might be conducted. For these tests, unlike those that preceded them, were no longer conducted for the mere sake of the perfection of certain armaments. The tests themselves were meant as an instrument of policy, and they were immediately understood as such. They gave the rather ominous impression of some sort of tentative warfare in which two opposing camps demonstrate to each other the destructiveness of the weapons in their possession. And while it is always possible that this deadly game of ifs and whens may suddenly turn into the real thing, it is not inconceivable that one day a hypothetical victory and a hypothetical defeat could end a war that never exploded into reality.

Is this sheer fantasy? I think not. We were confronted, potentially at least, with this sort of thing at the end of the Second World War, at the very moment when the atomic bomb made its first appearance. At that time, it was considered whether a demonstration of the potency of the new weapon on a deserted island might not be enough to force the Japanese into unconditional surrender. The advantages of this alternative have been argued many times on moral grounds, and I think rightly so. The decisive political argument in its favor was that it would have been much more in line with our actual and professed war aims; surely, what we wished to achieve was unconditional surrender, not extermination or wholesale slaughter of the civilian population.

Hypothetical warfare, it must be admitted, rests on at least two assumptions, both of which are actualities in the relationships between those fully developed powers which could enter into a nuclear war at all. It presupposes, first, a stage of technical development where risks can be calculated with almost perfect precision so that very little room is left to chance. Second, it presupposes an equality of knowledge and know-how among those who are at war. Thus, a chess game between two equally experienced players will end with one of them conceding defeat or with both agreeing on a stalemate long before all the moves leading to it have been made. The comparison of war with chess is old and has never been true, because the outcome depended to a high degree on chance and on personal factors—such as troop morale and military strategy. Technical warfare has eliminated these factors to such an extent that the old simile may unexpectedly acquire its measure of truth. Or to put this another way, mutual recognition of the results of a cold war which actually is a war would not imply a change in human nature; the demonstration of the A-bomb would have *forced* the enemy into unconditional surrender, it would not have *persuaded* him. For the experts, the results of the tests could be as conclusive and as compelling evidence for victory and defeat as the battlefield, the conquest of territory, the calculation of losses, etc. have been for the generals on either side in hot wars.

4. The trouble with these reflections is the same as with other discussions of the war question: they are idle, there is little we can do about the whole business one way or another. Even clarifications and attempts at understanding, though always tempting and, perhaps, necessary for the sake of human dignity, can hardly have any practical or even theoretical results. It is precisely a sense of futility which seems to haunt us whenever we approach this matter.

The same is not at all true for the other great issue confronting us, the issue of revolution. This issue can be clarified in the light of past and present experience, and such clarification is not likely to be futile. Its first prerequisite is to recognize and to understand what seems to be so obvious that no one is willing to talk about it, namely, that the inherent aim of revolution has always been freedom and nothing else. The chief obstacles to such an understanding are of course the various ideologies—capitalism, socialism, communism—all of which owe their existence to the nineteenth century and to social and economic conditions which were utterly unlike our own. We are in no position today to foretell what kind of economic system may eventually prove to be the best under the rapidly changing technical and scientific circumstances all over the world. But we can say even now that the West has long since ceased to live and to act in accordance with the tenets of capitalism, just as we can see that the chief obstacle to rapid progress in countries ruled by Communist dictatorships is precisely their rigid belief in an ideology. The truth of the matter is that West and East are now engaged in all kinds of economic experiments, and this is as it should be. The freer these experiments are from ideological considerations, the better the results are likely to be; and a competition between different economic systems, in view of the enormous objective problems involved, may eventually turn out to be no less healthy than competition has been within the more restricted framework of national economies. Politically, the only issue at stake between West and East is freedom versus tyranny; and the only political freedom within the economic realm concerns the citizens' right to choose their profession and their place of work.

If the ideologies of the nineteenth century constitute a severe handicap in understanding the dangers and the potentialities of the conflict which divides the world today, the two great revolutions of the eighteenth century—which politically, though not economically, are the origin, the birthplace as it were, of the modern world—may well contain the very principles which are still at stake. Since I cannot possibly hope to argue this matter at all plausibly within the framework of these casual remarks, I shall try and make a few points which seem to me to sum up what came to my mind when I read your questions. First, I must admit that I immediately interpreted or reformulated them until they seemed to be contained in a single question: What are the prospects of the West in the near future, provided nuclear war is avoided and provided, as I believe, revolution will remain the major issue of the century?

My first point would be that every revolution must go through two stages, the stage of liberation—from poverty (which is a liberation from necessity), or from political domination, foreign or domestic (which is a liberation from force)—and the stage of foundation, the constitution of a new body politic or a new form of government. In terms of historical processes, these two belong together, but as political phenomena, they are very different matters and must be kept distinct. My point here is not merely the truism (theoretically interesting enough) that liberation is the prerequisite of freedom and hence entirely different from it, but the practical truth that liberation, and especially liberation from necessity, always takes precedence over the building of freedom because of the urgency inherent in necessity. Moreover, liberation, even if successfully achieved, never guarantees the establishment of freedom; it does no more than remove the most obvious obstacle to it.

My second point would be that the whole record of revolutions—if we only knew how to read it—demonstrates beyond doubt that every attempt to abolish poverty, i.e., to solve the so-called social question with political means is doomed to failure and for this reason leads into terror; terror, on the other hand, sends revolutions to their doom. There has been not a single revolution that ever succeeded in the most important business of revolution, the establishment of a new government for the sake of freedom, except the American Revolution which also was unique in that it was not confronted with mass poverty but conducted, even then, under conditions of an otherwise unknown prosperity.

From this I would conclude that there would indeed be no great hope that revolution and freedom could ever succeed in the world at large if we were still living under conditions where scarcity and abundance were beyond the scope of human power. The American Revolution, that is, the experience of foundation on which the republic of the United States rests, would remain what it has been for so long, an exception from an iron rule and an incident of hardly more than local significance. But this is no longer the case. Even though the difficulties standing in the way to a solution of the predicament of mass poverty are still staggering, they are, in principle at least, no longer insurmountable. The advancement of the natural sciences and their technology has opened possibilities which make it very likely that, in a not too distant future, we shall be able to deal with all economic matters on technical and scientific grounds, outside all political considerations. Even today, in the fully developed areas of the West, necessity (and neither political nor humanitarian considerations) is pressing us into all sorts of Point Four programs for the simple reason that our economy produces abundance and superabundance in the same automatic way as the economy of the early modern age produced mass poverty. Our present technical means permit us to fight poverty, and force us to fight superabundance, in complete political neutrality; in other words economic factors need not interfere with political developments one way or another. This means for our political future that the wreckage of freedom on the rock of necessity which we have witnessed over and over again since Robespierre's "despotism of liberty" is no longer unavoidable.

Short of war and short of total annihilation, both of which I fear will remain actual dangers, the position of the West in general and of the United States in particular will depend to a considerable extent upon a clear understanding of these two factors involved in revolution: freedom and the conquest of poverty. Technically and economically, the West is in an excellent position to help in the struggle against poverty and misery which is now going on all over the world. If we fail to do our part in this struggle, I am afraid, we shall have occasion to learn by bitter experience how right the men of the French Revolution were when they exclaimed: "*Les malheureux sont la puissance de la terre.*" What we seem to fail to understand—in the West in general and in the United States in particular—is the enormous power inherent in wretchedness, once this *malheur* has come out into the open and has made its voice heard in public. This happened for the first time in the French Revolution, and it has happened time and again ever since. In a sense, the fight against poverty, though to be conducted by technical, nonpolitical means, must also be understood as a power struggle, namely, as the struggle against the force of necessity to prepare the way for the forces of freedom. In the United States the failure to understand the political relevance of the social question may have its roots in the history of the country, and especially in the history of the revolution which gave birth to the country's form of government. By the same token, the people of this republic should be in the best possible position to set an example for the whole world—and particularly to those new ethnic groups and peoples who in rapid succession are now rising to nationhood—when it comes to questions of founding new political bodies and establishing lasting institutions of liberty. There are, I think, two chief reasons why we have been found wanting even there, the one being our failure to remember and to articulate conceptually what was at stake in the American Revolution, and this to such an extent that the denial that a revolution ever had taken place here could become, for a long time, a cherished tenet of public as well as learned opinion. The second reason for our failure is perhaps even more serious because it obviously concerns a failing of the revolution itself and of the whole ensuing history of the country—i.e., the inability to solve the race question.

Let me point in conclusion to the last two major revolutions—the Hungarian Revolution, so quickly and so brutally crushed by Russia, and the Cuban Revolution which has fallen under Russian influence. After the American Revolution, the Hungarian Revolution was the first I know of in which the question of bread, of poverty, of the order of society, played no role whatsoever; it was entirely political in the sense that the people fought for nothing but freedom, and that their chief concern was the form the new government should assume. None of the participants—and they included practically the whole population—even thought of undoing the profound social change which the Communist regime had effected in the country. It was precisely the social conditions which everyone took for granted—just as, in vastly different circumstances, the men of the American Revolution had taken for granted the social and economic conditions of the people. Obviously, the Cuban Revolution offers the opposite example; up to now, it has run true to the course of the French Revolution, and for this very reason has fallen so easily under the sway of Bolshevism. If I reflect on our attitude toward these two recent revolutions, it seems to me that whatever we did, or rather did not do, during the Hungarian crisis—right or wrong—was based upon considerations of power politics but not upon a failure to understand what the whole business was all about. In the case of the Cuban Revolution, however, so much closer to us geographically, and yet apparently so much farther removed from our sphere of comprehension, our behavior, I think, demonstrates that we have not understood what it means when a poverty-stricken people in a backward country where corruption has been rampant for a very long time is suddenly released from the obscurity of their farms and houses, permitted to show their misery, and invited into the streets of the country's capital they never saw before. The mistake of the Cuban adventure did not lie so much in wrong information as in a conspicuous inability to comprehend the revolutionary spirit, to grasp what it means when *les malheureux* have come into the open and are told: All this is yours, there are your streets, and your buildings, and your possessions, and hence your pride. From now on, you will yield the road to no one, you will walk in dignity.

Ultimately and short of catastrophe, the position of the West will depend upon its understanding of revolution. And revolution involves both liberation from necessity so that men may walk in dignity and constitution of a body politic that may permit them to act in freedom.

Mary McCarthy

It doesn't seem to me meaningful to talk about "the West" as though it were a political or spiritual whole confronting "the East." The Western nations are divided and not just on what might be considered merely tactical questions, such as whether or not to admit Communist China to the U.N. or what terms to make on Berlin—assuming these are tactical questions and not questions of principle, though indeed this is one of the points of division, for there is a strain in American thought that does not care to distinguish between tactics and principle and regards any mobility vis-à-vis Communism as a "surrender" of principle or to put it in ad men's terms "assuming a posture of retreat," which may mean the same thing.

As far as principles goes, what principle unites the West? It cannot be the so-called Western values, for these values, if they include freedom and the usual democratic rights, are not prized by Spain or Portugal or even by the de Gaulle government. It cannot be a belief in God or in a transcendent power or idea. Can it be the Western standard of living—erected into a principle? Possibly. Yet this consumer well-being is not enjoyed by large parts of the Italian population, not to mention the Spanish and the Portuguese. Khrushchev, moreover, has been promising to give the Russians a standard of living that will equal that of the West, in terms of cars, television sets, frigidaires, mixers, etc., and I don't take it as an article of faith that he will be unable to do this—his meeting with Nixon in the model kitchen struck me as prophetic. Does it boil down to opposition to Communism? Is this the unifying principle? But opposition to Communism is not a principle per se. Anti-Communism in itself is scarcely a virtue—look at Hitler or Senator McCarthy or the average anti-Communist. Anti-Communism, to be principled, must base itself, surely, on some moral good. Thus it appears that reasoning on this subject goes around in circles. We have no *reason*, beyond mere prejudice or crude interest, to stand together against "the East" unless we stand together for something else—for political freedom, as well as material ease (on which America will not always have a monopoly). But this we don't do, and the more threatened we feel by Communism, the more we are encouraged to seek allies (and not only in foreign lands) who have an "interest" in opposing Communism, as though this "interest"—capital investments or an international religious network or maintenance of a ruling class in power—were the only human force we could trust.

It is claimed that what is at stake is survival: after the West has survived it can reopen its museum of values, some wings of which have been closed for the duration. But this is what the Russians claim too. They too have a museum of Western values. The "cultural heritage" of the Greeks, of the Romans, of the philosophers, poets, and painters, would not be lost if the West were to lose the battle for men's minds as it is called. And the Russians too promise freedom, not just culture in libraries, once capitalism has been finally defeated. . . .

My feeling is that political thought today would be less paralyzed if we stopped using terms like "the West," which are sheer cant at present, and said what we really meant, e.g., "nations friendly to capitalism," if that *is* what we mean. This would make our heads a little clearer in the argument we conduct with ourselves about nuclear war. While we prepare to die for the survival of the West, it would be reassuring to know what the West is or was, before we and it died for it. "He died for liber-r-ty," an old Irish saloonkeeper said to me one St. Patrick's Day, speaking of Robert Emmett. This was true, roughly speaking, of the Irish patriot, but it cannot be said of a nation of "patriots" herded hopefully in bomb shelters with a stock of canned goods. If we die it will not be for liberty but because we had no real choice in the matter. If you gave the ordinary man a free choice he would prefer a harsh life under Communism to death in a thermonuclear holocaust. Who wouldn't? And if the ordinary man were politically serious he would still more emphatically choose life under Communism to mass incineration. Alive, he could engage in political agitation, get arrested, go to Siberia; if he were shot eventually for his activities, his death at least would have some meaning.

This in fact is the difference. From the point of view of the ordinary conscript death in war has always been senseless as compared to death in bed. The drafted soldiers and the bombed civilians who died in the last war did not, for the most part probably, die for liberty as a matter of intention; nevertheless, their death served a purpose: the fall of the Nazis and the end of the concentration camps. Their deaths can be said to have been "worth it." But today no such clear and defined aim can be proposed for the extinction of most of the population of the world, to say nothing of the genetic consequences for the survivors. Neither Western values, nor the Western standard of living, nor capitalism in its present form, nor faith in God (I should think) would survive an exchange of hydrogen bombs. When war becomes total, war aims—that is, objectives apart from war itself—disappear. If we die, it will not be for freedom but out of a kind of inert necessity, in a chain reaction of challenge-and-response like the process of fission itself.

To say this is not to advocate surrender to Communism; that is really a scholastic issue like What-would-you-do-if-a-Negro-wanted-to-marry-your-sister? There is far more danger now of nuclear war than there is of what is called a "Communist takeover." It is on this issue—the issue of how to disarm—that we ought to try to regain our freedom of thought and hence our freedom of political action.

Hans J. Morgenthau

The cold war is being waged on two fronts: in Europe where the issue is Germany, and in Asia, Africa, and Latin America where the issue is the political orientation of the underdeveloped nations of the world.

In Europe, the cold war arose from the unsettled territorial issues of the Second World War. At the end of that war, a line of military demarcation was established between East and West which placed the Red Army a hundred miles east of the Rhine. The Soviet Union has consistently maintained that this line constitutes the definitive western boundary of the Soviet bloc, while the West has as consistently maintained that this line is only provisional and that the definitive boundary would have to run farther to the east. The West has successfully protected that line through the policy of containment. Stalin and Khrushchev have attempted by all kinds of devices to obtain from the West the formal recognition of the legitimacy of the territorial status quo in Europe; the raising of the Berlin issue by Khrushchev is but the latest of these attempts.

Two factors have prevented the West from considering such formal recognition: the trauma of the Yalta agreements and the fear of West German reaction. The Yalta agreements were an attempt to undo, at least in a certain measure, the political consequences of the conquest of Eastern Europe by the Red Army. This was to be achieved through free democratic elections. This being the intention of the West, it could hardly be expected that the Soviet Union would cooperate in dismantling its recently conquered European empire. Yet Western opinion has never recovered from the shock over the failure of the Soviet Union to live up to the Yalta agreements.

The issue of the European status quo has come to a head in the issues of German unification and the revision of the Oder-Neisse line. For if the Soviet Union has its way, Germany will remain divided in virtual perpetuity and the present boundary between East Germany and Poland will remain unchanged. But while the West has committed itself in words to German unification and the revision of the Oder-Neisse line, it has been unable to devise a policy in support of these objectives. Here is indeed the Achilles' heel of the Western position.

What the West pretends to be seeking in Europe can obviously not be obtained short of either a victorious war or irresistible diplomatic pressure. In other words, it cannot be obtained at all in the foreseeable future. The statesmen of the West know this, but they feel compelled to continue their verbal commitment to unattainable goals. For this verbal commitment provides at the very least the rationalization for the Western orientation of West Germany. West Germany has joined the Atlantic Alliance with the understanding that the Alliance will be used as an instrument for unification and the revision of the Oder-Neisse line. In the measure that it becomes obvious to West German opinion that the Alliance cannot be used for that purpose West Germany may turn elsewhere for the satisfaction of its national aspirations. It is this possibility of an Eastern orientation of West Germany which threatens the West with a danger and provides an opportunity for the Soviet Union.

The United States has fought the cold war in Europe with a considerable measure of success. While it has been unable to advance, it has not been forced to retreat. It has succeeded in doing what it originally set out to do: to contain the Soviet Union within the limits its power had reached at the end of the Second World War. Yet the positive goals of the cold war, unification of Germany and revision of her Eastern frontiers, not only were not achieved, but they were proven of being incapable of achievement, and our persistent verbal commitment to them threatens to jeopardize either the peace of the world or the success of our containment policy or both.

On the other cold war front, in the struggle for the minds of men in Asia, Africa, and Latin America, the position of the United States is both more complex and, even in the short run, less satisfactory. The United States must overcome a number of handicaps, some the result of objective conditions, others of its own making.

First of all, the United States is a Western capitalistic nation. Both in its civilization and social and economic structure, it belongs to that complex of nations which until recently were able to hold Africa, Latin America, and the more advanced areas of Asia in a condition of colonial or semi-colonial dependency. It has military alliances with these nations, and while it has generally shunned and even opposed outright colonial policies, it has actively and successfully participated in the semicolonial exploitation of backward nations. Thus the resentment against the former colonial powers attaches also to it, and its policies of foreign aid are frequently suspected as serving in disguise the traditional ends of colonialism.

Furthermore, the United States, by dint of its pluralistic political philosophy and social system, cannot bring to the backward nations of the world a simple message of salvation supported first by dedicated and disciplined revolutionary minorities and then by totalitarian control. In the nature of things, the advantage lies here with the Communist powers. They are, as it were, specialists in exploiting a revolutionary situation, which is bound to cause us embarrassment. For while the Communists are able to direct a revolution into the desired channels through their use of a disciplined minority, we, even if we are convinced that revolution is inevitable and therefore do not oppose it, tend to look with misgivings upon it since we cannot control the direction it will take.

The Communist powers have still another advantage over the United States in that their problems and achievements are more meaningful, at least on the surface, to the underdeveloped nations than are ours. The Soviet Union has achieved, and Communist China attempts to achieve, what the more enlightened underdeveloped nations seek: a drastic increase in the standard of living through rapid industrialization. The Communist powers use totalitarian control as their instrument and Communist doctrine as rationalization and justification. Seeking the same results, the underdeveloped nations cannot help being attracted by the methods which brought these results about elsewhere. In contrast, the slow process, stretching over centuries, through which the nations of the West achieved a high standard of living through industrialization must appeal much less to them. That appeal is lessened even more by the economic processes of the free market and the political processes of liberal democracy through which in large measure the Western industrialization was achieved. For these processes require a degree of moral restraint and economic and political sophistication which are largely absent in the underdeveloped nations. The simple and crude methods of totalitarianism must appear to them much more congenial.

While the United States must live with these handicaps which are not of its making, trying to overcome them by compensating for them, there are others which are the result of misconceptions in our thinking and errors in the execution of policy.

The United States is both domestically and internationally—and must so appear particularly to the underdeveloped nations—a conservative power. Abroad, it wants to preserve the territorial status quo and domestically it wants to protect and develop what it has achieved. In consequence of this general conservative outlook, the United States has tended to support abroad the most conservative elements because they seem to be "safest" in terms of the preservation of the status quo. This has proven to be a fatal miscalculation. For in many of the underdeveloped nations the choice is not between the status quo and change, but between change under Communist auspices and change which at the very least is not directed by Communists. For reasons mentioned above, the United

States has recently come to realize that it cannot help but support radical change. Yet this realization faces it with a new problem.

Change can be brought about by two different methods: through peaceful reforms or through violent revolution. Peaceful change requires the cooperation of the ruling groups, which has but rarely been forthcoming. For social and economic change is bound to threaten the foundations of their power. If these groups do not cooperate or, as they frequently do, actively oppose change, the United States must turn to alternative groups. Where they do not exist it must develop them. In this task, the United States has signally failed. Yet when worst comes to worst it must be willing to reconcile itself to revolutionary change, even at the risk that such change may take place under Communist auspices.

At this point, foreign policies and domestic politics merge. For the domestic climate of opinion constitutes at present a virtually insuperable impediment to American officials abroad pursuing such a novel and risky policy of promoting revolution. Communist successes abroad have in the past been equated with treason at home. Successive presidents have failed in the task, which only they can perform, of educating the American people in the facts of international life. If President Kennedy continues to fail to bring home to the American people what the facts of international life require of American foreign policy, he will have doomed to failure the cold war policies of the United States in the uncommitted third of the world.

On the level of the execution of policy, that failure is threatened by the deficiencies of our policy of foreign aid. The American theory and practice of foreign aid during the fifties was derived largely from certain unexamined assumptions which are part of the American folklore of politics. The popular mind has established a number of simple and highly doubtful correlations between foreign aid, on the one hand, and a rising standard of living, social and political stability, democratic institutions and practices, and a peaceful foreign policy, on the other. The simplicity of these correlations is so reassuring that the assumption of a simple and direct relationship between foreign aid and economic, social, and political progress is rarely questioned.

Thus fundamental questions like the following were hardly ever asked explicitly: what are the social, political, and moral effects of foreign aid likely to be under different circumstances? Does successful foreign aid require a particular intellectual, political, and moral climate, or will the injection of capital and technological capability from the outside create this climate? To what extent and under what conditions is it possible for one nation to transform, through outside intervention, the economic and technological life of another nation? More specifically, in terms of the political objective of keeping the uncommitted nations uncommitted, how is one to create that positive relationship in the mind of the recipient between the aid and its beneficial results, and the political philosophy, system, and objectives of the giver? As long as the recipient disapproves of the politics of the giver, the political effects of the aid are lost. These effects are similarly lost as long as the recipient remains unconvinced that the aid received is but a natural manifestation of the politics of the giver. Foreign aid, then, remains politically ineffective as long as the recipient says either, "Aid is good, but the politics of the giver are bad," or "Aid is good, but the politics of the giver have nothing to do with it."

Questions such as these require policies of extraordinary subtlety and intricacy to answer them. The simple correlation between foreign aid and what the United States desires in the uncommitted nations could not provide the answers. That correlation is a projection of the domestic experience of America onto the international scene. Capital formation and investment and technological innovation created the wealth and prosperity of America, and, so it was assumed, the export of American capital and technology into the underdeveloped nations would bring forth similar results there. The similarity between this and the Wilsonian expectation is striking. Wilson wanted to bring the peace and order of America to the rest of the world by exporting its democratic institutions. His contemporary heirs wanted to bring the wealth and prosperity of America to the rest of the world through the export of American capital and technology. Yet while the failure of the Wilsonian experiment was quick and drastically revealed, the failure of foreign aid, simplistically conceived, has been less obvious, albeit no less drastic.

The United States must start thinking of foreign aid not as a self-sufficient technical enterprise but as a political weapon to be applied to a great variety of situations with great subtlety and sophistication. The first prerequisite for the development of a viable philosophy of foreign aid is the recognition of the diversity of policies that go by that name. At least six such policies can be distinguished which have only one thing in common: the transfer of money and economic services from one nation to another. They are humanitarian foreign aid, military foreign aid, bribery, prestige foreign aid, subsistence foreign aid, and foreign aid for economic development. To identify each situation and the measures of foreign aid appropriate to it requires a political sensitivity both in understanding and action which thus far has been largely absent from the operations of our foreign aid. Yet without it much of our effort in this field will continue to be wasteful and even counterproductive in that it creates expectations which are bound to be disappointed.

To win the cold war on this second front or even to hold our own is bound to be much more difficult than to win it or hold our own in Europe; for there the problem has posed itself primarily in the traditional terms of military power and diplomatic manipulation. The cold war in Asia, Africa, and Latin America, once we have realized its true nature, will test not only our political inventiveness but also our moral stamina. For when we are faced with reverses, which will be inevitable, we will be tempted to seek military solutions to the problems that face us. Yet military solutions will not only be counterproductive locally, but they will also conjure up the possibility of the worldwide catastrophe of nuclear war. The Soviet Union will have to come to terms with the same temptation when it finds itself losing ground. The degree of the understanding of the issues which the cold war presents, and of the self-restraint in the choice of methods in dealing with them, will then decide whether the cold war will remain cold or else will degenerate into a shooting war which is likely to mean the end of all of us.

Norman Podhoretz

1–3. Though the West has obviously been losing ground in the cold war, I don't believe that this can be attributed either to Soviet successes in foreign policy or to failures of American statesmanship. The change in the balance of world political power has come about, very simply, as a result of the change in the balance of *military* power and has, in my opinion, little or nothing to do with the superior appeal of Communist ideology. There was no way, short of a preventive war while we still held a monopoly over the H-bomb, of stopping the Soviets from catching up—and surely American reluctance to wage a preventive nuclear war cannot be taken without further argument as a sign of weakness, structural or otherwise. Once the Russians caught up, the Western position in various places— particularly Southeast Asia—was bound to be challenged, for these positions had been maintained in the first place largely by an unambiguous nuclear superiority. So long as we are unwilling to fight a nuclear war to protect Laos or South Vietnam or—ultimately—Formosa [Taiwan] (and I personally hope this will be forever), we will continue to have great and perhaps insuperable difficulties in preventing Communist conquest of the "overextended" Western perimeter by subversion, infiltration, and guerrilla warfare. (This is not to say, of course, that the effort being made by the Kennedy administration to find ways of combating such techniques is necessarily doomed to failure. I myself am skeptical, but who knows?) In Europe, the change in the nuclear balance of power has mainly had the effect of destroying any remaining Dullesian illusions about roll-back and liberation. But the brilliantly successful economic recuperation of Western Europe has also destroyed any hope the Communists may have had ten or fifteen years ago of making further gains. As for Africa, what we have there is, in some sense, a totally new cold-war battleground or perhaps a testing ground of strictly political and economic competition between West and East. It is only the end of the first inning, and so far as I can tell, there is still no score.

This brings me to your second and third questions. I would certainly be in favor of a reorientation of American policy toward "movements and leaders of change throughout the world." I don't know how "decisive" the changes that have been made in this respect under Kennedy are, but I don't think there is any question that a new attitude exists in Washington. (Witness the stipulation of the Alliance for Progress that countries receiving aid under the plan must undertake social reform, and the pressure being put on Ngo Dinh Diem to democratize his regime.) But anyone who supports such a reorientation ought not to deceive himself into thinking that it would necessarily strengthen our position in the cold war. The extent to which Communist subversion of Laos, for example, might have been countered by a more enlightened policy under Eisenhower is a matter of speculation. Conceivably, the Communists might have maneuvered themselves into a strong position even if we had backed the most progressive elements in the country instead of the most reactionary and vociferously anti-Communist ones. Similarly, are we really so sure that the Communist assault on South Vietnam has profited from the undemocratic leadership of Ngo Dinh Diem? Even if Washington succeeds in pressuring Diem into behaving better, or even if a competent, forward-looking, democratic administration were to take over the country, the Communists would probably still peck away, and we would still be left with the problem of how to contend with infiltration and subversion in a far-off place and under unfavorable military conditions.

In other words, while we now know with reasonable certainty that past American policy in Southeast Asia was not only inhumane but stupid and futile from a cold-war point of view, we do not know that a more humane policy would turn out to be any less futile. I believe that a more humane policy is worth pursuing for its own sake, and I would support it on those grounds. If politicians are forced to construct *realpolitikische* justifications for actions that are good (or at least potentially good) in themselves, that is one thing. But the rest of us are better off with honesty and—shall I apologize for the word?—idealism.

4–5. I don't believe for a moment that "the intellectual values and freedoms and the political and civil liberties we all affirm" are inseparable from the particular complex of political and economic institutions that now exist in the West. On the contrary, I would even go so far as to say that certain of these institutions are positively hostile to the values and freedoms they purport to serve. The real problem here is the constant confusion in people's minds—a confusion that the cold war has done much to deepen—between the values presumably embodied in the institutions of our society and the values that are actually promoted and sustained by those institutions. What we need—and what until very recently the extraordinary willingness of intellectuals to think about everything in cold-war terms (which means precisely thinking in terms of the assumption that there is a rough identity between the institutions of American society and the values "we all affirm") has deprived us of—is an energetic and unremitting effort to keep a vision of the good society alive and to judge existing institutions *as they actually function* by the extent to which they further that vision. Let me point out that a commitment to such visionary ideals, no matter how utopian they may seem, is the best conceivable safeguard against being taken in by the lies of politicians and ideologues, West *and* East, who are in the business of persuading the credulous to accept what they do at face value. During the thirties, as everyone knows, many American intellectuals whose radicalism began with a commitment to a freer and more humane society allowed themselves to be persuaded—often against the evidence of their senses—that the Soviet Union was dedicated to furthering the values of the liberal-radical tradition. These intellectuals finally turned against Communism, most of them, when they decided that Stalin had betrayed the revolution, and some of them turned in the late thirties to Trotsky, believing that a true proletarian revolution would emerge out of the impending clash between the Fascists and the bourgeois democracies. (I recommend a glance at the back files of *Partisan Review* to anyone who doubts that this prediction was taken with the utmost seriousness by several of the most intelligent political minds of the day.) When the true revolution failed to develop and a new conflict began to shape up in the postwar period between the Western democracies and the Communists, these same intellectuals cried not "a plague on both your houses" (as might perhaps have been expected) but turned instead into vigorous supporters of the Western cause. Everyone, as I say, knows all this, but does everyone know what created the pattern? I think the pattern was created by the notion that values are "unreal" if they cannot be attached to power. This is a notion that grows directly out of the Marxist's contempt for "utopianism" (an attitude, incidentally, that many non-Marxist liberals have learned to share). There must always be a class or a party or a social force or a nation to supply a basis for effectuating values, and if none happens to exist and the energy is also lacking to send lonely cries into the wilderness in the hope that someone may some day listen—why then, one can always make a choice among the things that do happen to exist and then proceed to convince oneself that one is following the best and most "responsible" possible course. What becomes along the way of the values that started the whole process is pretty obvious: they turn into a dim memory, intoned mechanically, drained of all vitality, nothing in them left to inspire thought or passion, hatred or love. Or even, irony of ironies, political action.

To me, the most hopeful development in years is the recent reappearance of a body of utopian social criticism based on a very clear vision of what a decent life on this planet might look like and full of concrete ideas which, if they have little chance of being put into immediate effect, at least serve to refresh and nourish our fading sense of what the liberal-radical tradition has always stood for and how far short we still are of achieving it. The priests are forever distorting the prophets—sometimes by a successful pretense of being prophets themselves. And the only remedy is for the prophets to say them nay and remind them of what the Lord really demands of man.

6. It seems fairly well established that Khrushchev's objective is to spread Communism by any means he can find short of nuclear war. His foreign policy aims, in other words, differ from Stalin's only in the tactics he is using to achieve them. The objectives of the West, however, have changed. I don't think anyone in the West seriously entertains the hope of roll-back or liberation any longer; at most there is the dim and distant hope of forcing Khrushchev to renounce his imperialist aims or buying enough time through deterrence for changes to take place in the Communist world. In the shorter run, the West is committed to stopping the advance of Communism by any means short of nuclear war where it is possible to do so, and by nuclear war in certain areas (Berlin and Formosa). This, of course, puts the West continually on the defensive while Khrushchev is at liberty to probe, push, and swing at his own initiative. Since Khrushchev appears to be convinced that he can achieve his objectives without a nuclear war, I doubt that we need to worry about the Russians deliberately provoking us into one; the real danger is that they will provoke us into one without meaning to—that, in other words, they will impose one frustration too many on a sorely tried adversary. Therefore, if Khrushchev really wants to avoid a nuclear war, he would be wise to limit his own objectives and settle for what he has always claimed he wanted—namely recognition of the status quo, disarmament, and "peaceful" competition. The question is, if Khrushchev were willing to negotiate such a settlement (and I must emphasize that I am by no means sure that he is), would the West be ready to accept it? Would we, who are still unwilling or unable even to recognize East Germany and Red China, agree to ratifying the status quo in a treaty? Would we balk at nuclear disarmament, even with fairly adequate inspection, because—given Russian superiority in conventional forces—it would leave us at a great military disadvantage? Would we be afraid of losing out altogether in a disarmed world? I myself would happily take all these risks in preference to the dangers we are presently living with, and I would press for an unremitting effort to negotiate with that end in view. If it were to turn out that the Russians have no intention of limiting their objectives, we would at least have learned something. But we can never know without trying, and I doubt that we have so far tried very hard.

What I am saying, in effect, is that I am optimistic about the West's prospects in a disarmed world and altogether pessimistic about everyone's prospects under the policy of deterrence. Nuclear weapons have proved to be less than completely effectual in halting the advance of Communism (they have not even been able to keep it out of the Western hemisphere), and what frightens me most is that we might be pushed into a nuclear war as the inevitable frustrations of the next decade mount. First Cuba, then Laos, then Berlin, and soon, it seems, South Vietnam, and the Right cries Defeat and Humiliation at every turn, while Kennedy makes himself more and more vulnerable by pretending that he is indomitably holding the line instead of explaining that he is trying to effect a series of necessary strategic retreats. Thus the war party in this country (and I am convinced that that is what the radical Right is) moves from strength to strength, finding more and more arguments to bolster its belief (still not admitted) that a preventive war aimed at destroying Communism is the only answer. Certain other schools of anti-Communist thinking in this country suffer from what I would call inverse Bolshevism—that is, the secret belief that Communism really does represent the wave of the future and therefore can only be stopped by a forceful interference with the laws of history. I find the idea that Communism represents the wave of the future altogether incredible; the appeal of Communism, in my opinion, rests on its apparent ability to foster the rapid industrialization of backward countries. Communist ideals are, of course, powerfully attractive, but even Russian youth is beginning to learn that the Soviet system represents the betrayal rather than the fulfillment of these ideals. To the extent that we have also betrayed and continue to betray our own ideals—which are historically not very different from those of the socialist tradition—we are bound to suffer in political and ideological competition. We have not yet even begun to explore what a *real* belief in democracy and individual liberty implies, say, in the field of economic development. Suppose, for example, that the United States were to encourage and foster the discovery of techniques of industrialization that might result in prosperity without leading inexorably to alienation? Yet to try something of that sort means being sufficiently critical of our own institutions to imagine how they ought to be modified in the process of being transplanted; it means becoming aware of the extent to which a particular form of technology is in practice the enemy of our values. And that, in turn, means being very clear about what our values are. So the paradox is that we can probably halt the advance of Communism without nuclear war only by committing ourselves to a humanitarian and idealistic policy. Nor can we use the humanitarian impulse as a tactic and hope to achieve the same result. In short, everything depends on the prophets again. Do enough of them exist to make a real difference?

7. I don't think anything is worth a nuclear war, even though I would admit that the deterrence theorists have a point when they say that our willingness to fight such a war may be the best way of preventing it. Nevertheless, the willingness to fight draws nourishment from the debatable idea that recovery, or even victory, is possible. Herman Kahn offers a "complete description of nuclear war" which includes elaborate calculations of casualties, genetic damage, food contamination, and the like, and he argues that with proper preparations the United States could emerge from certain kinds of nuclear war relatively intact. What I would like to see is a similarly hard-headed and coldly objective description of surrender, with the same object of determining how long it might take to "recuperate" from Communist domination. How many would be shot, how many

deported, how many imprisoned in concentration camps, how much of the economic plant would be stolen, what sort of political institutions would be created and who would run them, how much resistance would be offered by the population, and finally, how long might it take for the Russians and/or Chinese to become "Americanized?" I know that this sounds unserious, but if we are being asked to make our choices on the basis of unflinching "realism" and rationality, I don't see why the alternative of surrender (which I do *not* favor) should not be made as "thinkable" as the possibility of nuclear war has been made in the last year or two.   1962, vol. 29, no. 1

• The National Style and the Radical Right
Daniel Bell

> The American has never yet had to face the trials of Job. . . . Hitherto America has been the land of universal good will, confidence in life, inexperience of poisons. Until yesterday, it believed itself immune from the hereditary plagues of mankind. It could not credit the danger of being suffocated or infected by any sinister principle.
> George Santayana, *Character and Opinion in the United States*

Every country has a "national style," its distinctive way of meeting the problems of order and adaptation, of conflict and consensus, of individual ends and communal welfare, that confront any society. The "national style" is a compound of the values and the national character of a country. And, as anyone who has read travelers' accounts knows, there has long been agreement on the characteristics of the American style.

The American has been marked by a sense of achievement, of activism, of being on the move, of an eagerness for experience. Europe represented the past with its hierarchies, its fixed statuses, its ties to antiquity. America was always "future-oriented." The American "makes" himself, and in so doing transforms himself, society, and nature. In Jefferson's deism, God was not a transcendental being but a "Workman" whose intricate design was being unfolded on the American continent. The achievement pattern was envisaged as an "endless future," a life of constant improvement. Education meant preparation for a career rather than cultivation. When Samuel Gompers, the immigrant labor leader, was asked what labor's goal was, he gauged the American spirit shrewdly in answering, simply, "more."

Hand in hand with achievement went a sense of optimism, the feeling that life was tractable, the environment manipulable, anything possible. The American, the once-born man, was the "sky-blue, healthy-minded moralist" to whom sin and evil were, in Emerson's phrase, merely the "soul's mumps and measles and whooping cough." In this sense the American has been Graham Greene's "quiet American," or, to Santayana, "inexperienced of poisons." And for this reason Europeans have always found America lacking in a sense of the aesthetic, the tragic, or the decadent.

American achievement and masculine optimism created a buoyant sense of progress, almost of omnipotence. America had never been defeated. America was getting bigger and better. America was always first. It had the tallest buildings, the biggest dams, the largest cities. "The most striking expression of [the American's] materialism," remarked Santayana, "is his singular preoccupation with quantity."

All of this was reflected in distinctive aspects of character. The emphasis on achievement was an emphasis on the individual. The idea that society is a system of social arrangements that limits the range of individual behavior was an abstraction essentially alien to American thought; reality was concrete and empirical, and the individual was the moral unit of action. That peculiar American inversion of Protestantism, the moralizing style, found its focus in the idea of reform; but it was the reform of the individual, not of social institutions. To reform meant to remedy defects of character, and the American reform movements of the nineteenth century concentrated on sin, drink, gambling, prostitution, and other aspects of individual behavior. In politics, the moralistic residue led to black-and-white judgments, and if anything was wrong the individual was to blame. Since there were good men and bad men, the problem was to choose the good and eschew the bad. Any defect in policy flowed from a defect in the individual, and a change in policy could begin only by finding the culprit.

This pattern of achievement, of optimism and progress, and the emphasis on the individual as the unit of concern, found expression in what W. W. Rostow has called the "classic" American style.[1] The American way was one of ad hoc compromise derived from an implicit consensus. In American political debates there was rarely, except for the Civil War, an appeal to "first principles" as there was, say, in France, where every political division was rooted in the alignments of the French Revolution or in attitudes toward clericalism and the Catholic Church. In the United States there were three unspoken assumptions: that the values of the individual were to be maximized, that rising material wealth would dissolve all strains resulting from inequality, and that experience would provide solutions for all future problems.

In the last fifteen years, the national self-consciousness has received a profound shock. At the end of World War II, American productivity and American prodigality were going to inspire an archaic Europe and a backward colonial system. But the American century quickly vanished. The fall of China, the stalemate in Korea, the eruption of anticolonialism (with the United States cast bewil-

---

1. In *The American Style*, Elting E. Morrison, Editor (Boston: Little Brown, 1960).

deringly among the arch-villains), the higher growth rates in the Western European economies at a time when our own growth has slowed considerably, and the continued claims of Khrushchev that Communism is the wave of the future, have by now shattered the belief which Americans had in their own omnipotence, and left almost a free-floating anxiety about the future. In a crudely symbolic way, the Russian sputniks trumped this country on its own boastful claim of always being first. Getting to the moon first may be, as many scientists assert, of little scientific value, and the huge sums required for such a venture might be spent more wisely for medical work, housing, or scientific research, but having set the "rules of the game" the United States is unable to withdraw even though, in its newly acquired sophistication, it has begun to realize that such competitions are rather childish.

But these immediate crises of nerve only reflect deeper challenges to the adequacy of America's classic national style. For that style, with its ad hoc compromise and day-to-day patching of problems rather than the formulation of consistent policy, no longer gives us guides to action. The classic notion was that the individual was the unit of action. But the chief realization of the past thirty years is that not the *individual* but *collectivities* — corporations, labor unions, farm organizations, pressure groups — have become the units of social action and that individual rights, in many instances, derive from group rights, or have become fused with them. But other than the thin veil of the "public consensus" we have few guidelines, let alone a principle of distributive justice, to regulate or check the arbitrary power of many of these collectivities.

A second sign that the classic style has broken down appears in the lack of any institutional means for creating and maintaining necessary public service. On the municipal level, the complicated political swapping among hundreds of dispersed polities within a unified economic region, each seeking its own bargains in water supply, sewage disposal, roads, parks, recreation areas, crime regulation, transit, and so on, makes a mockery of the ad hoc process. Without some planning along viable regional lines, local community life is bound to disintegrate under the burdens of mounting taxes and social disarray.

And, third, foreign policy has foundered because every administration has had difficulty in defining a national interest, morally rooted, whose policies can be realistically tailored to the capacities and constraints imposed by the actualities of world power. The easy temptation — and it is the theme of the radical right — is the tough-talking call for "action." This emphasis on action, on getting things done, on results, is a dominant aspect of the traditional American character. The moralizing style, with its focus on sin and on the culpability of the individual, finds it hard to accept social forces as a convincing explanation of failure, and prefers "action" instead. Americans have rarely known how to sweat it out, to wait, to calculate in historical terms, to learn that "action" cannot easily reverse social drifts whose courses were charted long ago. The "liberation" policy of the first Eisenhower administration was but a hollow moralism, deriving from the lack of any consistent policy other than the traditional need to seem "activist," rather than from a realistic assessment of the possibility of undermining Soviet power in Eastern Europe. Until recently, there has been little evidence that American foreign policy is guided by a sense of historical time and an accurate assessment of social forces.

Styles of action reflect the character of a society. The classic style was worked out during a period when America was an agrarian, relatively homogeneous society, isolated from the world at large, so that ad hoc measures were a realistic way of dealing with new strains. As an adaptive mechanism, it served to bring new groups *into* society. But styles of action, like rhetoric, have a habit of outliving institutions. And the classic style in no way reflects the deep structural changes that have been taking place in American life in the past quarter of a century.

II

The psychological stock-in-trade of the radical right is an "ideologizing" of the American style. It rests on a three-fold appeal: the breakdown of moral fiber in the United States; a conspiracy theory about a "control apparatus" in the government which is selling out the country; and a detailed forecast regarding the Communist "takeover" of the United States.

Central to the appeal of the radical right is the argument that old-fashioned patriotism has been subverted by the cosmopolitan intellectual. An editorial in the *National Review* on the space flight of astronaut John Glenn sums up this theme in striking fashion. Glenn, said the editorial, is an authentic American hero because he is unashamed to say that he gets a thrill when the American flag goes by and because he will openly acknowledge the guidance of God.

> It is "American" as in older storybooks, as in legends, and myths and dreams—brought up to technological date, of course—as, let's say it plainly, in the pre-1930 Fourth of July celebrations; and the *Saturday Evening Post* covers before they, too, not long ago, went modern; and a touch of soap opera. Yes, a bit corny—for that is the traditional American style. Too corny by far for the Norman Cousinses, Arthur Schlesingers, Adlai Stevensons, Henry Steele Commagers, Max Lerners, John Kenneth Galbraiths, and those others of our enlightened age—so many of them now fluttering around the Kennedy throne—who have long left behind the old provincial corn for a headier global view.

> Here one finds the praise of the "simple virtues"—they are always simple—the evocation of small-town life and the uncluttered Arcadia, against the modern,

the sophisticated, the cosmopolitan. But the Glenn flight, according to the editorial, proved more: it proved the victory of "man" against the "mechanical" and implicitly against the intellectual. "This and that went wrong, we all learned, with the unbelievably complex mechanism of Glenn's ship, as it whirled through the emptiness of Space," continued the *National Review*:

> The attitude control thingamajigs didn't work right. There were troubles in some of the communication instruments. . . . This and that went wrong with the mechanism, and man took over and brought Friendship 7 to its strange harbor. . . . And that is fine news, though it should hardly be news. It is good technically, because we Americans with our gadgetry obsession and our wish for too much convenience, safety, and comfort, tend to crowd all our machines and vehicles with too immensely many tricky devices. Every additional transistor in these automatic mechanisms means that many more connections to loosen, every valve can fail to open; every fuse can blow. . . . It is better news still, philosophically, we might say, because it reminds us that there is no such thing, and never will be, as a "thinking" machine. Only man thinks, wills, decides, dares. No machine, on land, in sea, air, or space, can do man's job for him: can choose, for good or ill.

The fact that "man" is also the one who designs the machine is, of course, beside the point of the editorial. Its implication is fairly clear: don't let anyone tell us that space (or politics, or economics, or life) is complicated; machines can never be perfect ("every valve can fail to open, every fuse can blow"); only "man" (not the scientist or the intellectual) can think. In short, America will be back on an even keel when the simple virtues prevail.

The theme of conspiracy haunts the mind of the radical rightist. It permits him to build up the image of the children of darkness and the children of light. It exempts him from having to specify empirical proofs. General Edwin Walker told a Congressional committee that a "control apparatus" was "selling out the Constitution, national sovereignty, and national independence," but when asked to specify the members of the control apparatus he replied that he could not name the individuals, but that the apparatus could be identified "by its effects — what it did in Cuba — what it did in the Congo — what it did in Korea." The irony of this reply is that it is cut from the same cloth as vulgar Bolshevik explanation: accident and contingency are ruled out of history, subjective intentions are the prattlings of "bourgeois morality," history is plot and objective consequence. Just as in a concentration camp — or any extreme situation — a victim adopts unconsciously the mode, manner, and even swagger of the aggressor, so men like General Walker seem to have become mesmerized by the enemies they have studied so assiduously and with such horrified fascination.

To round out their picture of horror, the radical right has given us an exact forecast of things to come. Just as the "enthusiastic" preachers of Baptist fundamentalism would predict with Biblical certainty the date of the end of the world, so the fundamentalists of the radical right make their own predictions of the end of liberty in the United States. Fred Schwarz, for example, has named 1973 as the date set by the Communists for the takeover of America. In his lectures, Schwarz builds up the picture of the ultimate fate in store for his audience once the Communists win. "When they come for you, as they have for many others, and on a dark night, in a dark cellar, they take a wide-bore revolver with a soft-nose bullet, and they place it at the nape of your neck. . ."

A more elaborate fantasy is provided in the *John Franklin Letters*, a Birchite novel that was circulated in 1959 and then withdrawn.[2] The novel pictures an America Sovietized by the Communists in 1970. The beginning of the end comes in 1963, when the World Health Organization sends in a Yugoslav inspector, under powers granted by the President of the United States, to search any house he chooses. The Yugoslav discovers in the house of a good American a file of anti-Communist magazines, seizes them as deleterious to the mental health of the community, and is shot by the American, who escapes to the woods. But the infiltration continues. By 1970, the United States, thanks to the global do-gooders, has become part of a World Authority dominated by the Soviet-Asian-African bloc, and this Authority suspends the country's right to govern itself because of the "historic psychological genocide" against the Negro race. United Nations administrators, mostly Red Chinese, are sent in to rule. Harlem, triumphant, arises and loots the liquor stores. The city proletariat, its sense of decency destroyed by public housing, begins to raid the suburbs. In short order, twenty million Americans are "done away with," while the people are subjected to torture by blowtorch and rock-n-roll—the latter on television.

Meanwhile, the good American begins to fight. As far back as 1967, John Franklin and his friends had been stockpiling rifles. And now they act. Franklin describes in gory detail a total of fourteen patriotic murders: two by fire, one by hammer, one by strangling, two by bow and arrow, one by defenestration, one by drowning, and the rest by shooting. These brave actions are sufficient to turn the tide—despite the atom bomb, a huge invasion army, and absolute terror. By 1976, the people all over the world go into the streets, and everywhere Communism falls. The assumption is that Communism is so inefficient it cannot build heavy tanks or heavy weapons. All that is necessary is the courage of a few determined men, practicing the "simple virtues," to overthrow this clumsy Moloch. As Murray Kempton remarks:

2. I am following here the account of Murray Kempton in the *New York Post*, October 26, 1961.

This, of course, is the Bircher's dream. America slides unresistingly into communism; a few Mike Hammers find their rifles; and in five years the world is free. The Birch mind is only the Mickey Spillane mind. There is that lingering over and savoring of pure physical violence, the daydream of the disarmed. Reading *The John Franklin Letters* we can recognize Robert Welch's voice. He is Charles Atlas saying to us again that we need only mail the letter and back will come the muscles which we will use to throw the bully off the beach and have the girl turn to us with eyes shining with the sudden knowledge of how special we are.

III

The distinctive theme of the radical right is not only that Communism is a more threatening force today than at any other time in the past forty years, but that the threat is as great *domestically* as it is externally. If one points out, in astonishment, that the American Communist Party is splintered badly, its membership at the lowest point since the mid-1920s, its influence in the trade unions nil, and that not one American intellectual figure of any consequence today is a Communist, the rightist replies do not confront these assertions at all. They range from the question of how, if this is so, it happened that the United States "lost" China, Czechoslovakia, and Cuba to the Communists, to General Walker's charge that the highest officials of the Democratic Party are members of the "Communist conspiracy," or Robert Welch's claim that former President Eisenhower was a "tool" of the Communists and that his brother Milton is an avowed one. Defeat can be possible in America only if sinister men are at the helm. Typical of this line is the question constantly reiterated by Reverend Billy Hargis: "How can you explain the mistakes of our leaders for the last thirty years if there aren't Communists giving them advice?"

In fact, so great is the preoccupation with the alleged domestic threat that only rarely in the press of the radical right is there any mention of Russia's military prowess, its scientific equipment, or its ability to propel intercontinental ballistic missiles. When such facts are raised, it is often asserted either that such strength is a sham or that whatever knowledge Russia has was "stolen" from the United States. (This claim is made, for example, by Medford Evans, now an adviser to General Walker, in his book *The Secret War for the A-Bomb*, Chicago: Regnery Press, 1953.) For a considerable period of time the magazines of the radical right refused to acknowledge that the Russians had sent a sputnik to the moon or that they had sent a man into space and, like the *Daily Worker* unmasking a capitalist conspiracy, they gleefully pounced on inconsistencies in news stories to assert that we were all being hoodwinked by a hoax (as were, presumably, the United States tracking stations).

The existence of an extreme *internal* threat is crucial to the ideological, if not the psychological, posture of the radical right. For if they admitted that such a threat is dubious, then the debate would have to shift to ground about which they have little comprehension, or they would have to admit—as Eisenhower did—that the area of maneuverability in foreign policy is highly limited. If the threat was conceded to be largely external, then one would have to support an expanded federal budget, large military expenditures, foreign aid to allies. And they would have to confront the intractable fact that American might alone is insufficient to defeat the Russians—or that victory for anyone would be possible once war began!—and that the United States has to take into account the forces working for independence in the former colonial world.

The unwillingness of the radical right to recognize Russian military strength as a prime factor in the balance of terror, and the compulsive preoccupation with a presumed internal threat, can perhaps be clarified by a little-understood psychological mechanism—the need to create "fear-justifying" threats in order to explain fright that is provoked by other reasons. A child who is afraid of the dark may tell his parents that the creaking noises he hears in the house indicate that there are burglars downstairs. It does not reassure the child if he is told that there is no burglar, or that the noises are harmless, for he needs the story to justify the fear he already feels. In fact, it upsets the child to be so "reassured." (The simplest answer is to tell the child that *if* there are burglars downstairs, his father is strong enough to handle them or that the police are close by.) An Indian study by Prasad a few years ago on rumors following an earthquake found that people in the areas adjacent to the earthquake, who had heard about the quake but had no direct experience of it, persisted in believing and spreading rumors that a *new* earthquake was coming. The function of such stories was to justify, psychologically, the *initial* apprehensions which had ambiguous basis in experience.[3] In a similar sense the radical right, having a diffused sense of fear, needs to find some story or explanation to explain or justify that fear. One can deny the external reality, and build up the internal threat, through such psychological mechanisms.

One sees among the radical right, particularly among sections of its upper-middle-class following who have never seen a Communist, the most extraordinary apprehensions about the extent of current Communist infiltration in government. If asked to explain these attitudes one is constantly reminded of Alger Hiss and Harry Dexter White. Yet whatever the reality of past Communist infiltration in the government—and its actual influence has been highly distorted—none of this is any proof about the current status of Dean Rusk or W. W. Rostow, or any of the present foreign policy advisers of the Kennedy administration. Yet

---

3. For a technical elaboration of this psychological mechanism, see A *Theory of Cognitive Dissonance*, Leon Festinger (Chicago: Row, Peterson, 1957).

the *internal* threat is the one that is largely harped upon, along with the suspicions of the "soft" attitudes of the current administration.

It is largely among the extremist fringes of the radical right that such paranoid views are peddled. But most of the radical right, uneasily aware of the difficulty of maintaining the position that the Communist Party alone constitutes the internal threat, has shifted the argument to a different and more nebulous ground—the identification of Communism with liberalism. "I equate growth of the welfare state," says Dan Smoot (a former FBI agent whose program, *The Dan Smoot Report*, is heard on thirty-two television and fifty-two radio stations), "with socialism and socialism with Communism." Thus it is argued that the Administration is unwilling (for ideological reasons) or incapable (for intellectual reasons) of "getting tough" with Communism. And in this fashion the foreign policy issue is tied in with a vast array of right-wing domestic issues, centering around the income tax and the welfare state.

But in so shifting the argument, the nature of the debate becomes clearer. What the right wing is fighting in the shadow of Communism is, essentially, "modernity"—that complex of attitudes which might be defined as the belief in rational assessment, rather than established custom, for the control of social change—and what it seeks to defend is its fading dominance, once exercised through the institutions of small-town America, over the control of social change. But it is precisely these established ways that a modernist America has been forced to call into question.

IV

Within the American consensus a meaningful polarity has always been part of the search for self-definition and self-identity: Jefferson versus Hamilton, Republicanism versus Federalism, Agrarianism versus Capitalism, the frontier West versus the industrial East. However significant such polarities may have been in the past, there seems to be little meaningful polarity today. There is no coherent conservative force[4]—someone like Walter Lippman, whose *The Public Philosophy* represents a genuine conservative voice, rejects the right as it rejects him—and the radical right is outside the political pale insofar as it refuses to accept the American consensus. Nor does a viable left exist in the United States today. The pacifist and socialist elements have been unable to make the peace issue salient. The radicals have been unable to develop a comprehensive critique of the social disparities in American life—the urban mess, the patchwork educa-

---

4. The *National Review*, which proclaims itself conservative, is a strange mash of Thomistic natural law (Buckley), Manchester economic liberalism (Hazlitt and Buckley), Burkean traditionalism (Meyer and Buckley), Platonic *virtu* (Bozell and Buckley), Haushofer geopolitics (Burnham and Buckley), and single-tax, agrarian, libertarian individualism (Choderov and Buckley). A heady brew indeed.

tional system, the lack of amenities in our culture. Among the liberals, only the exhaustion of the "received ideas," such as they were, of the New Deal remains. It is a token of the emptiness of contemporary intellectual debate that from the viewpoint of the radical right, the Americans for Democratic Action constitutes the "extreme left" of the American political spectrum, and that *Life*, in order to set up a fictitious balance, counterposes the tiny Council of Correspondence, a loosely organized peace group inspired by Erich Fromm and David Riesman, as the "extreme left," to the "extreme right" of the John Birch Society.

The "politics of conflict" in any country inevitably has an emotional dimension, but in the United States, which has lacked a historically defined *doctrinal* basis for emotional divisions, the politics of conflict—when economic interest-group issues are muted—takes on a psychological dimension. In this psychological polarity, the right has often been splenetic, while the mood of the left has traditionally been one of *ressentiment*. Today the politics of the radical right is the politics of frustration—the sour impotence of those who find themselves unable to understand, let alone command, the complex mass society that is polity today, while only the Negro community is fired by the politics of resentment—and this resentment, based on a justified demand for equity, presents no psychological polarity to the radical right. Insofar as there is no real left to counterpose to the right, the liberal has become the psychological target of that frustration.

One of the reasons why psychological politics can flare up so much more easily here than, say, in Great Britain is the essentially "populist" character of American institutions and the volatile role of public opinion. In the ill-defined, loosely articulated structure of American life, public opinion rather than law has been the operative sanction against nonconformists and dissenters. Though Americans often respond to a problem with the phrase "there ought to be a law," their respect for law has been minimal, and during periods of extreme excitement, whether it be the vigilante action of a mob or the removal of a book from a school library, the punitive sanctions of opinion quickly supersede law. The very openness or egalitarianism of the American political system is predicated on the "right of the people to know," and the Congressional committees, whether searching into the pricing policies of corporations or the political beliefs of individuals, have historically based their investigative claims on this populist premise.

It has always been easier to "mobilize" public opinion on legislation here than in England; and in the United States the masses of people have a more direct access to politics. In the elite structure of British politics, control is not in the constituencies (or, as here, among the hundreds of local political bosses who have to be dealt into the game), but in the small parliamentary caucuses which have a legal, as well as historic, independence from mass party control. The British elite, wedded to a "politics of civility," tends to dampen any extremism within the top political structure, while the control system keeps the masses outside and makes it difficult for them to be mobilized for direct pressure on the government. The presidential election system—as against a ministerial system—with the candidates appealing to every voter and, if possible, shaking every hand, involves a direct relation to the electorate. And in the Congressional system, individual constituents, through letters, telephone calls, or personal visits, can get through immediately to their representative to affect his vote. The Congressional system itself, with its elaborate scaffolding of Senatorial prerogative, often allows a maverick like Borah, Norris, or Robert La Follette to dominate the floor, or a rogue elephant like Huey Long or Joe McCarthy to rampage against the operations of the government.

But while the populist character of our political institutions and the sweeping influence of public opinion allow social movements to flare with brush-fire suddenness across the political timberland, the unwieldy party system, as well as the checks and balances of the presidential and judicial structures, also act to constrain such movements. In a few instances, notably the temperance crusade, a social movement operating outside the party system was able to enforce a unitary conception of social behavior on the country—and even then prohibition was repealed in two decades. Until recently, the party and presidential system have exerted a "discipline of compromise" that has put the maverick and the rogue elephant outside the main arena of the political game.

Within this perspective, therefore, what are the prospects of the radical right? To what extent does it constitute a threat to democratic politics in the United States? Some highly competent political observers have already written it off as a meaningful political movement. Richard Rovere has argued that the press treats the extreme right as though it were a major tendency in American politics, and that certain politicians are as much obsessed with it as certain others are with the extreme left. "If a day arrives when the extreme right does become a major movement," he writes "the press and the obsessed politicians may have a lot to answer for. For the time being, there seems no reason to suppose that its future holds anything more than its present. There is no evidence at all that the recent proliferation of radical, and in some cases downright subversive, organizations of a rightist tendency reflects or has been accompanied by a spread of ultraconservative views. On the contrary, what evidence there is suggests that the organizations are frantic efforts to prevent ultraconservatism from dying out."

In his immediate assessment, Rovere is undoubtedly right. In the spring of 1962, both former Vice President Nixon and Senator Goldwater had already dissociated themselves from the extremist right. Nixon repudiated the Birchites on the premise that they were already a political liability. Goldwater, treading more cautiously, expressed his concern that, if not the Birchites, then their leader, Robert Welch, may have gone too far.

Yet the future is more murky than Rovere suggests. It is in the very nature of an extremist movement, given its tensed posture and its need to maintain a fever pitch, to mobilize, to be on the move, to act. Lacking any sustained dramatic issue, it could quickly wear itself out, as McCarthyism did. To this extent therefore, the prospects of the radical right depend considerably on the international situation. If Laos and all Vietnam were to fall to the Communists; if, within the Western Hemisphere, the moderate regimes of Bolivia and Venezuela were to topple and the Communists to take over—then the radical right could begin to rally support around a drive for "immediate action," for a declaration of war in these areas, for a pre-emptive strike or similar axioms of a "hard line." And since such conservatives as Nixon and Goldwater are committed, at least rhetorically, to a tough anti-Communist position, they would either be forced to go along with such an extreme policy or go under. If the international situation becomes stabilized, it is then likely that the radical right may run quickly out of steam.

The situation in Europe, however, still presents in a very different and less immediate sense a threat to American liberties. Democratic consensus, as the sorry history of Europe has shown, is a fragile system, and if there is a lesson to be learned from the downfall of democratic government in Italy, Austria, and Germany, and from the deep divisions in France, it is that a crucial turning point comes, as Juan Linz pointed out, when extremist political parties or social movements can successfully establish "private armies" whose resort to violence—street fightings, bombings, the break-up of their opponents' meetings, or simply intimidation—cannot be controlled by the elected authorities, and whose use of violence is justified or made legitimate by the respectable elements in society.

In America, the extreme-right groups of the late 1930s—the Coughlinites, the German-American Bund, the native fascist groups—all sought to promote violence, but they never obtained legitimate or respectable support. The McCarthyite movement of the early 1950s, despite the rampaging antics of its eponymous leader, never dared go, at least rhetorically, outside the traditional framework in trying to establish loyalty and security tests. The Birchers and the small but insidious group of "Minutemen," as the epitome of the radical right, are willing to tear apart the fabric of American society in order to instate their goals; and they did receive a temporary aura of legitimacy on the right.

Barbarous acts are rarely committed out of the blue. (As Freud says, first one commits oneself in words, and then in deeds.) Step by step, a society becomes accustomed to accept, with less and less moral outrage and with greater and greater indifference to legitimacy, the successive blows. What was uniquely disturbing about the emergence of the radical right of the 1960s is the support it was able to find among traditional small-town leaders who have become conditioned by an indiscriminate anti-Communism equating any form of liberalism with Communism to judge as respectable a movement which, if successful, would only end the liberties they profess to cherish.   1962, vol. 29, no. 4

• Notes on "Camp"
Susan Sontag

Many things in the world have not been named; and many things, even if they have been named, have never been described. One of these is the sensibility—unmistakably modern, a variant of sophistication but hardly identical with it—that goes by the cult name of "Camp."

A sensibility (as distinct from an idea) is one of the hardest things to talk about; but there are special reasons why Camp, in particular, has never been discussed. It isn't a natural mode of sensibility, if there be any such. Indeed the essence of Camp is its love of the unnatural: of artifice and exaggeration. And Camp is esoteric—something of a private code, a badge of identity even, among small urban cliques. Apart from a lazy two-page sketch in Christopher Isherwood's novel *The World in the Evening* (1948), it has never broken into print. To talk about Camp is therefore to betray it. If the betrayal can be defended, it will be for the edification it provides, or the dignity of the conflict it resolves. For myself, I plead the goal of self-edification, and the goad of a sharp conflict in my own sensibility. I am strongly drawn to Camp, and almost as strongly frustrated by it. That is why I want to talk about it, why I can talk about it. For no one who wholeheartedly shares in a given sensibility can analyze it; he can only, whatever his intention, exhibit it. To name a sensibility, to draw the contours of it, to recount its history, requires a deep sympathy modified by revulsion.

Though I'm speaking about sensibility only—and about a sensibility that, among other things, converts the serious into the frivolous—these are grave matters. Most people think of sensibility or taste as the realm of purely subjective preferences, those mysterious attractions, mainly sensual, that have not been brought under the sovereignty of reason. They *allow* that considerations of taste play a part in their reactions to people and to works of art. But this is naive. And even worse. To patronize the faculty of taste is to patronize oneself. For taste governs every free—as opposed to rote—human response. Nothing is more decisive. There is taste in people, visual taste, taste in emotion—and there is taste in acts, taste in morality. Intelligence, as well, is really a kind of taste: taste in ideas. (One of the facts to be reckoned with is that taste tends to develop very unevenly. It's rare that the same person has good visual taste *and* good taste in people *and* good taste in ideas.)

There is no system in taste, and no proofs. But there is something like a logic of taste: the consistent sensibility which underlies and gives rise to a certain taste. A sensibility is almost, but not quite, ineffable. Any sensibility which can be crammed into the mold of a system, or handled with the rough tools of proof, is no longer a sensibility at all. It has hardened into an idea. . . .

To snare a sensibility in words, especially one that is alive and powerful,[1] one must be tentative and nimble. The form of jottings, rather than an essay (with its claim to a linear, consecutive argument), seemed more appropriate for getting down something of this particularly fugitive sensibility or taste. It's embarrassing to be solemn and treatise-like about Camp. One runs the risk of having, oneself, produced a very inferior piece of Camp.

These notes are for Oscar Wilde.

> One should either be a work of art, or wear a work of art.
> • *Phrases & Philosophies for the Use of the Young*

1. To start very generally: Camp is a certain mode of aestheticism. It is *one* way of seeing the world as an aesthetic phenomenon.

That way, the way of Camp, is not in terms of beauty, but in terms of style.

2. To emphasize style is to slight content, or to introduce an attitude which is neutral with respect to content. It goes without saying that the Camp sensibility is disengaged, depoliticized — or at least apolitical.

3. Not only is there a Camp vision, a Camp way of looking at things. Camp is as well a quality discoverable in objects and the behavior of persons. There are "campy" movies, clothes, furniture, popular songs, novels, people, buildings. . . . This distinction is important. True, the Camp eye has the power to transform experience. But not everything can be seen as Camp. It's not *all* in the eye of the beholder.

4. Random examples of items which are part of the canon of Camp:

Tiffany lamps
Scopitone films
The Brown Derby restaurant on Sunset Boulevard in LA
The Enquirer, headlines and stories
Aubrey Beardsley drawings
Swan Lake
Bellini's operas

1. The sensibility of an era is not only its most decisive, but also its most perishable, aspect. One may capture the ideas (intellectual history) and the behavior (social history) of an epoch without ever touching upon the sensibility or taste which informed those ideas, that behavior. Rare are those historical studies — like Huizinga on the late Middle Ages, Febvre on 16th century France — which do tell us something about the sensibility of the period.

Visconti's direction of *Salome* and *'Tis Pity She's a Whore*
certain turn-of-the-century picture postcards
Schoedsack's *King Kong*
the Cuban pop singer La Lupe
Lynn Ward's novel in woodcuts, *God's Man*
women's clothes of the twenties (feather boas, fringed and beaded dresses, etc.)
the novels of Ronald Firbank and Ivy Compton-Burnett
stag movies seen without lust

5. Camp taste has an affinity for certain arts rather than others. Clothes, furniture, all the elements of visual decor, for instance, make up a large part of Camp. For Camp art is often decorative art, emphasizing texture, sensuous surface, and style at the expense of content. Concert music, though, because it is contentless, is rarely Camp. It offers no opportunity, say, for a contrast between silly or extravagant content and rich form. . . . Sometimes whole art forms become saturated with Camp. Classical ballet, opera, movies have seemed so for a long time. In the last two years, so has popular music (post rock 'n' roll, what the French call *yé yé*). And movie criticism (like lists of "The 10 Best Bad Movies I Have Seen") is probably the greatest popularizer of Camp taste today, because most people still go to the movies in a high-spirited and unpretentious way.

6. There is a sense in which it is correct to say: "It's too good to be Camp." Or "too important," not marginal enough. (More on this later.) Thus, the personality and many of the works of Jean Cocteau are Camp, but not those of André Gide; the operas of Richard Strauss, but not those of Wagner; concoctions of Tin Pan Alley and Liverpool, but not jazz. Many examples of Camp are things which, from a "serious" point of view, are either bad art or kitsch. Not all though. Camp is not necessarily bad art. But more on that later, too.

The more we study Art, the less we care for Nature.
• *The Decay of Lying*

7. All Camp objects, and persons, contain a large element of artifice. Nothing in nature can be campy. . . . Nothing rural, either. Campy objects are urban. (Yet, they often have a serenity—or a naiveté—which is the equivalent of pastoral. A great deal of Camp suggests Empson's phrase, "urban pastoral.")

8. Camp is a vision of the world in terms of style—but a particular kind of style. It is the love of the exaggerated, the "off," of things-being-what-they-are-not. The best example is in Art Nouveau, the most typical and fully developed Camp style. Art Nouveau objects, typically, make one thing into something else. Generic examples: the lighting fixtures in the form of flowering plants, the living room which is really a grotto. A particular example: the Paris Metro entrances designed by Hector Guimard in the late 1890s in the form of cast-iron orchid stalks.

9. As a taste in persons, Camp responds particularly to the markedly attenuated and to the strongly exaggerated. The androgyne is certainly one of the great images of Camp sensibility. Examples: the swooning slim sinuous figures of pre-Raphaelite painting and poetry in the Art Nouveau style, the thin, flowing, sexless bodies in prints and posters, presented in relief on lamps and ashtrays; the haunting androgynous vacancy behind the perfect beauty of Greta Garbo. Here, Camp taste draws on a mostly unacknowledged truth of taste: the most refined form of sexual attractiveness (as well as the most refined form of sexual pleasure) consists in going against the grain of one's sex. What is most beautiful in virile men is something feminine; what is most beautiful in feminine women is something masculine. . . . Allied to the Camp taste for the androgynous is something that seems quite different but isn't: a relish for the exaggeration of sexual characteristics and personality mannerisms. For obvious reasons, the best examples that can be cited are movie stars. The corny flamboyant femaleness of Jayne Mansfield, Gina Lollobrigida, Jane Russell, Virginia Mayo; the exaggerated he-manness of Steve Reeves, Victor Mature. The great stylists of temperament and mannerism, like Bette Davis, Barbara Stanwyck, Tallulah Bankhead, Edwige Feuillière.

10. Camp sees everything in quotation marks. It's not a lamp, but a "lamp"; not a woman, but a "woman." To perceive Camp in objects and persons is to understand Being as Playing a Role. It is the farthest extension, in sensibility, of the metaphor of life as theater.

11. Camp is the triumph of the epicene style. (The convertibility of "boy" and "girl," "person" and "thing.") But all style is, ultimately, epicene. "Life" is not stylish. Neither is nature.

12. The question isn't, "Why travesty, impersonation, theatricality?" The question is, rather, "When does travesty, impersonation, theatricality acquire the special flavor of Camp?" Why is the atmosphere of Shakespeare's comedies (As You Like It, etc.) not epicene, while that of Der Rosenkavalier is?

13. The dividing line seems to fall in the eighteenth century; that's where the origins of Camp taste are to be found (Gothic novels, Chinoiserie, caricature, artificial ruins, and so forth). But the relation to nature was quite different then. In the eighteenth century, people of taste either patronized nature (Strawberry Hill) or attempted to remake it into something artificial (Versailles). They also indefatigably patronized the past. Today's Camp taste effaces nature, or else contradicts it outright. And the relation of Camp taste to the past is extremely sentimental.

14. A pocket history of Camp might, of course, begin farther back—with the mannerist artists like Pontormo and Caravaggio; or the extraordinarily theatrical painting of Georges de la Tour. Still, the soundest period to start with seems to be the late seventeenth and early eighteenth centuries, because of its extraordinary feeling for artifice, for surface, for symmetry, its taste for the picturesque and the thrilling, its stylish conventions for representing instant feeling and the

total presence of character—the epigram and the rhymed couplet (in words), the flourish (in gesture and in music). The late seventeenth and early eighteenth century is the great period of Camp: Pope, Congreve, Walpole, etc., but not Swift; much of Mozart; *les précieux* in France; the rococo churches of Munich. But in the nineteenth century, what had been distributed throughout all of high culture now becomes a special taste; it takes on overtones of the acute, the esoteric, the perverse. Confining the story to England alone, Camp continues wanly through nineteenth century aestheticism (Burne-Jones, Pater, Ruskin, Tennyson), it emerges full-blown with the Art Nouveau movement in the visual and decorative arts, and it finds its conscious ideologists in such "wits" as Wilde and Firbank.

15. Of course, to say all these things are Camp is not to argue they are simply that. A full analysis of Art Nouveau, for instance, would scarcely equate it with Camp. But such an analysis would not scant what in Art Nouveau allows it to be experienced as Camp. For Art Nouveau is full of "content," even of a political-moral sort; it was a revolutionary movement in the arts, spurred on by a utopian vision (somewhere between William Morris and the Bauhaus group) of an organic politics and taste. Yet there is also something in the Art Nouveau objects which suggests a disengaged, purely aesthetic, and unserious vision. This tells us something important about Art Nouveau—and about what the lens of Camp, which blocks out content, is.

16. Thus, the Camp sensibility is one that is alive to a double sense in which some things can be taken. But this is not the familiar split-level construction of a literal meaning, on the one hand, and a symbolic meaning, on the other. It is the difference, rather, between the thing as meaning something, anything, and the thing as pure style.

17. This comes out clearly in the most vulgar use of the word Camp, as a verb, "to camp," something that people do. To camp is a mode of seduction—one which employs mannerisms susceptible of a double interpretation; gestures full of duplicity, with a witty meaning for the cognoscenti and another, more solemn, for outsiders. Equally and by extension, when the word becomes a noun, when a person or a thing is "a camp," a duplicity is involved. Behind the "straight" public sense in which the thing can be taken, one has found a private witty experience of the thing.

To be natural is such a very difficult pose to keep up.
• *An Ideal Husband*

18. One must distinguish between naive and deliberate Camp. Pure Camp is always naive. Camp which knows itself to be Camp is "camping," which is usually less satisfying.

19. The pure examples of Camp are unintentional; they are dead serious. The Art Nouveau craftsman who makes a lamp with a snake coiled around it is not kidding, nor is he trying to be charming; he is saying, in all earnestness: Voilà! the Orient! Pure Camp—for instance, the numbers devised for the Warner Brothers musicals of the early thirties (*42nd Street; The Golddiggers of 1933; . . . of 1935; . . . of 1937*, etc.) by Busby Berkeley—do not *mean* to be funny. Camping—say, the plays of Noel Coward—does. It doesn't seem possible that much of the traditional opera repertoire could be such satisfying Camp if the melodramatic absurdities of most opera plots hadn't been taken seriously by their composers. One doesn't need to know the artist's private intentions. The work tells all. (Compare a typical nineteenth-century opera with Samuel Barber's *Vanessa*, a piece of manufactured, calculated Camp, and the difference is clear.)

20. Probably, intending to be campy is always harmful. The perfection of *Trouble in Paradise* and *The Maltese Falcon*, among the greatest Camp movies ever made, comes from the effortless smooth way in which tone is maintained. This is not so with such famous would-be Camp films of the fifties as *All About Eve* and *Beat the Devil*. These more recent movies have their fine moments, but the first is so slick and the second so hysterical; they want so badly to be campy that they're continually losing the beat. . . . Perhaps, though, it's not so much a question of the unintended effect versus the conscious intention, as of the delicate relation between parody and self-parody in Camp. The films of Hitchcock are a showcase for this problem. When self-parody lacks ebullience but instead reveals (even sporadically) a contempt for one's themes and one's materials—as in *To Catch a Thief*, *Rear Window*, *North By Northwest*—the results are forced and heavy-handed, rarely Camp. Perfect Camp—a movie like Carné's *Drôle de Drame*; the film performances of Mae West and Edward Everett Horton; chunks of the Goon Show—even when it rests on self-parody, reeks of self-love.

21. So, again, Camp rests on innocence. That means Camp discloses innocence, but also, when it can, corrupts it. Objects, being objects, don't change when they are singled out by the Camp vision. Persons, however, respond to their audiences. Persons begin "camping": Mae West, Bea Lillie, La Lupe, Tallulah Bankhead in *Lifeboat*, Bette Davis in *All About Eve*. (Persons can even be induced to camp without their knowing it. Consider the way Fellini got Anita Ekberg to parody herself in *La Dolce Vita*.)

22. Considered a little less strictly, Camp is either completely naive or else wholly conscious (when one plays at being campy). An example of the latter: Wilde's epigrams themselves.

It's absurd to divide people into good and bad. People are either charming or tedious.
• *Lady Windemere's Fan*

23. In naive, or pure, Camp, the essential element is seriousness, a seriousness that fails. Of course, not all seriousness that fails can be redeemed as Camp. Only that which has the proper mixture of the exaggerated, the fantastic, the passionate, and the naive.

24. When something is just bad (rather than Camp), it's often because it is too mediocre in its ambition. The artist hasn't attempted to do anything really outlandish. ("It's too much," "It's fantastic," "It's not to be believed," are standard phrases of Camp enthusiasm.)

25. The hallmark of Camp is the spirit of extravagance. Camp is a woman walking around in a dress made of three million feathers. Camp is the paintings of Carlo Crivelli, with their real real jewels and *trompe-l'oeil* insects and cracks in the masonry. Camp is the outrageous aestheticism of Von Sternberg's six American movies with Dietrich, all six but especially the last, *The Devil Is a Woman*. . . . In Camp there is often something *démesuré* in the quality of the ambition, not only in the style of the work itself. Gaudi's lurid and beautiful buildings in Barcelona are Camp not only because of their style but because they reveal—most notably in the Cathedral of the Sagrada Familia—the ambition on the part of one man to do what it takes a whole generation, a whole culture to accomplish.

26. Camp is art that proposes itself seriously, but cannot be taken altogether seriously because it is "too much." *Titus Andronicus* and *Strange Interlude* are almost Camp, or could be played as Camp. The public manner and rhetoric of de Gaulle, often, are pure Camp.

27. A work can come close to Camp, but not make it, because it succeeds. Eisenstein's films aren't Camp because, despite all exaggeration, they do succeed (dramatically) without surplus. If they were a little more "off," they could be great Camp—particularly *Ivan the Terrible I & II*. The same for Blake's drawings and paintings, weird and mannered as they are. They aren't Camp; though Art Nouveau, influenced by Blake, is.

What is extravagant in an inconsistent or unpassionate way is not Camp. Neither can anything be Camp that does not seem to spring from an irrepressible, a virtually uncontrolled sensibility. Without passion, one gets pseudo-Camp—what is merely decorative, safe, in a word, chic. On the barren edge of Camp lie a number of beautiful things: the sleek fantasies of Dali, the haute couture preciosity of Albicocco's *The Girl with the Golden Eyes*. But the two things—Camp and preciosity—must not be confused.

28. Again, Camp is the attempt to do something extraordinary. But extraordinary in the sense, often, of being special, glamorous. (The curved line, the extravagant gesture.) Not extraordinary merely in the sense of effort. Ripley's Believe-It-Or-Not items are rarely campy. These items, either natural oddities (the two headed rooster, the eggplant in the shape of a cross) or else the products of immense labor

(the man who walked from here to China on his hands, the woman who engraved the New Testament on the head of a pin), lack the visual reward—the glamour, the theatricality—that marks off certain extravagances as Camp.

29. The reason a movie like *On the Beach*, a book like *Winesburg, Ohio*, are bad to the point of being laughable but not bad to the point of being enjoyable is that they are too dogged and pretentious. They lack fantasy. There is Camp in such bad movies as *The Prodigal* and *Samson and Delilah*, the series of Italian color spectacles about the super-hero Maciste, numerous Japanese science fiction films (*Rodan*, *The Mysterians*, *The H-Man*) because, in their relative unpretentiousness and vulgarity, they are more extreme and irresponsible in their fantasy—and therefore touching and quite enjoyable.

30. Of course, the canon of Camp can change. Time has a great deal to do with it. Time may enhance what seems simply dogged or lacking in fantasy now because we are too close to it, because it resembles too closely our own everyday fantasies, the fantastic nature of which we don't perceive. We are better able to enjoy a fantasy as fantasy when it is not our own.

31. This is why so many of the objects prized by Camp taste are old-fashioned, out-of-date, *démodé*. It's not a love of the old as such. It's simply that the process of aging, or deterioration, provides the necessary detachment—or arouses a necessary sympathy. When the theme is important, and contemporary, the failure of a work of art may make us indignant. Time can change that. Time liberates the work of art from moral relevance, delivering it over to the Camp sensibility. . . . Another effect: time contracts the sphere of banality. (Banality is, strictly speaking, always a category of the contemporary.) What was banal can, with the passage of time, become fantastic. Many people who listen with delight to the style of Rudy Vallee revived by the English pop group, The Temperance Seven, would have been driven up the wall by Rudy Vallee in his heyday.

Thus, things are campy not when they become old—but when we become less involved in them, and can enjoy, instead of be frustrated by, the failure of the attempt. But the effect of time is unpredictable. Maybe Rod Steiger's acting will seem as Camp some day as Ruby Keeler's does now—or as Sarah Bernhardt's does, in the films she made at the end of her career. And maybe not.

32. Camp is the glorification of "character." The statement is of no importance—except, of course, to the person (Loie Fuller, Gaudi, Cecil B. De Mille, Crivelli, de Gaulle, etc.) who makes it. What the Camp eye appreciates is the unity, the force of the person. In every move Martha Graham makes she's being Martha Graham, etc., etc. . . . This is clear in the case of the great serious idol of Camp taste, Greta Garbo. Garbo's incompetence (at the least, lack of depth) as an *actress* enhances her beauty. She's always herself.

33. What Camp taste responds to is "instant character"; and, conversely, what it is not stirred by is the sense of the development of character. (This is, of

course, very eighteenth-century.) Character is understood as a state of continual incandescence—a person being one, very intense thing. This taste in character is a key element of the theatricalization of experience embodied in the Camp sensibility. And it helps account for the fact that opera and ballet are experienced as such rich treasures of Camp, for neither of these forms can easily do justice to the complexity of human nature. Wherever there is development of character, Camp is reduced. Among operas, for example, *La Traviata* (which has some small development of character) is less campy than *Il Trovatore* (which has none).

> Life is too important a thing ever to talk seriously about it.
> • *Vera; or, The Nihilists*

34. Camp taste turns its back on the good-bad axis of ordinary aesthetic judgment. Camp doesn't reverse things. It doesn't argue that the good is bad, or the bad is good. What it does is to offer for art (and life) a different—a supplementary—set of standards.

35. Ordinarily we value a work of art because of the seriousness and dignity of what it achieves. We value it because it succeeds in being what it is and, presumably, in fulfilling the intention that lies behind it. We assume a proper, that is to say, straightforward relation between intention and performance. By such standards, we appraise *The Iliad*, Aristophanes' plays, "The Art of the Fugue," *Middlemarch*, the paintings of Rembrandt, Chartres, the poetry of Donne, *The Divine Comedy*, Beethoven's quartets, etc., etc.; and—among people—Socrates, Jesus, St. Francis, Napoleon, Savonarola, and so forth. In short, the pantheon of high culture: truth, beauty, and seriousness.

36. But there are other creative sensibilities besides the seriousness (both tragic and comic) of high culture and of the high style of evaluating people. And one cheats oneself, as a human being, if one has respect only for the style of high culture, whatever else one may do or feel on the sly.

For instance, there is the kind of seriousness whose trademark is anguish, cruelty, derangement. Here we do accept a disparity between intention and result. I am speaking, obviously, of a style of personal existence as well as of a style in art; but the examples had best come from art—Bosch, de Sade, Rimbaud, Jarry, Kafka, Artaud, most of the important works of art of the twentieth century, that is, art whose goal is not that of creating harmonies but of overstraining the medium and introducing more and more violent, and unresolvable, subject matter. This sensibility also insists on the principle that an *oeuvre* in the old sense (again, in art, but also in life) is not possible, only fragments. . . . Obviously, different standards apply here than to traditional high culture. Something is good not because it is achieved, but because another kind of truth about the human situation, another experience of what it is to be human—in short, another valid sensibility—is being revealed.

And third among the great creative sensibilities is Camp, the sensibility of failed seriousness, of the theatricalization of experience. Camp refuses both the harmonies of traditional seriousness and the risks of fully identifying with extreme states of feeling.

37. The first sensibility, that of high culture, is basically moralistic. The second sensibility, that of extreme states of feeling, represented in much contemporary "avant-garde" art, gains power by a tension between moral and aesthetic passion. The third, Camp, is wholly aesthetic.

38. Camp is the consistently aesthetic experience of the world. It incarnates a victory of style over content, of aesthetics over morality, of irony over tragedy.

39. Camp and tragedy are antitheses. There is seriousness in Camp (seriousness in the degree of the artist's involvement) and, very often, pathos. The excruciating is also one of the tonalities of Camp; it is the quality of excruciation in much of Henry James (for instance, *The Europeans*, *The Awkward Age*, *The Wings of the Dove*) that is responsible for the large element of Camp in his writings. But there is never, never tragedy.

40. Style is everything. Genet's ideas, for instance, are very Camp. Genet's statement that "the only criterion of an act is its elegance"[2] is virtually interchangeable, as a statement, with Wilde's "in matters of great importance, the vital element is not sincerity, but style." But what counts, finally, is the style in which ideas are held. The ideas about morality and politics in, say, *Lady Windemere's Fan* and in *Major Barbara* are Camp, but not just because of the nature of the ideas themselves. It is those ideas, held in a special playful way. The Camp ideas in *Notre Dame des Fleurs* are maintained too grimly—and the writing itself is too successfully elevated and serious—for Genet's books to be Camp.

41. The whole point of Camp is to dethrone the serious. Camp is playful, anti-serious. More precisely, Camp involves a new, more complex relation to "the serious." One can be serious about the frivolous, frivolous about the serious.

42. One is drawn to Camp when one realizes that "sincerity" is not enough. Sincerity can be simple philistinism, intellectual narrowness.

43. The traditional means for going beyond straight seriousness—irony, satire—seem feeble today, inadequate to the culturally oversaturated medium in which contemporary sensibility is schooled. Camp introduces a new standard: the idea of style, theatricality.

44. Camp proposes a comic vision of the world. But not a bitter or polemical comedy. If tragedy is an experience of hyperinvolvement, comedy is an experience of underinvolvement, of detachment.

2. Sartre's gloss on this in *Saint Genet* is: "Elegance is the quality of conduct which transforms the greatest amount of being into appearing."

I adore simple pleasures, they are the last refuge of the complex.
• *A Woman of No Importance*

45. Detachment is the prerogative of an elite; and as the dandy is the nine-teenth century's surrogate for the aristocrat in matters of culture, so Camp is the modern dandyism. Camp is the answer to the problem: how to be a dandy in the age of mass culture.

46. The dandy was overbred. His posture was disdain, or else *ennui*. He sought rare sensations, undefiled by mass appreciation. (Models: Des Esseintes in Huysmans' *Là Bas*, *Marius the Epicurean*, Valéry's *Monsieur Teste*.) He was ded-icated to "good taste."

The connoisseur of Camp has found more ingenious pleasures. Not in Latin poetry and rare wines and velvet jackets, but in the coarsest commonest plea-sures, in the arts of the masses. Mere use does not defile the objects of his plea-sure, since he learns to possess them in a rare way. Camp—Dandyism in the age of mass culture—makes no distinction between the unique object and the mass-produced object. Camp taste transcends the nausea of the replica.

47. Wilde himself is a transitional figure. The man who when he first came to London sported a velvet beret, lace shirts, velveteen knee-breeches and black silk stockings could never depart too far in his life from the pleasures of the old-style dandy; this conservatism is reflected in *The Picture of Dorian Grey*. But many of his attitudes suggest something more modern. It was Wilde who formulated an important element of the Camp sensibility—the equivalence of all objects—when he announced his intention of "living up" to his blue-and-white china, or declared that a doorknob could be as admirable as a painting. When he empha-sized the importance of the necktie, the boutonniere, the chair, Wilde was antic-ipating the democratic *esprit* of Camp.

48. The old-style dandy hated vulgarity. The new-style dandy, the lover of Camp, is a lover of vulgarity. Where the dandy would be continually offended or bored, the connoisseur of Camp is continually amused, delighted. The dandy held a perfumed handkerchief to his nostrils and was liable to swoon; the con-noisseur of Camp sniffs the stink and prides himself on his strong nerves.

49. It is a feat, of course. A feat goaded on, in the last analysis, by the threat of boredom. The relation between boredom and Camp taste cannot be overesti-mated. Camp taste is by its nature possible only in affluent societies, in societies or circles capable of experiencing the psychopathology of affluence.

What is abnormal in Life stands in normal relations to Art. It is the only thing in Life that stands in normal relations to Art.
• *A Few Maxims for the Instruction of the Over-Educated*

50. Aristocracy is a position vis-à-vis culture (as well as vis-à-vis power), and the history of Camp taste is part of the history of snob taste. But since no authentic aristocrats in the old sense exist today to sponsor special tastes, who is the bearer of this taste? Answer: an improvised self-elected class, mainly homosexuals, who constitute themselves as aristocrats of taste.

51. The peculiar relation between Camp taste and homosexuality has to be explained. While it's not true that Camp taste *is* homosexual taste, there is no doubt a peculiar affinity and overlap. Not all liberals are Jews, but Jews have shown a peculiar affinity for liberal and reformist causes. So, not all homosexuals have Camp taste. But homosexuals, by and large, constitute the vanguard — and the most articulate audience — of Camp. (The analogy is not frivolously chosen. Jews and homosexuals are the two outstanding creative minorities in contemporary western culture. Creative, that is, in the truest sense: they are creators of sensibilities. The two pioneering forces of modern sensibility are Jewish moral seriousness and homosexual aestheticism and irony.)

52. The reason for the flourishing of the aristocratic posture among homosexuals also seems to parallel the Jewish case. For every sensibility is self-serving to the group that promotes it. Jewish liberalism is a gesture of self-legitimization. So Camp taste, which definitely has something propagandistic about it. Of course, the propaganda is in just the opposite direction. The Jews pinned their hopes for integrating into modern society on promoting the moral sense. Homosexuals have pinned their integration into society on promoting the esthetic sense. Camp is a solvent of morality. It neutralizes moral indignation, sponsors playfulness.

53. Nevertheless, even though homosexuals have been its vanguard, Camp taste is much more than homosexual taste. Obviously, its metaphor of life as theater is peculiarly suited as a justification and projection of a certain aspect of the situation of homosexuals. (The Camp insistence on not being "serious," on playing, also connects with the homosexual's desire to remain youthful.) Yet one feels that if homosexuals hadn't more or less invented Camp, someone else would. For the aristocratic posture with relation to culture cannot die, though it may persist only in increasingly arbitrary and ingenious ways. Camp is (to repeat) the relation to style in a time in which the adoption of style — as such — has become altogether questionable. (In the modern era, each new style, unless frankly anachronistic, has come on the scene as an anti-style.)

One must have a heart of stone to read the death of Little Nell without laughing.
• *In conversation.*

54. The experiences of Camp are based on the great discovery that the sensibility of high culture has no monopoly upon refinement. Camp asserts that good

taste is not simply good taste; that there exists, indeed, a good taste of bad taste. (See Genet on this in *Notre Dame des Fleurs.*) This discovery is very liberating. The man who insists on high and serious pleasures is depriving himself of pleasure; he continually restricts what he can enjoy; in the constant exercise of his good taste he will eventually price himself out of the market, so to speak. Here Camp taste supervenes upon good taste as a daring and witty hedonism. It makes the man of good taste cheerful, where before he ran the risk of being chronically frustrated. It is good for the digestion.

55. Camp taste is, above all, a mode of enjoyment, of appreciation—not judgment. Camp is generous. It wants to enjoy. It only seems like malice, cynicism. (Or, if it is cynicism, it's not a ruthless but a sweet cynicism.) Camp taste doesn't propose that it's in bad taste to be serious; it doesn't sneer at someone who succeeds in being seriously dramatic. What it does is to find the success in certain passionate failures.

56. Camp taste is a kind of love, love for human nature. It relishes, rather than judges, the little triumphs and awkward intensities of "character.". . . Camp taste identifies with what it is enjoying. People who share this sensibility are not laughing at the thing they label as "a camp," they're enjoying it. Camp is a *tender* feeling.

(Here, compare Camp with much of Pop art, which—when it is not just Camp—embodies an attitude which is related, but still very different. Pop Art is more flat and more dry, more serious, more detached, ultimately nihilistic.)

57. Camp taste nourishes itself on the love that has gone into certain objects and personal styles. The absence of this love is the reason why such kitsch items as *Peyton Place* and the Tishman Building can't be Camp.

58. The ultimate Camp statement: it's good *because* it's awful. . . . But one can't always say that. Only under certain conditions, which I've tried to sketch in these notes.   1964, vol. 31, no. 4

• The New Radicalism
Nat Hentoff

Michael Harrington's article on the "new radicalism" [*Partisan Review* 2, 1965] seems in many respects more like an exercise in wishful thinking than a political analysis. The piece also reveals his failure to understand the real nature of the new left. I referred—and I assumed he did too—to the core of the new radicalism, represented by such groups as SNCC, the Northern Student Movement, Students for a Democratic Society, a growing number of CORE workers and their putative allies on campuses and among radical intellectuals as well as among those of the poor who are starting to organize themselves. I'm sure we both agree that the Progressive Labor Party, which predictably (despite its minute numbers and influence) is given absurdly wide coverage in national magazines, is not part of a viable new left. Nor are any other neo-Stalinist or pro-Mao or ideologically quasi-totalitarian sects.

Harrington writes, "This new leftism is youthful, disrespectful of radical tradition, and, because of the civil rights movement, values personal commitment and involvement highly." But the young are not so much disrespectful of radical tradition as they are disrespectful of those aging radicals who try to counsel and influence them in the terms of the thirties. I have heard Irving Howe, for example, address himself to the new left, and I was saddened by his self-righteous conviction that he himself had nothing to learn from *them*.

It is true that the young, for the most part, have not yet thought through a comprehensive ideology or a strategy for basic social change, but it is also true that they quite rightly consider their situation to be qualitatively different from that of radicals in the thirties. For one thing, as I tried to show in my piece, the enemy is basically different. Second, these young people are not the children or the auxiliaries of already established parties or other "adult" ideological centers. (Even CORE, which was started and for a long time shaped by older radical-pacifists, is rapidly developing its own indigenous young leadership.) PLM (or, now, PLP), by contrast, *is* an offshoot of older ideologies (at least two of its leaders are former functionaries of the Communist Party, and that is one of the reasons for the Progressive Labor Party's rigid irrelevance).

Third, because of the strength of their commitment and because of the existential force of the experience of working in the ghettos, the youth feel secure enough to be unafraid of "takeover" by manipulators from totalitarian groups. Accordingly, they are disrespectful of what to them seems the hysteria of those older radicals who tried to "purify" the Students for a Democratic Society's April 17 March on Washington to protest the Administration's Vietnam policy. The young knew they could protect the content of their protest against infiltration by fellow travelers of one kind or another, and they succeeded. Most of the active young are not ingenuous about the dangers of takeover, but they are convinced that they are at the very least as able as their elders to guard against manipulation and that those elders are spending far too much time and energy drawing frightened parallels between the radicalism of today and that of their own youth.

Harrington goes on to say that this is "probably the first serious left in the last century which has ignored, or even rejected, the organized workers." But who has ignored whom? So far most of the prescriptions for a broad coalition which includes labor have been far too vague to make sense to the young. And the failure of the unions to protest our appalling adventures in Vietnam and the Dominican Republic hardly gives the new left confidence in organized labor as an ally. George Meany refers to critics of American policy in Vietnam as "intellectual jitterbugs and nitwits"; and David Dubinsky of the ILGWU takes exactly the same line. Walter Reuther, whom the coalitionists regard as a more flexible possible ally than Meany or Dubinsky, is silent.

Domestically, Harrington finds hope in the rising militancy of such unions as the American Federation of Teachers and the social workers' Local 371 in New York. A few other unions, like Local 1199 in New York which has been organizing hospital workers and other groups, are aware of the need for fundamental social change. But on the whole, organized labor is concerned with protecting its own. It has done far too little about organizing the marginal workers and the underemployed. And nothing about the unemployed.

Harrington says "the unions have the beginnings of a program to deal with the current situation. They are for national economic planning, for massive social spending to generate jobs, for upgrading various social benefits, etc." But he ignores the fact that organized labor is so intertwined with the Democratic party that it shows no signs of being willing to fight hard enough for its program. There is no indication that labor will dare risk a confrontation with the leadership of the "consensus party."

I do think that as cybernation cuts further into labor's strength and numbers more unions will be ready for a coalition with the underclass. But those who advocate broad coalition *now* forget that the groups they want to ally are moving at different speeds. In their analysis of the need for institutional change, those involved in action beyond civil rights (SNCC, the Northern Student Movement, etc.) are much more radical than organized labor, churchmen, and most white liberals. The young radicals can work with the older groups on specific projects. But for the young to form any strong alliance with labor as it is now would be to slow down markedly the process of any real change.

Harrington and many of the younger new radicals disagree more fundamentally about the very nature of the "unfinished revolution." What should the goals of the new left be? In the June/July 1965 *Liberation*, Staughton Lynd speaks for those who, like myself, are opposed to the coalitionism defined by Harrington and Bayard Rustin. "The civil rights movement, so often called a revolution," Lynd asserts, "is thus far no more a revolution than the trade-union movement of the 1930s. Presumably the definition of a revolution is that the direction of society's affairs shifts from one group to another, and the economic foundation of political power is transformed so as to make this shift permanent. A revolution in this sense—and not merely public works planning by an Administration whose power rests on private ownership and lack of planning—seem to me required both to prevent war and to satisfy the needs of the other America."

If Harrington's claim that "the unions are the largest, most politically significant force for economic and social change in the United States," is true, we are condemned to stumbling meliorism while the conditions of the poor worsen. Certainly Harrington does not maintain that present labor leadership is committed to the kind of revolution Lynd describes. Yet he adds, "in the political spectrum of this society, labor is as far left as the masses go." Which masses? What about the millions of the poor who might be willing to go much farther if they were organized? Harrington says the two largest groups of the poor and the deprived—the young and the old—are the "most difficult to organize." But we know so little about the dynamics of organizing the poor to organize themselves in the current situation. Harrington may be right. But it is too soon for him or anyone else to conclude that the future must necessarily mirror the past.

The new left has only begun to act as a catalyst among the poor. And other ghetto groups, which have sprung up without outside help, are also very new. A politicized underclass has not yet emerged nor, as Harrington says, can one "wish or exhort or romanticize it into existence." But one *can* work toward that goal, and this is precisely what more and more of the young are doing.

But what if the poor were to start to move? "Even a full mobilization of all the impoverished would . . . fall numerically short of a majority," Harrington claims: the poor and deprived together total no more than forty percent of the citizenry. But a numerical majority is hardly essential to create an effective thrust for basic change. After all, the other sixty percent, many of whom are in their own way insular and apathetic, does not share a community of self-interest.

Harrington is right when he says that the Negro "cannot make revolution by himself." The Negro will have to ally himself with the white workers, and with other groups. But because of the civil rights movement there is now more potential for self-organization among the black poor than among the white. And it is in the black ghettos that most attempts at community organization by the new left and by the poor themselves are taking place. As more workers come into community organization, intensive efforts will have to be made in white ghettos too, like those made in Kentucky. And I agree with Bayard Rustin's statement of a few years ago that more white activists should ask themselves whether this course will be the most effective role they can play in the movement beyond civil rights.

In any case, if larger and larger groups of the black poor do organize themselves to acquire political and social power, they will then be able to enter into a coalition on an equal basis. They cannot do that now, even if a real coalition existed. And one of the primary objections to the current theory of coalition is that the black underclass's lack of cohesive strength fosters elitism. Without leaders directly responsible to a mass base in the ghetto, what real voice can the black poor have in any coalition at present? Instead, the Negroes now have "national spokesmen" who, for example, equate political maturity with "compromise" in the seating of the Mississippi Freedom Democratic Party delegates at the

Democratic party convention in Atlantic City. But whom do these leaders represent—in Mississippi or in Harlem?

If the black and the white poor each organize, we can then talk of an effective coalition of black and white workers and of the black and white unemployed. To speak now as if either group were cohesive enough to join a coalition in which its members would have decision-making power is to compound illusions.

I do not think Harrington has gone beyond wishful thinking in his belief that "if the civil rights activists, the union members, the poor, the youth, and the rest of the population geared to social change could make the Democratic Party their party, that would be a tremendous step for the left of the Sixties." Of course it would but how is that to be done in view of the current state of the left? Who will begin the takeover? In many sections of the country that change in the Democratic Party will have to come through *black* organization. In some places, parapolitics may be the first step—as with the Freedom Democratic Party in Mississippi and the new Brooklyn Freedom Democratic Party. In other situations, people of the ghettos could take over the local Democratic Party from below and elect people who are fully responsible to their constituency.

I recognize the danger that local power structures may then be able to dilute and detour these community organizations by granting part or all of their most pressing demands. If that were to happen the kind of revolution and fundamental redistribution of power called for by Staughton Lynd would remain a fantasy. Much depends, therefore, on the degree of democracy and the depth of understanding about basic issues in newly created community groups. That the black poor have not yet shown that they can be organizationally and politically hip is only part of the story. So far no real choice has been offered them that would warrant their ceasing to be apathetic about voting and about organizing themselves. What the new left is trying to do is to help them find for themselves genuine reasons for organizing and for selecting their own leaders.

Once the black poor begin to move, other sectors of society may be spurred to action. Already the dynamism of the civil rights movement has led not only to civil rights bills but also to a new look at public education and to at least a rhetorical "war" on poverty. Successful political action among the black poor could extend beyond remaking the Democratic Party in the black ghettos to challenging white liberals and white "reformers" to organize *themselves* much more effectively. And with much more radical programs.

It's all too clear that these are difficult courses of action. But since organized labor, despite Harrington's overestimation of the value of its intermittent awakening, is *now* of little relevance to the underclass, I do not understand what immediate alliances for basic change Harrington has in mind. As a matter of fact, I expect that Ben Seligman is accurate in his picture of the kind of labor movement that *can* become relevant, both to its own increasingly vulnerable members and to the poor. "Ways must be found," Seligman wrote in the Winter 1965 *Dissent*, "to organize and represent workers thrown out of jobs by automation; ways must be found to organize and consider the millions of ill-paid 'marginal' workers who scrape along on the minimum wage and suffer the consequences of racial discrimination. Perhaps new structures will be needed, amalgamated unions of workers cutting across industrial lines, just as in the thirties the CIO cut across craft lines."

When—and if—this kind of labor movement begins to develop, a coalition of the underclass with labor will be a much more realistic goal. And when church-men and white liberals, instead of marching only from Selma to Montgomery, put real pressure on those who wield power in the North (many of them Democrats and self-labeled "liberals"), talk of a coalition with *them* will have some meaning. Take the city of New York. A "liberal" Democratic mayor, Robert Wagner, has for fourteen years presided over the steady deterioration of housing, jobs, and education in the growing slums. Had he chosen to run in this year's election, who would have supported him? Virtually every labor union, including the "liberal" unions; the Liberal Party, which is dominated by the ILGWU; and many, though not all, in the predominantly white reform movement in the city. And those few churchmen who recognize the costs to the poor of another four years of Wagner—would they have spoken up? What has Harrington to say to the new left in that situation? From what elements can one now construct Harrington's broad coalition for change in New York City? I will grant that if John Lindsay wins, he will probably not be elected by black and Puerto Rican votes. Out of habit, and mistrust of *any* Republican, they will probably still go Democratic. In this instance, what is to be done? Does the new left try to convert organized labor in New York, which is quite happy with its relationship to a Democratic Party that obstructs rather than facilitates social change? Or does it convert churchmen and white liberals? Isn't the real task—the most promising one—to focus on the ghettos and work with indigenous black and Puerto Rican leaders who are trying to organize their communities so that four years from now a Wagner will not be able to take the black vote for granted?

There are similar problems in most if not all large cities. To talk of a broad coalition now is too simplistic. In what Harrington calls a "brilliant" analysis of the new coalitionism in the February 1965 *Commentary*, Bayard Rustin is aston-ishingly simplistic when he writes: "the objective fact is that *Eastland* and *Goldwater* are the main enemies—they and the opponents of civil rights, of the war on poverty, of Medicare, of social security, of federal aid to education, of unions, and so forth." If the situation were that simple, a meaningful coalition, even with things as they are, would be possible. But for the urban poor—black and white—a more immediate and more serious enemy is the Robert Wagners, the labor leaders in alliance with him, those well-intentioned policy-makers of the "war" on poverty who are making that operation a cruel hoax, and the interlocking corporate structures which make so many basic decisions for all of us. The enemy is also those members of a Rustin-Harrington kind of coalition who are not protesting against a disastrous, let alone immoral, foreign policy, a policy which rationalizes allocating at least forty-five percent of our budget to military spending (54.5 billion dollars in 1964) and which may ultimately bring about an integrated crematorium of all classes and colors.

The problem of redistributing power is much more complex than Harrington admits. And helping the poor learn how to organize themselves to get power is extremely complicated. There are no formulas for the future. There will be all kinds of interim alliances, and if there is change, it will move at many different speeds in many different areas. But the new left is, I'm convinced, basically more in contact with reality than are Harrington and Rustin. The new left neither "idealizes" the poor nor does it believe that the past can be used to predict the future. And they do not allow themselves to be deluded into thinking that a broad-based coalition can be created *now* which, by some act of magic, will operate on an identity of interest between David Dubinsky and an unemployed black construction worker, between Walter Reuther and a youth who is sickened by what this country has done in the Dominican Republic, between a white churchman wearing his CORE button and the poor family on the next block whom he has never seen.

I am not optimistic about the chances for radical social change. To change the picture of the future that Donald Michael has chillingly—and unpolemically—drawn in *The Next Generation* will require a great deal of power. The blacks can't do it alone. The poor of any color can't do it alone. Nor can the young of the new left. But they can perhaps start things moving.

Harrington says the new radicals are looking for a "new proletariat." What actually is happening is that, as Sidney Lens has pointed out, the new left is attempting to group all the "left outs" rather than just the economic "have nots." The poor are left out, particularly the black poor. But so are the young who can find no personally relevant, honorable place for themselves in this society except in working to change it. Those clergymen who practice what they preach are also left out; but they too, if there are enough of them, can be effective. And as labor begins to recognize the insufficiency of its programs and its present political alliances—forced to do so by the changes in the definition of work that cybernation is making—it too can join with the left-outs and those soon to be left out. At that point, if it is not too late, the Democratic Party can be radicalized.

As Harrington says, "One need no longer be contented with the vision of a revolution. The more radical task of taking the next step is at hand." But for that task to be indeed radical, that next step must be taken before the broad-based coalition which he calls for can be formed.

Michael Harrington

Dear Nat,

I use the form of an open letter partly out of literary and political convenience, but also because I was puzzled and sometimes angered by your description of the new radicalism. So I find the informality and candor of a letter especially appropriate for my comments.

First of all, you draw a sharp and somewhat emotional line between the old and new radicals. You speak of the "irrelevancy of most traditional American styles"; Bayard Rustin, to whom you dedicated a book only last year, is now described as a "former radical"; you refer to the "retired radicals," and so on. Since I agree with most of Bayard Rustin's politics, I would be, by your definition, a "former radical."

But when I read your analysis, I found no basis for the anathema against people like Rustin and me. Your description of the substantive program of the new radicalism, with a few exceptions I'll note later, gives me a feeling of *déjà vu*. For these are precisely the ideas of many of the older, irrelevant, former radicals. The acrimony of the current discussion of old and new lefts does not make for clarity, but let me try as calmly as I can to point out how much what you define as the new radicalism agrees with what you call irrelevant or former radicalism.

The War on Poverty, you say, not only is inadequately financed but also does not recognize that technology is making current definitions of work obsolescent, and most important, is breaking the traditional link between production and income. "It is here," you say, "that the new radicalism as a political and economic movement differs from much of the American radicalism that has preceded it." This is the position, you note, taken by the statement of the Ad Hoc Committee on the Triple Revolution (which both Rustin and I signed). For this reason, you go on, there must be basic change. You find it wrong, therefore, to spend *"all* one's energies" fighting for full employment, massive public works, social investments, etc., although you recognize that demands for this kind of program do play an immediate, transitional role in the politics of the new radicalism.

But how does one get America to confront this new reality? You say "a new politics" must elect "a greatly changed Congress," which means you look toward a parliamentary (Congressional) transformation. To achieve this, you argue, a coalition will indeed be necessary. But, according to you, labor, the liberals, and the religious reformers—all of whom would be parts of the coalition you are calling for—are not "ready at this time to move beyond meliorism." Finally, you see that the tax dollars in the official antipoverty effort will not subsidize the poor in a revolution against the status quo.

From this grim perspective, you base the hope of the new radicalism on three developments. First: the young militants will go into the slums in every part of

America and help the poor find a voice. Second: you predict that the middle and lower-middle classes might be rendered useless by technological change and thus made receptive to united action with the organized poor (or to fascism, one might add). And third: you say that change in definitions of work may well push the labor movement to a much more radical position. Then a really effective coalition could be formed with the newly enfranchised poor and the radicalized middle, lower-middle, and working classes.

Such a coalition would allocate resources to satisfy social needs, improve the quality of education, and provide a material basis for new definitions of work, such as that represented by the job of teacher's aide. There would still be a planning, centralist sector, but as a result of changes in values and the greatly increased individual participation in the democratic process the voluntarist and decentralist sector would become dominant.

I would quarrel with some of your formulations and emphases (of that, more in a moment) but I certainly agree with the drift of your thought and even take pride in having helped popularize some of these ideas during the last few years. But where, then, is the chasm between the old radicalism and the new?

Except for a few sectarians, no American radicals, whether veterans of the thirties or recruits of the sixties, believe that the workers are, on schedule, more impoverished and more revolutionary or that nationalization alone solves everything. But more than that: to the extent that there are these new ideas which you attribute to the new radicalism, they are by no means the property or creation of the younger generation. Indeed, if you took the trouble to check, you would find that these programmatic innovations are, in almost every case, the work of "former radicals." I labor this point not simply because I want to set the historical record straight, but because it reveals that the real difference between the old and new lefts is not in their analysis of their proposals so much as in style, mood, and tactic. (Incidentally, it also makes me think that perhaps my radicalism is not so former, nor yours so new.)

What are these nonprogrammatic, tactical differences that divide the new radicals from the old? Your description corroborates my thesis that the best and worst in the young comes from their search for a new proletariat. In theory, you, and many of them, admit the need for a coalition of forces; in practice, you say you have found the force, the poor.

For example, you write that the new radicals "realize—as a number of older, retired radicals do not—that class cleavage in this country is deepening." If this means that there is poverty in the affluent society or that the poor, unlike the organized workers, do not share even the major benefits of the welfare state, or that one result of the intersection of cybernation and the baby boom is a "growth potential" for poverty, then you and I agree. (Every one of these points, by the way, was documented by "former radicals" in the fifties and early sixties in journals like *Dissent*.) But if you mean—as I suspect you do—that class conscious-ness and solidarity are developing among the poor, that is quite another matter.

Let me be very explicit. One is heartened by every tendency of the poor to organize themselves and to rebel, and the attempts of some of the new radicals who have gone into the slums and shared the daily life of those imprisoned there to speed this process are more heartening still. But this does not prove that "the steadily growing ranks of the speechless" are finding a voice. As I've been saying, poverty can drive people either to protest or to passivity. In the widely publicized Philadelphia election for a community action council, only 2.7 percent of eligi-ble voters went to the polls (13,500 out of 500,000). This hardly supports the the-sis of the growth of *conscious*, *political* class cleavage between the poor and the rest of society.

If the poor were becoming more militant and becoming aware of themselves as a group, that is, if some millions and tens of millions of people were becom-ing radical, then the rejection of coalition politics that is so often characteristic of the new radicalism would make some sense. If this were the situation, there would be no reason to subordinate the radical instincts of the masses to the meliorist bureaucracies of labor, liberalism, and church. To be sure, even then coalition would still be necessary in order to achieve a political majority, but the terms of the alliance would be dictated from below. I suggest to you that American life is not so simple and never will be.

Strangely enough, the new radicalism's ultra-left agrees with my analysis here. They too see no imminent prospect of revolutionary change—no new prole-tariat—within the United States. But their conclusion is a militant despair. In a vague and confused way, they look for eventual salvation from the revolutionary Third World forces. Domestically, they tend toward symbolic and even kamikaze-like action. This tendency is difficult to discuss, so let me return to the mood, the style, and the tactics which actually separate the old from the new radicals.

Your remarks, Nat, on the Mississippi Freedom Democratic Party at Atlantic City are extremely relevant here. For you, and most of the new radicals, have made of that issue a major dividing line. You even write that the MFDP's refusal of the convention compromise "will be seen in retrospect to have been one of the watersheds of the new radicalism . . . if this politics-by-the-poor approach proves viable." In arguing your case, like most of the new radicals, you confuse tactic and principle. It is certainly true that a dispute over tactics can get bitter and nasty, but that still does not justify your division of radicalism into two categories, the old and the new, the irrelevant and the relevant.

To have stayed outside Convention Hall would have been a defensible tactic. The civil rights movement could then have exposed the concessions and com-promises made by a party that still embraces New Dealers and slave dealers. It might even have called on the best people in that party to leave and join the movement in independent political action against *both* major parties. (This is the hallowed, spectacularly unsuccessful nostrum of traditional American radicals.) Or the movement might have picketed outside the convention hall in support of various programmatic demands. I would have disagreed with this as a strategy, but an argument could be made for it. In any case, the movement itself rejected it.

When the Mississippi militants decided to go inside the convention, their strategy was no longer one of protest; it became political. Outside the convention, the movement would have been able to control what was said and done and could have put forth its total program. But once the decision was made to organize as a *Democratic* party which would support the convention's candidate, if only to get a hearing the movement had to ally with labor, liberal, and reform forces. Thus the basic question was: how far would the movement be able to move its meliorist allies?

From the outset then, the argument at Atlantic City was not whether to compromise but what kind of compromise to accept. In all reports of the convention, it's agreed that the MFDP was ready to take something short of justice (justice would have meant accrediting the MFDP as *the* Mississippi delegation and taking the privileges of party membership, such as Congressional seniority, away from *all* racist Democrats). The MFDP did feel, however, that the compromise eventually settled upon (two at-large seats for the Freedom Party) not only was inadequate, but also blocked the larger victory that would have been won in a floor fight.

In the recrimination following the convention, a line of principle was drawn between "us" (the movement) and "them" (the white liberals and the "former radicals" who advocated a qualified acceptance of the actual compromise). In doing this, you and the young radicals mistook a bitter dispute over tactics for a question of fundamental perspective and morality.

Let me assume that the MFDP majority's analysis at Atlantic City was completely correct. (I do not believe this to be the case.) *Even so*, if the MFDP wants to change the life of the Negro in Mississippi and of the black and white poor in the United States, it—and the rest of the movement—will have to collaborate with those labor, liberal, and church forces that favored the Atlantic City compromise. Indeed, the support for the MFDP's challenge of the seating and Congressional status of the Mississippi delegation has come from those very labor, liberal, and church forces. For nothing that happens in Atlantic City can change the fact that there is no proletariat that makes up a present or potential revolutionary majority in America. There can be no "politics-by-the-poor" approach except within the framework of coalition. And the movement and the new radicals must look forward, perhaps sadly and warily, to cooperating with the liberal groups. You and I both hope that the case for radicalism and the inevitable course of events will drive those liberal groups beyond meliorism in time for us to confront our revolutionary technological world. But it would be a disaster to interpret the basic disagreement at Atlantic City as an expression of the division between the militant Negroes and their radical white allies and those you call meliorists. Yet that is what you and too many of the new radicals do. Your position is, I am sure, cathartic and bold; politically it is a sentence to permanent failure for the black and white poor.

Before concluding, let me talk about something neither you nor I really touched upon: foreign policy. The new radicalism certainly had roots in the peace movement, particularly in the ban-the-bomb campaigns of the late fifties and early sixties, but it has always been defined by its position on domestic issues—civil rights and poverty. And domestic questions led the new radicals to an analysis of society. As a result, there was a lengthy period, coinciding with the American-Soviet detente and the nuclear test ban, during which international issues were secondary. The new radicals had opinions about Fidel or Mao or Algeria, but these were much less important than their feelings about Mississippi.

But the recent disastrous escalation of American involvement in Vietnam and our crassly imperialist invasion of the Dominican Republic have changed this situation. One encounters new radicals who are so infuriated, and rightly, by Lyndon Johnson's foreign policy that they feel vindicated in their previous rejection of coalition on domestic issues with those who support the administration's international position. This mood is intensified by the *National Review*-like stand of the AFL-CIO, or more precisely, of the Meany-Lovestone team, on scandals like the Dominican invasion.

But how can the position taken by America in other parts of the world be changed? Internationalism has not been the strong point of the left since World War I and the collapse of European Social Democracy. But some steps in that direction might be possible. If there were to be a new political majority, if tens of millions were to have a sense of shaping their own destiny, if the economic underpinnings of the military-industrial complex were being challenged, then one could look toward a mass movement for a democratic foreign policy, and for peace. In other words, domestic change will have to precede international change. One has to make political alliances *on domestic issues* with forces that one might regard as confused, or wrong, on the question of Vietnam and the Dominican Republic. Those who refuse such coalitions in the name of internationalist principle help to keep their principle the property of a tiny group.

But to return to the main argument. Your article demonstrated that one cannot define the program of a "new" radicalism in terms of generations. The programs you cite were all developed and popularized by those you would call "former radicals." In theory, you and I and the more political of the young radicals can generally agree on the need for coalition. But when it comes to tactics, you act *as if* there were a new proletariat, a "politics-by-the-poor" which on its own can transform society. And you overestimate the degree to which the poor are a cohesive, conscious, and politically dynamic group.

In all of this, unfortunately, labels and denunciations have been thrown around; programmatic differences between the young and old radicals have been exaggerated; and tactical divergences have been blown up into issues of principle and morality.

There is, alas, no new proletariat, no simple way to change the most powerful nation in history. But still, I am heartened by the young radicals. We share so many ideas. And the disagreements which do exist on style and tactics I am sure will be resolved. Perhaps the most exciting thing about these new radicals is their personal commitment, which has taken them into the slum streets and the Mississippi Delta. This openness to experience has already given new life to the American left and eventually it will give it new theory as well.   *Fraternally,*
Mike

1965, vol. 32, no. 3

• On Vietnam and the Dominican Republic
Editorial Statement

We do not think that the present or past policies of the United States in Vietnam are good ones, and we lament the increasing and often self-defeating military involvements which those policies require. We have not heard of any alternative policy, however, which would actually lead to a negotiated peace in Vietnam or promote the interests of the people of Southeast Asia. This is not to say that the critics of American actions in Vietnam are therefore required to propose a specific policy. But it is not unfair to ask that their criticism be based on more than the apolitical assumption that power politics, the Cold War, and Communists are merely American inventions. Most of the criticism of Administration policy at the teach-ins and in the various petitions we have been asked to sign has simply taken for granted that everything would be fine if only the Yanks would go home. It is not clear whether these critics think Asia will not go Communist if American troops are withdrawn or whether they don't care. Nor is it clear whether they really care what happens to the people of Southeast Asia so long as America gets out.

The creation of a world in which free societies can exist should be the goal of any international policy. Our policies in Vietnam do not promote that end, even though it is claimed that they are justified because the United States is preventing a Communist takeover. Nor do the policies of North Vietnam, Communist China, or the Vietcong, however they are explained. As for our policies in the Dominican Republic, they cannot be justified even on the grounds that the

United States is preventing a Communist coup. They are a disastrous violation of any democratic principle, a violation likely to alienate the people of South America, especially the youth, or even drive them into an alliance with precisely those Communist forces our government claims to be combating.

The fiasco in the Dominican Republic illustrates, we think, what is basically wrong with our policies. So long as we are not able to understand the political and economic problems of rapidly changing countries and to support democratic revolutionary groups, we are bound to find ourselves in a false dilemma, always having to decide at the last minute whether to intervene, as though that were the only solution. Military action can be a substitute for political foresight only if we propose to police the whole world, and to imagine that we can do that is to lack even hindsight.

Obviously, the time has come for some new thinking. And some of it has to be about what's happening in different parts of the world, regardless of what the United States does or fails to do.

Eleanor Clark	Steven Marcus
Martin Duberman	William Phillips
Irving Howe	Norman Podhoretz
Alfred Kazin	Richard Poirier
Bernard Malamud	Richard Schlatter

1965, vol. 32, no. 3

• What's Happening to America
H. Stuart Hughes

In thirty years of concern with American politics and American society, I have never been so close as I am now to despairing of my country. The war in Vietnam has brought to the surface the latent ugliness in American life—the scorn for the weak and racially diverse, the acceptance of violence as something normal, the lack of imagination about the suffering of others—in short, a profound emotional and ethical insensitivity. When pressed, nearly every American of discernment will admit that the war is wrong; but he will add that there is nothing that can be done about it. Our people seem to be settling into a protracted neocolonial conflict as though it were their natural habitat.

Which is not to say that the war in Vietnam cannot be defended in rational terms. The Johnson-Rusk line of reasoning makes perfect sense if one grants its assumptions. And by these I do not mean the dubious analogy with Munich or the domino theory of subversion. I mean, rather, the idea that there must be a leader of the world and that this position, by right of both power and virtue, belongs to the United States. Now that the Soviet Union has fallen behind in the armaments race—and has simultaneously turned toward moderation in its foreign dealings—China remains as the only challenger. In the administration's reasoning the real point of the Vietnam struggle is not the defense of a small people against Communism; for the president and his advisers are quite prepared to see that people sacrificed in the process. The real point is that Vietnam marks the first round in a contest with China for world leadership.

In such a perspective, major reform at home has to be slowed down—as it has been in our country during all four of our twentieth-century wars. In the name of national unity, the existing system of economic power must be endorsed; the "Great Society" (if the goal indeed still exists) must slip as best it can into the interstices of a going concern; poverty and Negro rights must come second to national assertion on the foreign scene.

There can be scarcely any meeting ground between this perspective and a way of thinking such as my own, in which the problem of poverty—at home and in the underdeveloped countries—takes first place, in which the notion of world leadership is heady nonsense and in which the idea of holding an American bridgehead in Asia ranks as an affront to nonwhite peoples everywhere and a dangerous anachronism in the third quarter of the twentieth century.

To the extent that American intellectuals think as I do, the lack of understanding between them and the Johnson administration is perfectly natural. We and the president are living in two different ideological worlds.

This radical incompatibility was obscured for a time by the mediating rhetoric of the Kennedy era. Particularly in the last months of his presidency, when he sketched a new foreign policy in his American University address and when he signed the limited test-ban treaty, Kennedy seemed to be coming around to the point of view of his peace-minded critics. But the Kennedy rhetoric never cut deep enough. In what his biographers have described as his finest hour—the Cuban missile crisis—he was more concerned about winning a trial of strength with the Soviet Union than with the military threat the missiles posed to the security of his country. And his insistence on American primacy in the space race suggested that he was not above treating this vast expenditure of funds and scientific effort as an international sporting event.

The continuity of the space program from one administration to another and the fact that so few Americans find anything wrong with it epitomize the nationalist reflexes that seem to have become second nature among our countrymen. They further explain why it was comparatively easy for Johnson to shift over from the cautious approaches toward peace which he had inherited from his predecessor to a policy of steady military escalation. Nationalism among small peoples—and especially among recently humiliated and newly liberated peoples—

may well be an emotional necessity; for a country as rich and as strong as ours it is a luxury that the world cannot afford.

I am writing this from Paris. From here the United States looks very big and very threatening. I had occasion the other day to talk with a French friend just returned from America; his last trip to our country had been two years ago. Besides his anxiety about the war, what had now struck him most was the great leap forward—in power, in riches, in self-confidence—that the United States seemed to have made in the brief interval between his two visits. He, as I, had the impression of a productive and scientific machine of unparalleled strength and complexity which was under the guidance of men of little wisdom and in grave danger of going out of control.

Such a prospect is not new in our history. Several times in the recent past our national power has gotten ahead of our ability to manage that power. But these periods in which we have thrown our weight around on the international scene have been followed by pauses for reflection and for bringing official thought abreast of a new reality—such were the final months of Kennedy's presidency. Today, when the last intellectual dissenters have left the administration, it is hard to see where a similar corrective will come from.

Possibly from our young people—but I doubt it. America's radical youth prefers to opt out of the national consensus rather than to find realistic ways of influencing it. And in the present situation I cannot blame them. While the violent rhetoric of so many of the young grates on my nerves, I appreciate the desperation behind it. To be a young and sensitive and intelligent American today is not an easy experience. Or rather, it is so easy to join the national rat race and swallow the national bilge, and so difficult to find an alternative that has real promise for the future. As a teacher and a father I can think of no reassuring answers to offer the young. I can suggest only that they not be frightened, that they stick to what they believe, and that they try to live in such a way that the world outside will know that the America of President Johnson is not the only America there is.   1967, vol. 34, no. 1

• A Statement on the CIA

We, the undersigned, would like to make public our opposition to the secret subsidization by the CIA of literary and intellectual publications and organizations, and our conviction that regular subsidization by the CIA can only discredit intellectually and morally such publications and organizations.

Thus, in view of the facts so far disclosed, we must say we lack confidence in the magazines alleged to have been subsidized by the CIA, and we do not think they have responded appropriately to the questions that have been raised. We would have expected more serious and more searching statements than we have so far seen by responsible editors, and some indication of genuine reorganization of these publications. Instead they seem to be content to go on as though nothing had happened, either remaining silent, or acting as though the importance of the entire matter had been exaggerated, apparently on the assumption that the storm will blow over.

We are aware that many people were innocent recipients of various literary and travel grants to meetings and congresses, but we believe a distinction must be made between such occasional grants and continuous and secret subsidizations by the CIA of any intellectual publications claiming to be independent and open to all views however radical or critical of American policies and institutions. And in the case of the publications, we find the attempt to play down the whole issue a not very satisfactory way of dealing with the questions posed by the original deception about their financing. Obviously, intellectual and literary publications must have their biases; and they often receive contributions from various individuals and foundations who share these biases. But if they are to have the respect of an international intellectual community and any influence on it, it seems to us a basic principle that their steady support should be of a kind—and this may include grants from the government—which they are not ashamed to make public, so that there can be no question of their editorial bias being affected by surreptitious financial support.

Henry David Aiken	Steven Marcus
John Arden	Iris Murdoch
Hannah Arendt	William Phillips
Paul Goodman	Richard Poirier
Stuart Hampshire	V. S.Pritchett
Lillian Hellman	Philip Rahv
John Hollander	William Styron
Dwight Macdonald	Angus Wilson
Norman Mailer	

1967, vol. 34, no. 3

• June 6, 1968
William Phillips

It has been said that outstanding individuals die but mankind, civilization, the nation, all go on. Yet the assassination of Robert F. Kennedy is frightening in its implications about the state of the country.

Robert F. Kennedy was not a political saint, nor did he embody the more radical ideas of the future that sustain so many people—like myself. (Neither does

Senator Eugene McCarthy.) But in a sense larger than the specific records and personalities of these two men, together they offered some hope of a new politics, perhaps of a new national style, by galvanizing those Americans, especially among the young, who are tired of the old crap. Senator Kennedy particularly seemed to supply the power we ourselves lacked.

There are many stirring movements of dissent and of intellectual renewal here and abroad. But there is none strong or intelligent enough to become more than an expression of protest, none one could support all the way. In this situation, Senator Kennedy—and Senator McCarthy—may be said to have represented a heroic effort to work for a new world within the confines of the old one. Thus he became a symbol of the legitimacy of dissent.

There are too many facile generalizations about the spread of violence, which do not say anything about specific questions, and hence are easily absorbed into an empty and dangerous rhetoric about law and order, mouthed by people who would do little or nothing about the problems tearing the country apart. As usual, this plays into the hands of the more backward, the more repressive, the more demagogic currents and figures.

At the same time, there is something awful, and ominous, about the assassination of so many public men in this country whose charisma was a charisma of change. It almost looks as though some perverse historical forces were conspiring to polarize the country by removing those addressing themselves to some of its real problems. It is true that in each case only one, or, at most, several people were implicated. In a strictly logical sense, the whole nation has not been directly involved; and those who argue that it is all the work of a few nuts are technically right. But this is just a legalistic kind of logic and is being fed us by people who want to prove that there is nothing basically wrong, to lull us back into the past.

The one thing we do not need now is more rhetoric. Yet even the death of Senator Kennedy is being used to escalate the production of words, creating a sea of confusion and dissolving people's fears and doubts into the homilies of the status quo. All the political pieties Senator Kennedy stood against in his life are being invoked to memorialize his death.

Who knows what's coming?   1968, vol. 35, no. 3

• Remarks

William Phillips

On most questions, the left has been opposed almost on principle to the official position of the government. But by some strange convergence, Israel has become the victim both of the power politics of the Big Four and of the ultra-highmindedness of the left.

England and France, as well as the Soviet Union, have been playing the old power game in the Middle East, while America, stunned by its failure in Vietnam, has expressed its newly found caution by trying to play both sides.

On the other hand, many liberals and radicals, particularly the militant blacks, have taken pro-Arab or neutralist positions. Cleaver and Carmichael, for example, have identified the Arabs with North Vietnam and Israel with American imperialism. (If, as some charge, Israel is an "outpost of American imperialism," President Nixon seems not to have been informed.) And an internationalist like Chomsky, ignoring the patent Arab and Soviet provocations, has proposed a standard socialist solution. Put forward as a political abstraction, Chomsky's long perspective presents an appealing vision of a socialist community in the Middle East sometime in the future. Its meaning for the present is not so clear: so far as one can make out Chomsky seems to be demanding the instant withering away of the state of Israel while calling for no such revolutionary changes in the Arab countries.

Who can object to the investment of one's hopes in genuinely socialist societies? But meanwhile, back in the here and now, it's clear that the current level of military activity is being maintained not by Israel but by the Arabs, who, after all, invited the Six Day War, and the Soviet Union, who stimulated it. One might argue about the right of the Jews to be in Israel in the first place; but it is now a fait accompli and can be reversed only by the kind of extermination threatened by the Arabs.

The threat of war is an Arab threat. If the Arabs wanted to prove that Israel is the aggressor, all they have to do is control their guerrilla activities and then leave it to the rest of the world to discover whether or not Israel is still making punitive strikes.

As for the Palestine refugees, it should be obvious that a solution could be found if there were a will by both sides—as well as by the American and Soviet governments—to resolve the problem.

In the present situation, we feel Israel should have our moral and political support, whatever views we might have about an ultimate solution. And we see no reason why the revulsion properly felt about Vietnam should prevent the left from taking such a stand. Nor should the hope for socialism be taken as a license not to think.

1970, vol. 37, no. 1

• The Politics of Polemics
William Phillips

The level of discussion and debate today is so low that it is impossible to make any sense out of anything. Name-calling, ranting, cliché-mongering, argument by assertion, excommunication, posturing, appeals to one's radicalism or one's fear of radicalism—all these expressions of contempt for intellectual discourse have become the standard modes of disagreement. There are complex reasons, of course, but I think the main ones are the breakup of the old intellectual communities and the emergence of new figures and movements, wild, sprawling, dissident, chaotic. Everyone is busy taking sides, bouncing from issue to issue, frantically looking for solutions that aren't there. And as soon as two people get together they are polarized.

Going to extremes, that old American custom, has taken over: no sooner is a new idea or movement born than it develops a lunatic fringe, and it doesn't take long for the fringe to be mistaken for the center—or to become the center. And then there is the bad faith of those who claim to be defending civilization against the extremists when they are really just protecting their investments.

Some random examples, in no special order:

The Greening of America

It's hard to understand the success of a book so full of truisms and false hopes. Its best parts are simply a rehash of radical theories and criticisms of existing society, presented with a breathlessness and innocence that gives them the air of fresh discovery. The rest is a compendium of fashionable notions about youth culture and the new radicalism, all lumped together into one huge historical package. Perhaps Reich's success is due to the fact that he has concocted a soothing mixture for both radicals and liberals: his prescription for the new society involves little pain, less effort, and above all, no revolution. Even the style is simple and declarative, in keeping with the author's evident sincerity. It's the old wave of the future, with consciousness filling in for determinism.

Old and New Polemics

An old form of political polemic which proves its case simply by asserting it is being revived. For example: a one-dimensional, oversimplified piece by Dennis Wrong in a recent issue of *Commentary* ostensibly presenting a capsule history of New York intellectual life. Most of its fire is directed against the *New York Review of Books*, though many people get a going over and *Partisan Review* too is accused of deviating from an arbitrary political norm that is somewhat hazy but turns out to be right of center. True, many of the things Wrong said were right. But much of his argument rests on ignoring the differences between diverse people and positions, on a hasty disposal of complicated questions, particularly literary ones, and on a vague, underlying assumption that all forms of radicalism amount to intellectual betrayal. In this respect, Wrong's piece is typical of the new conservative polemics—it raises questions only about the left, not about the right, not about the state of the country, which is presumably what the left is responding to. The ideological justification for this kind of argument is the belief that the left is the main threat, an appraisal that exaggerates the power of the puny left and minimizes the massive power of big business, the force of backward and provincial opinion throughout the country, and the strength of various arms of the government.

The Vietnam Riddle

A number of commentators have pointed out how mad the Indochinese expedition is even from the point of view of the Pentagon and the administration—so mad it sometimes seems to lack the logic of madness. It's surprising, though, how restrained the far right has been in exploiting the dilemma of the government. (The Calley case may be the signal it has been waiting for.) For if the Asian Communists must be stopped, if the war is justifiable, then Washington could be accused of betraying the national interest in not going all out. Its plight is that it plunged into a war it cannot "win," because of its fear of escalation and its failure to comprehend the political situation in Indochina, yet one it thinks it cannot afford to lose. Hence the dragging on of the war is not just a blunder that the government is committed to but a predicament that it is trapped in by its continued policies of equivocation. The future of the country depends on whether this kind of political stupidity is accidental or built into the system.

Conservatism Is Catching

As if to prove the instability of thinking in this country the pendulum swings back and forth every few years. Recently there have been a number of attacks, some quite venomous, on the youth, the students, the left, and on newer trends in writing and painting, all part of a cultural swing to the right mostly on the part of middle-aged writers with special attachments to some period or movement in the past. It has been argued that this turn is of little significance, that it represents mainly the disgruntlement of a few aging people who refused to face the present. But I think it is a symptom of something deeper. And regardless of how much weight history eventually will assign to it, it does have an immediate importance, if for no other reason than that people are infected by what's in the air. Hence you can't refute the new conservatism the way you would a legitimate argument. In a recent review in *The New York Times*, Christopher Lehmann-Haupt, who is a very intelligent reviewer, made the point that responsive people are bound to be in the middle—between the new and the old—because we have something of each in our thinking. This is, of course, true, except for the new conservatives who, like the most extreme of the new radicals, are concerned with only one side of the equation. For despite their protestations that they are attempting to restore the balance between the past and the present, the new conservatives are actually using earlier positions and ideologies to assault the very idea of change and experiment.

For example, one of the symptoms of the new cultural conservatism is the argument that today's avant-garde is really a perversion of "modernism." But arguing this way is just clinging to *earlier* forms of modernism, unless—and this would mean hiding literary differences behind a verbal quibble—we limit the term "modernism" to the earlier period. There should be no difficulty in granting the monumental work of figures like Joyce, Kafka, and Eliot, whom we identify with the modernist surge of the early part of the century, without being fixated on them, without, that is, assuming that no further experiments or developments can come out of the modernist spirit. No one who lives in the present but has a sense of the past argues that everything being written today is as good as the great works of the earlier period, or even that everything being written today is good. Nor does anyone with a historic sense deny that the contemporary scene, like every period, is full of mindless, disruptive, arrogant, futile postures and works. But there are intelligent younger writers and thinkers; and there is a genuine concern for the quality not only of our art but also of our life among the best of the younger people; and the issue is really whether they too are to be dismissed in a wholesale condemnation of the "postmodernist era," that is, of everything going on today. As always, the critical job is to distinguish between genuine talent and experiment and those who trade on novelty and dissidence.

To use the past as a club against the present is to freeze the values of the past, to transform the achievements of modernism into historical showpieces, putting them out of reach of those to whom they might be live forces and examples for their own work. If figures like Joyce, Kafka, Eliot, Picasso have a meaning for us, it is because of their peculiar combination of restlessness, morbidity, and playfulness, of generalization and fragmentation, that we associate with the quality of modern life and art. They are certainly not the models of balance, moderation, sanity, and structural solidity they are made out to be by those who regard a change of sensibility as a sign of cultural barbarism. Of course, there is a more complex aspect of the question: namely that an older writer cannot authentically assume a younger sensibility. But that is no reason for him to assume that history stopped the minute he was born.

It is certainly discouraging to argue these questions over and over again. Has everyone forgotten that the innovations of the twenties were thought to be nihilist and that the abstract expressionist painters were dismissed as undisciplined and self-indulgent by the frightened defenders of the true modern tradition?

One Issue Politics

One of the symptoms of intellectual breakdown is the inability to see things as part of a total scene. Individuals and movements become fixed on a single target, usually to the exclusion of everything else. Thus the obsessive and exclusive concern with—for or against—Vietnam, pollution, black rights, women's lib, youth, drugs, etc. Some people can see nonsense only on the right, others only on the left. As though this were not absurd enough, we are all familiar with the reduction of the absurd *ad absurdum* which focuses not merely on one issue but on only one aspect of it: one trend, one organization, one publication. Do we need to be reminded that a distinguishing trait of crackpots is the inability to generalize?

Women's Liberation

The hottest, and touchiest, issue today is women's liberation. Nobody can quarrel with its aims. But what do you do with its nutty fringes, with the celebration of masturbation and lesbianism, with its man-baiting, its cultism, and all the ideological meanings that have been squeezed out of the shape of the vagina and the exact site of the orgasm? I suspect that the exotic questions have taken over quickly because questions like equal rights and opportunities are not so modish and require low-keyed, dull, plodding, humdrum work. All that smacks of namby-pamby liberalism while the orgasm has all the explosive resonances of revolution.

On the other hand, those who are always ready to pounce on any sign of weakness or foolishness on the left are using the sexist extravaganzas to dismiss women's liberation as a whole. I guess one can recognize women's liberation enemies, open or concealed, for what they are. But some of its friends make it difficult to remember that you are really for it.

Educational Recipes

Education experts are probably more polarized than any others. On the one hand, there are the standpatters who act as if education has been destroyed by the students, and as though inflated costs, fund cuts, Agnewesque attacks on intellectuals, the smugness and inertia of middle academia, and mass education have had nothing to do with it. On the other side, speaking in the name of freedom, enlightenment, and revolution are the nouveau-Rousseauists, whose position when you dig through the rhetoric of human fulfillment is not so new. It's the same old progressive notion of the student as gifted savage.

The new educational crusaders all agree on one thing: that the wrong subjects and wrong values are taught by the wrong teachers, particularly in the colleges which, they claim, are cluttered with the ghosts of the past, and that historical knowledge has been frozen into the bureaucratic mind of the academy. There is some truth to the charges. Only an apologist for old academic routines can deny that English studies needs to be revised. But this is not to say that the past is to be given up in a splurge of historical masochism, or that it is to be taught in a gimmicky fashion to satisfy an improvised principle of relevance.

Of course, it is difficult to talk about "relevance" because the term has been so sloganized and has led to simple-minded and ingenious correlations of older figures to current events and fashionable causes. Obviously in some sense rele-

vance is relevant to the act of writing and the study of literature, as it is to thinking in any field. After all, as T. S. Eliot pointed out, the past is not fixed; it is constantly reshaped by new ideas and new works. In this sense, the past is a retroactive version of our engagement in the present—cranky, biased, very selective.

If such a view of the past were applied to teaching, it would mean abandoning many academic conventions based on the idea that literature is a self-perpet-
uating body of knowledge that can be taught once it has been sorted out by qualified experts. The more scholarly teachers think of literature as a museum with
walls stocked with works to be studied and rearranged, the more literary ones as
a gourmet shop in which to cultivate one's tastes. But for both literature is identical with its history. (Comparative literature departments, which sound more
sophisticated, have their own baroque mystiques for correlating and extracting
aesthetic juice.)

Those of us who teach often forget that the whole academic enterprise is a vast,
semi-autotelic system, with its own conventions and traditions that are not the
same thing as critical thinking—a kind of academic counterculture. True, the
teacher is affected by currents from the outside. But he assimilates them into the
business of teaching and studying literature, so that while the body of teaching and
learning cannot be said to be totally independent of literature itself, it does develop
its own rules and intellectual habits. What it does is to isolate thinking about literature from writing. The best example of this process—or state of mind—is to be
seen in Northrop Frye. Mr. Frye does not represent the academic unconscious; he
set out to construct a paradigm for the academic approach to literature, freed from
the battle-scarred critical polemics of the literary marketplace. Frye may go too far
for some, but his dismissal of "literary taste" and "opinion," which includes all
nonacademic criticism, is essentially a justification of a self-enclosed intellectual
apparatus. But to give Frye his due: he is probably the best academic critic today,
and not always bound by the limitations of his scheme. Much of the other criticism coming out of the universities, lacking Frye's architectural vision, is little
more than an accomplished deployment of current academic assumptions.

Leavis once said that you cannot teach literature without critical values, that
is, without a critical mind. Otherwise you are teaching someone else's apprecia-
tions. And our graduate schools, through their emphasis on vocational training,
standardize and transmit secondhand evaluations to each new generation of students. But even if we assume that judgment rather than knowledge should be the
aim of English studies, the question remains how to translate live critical thinking into a curriculum. As with so many other questions, some of the difficulty
comes from the fact that the way we see the problem rests on assumptions that
themselves need questioning. But to reexamine the things we take for granted
about education is harder than to sound off about culture, counterculture, and
the liberation of the mind from learning.

It's not all just a question of intellectual tone, though that's not something we should be too quick to dismiss. It goes deeper. We're angry, we're frustrated, we're righteous, and we can't talk to each other anymore. In this situation, polemics are simply thwarted politics.

P.S. A notable exception to all this: I am reminded by an interview with Hannah Arendt I have just read that there is at least one speculative mind still around: bold, freewheeling, not looking to fashionable opinion but with an eye for the current scene, never petty, and always on the level of the subject. It's not her conclusions that matter; it's the freedom from contemporary cant—left and right— the universal language of those who know the solutions before they understand the problems. Miss Arendt is a unique, anomalous figure. She belongs to a time of strong thinkers and large theories, but could have a needed influence today. For though she is not herself a radical, in the usual sense of the term, the left could use some of her intellectual temper.   1971, vol. 38, no. 1

• America Today: An Exchange
Norman Birnbaum and Christopher Lasch

BIRNBAUM: I thought we might talk about our perplexities about politics and culture in America now. But perhaps I had best lay out mine, and leave you to speak for yourself. At the root of mine is the fact that our cultural resources—what's called the Western tradition—don't seem to have given us ideas of the kind of lives we might wish to lead, the kinds of values we might wish to pursue, the kinds of people we want to become. This is an eminently political problem because without such ideas there can't be effective movements for change.

　　In Western Europe, all we seem to have are the welfare state institutions, the socialists, and the presently reformist programs—regardless of their ultimate aims—of the Communists in France and Italy. (In Portugal the situation is of course different.) And whether these programs are adequate to the task of creating a just political and economic community is doubtful. In France and Italy where the Communists and socialists are close to entering government together, the parties themselves are currently rather conservative, and neither is eager to be called upon to administer the decline of capitalism.

LASCH: To play the historic role of socialism.

BIRNBAUM: Right. What ultimately disturbs me is that I can't easily recall a historical precedent for the universal bleakness of the intellectual landscape. There is no conviction that thought which is descriptively correct can have an impact, let alone belief that new ideas can in fact generate a different—or better—situation.

LASCH: Well, what would you say against the view that the decline of the Western tradition, and therefore, the West should not, after all, be looked on as a global catastrophe and that what we are sometimes tempted to regard as cultural exhaustion may signify nothing more than the exhaustion of the West's capacity to exploit the rest of the world.

BIRNBAUM: I don't know. If one were to study the history of antiquity—if I may advance what is certainly not a new comparison—when power passed to the Roman Empire, were not Greek ideas still very important? The political or economic decline of the West need not be accompanied by the decline of our cultural tradition. After all, many of the leaders of the so-called Third World did study at our Western universities, and have taken back to their homelands ideas from the Western tradition. Can one seriously say that Dakar, Beirut, Cairo, Jakarta, Peking are really centers of cultural creativity, much less a new world culture? Another heralded alternative, Latin American culture, has always struck me as a variant, an interesting provincial variant of European civilization—rather like Russia in the nineteenth century.

Perhaps I am wrong and it is merely my ignorance, provincialism, or ethnocentrism which lead me not to see it. You're the historian, though. What do you think about this generation of American intellectuals and their relationship to their culture and to their historical possibilities? Is our experience different from that of the intellectuals of the late twenties and early thirties?

LASCH: The twenties and thirties were different. Not only did the political possibilities seem to be much better, but in this country at least there was an exhilarating sense that the country had culturally come of age, in Van Wyck Brooks's famous phrase. While intellectuals found plenty to criticize in American culture and in American life as a whole, even those who expatriated themselves or later turned to revolutionary political solutions had the sense of contributing directly to cultural and political renewal.

Perhaps the present mood in the United States is more like the pessimism of certain European intellectuals in the years between the Franco-Prussian War and World War I. I wouldn't want to argue that this pessimism was very general, but the sense of cultural disintegration, for which Nietzsche is still seen as the most important spokesman, seems to have more in common with the current mood than anything one can find in the cultural history of the United States.

BIRNBAUM: Wasn't Nietzsche more than a negative critic? Didn't he propose a new model: man reconciled with himself? That's precisely the kind of model that is not now available with any conviction or with any program.

LASCH: Yes, that's the difference between Nietzsche's time and ours. What survives today, not only of Nietzsche's work but of the whole tradition of social thought he stood in, is only the negative and critical side, without any of the hopes that in part provoked this criticism of modern society. And even to uphold the negative side is becoming increasingly difficult without inviting charges of elitism and political irresponsibility.

BIRNBAUM: It's true that much of the populism of the American New Left, in particular, was of a breathtaking degree of simplemindedness and vulgarity. It itself represented the latest incarnation of the American philistinism which it thought it was opposing. Lionel Trilling recently published an article in *The American Scholar*. In it he announces with genuine regret that it is no longer possible in this society to promulgate notions of high culture with any conviction, at least in part because of a new property of modern American culture: a limitless search for a boundaryless self. He connects this development somehow with mass higher education and the mass diffusion of high culture, precisely those things which one would have thought an earlier generation of liberals would have welcomed.

It seems to me that you were onto something when you talked about the fear of being negative, but I would think there are two kinds of negativity. There is a global negativity which argues that everything now is terrible and therefore we can only defend old positions in an antiquarian way. And there's a negativity which argues that all the available solutions, even the old ones, are no good and new ones must be invented.

LASCH: I agree that there is a great difference between these two positions. The second refuses among other things to set up against the present disorder an idealized and nostalgically remembered past. Unfortunately, part of the trouble is that the difference is not always easy to perceive when there are no movements interested in inventing new solutions. In the absence of any real political alternatives—the absence of a left—it becomes difficult for many people to distinguish between the positions: both of them are opposed to slogans of cultural liberation when what the slogans really call for is impulse gratification, a kind of demand feeding of the self.

BIRNBAUM: Consider, however, this paradox. The Europeans have the kind of political movements you say America lacks. European socialism feels itself revitalized. Yet even there, the impression of cultural exhaustion is unchanged by a political context much more favorable than our own.

LASCH: You see political developments in Europe as much more hopeful than I do.

BIRNBAUM: At the least, one can say that the political space for certain kinds of cultural experiment or development, a protected cultural space, may be somewhat larger there.

LASCH: I'm not sure. That may be only a function of the backwardness of the culture industry in Europe as compared with the United States, where there are fewer forces to resist its almost total domination of public discussion. I don't mean that the media in America are necessarily hostile to cultural experiment. On the contrary, their receptivity to changes in cultural fashion instantly turns all cultural developments into marketable commodities, thereby nullifying their capacity to provoke thought, let alone action. Ideas and programs formerly promulgated by the avant-garde—the idea of alienation for example—have become objects of popular consumption, thanks to the efficiency with which not only the press and television, but also the universities, the advertising industry, and guardians of public morality reproduce almost all forms of culture for a mass market.

What I'm interested in is your notion that there may not, after all, be an organic connection between culture and politics. Does this mean you subscribe to Bell's theory of the disjunction between politics and culture?

BIRNBAUM: Bell's theory of the disjunction of politics and culture is clearly, I think, a theory of their conjunction. Bell has argued that our administrative and productive system has reached a point at which the cultural values of the elite—the bourgeois—are irrelevant to the functioning of the system. In effect, he has supplied us with a renewed or refurbished version of the theory of the exhaustion of bourgeois culture. At the end, he simply asks, "So what?" and demonstrates that the system which has reduced to impotence the purveyors of these cultural values can and must continue. It continues, of course, because those in command of the system have post-bourgeois values which are not modernist but technocratic. They may indeed be antivalues.

LASCH: Something he would deny, of course.

BIRNBAUM: I suppose that we should honor his denial, but the thrust of his thought points the other way.

LASCH: I must say I find compelling but hardly reassuring the argument that bourgeois culture or high culture in the contemporary economy is functionally irrelevant. It's quite compatible with a psychological analysis of modern society that stresses the obsolescence or dysfunction of conscience and the psychological processes that formerly shaped it.

We do seem to have a society that no longer requires, as psychological cement, authority and, in particular, paternal authority—at least, not in the same way an earlier form of bourgeois society required it. Nor does our society seem to require the kind of family structures that characterized not only bourgeois society in earlier stages but many of its predecessors.

BIRNBAUM: Your remark reminds me of one of Mitscherlich's: his was that a historical change requires three generations to work itself out. The grandparents experience the change but transmit (however unintendedly or unconsciously) older models of existence to the next generation, which in turn struggles with new experience which it has to confront with old models, historically inappropriate or maladapted psychic structure. Then a generation is born which can take all of this more or less for granted, can mobilize its psychic resources to meet the real problems of a changed historical situation. That's a very crude summary, but it is roughly what the analysis entails. When we apply it to our present situation however, we have to say that the new or third generation has few psychic resources with which to confront our history. We have few cultural resources. In the process something of ineluctable value has been lost which cannot be replaced.

LASCH: It could be argued, of course, that if it takes three generations for any far-reaching characterological changes to work themselves out, this particular process is only beginning, and that it is therefore too soon to come to any conclusions about it. This argument seems to me somewhat evasive. If it is true that conscience is being superseded by other forms of personality organization and social cohesion, I would agree that what is being lost, for all its own pathological side effects, is irreplaceable. This reorganization, or perhaps simply disintegration, of personality is the psychic foundation of the growing demand for immediate impulse gratification and also of the tendency to equate fulfillment of these demands with political and cultural emancipation.

BIRNBAUM: You're putting yourself (and myself) clearly in the camp of the cultural traditionalists. I don't mind being there—after all, for Marx, a major justification of socialism was that it was the only way to realize bourgeois cultural values. But if in fact we face a world in which new historical structures and new modes of gratification combine to propagate values we despise—and we can no longer imagine any social institutions that can generate cultural values we espouse—that is a very serious matter.

LASCH: It is a matter, however, insofar as it concerns the family, about which your colleagues in sociology provide very little guidance. Academic sociologists, until the seventies at least, have resisted the very proposition that the family is in some kind of trouble. The position they defend is that the family has gained in emotional services what it has lost in the way of economic, educational, and protective functions.

BIRNBAUM: What do you think that "emotional services" means to them? That the family does more for people, or that more is attempted?

LASCH: It does more for people, because it's lost its economic and protective functions and therefore can concentrate on serving as a kind of asylum for feelings that have to be suppressed elsewhere. The world of work is cold and impersonal, and the family provides consolation for deprivations suffered at work, goes the typical argument. Parsons, whose theory of the family still commands a good deal of respect, constantly compares what goes on in the family to psychotherapy.

BIRNBAUM: A therapeutic community in miniature?

LASCH: A therapeutic community; a haven in a heartless world.

BIRNBAUM: Others would argue that precisely this overloading of the family emotively is what is destroying it. The seventies rewrite of the suburban scenario of the fifties has the husband coming home to a wife who terms him an oppressor for monopolizing the exciting world of work. Yet the exciting world of work is one in which most men are dominated, frustrated, exploited.

LASCH: Parsons himself seems to admit that it causes more forms of sickness than it can cure. I suppose the usual way of dealing with this kind of information, from sociologists of the family to social workers, is to argue that familial therapy, and therapy in general, simply has to become more effective. The burden of the new psychiatric movements one might characterize collectively under the heading of psychiatric self-help seems to be that people have to "get in touch with their feelings" and to become more adept at performing therapeutic roles for each other. But what it often seems to come down to, at least for marriage and the family, is that the participants have to become more adept at absorbing various forms of abuse.

BIRNBAUM: Doesn't that impose moral demands upon the human personality which are excessive? Freud's critique of culture was that it imposed excessive demands on a humanity little able to bear them, and that for most persons the cost of what he termed "instinctual renunciation" was too high.

LASCH: He was right.

BIRNBAUM: This belief was connected not only with his critique of culture; it was part of something else in his philosophy, a critique of average humanity. Only a cultural elite found, in his view, the rewards of culture roughly in balance with the cost exacted from them. Where the very idea of an elite is suspect, who will honor those who pay the price? Perhaps the doctrine of limitless gratification is, as the traditionalists suspect, a not entirely subtle form of cultural class warfare—or psychological guerrilla action.

The chief injustice Freud himself thought about was injustice in the distribution of gratification, with the family imposing one kind of restraint and the idea of work another. If Freud was right, I do not see how you can erect a defense of traditional values that are being eroded by new developments. In fact, these values are based on illusions created by specific historical conditions—in sum, on a notion of humanity that is neither socially nor biologically tenable in the long run.

LASCH: I should have added that although I think Freud was right in saying that most people pay too high a price, it's becoming more and more clear that the alternatives are no better.

BIRNBAUM: I was going to say, not paying the price may be worse.

LASCH: In "The Most Prevalent Form of Degradation in Erotic Life," Freud's analysis of what he calls psychic impotence amounts to a damning indictment of civilized sexual morality, as he calls it elsewhere. But he immediately goes on to say that "unrestrained" sexual liberty is no better than the prolonged abstinence and deprivation formerly imposed by civilized sexual morality. It isn't just that some obstacle is necessary "to swell the tide of libido to its height." What Freud perhaps does *not* anticipate is the way in which glamour and sexiness have become themselves part of the apparatus of domination—the phenomenon aptly characterized by Marcuse as repressive desublimation.

BIRNBAUM: I am trying to think of some way to counter this pessimism. Let's suppose a kind of neo-Marxist utopia in which the Western and industrialized nations would have agreed to give some considerable share of their gross national product to underdeveloped societies. Then imagine that the world disequilibrium in resource and wealth accumulation was righted. A global sense of justice, or an anticipation of one, would then be at least possible. The material problems of existence having been solved, the inhabitants of the advanced societies could then turn in the classic Marxist sense to the cultivation of the new human personality and new cultural values. Of course, I've left out something critical to the Marxist argument, the reversal or revolution in property relationships and the devising of new communal institutions for economic production and distribution.

Let's say we're in the middle of the process. Would socialist revolution in the West give you more occasion to hope, or less? The cultural meaning of socialism, after all, is that it would create the possibility of a new human personality. Socialism does not claim to be the expression of a new human identity, to use that contemporary phrase. Socialism would create the conditions under which a new human identity could develop, or be developed, more or less self-consciously. If that is *not* true, then I can understand a great deal of cultural pessimism, including our own.

LASCH: Maybe the objectives of socialism have to be stated more modestly. You said Marx thought socialism was the only way to realize bourgeois values. In our own time it may become the only way of realizing any values at all. It may have become the only chance for human survival. I think I could live with your utopia, even if the development of a new identity remained problematic; and I do have questions about whether a change in the form of production invariably means a change in the human psyche.

I'm pessimistic now for two reasons. First, it is unfortunately impossible to say, except for the purposes of examining the implications of your neo-Marxist utopia, that we are in the midst of a revolution in property relationships. If anything, social and economic inequalities, both within the advanced countries and as between advanced countries and poor ones, are growing worse all the time. Second, we seem to be undergoing a process of cultural leveling in which the masses attempt to impose their own culture (actually the culture of the culture industry) on the elites—a very different process from the ideal envisioned by nineteenth-century democrats and even by apostles of high culture such as Matthew Arnold. They imagined a situation in which "the best that has been known and thought" would become available to anyone who cared to listen. Instead we have a situation in which the worst tends to dilute the best, and in which critical thinking becomes synonymous in the popular mind with privilege.

So we have the worst of everything, an ever-widening gap between rich and poor combined with a regressive egalitarianism in culture. Ultimately, the decay of critical thought makes it all the more difficult to mount a sustained attack on social and economic inequality.

BIRNBAUM: If we're to talk about socio-economic problems, or political-economic problems, three occur to me. First, of course, there is the internal crisis of capitalism. Second, we have to deal with the continuing confrontation between the developed and underdeveloped countries. Third, a fragmented capitalist is now opposed to an internally divided Communist world. These questions are obviously connected, but they have to be treated separately. What can we say about the first one? The United States, at least, faces its crisis without what the French call a *solution de rechange*, without a socialist alternative. Even the critique of capitalism is rather muted. How do we explain that, particularly after the sixties?

LASCH: One of the reasons is that the collapse and the lunacy of the New Left— the lunacy that always existed side by side with whatever was admirable in it— have done a good deal to discredit the possibility of any leftist solution. I'm struck by the lack of political interest on the part of students now coming into college. I can't document it, but I'm convinced that the New Left had something to do with turning students away not just from radicalism but from politics, partly because its own inflated expectations of what it could accomplish gave rise to inflated estimates of its failure and of the futility of any kind of political action.

As we get further away from the sixties, the New Left will probably be seen more as a cultural movement than as a political movement. Political radicalism has collapsed, but cultural radicalism has survived and is becoming more and more respectable. Historians looking back on this period will have to distinguish between long-range social and cultural tendencies and the immediate effects of the Vietnamese war. Speaking of which, what do you think will be its effect? Would you argue that there has been any real diminution of

American world power, not only vis-à-vis the non-Western world, but vis-à-vis other capitalist nations?

BIRNBAUM: There has been a change, though perhaps one which preceded Vietnam. Alain Touraine has recently spoken of a new hand in cards dealt out within the capitalist bloc. The fact that the West German standard of living is higher than our own is an indication of what is happening. The neo-capitalist societies, more modern than our own in many ways, have become stronger: they can sell better goods more cheaply on the world market. And though dollar devaluation and domestic inflation may assist our capitalists, it won't assist the working class, whose relative position is in decline. And by working class I also mean those who live as we professionals do, by selling labor.

Which raises again the question of the potential of American socialism. The legacy of the New Left surely is not exclusively cultural—it is mainly that, of course, but not entirely that. After all, there were millions of people in it who developed the idea, however crudely or incoherently, that our society is dominated by corporate capitalism which, as it were, industrially fabricated many of the values they abhorred. Surely, this has not been forgotten entirely. Can these people be remobilized for a more enduring form of political action?

LASCH: Well, at one time I thought that since many of them were returning to graduate school with the intention of becoming serious scholars, at least the New Left would have some intellectual impact. And I've been enormously impressed by the dedication of the young socialist scholars who came out of the sixties, and with the work they've produced, although not much of that work has so far been published. Unfortunately, the academic depression makes it more difficult than ever for such people to get a foothold in academic life. The depression is filtering out the best people and producing yet another generation of dull, respectable, young, conformist scholars. I still don't entirely exclude the possibility that people who received their political training in the New Left will eventually make some impact on the academic disciplines and the way in which issues are formulated. But there remains the question of whether such a development would in turn have any effect on national politics.

BIRNBAUM: What you are saying is that the New Left was a social movement that criticized affluence; it was not developed in a period of unemployment and economic crisis. After all, what we might have expected is a rapprochement of new and older modes of left thought during periods of recession or depression. But can one really conceive of a new working-class movement headed by leaders like Woodcock or Wurf, and the recent insurgents in steel abandoning a Meanyite politics? The radicalization of the working class—particularly of the young workers—the depression should have brought has not happened. For all the talk about new alignments in the Democratic Party, its response to the crisis of capitalism is a welfare capitalist response: increased federal spending, public job programs, and so on. Not a single Democrat in Congress has introduced a bill proposing nationalizing the oil industry.

LASCH: Still it could be argued that what you call the crisis of capitalism is only now becoming really acute and that its full effects are only now beginning to be widely felt. If welfare liberalism really rests on an assumption of continuing economic growth—an assumption which until recently most people found it unnecessary to question, even during the Great Depression—its days may be numbered. When the fact of continued expansion begins to be widely questioned, and when it becomes apparent that implementing traditional liberal programs will require an actual redistribution of wealth—cutting up the same pie instead of baking a bigger one—then welfare liberalism may cease to have any appeal to the working class, and more radical programs will begin to win adherents.

BIRNBAUM: But such responses are never produced mechanically by historical situations: they come, rather, in situations which have been anticipated ideologically. The question Robert Bellah raised recently as to whether the American ethos allows anything like the development of socialist political ideas becomes more and more interesting.

LASCH: Whatever else we can say about the prospects for American socialism, we can say that of the various capitalist countries, the United States is about the last place one would look for the development of a powerful and radical socialist movement. It's more likely that some serious attempt at a general transfer of power would take place in Western Europe, in some major industrialized country.

BIRNBAUM: I agree, and I think that we spend so much energy accusing the Western European socialists of being overly integrated with their capitalist societies that we overlook the extent to which certain transfers of power which would be regarded as revolutionary in this country have taken place there. The furthest we go here is that a senior partner in Lazard Frères, Felix Rohatyn, has called for economic planning in the U.S., and a bill calling for planning was proposed by Senators Humphrey and Javits—who have joined Rohatyn and some unionists in a committee to advocate planning in European neo-capitalist form. However, the most efficient way to run capitalism may be under the name socialism, with socialist parties to discipline the working class.

LASCH: But if the ultimate fate of socialist parties is to keep alive a moribund capitalism, it is no longer clear what the advantages are of being politically more advanced.

BIRNBAUM: In terms of the struggle between the developed and underdeveloped nations, it is difficult for any of us to see the Shah of Iran or the new King of Saudi Arabia as leaders of an embattled world proletariat—even though a crude Marxist interpretation of what has happened, say in the raising of oil prices, could be that proletarian nations or nation classes have resisted giving up raw materials at prices which impoverish them in world-market terms. What does this kind of action mean for the future of the industrial societies in general?

LASCH: We can envisage a world in which the major powers will find themselves increasingly unable to impose their will on the rest of the world. Presumably this will exacerbate the economic difficulties the capitalist countries, at any rate, are already beginning to experience at home.

BIRNBAUM: It also appears that within the so-called Third World, there is a Fourth World. The Third World consists of countries with raw materials to sell. But the Fourth World countries have neither adequate supplies of raw materials to sell on the world market nor enough resources for themselves. We have to transform our simple models of global exploitation into more complex ones, in which not only the industrialized countries including the Soviet Union but underdeveloped ones with resources combine somehow, together exploiting nations poorer still. And no political solution, no mediating mechanisms are in sight. The facts of international relations in this period are that the identities of the strong may change, but those who are strongest are going to impose their global will upon the others.

LASCH: Vietnam, the dissolution of the cold war power blocs, and the oil embargo itself all seem to me to call that proposition into question. At the very least these developments suggest, as you say, a change in the identity of the strongest; and we might ask whether this change makes any difference.

BIRNBAUM: Possibly some, and that leads us to the Communist bloc. I'm struck by how little magnetic power is exercised by China or the Soviet Union. For the advanced industrial societies, the Soviet Union is neither an inspiration nor a model—politically or economically, and certainly not in its philistine culture. The Chinese enjoy a certain amount of credit in the Third and Fourth Worlds for their modes of aid as well as for their own internal achievements, but there is little prospect of the Chinese assuming the leadership of the Third and Fourth Worlds, or any parts of them. Perhaps the secret of Chinese Communism is not that it is a new version of Leninism for backward countries, but a new version of Marxism, successfully fused with a very old and complex culture, which has been able to achieve national goals like independence, psychic and cultural self-sufficiency. And what this suggests is that there is no one global, much less revolutionary, model of development for the Third and Fourth Worlds.[1]

LASCH: Any more than there is a polarized structure of international power, dominated by the superpowers. At one time the dissolution of the wartime alliances and of monolithic Communist and capitalist blocs would have seemed an eminently desirable development. But now it is no longer clear that a politically fragmented world will be any more pleasant or safe to live in than one dominated by two or three great powers.

BIRNBAUM: If the picture of struggle is in fact a Hobbesian one, international society has been reduced to the state of nature from which we thought it had begun to emerge. The creation of a world market has not been accompanied by the creation of a world culture or a world polity.

LASCH: I'm wondering about the theoretical implications of that statement. We might view American history as a precedent for this curious situation. It wouldn't be a bad sketch of American history to say that the creation of a national market wasn't followed by the creation of a national or public culture or even, perhaps, of a very securely grounded political order.

BIRNBAUM: That's not an interpretation of American history I am prepared to dispute, but if it is accurate, imagine then what the chances are for a political or public culture in a world dominated by multinational corporations. Nor, as the left assumes, would the overthrow of the multinationals produce a better world polity, or restore the polity or culture that existed before. There is also a pseudo-evolutionary theory which argues that the spread of a certain kind of

---

1. The editors have asked us to comment, separately, on the Cambodian Revolution. Even this brutal, distant, and strange revolution has been accompanied by a comedy, a grotesque distortion of some of our own. In the last hours of the siege of Phnom Penh, a group of young bourgeois "revolutionaries" (their leader, a "general" in his twenties, was a playboy in the capital, son of one of Lon Nol's generals) put on red scarves, commandeered some armored cars and took the surrender of the last 30,000 "Republican" troops.

The comedy ended, of course, when the peasant army of the Khmer Rouge entered the city—and promptly evacuated it. Now I read of a decree that only Cambodian is henceforth to be spoken in the nation. Revolutionary purity and national cultural integrity, alike, are to be attained by an agrarian society, encapsulated from the world. The Maoists hold that the countryside will encircle and conquer the city, but they have not thought of emptying Peking or Shanghai or of renouncing industrialization. In a world of centrally fabricated cultures and ideologies, we may expect more primitivism of the Cambodian sort. Rousseau, it would appear, has triumphed over Marx.

We share responsibility for the Cambodian Revolution, in two senses. It was American power that ravaged the countryside. And the leaders of the revolution share some culture with ourselves: the theorists of agrarian purity have doctorates from the Sorbonne. NORMAN BIRNBAUM, June 30, 1975.

Shortly after the evacuation of Phnom Penh I wrote that the so-called peasant revolution in Cambodia would lead to another socialist dictatorship—a socialism of barbed wire, the forced march, the forced confession, the concentration camp, and "self-criticism." Friends have told me that this view is too gloomy. Emptying the cities as the prelude to periodic purifications of the social order, it appears, is an old tradition in Cambodia. A Cambodia friendly to China, moreover, might help to offset the close relation between North Vietnam and the Soviet Union. The first of these objections probably rests on the same kind of wishful thinking that welcomed the Chinese Communists in 1949 as "agrarian reformers." The second appears to assume that Southeast Asia and the rest of the world are destined to be dominated by great powers—a proposition that is by no means self-evident, as we have argued above. CHRISTOPHER LASCH, July 9, 1975.

technology and economic psychology will modernize everything, that is, make every place more like the United States. Am I right in saying that we hear less of "modernization" in our universities these days—it seems to me one last use of it was made by Samuel Huntington, who argued that "modernizing" rural Vietnam would deprive the national liberation movement of its popular basis. Perhaps that was a clue to some of the ideological sources of a certain kind of vacuity in academic social science.

LASCH: Unfortunately this vacuity has been enthusiastically inherited by the so-called new social history, which has taken over the concept of modernization from the social sciences and given it a new lease on life—or perhaps we should say, provided it with a final resting place. Even Marxist historians have taken over much of modernization theory—not surprisingly, since the theory itself, if it can be dignified by that name, originates in economic and technological determinism, often confused with Marxism. Whether in their Marxist or liberal version, all such theories are now proving their complete inadequacy in the face of a world that is clearly being neither Americanized, modernized, communized, nor otherwise inexorably transformed in accordance with some overriding principle of historical development.

BIRNBAUM: We're back where we started—facing an uncertain situation. We cannot say what will actually happen. Of all that can be said about the Chinese, maybe one of the wisest things they've done is that they've stayed out of things they could not control.

1975, vol. 42, no. 3

• The Decline of the West
Hans Morgenthau

Present concern with the decline of the West is caused by the obvious decline of American power. The defeat the United States has suffered in Indochina has not only been total but ignominious. Even if defeat had to be anticipated as inevitable, there was nothing inevitable about our inability to manipulate the modalities of defeat for the purpose of retreating from an untenable position with at least a modicum of poise. American power and influence used to be dominant in Turkey and Greece. The United States has succeeded in alienating both to the point where their effective membership in NATO is in question, and has failed in inducing them to compose their differences over Cyprus. We are reduced to watching passively the anarchy, threatening Communization, of our ally Portugal. We are unable to dissuade the Federal Republic of Germany, one of our closest allies, from selling a whole nuclear production cycle to Brazil, a transaction that, making the proliferation of nuclear weapons virtually inevitable, carries ominous implications for the survival of mankind.

The natural current concern with this decline of American power has obscured the relationship between that decline and the decline of the West in general. More particularly, it has obscured the fact that the United States owes its rise to predominance in the aftermath of the Second World War to the self-same decline of the West, of which it now appears as the prime example. In other words, the decline of the West, the United States included, was preceded by the decline of the traditional nation-states of Western Europe, of which the United States was the main beneficiary.

The first spectacular demonstration of that shift was the decisive intervention of the United States in the First World War, temporarily obscured by the American isolationism of the interwar period and the French military predominance in Europe during the twenties. The United States emerged from the First World War as the potentially most powerful nation on earth; but from the collapse of Wilson's foreign policy to the outbreak of the Second World War it acted as though it still were a power of the second rank. It was neither design nor choice but the ineluctable force of its circumstances that in the aftermath of the Second World War made the United States the most powerful nation on earth. On the one hand, the traditional great powers of Europe, having suffered the death of seven million of their most vigorous men in the First World War, became in the Second the victims of occupation, mass bombings, and genocide. Within a decade after the end of the hostilities, they had lost the bulk of their colonial possessions either voluntarily or in consequence of defeat in colonial wars.

On the other hand, the outcome of the Second World War was decided by nations either completely or largely outside Europe. The material productivity and technical ingenuity of the United States, undamaged—in contrast to all the other productive systems—but greatly stimulated by the war, was a decisive factor in victory and reconstruction. Thus, the conjunction of the absolute decline of the traditional nation-states of the West and the absolute ascendancy of the United States—both in consequence of two world wars—accounts for the rise of the United States in the context of the West's decline.

A similar shift from the traditional nation-states of the West to the United States can be observed on the moral plane. The First World War brought to the fore two challenges to the traditional moral order: Communism and Fascism. Faced with the choice, the ruling elites chose Fascism as protection against Communism or even radical reform. They chose Fascism even if it meant opening the gates to the enemy of the nation. "Rather Hitler than Blum" became the slogan of the French right, and the Vichy regime became the political manifestation of that moral preference.

The victory over Fascism in the Second World War by no means resolved this moral crisis but posed it in a new form. While it eliminated Fascism as a serious political force and discredited it morally, it established the claim of Communism as a legitimate political force both at home and abroad. During the Second World War, the Communists were in the forefront of the fight for national liberation from the national enemy. Close to one-third of the Italian electorate has consistently voted for Communist or pro-Communist parties; in France the corresponding figure is close to one-quarter. Yet the ruling elites of Italy and France have consistently treated the Communist parties as being unqualified to participate in the government. The consequence has been a distortion of the democratic processes through legal and political practices which have succeeded in excluding permanently a large segment of the electorate from active participation in the government.

The United States has been spared this moral dilemma of having to violate a basic principle of democracy for the sake of protecting the democratic processes. The United States has never had to choose between Fascism and Communism, for both threats to American democracy were always remote, however much the aberration of McCarthyism made it temporarily appear that Communism was the main issue America had to fight at home and abroad. Thus, while the nations of Western Europe risked national disintegration in the struggle to the finish between democracy and the two totalitarianisms, America was able to present a united national front against the two enemies from without: first against the totalitarianism of Fascism, then against that of Communism. The simplistic moral stance of Secretary of State John Foster Dulles, dividing the world into good and evil nations and the morally tainted neutral ones, expresses on the moral plane the simple political and military confrontation of the Cold War. Thus the United States became the "leader of the free world," both by dint of the actual distribution of political power and of the simple moral position it could afford to take vis-à-vis the enemies of the "free world." That ascendancy of the United States to unchallenged and seemingly unchallengeable leadership, not only in the "free world" but in the world at large, effectively concealed the actual decline of the collectivity called the Western world and the trends toward deterioration within the United States itself.

What sapped the moral strength of the United States was not the contradiction between national interest and class interest as it did in Europe, but, on the one hand, the reduction of complex political issues to a simple moral juxtaposition with Communism and, on the other, the spectacular demonstrations of moral obtuseness at home and abroad. What confronted the nations of Western Europe in the aftermath of the Second World War both as a threat and a challenge was the military presence of the Red Army one hundred kilometers east of the Rhine, the political presence of large Communist parties within their borders, and political, economic, and social structures and policies creating and maintaining the cleavages on which Communism thrives.

American simplistic anti-Communism was adequate to counter through containment the Soviet military threat. But the countersubversive programs America operated in the democratic countries of the West remained not only by and large ineffective but turned out to be counterproductive. What was difficult for the countersubversive technicians of the American secret services to understand was that the hold that Communism has over large masses of the Western peoples is not primarily, let alone exclusively, the result of the machinations of Communist governments from abroad, but of indigenous conditions exploited but not created from abroad. Thus, the rigid ideological commitment to a dogmatic anti-Communism, reducing a complex reality to a simple juxtaposition between good and evil, has been demonstrated to be untenable on philosophical and historical grounds and proven to be a political and moral disaster.

Committed in a largely revolutionary or prerevolutionary world to a precarious if not doomed status quo, the United States was forced by the very logic of the commitment to support or create the kind of government whose antagonistic rhetoric left nothing to be desired and which was willing to fight Communism by all means fair or foul. Thus, the United States found itself supported by, and supporting, governments throughout the world whose political philosophy and practice were completely at odds with what goes by the name of American principles of government. The protection of the "free world" from Communism became the main purpose of American foreign policy. In its name, or its alias, national security policies were pursued and outrages committed which could not pass muster before the moral standards by which the theory and practice of the government had been traditionally judged.

American moral and political commitment to anti-Communism succeeded only where the military and economic power of the United States could be effectively brought into play. It failed when its pure moral force was appealed to. Paradoxically, it failed not because the peoples whose freedom was at stake were not willing to listen to its message, but because America, the bearer of the message, did not know how to live up to it. The fear of Communism blocked the road to freedom. In the contest between the colonial powers of Europe and their colonies, the United States took the side of the former, not because it was in favor of colonialism, but because it was afraid that Communism might be the alternative to colonialism. The champion of freedom became the defender and restorer of the colonial status quo. Making common cause with the colonial powers, it shared with them the moral taint of colonialism. Thus America came to lose the peculiar moral aura that it thought had set it apart from all other nations.

Yet, while America's indiscriminate dogmatic opposition to Communism, or to what looked like Communism, compelled it to join the forces of the status quo, its libertarianism and anticolonialist tradition evoked its sympathies with the aspirations of the Third World. That world had painted a picture of its condition flattering to itself and disparaging to their former colonial masters and the industrial nations at large. Their miseries and failures are presented as the responsibility of the developed nations, who have the moral obligation to right the wrong they have done them. This moral dichotomy between the "good" members of the Third World and the "evil" colonial exploiters cut across the American dichotomy between "good" democratic capitalists and "evil" Communists. For many of the nations of the "free world" are sympathetic to one or the other brands of Communism, or at least to some brand of authoritarianism which bears the name of "Communism" or "socialism."

Thus what occurred on the moral plane was the opposite of what took place in the arena of power. In the latter, the United States benefited at the expense of its associates. On the former, it partook in the disrepute of its associates. Perhaps not surprisingly—considering the resentment that unchallengeable power evokes—the unprecedented power of the United States has not been matched by the reputation for the benevolent use of that power. That discrepancy produced the undoing of America's moral position. The Third World attacked the United States with the same arguments which America used to argue against colonialism, racism, and exploitation, perpetuated by its friends. Arguing within its traditional moral framework, the United States had no answer when its own arguments were turned against it. It had at least spoken as the champion of the downtrodden and the exploited in the name of equality and freedom, and now defended in its deeds the status quo of colonialism and exploitation in the name of anti-Communism. Foreign aid, parsimoniously and ineffectually dispersed, is a token tribute to the professed ideals of America.

This moral disarmament by an adversary invoking the other side's moral arguments for his own purposes was used brilliantly by Hitler in the Czechoslovakian crisis of 1938. Hitler invoked the principle of national self-determination for the purpose of destroying Czechoslovakia. Yet the Western allies, having invoked the very same principles on behalf of all oppressed nationalities, had no moral argument to counter Hitler. As the London *Times* put it in its comment on the Munich settlement:

> Self-determination, the professed principle of the Treaty of Versailles, has been invoked by Herr Hitler against its written text, and his appeal has been allowed.

The United States, threatened materially and weakened morally by its association with the traditional nation-states of the West, finds itself in the end weakened by the very magnitude of its material power. It is one of the paradoxes of the nuclear age that, in contrast to the experiences of all pre-nuclear history, an increase in military power is no longer necessarily conducive to an increase in political power. The threat of all-out nuclear violence implies the threat of total destruction. As such, it can still be a suitable instrument of foreign policy when addressed to a nation that cannot reply in kind. The nation armed with nuclear weapons can assert power over the other nation by saying: Either you do as I say, or I will destroy you. The situation is different if the nation so threatened can respond by saying: If you destroy me with nuclear weapons you will be destroyed in turn. Since the nuclear destruction of one nation would call forth the nuclear destruction of the other, both nations can afford to disregard the threat on the assumption that both will act rationally.

Thus the unprecedented power that modern technology has put into the hands of Western nations is useful only under extraordinary limiting conditions. Under most possible and actual circumstances, that power is an empty threat and is being disregarded by nations much inferior in material power. Thus the power that really counts, a few extreme exceptions to the contrary notwithstanding, is conventional power, and here the gap between the United States and the other Western nations, on the one hand, and the non-Western nations, on the other hand, is of course by no means as wide as it is if one puts nuclear power into the scales. Consequently, when one compares the conventional power of the West with the conventional power of the non-Western world, one notices that the nations of the West are much less powerful than they appear to be. That impression is strengthened when one examines the moral principles on behalf of which the Western nations may be willing to use conventional power and with a chance for success. The defeat of the United States in Indochina illustrates vividly the decline of Western power—material and moral.

It is one of the great ironies of contemporary history that the moral and material decline of the West has in good measure been accomplished through the moral and material triumphs of the West. The Third World has shaken off the Western yoke by invoking the very moral principles of self-determination and social justice which the West has proclaimed and endeavored to put into practice. That in the process national self-determination was to become the ideology of new imperialisms, and social justice the ideological disguise of servitudes new and old, was to be expected. What points to the moral exhaustion of the West is its inability to stipulate moral principles with which to justify its positions and interests against its enemies and detractors.

This moral helplessness whenever the West had to contend with the use of its moral principles on behalf of its enemies—dramatically revealed in the Czechoslovakian crisis of 1938—has been one of the main sources of its weakness in action. It is simple and convenient to identify this weakness with one particular man acting in a particular episode and thus isolate the "spirit of Munich" from the Western moral stance in foreign policy. It is equally simple and convenient to decry any kind of accommodation and compromise in foreign policy as "appeasement," relying instead upon the uncompromising containment of the enemy. Lacking credible moral standards that could guide his action, the actor is reduced to either denying the moral issue altogether or universalizing it to the point of irrelevance.

On the material plane the West has been made vulnerable to oil as a political weapon by its high technological development. The power that oil bestows upon oil-producing nations is the result of the technological development of modern industrial nations. Twenty or fifty years ago, oil did not bestow such power upon oil-producing nations because the use of oil as the lifeblood of modern industry was limited. The oil-consuming nations still operated in a buyer's market. If one source of oil was not available or was available only on conditions which were unacceptable to the consuming nation, that nation could go elsewhere and buy it there on more convenient terms. The contemporary situation is characterized by an imbalance between supply and demand to such an extent that the buyer's market has been transformed into a seller's market and nations which have large deposits of oil, cooperating as the oil-producing nations did during the fall of 1973, can apply a stranglehold to the consuming nations; or they can impose political conditions which the consuming nations can refuse to meet only at the risk of enormous political, economic, and social dislocations.

Thus the vulnerability of highly developed industrial nations of the West to the supply of oil is a function of their industrial advancement. The shift of power from the oil-consuming to the oil-producing nations is a byproduct of the former's industrial power. Industrial development has widened the gap between the advanced and backward nations in favor of the former, but it has supplied some of the latter with a new weapon: a quasi-monopoly of oil.

That weapon can be deadly, but it resembles nuclear power in that it is purely destructive. An oil-producing nation can bring an oil-consuming one to its knees, but it cannot govern it by virtue of its oil monopoly. Thus the potency of the oil weapon demonstrates dramatically the decline of Western power. Yet it indicates no substitute for that declining power—except the power of destruction.

The moral and material decline of the West is an observable fact. What is not observable is the kind of order that could take the place of the fading one created and maintained by the power of the West. Instead of the outlines of a new order created and supported by a new center of power, what appears on the horizon of the civilized world is the specter of anarchy, with legal arrangements, institutions, and procedures being utterly out of tune with the objective technological conditions of the age.   1975, vol. 42, no. 4

• While America Burns

EDITOR'S NOTE: *William Barrett's letter and William Phillips's reply are comments on the political and economic crisis in America and Western Europe.*

Dear William:
In trying to collect my thoughts on the present situation, I found myself persistently going back to the time more than twenty-five years ago when I was connected with the magazine. A great deal has happened in between; but it seems to me that the situation then, or the situation as *Partisan Review* then faced it, might serve as a channel-marker against the present turbulent currents. You were then both mentor and friend; and as my mind turns back in that direction, it seems only natural that I should be addressing my thoughts to you.

The great and overshadowing difference between then and now, it seems to me, is in the relative positions of power of the United States and the Soviet Union. America has become much weaker, markedly so after Vietnam and Watergate; and Russia much stronger. Everything else in the contemporary scene comes under the shadow of this shifting balance of power. If the United States were to go under, liberty would disappear for mankind. I don't say this out of any patriotic conviction of America's messianic destiny. History has simply dealt the cards in this way. If the American presence were to disappear, Western Europe would slide quickly into the Soviet bloc. Britain would be left an isolated island with a faltering economy and severe class conflicts; and Japan would be similarly isolated, with mounting internal pressures of its own. Anything, then, that weakens the strength of the United States weakens the cause of liberty.

In the past we had always nursed the hope, silently at least, that the Soviet regime might eventually liberalize itself. We were socialists, after all, and in some sense it was a socialist state. Perhaps we fixed too much on the person of Stalin as the evil figure responsible for the dictatorship. But now any such hope of liberalization is illusory. The iron law of a Communist regime is that its bureaucracy must not only perpetuate itself but expand its power as well. The permanent revolution is the permanent dictatorship. Security from external attack doesn't lead to any relaxation of its grip. We should have known this as early as 1946. At the end of the war, Russia had secured its borders and accumulated a fund of good will on the part of the Allies as a residue of wartime partnership—and it chose to launch the Cold War. One has to emphasize this point now against the distortions of our various revisionists. In 1946, when I joined you on *Partisan Review*, I found you already engaged in the Cold War, which I promptly joined. You were politically avant-garde then, ahead of the rest of the country. *Partisan Review* was engaged in trying to point out to liberals their illusions about

Russia and Russian expansionism. The response of the American government, which seemed to us so tardy and faltering, often left us feeling like climbing the walls out of frustration. That's the way it is to be politically avant-garde. The evil is not that the United States eventually responded to the Cold War, which it had not initiated, but that it carried it on so stupidly during the McCarthy era.

The Vietnam War was another stupidity on America's part. It could not have waged a more pro-Communist war if it had deliberately set out to do so. The struggle against Communism, which is bound to be long and protracted and will go on, détente or no détente, has to be a matter of much more limited commitments.

One thing that remains constant now as then is the presence of the fellow-traveler, though he has now changed his colors. Usually he professes to be thoroughly disabused and cynical about Russia, but the cynicism ends by equating the imperfections of American democracy with dictatorship. It's as if we were back with Orwell and Koestler arguing against the fellow-travelers of the late forties. China, or Cuba, is now the utopian and fair-haired darling. We have Park Avenue Maoists as we once had Park Avenue Stalinists. (The hostess at one fashionable party I attended wore a Chinese gown just to set the right tone.) Apparently we'll have to wait another generation until the Chinese dissenters begin to appear in order to change this attitude.

Fellow-travelling appears to be a permanent part of modern life, a condition of the modern spirit. It is "aesthetic" politics, "literary" Marxism, the lure of utopian thinking on the part of those who feel secure enough in their liberty to play around with it; a surrogate for the religion they have lost. In a back-handed way, Dostoevsky was right: the socialist question is above all the religious question.

Anyway, everybody else seems to be doing the old-fashioned fellow-traveler's work for him. The democracies are going through an orgy of self-destruction just as the Greek historians and philosophers described the process in the ancient world. We seem to have lost the sense of liberty as something connected with the continuing life of liberal institutions, which we have all been engaged in undermining in recent years. At this turn of history mankind (the intellectual most of all) seems hell-bent on enslaving itself. Sometimes I get the impression that nobody is really interested in liberty today except the Russian dissidents.

On the cultural scene: there is an awful lot of talent knocking around, but much of it, I'm afraid, goes to waste on the trivial and aimless. We've been in the midst of a cultural inflation for some time, worse in its way than the economic one. When we first knew DeKooning, he hadn't yet had his first one-man show, and was just scraping along. It was you — just to get the record straight on this — who opened the pages of *Partisan Review* for Clement Greenberg to push the Abstract Expressionists (the name didn't exist then). That was a first step in what later turned out to be a whole revolution in the artist's financial status. The artists who formerly had trouble getting galleries began to have income-tax problems. It's nice that with all the money flowing around some of it should drain off to the artists. Still, affluence has brought other problems—the commercial conniving of dealers, the bandwagons of taste, public relations promotions, etc., etc. In short, a cultural inflation, with its consequent debasing of real values. It's nice that Pollock's estate should have been able to get two million dollars for "Blue Poles," but is the picture really worth that much?

The more inflation the less seriousness about the art itself. The kinds of ambition for the individual work that the movement—and DeKooning particularly—had back in the late forties would seem strange nowadays. There is more trifling with the tricks of the medium, non-art as art, nihilism toward art—in a word, camp. As the substance becomes more minimal the rhetoric about it becomes more inflated. A recent ad in *Partisan Review* (I don't of course hold the magazine responsible for its advertisements) announced a collection of stories under the title *Superfiction*. Isn't it enough for the writer to aim at a good piece of fiction, which becomes all the harder as literary history accumulates, without seeking some new and inflated genre? "Super-colossal" used to be Hollywoodese, but the literary seem now to be aping that style.

In the history of art the great movements—the Renaissance (which was really two different movements), the Baroque, etc.—ran their course in less than a century. Their followers couldn't see, or didn't want to see, when the original wave had run out. As the imitations got more elaborate they became emptier, more inflated as they became more contrived. Similarly, nobody seems to want to face up to the fact that the great Modern movement has by now come to an end.

That should be an opportunity for the critics to reexamine that movement and find out what was really happening. They might be surprised to discover the traditional values that were always present in it. Art is, after all, one of the most traditional of human enterprises. Thus modern art taught us to see primitive art. Now that the superficial novelties have worn off, how Proust resembles Balzac or Joyce, Dickens, begins to interest us as much as the differences. Once DeKooning was trying to do the same thing as Giotto—to impart as much movement and tension to the pictorial surface as possible.

One great legacy of the Modern movement could be that it taught us to take experimentation in our stride. We're no longer shocked by it, but we're no longer taken in by it either. We allow the artist all the gimmicks he pleases; but when we have looked past them, we have to put to him the simple and central question: Does he have anything to say? We may discover he is empty. That might be enlightening. We might discover we are empty, too. That could be a beginning.

In short, we are caught in a difficult period of transition, of reassessment and rediscovery of values. That is bound to be painful, but it could be challenging work, a new world to discover, as we go about constructing the postmodern period. Unfortunately this adventure has to take place under the shadow of the awful and brutal political reality we cannot allow ourselves to forget: that we live in the time when the future of liberty may be decided for the whole of mankind.

Many years ago, William, you kidded me that I was "paranoid about the future." You could always beat me in an argument, but I've waited a quarter of a century to make this snappy retort: "Was I wrong?"

William Barrett

Dear Will:

It was always a pleasure to argue with you, regardless of who won, because both of us were interested in the truth almost as much as we were in arguing. And if you were paranoid about the future, still, as Delmore used to say, and he was an expert on this subject, one could be paranoid and right. Anyway, the future has not turned out so well, and it may be better to be paranoid than to be schizoid, as I am. I seem to have mixed feelings about almost every political question facing us, particularly the question of the role of America in the coming period. But I think my own uncertainties reflect the complexities of the situation.

One of the complications is the politically polarized atmosphere, which makes it difficult even to discuss the issue of American versus Russian power and the related issues of the preservation of freedom and the future of socialism. If one is anti-Communist, even from the left, one is tagged as a conservative; and if one is critical of America, he or she is lumped with fellow-travelers and apologists for Soviet policies. It has been particularly difficult to maintain a radical, socialist perspective—or conscience—in a time when a vocal part of the left confuses progress with backwardness, while the right has cast itself in the role of defending democracy.

Obviously, there are no simple answers. And though I agree with much of what you say, I think your argument is too syllogistic and hence leaves out many factors. Essentially, your point is that if America became so weak that it could not resist Soviet, or Communist, expansion anywhere, then the kind of freedom that we identify with Western democracy would almost surely disappear—unless Communism itself in these circumstances would develop into the free society that Marx envisaged. As things now stand, I believe you are right. If America could not defend Western Europe, no doubt it would go Communist and come under the Russian sphere of influence—again, unless it was strong enough to defy the Soviet Union. But what is assumed in this line of reasoning is that America and Europe are stable entities with well-defined interests, democratic commitments, and predictable developments.

The fact is that America cannot be counted on to defend even limited forms of democracy, as we have seen in Spain, Portugal, and Greece, for example, and as we can now see in the Middle East. If America is so dedicated to the defense of Western democracy, how can we explain the games being played with Israel and the Arabs? I need hardly remind you that in many, if not all, situations, the love of money is stronger than the love of liberty.

Besides, the strength and stability of Europe and America depend partly on the ability to solve their political and economic problems. The power of the Communist parties on the continent is not due simply to their clever propaganda or the craving of the intellectuals as well as the masses for political illusions.

And all this talk about America being the bulwark of democracy does nothing to ameliorate the conditions that deny it that role. On the home front, the notion of America's global mission, like most patriotic rhetoric, is actually a substitute for enlightened thinking and action. The truth is that the country has become a jungle of competing interests and pressure groups, corrupt and anarchic, unable to plan its economy, its ecology, its traffic, its control of crime, its foreign policy, its race problems, its urban decay. This state of affairs used to be rationalized by the myth that these contradictions were essential to democracy.

What I am saying is that the proposition that the decline of America will lead to the decline of political and intellectual freedom is a half-truth. It does not take into account all the other factors that create totalitarian parties and regimes. And it ignores the fact that the affairs of the country have been in the hands of those who seem least capable of dealing with them. Unless one has some alternative politics, one is simply putting one's faith in the people and ideas one never trusted much in the past. And if, as you imply, your position is that of critical support of the policy of the lesser evil—a position taken by liberals and radicals when their ideal, long-range program did not appear to be viable—then it seems to me your critical attitude should be both stronger and clearer.

But aside from the practical and immediate implications of an argument which is basically an appeal to realpolitik, I think one must have some larger vision if only for intellectual reasons, some idea of a better social order, which would provide a perspective from which to criticize both the Communist and our own societies. Otherwise one's political identity is dissolved in that jumble of opinions that can never extricate themselves from the assumptions of the status quo. Even if it is true that America is now the guardian of freedom, this is at best a reassuring observation, perhaps a fact, but scarcely a theory, and hardly distinguishable from the ready-made opinions of all the stalwarts of the popular media. No politics, other than support for America, follows from such an attitude, support, that is, in the event of a confrontation with Russia, which in any case few people would question. Obviously your own knowledge and insight, for which I have great respect, are incomparably greater, but they are not given an adequate outlet in a statement that confines the future of freedom to the limits of American power.

Hence the real question is not whether liberty is bound up with the American future, but how to evaluate American policies and motives. Obviously, reactionaries would have widely different estimates and programs from those of socialists, for example.

You speak of the change in the ratio of American to Soviet power, but of the persistence of the "fellow-traveling" mind as a constant. Here, too, I think you are right. However, I believe you are wrong in your assessment of its importance and its influence. In the thirties and forties, it seemed necessary to dispel the illusions about Russia and the Communists because so many people who should have known better were taken in. Now, on the other hand, with the exception of those who cling to a half-baked idealism, the whole country has no illusions about the Communists. Also, at that time, the unmasking of Stalinism was part of the struggle on the left to educate honest but mistaken radicals and liberals, and to free the left from the corrupting effects of its association with the Communists. Today, however, people may be muddle-headed, but no serious person on the left is pro-Communist. Neither on the right nor on the left can the problem now be said to be the failure to recognize the nature of Communism.

The problem for the country is not whether it understands the aims of the Communists, but whether there is a national interest and if so what its relation is to this understanding—in other words, whether the support of democracy is always in the national interest. As you know, Marxists have usually claimed that there is no national interest, that there are only class interests, and that the so-called national interest in this country is only a mask for the interests of the dominant economic class. This is probably too schematic and reductive a view of national motives. Nevertheless, many recent American policies certainly seem to suggest that the government has tried very hard to prove that Marx and Lenin were right. True, there have been instances when the country did not appear to act either in the interests of the nation as a whole or of any one class. I must confess that I see no explanation for this but stupidity—the kind of myopic stupidity that comes from the national addiction to empirical, day-to-day thinking. And I do think stupidity has been underestimated as a factor in history by right as well as left ideologues.

When you talk about the cultural decline, it is not clear whether you think this is connected with our political predicament and therefore with the question of freedom. If so, then what you take to be the signs of cultural decline must be seen as part of the political situation. For what are the cultural anarchy, the reign of pop, the popular distortions of modernism—what are these triumphs of the market if not products of the system of advertising and packaging. And this is the system that is supposed to save our freedoms and preserve our cultural values. I need not remind you that the serious art of this period has been critical and detached.

And in your dismissal of the art scene today I think you make the mistake of lumping fashionable versions of the avant-garde, tailored to the popular market, with work of genuine talent by writers and painters who have resisted the pressures of the time. Most poets, for example, perhaps because of the intractability of the medium, have kept their distance from pop taste. And a number of novelists might even be said to have become too eccentric in their effort to stay out of the entertainment business. Thus, in failing to distinguish between the conformist and noncomformist part of the culture, you are confusing the cure with the disease. I am sure you have no such political motives, but you must be aware that a favorite gambit of conservative critics is to blame the cultural slump on the radical sensibility, that is, on the sensibility that is opposed to all the things you are against.

What more can I say—except to deplore the situation in which people who have the same values and goals find themselves on opposite sides of the fence. In the "old days," which you refer to apparently with some nostalgia, there was plenty of nonsense, but one felt closer to those one was able to argue with. One can argue fruitfully only with those who share one's assumptions, but in the fragmentation and confusion of thinking today differences become barricades.

William Phillips
1976, vol. 43, no. 3

• The Neoconservatives
Amitai Etzioni

Among those anticipating, promoting, participating in, and benefiting from the past few years' shift to the right in the national mood is a group of social observers and essayists who are coming to be called "neoconservatives." For the past half decade and more they have dedicated themselves—often with considerable sense of mission, one might add—to elaborating the intellectual rationale behind public policies that would turn away from social activism, government intervention, and grand schemes to reform America—and rely instead on the private sector, the market mechanisms, and traditional institutions such as the family and local community. The group encompasses many of America's best known and most often quoted members of the intellectual elite including Irving Kristol, Daniel Bell, Nathan Glazer, Robert Nisbet, Daniel P. Moynihan, and James Q. Wilson, as well as less often cited Samuel P. Huntington, Edward C. Banfield, and Ernest van den Haag.

Despite significant differences of tone, style, and temperament neoconservatives qualify as a school because they all share the same basic views of society and human nature. Because neoconservatives are often in print and on the air, their basic position is well known: freedom and equality, far from being compatible values, are seen as frequently in conflict with each other. The main reason is that freedom to neoconservatives means noninterference by government with exercise of individual and group preferences and "natural" social patterns and tendencies. Equality, however, inasmuch as it fails to evolve naturally, tends to require a government to promote it; ergo, efforts to promote equality threaten freedom. More generally, neoconservatives are concerned about the oppressive encroachment of government bureaucracies on the spontaneous capabilities of individuals, families, communities, and voluntary associations—be it for purposes of consumerism, environmental or worker protection, or whatnot.

Also, neoconservatives see inequality, at least certain forms of inequality, as a positive social feature. They tend to see a society of equals as unwieldy and as unworkable as an army composed only of foot soldiers. Society may not require "a ruling class" but it can no more do without its various elites—cultural, political, economic, social—than followers can do without leaders. And, as long as inequality is based on talent and achievement, it is, according to neoconservatives, not only necessary but also quite fair.

As concerns human nature, neoconservatives are on the pessimistic side: human beings are not born "good," then mucked up by society's injustices (though still capable of being set right again via deliberate efforts ranging from social reform to individual psychotherapy). Quite the opposite: society is a continual struggle to impose qualities such as order and self-restraint on individuals whose inner drives press them toward disorder, insatiability, and selfishness. Thus neoconservatives are highly skeptical of educational, therapeutic, and rehabilitative efforts to tame and harness these drives. The best that can be expected is that authority may serve to keep a lid on man's psychic cauldron. Writes James Q. Wilson in *Time*:

> from the vantage point of 200 years we should have only modest expectations for what our institutions, facing these problems, can accomplish. We will not eliminate the causes of crime, nor will we rehabilitate offenders in any large numbers. But if prisons cannot rehabilitate, at least they can punish and isolate.

The sense that one is quite familiar with these positions quickly gives way when one ponders the political dilemma of neoconservatives: how is an ideology which openly embraces elites rather than masses, achievements rather than entitlements, "lids" rather than what comes naturally, to be sold to the masses? To put it differently, approximately thirty percent of Americans see themselves as conservatives; they need not be sold: they already subscribe to these views, although they may enjoy seeing them elaborated—the way people who have already bought Chryslers read chiefly Chrysler ads. But how is one to get to those attracted to the other brands—the nearly forty-two percent who see themselves as middle-of-the-roaders and twenty-nine percent who consider themselves liberals?

Some neoconservatives largely ignore this "marketability" issue; they are unabashedly ideological, adamant, hard-hitting, and let the chips fall where they may. Their appeal is typically sectarian, and they pay the price—they are *not* the mass media's neoconservative heroes. Other neoconservatives concern themselves much more with the values and views of non-neoconservatives and are in this sense less dogmatic, more pragmatic—and have a wider appeal, although their basic position is quite similar.

A typical unabashed, true-blue neoconservative is Samuel P. Huntington, who has never been bashful about baring the undemocratic premises that underlie his neoconservatism. In 1957 he closed his book, *The Soldier and the State*, by portraying West Point as the closest contemporary embodiment of the inegalitarian ideal. In a passage that comes about as close to poetry as any that claims to be political science, he writes of the military academy:

> There is ordered serenity. The parts do not exist on their own, but accept their subordination to the whole. Beauty and utility are merged in gray stone. Neat lawns surround compact, trim homes, each identified by the name and rank of its occupant. The buildings stand in fixed relation to each other, part of an over-all plan, their character and station symbolizing their contributions, stone and brick for the senior officers, wood for the lower ranks. The post is suffused with the rhythm and harmony which comes when collective will supplants individual whim. West Point is a community of structured purpose, one in which the behavior of men is governed by a code, the product of generations. There is little room for presumption and individualism. The unity of the community incites no man to be more than he is. In order is found peace; in discipline, fulfillment; in community, security.

His final stanzas counsel not only admiration but emulation, even if it goes against the American grain:

> West Point is a gray island in a many colored sea, a bit of Sparta in the might of Babylon. Yet is it possible to deny that the military values—loyalty, duty, restraint, dedication—are the ones America most needs today? That the disciplined order of West Point has more to offer than the garish individualism of Main Street?

In his bicentennial contribution to *The Public Interest* entitled "The Democratic Distemper," Huntington diagnosed America's sociopolitical ailments as stemming from "an excess of democracy," adding, "Al Smith once remarked, 'The only cure for the evils of democracy is more democracy.' Our analysis suggests that applying that cure at the present time could well be adding fuel to the fire."

Huntington is quite aware that such baldfaced conservatism could hardly lead to mass acclaim. In a letter to the *New York Times* he explains: "if I wished to 'forge a new base of power,' I could find much more productive ways to do it than to espouse a conservatism which has always been a minority stand in the American political tradition."

Another whose neoconservatism is unadulterated and too strong a brew for mass consumption is Edward C. Banfield. His *Unheavenly City* frankly espouses the view that urban poverty is much less the result of general economic and social conditions such as unemployment, exploitation, and the legacies of racism and discrimination than of characterological defects in the poor themselves. Poverty persists because society insulates such individuals from the negative consequences of their improper attitudes and actions—thereby, in effect, encouraging them. Writes Banfield:

> This principle implies that the individual should be allowed to suffer penalties (loss of the reward at the very least) if he does not behave as he should. Herbert Spencer was prepared to follow this principle to its logical conclusion, allowing those who failed to provide for the future to starve in their old age in order that others might see from their examples the advantage of saving. Few people today, however, would consider the issue settled by the principle that a cruel deterrent may in the long run be less cruel than the consequences of not deterring. Indeed, few people recognize that there sometimes *is* a problem of choice between these alternatives. The almost universal opinion today is that, both for his own sake and that of his society, an individual must not be left to suffer the consequences of his actions. If, for example, he has chosen a life of improvidence, he cannot for that reason be allowed to remain below the poverty line. To give him money, however, is to give him an incentive to persist in his ways.

The more bashful neoconservative basic message may be the same, but it is often espoused not as a matter of principle but of pragmatism. As a corollary, they typically write tentatively, as if pulled reluctantly toward conclusions by the overwhelming weight of logic and evidence. While ideological conservatives are more inclined to dispute the desirability of reform goals, pragmatic neoconservatives are more likely to claim that they favor these goals in theory but are forced to point out that attaining them is not feasible or exacts too high a price on resources or other values. In the same vein, pragmatic neoconservatives are more apt to criticize reform activists' means rather than their values, arguing that particular means are to be preferred as less costly or disruptive to other values—without explicitly noting that the means they favor happen to reflect neoconservative values.

Typical of these pragmatists is Nathan Glazer. His writing is careful and scholarly and his observations judicious. Thus, in his most recent work concerning affirmative action, *Affirmative Discrimination*, he does not attack outright the value of equality, nor, directly, even affirmative action. He favors "equal opportunity," a time-honored formula that fails to deal with the question of how to equalize opportunities for people who begin from largely different starting points, precisely where discrimination-in-reverse—at the core of affirmative action—enters. As for affirmative action, Glazer asks that it be "re-examined," because, he holds, it is not necessary for middle-class blacks (they make it, he says, without it) and does not work for lower-class blacks (among whom unemployment is rampant).

Similarly, it is instructive to compare pragmatic and popular James Q. Wilson's views on the proper societal approach to crime and punishment with those of ideological and controversial Ernest van den Haag. (Each has a recent book: respectively, *Thinking About Crime* and *Punishing Criminals*.) Van den Haag's position is that improving the conditions of the disadvantaged is no solution to the crime problem; indeed, it is more likely to promote than to deter crime by fueling the expectations, envy, and frustration of the poor. Wilson, in contrast, does not deny that poverty helps spawn crime and that overcoming poverty is therefore a useful way of combating it. Rather he argues that poverty alone does not account for enough of the "variance": the majority of poor people are not criminals. Hence, to focus on overcoming poverty as a means of reducing crime is to invest our resources and energies disproportionately to this factor's causative weight. Moreover, explains Wilson, those who insist on combating the "root causes" of crime—by which they often mean poverty, alienation, and associated family break-up—are also concentrating on the least tractable of crime's causes. However meritorious such strategies of societal reform and rehabilitation may be in theory, more is to be gained pragmatically by tailoring our corrective efforts to the immediate causes of crime which lie in individual motivation. Thus, by a different route, Wilson arrives at much the same concrete proposals for public policy changes as Van den Haag: i.e., concentrate on punishment and deterrence, making it clear that "crime does not pay" via such measures as mandatory jail sentences, restrictions on judicial discretion, and limits on plea bargaining.

Perhaps the most popular pragmatic neoconservative is Daniel Bell, who is most reluctant to accept the label, calling himself a "right-wing social democrat." Unlike other neoconservatives, Bell does not argue explicitly that the division of wealth and power in America is fundamentally a "reward system." In other words, "have-nots" are those who have not worked as hard or as long or have not demonstrated the requisite talent or accomplishment. The "have-nots" are entitled to a share, Bell says. The problem is that they refuse to be content. In their hunger for an even bigger bite of the societal apple, they have let their appetites grow to an extent that no apple can satisfy. Demands have become entitlements, a sense that each group has a right to a growing income, wealth, health, and all else that is to be had. Being "fanatic," the groups are unwilling to negotiate down their fantasies and they refuse to compromise, thus threatening the stability and ultimately the existence of the American society in their frenzy.

Voicing a related fear, Aaron Wildavsky warns in a *Commentary* article of "the manufacture of incompatible policy demands that impose burdens on government which no government can meet." Again Wildavsky does not say that the various groups—the poor, the blacks, all the other minorities—have no right to what they agitate government for. Rather he says, if they all try to cash in their moral chips at once—to collect on what they feel society owes them for past and present injustices—they will find not only not enough money in the bank, but no more bank.

Kristol writes, "neo-conservatism is not *at all* [italics mine] hostile to the idea of a welfare state. . . . It is skeptical of those social programs that create vast and energetic bureaucracies to 'solve social problems.' . . . it is opposed to the paternalistic state." While Kristol cites Social Security and unemployment insurance as acceptable examples of the welfare state, his fondness is for the market mechanisms that, he says, have the right "to respond efficiently to economic realities while preserving the maximum degree of individual freedom."

Bell similarly came to embrace the market as the way to bring into balance the explosion of social wants. "In many public-policy discussions, it is assumed that our choices are either administrative regulation to achieve those ends—or abandoning the ends. But the market can often be used to achieve them efficiently. The market provides for self-adjustment and self-regulation within a framework of rules."

One reads these and similar lines of the Harvard expert, unable to believe that he can really be either so naive or so disingenuous. Even a sophomore, and not necessarily in sociology, knows that the market, far from maximizing the freedoms of the individual, maximizes the range of choice only of those with a high buying power while restricting that of persons with low buying power. Unlike the polity in which the notion of one individual, one vote is at least very crudely approximated, the market offers individuals as many (or as few) votes as they have dollars. Moreover, an odd discount mechanism works by which the richer you are, the more you get per dollar; for instance, a small saver will get lower interest on his savings than a big saver, and will pay a higher interest on loans he takes. Though one can argue that both politics and market relations are bound to reflect overall the existing structure of power and privileges—inequities politics modifies, the market magnifies.

Kristol and Bell argue that you can use the market to introduce the social changes you desire, but this ignores the need to deal with the powerful people who oppose such changes, whose opposition can scarcely be countered without political mobilization of those who favor change. Societal stability is a classic conservative value. It was always a conservative line to call upon the underprivileged to sit still so as not to upset national unity, law, and order. These arguments gloss over the possibility that a class of people may find their needs better served in a different societal structure (hence one cannot assume that they will be scared off by fear of overly disturbing this one). Studies by William Gamson and others show that the fear of instability and violence is one of the main reasons those in power eventually come around to make concessions to the have-nots. As for the argument that if the underprivileged voice their needs or demand their entitlements the society will erupt in a war of all-against-all, the result of unreasonable, fanatic, intransigent minorities, the brief history of the turbulent sixties suggests quite the opposite: given rather limited concessions to minorities (and youth) violence (never all that high on a historically comparative scale) subsided and they returned to working within the system—rather than to overthrowing it.

Thus, after decades of relative neglect of the conservative position, we now have an articulate new group of advocates. They come in two wrappings, or more precisely, one quite unwrapped and one carefully packaged. Each to his own taste.   1977, vol. 44, no. 4

• **The Responsibility of Scientists**
Andrei Sakharov

Gorky
March 24, 1981

Because of the international nature of our profession, scientists form the one real worldwide community that exists today. There is no doubt about this with respect to the substance of science: Schrödinger's equation and the formula $E = mc^2$ are equally valid on all continents. But the integration of the scientific community has inevitably progressed beyond narrow professional interests and now embraces a broad range of universal issues, including ethical questions. And I believe this trend should and will continue.

Scientists, engineers, and other specialists derive from their professional knowledge and the advantages of their occupations a broad and deep understanding of the potential benefits—but also the risks—entailed in the application of science and technology. They also develop an awareness of the positive and negative tendencies of progress generally, and its possible consequences.

Colossal opportunities exist for the application of recent advances in physics, chemistry, and biochemistry; technology and engineering; computer science; medicine and genetics; physiology and hygiene; microbiology (including industrial microbiology); industrial and agricultural management techniques; psychology; and other exact and social sciences. And we can anticipate more achievements to come. We all share the responsibility to work for the full realization of the results of scientific research in a world where most people's lives have become more difficult, where so many are threatened by hunger, premature illness, and untimely death.

But scientists and scholars cannot fail to think about the dangers stemming from uncontrolled progress, from unregulated industrial development, and especially from military applications of scientific achievements. There has been public discussion of topics related to scientific progress: nuclear power; the population explosion; genetic engineering; regulation of industry to protect the environment; protection of air quality, of flora and fauna, and of rivers, lakes, seas, and oceans; and the impact of mass media. Unfortunately, despite the urgent and serious nature of the issues at stake, such discussions are often uninformed, prejudiced, or politicized, and sometimes simply dishonest. Experts therefore are under an obligation to subject these problems to unbiased and searching examination, making all socially significant information available to the public in direct, firsthand form, and not just in filtered versions. The discussion of nuclear power, a subject of prime importance, is an instructive example. I have expressed elsewhere my opinion that the dangers of nuclear power have been exaggerated in the West, and that such distortion is harmful.

With some important exceptions (primarily affecting totalitarian countries), scientists are not only better informed than the average person, but also strive for and enjoy more independence and freedom. Freedom, however, always entails responsibility. Scientists and other experts already influence or have the capacity to influence public opinion and their governments. (That influence should not be exaggerated, but it is substantial.) My view of the situation of scientists in the contemporary world has convinced me that they have special professional and social responsibilities. It is often difficult to separate one from the other—the communication of information, the popularization of scientific knowledge, and the publication of endorsements or warnings are examples of activities with both professional and social aspects.

Similar complications arise when scientists become involved in questions of disarmament: in developing strategy for or participating in international negotiations; in advancing proposals or issuing appeals to governments or to the public; and in alerting them to dangers. Disarmament is a separate, critically important issue which requires a profound, thorough, and scientifically daring approach. I realize that more detailed treatment is needed, but now I will simply outline a few ideas. I consider disarmament necessary and possible only on the basis of strategic parity. Additional agreements covering all kinds of weapons of mass destruction are needed. After strategic parity in conventional arms has been achieved, a parity which takes account of all the political, psychological, and geographical factors involved, and if totalitarian expansion is brought to an end, then agreements should be reached prohibiting the first use of nuclear weapons, and later banning such weapons.

Another subject which is closely connected to questions of peace, trust, and understanding among countries is the international defense of human rights. Freedom of opinion, freedom to exchange information, and freedom of movement are necessary for true accountability of the authorities which in turn prevents abuses of power in domestic and international matters. I believe that such accountability would make impossible tragic mistakes like the Soviet invasion of Afghanistan and would inhibit manifestations of an expansionist foreign policy and acts of internal repression.

The unrestricted sale of newspapers, magazines, and books published abroad would be a major step toward effective freedom of information in totalitarian countries. Perhaps even more significant would be the abolition of censorship—which should concern first of all the scientists and intelligentsia of totalitarian countries. It is important to demand a halt to jamming of foreign broadcasts which deprives millions of access to the uncensored information needed to form an independent judgment of events. (Jamming was resumed in the USSR in August 1980 after a seven-year interval.)

I am convinced that support of Amnesty International's call for a general worldwide amnesty for prisoners of conscience is of special importance. The political amnesties proclaimed by a number of countries in recent years have helped to improve the atmosphere. An amnesty for prisoners of conscience in the USSR, in Eastern Europe, and in all other countries where political prisoners or prisoners of conscience are detained would not only be of major humanitarian significance but could also enhance international confidence and security.

The worldwide character of the scientific community assumes particular importance when dealing with such problems. By its international defense of persecuted scientists and of all persons whose rights have been violated, the scientific community confirms its international mandate which is so essential for successful scientific work and for service to society.

Western scientists are familiar with the names of many Soviet colleagues who have been subjected to unlawful repressions. (I shall confine my discussion to the Soviet Union since I am better informed about it, but serious human rights violations occur in other countries including Eastern European countries.) The individuals I mention have neither advocated nor used violence since they consider publicity the only acceptable, effective, and nonpernicious way of defending human rights. Thus they are all prisoners of conscience as defined by Amnesty International. Their stories have much else in common. Their trials were conducted in flagrant violation of statutory procedures and in defiance of elementary common sense. My friend Sergei Kovalev was convicted in 1975 in the absence of the defendant and counsel, that is, with no possibility whatsoever for a defense. He was sentenced to seven years labor camp and three years internal exile for anti-Soviet agitation and propaganda allegedly contained in the *samizdat* news magazine *A Chronicle of Current Events*, but there was no examination of the substance of the charge.

Comparable breaches of law marked the trials of Yury Orlov, the founder of the Moscow Helsinki Group, and of other members of the Helsinki Groups and associated committees: Victor Nekipelov, Leonard Ternovsky, Mykola Rudenko, Alexander Podrabinek (and his brother Kirill), Gleb Yakunin, Vladimir Slepak, Malva Landa, Robert Nazarian, Eduard Arutyunian, Vyacheslav Bakhmin, Oleg Berdnik, Oksana Meshko, Mykola Matusevich and his wife, and Miroslav Marinovich. Tatiana Osipova, Irina Grivnina, and Felix Serebrov have been imprisoned pending trial. Yury Orlov's lawyer missed part of the trial proceedings when he was locked up forcibly in chambers adjoining the courtroom. Orlov's wife was frisked in a crude way and her clothing ripped during a search for written notes or a tape recorder, all from fear that the court's grotesque secrets might be revealed.

In the labor camps, prisoners of conscience suffer cruel treatment: arbitrary confinement in punishment cells; torture by cold and hunger; infrequent family visits subject to capricious cancellation; and similar restrictions on correspondence.

They share all the rigors of the Soviet penal regimen for common criminals while suffering the added strain of pressure to "embark on the path of reform," i.e., to renounce their beliefs. I would like to remind you that not once has any international organization such as the Red Cross or a lawyer's association been able to visit Soviet labor camps.

Political prisoners are often rearrested, and monstrous sentences imposed. Ornithologist Mart Niklus, poet Vasily Stus, physics teacher Oleksei Tikhy, lawyer Levko Lukyanenko, philologist Viktoras Petkus and Balys Gajauskas have all received sentences of ten years labor camp and five years internal exile as recidivists. A new trial is expected for Paruir Airikian who is still in labor camp. Within the last few days I have been shocked by the fifth (!) arrest of my friend Anatoly Marchenko, a worker and author of two talented and important books: *My Testimony* and *From Tarusa to Siberia*. Imprisoned religious believers include Rostislav Galetsky, Bishop Nikolai Goretoi, Alexander Ogorodnikov, and Boris Perchatkin. Imprisoned workers include Yury Grimm and Mikhail Kubobaka. Alexei Murzhenko and Yury Fedorov are still imprisoned. I shall name only a few scientists deprived of their freedom; many others could be added to the list: Anatoly Shcharansky, the young computer scientist now famous around the world; mathematicians Tatiana Velikanova, Alexander Lavut, Alexander Bolonkin, and Vazif Meilanov; computer scientist Victor Brailovsky; economist Ida Nudel; engineers Reshat Dzhemilev and Antanas Terleckas; physicists Rolan Kadiyev, Iosif Zisels, and Iosif Dyadkin; chemists Valery Abramkin and Juri Kukk; philologists Igor Ogurtsov and Mustafa Dzhemilev; and Vladimir Balakhonov.

A common violation of human rights, and one which especially affects scientists, is denial of permission to emigrate. The names of many "refuseniks" are known to the West.

I was banished without a trial to Gorky more than a year ago and placed under a regimen of almost total isolation. A few days ago the KGB stole my manuscripts and notebooks which contained extracts from scientific books and journals. This is a new attempt to deprive me of any opportunity for intellectual activity, even in my solitude, and to rob me of my memory. For more than three years Elizaveta Alexeyeva, my son's fiancée, has been arbitrarily prevented from leaving the Soviet Union. I have mentioned my own situation because of the absence of any legal basis for the actions taken and because the detention of Elizaveta is undisguised blackmail directed against me. She is a hostage of the state.

I appeal to scientists everywhere to defend those who have been repressed. I believe that in order to protect innocent persons it is permissible and, in many cases, necessary to adopt extraordinary measures such as an interruption of scientific contacts or other types of boycotts. I urge the use as well of all the possibilities of publicity and of diplomacy. In addressing the Soviet leaders, it is important to take into account that they do not know about—and probably do not want to know about—most letters and appeals directed to them. Therefore, personal interventions by Western officials who meet with their Soviet counterparts have particular significance. Western scientists should use their influence to press for such interventions.

I hope that carefully thought out and organized actions in defense of victims of repression will ease their lot and add strength, authority, and energy to the international scientific community.

I have titled this letter "The Responsibility of Scientists." Tatiana Velikanova, Yury Orlov, Sergei Kovalev, and many others have decided this question for themselves by taking the path of active, self-sacrificing struggle for human rights and for an open society. Their sacrifices are enormous, but they are not in vain. These individuals are improving the ethical image of our world.

Many of their colleagues who live in totalitarian countries but who have not found within themselves the strength for such struggle, do try to fulfill honestly their professional responsibilities. It is, in fact, essential to work at one's profession. But has not the time come for those scientists, who often exhibit their perception and nonconformity when with close friends, to demonstrate their sense of responsibility in some fashion which has more social significance, and to take a more public stand, at least on issues such as the defense of their persecuted colleagues and control over the faithful execution of domestic laws and the performance of international obligations? Every true scientist should undoubtedly muster sufficient courage and integrity to resist the temptation and the habit of conformity. Unfortunately, we are familiar with too many counterexamples in the Soviet Union, sometimes using the excuse of protecting one's laboratory or institute (usually just a pretext), sometimes for the sake of one's career, sometimes for the sake of foreign travel (a major lure in a closed country such as ours). And was it not shameful for Yury Orlov's colleagues to expel him secretly from the Armenian Academy of Sciences while other colleagues in the USSR Academy of Sciences shut their eyes to the expulsion and also to his physical condition? (He is close to death.) Many active and passive accomplices in such affairs may themselves someday attract the growing appetite of Moloch. Nothing good can come of this. Better to avert it.

Western scientists face no threat of prison or labor camp for public stands; they cannot be bribed by an offer of foreign travel to forsake such activity. But this in no way diminishes their responsibility. Some Western intellectuals warn against social involvement as a form of politics. But I am not speaking about a struggle for power—it is not politics. It is a struggle to preserve peace and those ethical values which have been developed as our civilization evolved. By their example and by their fate, prisoners of conscience affirm that the defense of justice, the international defense of individual victims of violence, the defense of mankind's lasting interests are the responsibility of every scientist.

P.S. After this letter was written, I received word of the tragic death of Juri Kukk in a labor camp. Tatiana Osipova was sentenced to five years labor camp and five years internal exile on April 2nd.   1981, vol. 48, no. 4

• Letter from Italy
Edith Kurzweil

August 1981

Italy is always full of surprise and chaos, but more so this time. I arrived on May 13, the day the Pope was shot, and before leaving two weeks later, the country had had a referendum, a major scandal had swept through the entire government and caused its fall, and the Christian-Democrats, with the "help" of the Socialist leader Bettino Craxi, were about to lose the premiership for the first time in thirty-five years. Not all of these events, of course, were causally connected, but there were many implicit relationships, if only because of the way Italian economic and political institutions are structured.

If, for example, Mehemet Ali Agca, whose deed shocked the world, had not been apprehended immediately, and had managed to disappear amongst the tourists and believers who surround the Pope whenever he leaves his Vatican chambers, everyone would have thought that the attempt on the Pope's life had been engineered by the radical left or by anti-abortionists who had good reason to be incensed by his interference in Italian politics—a breach of the Concordat between church and state—a few days before the May 17 referendum. Although the assailant was caught, the crime, of course, was not solved, and the only plausible motive might have been hatred of Catholicism by Muslim Turks, aggravated for Agca when the Pope visited Istanbul.

Yet as the Italian media continued to report and to comment around the clock, reality and fantasy often converged, and this was not surprising, given the possibilities of interpreting the absurdities and the horror of a terrorist act in a country with a number of right and left guerrilla organizations. For once, however briefly, politics was left aside, and Communist and Socialist leaders almost jumped the gun on the Catholics in condemning terrorism—in particular and in general— even before they discovered that Agca belonged to an international Fascist group. It still is not clear whether this group is not a cover-up for other connections.

Some Italians thought the left had to dissociate itself from this act immediately to win the five impending referenda, and particularly the referendum to retain the three-year-old law which legalizes abortion under very controlled and limited circumstances. In retrospect, one might argue that the large margin of their victory (sixty-eight percent on abortion) would indicate they could not have lost. But this is far from clear. The use of television, not only as propaganda, but as a means of education, turned out to be effective. And since the "right to life" movement got equal time, as did the forces for and against life imprisonment, the post-mortem editorial in *La Repubblica* concluded correctly that Italians had matured politically: nearly eighty percent voted; Christian-Democrats, though practicing Catholics, frequently disregarded their leaders' advice; and Italians— from industrialized northern cities to backward southern villages—talked about issues and convictions rather than party loyalty and slogans.

It has been argued that Italian democracy is too successful, that it is too open to anarchy, to fascism, to foreign influences, etc.; and that openness allows for the excesses of self-expression, for the manipulations leading to the perennial scandals, and ultimately, for the presence of terrorists like Agca. Though Agca himself is not an Italian creation, his presence in Italy does not seem fortuitous. It probably has been facilitated by the fact that Perugia's local government, for financial benefit, has allowed the construction of an Islamic center—including its own mosque—to accommodate approximately two thousand students, some of whom are members of extremist groups. But even before Agca's interrogations, where he would come off as a clever ideologue rather than as an ordinary fanatic, the Italian press spoke of "the presence of international organizations which aim to subvert civil life, to fuel and extend conflicts between people and nations, to generate fear and violence and thus obstruct open discourse and the democratic process." Other statements increasingly linked terrorism, which now transcends "right" and "left" politics, to special, and hidden, interests. And on May 23rd *La Repubblica* reported specifically how, and through what channels, the Libyan government and the PLO had provided bombs, machine guns, and other munitions, for the most part Russian-made, to such terrorist groups as Prima Linea and Metropoli "without charging a cent"—"in order to destabilize Italy's social-political situation."

Italians are particularly prone to believing in conspiracy theories. But it is quite possible that in a country where chaos is the norm, many people can easily remember that "something violent happens" before every election and before every referendum, because calamities abound. Certainly, this time the "something" did not influence the outcome of the referendum, that is, sympathy for the Pope was dissociated from papal politics. And there is enough evidence—from tourists' photos to false passport, from preassassination travel to unaccounted-for time, etc., to prove that Agca was backed by an organization, though we still don't know whether he served the PLO, Russian, Armenian, or Shiite interests, and whether he was paid by Gheddafi or by the proceeds from heroin traffic. For a few days, the Italian press speculated on all these possibilities, and a week later, while the police continued their inquiries, both Agca's motives and the Pope's health were relegated to page eight or twelve.

Nevertheless, international terrorism remained a major concern as representatives of police forces from seventeen countries began their yearly meetings in Milan, and as there seemed to be a growing awareness of the fact that unemployed youth—in many countries—have increasingly given up on Marx and instead, band together in Fascist activities, though fascism is illegal. Thus many Italians were glad that Agca turned out to be a foreigner, because very few of them would welcome another totalitarian regime such as Mussolini's; they value their freedoms, particularly of press and speech; many were shocked about reports that *Mein Kampf* was getting "popular" enough to be banned in Germany; and uneasy about their own right-wing youth.

One week after the attack on the Pope, the front page of every newspaper covered the imprisonment of seven of the most important Italian financiers—the first ones of that caliber to have been indicted for exporting large sums of money (at least one deal of thirty-six million dollars). Quite likely, the almost unexpected sophistication of the electorate—and especially its endorsement of the previously enacted emergency "law and order" decree against suspected terrorists—also encouraged the move against these powerful magnates, on the strength of information available for some time. Yet this turned out to have been only the outer layer of this scandal, which soon forced the resignation of the Forlani government. While looking into the "disappearance" of Michele Sindona, the failed financier, proof of the existence of a secret Masonic lodge—*Propaganda Due* (P2)—became public as did the list of its nearly thousand members which, as we now know, included the minister of defense, the secretary of the treasury, heads of police and the military, as well as other parliamentarians, bureaucrats, and functionaries of the state-run television network—mostly Christian-Democrats with a sprinkling of Socialists. Grand-Master Licio Gelli's organization chart— members had code names and knew only those belonging to their own cells— became available, although a suitcase of documents had been removed, leaving much room for speculation about the aims of P2. Later on, as witnesses began to testify, and Gelli had disappeared, he was not only linked to prominent Mafia bosses, NATO generals, and international bankers, but to former prime ministers Amintore Fanfani and Giulio Andreotti, so that membership in P2 seemed to be only the first step to the discovery of a larger political conspiracy. Essentially, the clandestine nature of this political organization, in a country where secret societies are outlawed, sparked the customarily vivid Italian imaginations. Personal histories of P2 members were being reexamined in line with the organization's scope, the combined power of whose "blood brothers" could easily effect a coup. At first it was speculated that even if no plan for such a coup would be found, the "lost" suitcase might contain one. Later on, the question was reversed: would it be worthwhile to set up such an elaborate network for any aim lesser than a government take-over? Already before the government was forced to step down, resignations had been demanded, and some were received. Many refused, protesting their innocence. When Gelli was reported to have been a confessed Fascist with underworld connections, the culpability of all P2 members seemed even more certain, especially as lists of "dues received" were produced, and as more and more festering scandals were examined from this new perspective.

Whereas some Italians perceived this super-scandal as no different from all the previous ones and expected that after a *rimpasto* (reshuffling) of the government, corruption would continue and increase, others likened it to Watergate. That the Forlani government resigned because the morals of some of its leaders were questioned indicates, in a subtle way, that Italy is turning a corner. There are other indications as well. The timing and the fact that the names were publicized at all appear to point to the loss of power of the Christian-Democrats. And the May 20 kidnapping of a Montedison director by the Red Brigades, for instance, engendered a joint protest strike by members of all the local and regional unions. (After he was found dead in the trunk of a car on July 7, both workers and managers staged a nationwide strike against terrorism.) In view of the strong condemnation of both far-left and far-right terrorism by the Italian Communist Party (PCI) as well as by all the other "legitimate" political parties, such strikes may not be surprising. But they would negate the frequent claim by some of the left that terrorism in crowded places and in daylight could not occur without the tacit consent or at least the widespread disaffection of a large number of citizens. The apprehension and trial of some of the Red Brigades seem to show that this organization is losing strength. Nevertheless, a number of kidnappers, including those of Aldo Moro, have not been apprehended and eradication of terrorism has been promised by campaigning politicians of every major party.

Accusations by the left against multinational corporations or against American imperialism also appear to have become less fashionable, and even the PCI has gone along with the proposed denationalization of Montedison. Five of the largest private holding companies, with the help of the government, had begun a complex maneuver to acquire an as-yet-undetermined percentage of the company's shares. Since nationalization of industry had always been pushed for by the PCI—the ideological justification that socialism is advancing peacefully—the party's increasing willingness to strengthen Italian economic structures would indicate that it has become "domesticated," has abandoned the revolution, and that it can now be trusted to further social democracy. All this would imply that the PCI, though internally split and responsive to signals from Moscow—at least in international politics—is attuned to an opinionated, involved, and for the most part informed electorate. Thus the revolutionary stance, I believe, is at least partly a response to the party's perceived chances at the polls. And Mitterrand's success in France, and his policies in relation to the Communists and to the nationalization of industries, is watched by all those Italians who are looking for radical change but don't quite trust the PCI.

Equally cynical about their politicians' and their bankers' honesty, many Italians expected that the recent disclosures, too, would be swept into the Tiber. So even as the proofs of inordinate greed for power and money kept mounting, many of them wondered why neither PCI nor PSI leaders had not long ago asked the "hard" questions that would have indicted dishonest bankers (for the most part Christian-Democrats) along with their government officials—inside or outside P2—and why only so few of the many culprits are being convicted.

Essentially, the Christian-Democrats miscalculated when they called for this recent referendum. Evocation of Don Sturzo's and De Gasperi's names no longer is helpful to politicians whose reputations are soiled, who have proven their incompetence, and who have been in the center of many scandals. The Communists, though considered more honest but less trustworthy, have lost some of their votes and their credibility since 1976, when Eurocommunism began to appear less independent of Moscow than had been claimed, and when it became clear that except for carefully formulated censures of, for instance, the Soviet invasion of Afghanistan, the PCI's foreign policy does not really differ from Moscow's. Italians, it is said, have become too enamored of democracy to swing to the far right, and too disenchanted with the post-1968 left to follow the radicals or the PDUP (a left splinter of the PCI) in large numbers. The Liberals

(PLI) and the Republicans (PRI)—the only parties to have been on the winning side of every one of the five referenda—all along have been considered too parochial, local, or narrow to draw a large constituency. When President Pertini convoked the party leaders to discuss a reshuffling of the government, Craxi, who had discharged PSI functionaries belonging to P2, refused to participate. He wanted to demonstrate that his party stands for honesty, social progress, and Western-style democracy.

Neither Pertini (a Socialist) nor the Christian-Democrats wanted to call a general election, or to be without a government during the June administrative elections—the former because the country would be too long without leadership, and the latter because this would favor the Socialists. They could not manage to form another government, but did prevent Craxi from becoming premier—by favoring PRI's Spadolini. Still, Craxi's tactics paid off: in the June elections he "detached" over 4.5 percent of the voters from the "right" wing of the PCI—Italian Communists who distrust the Soviet Union—and from the "left" of the Christian-Democrats—"progress-oriented" Catholics—to enormously strengthen the PSI. As the trial of the bankers and of other P2 personages progressed, as more and more evidence of corruption surfaced—implicating the heads of banks including the central Banca d'Italia, and connecting Christian-Democrat leaders and party finances to Sindona and Gelli—the need for the type of political and economic policies Craxi advocated became ever more evident. A major shakeup, of course, was long overdue; Italians had talked about it for years; and some of them had even known about P2. But this time there was too much proof, and the press (one of the most prestigious papers, *Corriere della Sera*, and the publisher Angelo Rizzoli had also been implicated) had furnished too much irrefutable evidence. Craxi's enemies—the Communists and radicals who accused him of being a minimalist and a social-democrat, those Christian-Democrats who perceived him as too "socialist," and big entrepreneurs who disliked his egalitarian slant—now attacked him for pushing his own career. He might have made a few more friends recently, by actively backing the Spadolini coalition, and by biding his time. Chances are that he will be asked to form the next government (the present one *is* shaky), or that the PSI will continue to gain adherents should the "anticipated" elections be necessary.

In any event, much will depend upon what happens under French socialism. For Craxi, who was summoned back from Mitterrand's inauguration, is likely to embrace the latter's policies, and to learn from his successes and failures. Because not only is Italy linked to the dollar, but Italians are sensitive to declarations by the American government; much will depend on the ability of our officials to refrain from foolish pronouncements. The perseverance of the prosecutors and the judges in the corruption trials also will be most crucial. But the real decisions, ultimately, are with the Italian electorate, with the same people who, in the recent referendum and in the administrative elections, voted with their conscience and intelligence. The question, basically, is to what extent a maturing electorate can eradicate the chaos and corruption at the top which has been going on for decades.   1981, vol. 48, no. 4

• **Thunder on the Left**
Morris Dickstein

In the middle of October, two momentous though unrelated events took place which may have long-range consequences for the American left. On Columbus Day weekend more than three thousand people jammed the Roosevelt Hotel in New York for the first American Writers Congress since the days of the Popular Front. Ten days later several members of the Weather Underground and the Black Liberation Army were seized after a bloody armed robbery in Nanuet, New York, which left three men dead and many in the radicals' own student generation in a state of shock and revulsion.

Neither event should be discussed in strictly political terms. The Writers Congress, the brainchild of Victor Navasky and his colleagues at *The Nation*, was cosponsored, at least in name, by a wide variety of writers' organizations and periodicals, including *Partisan Review*. Its concerns were divided between bread-and-butter issues affecting writers and more political problems exacerbated by the Reagan administration and the new conservative thrust across the country. As for the robbery and murders, as of this writing no political rationale whatever has been suggested, except for the crude logic of guerrilla warfare and violent confrontation to which these marginal groups, which had seemed dormant and decimated, had long been committed.

But politics involves symbolism along with programs and positions. Part of the success of the early months of the Mitterand presidency in France came from his adroit appeal to the venerable symbolism of the European Socialist tradition and the French left, with its martyrs like Jean Jaurès and Jean Moulin and its watershed moments like the Popular Front victory of 1936. The Brinks robbery was a reminder of a period which many on the left would prefer to forget—the disintegration of the student movement into random violence and destructive rage at the end of the sixties. "The bloody shootout walks into our consciousness like a ghost," Paul Berman wrote in the *Village Voice*. "These bandits are the Miss Havishams of the left, living in the past to the point of madness." In the same issue Alexander Cockburn, trying even harder to distance the Weatherpeople from the legitimate left, compared them to the Japanese soldiers still fighting World War II on some remote Pacific island. Except that those model warriors were not killing anyone, merely waiting for new orders from their emperor.

The symbolism of the Writers Congress proved far less interesting to the mass media, though it was fraught with meaning for those who knew the history of American radicalism. In its meager coverage, the *Times* gave almost as much space to the preemptive salvos of Midge Decter, that tenacious watchdog of the left, as to this extraordinary meeting of three thousand American writers gathered together for the first time in forty years. Like Midge Decter, the organizers of the Congress were well aware that the congresses of the thirties were manipulated by the communists, that they had, as Navasky put it, a "covert political agenda." But a line of continuity was established nonetheless in a keynote address by Meridel LeSueur, an 81-year-old writer who began by recalling the first Congress of 1935 and ended—in a progressive dithyramb to the American heartland—by embodying it. Miss LeSueur, who has labored and languished in obscurity since the thirties, obviously had a knotty integrity of her own. But too many other Congress speakers dampened the enthusiasm of their youngish audiences with a rhetoric as stale as the revolutionary jargon of urban guerrillas. Only an eloquent keynote speech by Toni Morrison rescued the eagerly attended opening session, from which a thousand people had to be turned away. Here at last was a real *writer*, someone with a finely sensual feeling for words.

The favored rhetoric at the Congress was not really Marxist; it was a rhetoric of crisis, less historical than hysterical. Yet the Reagan policies on First Amendment rights, on the domestic role of the CIA and FBI, on the Freedom of Information Act, on Latin America, on the regulatory agencies, on the environment, on taxes, on social programs, on affirmative action, on military spending, and on nuclear weapons lent plausibility to apocalyptic statements that would have seemed grossly exaggerated a year earlier. The political energy of the Congress came less from a resurgent left than from a left up against the wall, angry, frustrated, fighting battles that seemed won thirty years ago. Yet the gathering also demonstrated what a large reservoir of impassioned liberal and radical sentiment survives from the sixties—though, like the Congress itself, it remains below the threshold of media attention. The stingy press coverage only proved what Toni Morrison and others had repeatedly asserted, that as writers the participants were marginal to the life of the country. "We are toys," said Morrison, "things to be played with by little kings who love us while we please, dismiss us when we don't."

The contrast with the sensational coverage of the Brinks holdup was instructive. Without a trace of political theater, with nothing to attract the camera eye but words and more words, the Writers Congress was more old left than new, more interested in mobilizing its participants than in manipulating the media. Yesterday's radical celebrities like Abbie Hoffman passed through the halls of the Congress almost unnoticed. Instead speakers strained, sometimes persuasively, to link the worsening lot of writers with social and economic trends in the nation, especially the concentration of power in the hands of fewer and fewer large corporations.

The most damning testimony against the publishing industry came from those inside it, like Faith Sale, an editor at Putnam's, who eschewed ideological rhetoric but itemized the baleful impact of conglomerates, of large-scale bookstore chains monopolizing distribution, of huge advances to a few books and bottom-line pressures on all the rest. At the end of the Congress an overwhelming majority voted to support the formation of a writers' union. The Congress also took a stand on many political issues, only a few of them—book-burning, censorship, the First Amendment—directly impinging on writers as writers. It left unsettled the question of how those who had been reduced to cogs of the culture industry or dispensable toys would go about saving the world. There was something infectious about the sentiment of solidarity that seized many incorrigible individualists in the course of the proceedings. But it's hard to visualize how these elevating impulses will be translated into action.

Action was what the cohorts of the Weather Underground were presumably committed to, but did any still have the illusion that their hit-and-run tactics, their paltry numbers, and their wanton brutality still contributed to saving the world, or to any other unselfish goal? Whatever the attempts of organizers to mobilize the Congress towards prepared positions, whatever the woolly, politicized language of some of the panelists, the Writers Congress—with a thousand fringe groups clamoring for attention—was as open and disorganized as the cadres of crazed militants were clannish and conspiratorial. Instead of advancing the cause of justice and human dignity, the Brinks murderers have only swollen the arsenal of the right. The specter of a terrorist network will long outlive the network itself.

As always, writers in America are in an isolated position. Insofar as they aim to defend their own interests they are on solid ground. But writers are no more unified on political issues than most professionals; as an organized pressure group they are likely to remain where they began: on the fringe. But that's no reason for them to stop trying.   1982, vol. 49, no. 1

● **Letter from Israel**
Shlomo Avineri

For many observers the Israeli elections of 1977, which brought Menachem Begin to power, seemed like an aberration. Labor's defeat, after thirty years of continuous control of Israel's political life, appeared to be no more than an unfortunate combination of a number of unrelated elements: Rabin's mediocre qualities of leadership, the discovery of corruption among some members of Labor's elite, the internal squabbles between Rabin and Peres, Rabin's own illegal dollar account, the emergence of Yigael Yadin's attractive reform-oriented Democratic Movement for Change—all these contributed to the loss of Labor's plurality. Without any great increase in its own vote, the Likud thus became Israel's largest party and Begin, so it seemed, inherited the premiership not so much due to his party's own strength as to Labor's weakness. The fact that Begin himself was incapacitated during most of the election campaign because of a heart attack contributed to this general feeling that he might not be more than an accidental Prime Minister.

The election results of 1981 have dispelled these illusions almost completely. Just like the 1977 elections, the 1981 campaign had its own paradoxes: the Labor Alignment managed to bounce back, from thirty-two to forty-seven members of Knesset, but this remarkable recovery was not strong enough to unseat Begin. Moreover, Begin participated vigorously throughout the whole campaign and his oratorical skills as a populist tribune became more than evident. The Likud proved itself to be immensely popular among many of the so-called Oriental Jewish voters—the "ethnic" vote made up of immigrants from Muslim countries and their descendants: Moroccan, Iraqi, Yemenite Jews tended to vote for Likud rather than Labor despite their generally lower socioeconomic status. Younger people also tended to vote more for Likud than for Labor, and very strong anti-Labor groundswells were visible and audible during much of the campaign, which became vicious and occasionally even violent in its last stages.

Obviously, some fundamental changes are occurring in Israeli politics, and it is the aim of these comments to put them in some sort of historical perspective. For what occurred in 1977 and then again in 1981 should have come as no surprise. The tendencies that culminated in two Likud electoral victories were visible, albeit on a smaller scale, for several years. They were, however, dismissed as marginal phenomena, and since Labor continued to win all elections until 1977, they were conveniently pushed under the carpet.

Yet as in so many other cases of political change and upheaval, the shift of the periphery to the center of the political scene was a drawn-out process whose first expressions were hardly noticeable and even less appreciated.

There seem to be two major structural developments which have contributed to this realignment of Israel's political forces. The first is a shift in the demographic balance between "European" (Ashkenazi) Jews and "Oriental" (Sephardi) Jews in the country's population. The second is the shift in the political agenda of Israeli society since the Six Days War of 1967. In both cases, the first signs became apparent some years ago: 1977 and 1981 only registered them dramatically on the political map.

First, the demographic shift.

When Israel was established in 1948, its Jewish population numbered about 700,000 people. Out of that number, about eighty-five percent were immigrants from European countries and their descendants, while about fifteen percent were immigrants from Muslim countries and their descendants. Today, Israel's Jewish population is close to 3,500,000: about fifty percent of these are "Europeans," and the other fifty percent are "Orientals." (There is, of course, also the Arab population within Israel's pre-1967 borders which participates in parliamentary elections and makes up between twelve and fourteen percent of the electorate: but the shifts in its voting patterns would require a separate discussion which is outside the scope of these comments.)

Thus the non-European population, which has been marginal in Israeli political life in the first years after its establishment, has now reached the fifty percent mark of Israel's Jewish population. Most of this increase is due to immigration: but because non-European families are generally larger than European ones, the percentage of non-Europeans continues to rise even more among the younger age cohorts in the country. Insofar as this influx of non-European Jews has caught the attention of the media and public opinion outside of Israel, this has generally focused on the socioeconomic dimensions posed by this immigration with its lower socioeconomic status. Yet, despite the fact that, generally speaking, most non-European immigrants are today better off economically and socially than they have been when immigrating, and many of the socioeconomic gaps have been visibly closed, the impact of this new immigration on Israeli life is much wider than can be expressed merely by economic or educational statistics.

The liberal, social-democratic nature of much of Israeli society as it has evolved prior to the establishment of the state and in its first decades owes most of its impetus and character to the European immigrants who were the Founding Fathers (and Mothers) of Israeli society. Labor Zionism was a product of this Eastern and Central European immigration: most of these immigrants came from a more or less secularized background, were imbued with the ideas and heritage of the European enlightenment as reflected in the reawakened Jewish self-consciousness of the massive Jewish communities in and around the Pale of Settlement. Liberal, democratic, and socialist ideas were dominant, and since the 1920s the major political struggles in the Jewish community in Palestine and later in Israel were among the various brands of Labor Zionism. The kibbutzim and moshavim, the Histadruth and the Hagannah were the various expressions of this socialistically oriented tradition, which over the years became synonymous with the emerging "Establishment" of Israeli society. A mixed economy with a strong public and cooperative sector, an egalitarian wage structure, and a basically moderate policy vis-à-vis the Arab population became the hallmarks of this tradition. Out of this ambience, identified with the hegemony of the Labor movement, grew the willingness to accept partition in 1947 and to abide by a situation in which the realization of the Zionist dream would be achieved at the cost of not claiming Jewish control over all of the historical Land of Israel. A vision of social reconstruction coupled with pragmatism in foreign policy emerged as this unique blending of social vision and national moderation.

True, even during the halcyon years of Labor ascendancy there always existed the right-wing nationalism of the Revisionist Party under Jabotinsky, the Irgun, and after 1948, Begin's Herut party (later to become the main component of the Likud). Yet while the Hagannah was a people's militia numbering almost 100,000 members, the Irgun never had more than 5,000 activists; and after Independence, when Begin emerged as a head of a political party, he always remained at the margin of Israel's political life. His party numbered between eight to twenty members in the Knesset, losing eight parliamentary elections in a row between 1949 and 1973.

The emergence of the non-European electorate as a major force in Israeli politics in recent years introduced into the center of the political scene of the country a population coming from a completely different social and intellectual culture. In brief, most non-European immigrants came to Israel from a background that was much more Third World than European.

It is this different cultural background that is sometimes overlooked in many accounts of the changing Israeli scene. The non-European immigrants, coming as they do from "Third-World" Middle Eastern countries, came from highly traditional cultures. Unlike Jewish communities in Europe (and America), the Jewish communities in the Middle East have not gone through 100 or 150 years of secularization, emancipation, and enlightenment; their leadership is still primarily religious and traditional; socialist, revolutionizing Zionist Labor parties were not active among these communities as they have been among Eastern and Central European Jews; most of the "Oriental" immigrants are religiously orthodox, and their family structures remain hierarchical and male-oriented. Egalitarian ideas advocating equality between the sexes as well as between the elders and the youngsters never took root among them; nor did these "Oriental" immigrants come from a political culture in which party politics ever played a significant role. Hence the egalitarian ideas immanent in the Labor ethos never really appealed to many of these immigrants; they react much more positively to the style of hierarchical leadership like that of Begin and are mostly lost in the labyrinthine ideological divisions among the squabbling wings and factions of the Labor Party.

Similarly, a simple, if not simplistic, attitude to the Arab-Israeli conflict such as the one offered by Begin—"This country is either ours, or it is theirs"—strikes a much more responsive chord among the non-European, traditional, and ethnocentric voters than the tortuous compromises of Labor's attempts to square its Zionism with universalist and humanist ideas.

There is a further element, sometimes submerged even in the political consciousness of Israel itself, and this has to do with some general attitudes vis-à-vis the Arabs which can be found among many Jews coming from Arab countries. Some pious hopes have been expressed in the past that with the growing "Sephardization" of Israeli society, new avenues will be open for Jewish-Arab understanding, since "Oriental" Jews, coming themselves from an Arab environment, would be better suited than their Western brethren for an accommodation with the Arab world. PLO propaganda sometimes gave expression to a more malignant version of the same idea, namely, that all the trouble in the Middle East stems from the "European" and "Western" nature of "Ashkenazi Zionism": with the ascent of the "Arab Jews," as the PLO calls them, peace and understanding would triumph.

Reality, however, proved to be much more complex and recalcitrant. Jews coming from Arab countries do come from an Arab environment: yet they bring with them not only knowledge of the Arab language and acquaintance with Arab music, but also memories, personal and collective, of centuries of persecution and discrimination at the hands of Arab and Muslim majorities. Though the Muslim world was generally free from anything like the rabid brands of European anti-Semitism, Jews in Muslim countries—like all other non-Muslim minorities—were subjected to discrimination, humiliation, and occasional persecution. The civic discrimination of non-Muslims is basic to Muslim societies and codified in Islamic law, and anti-Jewish pogroms became even more frequent with the rise of Arab radical nationalism which sometimes took on quite xenophobic features. Jews coming from Iraq or Yemen have carried with them the scars of these personal and historical memories just as European Jews carried with them the imprint of Ukrainian pogroms and Nazi persecution.

While for most European Jews in Israel the Arab-Israeli conflict remained primarily a political conflict, basically free from the bitterness of historical memories and resentments, for many "Oriental" Jews the conflict is imbued with overtones of precisely such historical dimensions. And just as European Jews can be understood—if not necessarily forgiven—for not harboring particularly fond emotions about Cossacks, so many Jews immigrating from Arab countries continue likewise to carry with them an anti-Arab resentment which is then translated into more hawkish attitudes about the Arab-Israeli conflict. Bluntly put, for many Middle Eastern Jews the Arabs are the historical oppressors, the *goyim*. No wonder that while many European Jews do agonize about the degree to which the PLO may represent some elements of the Palestinian right to self-determination despite its terroristic activities, for most "Oriental" Jews the PLO is nothing else than a continuation of a familiar Arab enmity towards the Jews. And when an Iraqi nuclear reactor is hit by Israel, few European Jews in Israel view it in a context of a complex and long reckoning between the Jews and Iraqi nationalism that has ousted 100,000 Jews from Iraq and sequestered their property: for many "Oriental" Jews this is precisely the context in which such an Israeli act should be viewed. No wonder that the bombing of the Iraqi reactor was immensely much more popular among non-European voters than among European ones; nor should it come as a surprise that the "Peace Now" movement has yet to show any significant support among the Sephardi population: it is almost exclusively made up of "Europeans."

Public opinion polls suggest that on all issues related to the Arab-Israeli conflict, "Oriental" Jews tend to hold much more hawkish attitudes than "European" ones. With the spread of secondary and higher education among the "Oriental" population, such hawkish views tend to diminish somehow, yet they remain still more hawkish than the views of "Europeans" with comparable education. Even within the Labor Party, most "Oriental" members of Knesset belong to the more hawkish wing of the party.

All these elements combined together to bring about the situation in which Labor tended to be much weaker in recent elections among "Oriental" voters than among "European" ones, and Likud tended to draw most of its support from the "Oriental" vote. In the 1981 elections, seventy percent of the Labor vote came from the "European" electorate, and only thirty percent from "Oriental" voters. In the Likud, the obverse picture obtains: sixty-eight percent of the Likud voters were "Oriental" and only thirty-two percent were "European." These trends have been visible for more than a decade, but with the growth of the "Oriental" vote, as well as with their growing emancipation from the Labor-dominated bureaucracy, which to a large extent influenced and directed their vote in their first years of immigration, when they were still newcomers and not always familiar with the mechanics of election, the decisive impact of this shift has only now come to be felt as perhaps the dominant feature of the Israeli political scene.

The paradox of this is, of course, that Menachem Begin, the idol of the "Oriental" electorate, could not be less of an "Oriental" himself. With his conservative suits, his proper ties and cufflinks, his frequent Latin quotations ("*status quo ante*," "*pacta sunt servanda*," "*habemus pacem*"), nobody could be further removed from the ambience of the "Oriental" masses than this scion of the Russo-Polish Jewish Pale of Settlement. The nationalist, ethnocentric, tradition-oriented, and hierarchical style of leadership projected by Begin is nonetheless admirably suited to the emotional and cultural horizons of the "Oriental" electorate whose power is growing and will continue to grow in Israeli politics. To those who always bemoaned Israel's "Western" nature and hoped for its integration into the Middle East, Begin is the cruel answer: Israel now has a leader better suited to the nature of its growing Middle Eastern Jewish population, and is thus more "integrated" into the Middle East than under Ben Gurion, Eshkol, and Golda Meir, with their Western, social democratic, and universalist ideas. It is, though, an integration into the real not the imaginary Middle East, into a Middle East that prefers hierarchical styles of leadership, into a Middle East where populist nationalism is much more popular than universalist humanism. With a vengeance, Israel has been integrated into that Middle East, and Begin, incredible as it may seem, is the symbol of this Israeli relative integration into the Third World. What a cruel twist to the hidden hand of the Cunning of Reason.

The second fundamental change in Israeli politics in recent years has been the shift in the focus of the political agenda of the country.

Until 1967, there existed a widely held consensus on foreign policy issues in Israel. The partition of Palestine has been widely accepted as the best possible deal open to Zionism, and even Begin and his party have toned down over the years their claims for the whole of Eretz Israel. Before Nasser's catastrophic moves in May 1967, nobody in Israel seriously challenged the frontiers that were established in the wake of the 1949 armistice agreements between Israel and her Arab neighbors. Had the Arab states agreed before 1967 to transform these armistice lines into permanent and recognized borders, there would have been an overwhelming consensus in Israel for the acceptance of such a proposal.

The political debate in Israel between 1949 and 1967 was consequently focused on internal issues. Occasionally, as in 1956 during the Suez campaign, foreign affairs came up, but even then a widely held consensus ruled supreme. The main public concerns, as reflected in the press, in public debates, election campaigns, and the like, were problems of immigration, integration, nation-building, economic development, housing, education, retraining of newcomers, the development and opening up of new areas (like the Negev)—in short, the focus was on those issues of internal policies in which a social-democratic party with a strong commitment to nation-building enjoyed an obvious advantage. To an immigrant just freshly arrived either from the Displaced Persons camps in Europe or from a ghetto in Yemen, these were the issues that appeared pressing and relevant for him and his family. Labor had both the machinery of government at its disposal as well as the ideological and symbolical language to tackle these problems: the Ingathering of the Exiles, the Melting Pot, Making the Desert Blossom—these were the public slogans widely accepted in those years. For a newcomer still struggling to read the roadsigns leading from Tel-Aviv to Haifa, an impassioned plea by a person like Begin for the inalienable historical rights of the Jewish people to Jericho or Tul-Karm did not make much sense. And indeed, between 1949 and 1967 the Begin-style nationalist appeal appeared mostly irrelevant, and while Begin's party managed to hold on to the stalwart support of most erstwhile Irgun members, it never broke through on a massive scale.

The year 1967 changed all this very drastically: with Israel in control of all his-torical Eretz Israel west of the Jordan River, the questions that had appeared to have been settled once and for all in 1948 were reopened again. Domestic issues were put on the back burner, and ever since 1967 the constant debate in Israeli public life has centered around issues dealing with problems of nationalism. Since the aftermath of the Six Day War is still open-ended, and the issues—ter-ritorial and other—raised by the war have not been settled, they are constantly at the center of Israeli public debate: what are the justifications for Israeli claims to Judea and Samaria; what should be Israel's policies towards the Palestinians; what should the future boundaries of Israel be; should Jewish settlements be set up in the "territories"; how should Israel react to PLO terrorism—through a willingness to negotiate with the Palestinians or through the iron fist, etc.

In all these questions, the simple "Us versus Them" approach expressed by the Likud has—on balance—a much greater chance of getting across than the complex approach of Labor, which tries to balance Zionism with universalist values and strike a middle road between socialist ideas and defense considera-tions. Young people who have grown into maturity since 1967 have been exposed to the constant barrage of public debate on these issues rather than on internal problems, and have been sensitized to the centrality of these problems to the concerns of the nation rather than to the centrality of questions of social justice. For young people, the psychological map of Israel is that of the post-1967 situation, in which you roam freely over the West Bank, Sinai, and the Golan: older people, whose psychological map of the country was molded in the 1949–1967 period, are much more conscious of the pre-1967 borders and their political and demographical consequences. Nor are exhortations about the Jewish historical rights to Jericho and Tul-Karm merely abstruse claims any more, as they were before 1967: these places are real and visible, many young Israelis spent their army years in their vicinity, and the newcomers have been absorbed into society in a way that makes it possible for them to follow these debates with comprehension.

One of the results of this shift in the political agenda is that people who grew up in the post-1967 atmosphere tend to support Likud on balance more than older people. Israeli universities offer an unusual paradox: most of the faculty tend to be liberal and left-wing, while the student activists, who managed to capture most of the student organizations at the universities, are right-wing supporters.

Those Labor supporters who tried to console themselves after the elections that Likud's victory was merely an outcome of Begin's personality, now have to contend with these long-range developments. They also have to face the fact that after Begin's disappearance, the Likud will possess a number of popular possible successors: Ariel Sharon, the Minister of Defense, is certainly not the darling of the Israeli left wing, but he is immensely popular in the country; David Levy, the deputy prime minister and minister of housing, is a young Moroccan textile worker from a development town in the north, who represents the populist support for the Likud among "Oriental" blue-collar workers; and Yoram Aridor, the minister of finance, who through the introduction of tax cuts and reduction of import duties helped to create a consumer boom in the country, albeit at the cost of long-range problems. This is a powerful trio, and Labor is still at a loss to supply new faces to counter them: the old, tired leadership of Labor is not exactly appealing to those who really want a change.

Does all this mean that Labor has no chance in the future? Certainly not. After all, the parliamentary strength of Labor is almost equal to that of the Likud, and Begin's coalition has a threadbare majority in the Knesset. Yet even were Labor to win the next elections, it would not return to its former position as an unchallenged hegemonic party with no viable opposition to replace it—as Labor has been for almost three decades under Ben Gurion, Eshkol, and Golda Meir. Now a very strong populist right wing would face such a Labor-dominated government, and Labor has not yet found an adequate answer on how to address itself to the new electorate and the new political agenda. Since their defeat in 1977, Labor's leaders have been too preoccupied with their return to power and have consequently neglected the onerous task of rebuilding the party and revamping the whole Labor establishment. The Histadruth, the kibbutzim, the moshavim—all these flowers of Labor Zionism—have, over the years, become top-heavy with conservative and unimaginative bureaucracies; Peres and Rabin have come to leadership positions through bureaucratic in-fighting, not through public confrontations with popular tribunes like Begin.

Obviously, the present leadership does not have the qualities, and the stomach, for such an excruciating fight; it reacts bureaucratically and diplomatically to each new surprise Begin is able to bring up—the bombing of the Iraqi reactor, the Golan Law—without imagination and vigor. By trying to sound *ministeriable*, it neglects to deal with the changing infrastructure of Israeli society.

It took the French left wing twenty-three years to come back to power in France after de Gaulle's coup in 1958. It will probably take less time for the Israeli left wing to do so: but it will not be a return to the idyllic unquestioned hegemony of the historical Labor establishment. Something fundamental has changed in Israeli society, and the Likud with its populist nationalism gives it—for better or for worse—an authentic expression. A different Israel has emerged from the Ingathering of the Exiles which took place in the context of a Thirty Years War. None of the dreamers of Zionism had ever thought that such would be the context of their dream's realization: but this is the real Israel, with half its Jewish population being more Third World than European, living in the real, and not always very pleasant, Middle East. It has not become a Sparta or a Prussia, but obviously some of its Athenian or Weimarian qualities have been attenuated.

It is to this changing nature of Israeli society that a new Israeli left-wing movement will have to address itself. The historical Labor movement does not seem at the moment able to carry this burden, and a new left has not yet appeared. Depressing as it may sound, Begin's Second Republic does not appear at the moment to be seriously challenged.   1982, vol. 49, no. 1

• Israeli Letter
Robert S. Wistrich

The orgy of denunciation that has greeted Israel's actions during the recent Lebanese war, and in particular the concerted campaign to brand Zionism as a new type of Nazism, confronts Jews everywhere with a difficult challenge. The accusations are not in themselves novel—indeed, for many years Soviet and Arab anti-Zionist propaganda has sought to stigmatize the Israelis (and those who identify with them) as "heirs to Hitler"—but never before have they obtained such a sympathetic hearing in the Western media. There is no doubt that this campaign has been politically motivated and that it is part of a persistent, remorseless strategy by the enemies of Israel to undermine the legitimacy of the Jewish state, its moral basis, and the support it still enjoys among Jews and non-Jews alike. The campaign would not have enjoyed such resonance, however, were it not for the more long-term shift that has been taking place in perceptions of Israel and the Jewish people by the outside world. If one is to combat the new anti-Zionism effectively, it is imperative to understand the deeper reasons for this shift and the extent to which one can hope to bring about a fairer and more sympathetic attitude toward the raison d'être of the Jewish state. In particular, it is important to focus our attention on the uses and abuses of the Holocaust trauma, not only by the enemies of Israel but also, at times, by its supporters.

The Lebanese war, it must be admitted, has seriously eroded the image of the Jew as an underdog or persecuted victim, an image that reached its peak in the aftermath of the Holocaust but began to disintegrate after Israel's lightning military victory of 1967. In the eyes of the world David has now become Goliath, the oppressed Jew has become the oppressor of Palestinians, the paradigmatic victims of history have become ruthless victors. As a result, contemporary anti-Semitism centers on the theme of Jewish arrogance, and hatred of Israel expresses itself in the name of the "wretched of the earth," the humble, the suffering, and the vanquished. But the new anti-Semitism is still sufficiently embarrassed by the term *Jew*, with its emotive historical associations of Holocaust and mass murder, to avoid its use where possible. Zionism, especially in its current incarnation, has in this sense been a godsend, for it makes possible a sense of self-satisfied innocence among those enemies of Israel who claim only to be against imperialism, racism, oppression, etc. That this anti-Zionism is nothing but an alibi is apparent when one looks at the indiscriminate terrorist attacks against Jewish synagogues and other targets in Paris, Brussels, Antwerp, Vienna, Milan, Rome, and other European cities—a murderous violence against defenseless Jews unprecedented since World War II. This terrorist nihilism threatens the very fabric of the Western democracies more than it does Israel itself and is the inevitable price that the West will continue to pay as long as it pursues its politics of appeasement of the Arab world. It seems to me that, in fighting such forms of anti-Zionism (which is a life-and-death interest for the democracies as well as for Israel and the Diaspora), not enough has been done to expose the fact that terrorism is a *universal* threat for which Israel merely serves as a convenient pretext. The fashionable anti-Zionism currently trumpeted by the Western media, which subliminally legitimizes terrorism, is in effect no less of a destabilizing, antidemocratic, and corrupting factor than was the antisemitism-for-export of the Third Reich in the 1930s and 1940s. In the long term the only beneficiaries of this vicious campaign can be the enemies of the West—the Soviet Union, the Islamic fundamentalists, and the radical forces of the Arab and Third worlds.

Apart from the issue of terrorism and the struggle for world opinion, there is no doubt that the Holocaust, more than any other past event, has become a political card, though one that in recent years has begun to rebound against Israel and Diaspora Jewry. From the standpoint of Israel's enemies and of anti-Semites everywhere, the mass murder of European Jewry and the backlash of sympathy it created after 1945 has always constituted an intense irritant to their objectives, conferring a kind of maddening immunity from criticism or attack on the objects of their hatred. For Israel's own leaders it provided, if not the raison d'être of the Jewish state, at least a major argument in favor of Zionism and a source of support (much of it admittedly guilt-ridden) from Western Christians. For Jews all over the world, the Holocaust's message was also essentially a pro-Zionist one. Never again must the Jewish people be defenseless, never again must they rely solely on the goodwill or "toleration" of non-Jews, never again should Jews take lightly the verbal rhetoric of anti-Semitism—the avowed intent to destroy them as a nation.

Today, there is no denying the sad fact that Hitler's crimes have become part of the merciless propaganda struggle between partisans and adversaries of Zionism. The latter have generally and one-sidedly emphasized the innocence of the Arabs in the Nazi crimes against Jewry and the injustice committed by the West in making them pay for its own guilty conscience. More recently, however, both the Arabs and the West (especially Europe), by comparing Israel's treatment of the Palestinians with Nazi oppression of Jews, have conspired to turn the Holocaust *against* its victims, both parties thereby trying to free themselves of their historic guilt. The genocide of World War II has been turned in obscene fashion into a metaphor for Israeli actions in Lebanon and against the Arabs in general. All Hitler's sins, including racism, are being projected onto the Jewish state, which is described as holding itself above the law, acting with absolute impunity and disdain for moral values, and wreaking vengeance on its "innocent" Arab neighbors, driven by the conviction of its own superiority and divine chosenness.

This inversion of history, this imprisonment of the present in the past, is not easy to combat, because it clearly fulfills deep needs in the Western world, which, despite its democratic values, remains essentially Christian in its culture and its perceptions of the Jewish people. The continuing orgy of accusations against Israel postulates a kind of a priori guilt of the Jews—in this case the "Christ-killers" have become "mass murderers" of Palestinians. Just as Roman guilt for the crucifixion of Jesus was transferred to the Jews, so Israel was blamed by large segments of world opinion for the murders carried out by Christian militias in Sabra and Shatilla. For a part of the Christian West, as for the Arabs, the Soviets, and the Third World, the Israelis are the new Romans in Palestine or, rather, the new Nazis. Israel control of the West Bank becomes the Occupation, calling to mind the Nazi occupation of Europe in World War II; the PLO becomes the Resistance fighting the Occupiers; Beirut becomes the Warsaw ghetto; Lebanon itself is transformed into Lidice, the Czech village wiped off the earth as a reprisal by the Nazis, or else into Oradour-sur-Glâne, where the SS massacred innocent French civilians in 1944.

By force of repetition, banalization, and trivialization, the reality of the Holocaust is slipping away and losing its substance. Every brutal action is reduced to the same level; every massacre, bombardment, or military operation in which civilians lose their lives becomes a "genocide." We have reached a point where, in the West, every minority group that wants to be taken seriously— blacks, homosexuals, women, etc.—must claim that it has experienced its own unique version of cultural genocide—not to mention the many national and political causes that use the same hyperbole. The Nazi Holocaust, an *exceptional* phenomenon by any standard, even in the long history of anti-Semitism, thus becomes *typical*—the touchstone and archetype by which others, first and foremost the Palestinians, stake their claim on the world's conscience. Unless it fights this parody of the past, which mocks the Holocaust and reduces it to a mere metaphor, Israel will inevitably lose one of its most precious assets in forging its own consciousness of a common fate—namely, the sense of the uniqueness of Jewish suffering and of the unique wickedness of the total extermination directed against the Jewish people. No other people, before or since, not the Russians,

Poles, Czechs, Gypsies, or Armenians—and certainly not the Palestinians today—have had to face the threat of complete physical annihilation. Only in the case of the Nazi "Final Solution" were all utilitarian considerations of loss or gain, of *Realpolitik*, military strategy, and economics, utterly disregarded in pursuit of an uncompromising exterminatory drive.

All attempts, therefore, to transpose the Nazi horror to the Middle East, to fantasize the Israelis as Nazis, or the Palestinians as hunted Jews, are the product either of sheer ignorance and stupidity, cynical political calculation, or deliberate anti-Semitism. No one has imposed the Yellow Star on the Palestinians in Lebanon or in Judea and Samaria; they are not forcibly kept and starved to death in ghettos; sentenced to exhausting hard labor, or methodically gassed in extermination camps. (Indeed, when Lebanese Christians carried out a small-scale massacre of Palestinians in Sabra and Shatilla, this provoked the largest protest demonstration in Israel's history, much to the astonishment of the Phalange and the Arab world as a whole.)

Why then the special fervor of the mass media in stigmatizing the Lebanese war as a calculated act of "genocide" and implying that this was Mr. Begin's "Final Solution" to the Palestinian problem—which can only mean the physical liquidation of the Palestinian people? Is not this brazen mendacity a form of anti-Jewish blackmail, an attempt to taint and intimidate in advance any supporter of Israel with the odium of siding with executioners? The sad truth is that a significant number of Jews throughout the Diaspora, many of them sensitive, well-intentioned, and by no means unintelligent, have fallen for this maneuver and prematurely rushed to produce their certificates of divorce from Israel.

What appears to have affected such Jews, apart from the audiovisual spectacular of nightly Israeli bombing raids on color television, was the charge, shrewdly if hypocritically laid by the Western quality press, that the Jewish state was somehow no longer "Jewish." Suddenly the *idea* of Judaism, its universalist ethics and moral standards, became a matter of intense concern to non-Jews, insofar as it could be turned *against* Zionism. An Israel flexing its muscles must by definition be a betrayal of the Jewish "mission" even if military might, in the volatile conditions of the Middle East, proves to be a sine qua non of Jewish physical survival. Admittedly, the Israel of Mr. Begin and Mr. Sharon is some considerable distance removed from the visions of the Hebrew prophets, the ethics of the Baal Shem Tov, and the prudent maxims of our Jewish sages and rabbinical scholars. Indeed, not a few people within Israel would also argue that even by the standards of secular Zionism the present government has "betrayed" much of what was truly liberal, tolerant, and humanistic in the Jewish national renaissance. Whether this is really the case is not the purpose of this article to judge. What can be fairly charged against Mr. Begin is that his demagogic misuse of the Holocaust is *one* (though by no means the only or even the central) reason for the readiness of many non-Jews (and even Jews) to believe the wildest charges made against Israel. For many years Mr. Begin has used the Holocaust as a political weapon, encouraging the equation of Arafat with Hitler and of the PLO with the Nazis—the kind of false analogy that has now so cruelly backfired against Israel. Certainly Arafat and Hitler have had one aim in common—to kill Jews. But in terms of their general ideology, the means at their disposal, the balance of forces, and the basis of their conflict with the Jewish people—all comparison is gratuitous and an insult to the capacity of the Israel Defense Forces.

The propagandist inflation of the PLO into an omnipotent monster is in its own way symmetrical with the anti-Zionist obsession with an occult Jewish power and ironically obscures the central lesson of the Holocaust for the Jewish people—namely, that the existence of a strong Israel is the main shield against its recurrence. From a condition of total powerlessness the Jews have within less than forty years acquired a healthy modicum of power through the State of Israel, without which national survival would have proven very problematic in the modern world. This power, if used wisely, can forge the basis for coexistence with the Arab nations and the Palestinians in the Middle East. For such a *modus vivendi* to take place, it is incumbent on Israeli leaders as well as the Arabs to free themselves from the traumas of the past, from the mythologizing of history and the "demonologizing" of the enemy. It is no less the duty of the Western world to atone for its long history of racist oppression against Jews and Arabs by building confidence between the two sides instead of abjectly succumbing to anti-Zionist myths and unforgivably legitimizing a new wave of anti-Jewish violence on European soil.

The connection between the Holocaust and the Arab-Israeli conflict is a complex one that has not yet reached its conclusion. But unless the correct conclusions are drawn and the parties concerned succeed in extricating themselves from its shadow, we are likely in this age of thermonuclear war to arrive at a final solution to end all final solutions—one in which there are no victors and no vanquished.   1983, vol. 50, no. 1

• ### Gratitude to Our Former Rulers
Vassily Aksyonov

(excerpted from *Writers in Exile: A Conference of Soviet and East European Dissidents*, May 7 and 8, 1982, at Boston University)

It seems I was once a young writer and I am still a young writer. Some are so lucky to be ever-green writers.

Thinking of my own destiny as a writer and of my own past, I feel I should confess my feelings of gratitude to the Communist rulers of my country. First of all, I thank them for the frustration they suffered after the death of their idols in 1953. For a period of fifteen years after that time, they could not find a new style. Thanks to this frustration, my generation had the opportunity to express itself in literature, in art, and even in politics. While they discussed questions like the "cult of personality" and its aftermath, "socialism with or without a human face"—or with or without human maxims—socialist realism with shores or without, etc., we were writing books, sculpting, painting, playing jazz. The post-Stalin Communists were so diffident that they saw, even in the armed crackdown in Budapest, an "overbending of a stick"—the dreadful consequences of the personality cult that could have been avoided if . . . if . . . if . . . . Not to mention Krushchev's hooligan attack on young literature and art in 1963. That was a definite mistake of the so-called voluntaristic leadership, accused the collective wisdom of our Party. Even in 1966, when Siniavsky and Daniel were on trial, some of the rulers were uncertain about what they were doing.

They were frustrated even more after the unexpected protests by many of the new intelligentsia. The frustration was so deep that some of the rulers were reluctant to see the KGB as the best tutor for writers. The KGB of that time was rather timid in its relationship with literary circles. The criminal persecution of disobedient authors has generally been regarded as the survival of the old style rather than the brilliant discovery of contemporary life, the new splendor of the so-called highly advanced and ripe socialism.

In other words, I would thank them for the happiness I experienced. I experienced this fantastic state of mind, this happiness, taking part in the movement of the Soviet sixties. I was twice as happy as long as this unbelievable period of Soviet life coincided with my youth. I belonged to a generation born in the thirties, on the crest of revolutionary violence, when in Russia and Germany two kinds of socialism were simultaneously blooming. Should I thank and praise those "Cheka" officers who had taken my parents to jail and put me in an orphanage? Probably I should, because otherwise I would have run the risk of becoming one of them—either a ruler or a watchdog. After the great purges of the thirties, we—a thoroughly edited generation—were supposed to become the ideal slaves, but thanks to this loss of style, the result of the editing turned out to be the opposite of what had been expected.

In the sixties, the writers of our generation became known as the new voices of Russia. We looked to world literature, already mesmerized and inspired by the new ideas, new sounds, new smells, and all that jazz of the renaissance. Sure, it was a timid and feeble one, but nonetheless a renaissance indeed. And those who lived during those exciting periods of human history might know the touch of Fortune's wing. I read in an article by a surprisingly young Moscow writer that during the sixties he got up every morning with a strong feeling of the growing feast—a feeling of freedom broadening and deepening one's perception of independence. Formerly, it went without saying that a Soviet writer had to develop a sort of deviant conscience; to submit to the countless Soviet prejudices as if it were necessarily a big handicap for him to live in the ethical sphere; to omit any painful questions; to be an inspiring liar for the sake of the great idea. Our generation entered the literary stage with a vague perception of honesty, and—what is probably more important—without a clearly formulated aesthetic, without which you can hardly achieve a full scale of expression of anything, including honesty.

It sounds paradoxical, but while the years were passing by and the writers were getting older, any possibility for compromise was shrinking. And the feeling of freedom was also growing. Maturity brought about more courage and more determination. From time to time, it even seemed that we would overcome. I thank our watchdogs for their weakness in those times, which produced such happy false feelings. For surely our life has consisted of a mixture of false and true feelings, which is, believe me, the great fertilizer of poetry and prose. Alas, our generation has left behind a horrible memory of terror and Gulag, and it is hard to sustain the carnival mood of renaissance with a memory like this. Alexander Blok has written:

Those who were born during the deaf times
fail to recall their path.
We, the children of Russia's horror years,
cannot forget anything.

The contraposition of "the deaf times" and "the horror years" implies that by *deaf*, the poet meant the quiet, peaceful years. Without memory, literature is dead. "Old wounds are hidden treasures," Yuri Trifonov once said. From this perspective, I would dare say that Russia is not a bad country for a writer: we've never suffered from a surplus of tranquility. There is definitely a lack of "deaf times," and a good deal of wounds and of "horror years." So, once again, we have sufficient reason to thank our rulers.

One can hardly regard that false renaissance period as deaf. Nevertheless, our memory has not been totally awakened. I have often asked myself, Why was I so reluctant for so long to put my memory into motion? Why did I not recall the landscape of Magadan, with its watchtowers, the thousands of prisoners under escort, my mother's [Evgenia Ginsberg] face in the window of the KGB car. . . ? I used to lull myself: "It's not yet time for recollections like these." And apparently it wasn't. Obviously I had a sort of subconscious feeling that this gloomy memory would be out of place in our village feast; it could damage the carnival mood of our generation.

The end of this Soviet serenity has an exact date: August 21, 1968, the night of The Fraternal Assistance for our Czechoslovakian Brothers. That was a turning point for post-Stalin Communists; they reached the end of their search for a new style. That was also a great moment for us. The invasion brought about some advantages for the writers: it killed our naive illusions and Don Quixotic dreams, and, at the same time, it renewed our memory, revived those old hidden wounds which were necessary for the next step in our writing. Needless to say, not all writers have dared to take the next step, and those who did not extended their self-indulgence to a recipe for supreme happiness.

Not very long ago, I watched on Moscow television a ceremony honoring some talented writers and artists with highly distinguished state awards, formerly known as the Stalin awards. I was struck by a statement made by one of those honored, a former friend of mine: "The supreme happiness for any creative man is reached when his intentions coincide with the intentions of his government." This is a really fresh, fruitful idea, isn't it? If you tried to develop it from different positions, you would find, surprisingly, a utopian core. But eventually you would get tangled up in a number of contradictions. I really thank the rulers of my country for making their intentions and deeds so ugly that I never had any desire to make my intentions coincide with theirs. I used to consider myself a Western type of writer—a storyteller, an entertainer, a belle-lettrist rather than a master of thoughts in traditional Russian fashion. Thanks to their bloodthirsty slogan— "Those who are not with us are against us"—many authors became more Russian in regard to the "civic emotions."

What about politics? Unfortunately, you cannot avoid it if you are a Russian writer. Whatever we write turns into politics—if it is not "with them." On the other hand, thanks to their hyperbolic stupidity, it becomes advantageous to develop that wonderful style of "the empty page." Here is one of the newest jokes from Moscow, via satellite: One fellow decided to spread anti-Communist leaflets in Moscow. But when he was captured by the KGB agents, the leaflets turned out to be empty. "Why didn't you put down anything in your leaflet?" he was asked by an interrogator. "What for?" he shrugged. "Everybody knows everything."

By the beginning of the seventies, this period of frustration was over; a new style of leadership was found. It was named "the highly developed and ripe socialist society." And once again we had an occasion for more thanksgiving. Thank you for crossing *t*'s and dotting *i*'s, dear comrades. We used to think that your favorite activity was tightening screws; now we realize that you are really working for the future. Once and for all we realize that you mean business when you talk about "the creation of a new man." Thanks to your contemporary style, everyone can easily recognize the face of this new creature.

Our writers used to go to distant lands looking for new adventures. Under the Communists' sponsorship, literature itself has turned into a dangerous adventure—a sort of conspiracy, a matter of smuggling. So if you've heard something about the Russian Connection, please keep in mind that it concerns books rather than drugs. If one were to read a mere chronology of the so-called Metropol affair, one would be carried away as if by a thriller. From time to time, the rulers fight literature fiercely, as though the whole existence of their system were at stake. Whether we should thank them for this parochial overestimation of literature or not. . . . Anyway, I indulged myself by talking with high-ranking officers who came to warn me about one of my books. I thank them for so many privileges, as well as for kicking me out of their society and depriving me of their so-called citizenship.

One can imagine that the process of turning from an internal émigré into an external one is pretty natural in these days of wild metamorphoses. After emigration, you find yourself in a deafening silence, as if you had left behind a sound barrier in a jet flight. At first you feel discharged, but on second thought, you may suppose that emigration came to you on time. At last you are out of this damn Marxist ideological debauchery, as well as out of your indecent, clumsy struggle against it. For the first time in your life, you are able to feel the sweet temptation of being out of any recruitment—an adventure of solitude, the life of a vagrant juggler. Alas, you are not young anymore! But even so, from time to time at least, you can listen to the tune of that music you always dreamed of. So once again, I would like to express my profound gratitude to my former rulers, as well as to Marx, Engels, Lenin, Stalin, Krushchev, and Brezhnev, for helping me to become a writer. I have never desired any other destiny.

(Translated by John Glad)

1983, vol. 50, no. 3

• The Polish Spring
Jeffrey Herf

(This essay was delivered at Jagiellonian University, Cracow, Poland, on May 5, 1989.)

In 1964, the American new left adopted the slogan "a free university in a free society." In that time and place, it was a highly inappropriate slogan. We already enjoyed free universities in a free society. But here at Jagiellonian University in Cracow in spring 1989 it is appropriate for us to express the hope that you will attain a free university in a free society.

This year is the bicentennial of the French Revolution, an event which casts its spell on Poland and on the United States. It gave to modern politics the idea of revolution, of a sudden, dramatic, and violent—above all violent—break with the past. From this break was supposed to emerge a wholly new society and new man and new woman. Today, after the catastrophes of twentieth-century revolutions, the luster of the revolutionary idea has worn off in the West, not least of all in France itself. Nevertheless, outsiders may be tempted to interpret change in Poland in light of the two-centuries-old image of revolution, the sudden and violent break that denotes the "before" and "after."

You know better. Assuming that the changes of this spring become a permanent feature of Polish politics and society, the Polish spring of 1989 will cast its spell around the world as well. Your country has shown itself and the world that meaningful change from dictatorship to greater democracy can take place without "the revolution," without political murder, without the myth of human beings remade, and without dehumanizing hatred justifying violence. What message could be more important to people now seeking to free themselves from dictatorship? How much better it would be if Poland of 1989 were to displace France of 1789 in the political imagination of those all over the world who seek to displace dictatorship and poverty with democracy and economic well-being.

In the iconography of politics, you have replaced the violent mob and machine gun with the conversation and the conference table as effective means of political change. You have shown that there is a heroism and intelligence to a policy of many small steps, of moderation, and of talking rather than shooting. You have demonstrated political possibility where cynical realists would abandon hope. These are images and messages that need to be heard, especially where the romance of 1789 and 1917 has not yet expired. So at the outset, I want to express our admiration for your courage and persistence, and our congratulations for your accomplishment.

All of us who have come to talk to you this week share a youthful leftist radicalism from which we have distanced ourselves. We have "deradicalized" ourselves. That means that we, too, came to reject the images of 1789 and 1917 for the more prosaic and humane practices of classical political liberalism, practices such as talking, arguing, compromising, and tolerating those who disagree. On the path of deradicalization, we read a great deal, just as we had on our previous path of radicalization. The difference, of course, is that we read better books the second time around, books like Czeslaw Milosz's *The Captive Mind* and *Native Realm* and Leszek Kolakowski's *Main Currents of Marxism* and his superb response to the British and American new left of the 1960s, "My Correct Views on Everything." Both Milosz and Kolakowski, in piercing the totalitarian faith in History and the total reshaping of human beings at the hands of a political project, found common ground with deradicalizing American intellectuals of the 1950s, and with us deradicalizing intellectuals of the 1970s and 1980s.

Our intellectual debts to the Polish struggle against totalitarianism began long before 1989. In the 1960s, when Jean-Paul Sartre was setting the intellectual fashion and "revolutionary violence" was in vogue, it was Milosz, Kolakowski, and other Polish intellectuals who came to the defense of the then out-of-fashion liberal values of European civilization. In the 1960s, when Western intellectuals were turning against liberal values of tolerance and peaceful change, Polish and Eastern European intellectuals reinvigorated those traditions. In the early 1980s, when many Western intellectuals, especially in West Germany, Britain, and the United States, found it difficult to make moral distinctions between "both superpowers," Solidarity was a constant reminder that the issue of peace could not be separated from the issue of freedom. When these same intellectuals took political freedom for granted, dissidents from Eastern Europe and the Soviet Union were a constant reminder of how precious it is. Now, let us hope, political realities will catch up with the temporarily suppressed but never extinguished sense of European civilization. This "common European home" stretches across the Atlantic to include the United States. It is really a common Western home, though its values have been institutionalized most firmly in Western Europe and the United States.

We Americans with our "second thoughts" about the new left have drawn conclusions about capitalism, democracy, and the role of the United States in international politics that parallel some of the thinking in Cracow, the center of political and economic liberalism in Poland. The memories of Auschwitz-Birkenau that have haunted us must haunt you as well, offering yet another common ground on which a freer and more democratic Poland can reach out to the United States, and to Israel. It is to this common ground, to these glimmers of hope after so much catastrophe, that I will now turn.

Capitalism and Democracy

Discussion of dissidence in Eastern Europe in recent years has understandably concentrated on the realization of human rights and political freedom. If these rights continue to be realized, the issue of how politics and economics are related to one another will move closer to center stage. You are and will be faced with having to decide what you think about capitalism. For the past century in the West, many intellectuals, both inside and outside the Marxist tradition, assumed that capitalism was a barrier to the realization of genuine democracy because political institutions merely reflected the interests of dominant classes. For leftist intellectuals in the United States and Western Europe one of the appeals of East European dissidence and opposition, including Solidarity, was that such movements would bring into being the long hoped for "third way" of blending socialism and democracy. If by socialism we mean only "social democracy" as practiced in Western Europe or in the Democratic Party in the United States, then, of course, it is perfectly compatible with parliamentary democracy. But we deradicalized intellectuals concluded that if socialism meant state-planned economies, then it certainly was not compatible with democracy.

Max Weber, writing in 1919 with Lenin and the Bolsheviks in mind, argued that expropriation of the means of production by the state would give it unparalleled power over society. The superstructure would come to dominate the base. Elimination of independent centers of economic power and decision-making in society would eliminate an indispensable source of countervailing power to the state. Weber insisted that either socialism would be consistent, in which case it would end in dictatorship, or it would evolve into social democracy. However, if it became social democracy, it would have to come to terms with the central hate object of Western intellectuals: capitalism.

Capitalism is not lovely. It does not generate a heroic ethos, at least not one that appeals to intellectuals. It can bring out the worst in human beings. It can be heartless. Its impact on culture has been a mixture of support and corruption. It does generate inequality. A society totally organized around the market is a destructive utopia, one that erodes a common set of principles that every polity requires in order to address its problems. But for all these unlovely qualities, it is the only economic system compatible with the existence of pluralist democracy in which political parties can peacefully win political power and no less peacefully agree to give up political power.

Capitalism is a necessary but not sufficient condition for pluralist democracy because, as Frederick Hayek argued, it is an economic system that shares political liberalism's attitude toward knowledge. Capitalism and free markets rest on millions and millions of uncoordinated decisions made by individuals. The spontaneous and uncoordinated nature of these decisions maximizes the amount of intelligence in a society. It is impossible for any centrally planned economy to match the creativity unleashed by markets and independent capitalists. In a similar fashion, pluralist democracy maximizes intelligence and knowledge by rejecting the notion of an omniscient state in favor of political competition between political parties. Just as a capitalist economy derives its dynamism from competition, so the dynamism and strength of democracies comes from competition between political parties. Only where political parties stand a chance of losing power in an election can the process of political learning be peacefully institutionalized. In both politics and economics, stagnation is the product of the absence of effective competition.

Capitalist economies are also compatible with totalitarian rule as in Nazi Germany, and with authoritarian rule, as in some of the Asian capitalist economies today. However, few historians in Western Europe and the United States today would defend the Comintern's view of the 1930s and the still current East German view that National Socialism was a product of monopoly capitalism. The American historian Henry Turner, in *Big Business and the Rise of Hitler,* has effectively laid to rest the notion that Hitler was a tool of big business. In a book called *Reactionary Modernism,* I have argued along lines similar to historians such as Karl Bracher, George Mosse, and Fritz Stern that Nazi ideology, not German capitalism, accounted for the racist war waged in Eastern Europe and the Soviet Union, as well as for the Holocaust against the Jews.

From a glance at the variety of regimes in German history—constitutional republic, totalitarian dictatorship, and parliamentary democracy—that coexisted with a capitalist economy, it is clear that no necessary connection exists between capitalism and dictatorship. On the contrary, every pluralist democracy with meaningful, peaceful competition between political parties in the last century has coexisted with a capitalist economy. Because of the dispersal of power in society it brings about, capitalism is a necessary, though not sufficient, condition for democracy.

Capitalism and Culture

A second issue I'd like to raise concerns capitalism and its cultural prerequisites. The Polish opposition has dealt with the issue of a democratic political culture. I ask if you have also examined the question of cultural prerequisites of capitalism. You need no lessons from us about human rights, or the value of pluralism, and certainly not about the value of elections. One question I have about Poland's future is whether or not is has a culture that is conducive to economic growth, as well as to political democracy. In Britain, P.T. Bauer, and in the United States, Peter Berger and David Landes, have placed renewed emphasis on the importance of the cultural prerequisites of economic growth. They all ask a most embarrassing question: "Why are some nations rich and others poor?"

Since Rosa Luxembourg and Lenin developed their theories of imperialism, and since the coining of the term "third world" at the Bandung conference of 1955, many development economists thought they had the answer. "They," meaning the countries of Asia, Africa, and Latin America, were poor, because "we," the capitalist countries of Europe, the United States, and Japan were rich. Conversely, "we" were rich because we had exploited "them." Proposals for global redistribution in the form of a new world economic order in the United Nations rest on this tale of good and evil. From the end of World War II to the 1970s, this myth of a unitary Third World remained intact, until it fell to pieces under the impact of the OPEC cartel and the Asian economic miracle.

P. T. Bauer, in works such as *Equality, the Third World, and Economic Delusion* and *Reality and Rhetoric,* and Peter Berger, in his recent book, *The Capitalist Revolution,* have criticized the idea of a "third world." The idea of "the third world," they argue, is condescending and racist, ignoring as it does the multiplicity of over one hundred different nation states. By ignoring this multiplicity, such a blanket notion obscures the embarrassing fact that these one hundred or so countries are not equally poor. Instead, they mark points on a gradation of wealth. Moreover, some of the wealthiest are those that had most contact with former colonial powers, while most of the poorest were never colonized at all. Rather than seek the causes for their economic misery or success in the international economic system, Bauer and Berger examine the specific national economic cultures to understand why some nations are richer than others.

The short and simple answer is that where governments allow markets, encourage entrepreneurship, and foster private investment decisions and the free movement of labor, economic growth takes place. Where, on the other hand, government bureaucrats have tried to plan economies, discourage entrepreneurship, concentrate investment decisions in the state, and prevent the free movement of labor, economic growth does not take place. The phenomenal economic success of South Korea, Taiwan, Singapore, and Hong Kong has been a huge embarrassment for Latin American intellectuals accustomed to blaming all their problems on Yankee imperialism, and to African leaders whose visions of state socialism have crumbled in war and economic disaster. Today, the argument that socialism denies freedom in order to bring about economic growth is in shambles. It cannot offer either.

The work of Bauer, Berger, and Landes raises the issue of how a nation's cultural attitudes towards capitalism affect its capacity for economic growth. One of the most famous hypotheses of modern social science was Max Weber's argument that there was an affinity between the spirit of capitalism and Protestantism. He began with the observation that in Europe, capitalism was most advanced in those places where Protestantism was strongest. His explanation was that Protestantism fostered an ethic of individualist asceticism which legitimated in the eyes of believers the accumulation of capital. It broke through Catholicism's disdain for money-making and capitalist enterprise. Today, Berger argues that the Asian capitalist economies benefit from an Eastern form of asceticism which initially lacks the individualism of Western capitalism. In both cases, what is decisive is a cultural outlook that breaks through traditional hostility to the methodical accumulation of wealth and its use for long-term investments.

I've digressed a bit into this discussion because the historical moment of political change in Eastern Europe is placing the distinctive features of the countries of Eastern Europe into sharper relief. "Eastern Europe," like the term "Third World," gives way to more tangible historical communities, to the individual nation-states of Poland, Hungary, East Germany, Czechoslovakia, and Yugoslavia. The question for each of these states, including Poland, is what cultural resources exist on which a thriving and dynamic economy can be built. If newspaper reports are to be believed, there are more Marxists in Western universities than in Poland, but assuming a few remain here, Marxism is an important cultural barrier to economic growth. Yet European anticapitalism is much older than Marxism. One of its oldest homes is the Catholic church. Internationally, the Church has generally spoken more about redistribution of wealth than it has about the conditions for its creation. How Polish Catholicism responds to capitalist economics will be a central question in your future.

How will people who have participated in a movement entitled "Solidarity" respond to the quite different, at times contrary, pulls of individualism and competition? Where, in your national culture, are the resources for economic individualism which every capitalist economy requires? I should think you would want to talk a great deal to people from Catholic Italy and Spain, both of which emerged from dictatorships, have experienced rapid economic growth, and have managed to reconcile Catholic traditions with the development of capitalism. How have they become richer without losing their souls? The historical and contemporary evidence is that countries do not become wealthier if they have a national culture hostile to capitalism. The issue of how you reconcile Western political and economic liberalism with Poland's national culture is as important as any you face.

I would like to make one last point about capitalism and culture. Daniel Bell, one of America's foremost sociologists of the postwar era, in works such as *The Coming of Post-Industrial Society* and *The Cultural Contradictions of Capitalism*, has reiterated an important point made by Tocqueville, John Stuart Mill, Emile Durkheim and a host of other social theorists: Capitalism as an economic system may undermine values that serve to hold a society together and that create a basis for defining shared sacrifice and just reward. Our budget deficit is a monument to the erosion of a shared national culture upon which our government could ask us all to carry our fair share of taxation. Unfortunately, George Will has been one of the few American conservative and centrist intellectuals in the past decade to point out that the American people are undertaxed, not overtaxed, in relation to the tasks they want government to perform. The root of this undertaxation, as great liberals such as Tocqueville and John Stuart Mill understood, was the deficiency in a common culture raising individual concerns beyond those of self-interest. My point is that a functioning capitalist economy requires a culture whose origins do not lie in capitalism, and which preserves values beyond those of self-interest.

In this sense, you may very well be able to turn your Catholic traditions, and—who knows—maybe even elements of your socialist traditions into a set of national values that address political issues, such as protection of the global environment, that the market alone will not address. Capitalism, unlike communism, does not promise an end to politics. The politics of countries have made capitalism rather different in each. Contrary to the rhetorical flourishes of the *Communist Manifesto*, according to which capitalism would eliminate all national differences in favor of one universal culture, it has everywhere borne the stamp of the national cultures and polities in which it has emerged. Polish capitalism would be quite different from capitalism in the United States, Japan, or West Germany.

I can summarize what I've said as follows: If you want democracy over a long period of time, and if you want to improve the standard of living in this country, you must, sooner or later, develop a capitalist economy. Conversely, if you do not develop a capitalist economy, the democracy for which you have struggled so courageously will not be secure. But, if you do find yourself living with capitalism, your own precapitalist or noncapitalist traditions will be very important in addressing the political dilemmas that even the best functioning capitalism cannot resolve.

Peace and Freedom in Europe

I would now like to turn to questions of international politics, in particular to the impact of the *asymmetry* of democracy and dictatorship, and the impact of this asymmetry on relations between states. There is an argument, which I assume you have heard, according to which the postwar order has been the best of all possible worlds. The postwar order, in this view, "solved" the German question. Before 1945, Germany was too strong, especially in regard to the many weak governments to her east. If the United States had left Europe after 1945, or if a neutral, reunified Germany had emerged, there would have been a power vacuum in Central Europe which would have been filled by the Soviet Union. The division of Germany into two Germanies prevented the emergence of a Germany that was too strong or too weak.

While the division of Germany upset the Germans, it calmed the nerves of the neighbors that German armies had invaded in 1941 and 1939. Unfortunately, this elegant solution to the German question was purchased at the price of freedom in Eastern Europe. Like the Congress of Vienna in 1815, the postwar order has preserved peace at the price of the nonsatisfaction of the desires of the small powers of Eastern Europe. But peace is more than Europe could claim in the first half of the century. A free Eastern Europe, it was said, would reopen the German question and bring us back once again to cycles of instability and war. Who knew what the ethnic and national conflicts of Eastern Europe would produce? Just as the United States "pacified" Western Europe to such an extent that the French and West Germans became friends, so the Soviet Union united Eastern Europe in antagonism to itself. What, such analysts ask, would happen if the big bullies left town? Would the local citizens open up old quarrels that could draw the great powers into a fight? So while Western politicians express delight about freedom in Eastern Europe, some also quietly wonder how it can grow without destabilizing the postwar peace.

Such perspectives are in line with the balance of power tradition: peace requires satisfaction of the great powers, if necessary at the expense of the small powers. In times of great political change, geopolitics reminds us that states are "cold monsters" of international politics, but it does so too often without appreciating the importance of the nature of regimes in question. As Raymond Aron put it in his very important work, *Peace and War: A Theory of International Relations*, the essential point about Athens and Sparta was not that there were two great powers but what they concretely were. Democracies do go to war, but not with one another. In the twentieth century, no fully functioning democracies have gone to war with one another.

This has been the case because democracies share both values and social and political transparency. They pride themselves on openness, and this openness "builds confidence," to use a much overused term. The existence of dictatorship in the Soviet Union and Eastern Europe, far from being a source of postwar stability, has been the primary source of tension in Europe. The "peace" movements of the early 1980s in Western Europe equated both superpowers because of their possession of nuclear weapons, but these movements neglected the differences in their political regimes. They separated the issue of peace in Europe from that of freedom in Eastern Europe. They were wrong on both counts. Democratization of Eastern Europe and the Soviet Union reinforces, rather than undermines, the stability of peace in Europe. Democracies can never fully trust dictatorships because the latter make or try to make themselves invulnerable to outside influence while seeking to influence democracies, which are open to such pressures. Regimes that do not respect the human rights of their own citizens, and that do not have an institutionalized free and open public debate about their foreign and defense policies, will always arouse in democracies mistrust that no arms control agreement can ever fully overcome. Because this *asymmetry of regimes* is so important, democratization of dictatorships, far from being a threat to peace, promises to place it on a more secure foundation.

During the American engagement in the war in Vietnam, the Euromissile dispute of the early 1980s, and the recent controversies over Central America, public debate took place only in the democracies, in the United States and Western Europe. Neither the North Vietnamese, the Soviet Union and Warsaw Pact governments, and more recently the Sandinistas, faced effective pressures from a public debate at home. North Vietnamese negotiators in Paris, Soviet negotiators in Geneva, and the Sandinistas in Managua were able to take the political offensive and fight their battles in the public opinion of their democratic adversaries. In each case, the vices of dictatorship became strategic virtues, while the virtues of democracy became potential strategic vices.

But it is important not to overstate the case or to underestimate the powers of democracies. Democratic governments have formidable powers, powers often underestimated by friends and adversaries. The growth of democracy and free-dom in Eastern Europe has a potentially profound impact on international poli-tics in Europe. Public debate over foreign policy in the Soviet Union, in Poland, and in Hungary is potentially one of the most important changes in international politics since World War II. The mere existence of a Polish parliament free to debate foreign and defense policy offers the opportunity for ending the asym-metrical pressures on democratic and dictatorial regimes of the postwar era. Public debate, an inquiring press, governments accountable to parliaments, mean that the Polish and Hungarian governments will have to justify their poli-cies at home, and that the Soviet Union will have to be accountable to its alliance partners in Europe. We do not come to Cracow to call for apocalyptic and point-less gestures about dissolving the blocs. But the normalization of public debate over your own foreign and defense policies would be a most welcome change from the postwar system. The character of regimes, more than weapon systems alone, is decisive in how states relate to one another.

The strictly geopolitical approach is too narrow. It cannot adapt to political change. Forty-five years ago, it would have been hard to imagine a democratic West Germany, not to mention a democratic Italy, Portugal, and Spain. In 1945, who would have predicted that France and West Germany would be the closest of allies, or West German *Ostpolitik?* More freedom and democratization in Poland and Eastern Europe, and in the Soviet Union, should they continue, can be a stabilizing factor for peace in Europe because it increases trust between states. How, for example, can West European democracies fully trust Warsaw Pact countries, so long as political opposition in regard to all questions, includ-ing foreign and defense policy, is not permitted? Imagine how different East-West politics might look with free elections, functioning parliaments with effective power, a free and skeptical press, and public opinion and public opinion polls, in East Germany, Hungary, Poland, and the Soviet Union? If that were to be the case, the basic asymmetry of regimes of the postwar peace would be surmounted. Public controversy and debate over foreign and defense policy would take place in Eastern Europe and the Soviet Union no less than in Western Europe and the United States. The pressures on governments to compromise would, for the first time, be equal. I look forward to seeing the expression on the Soviet negotiator's face as he or she faces critical questions from Soviet and East European journal-ists asking why the Soviet Union is being so stubborn and unreasonable in nego-tiations with the West.

I think there is a tacit understanding in the United States that deployments of American intermediate-range nuclear weapons in Western Europe in the fall of 1983 was a turning point in postwar history. They meant the defeat of the Brezhnev-Gromyko-Andropov effort to drive the United States out of Europe through a policy of accumulating ever more military force in the form of the SS-

20 arsenal. That defeat led the Soviet Union to reassess its policy, and, in 1987, to accept the famous "zero-zero" option offered by President Reagan in November 1981 which the Russians had previously denounced as a propaganda ploy. The INF treaty eliminating medium-range nuclear weapons in Europe is the best evidence that diplomatic relations with the Soviet Union improve when the West is consistently firm about preserving a balance of military forces.

A dissolution of the Western alliance would be a severe, perhaps fatal, blow to prospects for greater freedom and democracy in Eastern Europe. A neutralist Western Europe without Atlanticist ties to the United States would be divided, weak, and unable to influence developments in Eastern Europe if the Soviet Union did not want it to do so. Hopes for continued democratization in Eastern Europe rest on a continuation of the Atlantic Alliance. Just as the Western alliance was decisive for the westernization of West Germany, so can it contribute to the political and moral strengthening of Western traditions in what is now called Eastern Europe. Mikhail Gorbachev is right to speak of a common European home, but the common Western values resting on the dignity of individuals and political freedom have found their home in a Western Europe. The facts of political, moral, and cultural tradition outweigh those of geographic proximity in thinking through what a common European home is. Without doubt, it stretches across the Atlantic.

Whether the Atlantic Alliance continues depends as much on decisions made in London and Bonn, in particular, as in Washington. It is not at all out of the realm of possibility that a combination of Gorbachev's arms control initiatives with a Labour government in Britain, and even more important, a Social-Democratic-Green government in West Germany, could lead to irreparable divisions, and an American exit from Western Europe. An influential part of the West German intellectual and political elites have already convinced themselves that the Soviet Union poses no threat at all while focusing their criticism on the United States and on the centrality of West Germany's Western ties. I would urge you to seek contact with that beleaguered but determined part of the West German intellectual and political establishment which retains Adenauer's wisdom that only a firmly Western-oriented West Germany could lend assistance to strivings for freedom and democracy in Eastern Europe.

Poland and Israel

Speaking here in Cracow, less than one hundred kilometers from Auschwitz-Birkenau, it is important to say we assume that you who defend principles of political freedom will also be loyal to the claims of memory, the memories of the Holocaust of European Jewry. No task could be more urgent in the creation of a democratic political culture in Poland than a truthful and complete recollection of the Jewish catastrophe. If they are not already translated into Polish, I would urge you to translate the great postwar historiography on the Holocaust, such as works by Lucy Dawidowicz and Raul Hilberg, and the essays by Primo Levi and Elie Wiesel. At Auschwitz and Auschwitz-Birkenau today, school children and visitors should be told the clear, unambiguous truth about the destruction of European Jewry, rather than the euphemisms of the official interpretations of "victims of fascism," interpretations which themselves are an enduring inheritance of European anti-Semitism.

Speaking honestly about the past has consequences for your country's foreign policy today. Assuming that democratization in your country proceeds as we all hope it does, Poland will become even more of an actor in world politics, a state with its own foreign policy. I would make a plea that as soon as possible, a freer and more democratic Poland would restore diplomatic ties with Israel. It is wrong, morally wrong, for this country, whose three million Jews were murdered by the Nazis, to participate in the world's hostility to Israel. As you emerge as a state that can speak with its own voice, I hope that you will take every opportunity to tell the PLO what successes a policy of compromise, of many small steps, and moderation can bring. Who knows better than Poles and Jews what devastation fanatics produce? As you have struggled for the right for free elections, I hope your government will urge the Palestinians not to throw away yet another opportunity to participate in elections, and to solve their problems through peaceful compromise. With your accomplishments, you are able more than ever to consign Poland's anti-Semitic tradition to the past. In 1989, your affinities with Israel include not only the darkest days of Polish and Jewish history. As you move toward democracy it makes no sense at all for your country not to have good relations with the only liberal democracy in the Middle East.

We deradicalized American intellectuals with our "second thoughts" about the new left of the 1960s share with you a fresh appreciation of a Western tradition of freedom and equality. It is a common heritage. Wherever people value conversation and roundtables over violence and hatred, they will cherish the Polish spring of 1989.   1990, vol. 57, no. 1

• No Third Way
Ralf Dahrendorf

As I allow my enthusiasm for the open society to run away with rational argument, it occurs to me that you may be a little too pleased with some of my remarks. You too have your doubts about Hayek, and you want some mixture of socialist achievements and liberal opportunities to prevail. Unbridled capitalism, you think, is not such a good thing, and you may therefore wish to enlist me as one of your supporters on the road to social democracy. I do not share the widespread obsession with labels and am therefore not particularly upset about being called a social democrat, though I have difficulties with the Italian epithet, *liberalsocialista*, because I prefer to think of myself as a radical liberal for whom the social entitlements of citizenship are as important a condition of progress as the opportunities for choice, which require entrepreneurial initiative and an innovative spirit. But before we get to normal politics, the point has to be made unequivocally that socialism is dead, and that none of its variants can be revived for a world awakening from the double nightmare of Stalinism and Brezhnevism.

Lest you think such language unnecessarily cruel, let me tell you about a book which has to do with my own political philosophy, George Dangerfield's *The Strange Death of Liberal England*, which first appeared in 1935. Dangerfield traces the curious story of the great triumph of the British Liberals under the Asquith ministry after 1908, and the hubris which led to their rapid decline from 1913 onward. "It was in these years that that highly moral, that generous, that dyspeptic, that utterly undefinable organism known as the Liberal Party died the death. It died from poison administered by its Conservative foes, and from disillusion over the inefficacy of the word 'Reform.' And the last breath which fluttered in this historical flesh was extinguished by War." Dangerfield is not naive; he knows that political parties can appear to survive their death. "I realize, of course, that the word 'liberal' will always have a meaning as long as there is one democracy left in the world, or any remnant of a middle class: but the true prewar Liberalism—supported, as it still was in 1910, by Free Trade, a majority in Parliament, the Ten Commandments, and the illusion of Progress—can never return. It was killed, or killed itself, in 1913." Dangerfield adds, for good measure, "And a very good thing too."

It is hard to resist the temptation to replace the year 1913 in these observations by 1989, and the word "liberalism" by "socialism," or at any rate "social democracy"—supported, as it still was in the 1970s, by economic planning, a majority in parliament, the creed of social service and the illusion of "progress." But (you will point out immediately) is this not conflating two different things? There is socialism in its Communist version—which collapsed dramatically in 1989, when country after country took the word out of its official description ("Socialist Republic of"), and parties like your own and those of Hungary and even of Italy sought a less offensive label—and there is social democracy, which if it died at all "perished in the dark" (thus Lord Selborne during the debate on the Parliament Act in 1911), unnoticed by many, because to all intents and purposes it is still very much around. Many other socialisms have cropped up in the last century and a half, but Communism (which has also been described as "really existing socialism" while it really existed) and social democracy (sometimes called, *pour épater les bourgeois*, "democratic socialism") are the only two of any historical weight.

Their story needs to be told, however briefly, in order to sort out what it means to speak of the strange death of socialism in the 1980s.

I suppose it all started in post-Napoleonic Europe, or more to the point, in the second phase of the industrial era, notably in England and France. Thoughtful people—bourgeois, no doubt—were upset by the plight of the laboring classes and began to think of remedies. These had certain ingredients in common. One was that there was something wrong with the way in which private property had come to be used; to redress such wrongs, property had to be "socialized" in one way or another. Another feature was that people's positions in society had become altogether too unequal; variants of egalitarianism accompanied socialism from its earliest days. The notion that things could, and had to, be done by deliberate planning rather than left to their own resources, to the "market," follows naturally. The cool rationality of such analyses was invariably coupled with more intangible and emotional hopes for a different way of living together, a sense of brotherly love, a desire to break the vicious cash nexus by voluntary cooperation, and the spirit of solidarity. An alliance of intellectuals and the working class turned this mix into the vision of an altogether different world—Henri de Saint-Simon's "New Christianity," Robert Owen's "New Society." Moreover, the new world had to be fought for by organizing either islands of a better future or movements to transform the present.

Marx did not like these notions of the Saint-Simons and Owens, Cabets and Fouriers, Proudhons and Weitlings. He scorned the attempt to confront the miseries of the present with alternatives which were mere "phantasies." Instead, he invoked the inexorable march of History with a capital H. The New Society was not a desirable prospect but the necessary outcome of the contradictions and conflicts of bourgeois capitalism. This is where the notion of systems crept into socialism and allied itself with the Utopian vision which had been there all along. It does not matter what people want or visualize for themselves—indeed, people do not matter—for they merely execute the will of History, and History has chosen the proletariat to become the agent of productive forces that will overcome the capitalist mode of production and create the New Society, socialist first and Communist when it has fully matured.

The parties formed in the name of the *Communist Manifesto* liked to threaten the powers that be with the inevitability of their downfall and the victory of socialism, but they were never strictly Marxist. It would actually be rather difficult to set up a trade union or a political party on the assumption that such movements are mere puppets of great impersonal forces. To have history on one's side—rather, to hear leaders tell one that this is the case—may sound encouraging to some, but an un-Marxian element of voluntarism crept into the socialist movement from the start. In England it was dominant from the Chartists to the Fabians and further to the Labour Party. With the formation of parties and a growing belief in their capacity to change things here and now came social democracy, that is, the grudging yet sincere acceptance of the rules of the open society. Versions of positivism entered into a curious marriage with socialism. By 1914 liberalism may have died, but socialism was alive and kicking in the democracies of Europe, and its parliamentary representatives voted for the war loans of their respective governments just as proletarians of all countries went to war against each other instead of uniting behind the red flag.

The events of 1917 do not mark just another stage of the same development. While Lenin obviously belonged in the tradition to which I have alluded here with almost frivolous lightness, the framework of his analysis owes little if anything to the growth of social democracy in Europe, a great deal to uniquely Russian traditions, and an important impetus to Marx. The reason for this particular debt is in many ways perverse, because it derives from an error of theory and of history which needs to be exposed. As you know, Marx tried to link the struggle of classes to underlying socioeconomic forces. The suppressed class draws its strength as well as its rhetoric from forces of production that are held back by the ruling class and by the mode of production which it represents. Marx needed the conflation of politics and economics to make the case for the inexorable march of History, but he had little history to go on. Some kind of class struggle had (perhaps) provided ammunition for the French Revolution; the Industrial Revolution can (probably) be described as the unavoidable removal of an older mode of production in order to make way for the new forces of technology, enterprise, and wage labor. The two revolutions, however, did not happen in the same place or at the same time, except in the books of Marx and Engels, where the revolt of the Third Estate and the breakthrough of industrial production were superimposed by the strokes of two pens.

Marx was more interested in the revolution of the future than in those of the past. However, his theory in all its abstract splendor made little sense for this prospect either. The proletariat never represented a new force of production; it was a class of exploited and downtrodden industrial workers who needed to find a place in the sun of this world here and now. Marx himself was hard-pressed to identify the underlying socioeconomic force of the revolutionary movement which he tried to promote, for "associated producers" and "socialized ownership" are hardly compelling motives for change (especially if joint-stock companies are regarded as "a necessary transitional point" on the road to socialism). Yet by a curious fluke, Marx's theory made sense for Russia. Indeed, it made sense for all countries which entered the modern world late and had to achieve political and economic modernization simultaneously and quickly. As older feudal or colonial elites were removed, those who took over could claim to do so in the name of hitherto repressed opportunities for economic growth. Contrary to the early English or American or French or Dutch bourgeoisie, they had no past economic achievement or wealth to rely on, nor were they a *Bildungsbürgertum* in the German sense, an "educated bourgeoisie" (to use a term by which Keynes described his own origins); instead, political power was the sole base of their position. Thus, it came about that a class rose to hegemony which had nothing but the Party to support it, but which set in motion a slow and ultimately ineffectual process of industrialization. "Communism," as Lenin put it crisply, "is Soviet power plus the electrification of the whole country."

Socialism of this brand—Communism—is in other words a developing-country phenomenon. Despite some islands of sophistication and even of capitalism, Russia in 1917 was by and large a developing country in this sense. So was China in 1949, as were the many third world nations which found it convenient to rely on the Soviet model, and on support by the older second world nations to boot. *Nomenklatura* socialism—some call it "administrative centralism" or even "democratic centralism"—became the preferred mode of late modernization.

It was, as we know today, not a very effective method. Its effectiveness remained largely confined to the destruction of the old authoritarian regime. This was accomplished with utter ruthlessness. The "harvest of sorrow" in the Ukraine and beyond (to use Robert Conquest's description) and the Chinese Cultural Revolution are two unforgettable and unforgivable examples, though Idi Amin and "Emperor" Bokassa and Pol Pot and other third world "modernizers," often in the name of socialism, will not be forgotten and forgiven either. The destructive part of the process did lead to a certain leveling of inherited social hierarchies and the creation of the institutions (though often merely the trappings) of modern states. It also laid certain foundations of modern economic development: elements of infrastructure (though often more symbolic than useful), generalized education (though often for purposes of mobilization as much as skill formation), large industrial complexes (though often geared to state, above all, military, purposes rather than consumer demand). But the process failed to do that crucial trick which the "Protestant ethic" achieved in some parts of the Western world, that is, to provide an incentive for saving, and for that deferred gratification that is a condition of early industrial success. People must be prepared to allow an accumulation of capital that sets the growth machine in motion. They may do so voluntarily—because they believe it is morally right, or because they can see the light at the end of the tunnel—but if they do not, they must be compelled to consume less than they produce. This is how forced labor came to be an indispensable ingredient of really existing socialism, as well as shortages and queues and in the end a huge and useless "overhang" of worthless money. The logic of Communist regimes made exploitation and suppression as inevitable as scarcity and pretense.

The promise of socialism of the Communist variety was a quick and painless way out of authoritarian rule and preindustrial poverty. Modernity without

Napoleon and the ginhouses, as it were. In fact, the peoples of the third world, including the Soviet Union, got both dictators and misery. Above all, they got what Milovan Djilas first called a "new class" of party officials. This class increasingly hardened into a large *nomenklatura*. The more rigid it became, the less sustainable was its rule. The combination of ineffectiveness and suppression eventually set in motion the process of self-destruction which we have watched in recent years. In other words, socialism is not only a developing-country phenomenon, but it is also one that cannot be upheld beyond the initial stages of development. Sooner or later it has to give way to more open and effective modes of economic advancement and probably political involvement as well. Really existing socialism cannot last.

There are those in the Soviet Union and elsewhere in the post-Communist world who speak today of a "return to capitalism." They are wrong in more ways than one, but above all inclining to Marx's mistaken assumption that socialism succeeds capitalism. In fact, the opposite is the case. Market-oriented economies based on incentives rather than planning and force represent an advanced stage of modern development. In this sense capitalism succeeds socialism—in those countries where the socialist option was the chosen method of entering the modern world. This is of course not the case in your country, let alone in East Germany and Czechoslovakia, where really existing socialism was the result of the hegemonic aspirations of the Soviet Union and stunted the hopeful saplings of the process of modernization. One can understand that, faced with the rubble left behind by the Second World War, large numbers of people were prepared to embrace any promise of progress on offer, including *nomenklatura* socialism, but after forty years the balance sheets of the regimes under its yoke show almost exclusively red figures. Soviet-style socialism in the advanced countries of East Central Europe was a tragedy without relief.

The year 1917 had more than one effect. It established really existing socialism of the developing-country variety, but it also encouraged those in more developed countries who were unhappy about what they saw as the accommodation of socialist parties to the status quo to remain on a more absolute course. Communist parties came into being which have played a horrific and often murderous part in the long-running battles with social democrats, notably in the Spanish Civil War, during the years of the Hitler-Stalin Pact, and in some European countries during the immediate postwar period as well. When the Soviets forced the countries of your region under their rule by forming "popular fronts," "unity parties," or merely Communist-dominated "coalitions," they could rely on Communist parties of varying but not inconsiderable strength. The fifth column was there to support their claims, and while the false god of Communism failed most of its believers (as Arthur Koestler, Ignazio Silone, Stephen Spender, and others have told us), it failed too late and too slowly.

It is important to remember this nightmare from which we are waking up today. I remember it well, for I was a young man in Berlin when the Russians came at the end of April 1945. Our family welcomed them warmly because I had been hiding for weeks after my unexpected release from the concentration camp in which I had spent the previous winter, and above all because we were waiting for my father, who was in prison for his involvement in the Resistance—notably in the plot to assassinate Hitler on July 20, 1944. He survived, but his friends who were killed by the Nazis had left him the message that there must never be disunity in the labor movement again. At first, the Communist leaders who had returned from their Soviet exile did not want to hear this message. They thought that they could go it alone, and in any case they did not like the social democrats, whom they had denounced as "social fascists" a mere five years before. Within a year, attitudes turned full circle. Soon the Communists realized that they would not win free elections; apart from the Italian city of Bologna, the Indian state of Kerala, and one or two other places, Communists have never won free elections anywhere, and so they put pressure on the social democrats to form a "Socialist Unity Party." By that time my father, who never succumbed to the pressures or the temptations of totalitarianism of any ilk, had made up his mind. As vice-chairman of the Central Committee of the East German Social Democrats he voted against the forced merger and had to flee to the West. I confess that while *Schadenfreude* is not the most noble of emotions, I watched with some pleasure the disintegration of that miserable assemblage of privileged cowards that called itself the SED.

On all this, however, you probably agree. But what about the other, the social democratic, thread of development since 1917? One key difference is now apparent. Whereas Communism and really existing socialism engaged in their own constitutional politics and set up monopolies of unfettered party power wherever they could, social democracy after 1917 became clearly and (except for some fringe groups) unambiguously a part of normal politics in the democracies of the world. Some thought that this was exactly what was wrong with it. It has to be admitted that Ramsay MacDonald and Hermann Müller and perhaps even Léon Blum were not the most inspiring leaders of political parties committed to radical reform. But it is also true that by involving themselves in normal politics, social democrats became staunch defenders of the constitution of liberty. Democracy and the rule of law were in good hands with them. As newcomers to its pastures, they showed if anything a greater commitment to the values and institutions of the open society than older liberals.

So what went wrong? Did anything go wrong? You reminded me of the article I wrote a few years ago called "The Misery of Social Democracy," which obviously caused you some heartache. (In this you are not alone; Willy Brandt, in his farewell speech as leader of the West German Social Democrats, expressed pained bewilderment: "I have asked myself time and again which decades those contemporaries had in mind who thought that the social democratic century is over. Have they overlooked the two wars, Fascism and Stalinism, the great economic crises and the new existential threats?") At the time, I started with the straightforward observation that social democratic parties all over Europe were not doing very well, and those that were doing well, like those of Spain and perhaps Italy, were not particularly social democratic. Advocating a decent society was evidently no longer good enough for the electorate of advanced societies. What had brought about this change of fortune for the dominant political force of a century?

The simplest answer is victory. Like the British Liberals in 1911, Social Democrats had conquered Europe by the end of the 1970s. Their combination of democracy and planning, of economic freedom and demand management, of individual choice and redistribution, of liberty and justice, had become the dominant reality of the OECD world (though the United States went partly its own way and never fully recognized the social rights of citizenship). We were all social democrats then, and in important respects we still are.

For the people of the developed world, this was fine, but for social democracy it was fatal. The creation of a large majority of those who could hope to satisfy many of their aspirations within existing conditions—a majority class—made Social Democratic parties either a protective, not to say conservative, force, or dispensable, or both. The emergence of a majority class (sometimes called a middle class, thought the concept is misleading in the absence of an upper class that sets the tone, and a cohesive working class) meant above all that the traditional social base of social democracy had melted away. The working class had disappointed its intellectual leaders; contrary to their assumptions, it was actually not a particularly progressive social force but one that sought "law and order" as much as social and economic advancement, and whose members were in the end quite pleased to make it for themselves and their families, never mind all the others. Class conflict was transformed into individual social mobility. The prevalence of this pattern in America in the form of the "American dream," if not always its reality, has often been cited as the reason for the absence of socialist parties in that country; now the same behavior began to spread in Europe. As the process went on, the working class not only lost its cohesion but began to shrink. A new middle class of white-collar employees emerged, and while their market position may have seemed similar to that of workers, they never saw themselves as a part of the proletariat. The shift from manufacturing to services reduced the industrial working class to a minority, and one whose status could no longer be described as neglected or downtrodden.

The crumbling traditional base of social democratic parties was accompanied by another effect of their victory. Social democracy has had a peculiar affinity to the state. Far from fighting it as the "body which administers the common business interests of the bourgeois class" (in Marx and Engels's formulation), social democrats used it to redress the injustices of capitalism. John Maynard Keynes and William Beveridge were both liberals by party affiliation, but Keynesian economic policy and Beveridge-type social policy became hallmarks of social democracy. "Policy" always means a greater role for government. This in turn led to the expansion of the planning apparatus, of bureaucracy. Social democracy became increasingly associated with bureaucracy to the point where, in some countries such as Sweden, it turned into the party of public servants. Elsewhere it has been described as the "teachers' party" (teachers being public servants in most European countries) or the "party of local government employees," which amounts to the same thing.

The quandary is evident. While there may still be much to do in order to complete the social democratic project, its traditional support has dwindled as a consequence of its success. Moreover, the link of social democracy with bureaucracy puts the old reformist force into a strange predicament. After all, bureaucracy is in a sense the democratic *nomenklatura* which, if we follow Max Weber's fears, may yet imprison us all in a new "cage of bondage." One aspect of the 1980s in the OECD world is the protest not only against the economic stagflation of the 1970s but also against the political dependence on bureaucracy. People have an elementary desire to do things their way rather than be pushed about by characters in offices who make them fill out forms and wait in queues for unsatisfactory answers.

I realize, of course, that the phrase "social democratic" will always have a meaning as long as there is one democracy left in the world, or any remnant of a working class. This is paraphrasing Dangerfield yet again, but so far as the working class is concerned, I am not even sure it is true. The remaining working class is by no means a safe reservoir for social democratic votes. Anyway, social democracy is in trouble, and it is in trouble at the very time at which more absolute versions of socialism have run aground. Does this mean (you asked me) that the social democratic option is foreclosed for those who have abandoned Communism?

The time has come to face squarely one issue which vitiates much of the debate about democratization in Europe. It has somewhat awkward names, all of which aim at describing a halfway house between the realities of what used to be the West and what used to be the East. Some speak of a "middle way," some of a "third way," and all believe that it would be wrong to shed the achievements of forty years of socialism and swallow capitalism lock, stock, and barrel. Surely—you seemed to say when we talked—there must be a place for a decent social and democratic or even democratic-socialist policy somewhere in between the extremes of what you had and what we have. This sounds good, even plausible, yet it is the wrong way to approach the tasks that lie ahead both in theory and in practice.

Instead of taking up Milovan Djilas, Ota Sik, Rudolf Bahro, or other writers from socialist countries, or the great advocate of humane capitalism in the 1960s and 1970s, Andrew Shonfield, let me use a Swiss author to make my case. The said author recently wrote a calm and reasoned article in the liberal *Neue Zürcher Zeitung* on "the possibility of a third way for Eastern Europe." He cautions the West against the self-important arrogance of the view that the collapse of really existing socialism leaves no alternative to its victims but to adopt all features of democratic and capitalist market economies on the grounds that one cannot be "a little pregnant." The author reminds us of the "pure doctrine of capitalism": self-organization, private property, the market, reliable rules of the game. He adds that the reality of the West is often far from this doctrine, and he makes a number of points. Private property has changed its complexion in giant enterprises which are run by people who do not own them; at the other end, small family-owned firms are by no means a model of efficiency. Planning and market forces have long ceased to be incompatible; the real question is where to draw the boundary between the two. Transparent cost and price structures are a good idea, but very far from the murky reality of the "markets" for agricultural products or the labor "market." The free movement of people, or even of goods, is as much a promise as it is a reality. "Let us not be more popish than the pope," he counsels.

So far so good. But the author then links his observations with a plea for "Utopian visions" that "transcend systems." There is much space for reform everywhere (he argues), and the analogy to being "a little pregnant" is a misleading description of economic structures in view of the need to seek complex mixtures of elements. This need has to be explored "across the systems without ideological prejudice and self-important arrogance. Liberal and socialist Utopias might thus be turned into a synergetic third." The "socialist Utopia" could be enriched by entrepreneurial initiative, and the "capitalist Utopia" by the insight that the economy serves human beings, and not vice versa. Thus, we should begin "the kind of intercultural dialogue that might lead to a variegated and dynamic path to Central Europe."

"No" is the simple answer to this demand. We should not engage in this "intercultural dialogue," and more, the very idea needs to be quashed. It is wrong because it is another version of system thinking, and thinking in terms of systems lies at the bottom of illiberalism in all its varieties. It is no accident that our author uses notions like "transcending systems," or exploring ideas "across the systems." This is how he sees the world. The only difference from, for instance, Fukuyama, is that he wants to introduce a third system, "Central Europe" as it were halfway between socialism and capitalism. (I know that you like the notion of Central Europe because you do not want to be labeled East European; indeed Poland has set its clocks to Central European Time throughout all these years and against Soviet pressure as well as the logic of geography; but the concept is nonetheless laden with ideological baggage—especially in its German incarnation, which brings back the "National Socialist" Friedrich Naumann and his *Mitteleuropa* as well as other unsavory characters—so let us be careful in using it!) Our Swiss author fortunately calls the system "variegated" but is nevertheless taken by its "Utopian" qualities. His is a kind of Rousseauean Utopia in which the "ritual competition between majority-forming pseudoalternatives" is replaced by "committed discussions of political programs" and of course a good dose of "human warmth, empathy, and solidarity."

We must beware of Utopia too, and not only if it is of the Rousseauean variety. Utopia is, in the nature of the idea, a total society. It may exist "nowhere," but it is held up as a counterproject to the realities of the world in which we are living. Utopia is a complete alternative, and therefore of necessity a closed society. Why did I not write the planned anti-Orwell book, *Nineteen Eighty-nine*? Because I could not find a way out of Big Brother's *Nineteen Eighty-four* for Winston Smith. Benevolent Utopias are no better. Karl Popper's demolition of Plato's *Republic* has precisely this theme. Whoever sets out to implement Utopian plans will in the first instance have to wipe clean the canvas on which the real world is painted. This is a brutal process of destruction. Second, a new world will have to be constructed which is bound to lead to errors and failures, and will in any case require awkward transitional periods like the "dictatorship of the proletariat." The probability must be high that in the end we will be stuck with the transition; dictators are not in the habit of giving up their power. The Utopian, writes Popper, "may seek his heavenly city in the past or in the future; he may preach 'back to nature' or 'forward to a world of love and beauty'; but the appeal is always to our emotions rather than to reason. Even with the best intentions of making heaven on earth it only succeeds in making it a hell—that hell which man alone can prepare for his fellow-men."

All this applies to the Utopia of the middle way as it does to all others. As a complete "third system" it remains primarily a system, never mind the "third" or "fourth" or "fifth." In the conflicts between advocates of systems and defenders of the open society, it therefore belongs on the side of illiberalism where all systems have their place. Neither Central Europe nor social democracy nor any other euphemism for the "middle way" must be thought of as a system, or indeed a Utopia, if liberty is what we want. The choice between freedom and serfdom is stark and clear, and it offers no halfway house for those weaker souls who would like to avoid making up their minds.

All this time we have been talking constitutional politics, of course. It is therefore necessary to define more precisely the ingredients of the open society. Since at this stage the issue is social and economic, we must ask which elements of economic organization are constituent parts of the open society and which others can be left to normal politics. Capitalism has often been defined in this context. Most definitions contain three elements: *private actors* coordinate their economic activity through the *market* in order to achieve accumulation and *growth*. How much of this is a part of the definition of an open society?

The question is extraordinarily difficult to answer, but it is undoubtedly a legitimate subject of debate and we can have a go at it. Take property. John Locke and his contemporaries would have had no doubt that private property is a constitutional requirement. Indeed, it probably is, though that does not mean that all property has to be private. State-owned railways are perfectly compatible with the open society. The key is that private property must be available as an option and it must be protected. Then there is the market. It has many implications, some constitutional and some not. Without legally protected contracts there can be no market; this is a constitutional need. Monopolies restrict the market, though this raises, even apart from the railways, the question of "natural monopolies"—for example, of air and of water. It is a constitutional condition of the open society that the generalization of monopolies be prevented. The burden of proof must always be on the defender of monopoly rather than on the advocate of pluralism and competition. Further, accumulation and growth. One ancient open society, Great Britain, has experienced many decades of indifferent or even "negative" growth without becoming illiberal. One can understand those who worry that economic growth may have become an almost constitutional postulate in a number of countries. Harold James had made the point for Germany, where "economic advance" has only too often in the last two centuries appeared to be the purpose "without which the nation could not exist." The constitutional requirement in this respect probably lies with the availability of incentives. Freedom to choose one's profession, freedom of movement, and arguably, limits to the progression of taxation belong in this category.

This is to say that neither demand management à la Keynes nor social security à la Beveridge is constitutionally incompatible with an open society. Indeed, many economic patterns which no textbook would describe as capitalist exist in democracies. The Japanese economy is hardly capitalist, with its large companies and their organized relations within the Ministry of International Trade and Industry. In Germany the role of the big banks, and of an informal network of major employers and trade unionists, coupled with codetermination and a highly developed welfare state, is hardly compatible with the publicly professed market economy. Sweden is in no strict sense a capitalist country. Yet these and others with their own idiosyncrasies are—with reservations in the case of Japan—open societies. The constitutional prerequisites of democracy are present.

The examples suggest an answer to your questions (and to the Utopian visions of the Swiss author whom, for the sake of clarity, I have perhaps treated a little harshly). There do exist aspects of economic order which belong to the constitution of liberty. They are, as it were, non-negotiable. In your own country, as in others under Communist domination, some of them were absent. There was no law of monopoly. There was instead a near total state monopoly. Private property was absent or severely restricted. Basic economic freedoms were missing. Without any "intercultural dialogue" aimed at compromise, and with a mish-mash of systems, these missing elements of the open society will have to be estab-lished if liberty is to stay. Like the common language which we speak again, such elements are neither East nor West nor Central European, but universal prereq-uisites of freedom.

Then there is normal politics. If you want your country to be not only a home of free speech and political choice, but also a place of prosperity and economic opportunity, I strongly recommend many of the liberal policies which your courageous Minister of Finance Balcerowicz—or his Czech counterpart Vaclav Klaus, and some others elsewhere—are pursuing. Some elements of this policy border on the constitutional, but most are the legitimate subject of political debate and therefore of divergent views. American-style capitalism is only one way forward; few countries anywhere in the world have opted for it. Britain may have displayed some similar traits in an earlier phase of modern economic devel-opment, but the two reformers whom I like to quote, Keynes and Beveridge, were after all British, and of Keynes it has been said that he saved capitalism by destroying it. The economic structures of France and Germany, of Italy and Spain, of the Netherlands and Sweden, are different in dozens of significant respects. There is no Central European model; there are as many models as there are countries.

Thus, the notion of a third or middle way is not only wrong in theory because it arouses the totalitarian potential of all Utopias; it is also wrong in practice. In constitutional terms, there are only two ways: we have to choose between systems and the open society. In terms of normal politics there are a hundred ways, and we can forever learn from one another in framing our own—your own, my own, everybody's, or at least every country's own—pattern of economic and social progress. None of these patterns is a model for others, let alone a system. Reality is infinitely varied. It may be a nightmare for the conceptual purist, but this must not mislead us into elevating it to a system. As long as the constitution of liberty is safe and sound, real people thrive in a real world for which all tidy concepts are inappropriate.

One other point needs to be made, although it is painful. The Swiss author rightly warned against arrogance on the part of those of us who were fortunate enough to live in conditions of liberty and prosperity while your people were suf-fering the leaden hand of *nomenklatura* socialism. His laudable compassion led him, as it does many others, to demand that the "achievements" of forty years of socialism be preserved even as its errors are undone. But what are these achievements? In terms of constitutional politics, I am afraid that I cannot see any. The much-quoted social rights embodied in your constitutions are not worth the paper on which they are written. No constitutional "right to work" can prevent unemployment; all it does is to discredit the constitution because it promises something which no judge can provide. A policy of full employment may rank high among the priorities of normal politics, but an article in the constitution is no substitute for it. (The right not to work is a more plausible candidate for constitutional guarantee, because it protects people against forced labor.) Nor can I see much in the field of normal politics that one would wish to preserve in the formerly socialist countries.

Something else remains, on which you placed great emphasis in our conversation. It has to do with the deep sense of loss felt by some in the post-Communist world because it appears that a style of life is irretrievably passing away which had much to recommend it. It was a less hectic style than that of the "capitalist" West, more sociable, more concerned with cultural values than the materialistic hedonism of the consumer society. You were quite specific on this point. It was right, you said, to subsidize good films rather than rent out video porn, indeed to make sure that inexpensive books of value (you said "classical" books) are available to everybody. I appreciate your intentions but cannot follow your conclusions. To some extent people's predilection for culture in totalitarian regimes is a substitute for other desires whose fulfillment they are denied. Once the pressure lifts, they go for tabloids and hamburgers and dishwashers and shiny motorcycles and holidays on the Costa Brava. It would be nice if some of the less shallow values could be preserved, but it is hard to see how this can be done. I suspect that even if your government continued to subsidize "good" films and "classical" books, people would prefer to see cheap romance and read trash, or no longer read at all.

The reason is simple, and important in this context. As one looks at our world from a distance, one would like to see the objectives in which one believes achieved directly and without detour or distraction. Perhaps what you call social democracy is an example of such an objective. But short of the horror of a "benevolent" dictatorship, this is not the way the world works. At least open societies do not work that way. Whether we like it or not, the pendulum swing from one side to the other—and it need not swing all the way from one extreme to the other—is the more likely rhythm of change. After the victory of social democracy in the OECD world, people wanted a new splurge of individualism, of innovation and initiative, and of consumerism. They elected Margaret Thatcher prime minister of Britain and Ronald Reagan president of the United States, and even their "socialist" leaders such as the prime ministers of Spain and Australia and New Zealand turned out to be what some called "left Thatcherites."

Now, at the beginning of the 1990s, the time may have come for us to turn back from the provisions party to the entitlements party, that is, from obsession with economic growth to recognition of the requirements of citizenship. Even the Republican president of the United States has promised a "kinder, gentler America," and in Europe the change of mood is unmistakable.

At the same time, it would not be surprising if your compatriots and your neighbors want to have their share of Western individualism, including consumerism and all that, before they remember the social needs of those who will be left behind. Some may regret this, but it is the price you pay for decades of glum and gray collectivism. I wish you well in your attempt to stem the tide of trash and glitter, but I suspect that it will sweep you away. Yours will be a minority position for a while, and as you undoubtedly perceive, I do not feel very sorry for you. At least I do not feel sorry as long as the swing of the pendulum remains contained by the limits of the open society. In practice, this means that it must be possible to vote Balcerowicz out of office (not too soon, I hope; in eight years' time perhaps) and replace him by a more social democratic politician.

This takes me back again to your question of political parties and their social bases. Who is going to support what in the years to come? What political structures are going to emerge from the collapse of the Communist monopoly? The question has vexing dimensions, for while it is clear that the party systems of the European democracies, and of North America for that matter, would sit uneasily on the post-Communist countries, your predicament reminds us of the fact that our own parties are out of date and out of tune with the times. The German experience has made the point perfectly. While West German parties have gone to great lengths and expense to restructure the numerous East German movements and sects along their lines, no fewer than thirteen groupings are represented in the freely elected parliament, and in many cases it is difficult to make sense of them either in terms of their programs or their electoral support.

One wonders whether, if we were in your position and had to build our party structures in the old democracies from scratch, the same would happen here. Along with class conflict, the two-party system has crumbled. Everywhere new groups seek a place among the old. Many of these are social movements, such as the Greens, or one-issue parties, like the Five-Eighths Party in Luxembourg (which demands that a retirement pension be five-eighths of a person's final income). Some try to cut across traditional divisions, such as the Alliance in Britain, now called the Social and Liberal Democrats. In the United States it has been observed that politics is now conducted by 536 entrepreneurs: 435 representatives, 100 senators, and one president. (The cynic might add that members of the House have a "turnover" of $1 million per election, members of the Senate $10 million, and the president $100 million.) You were thus quite right to raise the question of party after class, and I am not sure that my answer will satisfy you.

In your country, of course, as in others in the post-Communist world, you still have some way to go in order to join the great social democratic consensus. I suspect that if developments in East Central Europe remain undisturbed from out-side, or from antidemocratic forces within, the pendulum of normal politics will have to swing once in the liberal and once in the social direction before you feel that you have made it. The liberal direction means of course Balcerowicz if not Friedman (though I hope not Hayek); it involves the jump-start of economies whose batteries have been low for a very long time, with I hope the more fortu-nate countries of Europe and North America providing the lead with the nec-essary energy. The next steps can be taken in a variety of ways; *perestroika* too has as many variants as there are countries and organized views within them. They range from monetary union in Germany to massive privatization in Hungary. All of these steps will—and should—be taken as a part of the initial momentum of constitutional change, that is, before there are fully formed polit-ical parties. Opposition to this process is bound to arise, and it will be about the social cost of economic growth. At some point in four or even eight years' time (how I hope that you will have that time for reform which must seem endless and threatening now!), other groups will take over. They may even be called Social Democrats.

All the while, however, our own problem will be a lingering reality for you as well. Here the forces for change are fragmented and often weak. On the one hand, the place of class has been taken by what some have called "disparities of realms of life." This means that all of us have certain interests in common in one of our "realms of life," such as the integrity of the physical environment, whereas we may have divergent interests in other "realms of life," such as the distribution of wealth. Thus, trade unionists and employers can both be "green" at times, but they remain on opposite sides of the table when it comes to wage settlements. Special interests, and social movements built around them, take the place of political parties; individuals no longer "belong" to one group which combines most of their concerns, but they switch allegiances depending on the priority of one or another theme at different times. We have not yet invented institutions to accommodate this change. Not only parties but parliaments too were built around the idea of the class struggle, with the "right" and the "left" in their respective places if not on opposite sides. In any case, as you sit down to think about the rules of the game of your political process, you will wish to take the facts of conflict after class into account. Here too *The Federalist Papers* are rele-vant, not least because the United States Constitution was never constructed or applied to accommodate class cleavages in the European way.

The other force for change is even more problematic, and you may not like it at all. It consists of active minorities of people who have thought about things and have advice to give to those who are in a position to act on such advice. You prob-ably do not regard yourself as an intellectual, but I am one. I can therefore see that the demise of socialism not only has many practical consequences and raises questions such as those which you asked, but it also threatens the very existence of a group that has played a major role in the recent history of Europe. Perhaps intellectuals are not a group; they are a gaggle, a motley assortment, a category at best, but many of them have had a special affinity to socialism. Socialism was an intellectual invention, from Saint-Simon to Lassalle, from Marx to Gramsci, and through the hundreds of byways of Marxism which are now all ending in the sewers of discarded history.

One influential posture of intellectuals in Europe over the last hundred years had three ingredients. (In a halfhearted way they are still present among the bureaucratized intelligentsia in the universities and the media.) One was the outright rejection of present conditions as endemically rotten and incapable of repair. The second was a more or less elaborate vision of a totally different world in which the ills of reality are remedied. And the third was a great sense of certainty about both the rejection and the vision. Alienation, Utopia, and dogmatism do not form a very attractive triad, though it is one that leads almost naturally to versions of socialism which are not of the social democratic variety.

I say this without any sense of delight or superiority. After all, I grew up in this world, and have feelings of friendship for some of those who manage to combine their socialist certainties with a personal decency that belies their creed. One or two have even turned out to be reliable "constitutional patriots" without abandoning their claims to the rejection of the present and to a Utopian future. I feel much more alien among the new "intellectuals" of the right, notably among those who have embraced an unconditional and often vicious defense of Thatcherism with the same total devotion they once gave to socialism and even Communism. It is true that in recent years the unusual has happened, and *der Geist weht rechts*, creative minds have espoused right-wing causes. Some of these are of lasting importance. While John Rawls may survive Robert Nozick and others who were prepared to shed "justice as fairness" in favor of the "minimal state," public-choice theorists and constitutional economists have a great deal to offer when it comes to the issues with which I am dealing in this letter. But having said that, there remain the many for whom the demise of socialism means that a chasm has opened up, a great vacuum which is as disconcerting emotionally as it is intellectually. They no longer know where to go, and like the Italian Communist Party (of blessed memory) or the magazine *Marxism Today* in Britain, they combine a courageous preparedness for change with a remarkable confusion of ideas.

Some of these doubly homeless intellectuals—"free-floating" in any case and now robbed of their socialist mental home as well—try to keep a dream of some "real" socialism alive. They claim that none of the really existing versions had anything to do with the real thing; indeed, they were all betrayals of the true socialist ideal. They speak of "socialism with a human face," but the attempt is pathetic and will not lead anywhere. Kjell-Olof Feldt, a social democrat and former Swedish minister of finance, has put it succinctly: "If it is that difficult to give a concept a human face, I want nothing to do with it." I would recommend to those who still cannot get socialism out of their minds an intellectual tradition which is admittedly less impressive in numbers, but includes some upright individuals who have proved immune to the temptations of dogma and Utopian fantasies when these were strong. Karl Popper belongs squarely in this tradition. So does Raymond Aron, and perhaps Norberto Bobbio. John Maynard Keynes and William Beveridge have a place in this gallery. Max Weber can be found in it despite his early forays into nationalist pastures. The authors of *The Federalist Papers*—Alexander Hamilton, John Jay, and James Madison—were not tempted by tyranny, and likewise belong in this tradition (although I wonder what they would have said about being called intellectuals). And there are others, fortunately. They are all children of Kant, and of Hume and Locke before him, but emphatically not of Hegel or even of Rousseau. They are passionate defenders of the open society and at the same time committed reformers. One would be hard-pressed to place them on the left-right spectrum that the French Revolution has bequeathed us. Keynes put it well. He could not be a conservative—"I should not be amused or excited or edified." He could not be a socialist because he worried about "the party which hates existing institutions and believes that great good will result merely from overthrowing them." Rather, he wrote, "I incline to believe that the Liberal Party is still the best instrument of future progress—if only it had strong leadership and the right programme." Today the liberal *party* is just as likely to be a minority of active reformers who believe in the constitution of liberty.

All this is in some sense, by the way, more to amuse you than to answer your questions. Perhaps it helps to explain why I am so skeptical about social democracy, and also about the third way. My own liberal position is that of a constitutional liberalism in which the realm of normal politics advocates radical reform. I want to see entitlements of citizenship raised as well as the spirit of innovation and entrepreneurship aroused. Naturally, I believe that this is a helpful position both in your predicament and in ours. Communism has collapsed; social democracy is exhausted. We may have to live for some time with the shells of yesterday's politics, whatever their names may be. Thus, you will probably adopt the labels of political parties familiar from the older democracies. But the old politics is spent. Constitutional liberalism and social reform need to build a new alliance. This is neither just your problem nor merely ours; it is a European problem which we have to resolve together.   1990, vol. 57, no. 4

• The End of Communism?

Paul Hollander

The recent collapse of Communist states provides an unsurpassed opportunity to recall how long and tenacious the Western misperceptions of these systems had been, how confidently misjudgments were paraded, and how much resistance against revising these misconceptions still remains. This is an especially good time to ponder once more the relationship between theory and practice, that is, between the ideas and ideals of Marxism and the character of societies which were allegedly guided by or fashioned on behalf of, or in conjunction with, these ideals—in short, the relationship between "existing socialism" (the Communist states in Eastern Europe and elsewhere) and the ideals of socialism.

Did Communist practices merely give a bad name to socialist ideals (as some maintain) or were the ideals themselves defective or inherently difficult to realize? At last the collapse and total delegitimation of Communist systems also invites reexamination of the longstanding dispute in the West, and especially in the United States, between those who have been unembarrassed critics of Communism and those who brought us anti-anti-Communism.

Let me say something first about the reactions of the card-carrying anti-Communists, conservatives, and neoconservatives to the decline of Communist systems. Their aversion to these systems has been further validated by the new revelations following the reestablishment of free expression in Eastern Europe; we now have more evidence than ever about the specifics of political crimes and repression perpetrated by these systems (along with upwardly revised figures of the number of their victims); we have more inside information about lies routinely disseminated by their agitprop machinery; there is new, more detailed knowledge of their unsolved social problems and unsurpassed record of environmental degradation; there is even new revelation of the assistance (for long doubted by many in the West) these governments gave Western and Arab terrorist groups. Most important, anti-Communism has also been fully vindicated by the massive rejection of these systems by their own people and by the fresh evidence indicating not only their ruthlessness but also their inefficiency and inability to satisfy basic and modest material and human needs.

American and Western anti-Communists (myself included) were wrong only in one important respect: they attributed more strength and staying power to these systems than they actually possessed. They credited their leaders with a stronger grip on power; they thought their peoples more docile, helpless, or intimidated than was actually the case. Perhaps this had something to do with the totalitarian model (which I also regarded useful for understanding these systems through much of their existence) or simply with lack of imagination. In any event nobody in the West had anticipated the rapid unraveling of these systems—it was not a singular failing of their anti-Communist critics. On the other hand this unraveling does not justify the retroactive claim that these systems, and the Soviet Union in particular, have *never* represented a threat to the West or the United States, that Soviet aggression was a cold-war myth invented by Senator Joseph McCarthy and the military-industrial complex.

At the same time I am not sure how much the military build-up of the Reagan administration and its support for anti-Communist guerrillas hastened the decay of the Soviet empire, as is often claimed by conservatives. The Soviet Union shouldered huge military burdens throughout its existence, and its leaders did not flinch from imposing the attendant hardships on their people. Afghanistan was more important, and without American help the guerrillas would not have inflicted significant losses on the Soviet forces; in turn the failure to impose a military solution in Afghanistan was a notable factor in Soviet demoralization, both a cause and symptom of the loss of political will.

I do not believe that a more accommodationist American policy—such as was incessantly recommended by the liberal-left and the peace movement—would have been helpful in reducing Soviet expansionism, let alone would have contributed to domestic liberalization. (For example, not installing intermediate missiles in Western Europe was such a key demand; for others even Radio Free Europe and Radio Liberty were unwise "irritants" in the relationship between the United States and the Soviet Union.) Today everyone agrees that the domestic changes in the Soviet Union came about under the pressure of immense economic problems and not because of a sense of political security and material well-being that many Western sources stipulated as the only basis of democratization.

Much as I rejoice in the failures of Communism, I find the "end-of-history" viewpoint also bizarre; I believe that while Western pluralistic political systems and in a large measure contemporary capitalism too have been vindicated, we have no idea what the future will bring and no assurance that other, new varieties of authoritarian beliefs, movements, or political systems will not emerge.

Perhaps the most interesting reactions to the failure of Communist systems are coming from those for whom these developments should have provided an especially rewarding occasion for informed self-examination—those on the left who for decades have given every benefit of the doubt to political systems claiming socialist credentials and vigorously disputed (or muted) the critical assessments of these systems. We might designate this sizable and vocal group as the professional anti-anti-Communists, influential since the late 1960s and nourished by the lasting discredit Senator McCarthy brought to outspoken anti-Communism. They are mostly intellectuals and other educated groups, brought together by their aversion to American culture, the American political system, and American capitalism, as well as by their belief that no other society can match the corruptions of this one. These views have been most visibly and vocally expressed on our elite campuses and adjacent enclaves.

Anti-anti-Communists, radical leftists, and left-liberals responded in a rather predictable way to the collapse of "existing socialist systems" in Eastern Europe and Nicaragua. Their responses confirm once more that groups and individuals do not surrender lightly the beliefs which provide them with a sense of identity, meaning, communal ties, and the underpinnings of a moral universe. If, in addition, the public and private embrace of these beliefs also helps to make a living — as it has for many in the flourishing social criticism industry (in academia, the mass media, publishing, and so on) — there are still more substantial reasons for clinging to them.

We can better understand these attitudes by recalling that — besides the increasingly reflexive rejection of American society — the other centerpiece of this adversarial outlook has been a belief in some sort of socialism or "socialist alternative," often informed by what I have called elsewhere a "god-seeking Marxism." (I will not attempt here to improve on the insights into the religious functions and dimensions of Marxism provided by Raymond Aron and Leszek Kolakowski.) These beliefs survived notwithstanding the difficulty of finding countries that lived up to the hopes of those in the West waiting for the arrival of authentic socialism, and who from time to time thought that it had finally materialized (first in the Soviet Union, then in China, Cuba, Vietnam, or in the undifferentiated wonderland of the third world, and finally in Nicaragua), only to turn away, sooner or later, in disappointment from these flesh and blood incarnations of the ideal.

Still, the desire for a "socialist alternative" (to the corruption, injustice, and inhumanity of Western capitalist systems) persisted. Although the political systems now utterly discredited and collapsing in Eastern Europe and the Soviet Union have not been greatly admired by the critics of Western societies since the death of Stalin, they were not subjected to the type of searching and merciless criticism these critics so eagerly aimed at their own social systems. After all, these systems expunged capitalism.

The American (and Western) critics of capitalism could not quite believe that Soviet-type systems were totally lacking in legitimacy among their own people; they subscribed to the belief that while they did not excel in the provision of political liberties, they did provide their people with material security and a commendably egalitarian income distribution. The critics of the West did not know or found it difficult to believe that these socialist countries developed new forms of inequality which became deeply entrenched and that they were also riddled with social problems identical or very similar to those found in the decadent West. As far as the Soviet Union was concerned, its deficiencies were often ascribed to and excused by American intrigues, the arms race, a troubled history, and so on.

Thus certain illusions about these systems persisted even after they were no longer revered; the Western (and especially the more radical) left never really took their full measure because it was never much interested in them and their defects. Social democrats were the major exception; they remained unrepentant critics of Communist systems at a time (between the late 1960s and throughout the 1980s) when anti-anti-Communism was the proper attitude among people who thought of themselves as enlightened liberals.

It should be emphasized that those of left and left-liberal persuasion had ample opportunities to rethink their beliefs regarding "existing socialist systems" well before their recent collapse—but they were not terribly interested in those in Eastern Europe. They preferred the newer socialist states in the third world which more readily gratified their longings for some uncorrupted, harmonious, preindustrial realm, populated by poor but pure, happy, and unpossessive peasants thriving on authentic communal bonds. But then the supply of such countries began to run out as their images became tarnished: Cuba persecuted homosexuals, China was receptive to capitalism (and massacred students on television), Vietnam presided over the flight of the boat people. Nicaragua through the 1980s inspired great hopes but that too came to an end when in 1990 its benighted masses "voted with their bellies and not with their hearts" (in the words of William Sloan Coffin)—as the event came to be described among erstwhile supporters. At last came the spectacular collapse of the East European Communist states and the accelerating change (and decay) in the Soviet Union.

The adversarial (or radical) left could not ignore the demise of existing socialist (or Communist) systems because of its justified apprehension that their collapse could be used to enhance the legitimacy of the United States, capitalism, or Western culture, and to vindicate anti-Communism—the most troubling prospect for the upholders of anti-anti-Communism. So the battle was joined not merely by the contributors to The Nation or The Village Voice and many "alternative" publications, but also by many academic Marxists, well-known New York Times columnists, and various op-ed page authors seeking to minimize the damage to anti-anti-Communism.

Several approaches and arguments emerged in these apologetics and rationalizations designed to salvage deeply held beliefs threatened by the new developments. One recurring theme has been that whatever happened in Eastern Europe proves nothing about the ills and evils of capitalism and American society or should be understood to suggest that Western systems are in any way morally superior to Communist ones. Often each new revelation of the misdeeds or failures of Communist systems was instantly paired with some allegedly similar American vice or flaw. The improvements associated with glasnost came to be used to highlight the lack of change or reform in the United States. We have been inundated with warnings against American (or Western) self-righteousness and gloating and reminders of how many things are wrong with American (Western, capitalist) systems. Those particularly energetic or imaginative in this salvaging enterprise have insisted that developments in Eastern Europe merely show that Stalinism but not authentic Marxian socialism was rejected. When in the autumn of 1989 East Germans began to pour out in record numbers, an editorial in *The Nation* seriously suggested that this merely represented their going "from Stalin back to Marx"—the evidence being their choice of West Germany over Thatcher's England or "aprés-Reagan America"! It also has been proposed that even if it were true that East Europeans actually preferred capitalism to socialism, this may be a short-lived aberration, a form of false consciousness, or (as a British writer put it) manifestation of being "besotted with consumerist glitz"; or as an American kindred spirit observed (in the context of Nicaragua), "A few Nicaraguans will again enjoy the freedom of the shopping mall."

Much energy has been invested in claiming that no matter what happened in Eastern Europe (or the Soviet Union, Nicaragua, Mongolia, and so on), it had no relevance whatsoever to the riches and inspiring qualities of Marxist theory, since the systems in question had nothing to do with Marxism. Actually the Western left for some time has been divided on this matter; there have been many who took the above position while others thought that these systems at least tried to implement or apply Marxism, or parts of it (often under difficult conditions as in the Soviet Union, China, or Cuba), for which they should be given some credit. The currently popular argument—rapidly approaching the status of conventional wisdom—that these systems had nothing whatsoever to do with Marxism is, however, not tenable. While the gap between theory and practice has always been deep, this has more to do with *the intended and hoped for results* of particular policies and institutional transformations derived from the *theory* than with the distance between the policies themselves and the theory. The issue was aptly summarized well before the recent events, by three authors by no means unsympathetic to Marxism—Ferenc Feher, Agnes Heller, and Gyorgy Markus: "since socialism does not exist except as the sum of its historically existing varieties, nineteenth and early twentieth-century socialist doctrines are at least co-responsible for the 'real socialism' of today, even if we reassert . . . that the upshot is not socialism in any meaningful and acceptable sense of the term."

Let me note a few matters which suggest that Marxist theory and the Communist practices had *something* to do with one another, that the theory/practice divergence was far from total: most Communist leaders—Lenin, Stalin, Mao, and Castro as well as lesser figures—invested a great deal of energy in the study and theoretical development of Marxism (never mind the results) and gave many indications of being inspired and motivated by it; they found these ideas eminently suitable for legitimating their policies. The populations under their rule were compelled to familiarize themselves with Marxism or large chunks of it, and a vital core of Marxism, anti-capitalism (or hostility to private enterprise), was institutionalized in all these systems. The means of production were taken out of private hands; central planning was established; antireligious consciousness-raising campaigns were introduced, and institutional religion curtailed. The personal intolerance of Marx found institutionalized expression in political intolerance, and Marx's hostility to peasants became official policy. The political systems inspired by Marxism also absorbed the collectivistic ethos which pervades Marxism and which had an affinity with the authoritarian practices undertaken in its name. In brief, as David Horowitz put it recently, Marxist ideas and prescriptions exercised a "gravitational pull" on these systems. The salvage operation regarding the responsibility of Marxist theory for Marxist-Leninist (Stalinist, Maoist, and other) practices is also undertaken by focusing attention on the most general, humanitarian aspects and messages of Marxism (that is, the early Marx) the furthest removed from any application.

It is particularly important to address the parallel often drawn these days between Christianity and Marxism and the associated rhetorical question: should we also discard Christianity because of the Inquisition, corrupt popes, and other unappealing practices which were linked to it, or legitimated by it? Reject Christian values because of the small number of true Christians among us? But Christianity (and its various incarnations) did not make the same inordinate demands on human lives and social arrangements, nor did it seek to overcome (except on rare historical occasions) the division between the private and public realm; nor did these beliefs (obviously) claim to be scientific truths. And while religious intolerance too has been the source of conflict, bloodshed, and repression, Christianity did not inspire or legitimate slaughter and enslavement on a scale comparable to those Communist systems perpetrated. After all, a good deal of Christianity devalued existence here and now, hence its involvement with transforming life on this earth — its involvement with "theory and practice" — was inherently more limited, as was therefore its capacity to do damage. (Another difference of lesser moral importance: Christianity, unlike Marxism, inspired a vast amount of good art and music; it has also inspired enduring forms of charity and service to existing human beings, rather than to abstractions.) Also of some interest and relevance, as we pursue these parallels, unlike Marxism, Christianity has provided a sustaining worldview for hundreds of millions of people; Marxism and its varieties nourished intermittently small, elite groups, more often than not legitimating their power drives.

The argument that Communist practices discredited praiseworthy socialist ideals also has been advanced by people who are not Marxists. But what precisely is the socialism that Communism — the attempted applications of Marxism —

besmirched? Here the responses may divide between those who might point to Scandinavian countries as existing examples of a humane socialism and those who admit that socialism has not had so far any authentic or appealing incarnation but argue that this need not mean that we give up on awaiting or seeking its arrival. For the latter group "socialism" has become something of a code word for good intentions, decency, caring, a generalized affirmation of social justice, humane welfare-state policies, respect for a wide range of individual rights — values and policies not especially distinctive and already discernible in a number of Western societies which are more capitalistic than not.

Recent reflections of a Polish writer, Jerzy Surdykowski, suggest that those who had witnessed the attempts to realize socialism are less than sanguine about it *even as an ideal*. He wrote:

> . . . the most dangerous myth of the left, especially the Communist left, and one that it shares with many who are by no means leftists is: the desire to construct on earth an ideal state, one of the oldest dreams of humanity.
>
> Some socialists who consider themselves democratic and antitotalitarian have also become "enchanted with Plato" by nurturing hopes for a "better kind of socialism." No one has ever succeeded in constructing a system that would both deserve this name and give people at least a little more spiritual satisfaction and material prosperity than any other system. . . . Today when many people are searching for a "third way," a "self-governing republic," or similar constructs formulated under the slogan of "the democratic left," they are too echoing, however faintly, Plato.
>
> If socialism . . . does not contain within itself a gnostic faith in the inevitability of a Brave New World, if it does not promise all other kinds of happiness, what is left? . . . the notion of a socialist system or even socialist ideology is simply an illusion.

It may also be noted here that the most left-wing social critics in the United States have shown little interest in or enthusiasm for the Scandinavian systems, while they readily conferred the "socialist" title upon an impressive number of one-party dictatorships in the third world that legitimated themselves with some variety of Marxism-Leninism but failed to provide their people either with political rights or material-economic gains.

The Nicaraguan election was the last straw for the American left, far more devastating than the events in Eastern Europe and the Soviet Union. Nicaragua was for a decade the new hope and the most cherished setting for those anxiously waiting for the emergence of an inspiring socialist system. While its collapse was blamed on the United States (economic blockade, support for the *contras*, false promises of economic assistance if the opposition won), the popular rejection of the system removed the country from the itinerary of those who had difficulty rejecting the United States without being able to project their longings on an existing redemptive political system. That these attitudes had a utopian or quasi-utopian flavor is also suggested by the fact that according to recent reports the most committed supporters who used to live and work in Nicaragua are abandoning it. They do so not because the new government is expelling them, or because there is no longer need to help Nicaraguans to harvest coffee beans, dig wells, or build rural clinics and schools. "The concept of construction brigades lost its flair" is how a former volunteer put it. According to a coordinator of the Witness for Peace Delegations, "Folks are finding themselves moving to other countries where there is a lot of conflict, like the Middle East and South Africa." If so, the impulse to help Nicaragua and its people had more to do with the mystique of participating in the (presumed) redemptive revolutionary transformation of a society and the excitement generated by it than with helping flesh and blood human beings in their prosaic day-to-day existence.

I think that one effect of the events here discussed on the American (and Western) left and especially the radical left will be a further intensification of social criticism aimed at the United States, as if to confirm the claim that just because putative socialist systems failed, the United States or capitalism does not have a moral edge over them, or over the unfulfilled ideals of socialism. I believe that this trend has been with us since the early 1980s, stimulated in part by the anger and frustration the Reagan presidency had created in these circles.

Support for the African National Congress will remain on the agenda (and the corresponding demands for divestment); sympathy and support for the Communist guerrillas in El Salvador (and the associated criticism of United States foreign policy) will also persist; the overextended and disfigured concept of "racism" will continue to be used as perhaps the single most devastating (and intimidating) critique of American society (and of particular individuals); other critiques in part modeled after attributions of racism (and perhaps also stimulated by the institutionalized rewards provided to its real or putative victims) will continue to be voiced by other certified victims groups—feminists, homosexuals, AIDS victims, and their more privileged supporters and advocates, and others.

American society will continue to inspire and nurture a vast array of discontents and frustrations which will be blamed either on capitalism or on the more unique deformities of American culture. In doing so, the critics will persist in confusing the sources of their discontent which are stimulated by capitalism (or American social institutions) with those which are rooted in the far more general afflictions of modernity, including freedom, individualism, and affluence, all of which are at once intensely desired and bitterly denounced.

1991, vol. 58, no. 1

• Intellectuals and the Failure of Communism
Walter Laqueur

The intellectual impact of the collapse of Communism in the Soviet Union and Eastern Europe may well be less palpably felt in America than in Europe or the Far East for some time to come. There are a number of reasons why this is so. The study of the Soviet Union, of Eastern Europe, and of the third world has been strongly influenced for about two decades by a school of thought that in many articles and books, conferences and seminars has exaggerated the achievements of Communism and belittled its failures. While Lenin's mistakes and Stalin's crimes were not denied, it was argued that by and large, and in a long-term perspective, these were less significant than the political, social, and economic achievements of the Communist regimes.

Such misjudgments have been by no means limited to the left; they have extended to the political and academic establishment, the media, and even Western intelligence—as shown, until very recently, by the erroneous estimates of the Soviet and East European economies. The doctrine of equidistance between East and West was fashionable, and in the 1970s it became bad form to use the term *totalitarianism* in the political discourse about the Soviet system. Even today this is widely considered a "loaded," that is to say "propagandistic," term. In the Soviet Union, firsthand experience has lent wide currency to "totalitarianism," and comparisons between Nazism and Stalinism are considered perfectly legitimate even among Communist Party members. Many such examples could be adduced: Soviet and East European comments on their recent history and on Marxist and radical ideology are far more outspoken and truthful today than those still heard in Western circles.

Why should Western thinking have been mistaken so often? This is a question of considerable importance that will be studied in the years to come. Yet it would be quite unrealistic to assume that events in the Soviet Union and Eastern Europe will produce a collective admission of guilt in Western revisionist thought. To own up to mistakes is a painful process and, just as in daily life many prefer to think of justifications and excuses for their past behavior rather than admit error, many will think very hard of reasons why they might have been right after all. This kind of reaction is true even in the natural sciences, where ideology and political bias play only a minimal role. Max Planck, of quantum theory fame, once noted that the great controversies in the history of science have not been resolved by persuasion and admissions of mistakes but by the disappearance of the party that happened to be wrong. Since many "revisionists" are in their forties, the day of reckoning may be some considerable time off. A visit to almost any university bookstore in the United States and in Great Britain tends to show that, to give but two examples, Isaac Deutscher's *Stalin* (first published in 1949) and Geoffrey Barraclough's *Introduction to Contemporary History* (published in the early 1960s) are still used as basic textbooks for new generations of students. Their teachers obviously grew up with these books, and it does not make the slightest difference that these books were proved hopelessly wrong in the light of what has happened since then in the Soviet Union and the third world.

Even if socialism were officially abolished in the Soviet Union and the other East European countries, this would not necessarily bring about the total collapse of Marxism as an ideology in the West. For it can always be argued that while the idea per se was correct and productive, it was a mistake to try to build Communism in backward countries, and that the result elsewhere would have been quite different. It could be maintained that while the October Revolution was inevitable, Lenin erred grievously by suppressing democracy in the Soviet Union and Stalin compounded these errors by setting up his machine of terror. In brief, it is argued, Communism is no more disproved by Stalinism than is Christianity disproved by the Inquisition and other similar aberrations.

Most of those who have argued for many years that America was as much (if not more than) to blame for the Cold War as the Soviet Union will no doubt continue to stick to their guns. It has already been said that there have been no winners and losers, for America has ruined herself in the course of an unnecessary arms race—not to mention the domestic political and psychological damage that has ensued—resulting in the militarization of our thinking and our political culture.

I find it impossible to discuss such views seriously; their proper place is in a satirical novel in the tradition of David Lodge or Malcolm Bradbury. (I wish that Robyn Penrose, Lodge's *Nice Work* character, a lecturer in English literature at the fictional Rummidge University, would travel one of these days accompanied by his Professor Zap to the strange world of the "revisionists.") Nor will they cut much ice beyond those in the media and *academe* who feel that they have to defend their record.

There are other, more weighty factors likely to limit the impact of the collapse of Communism. This refers both to developments in the Soviet Union and Eastern Europe in the post-Communist era and the events in the West, more specifically in the United States. It cannot be taken for granted that the transition towards a democratic order in these parts will be relatively smooth and uncomplicated and that it will be accomplished in the not too distant future. Some countries may make decisive progress on the road to freedom, but in most, including the Soviet Union, prospects are far from brilliant. As long as there is no substantial economic progress, social tensions will not be resolved but on the contrary may grow more acute. (In fact, such tensions may become more acute irrespective of economic progress.)

Nationalist passions may be running high and may become even more intense in the years to come, leading to violence on a massive scale. While Communism is at present deeply discredited, it may well look better at the distance of a decade or two unless considerable progress is made. It will be argued, for instance, that for all their other sins, Stalin and his successors at least suppressed national strife in their empire. And if the Soviet Union should disintegrate can we be sure that the emergence of a dozen sovereign Turkmenistans and Tadjikistans, much of the time battling each other, will be a major step to global peace and progress?

The failure of Communism in Eastern Europe (or in Cuba, China, Vietnam, and elsewhere) will not have an immediate decisive impact on radical criticism of democratic societies. This is obviously because political views are shaped above all by events at home rather than abroad. Whether America will remain the greatest exporter of goods and services or whether its net savings rate will continue to slip, or whether high-tech exports continue to decline, may be of less importance than the doomsayers claim. But one needs hardly to enumerate all the major social ills from inner city ghettos, the crime rate, the widening gap between rich and poor, to the sad state of American education and the scandalous backwardness as far as health and other social services are concerned, to realize that there is no room for complacency. To state that American capitalism has performed better than Soviet Communism is a backhanded compliment. The complacency will probably give way in the coming years to an equally unjustified pessimism: if there has been an American decline, it is not irreversible.

It is quite unlikely that the collapse of Communism will strengthen conservative parties in Europe. True, socialist parties in Sweden and the Netherlands have lost influence over the last few years, but France and Spain are ruled by social democrats, and their chances for electoral victory in Germany and Britain have improved in recent months. If their prospects are now better than a year or two ago, it is precisely because they have dropped much of their extremist and utopian ballast. The differences between the social and economic policies of the social democrats and the conservatives (which in the European context more often than not are really centrist parties) are less and less important: both are in favor of the market; both want to keep the welfare state. In essential respects, Europe has moved into a direction of which the early Fabians and Eduard Bernstein would approve.

In a recent issue of *Partisan Review* (1990, no. 3), William Phillips quoted an American professor to the effect that recent events in Eastern Europe will "not reverse the impressive growth of leftist faculty in universities." I do not find the statement surprising at all, and Mr. Bowles is probably right, at least in the short run. Ever since Talleyrand wrote to Mallet du Pan about the Bourbons, *ils n'ont rien appris, ni rien oublié*, there are countless examples for the astonishing capacity of survival of Bourbonic ideologies. The fact that pan-Germanism had been defeated in the First World War did not affect the political views of large sections of the German middle class after 1918; Trotskyism continued to exist in various parts of the world long after it had lost any relevance to the real world. One could think of many other examples; sectarianism has almost always flourished. A not inconsiderable part of the Soviet intelligentsia continues to pay respect, after all that happened, to Stalin or, alternatively, has been converted to belief in the Judeo-Masonic conspiracy, *The Protocols of the Elders of Zion*. A price, of course, has to be paid for sectarianism—political influence will be beyond its reach. But most sectarians do not even want political influence; they are perfectly content in their own little ghetto.

Isolation is part of the price they will pay, boredom the other. I find the literary and political magazines published in the Soviet Union infinitely more interesting these days than anything published in the West. The Western radicals have had their say, and for years they have been repeating themselves. Among Soviet intellectuals, on the other hand, there is an openness to new ideas, a willingness to confront past mistakes, an intellectual curiosity and sophistication for which one looks in vain nearer home.

With all this one should end perhaps on a note of cautious optimism. What Max Planck said about the outcome of great intellectual controversies may apply more to Europe than America. Intellectual fashions have a shorter life in this fickle country than elsewhere, perhaps because ideas (and ideology) are still not taken as seriously as in other parts. This may have sometimes welcome consequences; perhaps we shall be spared some of the intellectual agonies of the latter-day Bourbons.

There is another, more positive aspect. What our American professor calls "leftist" can mean a great many things. He mentions "scholarship critical of American capitalism"—something which Mr. Kevin Phillips has been doing of late with great effect. He also refers to Norway and Austria as role models for socialists. This is very tame stuff; who does not admire Norway? A year or two ago, I suspect, we would have been offered far more radical fare. If so, recent events did perhaps have, after all, some effect.

In the Soviet Union "leftist" or "left-wing" refers to the party of reform, even of revolution, against the existing order and doctrine; "right-wing" and "conservative" refers to neo-Stalinism and ultranationalism, as indeed it should. Despite decades of indoctrination, Soviet intellectuals eventually came to question the basic tenets, first Stalin, subsequently Lenin, and eventually Marx. I find it difficult to believe that a similar process will not take place sooner or later in American universities. The year 1989 was not the end of the socialist idea and the final, irrevocable triumph of the American way of life. The socialist idea may well have a future but only if those subscribing to it are ready to examine search-

ingly and honestly what went wrong and why. This is bound to lead them away
from most of the gods worshiped only yesterday, away from scientific claims and
utopian extremism to the revisionism of a century ago. These revisionists of 1900
have long been discredited among the neophiliacs and considered intellectually
unexciting. But, in retrospect, they are infinitely more relevant for those who
have embraced the cause of political freedom and social justice.

1991, vol. 58, no. 3

• Soft Totalitarianism
Steven Marcus

It may only be another confirmation of the discouraging state of affairs in society
today, but a good part of the phenomena that fall into the category of political
correctness was already clearly described in its general outlines more than forty
years ago. I am referring of course to George Orwell's classic essay of 1946,
"Politics and the English Language," and to his expansion and elaboration of its
insights in 1984, particularly in the appendix on Newspeak. Although the epoch
of Hitler and Stalin has long since passed, and totalitarianism in the forms associated with those two incomparable tyrants no longer prevails as an immediate
threat to the world, or to large portions of it, some of the qualities and attributes
that characterized the cultural life of the age of totalitarianism linger on and
remain with us yet, in modulated, mitigated, or attenuated forms, a kind of soft
totalitarianism — along with a residual totalitarianoid sensibility. In particular the
corrupted language that emanates nowadays from our institutions of culture and
intellect expresses at point after point its affiliation with the historic experience
of totalitarianism out of which we are still emerging — or from which, one might
more austerely suggest, we have not yet fully emerged. Totalitarianism is, after
all, the twentieth century's contribution to the forms of extreme orthodoxy.
Orthodoxies of one kind or another have enjoyed a long and sustained existence
among human societies. Sometimes they act to create order and hold groups of
people together. As a rule they also tend to muzzle, stifle, or suppress dissent, and
create anxiety and fear in those whose thinking deviates from their prescriptions.
The situation as it exists today represents a continuation of the state of things represented by Orwell, but by other means and in other dimensions.

The orthodoxies in question are chiefly those that are loosely associated with
the liberal left in a variety of areas and discourses and are organized around a variety of causes or projects. One major difference that has occurred since Orwell
published his indictments of the political abuses of language and intelligence is
that there is at present no single party or group of sub-parties or shadow parties

with a unified, centrally-controlled party line and apparatus of propaganda to which believers and adherents can refer their allegiances. Another difference is that the focus of such cultural-political goings-on has, at least in America and some other parts of the West, shifted from the region of politics at large to the more confined though still spacious precincts of our institutions of higher education, our colleges and universities, our learned societies and professional organizations, our philanthropic foundations, museums, and other centers of cultural activity. What this transposed location registers, among much else, is the immensely increased importance of higher education in Western societies—an importance that touches almost every locus of human enterprise—scientific, technical, technological, economic, social, cultural. Universities as institutions have become central to the workings of our societies in a wholesale variety of new senses. And as a matter of course, many of the conflicts, inequities, injustices, and abuses of those same societies have found new registries and appeared in novel but recognizable forms within these institutions. The ideological orthodoxies referred to by the term "political correctness" and its variations have largely to do with attitudes and movements that have arisen in opposition to such inequities and injustices and have as their purpose the countering and rectification of their harmful influences. Moreover, the corruptions of both language and thinking that are associated with this group of phenomena have become densely entangled with the organizational structures taken by these virtuous causes themselves. As a result, those causes tend to be reciprocally influenced, not for the better, by the means they are articulated through, by the language in which they are prosecuted and promoted, by the cultural styles of their representations—and as in the past, the republic of virtue, even before it is realized, has begun to take visible shape as a congregation of dunces, or something even less savory.

A fundamental assumption of these loosely associated cohorts is, to cite the ongoing cliché, that "everything is political." In this axiomatic presupposition, they appear to agree with Orwell. "In our age," he wrote, "there is no such thing as 'keeping out of politics.' All issues are political issues." But he then went on to add what few of our contemporaries would, I believe, acknowledge in a similarly convincing self-inclusive and self-incriminating sense: "and politics itself is a mass of lies, evasions, folly, hatred, and schizophrenia. When the general atmosphere is bad, language must suffer." Orwell was making his declaration from a restrictive and specific historical perspective; he was not asserting that politics were universally and at all times as debased as he believed, with justification, the politics of his time to be; indeed, he felt trapped in the poisonous political universe of the thirties and forties and longed, often nostalgically, for a world and a time in which political life had a less lethal character to it—his novel of 1939, *Coming Up for Air*, is all about such a daydream. But when our orthodox contemporaries affirm that "everything is political," they are speaking in error and in

contradiction of certain of their own philosophical convictions: they are universalizing, absolutizing, and essentializing, to use a few choice fragments of the
current jargon. They are, in addition, repeating, in a different region of discourse,
an error that certain of their predecessors had made earlier.

One of the historic disabilities of vulgar Marxism was its tendency toward economic reductionism. All human phenomena, including such cultural artifacts as
poetry, music, and logic, could be "explained" by reference to the economic
base, or modes of production and ownership, out of which different societies created and perpetuated themselves. This species of reductive explanation was not
to be confused with other kinds of analysis that strove to demonstrate the socially
or historically contextualized nature of cultural artifacts, and that insisted upon
multiple determination in any explanatory account of social eventuations. Such
analyses sought to anatomize simultaneously both the historically grounded circumstances that were almost inevitably refracted in most cultural objects along
with the relative autonomy of the so-called superstructure, its loose and incom-
pletely determined nature as well. And it was with the purpose of modulating
reductive simplicities and addressing more adequately the complexities of cultural and mental life that such projects as the sociology of knowledge and
Gramsci's reflections on hegemony were undertaken. The spirit of these essays
in ideological analysis was anti-reductive and anti-totalitarian, even as both
worked toward a larger inclusiveness of explanatory purview. Hence the assertion
that "everything is political" is at the level of intellectual and cultural pathology
the functional equivalent of the return of the repressed; perhaps it would be more
salient to remark that it is like a bad penny turning up again.

What moves large numbers—if not all—of those who adhere to soft totalitarian convictions is first a shared sense of victimhood. Such presentment of ill-usage
is what tends to join and shape those who share it into a group. The form favored
by such groups is extremely likely to be that of a "community," a *Gemeinschaft* no
less. Those unfortunate members of our society who have been born with or who
have acquired—through whatever agency or combination of natural and human
causes—physical handicaps now belong to what they themselves describe as "the
disability community." No one can or should blame them for the anger and
resentment they bear against nature for their disadvantaged physical state, and
against social institutions for treating them as being less than fully endowed in
their humanity. At the same time, and in the next breath, that "community" of the
disabled rejects the idea of disability itself and demands that it be publicly
renamed as the "differently abled," as if the altered nomenclature had some inde-
scribable power to abolish the condition by renaming it. At the end of this line of
inelegant variations is the by-now-famous suggestion that very short people are
hence forward to be thought of, and referred to, as "vertically challenged"—perhaps "specially non-tall" might have done almost as well. One of the striking

things about such examples is the extraordinary insensitivity to language and the common idiom that they reveal; it's almost as if there were a counter-linguistic spirit impelling such locutions and ensuring that they be obtrusive, inept, and self-defeating. Another is their immunity to the apprehension that such expressions, in their awkwardness and absurdity, are often open invitations to harsh and virtually irresistible humor and ridicule. Indeed it is the humorlessness, the lack of comic or ironic self-awareness, that is often most arresting about politically correct language, rhetoric, and terminology. It shares this incapacity with other historical orthodoxies, one of the compelling characteristics of group thought apparently being that it does not come with a sense of humor as standard equipment.

Even more, orthodoxies tend to be aggrieved by and resentful of humor, jokes, and comedy, and regularly respond with clamorous hostility to all three, as if they were exclusively enjoyed at their expense. To be sure, cruel and offensive humor is often used by dominant groups to diminish and render ineligible the claims of those whom they exclude from membership. But jokes and comedy can also be anarchic, aggressive, lawless, and individualistic repudiations of the normative assertions made by any group; they can and have been regularly used to resist and expose the pieties that group allegiances are likely to express themselves in. Hence the formidable humorlessness of much politically correct language is in part an understandable counterpart to the aggressive, individualistic resistance of irony, comedy, and humor to collective claims.

The reader will also have noticed, as Orwell himself had noted before, that there is a tendency in this kind of language toward euphemism. Insincerity breeds contempt. Vague and blurred language permits one to ignore the gap between "one's real and one's declared aims." It also permits one to express malice in an ostensibly neutral manner. I recently was indirectly a witness to a minor incident that illustrates this last point. It was reported to me that a male colleague had been guilty of making a sexist remark to a younger female colleague and that he had done this while committing substance abuse. What happened was that a senior male had indeed said something both unpleasant and disrespectful to a younger female after he had had too much to drink. What I want to call attention to is the use in this situation of "substance abuse." Scientific in provenance, dispassionate in tone, Latinate in derivation, it is supposed on the surface to supply us with an appropriately impersonal and non-moralistic descriptive context for the behavior in question. But what it does in fact is to assimilate several glasses too many of wine (the substance in question) to lines of cocaine, to the drug trade, Alcoholics Anonymous, potential violence, and heaven knows what else. And "substance abuse" becomes itself, in the course of this politically adaptive recontextualization, a term of abuse.

An analogous fate seems to have overtaken such a word as "diversity," which has mutated from a general term referring to formal ideas about the desirability of what used to be thought of as pluralisms of goals, ideas, and representatives of groups to certain specific and even quantifiable results. In this setting, diversity can come to be compatible with—if not the same thing as—separatism, isolation, and bureaucratically mandated quotas. From the relatively safe and insulated perspective of the American campus, one can see the further playing out on the larger international scene of such ideas in the atrocities that are being committed in the name of "ethnic cleansing." And as part of this latter process, one witnesses the creation of "safe havens," an Orwellian term for extensive concentration camps, which are, to boot, safe to bomb at will. It is difficult not to be reminded of Newspeak and doublethink forty years later. The lines of causal influence run in both directions. Bad, sloppy, careless language is the vehicle of and conduces to careless, foggy, imprecise, and manipulated thinking, and both in turn make it easier to do things and support causes that one would otherwise steer clear of, or at least be more cautious in approaching.

The current language of political "struggle" tends to anesthetize the intellect. Out of thousands of examples, here is one chosen almost at random from the writing of a student political leader. "It's about time that we stop apologizing for being hostile, emotional, and militant. It's about time we take sweeping actions to send a message to the racist oppressors that we are tired of your shit." On the one hand virtually every word or phrase in these two sentences—including shit— is a cliché. Terms such as racism, colonialism, sexism, and equality have tended to lose most of their specific meanings; like fascism in the thirties and forties, they only signify something general that one feels entirely justified in disapproving of without qualification. On the other hand, such language can be deployed in a tactical sense to useful destructive ends. If in some familiar situation of academic dispute, an ancient fogy of a professor or a dopey administrator rises up and suggests something to the effect that reason and compromise are preferable to intimidation and coercion, such vaguely incendiary expressions as I have quoted can be conveniently brought out to shut him up. Reason and compromise are after all the shit handed out by racist oppressors, and it is we, on the contrary, who are being intimidated and coerced, even as we write and publish these very utterances—indeed such utterances are themselves the proof and warrant of our continued oppression. And there should be nothing surprising in the circumstances that the broad context that originally gave rise to such remarks happened to be a discussion about the curriculum.

Moreover, it is the curriculum that has provided occasions for some of the better illustrations of politicizing language that has been put into anesthetic slumber through overuse, misuse, and displacement. Here, for example, is part of a statement outlining the new aims of American studies. "Freed from the defensive constraints of cold war ideology, empowered by our new sensitivity to the distinctiveness of race, class, and gender, we are ready to begin to understand difference as a series of power relationships involving domination and subordination, and to use our understanding of power relationships to reconceptualize both our interpretation and our teaching of American culture." Apart from the idea that American studies should henceforth have an overt politically driven academic agenda, thinking in such a passage is in a state of indefinite repose. "Ideology," "empowered," "sensitivity," "r, c, g," "difference," "power relationships," and "reconceptualize" are all within this context of airless prose as inert as last semester's notes.

Part of the point of such language is that it asserts one's goodness of will, intentions of virtue and benignity, radical courage and solidarity of sentiment with the oppressed, the deprived, the needy, and the mistreated. It is very difficult, indeed it would be wicked and perverse, to disparage these motives; they are indeed impeccable. But the results they can lead to are something else. For example, some scholars' *engagés* have undertaken to explore how the English language itself has been the unconscious vehicle for racist and colonialist thinking. "Snow White" as the name of the heroine of a fairy tale is one frequently-cited example of such an unwitting if baleful tendency. I recently ran across another instance brought forward by an anthropologist who is studying American political and cultural colonialism. As evidence of this pervasive social disposition, the anthropologist referred to the candy Mars Bars as a confectionery embodiment of America's indefensible impulse to colonize everything, including extraterrestrial planetary space. It was not a relevant consideration that 1) the candy was named and marketed long before space flight had ever occurred; or 2) that the name belongs to the family that owns the candy manufacturing company. In this instance, as in many others throughout our history, silliness and scholarship consort in happy tendentiousness.

As does ignorance consort as well. A colleague recently recounted to me that she had been teaching Keats's "The Eve of St. Agnes" to a class of students who were by and large studying poetry for the first time. She asked the students what their first responses to this marvelous early nineteenth-century rendering of a romance were, and, after some hesitation, a bright young woman responded, "Date rape." Soft totalitarianism can occur in moments that are almost winning in their poignancy.

I close with these two illustrations that are amusing in their fatuity and triviality. And I do so not because I think that the situation in our universities is a good one or that their condition is not serious. Far from it. But I do not believe either that it is catastrophic or beyond redemption. A good deal of damage has been done, to be sure, to both these institutions and to individual persons as well; and the general intellectual tone has become worse than ever, while standards and judgments of quality, in the humanities and the social sciences, have continued to go more or less out the window. But the long-term prospects may be something else again, and here we have to stand back and regard things in historical perspective. For America as a national society seems in the last generation or two to have arrived at something like a common decision: to use institutions of education—and in particular higher education—as a means for accelerating social change and mobility, redressing injustices, promoting various equalities, and enforcing cultural relativism. In other words, universities have become the contested sites on which certain social ideals are being tested, tried out, or getting a dry run. They are contested sites for several reasons. First, although the decision (or group of decisions) seems to have been made, not everyone agrees with it, nor is there adequately convincing concurrence on the appropriateness of the means that have been enlisted to realize the worthy goals that are at stake. Second, universities by historical tradition and, in some degree, by necessity are not democratic institutions. Scientific problems are not decided by votes; they are often not decided by entirely scientific procedures either, but the social processes that govern the way in which decisions are reached in communities of scientists are not by any stretch of the imagination democratic. And in the social sciences and the humanities, idiosyncratic mixtures of tradition, authority, personal persuasiveness and charisma, along with external social and cultural pressures, appear frequently to act as decisive influences in dealing with both intellectual and scholarly issues.

Institutions of higher education tend, in the main, to be intellectual aristocracies. In their corrupt versions they become ossified and oligarchic. When they work well, they tend to be meritocratic and allow talent to rise to the top, while reproducing at the same time many if not most of the inequities of the social matrix in which the talented unevenly begin as well, and out of which they also unevenly arise. The great European systems of secondary education, for example, were created in the wake of the French Revolution and functioned to enforce the larger aims of the socially dominant middle and upper-middle classes or bourgeoisie. Those systems offered to the sons of those classes an education that would prepare them for leading positions in nineteenth-century society—in the professions, politics, the civil service, and other institutions of social and cultural reproduction—while safely isolating them at the same time from the different destinies laid out in advance for the majority of those who were stationed or situated beneath them. In America, our institutions of higher education functioned almost from the outset in ways that were analogous to continental secondary education—but with appreciable differences. American class society was always more permeable, fluid, and loosely articulated than its European counterparts, and as a result American colleges and universities were earlier and more easily transformed into institutions that also promoted social and cultural mobility than was the case in Europe. What we are seeing today, among many other things, is a further evolution in that tendency as universities are becoming one of the most visible locations for the agencies of particular kinds of social change.

These changes have largely to do with interpretations and versions of equality, and in the name of equality and related social values, I have been arguing, quasi- or soft totalitarian ideas, formulations, persons, and arrangements have in recent years made themselves felt as important influences within our colleges and universities. The connections between the two are neither accidental nor inevitable. And the outcome of the conflicts that are entailed in the term "political correctness" and what it refers to is uncertain as well. For the present, however, one must as an individual continue to resist the decay of language, the decay in question at this moment having to do with the discursive occupation of university life by a variety of political and cultural orthodoxies and their thought-stifling idioms. The discourse of political correctness is political in the bad sense, and we could do worse than to recall Orwell once again. "Political language," he wrote, "and with variations this is true of all political parties, from Conservatives to Anarchists—is designed to make lies sound truthful and murder respectable, and to give an appearance of solidity to pure wind." That wind continues to blow, and I believe that one still doesn't have to be a weatherman in order to figure out what one's responsibilities are.   1993, vol. 60, no. 4

• American Identities
Conor Cruise O'Brien

Identities, yes. But singularity, as well. Foreign governments having dealings with America in the post–Cold-War period—as in earlier periods—are conscious mainly of having to face a single entity. Not a monolithic entity, indeed, but not, either, some kind of loose coalition of diverse identities. Rather, a complex, highly-structured polity: a Union, the United States of America. This is a trite enough train of thought, I confess, but one should not get altogether out of earshot of it. There is always some danger of losing sight of the obvious in dealing with a vast and complex subject matter.

"Out of many, one." *E pluribus, unum.* Not a very fashionable idea, but I think one with more life in it than might be supposed. The current emphasis among those who engage in the discussion of such matters is on diversity, the multicultural agenda, on race and gender differences, on efforts to downgrade both the English language and standard English in particular. The salience of identities, plural, seems at times so strong that one might think there could be no possibility any more of an American identity, a common sense of being American. If this is so, what will become of the Union, that is, of the United States?

Some activists, speaking on behalf of minority groups, have shown a tendency to disparage the whole idea of the Union as irrelevant to their concerns. This is not at all surprising, in view of the record of the federal government and federal institutions regarding what was happening to blacks in the South from the 1870s to the 1950s. But to dismiss the Union itself on account of that period of occultation is historically unsound. It was the Union that abolished slavery. It is within the framework of the Union that all later racial progress has been achieved. It is within that framework that what needs to be won can be won. The breakup of the Union into separate states and groups of states would have brought about a certain multiplication of identities indeed, but one which would have been fatal to the hopes of racial minorities and many others as well. So people should think twice before they disparage the Union.

I think the present forms of emphasis on diversity are actually both a mask for, and perhaps an unconscious mode for achieving, a unity which would be broader-based and to that extent stronger. For listening to some of those Americans who lay most stress on multiculturalism, I have been struck by the fact that their culture is in fact American, based on generations of American experience and on the primacy of American values and professions.

The relation of racial minorities to their own original homelands and to America is not so different, as is often suggested, from the equivalent relations of minorities of European origin. Few of those engaged with the multicultural agenda know much about any culture outside the United States, and most would be extremely unhappy if they found themselves constrained to live in any of the cultures for which they have a vague, theoretical enthusiasm.

What is really going on, under the multicultural agenda and related enterprises stressing distinct identities, is something more practical and more American than appears on the surface. The real agenda is the enlargement of the American national elite to include groups of persons who have traditionally been excluded from the same, mainly for reasons associated with race and gender. What is in view is the enlargement and diversification of the composition of the future governing class of the United States of America. I hope the expression "governing class," which is certainly not politically correct but which does refer to a reality, will be forgiven.

That enlargement is a legitimate objective, and it is in the interest of Americans generally that it shall be attained, as I believe it will. But those who are in fact doing most to bring about this change do not define their objective in these terms, even to themselves, I think. What I am talking about here is the circulation of elites. As a concept, this is not merely politically incorrect but even perhaps superficially un-American, and it is particularly offensive to the multicultural elite, which is opposed, in theory, to all elitism. Yet the circulation of elites, however un-American it may be as a concept, is part of American society and American history, and what the multiculturalists and their allies are actually trying to do is to remove a block in the way of that circulation: specifically a block to upward mobility by members of their own groupings, including themselves, into the national elite.

At a discussion I attended recently on "cultures," the thought was offered that the distinctive characteristic of American society is "equality." No one challenged this, yet there is some rather weighty evidence against the proposition. America's is an intensely competitive society, in business, in technology, in politics, in sport, and in all forms of communication. It is a society with great extremes of wealth and poverty, and a huge range of gradations between the extremes; gradations closely monitored and used by those with goods to sell, and, consequently, by the media. It's not obvious that equality is the distinguishing characteristic of such a society.

Yet, of course, one knows what is meant by the point. What is meant is equality of opportunity, not that it exists or can exist, here or elsewhere, in a pure condition. But there is more of it in this country than in most other countries, and it does produce a pleasant social breeziness lacking in other cultures. The breeze is produced by the circulation of elites, not only up and down, but sideways as well. What I mean by "sideways" is that people can move out of their neighborhoods, and the culture of their neighborhoods, and go elsewhere. And this is not the least precious aspect of American freedom.

At the same discussion I have just mentioned, there was considerable talk of ethnic cultural identities, amid a general assumption that these are invariably a good thing. One of those present happened to be a citizen of former Yugoslavia, a Bosnian, and a resident until recently in Sarajevo. She intervened to suggest that ethnic solidarity can be a trap. This thought was dismissed, rather summarily. She was given to understand that ethnicity might perhaps take an ugly turn in backward places like former Yugoslavia, but that it had no such potential in the United States.

I think there are quite a lot of young American students, those living in various ghettos and anxious to get on with studies related to a wider culture, who would not agree. There are some in the ghettos, and among their toughest denizens, who resent such students, quite understandably, precisely because of the upward mobility these students are acquiring. And when the national elite is expanded to include more members of racial minorities, those recruits will indeed be products of the ghetto culture, but mainly in the sense that they have managed to escape from it, generally both sideways and upward.

Two questions arise here concerning the possible effects on policy of the kind of expanded elite I have been discussing. Will it be more capable of handling America's domestic problems than the current still fairly narrow elite has shown itself to be? And will it be better able to handle America's international relations in the post–Cold-War arena than that older elite has been?

On both scores, I am inclined to return relatively optimistic answers. This is more obvious in the first case than in the second. It is true that white racism has done an enormous amount, historically, to create the ghettos and their problems. White guilt—a later growth and often mixed, consciously or unconsciously, with white racism—has done little to alleviate the problems. To throw money at ghettos, watch it get stolen, and then shrug one's shoulders at the impossibility of helping "them," pretty well sums up much of the relevant history. Yet it is also true that black demagogues, often themselves on the take, have compounded the damage. Already a black leadership is emerging which is facing the fact that, in the late twentieth century, most of the oppression of blacks in America is the work of other blacks. But the kind of approach with which Jesse Jackson, his assiduous work in the high schools, and his associates are now identified can, if resolutely sustained, do more to help than anything previously tried has accomplished.

In post-Cold-War foreign affairs, I think the implications of a significantly expanded American elite are likely to be benign, though not dramatically so. This development should tend to diminish the self-righteousness in the formulation of American foreign policy and thereby be conducive to somewhat greater realism in the framing of actual decisions. In this connection Henry Kissinger's new book, *Diplomacy*, is relevant. It is a rather curious book. Its main thrust is against the moralistic, Wilsonian element in the making of foreign policy. To be against this is all right, at least by me. But Kissinger's way of being against it is peculiar and largely unrealistic. He tends to take this stuff at its face value, to exalt it, even to flatter it, as an actual and peculiarly American force in history, quite distinct from the pursuit of self-interest. He tends to ignore the distinction between rhetoric and policy although, as President Nixon's chief adviser, he must know more than most people about that. In fact, neither self-interest nor self-righteousness is either absent from or peculiar to American foreign policy. Most countries tend to combine the two, often without being quite aware of what they are doing. Universally, self-interest shapes most of the policy, while self-righteousness tends to dominate the formulation.

America is not an exception to this law, though Kissinger incessantly seeks to suggest that it is. Thus, he suggests that the Treaty of Versailles was shaped by the ethical and moralistic concerns of President Wilson as expressed in the doctrine of self-determination. But self-determination as practiced at Versailles was simply the disintegration of the Austro-Hungarian and Ottoman Empires at the hands of the victorious French and British Empires, to the mutual advantage of the latter, except when one of them saw some advantage in a doublecross, as Britain did with France over the Sykes-Picot Agreement. The moralistic Wilsonian bit no doubt meant a lot to Woodrow Wilson personally. But in terms of international politics, it was no more than a way of attempting to make the realpolitik of the Versailles settlement acceptable to the American public.

Wilsonianism is not as important as Kissinger suggests; it is always mostly a matter of formulation, of rhetoric. But especially in conditions of confusion and rapid change, such rhetoric can have dangerous effects on the making of actual policy, leading to excessive commitments at variance with interests, and then precipitating retreats from such commitments also damaging to interests and to the stability of alliances in particular. This was evident in the first phase of the post-Cold-War period, at the beginning of our decade. The idea of the End of History and the New International Order blended together in a kind of woozy millennium, without moorings in global reality. Democracy and freedom of expression were seen as on the march everywhere, and if they should seem to get stuck anywhere, for a time, America would just give them a good shove and they would get moving again.

That was the mood of those days. Heads were so swollen in the West, among politicians and commentators alike, that feet could be no longer kept on the ground. The mood of 1994 has to be more chastened than it was then, but habitual rhetoric, especially in America, keeps the Fukuyama mood alive, or half-alive, despite what four years of unremitting historical continuance should have done to the theory of the end of history. The rhetoric, therefore, remains dangerous. The great continuing illusion of the post–Cold-War period is that America, working through NATO and the United Nations, or the UN alone, can convert other cultures into something different from what they are. Examples of that illusion in practice are: the illusion that China can be made amenable to the First Amendment; the illusion that the whole of the former Soviet Union can be made safe for democracy, and safe also from both further disintegration and restored centralism; the illusion that some form of external intervention can eliminate ethnic strife from former Yugoslavia. The most pervasive illusion of all is that nationalism can be made to fade away, yielding place to a new universal order.

The trend has of course been the other way in recent years in the former Soviet Union and the former Yugoslavia, with the supranational yielding place to the national. That trend in itself, however, is not necessarily or universally irreversible. In the former Soviet Union, for example, we can now discern a centripetal pattern beginning to prevail over centrifugal ones in some places, while interacting unpredictably with them in others. Many groups in the former Soviet Union would rather be in the Russian Federation than subjected to new ethnic or religious masters in an independent state.

In short, some nationalists can seek refuge from other nationalists within a supranational entity. Various examples are Crimea and the Eastern Ukraine; Abkhazia, Moldova, and Tadjikistan. In some ways, the processes at work in the former Soviet Union resemble those through which the original Soviet Union was created, under the auspices of Lenin and Stalin, three-quarters of a century ago. Such a trend exists today, but it is a product of autonomous forces which include the often frantic interactions of nationalism mixed up on the ground. There is very little that Americans, or other outsiders, can do about it all, one way or another. It is unlikely that the outcomes, whether centralized or decentralized, will be democratic or otherwise congenial to American values. It was *glasnost*—freedom of expression—that blew the old Soviet Union apart. It is unlikely that the consolidation of *glasnost* will be high among the priorities of a restored Soviet Union.

Contemplation of what is now going on in the former Soviet Union should concentrate the minds of the United States and its allies on the state of their defenses, rather than on the possibilities of such an unlikely contingency as the indefinite extension of democracy. It is evident from the rise of Zhirinovsky and other related developments that humiliated nationalism is a major force today in the former Soviet Union. Humiliated nationalism is the most dangerous force in history. More than anything else it gave rise to the French Revolution, the Russian, the Nazi, and the Chinese revolutions. Its emergence in a dilapidated country still possessing nuclear weapons should hardly be regarded with the complacency which the progress of disarmament in the West seems to register.

In general, post-Cold-War conditions seem to point to the need for a more sober, alert, modest, and realistic posture than the present still-inflated state of American official rhetoric yet seems to point to. No doubt the calculations are more realistic, but the rhetoric has a tendency to outrun these. I believe that, in time, if events in the interim allow room enough, the expected expansion of the American elite may have a healthy effect on this. The groups which have so long been left out, even far out, can hardly be quite so complacent as those who have long been in. Racial minorities in particular have been listening to that rhetoric for a long time from the outside, where it doesn't sound so good.

A greater role for women, including black women, in international decision-making could also have a major positive influence on international social priorities, especially in the field of human reproduction. For many years now, the international influence of the United States has been on the side of the Vatican in deemphasizing the importance, and even denying the existence, of the population explosion. At the Rio Conference on the Environment, for example, the question of population was played down, in comparison with matters of great but still subordinate significance such as the state of the rain forests. The destruction of the rain forests and so much else in the environment is a direct result of the still-continuing population explosion. Yet the United States, throughout the last three presidential terms, has helped the Vatican and other interested parties to block the dissemination of contraception and abortion information.

I believe women may already be beginning to alter those priorities, but the need for change is urgent, and there are small signs of it so far. Most of the great and growing evils of the post-Cold-War era around the globe are connected in some way with this, the greatest of all human problems. South Africa is a major case in point. While most discussion of South Africa's future still tends to center on race relations, problems connected with the population explosion such as mass unemployment, a great increase in violent crime, and destruction of the environment pose greater threats to the future of South Africa than even any form of racism does. By giving a clear, consistent lead on the population explosion, the United States could do far more to help the human race, including the West, than with an indefinite number of well-intentioned but unsustainable—and often counterproductive—local, piecemeal military and quasi-military interventions.

I have noted that there have indeed been small signs of positive change in the attitude of the United States toward the population explosion. As it happens, the largest sign of such change that has yet come to my notice is one reported in the *Wall Street Journal* of April 8, 1994: "Washington is seeking revisions in a U.N. draft document on stabilizing global population growth, with the U.S. hoping to include stronger language on the importance of access to abortion services. The draft is already under attack by Roman Catholics and antiabortion activists."

If the United States maintains its position in relation to that United Nations document, it is likely to find itself in confrontation with the Vatican during the relevant international conferences. This would be a most healthy development and an overdue one. It would lead to an open and sustained debate on this great matter and eventually to a much-expanded allocation of resources toward checking the population explosion. The Vatican, with the aid of the pro-life lobby in the United States, will try to get the Clinton administration to back away from the position it has taken in relation to that draft document. But if the Vatican fails in that attempt, it will not wish to sustain confrontation with the greatest power on earth. It may not formally change its basic position, but it may cease to lead the obstruction of discussion and action in this domain.

In short, if the United States maintains its present position, the whole climate of international relations with regard to the population explosion will change almost overnight, and vastly for the better.   1994, vol. 61, no. 3

• Romania's Mystical Revolutionaries
Vladimir Tismaneanu

Few stories in this century are more fascinating than the intellectual history of Romania's mystical revolutionaries of the 1930s. Until recently, the activities of the intellectuals associated with the "legionnaires of the Archangel Michael" have almost universally been glossed over with a veil of silence and presented as an ephemeral, almost insignificant episode in their tumultuous *Lehrjahre*. Nor have any of the participants engaged in soul-searching to detect the reasons for their youthful obsession. What followed after 1940 has been a long, and one must say, successful exercise of willed amnesia. Yet in the preceding decades the fascist commitment of the "Young Generation" and its identification with the Iron Guardist movement was the most straightforward expression of nationalism and anti-Semitism to be found in Eastern Europe.

Mircea Eliade wrote in "Itinerar spiritual," a 1927 series of essays published in *Cuvintul*, what became the group's credo: the old generation created Great Romania, the young one would create a great culture. Political geography was insufficient: a spiritual realm was required for a nation to exist. Although influenced by the apostles of traditional Romanian nationalism, from Mihai Eminescu and B. P. Hasdeu to Nicolae Iorga and Vasile Parvan, the members of this group were nevertheless attracted to Europe's then new cultural trends: surrealism, expressionism, syndicalism, psychoanalysis, and the study of esoteric creeds and religions. Spellbound by their readings of Pascal, Joseph de Maistre, Schopenhauer, Berdiayev, d'Annunzio, Sorel, Maurras, Klages, Spengler, Bakunin, and Papini, they dreamt of a new Middle Age, exalting the values of organic community based on a heroic sense of sacrifice and martyrdom. The cult of excess was the hallmark of their *Weltanschauung*. The tradition of the dissatisfied, skeptical, tragically depressed writer was internalized and embellished by them.

They represented a Balkan counterpart to the revolutionary aristocratism preached by Ernst Jünger and other proponents of the Germanic resurrection: they were anti-bourgeois, anti-mercantile, anti-democratic. The centrality of anti-Semitism in this philosophy was linked both to the rejection of the economic and political forms associated in East-Central Europe with Jews as agents of capitalist transformations and to the perception of Judaism as inimical to the Christian Orthodox cement of Romanianism. In a country like Romania, with its predominantly agrarian and illiterate population, with a corrupt and often irresponsible political class, the anti-liberal and mystical revolutionary rhetoric of the far right was bound to excite and galvanize the intellectual elite.

In *Romania's Transfiguration*, published in Bucharest in 1937, the young E. M. Cioran wrote: "The Jews are unique in every way. Bent by a curse for which only God is responsible, they are matchless. If I were a Jew, I would commit suicide immediately." (He would later recall his words as an expression of a love-hate relationship with the Jewish people and tradition.) Cioran had triumphantly entered the Romanian literary world in 1934 with his book *On the Heights of Despair* (recently reissued, in a masterful translation by Ilinca Zarifopol-Johnston, by the University of Chicago Press). The book is full of overblown metaphors, linguistic somersaults, and conceptual precipices. It was not a banal debut. Nothing in Cioran's intellectual life had been banal. Indeed, the angry young man's nihilistic creed was crowned with the prize of the Young Romanian Writers' Association along with *No*, Eugène Ionesco's first and only volume written in Romanian.

The third recipient of this prestigious award was Constantin Noica, born in 1909, who was to be the only member of the Generation to remain in Romania, survive Communist jails and harassment, and become, at the end of his life in 1987, a cultural model for Romania's young intellectuals. To his credit, Emil Cioran, who left Romania for France in 1938 and never went back, has been the only member of the Generation to have dealt, albeit in an delphic way, with his initial Fascist commitment. In a famous essay, actually an open letter addressed to his friend the philosopher Constantin Noica in 1957, "Lettre à un ami lointain," Cioran insisted on the Generation's marked hostility to and even scorn for parliamentary democracy:

> Happier than me, you have resigned yourself to our native dust; in addition, you have the faculty of being able to bear all regimes, even the most rigid ones. Not that you don't have the nostalgia for fantasy and disorder, but I don't know a spirit more opposed than yours to the superstitions of "democracy." True, there was a time when I detested it as much as you did, probably even more: I was young and I could not admit other truths than mine, neither could I concede to the adversary the right to have his truths, to invoke or to impose them. The fact that parties could confront each other without annihilating each other went beyond my capacity for comprehension. . . . The systems that tried to supplant it seemed to me beautiful without exception, attuned to the movement of Life, my divinity of those times. For the one who, before thirty, did not experience the fascination with all forms of extremism, I don't know whether to feel admiration or contempt, whether to consider him a saint or a cadaver.

Years later Cioran further emphasized his distance from the Iron Guard by speaking with undisguised contempt for the movement. The problem, however, is not whether Cioran ever pledged the membership oath to the Iron Guard. Too anarchic, too self-centered and undisciplined to accept the Legionary rituals, Cioran and many others nevertheless were intimately linked to the intellectual climate of unbound national fanaticism and antidemocratic furor that accompanied and favored the Guard's activities. Although later Mircea Eliade would deny having been enrolled in the Iron Guard, in 1937 he published an article in the Guardist newspaper *Buna Vestire* titled, "Why I Believe in the Triumph of the Legionary Movement," a most vibrant endorsement:

> I believe in the destiny of the Romanian people. That is why I believe in the victory of the Legionary movement. A nation that has demonstrated huge powers of creation at all levels of reality cannot be shipwrecked at the periphery of history in a Balkanized democracy, in a civil catastrophe. . . . I believe in the destiny of our nation. I believe in the Christian revolution of the new man. I believe in freedom,

personality, and love. Therefore, I believe in the victory of the Legionary movement, in a proud and powerful Romania, in a new way of life that will transform the riches of the Romanian soul into universal spiritual values.

In truth, Eliade, the recognized spiritual leader of the Young Generation, was not alone in his Guardist exaltation. Cioran himself contributed to the ultranationalist and Guardist newspapers with articles eulogizing Hitler and Nazi Germany and urging Romanians to relinquish their lukewarm psychology and enjoy the politics of delirium. While young Eugène Ionesco remained a true democrat, equally opposed to Bolshevism and Nazism, the great French *moraliste* E. M. Cioran—the worshiper of Vladimir Soloviev and Leon Shestov, the man who later would write superb pages about the Romanian-born Jewish poet Benjamin Fondane who was gassed at Auschwitz—unambiguously endorsed the totalitarians of the extreme right.

In their support for the Iron Guard's ideology, philosophers like Nae Ionescu, Mircea Eliade, and Emil Cioran illustrated what Hannah Arendt once rightly called "the temporary alliance between the mob and the elite." With few exceptions, they never used the scurrilous language of the rank-and-file Guardists: they were too refined for that. What they did was to convince the boys and the girls of the Legionary death squads (*echipele mortii*) that dying for the "Capitan" (as the Guard's leader Corneliu Zelea Codreanu was called) meant dying for Romania. In an ironic twist, what started as the cult of creative life culminated in the mystique of heroic death. Eugène Ionesco recalled in an 1970 interview the spiritual-political atmosphere in Romania of the 1930s and the "ideological contagion" of the Nazi virus:

> University professors, students, intellectuals were turning Nazi, becoming Iron Guards, one after the other. We were some fifteen people who used to get together, to discuss, to try to find arguments opposing theirs. It was not easy. . . . From time to time, one of our group would come out and say: "I don't agree at all with them, to be sure, but on certain points, nevertheless, I must admit, for example, the Jews. . . ." And that kind of comment was a symptom. Three weeks later, that person would become a Nazi. He was caught in the mechanism, he accepted everything, he became a rhinoceros. Toward the end, it was only three or four of us who resisted.

To be sure, Cioran and Eliade wrote their ignominious pro-Nazi pieces before Auschwitz. Still their lack of awareness about what was in store for Jews in the Nazi-controlled Europe dumbfounds. For instance, writing in February 1937, after the promulgation of the Nuremberg racist legislation and one year before *Kristallnacht*, Mircea Eliade justified his sympathy to National Socialism by

invoking Bolshevik anti-religious zeal: "Whatever I am told about Hitlerite terrorism, I cannot forget that in the very center of Berlin there stands a synagogue,
solemn and untainted—unlike any church in Russia." This strategy of "comparative trivialization" (as Peter Gay calls it) is subliminally linked to the fallacy of a
Judeo-Bolshevik conspiracy. More recently, this vision has resurfaced in Ernst
Nolte's attempt to explain the Jewish Holocaust as part of a "European civil war"
in which Hitler's perception of a presumed Jewish-Bolshevik threat to subjugate
the Germans motivated his "preemptive" mass-murderous program.

In December 1933, almost a year after Hitler's takeover, young Cioran glow-
ingly celebrated the Nazi neo-pagan dramaturgy: "I like the Hitlerites because of
their cult of the irrational, their exaltation of vitality as such, their virile expansion of energy, without any critical spirit, without reserve and without control."
By mid-1934, following a trip to Munich (during his 1933-35 Humboldt scholarship study in Nazi Germany, where he went together with Noica, who studied in
Freiburg under Martin Heidegger), Cioran went even further with his frantic
encomia for the Nazi revolution:

> There is no politician in the world today who inspires my sympathy and admira-
> tion to a greater extent than Hitler. . . . The mysticism of the Führer in Germany
> is fully justified. . . . It is Hitler's merit that he has ravished the critical spirit of a
> nation. . . . Hitler has poured a fiery passion into political struggles and dynamized
> an entire domain of values, reduced by democratic rationalism to platitudes and
> trivialities, with a Messianic spirit. All of us need mysticism because we are tired
> of so many truths which do not spark a flame.

Such Cioran texts have been ignored by those seduced by the elegant (though
somewhat pompous and grandiloquent) aphorisms that were later to ensure his
French and international glory. Once he left Romania, it was as if Cioran had
also left behind a world of frightening deformities, irresponsible vagaries, and
devastating nightmares. According to his confessions made in different interviews published in Germany, Italy, and Spain (he systematically shunned interviews in the French media), this "transfiguration" took place during the years he
spent in Nazi-occupied Paris. What he did during those years in terms of professional occupation is still unknown. However, it is known that until 1944, he continued to receive a fellowship from the French Institute. France had ceased to
exist as an independent country, so the logical conclusion is that the money
came from the Vichy regime. During those days Walter Benjamin committed
suicide, and Benjamin Fondane, Cioran's personal friend, died at Auschwitz.
Did he know about the scope of the horror? Was it possible for an intellectual of
his caliber to simply ignore the Nazi anti-Jewish measures, including the notorious *rafle* at the Velodrome d'Hiver in 1942?

While Cioran was not a Guardist himself, his mentor Nae Ionescu was, and so were (for short periods of time, to be sure) other members of the Generation, including Constantin Noica. The best analysis of Nae Ionescu's political demonism and the relationship between the Professor (as he was revered by his disciples in the Generation) and the Iron Guard has been provided by Mircea Vulcanescu, a philosopher belonging to Cioran's generation, in a book written in 1942, completed in 1945-46, but published in Romania only in 1992. Never an Iron Guardist, Vulcanescu served in Marshal Ion Antonescu's pro-Nazi government as undersecretary of state at the Ministry of Finances and died in 1952 in a Communist jail. For him, Nae Ionescu was a consummate Machiavellian who managed to beguile a whole generation and thus change its destiny. The Professor's post-1933 idyll with the Iron Guard was part of his search for the political force that could fulfill his ethno-theocratic ideal. Regarded by some as an intellectual crackpot, adored by others as a metaphysical genius, Ionescu died in 1940 at the age of fifty, shortly before the triumph of the Iron Guard.

A religious thinker, Nae Ionescu yearned for the figure of the national redeemer, the charismatic leader who would restore the spiritual value of human existence and make possible the country's "resurrection" from the execrated democratic shambles. But he was too profound a philosopher, Vulcanescu argues, not to doubt the ultimate legitimacy of Corneliu Zelea Codreanu, the Iron Guard's captain, to claim such a mystically privileged status.

In short, Nae Ionescu embraced the Guard's political views because of the affinities between the movement's visceral anti-democratism and his own distrust of Western liberalism. Nae Ionescu's theoretically founded anti-Semitism was rooted in his conception of an immutable ethnic structure: Romanianness was almost a genetic given, and no effort to acquire this status could succeed. In 1934, the novel *For Two Thousand Years* by Iosef Hechter (under the pen name of Mihail Sebastian), which was a parable of the dilemma of Jewish assimilation in the Danubian and Carpathian space as well as a *roman à clef* about the intellectual debates among the Young Generation's members, was published. Nae Ionescu responded to it by publishing a "Preface" to the novel in which he admonishes:

> You are sick, Iosef Hechter. You are essentially sick because you cannot but suffer; and because your suffering does not lead anywhere. Everybody is suffering, Iosef Hechter. We Christians also are suffering. But we have a way out, because we can redeem ourselves. I know you are hoping, hoping that he for whom you wait will come. The Messiah, on his white horse, and then you will rule the earth. You are hoping, Iosef Hechter. This is the only thing left to you. But I cannot do anything for you. Because I know that the Messiah you wait for will not come. The Messiah has already come, Iosef Hechter, and you did not recognize him. All you were

asked to do in exchange for all the good things God offered you was to be on the watch. And you did not watch. Or you failed to see, because vanity covered your eyes with scales. . . . Iosef Hechter, don't you feel the grip of the cold and darkness?

Jehuda semper patet: Thus spoke Nae Ionescu. More disturbing was that the paragons of the Young Generation took his arguments at face value and engaged in a theological dispute about the Jewish chances for salvation. With his extraordinary magnetism—remembered by Eliade in his memoirs—Nae Ionescu contributed decisively to the "Guardist Conversion" of the Generation. In the context of the Nazi racial revolution and the murderous actions of the Iron Guard, Nae Ionescu's lines represented a pseudo-theological warrant for genocide. To exonerate him and present his views as a legitimate dogmatic stance, as some Romanian intellectuals have lately done, is morally idiotic and intellectually dishonest. I totally agree with Matei Calinescu, who considers that the "Preface" to *For Two Thousand Years* was one of the first major cases of "rhinocerization" among the Romanian intellectuals of the time, "serving as an unfortunate but mesmerizing example to many of the younger writers, journalists, philosophers, professors, and artists who, after 1933, but particularly after 1934, joined the Iron Guard in droves."

Such exoneration is particularly disquieting today in post-Ceausescu Romania, where many within the new generation of students and intellectuals identify themselves with the spirit of the rebellious radicals of the thirties. For instance, student leader Marian Munteanu has founded an organization called *Miscarea pentru Romania* (The Movement for Romania) and invoked Nae Ionescu and his school as his models. Both Ionescu's "Preface" and Cioran's *Romania's Transfiguration* have recently been reprinted by Humanitas Publishing House in Romania. The head of Humanitas is Gabriel Liceanu, Constantin Noica's main disciple and anointed heir (and currently an adamant critic of the Iliescu regime). In 1992, Liceanu himself published a book called *Cearta cu filosofia* (The Quarrel with Philosophy), in which he performed a lengthy tour de force in examining Cioran's theoretical tribulations without any reference whatsoever to Cioran's Fascist past. Not surprisingly, one cannot find any anti-Semitic fulminations in the meticulously revised edition of *Romania's Transfiguration*, whose updating Cioran personally supervised. The whole fourth chapter, titled "National Collectivism," as well as the long aforementioned passages referring to the need for more fanaticism in Romania's politics, has been carefully deleted. The preserved passages on Jews do not lend themselves to moral objections in the light of the Holocaust. The reader who might have expected Cioran to have elaborated on these problems will be disappointed. Neither he nor Liceanu found it necessary to offer a critical introduction to a book that was one of the main manifestos of European Fascism in its "National Bolshevik" version.

The truly odd thing is that instead of the usual copyright notice, Humanitas (certainly with Cioran's blessing) printed the following: "The first two editions appeared in 1936 and 1941. The current edition is the only authorized version." To make things more explicit, the octogenarian Cioran composed the following caution: "I wrote these divagations in 1935-36, at the age of twenty-four, with passion and *orgueil.* Of all I have published in Romanian and French, this text is perhaps the most passionate. It also is the most alien to me. I do not rediscover myself in it, although the presence of my then hysteria strikes me as obvious. I saw it as my duty to suppress some pretentious and stupid pages. This is the definitive edition. Nobody has the right to change it." Cioran may have changed his mind (it was Claudel who once wrote that *ce sont seulement les imbéciles qui ne changent pas d'avis*), but his early Romanian writings exist and should be freely examined. With its lionization of the hysterical crowds, his book belongs to the impetus that helped establish the Fascist dictatorship in Romania, the bloody prelude to the next, no less ruthless, Communist tyranny. Although subdued and cryptic, Cioran's short warning at least does imply that he repents for his juvenile aberrations. In contrast, Eliade, as Norman Manea rightly pointed out in his essay "Felix Culpa," never explicitly abjured his Guardist commitment.

The reissue of Cioran's first book shows it still to be the *cri de coeur* of a metaphysical dandy, a collection of spasmodic aphorisms and reflections written by a young epigone of Nietzsche during insomniac crises of misanthropy and narcissism. The translator's introduction is a perceptive piece of literary history, showing that, from title to conclusions, Cioran's book has a deep ironical dimension, but there is no information about Cioran's fateful political wager. Thus in the new edition Cioran's metaphysical lyricism has been artificially distilled and purified from his no less significant political radicalism. One can, of course, accept Cioran's repudiation of his early political blunders, but intellectual history requires some reflection on the relationship between Romania's spiritual elite and the pseudo-Christian, ethnic fundamentalism of the Iron Guard.

The espousal by Cioran and other members of the Young Generation of the Guardist tenets was linked to their entrenched anti-intellectualist and anti-liberal beliefs. Part of the allegiance to the Guard was linked to their cultural inferiority complex: as Cioran once put it, the "vanity of a man born within a small culture is forever wounded." Anti-Semitism was adopted as part of the creation of a much-needed "national myth" which could not be conceived in the absence of an enemy figure. For them the Jews became the symbol of the plutocratic-commercial values they had so much decried in their earlier but not manifestly anti-Semitic writings. In times of historical catastrophe, with the Iron Guard singling out the Jews as the main enemy of Romania's renascence, these intellectuals "respectabilized" a direction and a movement that under any circumstances could only be called barbaric. The more they talked about Christian values, the less were they ready to feel any empathy with those who were suffering real persecution.

With their contempt for the idea of natural rights and the Western contractualist tradition, with their glorification of the ethnocratic state and the wild, often insane generalization about national characteristics (more often than not egregious stereotypes rooted in envy, fear, and resentment), they paved the ground for the extreme racist legislation after 1940 and the forcible deportation and vanishing of Romania's Jews in the Transnistrian camps. The more they insisted that the nation had to assert its purity by contrasting alleged Judaic materialism to Christian Orthodox idealism, the more they anesthetized the population and allowed for insensitivity to real, palpable, and murderous forms of "ethnic cleansing."

Leon Volovici's book *Nationalist Ideology and Anti-Semitism: The Case of Romanian Intellectuals in the 1930s* (Pergamon Press) is the first systematic attempt to tell the convulsive tale of Romania's inter-war young intellectuals. As he puts it, the theorists of the Messianic national revolution created a climate in which the "Jewish question" became "an acute theme of intellectual life." Fortunately, he places this history against the background of Europe's ideological battle between Enlightenment and counter-Enlightenment, with its often misleading images of "total revolution" and frozen archetypes of Left and Right. The merit of Volovici's book is that it offers the Western reader an introduction to the early stage of a thinker who was later to be lionized as the distinguished successor to the lyrical, aphoristic, and anti-systematic tradition of philosophizing exemplified by Kierkegaard, Nietzsche, and Wittgenstein. When Susan Sontag praised Cioran's "radical will," she was unaware of his intellectual metamorphoses: the little *tache honteuse* in Cioran's biography eluded this proponent of absolute candor and supreme authenticity. Volovici's book is not an indictment. His sober (and somber) conclusion is worth quoting:

> Between the two world wars, few of Romania's intellectuals were extremist anti-Semites, but attachment to a certain idea of national awareness, with a somewhat latent perception of the Jew as an alien, and in certain circumstances as even dangerous, characterized most of them. For this reason there were very few intellectuals who, in the most critical days, adopted the rejection of anti-Jewish discrimination as a cause of their own that they would willingly defend in public. In the 1930s, a "Dreyfus affair" was unimaginable in Romania.

The strength of Volovici's book lies in its demonstration of how a group of outstanding writers inspired by an intellectual guru with Christian pretensions and Mephistophelic influence made their pact with the darkest forces of this century and never engaged in a serious coming to terms with their own past. Like Martin

Heidegger and Carl Schmitt, Cioran has avoided any direct avowal of his Fascist past. The issue of responsibility is not part of his ethical concern. While Volovici offers the first comprehensive and remarkably balanced analysis of this fascinating chapter of intellectual and political history, there is, however, a missing epilogue: the story did not end in the 1930s and 1940s, and the Generation has made a spectacular comeback in post-1989 Romania. For instance, former Ceausescu sycophant Dan Zamfirescu re-edited Nae Ionescu's volume *Roza vinturilor* (The Wind Rose) with an afterword by Mircea Eliade, and he stated in the foreword that "no other book is more urgently needed to be known and revalued into a direction vital for the national existence of the Romanians." The truth is that no other book, with the exception of Cioran's *Transfiguration*, has had such deleterious effects on the minds and souls of the young Romanians.

Radical ideas do not exist in a vacuum, and their impact on human existence can often be disastrous. Whatever the reasons for young Cioran's moral dissatisfaction, his political wager was tragically wrong. During those times of shame and horror, Cioran, Eliade, and their fellow mystical revolutionaries were impervious to what was indeed the revelation of sorrow: the coming of the statistical murders and the appalling realities of the concentration camps. Later, they continued to remain silent, prolonging an abysmal moral error and perpetuating nebulous ambiguities.   1994, vol. 61, no. 4

Index